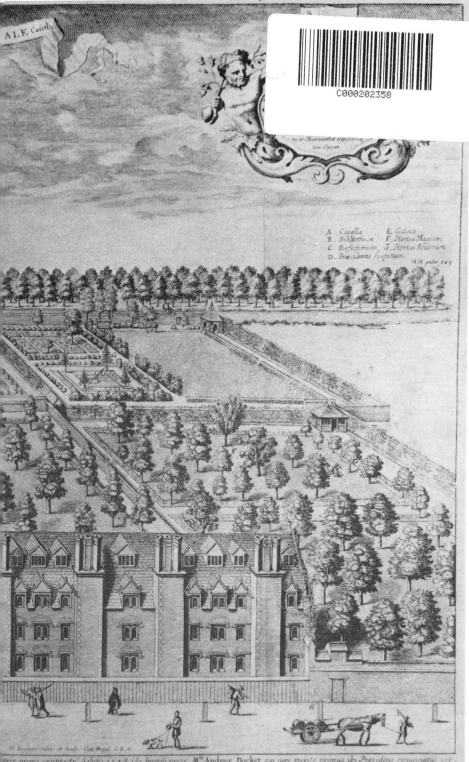

A.L.F. Cantb.

ru et Obseruantia eriqeretur
tum Logan

A. Capella   E. Culina
B. Bibliotheca   F. Hortus Magistri
C. Refectorium   G. Hortus Socierum
D. Præsidentis hospitium
                           H.H. pag. 245

D. Logan delin. et sculp. Coll. Regal. ad B.M.

trix prima extitit An.ᵒ Salutis 1448. idq humili prece Mᵈ Andreæ Docket qui jure merito primus ibi Præsidens renunciatus est
a hac Suum, etsi non usquequaq par. Maritali tamen Illi alteri, aliquatenus responderet. Operum coacte Fundatrices non ita multo
antium invenerat, uti jure Successionis vera Fundatrix, feliciter absolvit, muruvit legibus, privilegijs auxit &c evocurantz
RICH. III serenissima Anna, ad cujus singulares contemplationem & requisitionem (sunt ea Diplomatis Regii verba)&c ita innui
um fundis quibus, cum Glocestriæ esset Dux, Collegium dotarat, ANNAM vero excepit HEN. VII ELIZABETHA Fundatrices
ns 19 Socij singuæ Hebreæ, Græcæ, Rhetorices, Geometriæ, Arithmetices, Prælectores, 5 Censores 2, alter Theologicus, Philosof
s visum est silentio premere quam plurimis in hac pagella necessario pretereundis injuriam facere Collegii hodie floret Præs.Reg vero HEN.IAMES S.T.P

for Mary Connell,

with every good wish,

John Twigg

A HISTORY OF QUEENS' COLLEGE, CAMBRIDGE
1448 – 1986

A HISTORY OF
QUEENS' COLLEGE, CAMBRIDGE
1448 – 1986

John Twigg

THE BOYDELL PRESS

First published 1987 by The Boydell Press
an imprint of Boydell & Brewer Ltd
PO Box 9, Woodbridge, Suffolk IP12 3DF
and Wolfeboro, New Hampshire 03894-2069, USA

ISBN 0 85115 488 3

British Library Cataloguing in Publication Data

Twigg, John
    A history of Queens' College, Cambridge
    1448 – 1986.
    1. Queens' College, Cambridge – History
    I. Title
    378.426'59   LF235
    ISBN 0-85115-488-3

Library of Congress Cataloging in Publication Data

Twigg, John, 1957 –
    A history of Queens' College, Cambridge,
    1448 – 1986.

    Includes Index.
    1. Queens' College (University of Cambridge)
– History. I. Title.
LF235.T95 1987 378.426'59 87-10271
ISBN 0-85115-488-3

Printed in Great Britain by St Edmundsbury Press,
Bury St Edmunds, Suffolk

Contents

List of illustrations   vii
Abbreviations   ix
Preface   xi
Acknowledgements   xvii

Part I. The outline history of the college in its times from the foundation until 1660.
Chapter 1.   Founders and foundresses (1446 – 85)   1
Chapter 2.   Renaissance men (the early 16th century)   13
Chapter 3.   The Reformation (1520 – 1603)   25
Chapter 4.   The early 17th century (1603 – 60)   42

Part II. The college and its society from the 15th to 17th centuries.
Chapter 5.   The early presidents   64
Chapter 6.   College Fellows   74
Chapter 7.   Students and student life   86
Chapter 8.   Studies and degrees; the college library and theatre   98
Chapter 9.   College estates and finances; benefactions; charity   110
Chapter 10.   Miscellany: servants and tradesmen; the college
              and the town; the buildings; visits; health and
              disease   123

Part III. The 18th century and early 19th centuries
Chapter 11.   Prologue: the Restoration and the reigns of
              Charles II and James II (1660 – 88)   141
Chapter 12.   The 18th century – introduction; politics; religion   153
Chapter 13.   Presidents and Fellows   179
Chapter 14.   Eighteenth century students   192
Chapter 15.   Study and the curriculum   203

Part IV. The age of reform: the later 19th and early 20th centuries
Chapter 16.   College Fellows   220
Chapter 17.   Students   234
Chapter 18.   Religion   267
Chapter 19.   The educational revolution   287
Chapter 20.   College finances (18th and 19th centuries)   300
Chapter 21.   College buildings (18th and 19th centuries)   310

Part V. Modern times.

Chapter 22. The college and the first world war 317
Chapter 23. Aspects of college society, 1919 – 1939 325
Chapter 24. The college and the second world war 355
Chapter 25. The modern college (I) – introduction;
government; finance 363
Chapter 26. The modern college (II) – college buildings
in the 20th century 369
Chapter 27. The modern college (III) – the curriculum;
the library; presidents; Fellows; religion 380
Chapter 28. The modern college (IV) – students and student
life 394
Chapter 29. The admission of women 434

Appendices

Appendix 1. Matriculations and degrees, 1639/40 – 1664/5 444
Appendix 2. Size of college fellowships, 1564 – 1727 445
Appendix 3. Fellows ejected in the parliamentary purge of
1644 – 5 446
Appendix 4. Presidents of Queens' 447
Appendix 5. Status of Queens' students on entry, 1500 – 1751 449
Appendix 6. Numerical size of colleges, 1564 – 1727 450
Appendix 7. Geographical origins of Queens' students,
1500 – 1751 451
Appendix 8. Examples of family connections with Queens'
over more than two generations 452
Appendix 9. Ecclesiastical offices held by former students
of Queens', 1448 – 1751 454
Appendix 10. Scholars and bible-clerks at Queens',
1535/6 – 1639/40 455
Appendix 11. Degree-taking at Queens', 1448 – 1751 456
Appendix 12. College finances, 16th – 18th centuries 457
Appendix 13. Incomes of Cambridge colleges, as presented
to the crown, 1535 and 1546 459
Appendix 14. Daniel Nichols' poem welcoming the restoration
of Charles II in 1660 460
Appendix 15. The Plumptre family at Cambridge 461
Appendix 16. Size and social composition of the 19th
century student body in Queens' 462
Appendix 17. The 'ten year man' 464
Appendix 18. Subjects for debate in the St Bernard
society, 1886 – 1914 466
Appendix 19. Contingency plans for dealing with student
agitation 1969/70 475

List of illustrations

Colour plates   *Between pp. 142 and 143*

1   Detail of centre panel of triptych in new Chapel. Attributed to the 'Master of St Gudule', Brussels, 1480s.

2   Margaret of Anjou, with her husband, Henry VI, receiving presentation by John Talbot, Earl of Shrewsbury, of his book of *Poems and Romances*, 1445 [British Library, Royal MS II 15 E VI, fo. 2b].

3   Carved keystone over old Main Gate of College, 1450, traditionally thought to be Andrew Doket holding the College's foundation charter.

4   Elizabeth Woodville, queen of Edward IV. The best surviving panel portrait of her, traditionally thought to be the original from which the other portraits derive.

5   (top) Sir Thomas Smith, contemporary portrait panel.
    (bottom) Isaac Milner, by G. H. Harlow, 1798.

6   Fireplace Tiles from Old Hall, 'April' and 'June' by William Morris, c. 1862.

7   (top) Arthur Wright, by G. Henry, 1915.
    (bottom) Sir Harold Bailey, by Ronald Way, 1972.

8   Final phase of Cripps Court. Model of winning design by Bland and Brown.

Black and white plates   *Between pp. 302 and 303*

1   Old Court, built 1448 – 9

2   (left) Old Hall in use for May Ball, 1913.
    (right) Old Kitchens, 1912.

3   Old Hall — detail of roof, as repainted by William Morris, 1875.

4   President's Lodge and Long Gallery, c. 1890.

5   President's Lodge and Long Gallery.

6   Interior of Long Gallery.

7   Interior of Old Library.

8   Walnut Tree Court, c. 1855/60.

9A   Essex Building, as originally planned.
 B   Essex Building, as built.

10   Old Chapel, pre 1890.

11   New Chapel, before completion of decoration.

12   River Front, Le Keux, c. 1837.

13   Queens' undergraduates manning trams during General Strike, 1926.

14   Tied Cottages for College Servants on site of present Fisher Building.

15   Fisher Building when new.

16   Planning the Erasmus Building: Rejected design by S. Dykes Bower.
        Original version of design by Sir Basil Spence.

Front Endpaper   Queens' College c. 1687 by David Loggan
Back Endpaper   Queens' College 1986.

Acknowledgements for illustrations

Dust jacket by Leonard Beard.
Colour photographs 1, 3, 4, 5A and B, 7A and B by Christopher Hurst
Colour photograph 2 by British Library.
Colour photograph 8, and model, by Thorp Modelmakers
Black and white photographs 3 and 7 by Wim Swaan
Black and white photograph 8 from Cambridge University Library Collection
Black and white photograph 14 from City Library, Cambridgeshire Collection E.Q.K3.8486
Black and white photographs 2A and 13 from *The Dial*, 1913 and 1926

Abbreviations

AC	J. and J. A. Venn, *Alumni Cantabrigienses*, Part i, Cambridge, 1922 – 7; Part ii, Cambridge, 1940 – 54.
BA	Bachelor of Arts.
BD	Bachelor of Divinity.
CAS	Cambridge Antiquarian Society.
CB	Conclusion Book.
CM	College Minute.
Cooper	C. H. Cooper, *Annals of Cambridge*, Cambridge, 1842 – 1908.
Courier	*Queens' Courier* (college magazine).
CR	*The Cambridge Review.*
CSPD	*Calendar of State Papers (Domestic series)*, London, 1856 – 1972.
CU	Cambridge University.
CUA	Cambridge University Archives.
CU Cal.	*The Cambridge University Calendar.*
CUL	Cambridge University Library.
DD	Doctor of Divinity.
DNB	*Dictionary of National Biography.*
DSB	*Dictionary of Scientific Biography.*
Emden	A. B. Emden, *A Biographical Register of the University of Cambridge to 1500*, Cambridge, 1963.
Fuller, *History*	T. Fuller, *The History of the University of Cambridge* (ed. J. Nichols), London, 1840.
GB	Governing Body minutes.
Gray	J. H. Gray, *The Queens' College of St Margaret & St Bernard in the University of Cambridge*, Cambridge, revised edition, 1926.
JB	Junior bursar/Junior bursar's files.
MA	Master of Arts.
MS(S)	manuscript(s).
MS u/c	unclassified manuscript in room S2C.
OPR	Old Parchment Register.
QC	*Queens' College* (college magazine/record).
QCBC	Queens' College Boat Club.

RCHM	Royal Commission on Historical Monuments, *An Inventory of the Historical Monuments in the City of Cambridge*, London (HMSO), 1959.
Record	*Queens' College Record.*
SBSM	Minutes of the St Bernard Society.
Searle	W. G. Searle, *The History of the Queens' College of St Margaret and St Bernard in the University of Cambridge. 1446 – 1662*, Cambridge, 1867 – 71.
TB	Tutor's Book.
VCH	*Victoria County History.*
W&C	R. Willis and J. W. Clark, *The Architectural History of the University of Cambridge*, Cambridge, 1886.

Preface

In 1983, the governing body of Queens' College agreed to admit a BBC film crew to make a series of documentary programmes about the college. Most of the filming was done during the academic year of 1983 – 4, and ten weekly episodes of 'Queens': A Cambridge College' were broadcast on BBC 2 at the end of 1985. Although the television series inevitably raised the college's public profile, it also, perhaps equally inevitably, produced mixed reactions among its viewers. The programmes appear to have been judged from two main standpoints: first, how much did they benefit the college (this was a consideration which concerned college members, principally); second — and this concerned many outside the college, too — how fairly did they represent college life?

Both of these aspects were considered by the college when it discussed whether or not to allow the cameras in. A governing body committee reported in April 1983 that although the benefits 'cannot be guaranteed', the programmes could stimulate an increase in applications for student places, and provide 'an opportunity maybe to better Cambridge University's standing in the world outside'.[1] A further report in the following month, after a JCR referendum had shown overwhelming student support for the proposal, elaborated upon these two themes.[2] It suggested that the publicity value of the series would be 'medium-term' only, but although 'the overall increase in the number of applications might be transient, the changes in the population groups which apply could be more long-lasting' — in other words, it might encourage applications for places from schools which would not normally think of sending pupils to Oxbridge. It was also felt that the programmes might help to 'demystify' the university: 'by showing that we work within what is (on the whole) a serious-minded and balanced intellectual community, we are better placed to rebut charges of unwarranted privilege and élitism'.[3]

To what extent have these expectations been fulfilled? Those who

[1] CM 760; GB, 18.4.1983.
[2] Of 312 votes cast, 230 supported the proposal, 73 were against, and there were 9 abstentions, CM 769; see also Stop Press, 29.4.1983.
[3] CM 769; GB, 25.5.1983. The report recognised that Queens' could be portrayed in an 'unfair, misleading or harmful way' — especially since it did not have any editorial control over the series — but was confident that the producer would create programmes which would be 'honest as well as entertaining'; this was also stressed in statements to the press.

xi

maintained that any publicity was beneficial are presumably satisfied: the programmes were watched by a large number of people,[4] and generated a considerable press response. The effect on admissions is probably incalculable: applications made in 1986 for admission in 1987 are well down from those of the previous year — significantly further than the general fall in Cambridge applications caused this year by a change in the university's admissions procedure; although there has been a broadening of the range of schools sending applicants. But it is impossible to tell how much of this decline in applications is due to the television programmes.[5]

Most of the criticism of the BBC series came from those who felt that the programmes had not given a balanced or objective picture of college and university life. This was surely unavoidable from the start. The first aim of the film-makers was to create good entertainment for the viewing public, and all aspects of college life do not lend themselves equally well to the medium of television. The series was a 'documentary', but the film seen on television was only a small proportion of the amount shot in Queens' over a long period; the considerable editing which was required reinforced the process of selection.[6] However, the crux of the critics' objections did not concern these largely formal weaknesses: it was that, far from demystifying Cambridge in the way the governing body report of May 1983 had hoped, the series had exploited and reinforced the popular Oxbridge myths and stereotypes.[7]

All this will be of great relevance for future historians of the university, and of Queens'. The BBC television series is in a sense an historical document — and a significant one — but as such it must be treated with caution. It testifies to the hold which the Oxbridge 'myth' exercises over the public's imagination, a mythology which has often been fostered as assiduously by those within the two universities as by those outside. The temptation to embellish or idealise the history of Oxford and Cambridge has been felt by many generations of university men; such a desire probably stems from a strong sense of the universities' importance, and the creation and spread of Oxbridge

---

[4] The episode shown in the week ending 20.10.85 attracted an estimated 4.10 million viewers (figures from the press cuttings cited in note 6).

[5] I am grateful to Andy Phillips, the college's admissions tutor, for this information. Even if the fall in applications has been due to the television series, it is impossible to say why: was it because prospective candidates were unimpressed by the college as it was portrayed, or because they believed that the publicity would attract too many applicants of high quality? One Cambridge senior tutor believed, however, that the series 'must have tarnished the progressive image which the Queens' senior tutor believes his college has', *Times Higher Educational Supplement*, 3.1.1986.

[6] The college has a collection of press cuttings concerning the series, from which these observations are taken. See also *CR* (November 1985), 173–6.

[7] This can be seen from the press cuttings. Stereotyping was also evident in the press commentary on the series; certain newspapers dwelt on those aspects which were felt most likely to touch a responsive chord in their readers.

mythology strengthens that self-important feeling. The same may be said of colleges: it is a trap which the potential college historian should be aware of.

Conventional — one might even say, traditional — college histories have come under attack in recent years; it has been asked if they are not in fact 'an outdated genre'[8] Present day research on the history of Oxford, Cambridge, and their colleges still owes much to the work of dedicated antiquarians, who, from at least the 16th century onwards, gathered documentary evidence of all kinds relating to the history of these institutions; in many cases, the sources from which the antiquarians made their copies have since been lost. The antiquarian tradition endured into the 20th century.[9]

In the 19th century, interest in university and college history flourished, based on and evidently inspired by these antiquarian researches. One of the many expressions of this interest was the publication of a series of histories of all the Oxford and Cambridge colleges around the turn of the century.[10] J. H. Gray's *The Queens' College of St Margaret and St Bernard in the University of Cambridge* appeared in this series in 1899; its early chapters were based extensively upon W. G. Searle's lengthy, essentially antiquarian work, *The History of the Queens' College of St Margaret and St Bernard in the University of Cambridge. 1446 – 1662* of 1867 – 71.[11]

The volumes in the college history series were very much alike: relatively short, usually semi-scholarly, readable narratives. Their range and depth were limited by their restricted length and the need to secure a wide readership among college members and old members, many of whom would have had little time for severe scholarship. This meant of course that, especially in the case of the older colleges, the histories could not hope to do justice to the mass of evidence at their disposal, and one criticism levelled at several of the volumes when they first appeared was that they tended to degenerate into catalogues of names and dates; this was perhaps also a legacy of the antiquarian tradition from which they derived.[12]

There were other, more fundamental, failings in these books. That they embodied many of the prejudices of Victorian historical scholarship

---

[8] Feingold (1981).
[9] Perhaps its last major representative was J. A. Venn, president of Queens', 1931 – 58. The *Alumni Cantabrigienses*, compiled by him and his father, is an invaluable work of reference.
[10] Published by F. E. Robinson of London.
[11] The extent to which this history is also indebted to Searle's work can be seen from the frequency with which it is cited in the following pages.
[12] e.g. the reviews in *CR* (7.3.1901), 226; (4.12.1902), 117; a review of the history of Emmanuel felt the author had 'achieved what some of his fellow authors in the same series have markedly failed in — he has written a really interesting book', *ibid.* (16.3.1905), 262 – 3.

cannot, of course, be held against them, but a contemporary reviewer warned of 'the extravagant panegyrics that are so often mistaken for college patriotism', and a more recent commentator has observed the temptation to 'claim for a college an exaggerated part in the world outside, through the later achievements of its sons' — a method characterised by one historian as the 'pious memorial' approach, which places undue emphasis on the biographies of famous college *alumni*, to the detriment of a broader, more representative study of college society.[13]

Recent critics have also pointed to another danger: that of taking too parochial a view of the college and failing to set it in its context, be it local, social, cultural, intellectual, religious or political.[14] The result of these failings is to produce less a college history than a sophisticated college guide, and many of the traditional college histories have fallen into this trap to some degree.[15] Many histories have been commissioned by the governing bodies of the colleges themselves, and intended primarily for internal consumption rather than for study by professional historians,[16] but there is no intrinsic reason why a college history cannot be both readable and scholarly, as histories of Oxford and Cambridge colleges in the last decade or so have demonstrated.[17]

There is no single 'correct' way to go about writing such a history, for the subject, if treated properly, is not a simple, narrow one, but complex and broad. There are many layers in college society, and many facets of college life, nearly all worthy of serious investigation. The proper emphasis to be placed on each of these features within the history of the college as a whole will be judged differently by different historians according to their understanding and expertise, and — most importantly — to the quantity and quality of the available evidence.[18] To write a truly adequate college history requires a wide range of specialist knowledge, not just of the different aspects of college life, but also of many different historical periods — in the case of Queens', over 500 years. Perhaps a collaborative effort, with several specialist authors, would serve the purpose best.[19] Such a study might also benefit from the different

[13] *ibid*. (4.12.1902), 117; G. Storey in Crawley (1976), ix; Cobban (1975), 122.
[14] Cobban (1969), 2–4; Storey in Crawley (1976), ix.
[15] Feingold (1981), 207.
[16] *ibid*.
[17] Such as Crawley (1976); Green (1979); Buxton and Williams (1979); Brooke (1985). Other histories are on the way.
[18] Both primary and secondary sources, and both evidence directly concerning the college and that concerning the background or context.
[19] This was employed in Buxton and Williams (1979). J. H. Gray noted in the preface to his history of Queens': 'a really adequate History of Queens' College . . . would require an amount of time, and also of knowledge, historical, antiquarian and architectural, which it is wholly out of my power to command', Gray, viii. Every honest college historian must share this sentiment.

methods of investigation pursued by other branches of the social sciences: as a community with clearly definable boundaries, an Oxbridge college, with its distinctive hierarchies, sub-cultures and rituals, would surely make an interesting study for a social anthropologist, and a fascinating piece of evidence for a future college historian.[20]

---

[20] My understanding of anthropological perspectives owes much to several stimulating ideas given to me by Peter Wade; I am sorry not to have been able to expand on some of these here. College archives might not be able to supply sufficient data over long periods of time for that 'very intensive study of daily interactions and everyday thoughts which is the hallmark of social anthropology and micro-social history', MacFarlane (1977), 8, and chapter 1; but a study of a contemporary college would be illuminating.

Acknowledgements

Although its faults are the author's responsibility alone, this book, no less than any other work of historical research, owes much to a large number of collaborators. Many people have given me their advice and assistance on a wide range of matters, great and small, connected with the book. They are: the Rev. H. C. Alexander, the late Mr T. H. Aston, Prof. G. E. Aylmer, Dr J. M. Black, Steven Botterill, Prof. D. W. Bowett, Brendan Bradshaw, Dr B. A. Callingham, Miss D. M. Cannell, Rachel Clifford, Andy Cosh, Prof. J. M. Crook, Eric Davison, Dr J. Diggle, Dr J. H. Dowson, Richard Fentiman, Mr L. Fowler, John Gascoigne, the Rev. J. B. Geyer, Judith Glynn, Dr J. T. Green, Dr W. P. Griffith, Mrs C. Hall, Prof. G. B. Harrison, Allan Hayhurst, Brian Hebblethwaite, David Hoyle, Dr E. S. Leedham-Green, Stephen Lees, Elisabeth and Ken Machin, Clem Macintyre, Tony Mangan, Dr E. A. Maxwell, Mr J. F. Mills, Anne Munro, Bishop Lesslie Newbigin, Dr D. Nicol, Mr A. P. R. Noble, Mr A. E. B. Owen, Dr D. M. Owen, Prof. E. R. Oxburgh, Harry Porter, Dr W. A. Phillips, Dr J. M. Prentis, Jonathan Riley-Smith, Mrs C. Smale-Adams, Dr R. A. Smith, the staffs of the Manuscripts Room and Rare Books Reading Room in the Cambridge University Library, Rex Thorpe, Sarah and Giles Tillotson, Peter Wade, Robin Walker, and Tim Wales. Iain Wright, as one of my two official 'editorial advisers', and as college archivist, has given a great deal of assistance. I am grateful to all of them for their help, and in particular to those who were kind enough to read parts of the book in typescript and suggested a whole host of improvements. The project was funded by Queens' College.

I owe two very special debts of gratitude. It was at Peter Spufford's instigation that the college commissioned this history; he has managed the administration of the project and arranged for its publication; and his editorial comments have been invaluable. Christopher Brooke has been a formidable critic and a constant source of expert advice. Both have been more than generous with their assistance in practical matters; and their encouragement and moral support has been no less valuable.

1

Founders and foundresses (1446 – 85)

Both Henry VI and his queen, Margaret of Anjou, had to send proxies to lay foundation stones at their new colleges in Cambridge. In September 1444 the king's chief minister, the marquis of Suffolk, laid the foundation stone of the first chapel at King's College, 'the aier and the Pestilence' having frightened Henry into staying away.[1] Four years later Margaret, citing only *'diversas causas'* for her absence, despatched her chamberlain, Sir John Wenlock, to lay the foundation stone for her college of St Margaret and St Bernard.[2]

By founding King's College in 1441, Henry VI helped to set in motion a new enthusiasm for collegiate foundations which was not exhausted until the end of the 16th century.[3] King's was a grand design: Henry's ambitious building plans were to be financed to the cost of £1,000 *per annum* (then a considerable sum) from the revenues of the Duchy of Lancaster, and by the time of Henry's deposition in 1461 the college's own income from landholdings in 21 counties also exceeded £1,000 annually.[4] It was to provide for seventy fellows and scholars; ten priests, six clerks and sixteen choristers were to serve the chapel (Queens', in contrast, began life with four fellows and a president, and was permitted to own lands worth £200 *per annum*).[5]

Henry regarded the foundation of King's as 'the prymer notable werk' of his reign, and was closely involved in all that went on.[6] He himself undertook the task of drawing up the college statutes, dismissing an expert committee previously summoned for that purpose (though the finished code owed little to Henry, being slavishly modelled on William of Wykeham's statutes of 1382 for New College, Oxford.[7] He seems to have been obsessed with grandeur. The avowed aims of the foundation — to glorify God and the church, educate the clergy, and fight against

---

[1]   Wolffe (1983), 141 and n. 31; Cooper, i.199. Henry laid the foundation stone of the second (present) chapel of King's in July 1446, Wolffe, *loc. cit.*.
[2]   On 15 April 1448, Searle, 42 – 3. Searle's suggestion that 'plague' kept Margaret away is unproved.
[3]   For a list of collegiate foundations and their dates, see Fowler and Fowler (1984), 11.
[4]   Wolffe (1983), 141 – 2.
[5]   *ibid.*, 140; Searle, 25. In the earliest charter of 1446 the college was only permitted to own lands worth £100 *per annum*, Searle, 14.
[6]   Quoted in Saltmarsh (1972), 4.
[7]   Wolffe (1983), 140, 145.

heresy — were plainly laudable,[8] but his plans for King's underwent several changes, with a much greater emphasis on scale, a resolve to surpass the great works of Wykeham; this was ostentatious piety, regardless of expense.[9] After Edward IV's seizure of the throne in 1461, the college suffered greatly from Henry's failure to provide statutory guarantees of constant funds; he was enthusiastic, but not notably practical.[10]

Henry's queen was, in her own way, just as much an enthusiast as her husband. The example of Margaret's later political career lends some weight to John Bocking's contemporary description of her as a 'grete and stronge labourid woman, for she spareth noo peyne to sue hire things to an intent and conclusion to hir power', and Henry's most recent biographer has characterised her political intervention from 1456, when she took control of the king and royal policy, as 'rash and despotic'.[11] But Margaret's tenacious, often ruthless defence of the Lancastrian cause lay well in the future at the time of her marriage to Henry in 1445: she was then only fifteen years old, high-spirited and impetuous.[12]

These characteristics helped prompt her to request the king in 1447 – 8 that she might be allowed to become the first queen to found a Cambridge college, to be known as 'the Quenes collage of sainte Margarete and saint Bernard, or ellis of sainte Margarete vergine and martir and saint Bernard confessour'.[13] If the 17th century historian Thomas Fuller is to be believed, Margaret was inspired by Henry's designs, and 'restless in herself with holy emulation, until she had produced something of the like nature'.[14] The example of the king's 'mooste noble and glorieus collage roial'[15] was mentioned in her request, but Margaret was particularly inspired by previous foundresses: in the 14th century, the countesses of Clare and Pembroke had each founded colleges,[16] 'the wiche are of grete reputation for good and worshipful clerkis that by grete multitude have be bredde and brought forth in theym'.[17]

Although Margaret wished to found a college, she did not choose to

---

[8]   ibid., 137.
[9]   ibid., 137, 139, 145; Saltmarsh (1972), 7. Eton, the linked foundation (like Winchester with New College) also grew, Wolffe (1983), 140.
[10]   ibid., 144 – 5. The Eton statutes did make adequate provision, ibid.; c.f. Lovatt (1981), 419 – 424, 435 – 444, for Henry's work at Eton.
[11]   Wolffe (1983), 301 – 3.
[12]   ibid., 182; Bagley (1948), 56 – 7.
[13]   Searle, 15. The request must have been made between the dates of issue of the second and third charters, as shown below.
[14]   Fuller, History, 120.
[15]   Searle, 15.
[16]   In 1338 and 1347 respectively, Fowler and Fowler (1984), 11.
[17]   Searle, 16; see also ibid., 47.

create one from nothing, as Henry had done at King's. Instead, she refounded an existing college in her own name. The first foundation charter for a college of St Bernard had been issued by the king in December 1446;[18] a second, refounding it on a different site, was issued in August 1447, when Henry referred to it as *'de fundatione nostra'*;[19] Margaret's almost identical charter followed in March 1448.[20]

Documents such as these charters, together with Margaret's letter of request, help to explain why the king and queen promoted the establishment of the college. The reasons given — 'the extirpation of heresies and errors, the augmentation of the faith, the advantage of the clergy and the stability of the church' — closely resemble those given for the foundation of King's. The new foundation was to train and send forth suitable clergymen to teach the people 'by learning and example alike'.[21] An anonymous manuscript, written perhaps in the 1470s, purports to explain Margaret's motives further, describing the condition of the times: an age in which virtue had declined, popular devotion to God had grown lukewarm, and divine worship was neglected.[22]

The college was said to be established 'for study and prayer', and particular prayers were specified for the well-being of the king and queen during their lives, for their souls after death, and for those of their ancestors.[23] The idea of intercession for the living and the dead was central to medieval pious foundations, and in the late medieval period it became common to provide for masses specially for the souls of the founder and his or her family. Such provisions, known as chantries, often took the form of chapels attached to churches, with chantry priests paid to say the masses; sometimes a whole college of chantry priests might be established.[24] Similar aims can be seen in the foundation of St Catharine's Hall in 1473 by Robert Wodelarke, provost of King's. Here too was a pronounced chantry motive, emphasised even more strongly

[18] *ibid.*, 3.
[19] *ibid.*, 7, 8 – 15.
[20] *ibid.*, 18 – 26. It has been suggested that William Waynflete, bishop of Winchester, founder of Magdalen College Oxford, and an influential figure at court, was also involved in the foundation of Queens', and there are indications in the college's foundation charter that he may have given some advice about its provisions, Mills (unpublished thesis, 1977), 6 – 7, 10. But the argument fails to understand the development of St Bernard's College, or that the real impetus and creative force behind the scheme came from Andrew Doket, for whom see below, pp. 5 – 6.
[21] Searle, 4 (charter of 21 August 1447). For other similar expressions of her aims, see *ibid.*, 10, 15 – 16 (when Margaret refers to the 'conservacion of oure feith and augmentacion of pure clergie'), 46 – 7.
[22] *ibid.*, 45 – 6. This decline was said to have come about recently.
[23] *ibid.*, 8 ('*ad studendum et orandum*').
[24] Myers (1971), 176 – 7. A deed of Edward IV in 1465 required Queens' to pray for his family and ancestors, and those of his queen, Elizabeth, Searle, 70.

than in other collegiate foundations.[25] There was similar stress on the defence and improvement of the church, and recognition of the potent threat of heresy.[26] Cambridge was free of heresy at this time, whereas Oxford was still tainted by its association with John Wyclif (a former Merton don and master of Balliol) and the anti-sacerdotal, anti-authoritarian Lollard movement which he had inspired in the late 14th century;[27] this connection was one reason for Henry's choice of Cambridge as the site for King's.[28]

In supporting the foundation of Queens', Henry and his wife were expressing the orthodox piety of 15th century England. Yet the creation of Oxford and Cambridge colleges was but one means of such expression, and colleges had not hitherto played a major rôle in university life. The University of Cambridge had been founded in 1209 by academic refugees from troubles at Oxford, and it advanced steadily during the 13th century. In 1318 Pope John XXII set the seal on this development by formally recognising Cambridge as a *studium generale* — in other words, confirming its status as a fully-fledged university.[29] Only one college had been founded so far — Peterhouse, in 1284 — but the next forty years saw the first great period of college foundations: a further eight were established between 1324 and 1352.[30] There was only one more new college before the building of King's inaugurated a second wave of foundations and refoundations; like the first series, this reflected the growing repute and well-being of the university, particularly its independence from the control of the bishop of Ely, confirmed in 1430.[31]

Most medieval undergraduates lived in hostels, which were lodging houses of students formally controlled under the authority of the university. They were numerous and had a reputation for rowdiness.[32] There were considerable variations of size and facilities among them, although our knowledge remains sketchy. The simplest were single tenements; larger ones might consist of a group of houses enclosed by a wall. Some had libraries, and two are known to have had chapels.[33]

---

[25] Cobban (1973), 7 – 9.
[26] *ibid.*, 12.
[27] Moorman (1952), 112 – 114. See McFarlane (1972), *passim*, esp. 107 – 168 for Lollardy.
[28] Cobban (1973), 11 – 12; Cobban also sees a concern for the state of society as a whole, *ibid.*, 13.
[29] Roach, 'University of Cambridge', 151 – 4. The 1318 recognition merely set the seal on a status already effectively attained in the 13th century, Cobban (1975), 113.
[30] Roach, 'University of Cambridge', 154; Fowler and Fowler (1984), 11.
[31] Roach, 'University of Cambridge', 155 – 6, 164 – 5; Moorman (1952), 118 – 9; Fowler and Fowler (1984), 11.
[32] Roach, 'University of Cambridge', 160 – 1; Stokes (1924), 39 – 42, 60 – 136.
[33] Stokes (1924), 38 – 9; Aston *et al.* (1980), 15 – 19; Brooke (1985), 24.

They might house up to a hundred students, but tended to be smaller.[34] Although all students were supposed to live in a licensed hostel or hall, many had to live where they could, according to their means.[35] Most of the few colleges then in existence were also small, with limited financial resources. They were designed for a few select graduate students reading for higher degrees, not for undergraduates.[36] This balance did not shift fundamentally until the 16th century, but during the second half of the 15th century changes were set in motion: colleges began to look to fee-paying undergraduates as a useful source of income, and the unendowed, insecure and often turbulent hostels suffered by comparison.[37]

One of the more successful hostels in the mid-15th century, to judge from its physical appearance, was St Bernard's Hostel, which stood close to the site of the present gateway of Corpus Christi, with grounds reaching to St Botolph's churchyard. It possessed extensive buildings, a chapel, a hall and a gallery.[38] In the mid-1440s its principal was Andrew Doket, who also seems to have owned the property, and who subsequently became the first president of Queens'. Nothing is known of the foundation and establishment of St Bernard's Hostel, and there is no mention of it before this time.[39]

Doket's own past is equally obscure. Thomas Fuller believed that he was 'formerly a friar', but there is no evidence of this.[40] He became vicar of St Botolph's in about 1435, and was promoted rector between 1439 and 1444; the living was then in the gift of Corpus Christi, but we do not know if he was a Corpus man.[41] There were another two Dokets at Queens' during the 1480s — one a Fellow — and this, coupled with the rarity of the surname, suggests that they may have been relations, but we know nothing of their origins either.[42] Professor Ross argues that Andrew was related to, or even the brother of, John Doket, who was sent on diplomatic missions by Edward IV, was Richard III's private chaplain, and became provost of King's under Henry VII. John Doket was educated at Eton and King's; he came from Sherborne in Dorset and was a nephew of Thomas Bourchier, archbishop of Canterbury.

[34] Aston *et al.* (1980), 18, where it is tentatively suggested that there were an average of 25 – 30 students living in arts hostels, and an average of 80 in law hostels.
[35] *ibid.*, 19; Cobban (1969), 43.
[36] King's Hall was a significant exception, *ibid.*, 43.
[37] *ibid.*, 49 – 50, 53.
[38] Stokes (1924), 39, 63; Goodman (1922), 31; *W&C*, i.xxii.
[39] Stokes (1924), 63; Searle, 2. See also Doket's will, *ibid.*, 56.
[40] Fuller, *History*, 120; see also Searle, 55. The view was widely accepted in the early 17th century, see Book 87; Parker (1721), 110.
[41] Goodman (1922), 97 – 9.
[42] Emden (Robert, commoner in 1485; William, Fellow 1484 – 8). Only five Dokets are known to have been at Cambridge before 1500, *ibid.*

However, there is only the coincidence of surnames to support this argument.[43]

The king and queen contributed enthusiasm, charters and endowments to Queens' and its predecessor college of St Bernard, but Doket was the creator of the project, and its driving force. In 1574 John Caius wrote that 'his service in building the college and procuring the money was so great that some consider this college to have been the most glorious work of him alone'.[44] Doket was an ambitious and energetic man. Though we do not know if he founded St Bernard's Hostel, he was certainly responsible for altering and enlarging the buildings there.[45] His incumbency at St Botolph's was marked by a substantial programme of building and improvements to the church.[46] Deeds concerning the site of Queens' reveal him to have been a property owner, and he was among those who gave land to Henry VI for King's.[47] The first foundation charter of 1446 was for a college on part of the present site of St Catherine's, but when a larger and better site next to the river became available, Doket was quick to secure this, and petitioned the king for another charter.[48] Two of his parishioners, Richard Andrew and John Morris, were influential in the acquisition of lands for both sites; and a third, the master mason Reginald Ely, was the architect of the earliest buildings at Queens'.[49]

Margaret's foundation charter was confirmed by letters patent in April 1448; work on the buildings began; and the pope gave the scheme his approval.[50] The college was sufficiently endowed, with the prospect of further benefactions. But it still had no statutes by which to regulate its life. Each of the three foundation charters appointed a committee to frame a set of statutes, and the three committees had several members in common. The final committee consisted of seven men, of whom four had served on the previous two committees, and one on the second. Three were, or had been, heads of houses; another subsequently became one. The two leading members were William Booth, bishop of Coventry and Lichfield, and John Somerseth, the king's chancellor, who

---

[43] Ross (1981), 134; Weiss (1967), 165; Emden. It has been suggested that Andrew was the younger son of a Westmorland knight, but the claim is not substantiated, Duckett (1960), 27. A more likely lead comes from the several Dokets and Dogets known to have been living in Suffolk and Norfolk in Henry VI's reign and (in Norfolk) into the 17th century, Rye (1896), 41; Rye (1900), 278, 289, 296, 300, 306.

[44] Quoted in Oswald (1949), 11. This view was echoed by Thomas Fuller in the 17th century, Fuller, *History*, 120.

[45] Oswald (1949), 11, citing *W&C*, i.248, 259.

[46] Goodman (1922), 67, 79.

[47] Searle, 9 (he owned land adjoining the site of Queens'); Cooper, i.192.

[48] Searle, 4 – 6.

[49] Oswald (1949), 12 – 14.

[50] Searle, 26, 27.

had also served on the committee for the King's College statutes.[51] This was an expert committee, and Somerseth's presence shows the crown's continuing interest in the college.

Yet no statutes were issued during Henry VI's reign, although they were needed for the orderly government of the college. The foundation charters established certain basic provisions: the college's title, its corporate status (*'unum corpus in se in re et in nomine'*) with a common seal, its right to own lands and to initiate and defend legal actions. There were to be free elections of new presidents and Fellows, but these would have to be regulated by the still unwritten statutes.[52] We do not know why the committee failed to complete its task; certainly it was one which required time and careful thought. The King's College committee had pleaded that it was *'negotiis et occupationibus impediti'* when explaining its slowness in framing statutes there; the Queens' committee was not pressed by Henry in the same way.[53]

The easiest answer, though unprovable, is to blame the growing political troubles nationally for this inability to see the project through. The early history of Queens' is clearly linked to the power struggle in England during the middle and later years of the 15th century: the Wars of the Roses. Opinions still differ over the extent to which this conflict affected the everyday life of the nation.[54] It can be seen as a short-term dynastic squabble, or as the result of a deeper breakdown in the structure of politics and society, exacerbated by Henry VI's inability to govern.[55] The direct effects of the wars left social, economic and religious life mostly untouched; the armies involved tended to be small, and campaigns were short. Some areas, such as East Anglia, hardly saw any fighting.[56] But war imposed indirect, more widespread, financial burdens, and it had a deep psychological effect, engendering fear, uncertainty and despondency.[57] There was a strong sense of insecurity at both Oxford and Cambridge, shown in the practice of electing non-resident courtiers and royal officials as chancellors, to defend their interests.[58] The colleges connected by foundation with Henry VI's Lancastrian interest were potentially vulnerable after Henry's over-

---

[51] *ibid.*, 32 – 6; Emden. The others were Richard Cawedray, Peter Hirforde, Hugh Damlett, Thomas Boleyn, and William Millington. Hirforde (or Irford) had acted as arbitrator in a dispute between Pembroke Hall and St Thomas's Hostel in 1446.

[52] Searle, 10 – 15.

[53] Mullinger (1873 – 1911), i.306, 315; Searle, 64. 'Men in the Middle Ages were intensely legalistic, and corporate bodies never felt happy until the lives of their members were regulated', J. S. C. Riley-Smith in *Record* (1975); Riley-Smith also speculates that the Wars of the Roses interrupted any plans that might have been laid.

[54] See Gillingham (1981), and Goodman (1981), for the most recent interpretations.

[55] Gillingham (1981), 254 – 7; Goodman (1981), 196 – 226.

[56] Gillingham (1981), 255; Goodman (1981), 208 – 9, 213 – 4.

[57] Goodman (1981), 213, 218 – 220.

[58] Storey (unpublished, 1981/forthcoming).

throw in 1461 and the accession of the Yorkist Edward IV to the throne.

Henry V and Henry VI had been exceptional among English kings for the wide range of their interests in scholarship and theology, and Edward IV was far from uncultured. He was the first English king to assemble a large and permanent royal library, and, in the words of one chronicler, was 'a most loving encourager of wise and learned men'. The royal entourage included men interested in educational questions, and a few who were interested in the classics and contemporary humanist ideas.[59] In these matters, Edward resembled many other European princes of the period, and was representative of the English lay aristocracy: not an intellectual, but certainly literate and educated.[60]

Unlike Henry VI, he was not anxious to be remembered as a patron of learning: his sole significant educational benefaction was the founding of a lectureship in divinity at Oxford, where his wife's brother was chancellor.[61] Though he showed no hostility towards Queens' College, he was harshly vindictive towards Henry's linked foundations of Eton and King's: the former was virtually closed down for a time, and Edward was bent on its abolition; the latter suffered badly from seizure of its estates and revenues by the crown. From 1467 onwards, Edward relented, but we do not know what induced him to change his mind.[62]

Elizabeth Woodville, Edward's queen and the second foundress of Queens' College, was a more mature woman at the time of her marriage to the king than Margaret had been when she married Henry — in fact, she was a widow: her first husband, Sir John Grey, had been killed fighting against the Yorkists at the second battle of St Albans in 1461.[63] Edward married her 'In moste secrete maner' in May 1464. Secrecy was necessary, for he was marrying beneath him; the king's counsellors, when they learned of the marriage, admonished him 'that she was not his match, however good and however fair she might be'.[64] It was definitely a love match, although rumour had it that Edward, who enjoyed a reputation as a womaniser, married her as the only way to obtain her favours.[65] The king's most recent biographer believes her to have been ungenerous, designing and grasping; more relevant perhaps to her involvement with Queens' is her known love of books, and she was a patron of William Caxton.[66]

She was quick to take an interest in the college's affairs. In March 1465 Edward granted it a licence to hold property to the yearly value of £200,

[59] Ross (1974), 264 – 5, 268.
[60] ibid., 267 – 8.
[61] ibid., 270.
[62] ibid., 269 – 70; Ross wonders if his wife persuaded him to change his mind.
[63] Smith (1975), 29.
[64] ibid., 33; Ross (1974), 85, 89.
[65] Ross (1974), 86 – 7.
[66] ibid., 87 – 9; MacGibbon (1938), 208.

thereby confirming the allowance made in Margaret's foundation charter of 1448. In this licence, the college was said to he *'de patronatu Elizabeth regine Anglie'*, and its members were expected to pray for the souls of both the king's and queen's families. Elizabeth is said to have given money at this time, but as with Margaret of Anjou, there is no record of any gift.[67]

Elizabeth had strong Lancastrian connections through her first husband, and she had been one of Margaret's ladies in waiting, but it is fanciful to suggest that sympathy for her former mistress caused her to take an interest in the college.[68] We may assume that she knew of Queens' through Margaret's involvement, and also that on this occasion she was approached by Doket, who hoped to make what he could of an awkward situation. Although Elizabeth was still styling herself as patroness in 1473, two years later she assumed the title of *'vera fundatrix'*, thereby disregarding Margaret's former rôle.[69] At some time the college seal was changed: Margaret's coat of arms was replaced by that of the new queen and the arms of England.[70]

Elizabeth's assumption of the title of foundress was announced in her issue of a set of statutes for 'the consolidating and strengthening' of the society, which was prompted by Doket and compiled with the assistance of unnamed royal councillors. Piety, natural reason and her duties as queen combined to make her 'specially solicitous concerning those matters whereby the safety of souls and the public good are promoted, and poor scholars, desirous of advancing themselves in the knowledge of letters, are assisted in their need'.[71] This explanation contrasts with the more generalised notions, and the more alarmist tone, of Margaret's letter of request in 1447 – 8.

The statutes themselves were straightforward. There were to be a president and twelve Fellows (which indicated that the college had grown since the first foundation), and arrangements were made for the regular organisation of college life.[72] Most notably, the statutes reflect

---

[67] Searle, 62, 70, 71.
[68] MacGibbon (1938), 15. Mullinger does suggest such sympathy, Mullinger (1873 – 1911), i.316.
[69] Searle, 82, 84. The view that Elizabeth claimed to be foundress 'by right of succession', which is frequently repeated in the literature, is not based on her own words, but on the manuscript account from the 1470s cited above (Searle, 71 – 2); she referred to herself as *'vera fundatrix'* without any qualification.
[70] L. Galley in *Dial* (Michaelmas 1921), 1 – 4; P. R. N. Fifoot in *ibid.*, (Easter 1948), 50 – 3. Both Galley and Fifoot believe that the new seal was issued in 1465, but there is no evidence for this.
[71] Book 79, f.2; printed in Mullinger (1873 – 1911), i.316.
[72] Book 79, fos.2 – 2v, and *passim* to f.12v for the 1475 statutes; Mullinger (1873 – 1911), i.316. Earlier charters had provided for an increase in the number of Fellows according to the college's means, Searle, 7 – 15. The statutes are discussed in more detail below, chapters 5 – 7.

continuing concern for the well-being of the church and the quality of the clergy, in that Fellows were encouraged to study theology, and discouraged from studying law: the latter was forbidden until three years after taking the MA degree, and then only with the consent of the president and a majority of the Fellows.[73] Such a reaction against the legalist outlook of the church — most bishops of the time had been trained in law rather than theology — is echoed in other 15th century foundations. The number of scholars permitted to study law at King's was limited to six (out of seventy); and the statutes of St Catherine's, issued in the same year as those of Queens', imposed an extremely restrictive scheme of study upon the Fellows, effectively prohibiting any serious study of either law or medicine. Bishop Stanley's statutes for Jesus College in 1514 – 15 required that four of the five foundation Fellows should study theology.[74]

By 1475, therefore, the college was securely established. Doket had, in Fuller's words, 'with no sordid but prudential compliance, so poised himself in those dangerous times betwixt the successive kings of Lancaster and York, that he procured the favour of both'.[75] The college insured itself further by procuring two general pardons from Edward IV in 1470 and 1473 (Edward was deposed briefly in 1470 – 1). In 1473 the king ordered the barons of the exchequer to respect these pardons and not to trouble the college; and when the second pardon was lost, a copy was issued at the college's request in 1480.[76] Clearly, these documents afforded some security.

Edward died in April 1483, and his brother's seizure of the throne as Richard III in the summer of that year inaugurated a further two years of civil war. This was brought to a close by Richard's death at the battle of Bosworth in August 1485, and the subsequent accession of Henry VII. In theory, the events of 1483 threatened the college's standing: its foundress and patroness had been displaced from her position of authority, and Richard's supporters argued that her marriage to Edward had been invalid, because he was already engaged to another woman at the time.[77]

In practice, Richard proved to be a more enthusiastic supporter of the college than his brother. He was interested in educational matters, and enjoyed the company of scholars, being particularly associated with a group of Cambridge-educated humanists, some of whom he pro-

---

[73] Book 79, fos.5v – 6; Mullinger (1873 – 1911), i.316 – 7.
[74] Cobban (1973), 14, 17; Mullinger (1873 – 1911), i.308; Gray and Brittain (1979), 24. Doket may have been a friend of Wodelarke, Cobban (1973), 16. The study of theology had also been encouraged in 13th and 14th century foundations, Brooke (1985), 12, 19, 30 – 33; Fowler and Fowler (1984), 12.
[75] Fuller, *History*, 120.
[76] Searle, 78 – 9; *Calendar of the Patent Rolls* (1476 – 85), 220.
[77] Ross (1981), 88 – 9.

moted.[78] He had already a fine record of religious foundations and benefactions to his name, and in 1477, as duke of Gloucester, had founded four fellowships at Queens'.[79] As Richard III, he was free of Edward's vindictiveness towards Henry VI's foundations: King's received a series of cash presents to resume the building programme which had come to a halt in the previous reign, and in 1484 the university thanked him publicly for his generosity towards that college, and the 'many benefits' he had conferred on them in general; he, and the queen, were also thanked for their considerable benefactions to Queens'.[80]

In March 1484, he granted a licence to the college to hold property to the annual value of £466, more than double the previous limit.[81] This paved the way for a huge grant of lands and rents in five different counties, four months later; some of this property was given by his queen, Anne.[82] Queens' did not enjoy the benefits of this generosity for long, but the annual value of the gift amounted to £265, a considerable increase in the college's income.[83] After Richard's overthrow in 1485, and despite college lobbying in London, parliament returned some of the lands to the earl of Oxford, whose mother claimed to have made them over to Richard when he was duke of Gloucester 'in Salvacion of her Lyfe'.[84] Three years later, parliament annulled the act of Edward IV which had enabled Anne to possess the other properties given to Queens', and these were restored to the countess of Warwick.[85]

The manner in which Richard's benefactions had been made also demonstrated the extent of his support for the college. The grant of July 1484 not only acknowledged Queen Anne's concern for the college, but made plain that Queens' was *'de fundatione et patronatu prefate consortis nostre'*, thereby assuming at once two positions which Elizabeth had delayed for ten years before combining.[86] Richard also intended to give the college new statutes, or amended statutes to regulate his new endowment, but his reign was too short and troubled for anything to come of this; nor would it have made the properties proof against Henry VII's act of resumption.[87]

Henry at least bore the college no ill will for its Yorkist assocations, but

[78] *ibid.*, 132 – 4.
[79] *ibid.*, 129, 135; Searle, 87 – 8.
[80] Ross (1981), 135 – 6; Cooper, i.228 – 9.
[81] Searle, 95 – 7.
[82] *ibid.*, 97 – 9, 100. A university decree of 16 March 1484 also thanked Anne for having 'augmented and endowed' Queens' with 'great rents', Cooper, i.228 – 9; yet the grant itself was not until July 1484, Searle, 100 – 1.
[83] Searle, 110 – 11; Book 1, f.1.
[84] Searle, 114, 118.
[85] *ibid.*, 117. The countess of Warwick was Anne's mother; the full story is in *ibid.*, 100.
[86] *ibid.*, 97 – 8.
[87] *ibid.*, 111.

he was largely indifferent towards its welfare, despite being an educated man with some interest in books. His wife, Elizabeth of York, was apparently well liked, and contemporaries remarked on her humanity and charity, but she did not become the college's patroness as the three queens who preceded her had done, and she had almost no contact with it up to her death in 1503.[88] A few years later, royal interest in Queens' was resumed by the king's mother, Lady Margaret Beaufort, but it was to be of a different kind.[89]

[88] Chrimes (1972), 302, 307; Searle, 124.
[89] Below, chapter 2.

2

Renaissance men (the early 16th century)

John Fisher was elected chancellor of the university of Cambridge in 1504, and held that office for almost thirty years. Fisher's chancellorship is said to have 'marked the spring of Renaissance Cambridge, no less surely than it witnessed the Indian summer of the medieval university'.[1] The study of early 16th century Cambridge is easily dominated by the theme of Renaissance humanism, seen as a clearing of the decks before the storm of the Reformation. The story of Cambridge humanism itself is dominated in turn by two men, Desiderius Erasmus and John Fisher, both of whom were connected with Queens'. Such preoccupation with individuals, and with what was then avant-garde intellectualism is an excessively narrow approach to university history; moreover, both Fisher and Erasmus have often been given a prominence in the history of the college which is quite out of proportion to their real influence.

Humanism

The word 'humanism' denotes a particular intellectual movement which reached England from the continent in the mid-15th century, and became well known during the 16th. It is sometimes called 'Renaissance humanism' to distinguish it from the word's broader modern meanings. Contemporaries generally referred to humanism as the 'new learning'; the term 'humanist', originating from student slang, was used to describe a professional teacher of the humanities, or *studia humanitatis*. These consisted of grammar, rhetoric, poetry, history, and moral philosophy, taught in order to train students to speak and write well, especially in Latin.[2] Although it took many forms, the distinguishing marks of humanism were its stress on classical literature, both Greek and Latin, and the consequent urge to step beyond the confines of traditional scholastic teaching — 'an interest in the ancients (especially the Greeks) and in philological soundness, a concern to study the sources of the faith in human fashion, a revulsion against the methods and views of the prevalent thinkers of the schools'.[3]

[1] Lamb (1838), lxvii; Porter (1958), 6 – 7.
[2] Quoted in Jardine (1975), 17.
[3] Elton (1977), 12 – 13.

13

Although there was a growing interest in the classics in 15th century England and a 'slow maturing of change in institutions and attitudes', this involved only a small number of people.[4] Oxford was more advanced than Cambridge in this respect, thanks to the patronage of Duke Humphrey of Gloucester, and by the middle of the century there are signs of an interest in the new ideas emerging from Italy; Cambridge patrons were more concerned with the foundation of new colleges than with new intellectual movements.[5] Two Italians are known to have held university posts at Cambridge in the late 15th century: one was specifically concerned with improving the standard of written Latin — a decidedly humanist concern — and the other wrote a popular book on rhetoric which displayed a modern outlook. John Doket, who was appointed provost of King's in 1499, was a leading early English humanist.[6] But these men represented a limited and largely superficial movement which was unlikely to broaden and deepen unless supported by the establishment of lectureships in humanist areas of study.[7]

Humanism put down roots in Cambridge in the early 16th century principally through the foundations of Lady Margaret Beaufort, Henry VII's mother, and the work of John Fisher, who was closely involved in establishing her benefactions; he had become her chaplain and confessor in the late 1490s. Lady Margaret was deeply pious, and Fisher deflected her desire to endow religious institutions away from the monasteries and towards the university.[8] There was more to this patronage than enthusiasm for new intellectual theories, for the growth of English humanism was also connected with contemporary concern about the quality of the nation's clergy. By the 16th century it was increasingly recognised that it was not enough to endow new colleges and encourage the study of theology against that of law, and that there was a need to improve the quality of the education which was provided. In 1510 William Melton, a former master of Michaelhouse (where he had taught Fisher in the 1480s) published a book on clerical education, the *Sermo Exhortatorius*, stressing that most priests had an inadequate grasp of Latin.[9]

Crucial to the development of Cambridge humanism were the foundations of Christ's (1505) and St John's (1511) colleges by Lady Margaret and Fisher. These were innovative in seeking reform through the 'infusion' of new learning into clerical studies, particularly at St John's, where Fisher's revisions of the statutes show a growing

[4] Simon (1967), 57.
[5] Weiss (1967), 160.
[6] *ibid.*, 162 – 5. For John Doket, see above, p. 5.
[7] Weiss (1967), 167, 182 – 3.
[8] Simon (1967), 81.
[9] Dickens (1967), 72 – 3.

14

humanist influence.[10] In 1503 Lady Margaret had founded lectureships in divinity at Oxford and Cambridge, in an attempt to improve the quality of religious instruction, and in the following year she endowed a post of university preacher at Cambridge; the first man known to have held the preacher's post was John Fawne, a Fellow of Queens'.[11] By 1520 both universities had public lectureships in Greek and mathematics.[12]

Although such foundations demonstrate that humanism had the support of influential patrons, it is difficult to discover how much effect the movement had on university life and thought in general. Formal records are of little help, being concerned with property and privileges.[13] Those statutory changes which affected teaching in the 16th century were made mainly to suit religious policy, not to alter educational methods.[14] College statutes did establish college lectureships here and there in humanist fields, and a tutorial system began to evolve outside the formal system of university teaching, but whilst this offered opportunities for more flexible schemes of study, we do not know how many benefited from such opportunities; tutors were not necessarily humanists.[15] On the other hand, the endowment of lectureships associated with the new learning — a movement which culminated in the creation of the five Regius professorships in 1540 — offered considerable opportunities for those interested in humanism, even if such lectureships were not always as successful as their founders hoped.[16] There was a 'closely knit community of interest' behind the establishment of humanism in the early 16th century, and a considerable interchange of students between the two English universities and those on the continent.[17]

Some of the most telling evidence for the impact of humanism comes from inventories of books. College libraries tended to be conservative buyers — insofar as they bought at all, depending mostly on donations — preferring to acquire standard texts rather than to follow the latest trends; given the high cost of books, this is not surprising. Booksellers' lists and inventories of private libraries are a more reliable pointer to contemporary tastes. The former show a wider, and more modern range of reading than the college libraries;[18] the latter, which in Cambridge

---

[10] McConica (1968), 78 – 80. The Christ's statutes are discussed in Rackham (1959), 430 – 1. See also Surtz (1967), 137 – 8, 183 – 8.
[11] McConica (1968), 78 – 9 (who also notes the preaching function of the divinity lectureships); Roach, 'University of Cambridge', 166 – 7; Underwood (1982), 71 (Underwood shows that Fawne was a protégé of Lady Margaret).
[12] McConica (1968), 84; see below, pp. 21, 99 – 100.
[13] McConica (1968), 77.
[14] Charlton (1965), 141.
[15] ibid., 144 – 8.
[16] ibid., 141 – 2 (in divinity, Greek, Hebrew, civil law, medicine).
[17] McConica (1968), 85 – 6.
[18] ibid., 88 – 9 (evidence from Oxford).

have survived in large numbers, show a decisive emphasis in favour of books associated with humanism: classical texts, works by modern humanist authors, and Greek grammars, for example.[19] Erasmus seems to have been an extremely popular author.[20] It is clear from this that both universities were strongly influenced by humanism, at least in an informal manner, during the period after 1530,[21] under the influence of these new foundations and endowments. As will be seen, Queens' may have been precociously humanist.[22]

John Fisher

'Renaissance Cambridge' was not a brand new institution: it was an old establishment with humanist features grafted onto it.[23] The collegiate movement which flourished at this time had recommenced in the middle of the preceding century. There were new foundations, but also refoundations which reshaped existing materials. The men responsible for the introduction of humanism into Cambridge were products of the 15th century university.

John Fisher was one such man. He arrived as an undergraduate at Michaelhouse in the 1480s and his subsequent career was that of a successful don: Fellow of Michaelhouse in 1491, senior proctor in 1494, master of Michaelhouse from 1494 – 8, vice-chancellor 1501 – 4, president of Queens' 1505 – 8, and chancellor 1504 – 33.[24] In 1504 he was also appointed bishop of Rochester, but he rose no further in the ecclesiastical hierarchy; although Rochester was a poor diocese, he chose to remain there, and it has even been argued that he resisted promotion to more prestigious sees.[25] He was nonetheless influential as a scholar and patron of scholars, as chancellor of Cambridge, and as a religious reformer and controversialist.[26] He was an important figure in Cambridge for some forty years.[27] He was re-elected chancellor every year from 1504 until, in 1514, he suggested to the university that it should attach itself to the rising fortunes of the bishop of Lincoln, Thomas Wolsey. When Wolsey unaccountably declined the offer, Fisher

---

[19] Jardine (1975), 16 – 17; Smith (1974), *passim*; see also below, p. 99.
[20] Jardine (1975), 16 – 17; McConica (1968), 88 – 9.
[21] McConica (1968), 92, 104; Jardine (1975) surveys 150 booklists from c. 1535 – 1590.
[22] Below, pp. 99 – 100.
[23] Such a combination of old and new was characteristic of the religious life of Tudor England, Porter (1958), 6 – 7.
[24] Surtz (1967), 181; Emden.
[25] Reynolds (1972), 25, 28.
[26] In the last rôle Fisher was more famous in Europe than Thomas More, Surtz (1967), v.
[27] According to Porter, 'perhaps at no other time has the university owed so much, for so long, to one man', Porter (1958), 3.

was elected chancellor for life, a unique honour at that time.[28]

As has been shown, some of his major achievements in Cambridge were in conjunction with Lady Margaret Beaufort, and in 1529 the university recognised these achievements by declaring him a founder and promising an annual requiem after his death. Fisher's modest reply that he had merely been Lady Margaret's servant understated the extent of his own contribution in directing her pious inclinations, and the considerable efforts required in implementing her projects. He was well equipped for this, having great experience of university administration; he was a prudent, sensible man with great business ability.[29]

He worked hard, supervising the creation of the new colleges, securing royal support and approval from Henry VII, fighting doggedly with Henry VIII over Lady Margaret's legacy to St John's, rewriting college statutes and attracting the interest of fellow humanists such as Erasmus and Thomas More.[30] The results were plain: new colleges and lectureships, the firm establishment of humanism as a powerful intellectual force, and the general revival of the university's prestige. The dominance of the episcopal bench by Oxford men was ended: during Henry VIII's reign, every see was held by a Cambridge man at one time or another.[31]

Fisher's humanist reforms were inseparable from his pastoral enthusiasms. In 1502, as vice-chancellor, he procured a papal bull enabling the university to appoint twelve preachers annually to any part of the kingdom; two years later Lady Margaret endowed a university preacher; her lecturer in divinity was expected to preach; and the statutes of St John's required one quarter of the Fellows to deliver sermons in English at least eight times a year.[32] These were an extension of the concerns expressed in the terms of the 15th century college foundations, and in many ways the new creations were evolutionary developments of earlier forms. Humanism was not a static imprint: it operated within an established and changing social framework, and was itself evolving and subject to change. The statutes of St John's were revised twice by Fisher, expanding and improving the humanist programme and taking into account similar programmes for new Oxford foundations. The final version shows elements of renewed conservatism: a greater emphasis on depth rather than breadth of study, possibly a recognition that humanism still needed the rigour of scholastic

---

[28] Reynolds (1972), 44; see also Cooper, i.296.
[29] Surtz (1967), 181, 191 – 2; Porter (1958), 6.
[30] More became High Steward of Cambridge in 1515, Surtz (1967), 4, 182 – 3; Scarisbrick (1971), 664 – 5.
[31] Surtz (1967), 180.
[32] ibid., 56 – 7; Reynolds (1972), 16 – 17.

training.[33] The *Life* of Fisher written in the late 1560s or early 1570s speaks of him 'endeavouring himself by all the means he could to reduce the University to their ancient rules and statutes, which began even then to grow out of frame', an obvious reaction to the heretical Lutheran ideas coming out of Germany at that time, which were later to exert a great influence on the university.[34]

But for his involvement with Lady Margaret's works, Fisher would have had no connection with Queens'. His appointment as bishop of Rochester in 1504 took him away from Cambridge, and it was considered acceptable for chancellors to be non-resident by that time. He became president of Queens' because he needed a base from which to supervise the building and establishment of Christ's College; when that had been accomplished, he resigned. His commitment to Queens' was largely a token one.

In 1505 Thomas Wilkinson, Doket's successor since 1484, resigned the presidency of Queens'; his reasons for doing so are unknown, but Lady Margaret seems to have been instrumental in the decision.[35] The anonymous author of the *Life* believed that the Fellows elected Fisher 'respecting the present necessity of this good prelate and considering his continual diligence and care for the whole state of the University'; the first reason given indicates Fisher's desire for a Cambridge base.[36] He had already been recommended to the Fellows by Wilkinson, acting under Lady Margaret's instructions.[37] 'And so at times convenient' he would appear in Queens' to check on the progress at Christ's.[38] He was also present for the royal visits of Henry VII and Lady Margaret to Cambridge in 1505 and 1506, visits which demonstrated royal interest in the university and which must have greatly enhanced Fisher's prestige.[39] But for most of the time, he remained in his diocese, and it was sometimes necessary for the Fellows to send one of their number to Rochester to consult him.[40] His letter of resignation in 1508 (sent from Rochester with one of the Fellows) offered non-residence as the reason for his decision, and he remained adamant despite the Fellows' protestation that they did not regard this as a difficulty.[41] Yet a major

---

[33] Surtz (1967), 186. The Oxford foundations were Corpus Christi and Cardinal (later refounded as Christ Church) colleges.
[34] Hughes (1935), 8 – 9, 40 – 1; see also Surtz (1967), 188, for the reaction to this threat as shown in the St John's statutes of 1530.
[35] Searle, 125 – 6.
[36] Hughes (1935), 47.
[37] Searle, 126.
[38] Hughes (1935), 47.
[39] Reynolds (1972), 34 – 5; Searle, 133 – 6.
[40] e.g. Searle, 133.
[41] *ibid.*, 137 – 8; Gray, 51 – 2.

reason must have been that the work at Christ's had by then been completed. Robert Bekynsaw, another protégé of Lady Margaret, was elected president on Fisher's recommendation.[42]

Lady Margaret may have assumed the rôle of *de facto* patroness of Queens' after the death of Elizabeth of York in 1503, and she was influential in procuring one major benefaction for the college.[43] But apart from this, she took no marked interest in Queens', saving her own benefactions for Christ's and St John's; nor was Fisher a benefactor, though he kept up contacts with the college.[44] Erasmus, writing many years later, referred to Fisher as having set up three colleges, 'out of which could proceed theologians not so much fitted for battles of words as equipped for the sober preaching of the Word of God'.[45] Two of these were Christ's and St John's; Erasmus may have elevated Queens' to be a third because of his own presence there. The *Life* claims that Fisher was prevented from building a third college by 'the iniquity of the time that shortly after followed', but this is based on a misreading of Erasmus.[46] The third college remains mysterious, therefore, but it is clear that Fisher did not attempt to introduce any major reforms at Queens', in contrast with his involvement elsewhere in the university. He was responsible, however, for introducing to the college the greatest humanist scholar of the age.

Erasmus

In 1908 P. S. Allen, the editor of Erasmus' complete correspondence, visited Queens' and reported that 'the most grotesque traditions were afoot, even among the servitors. The butler showed us Erasmus' corkscrew'.[47] Although this tradition has expired there are many others,

---

[42] Searle, 139–40; Bekynsaw was Lady Margaret's almoner.
[43] The duke of Buckingham gave 31 acres of land in Essex to Queens' in 1505, *ibid.*, 133; Underwood (1982), 74–5.
[44] Searle, 142.
[45] Porter and Thomson (1963), 188, and see *ibid.*, 189.
[46] Hughes (1935), 55.
[47] Porter and Thomson (1963), 36 n. 101. There is no record of this tradition before the 19th century. A visitor to the president's lodge in 1814 was told by the president, Isaac Milner, that 'We have no relique of him [Erasmus] at Queen's except a huge corkscrew, and I am afraid that there was nothing in his principles to keep him from making very assiduous use of it', Milner (1842), 596 and n. Another visitor to Queens' at about that time described the corkscrew as 'about a third of a yard long', Pearson (1817), ii.343. The early 19th century historian of the university, George Dyer, dismissed the story that it had belonged to Erasmus as 'an idle conceit', Dyer (1814), ii.161. It is not clear what became of the corkscrew.

equally apocryphal, concerning him.[48] In part this is due to his great fame: he was known throughout Europe; the new learning went hand in hand with his ideas; his critique of the established church was enormously influential; by the 1520s he was 'part of the accepted order', admired by kings.[49] That Queens' should have appropriated him as one of its great *alumni* is understandable, yet his contacts with the college were relatively limited, and are now almost intangible. There are no references in the college archives to his stay; the little that we know is derived from his own letters.

He was, it must be conceded, a man of 'harmless vanity', who 'loved his comforts dearly',[50] and Cambridge did not minister to these indulgences as much as he would have liked — certainly not to the latter; some of his complaints, particularly his criticism of English ale, have become famous.[51] Cambridge was a temporary port of call on his travels, which were extensive by contemporary standards. He belonged to no country: although he hailed from the Netherlands, he lived in France, England and Italy before settling down, more or less, at Basle.[52] He visited England several times between 1499 and 1517, staying at Oxford and London, as well as Cambridge.[53]

His personal contacts with Cambridge are known to date back to the late 1490s, when he was studying in Paris. In 1497 he was living at the English hall of residence there, as was Robert Fisher, a relation (perhaps brother) of John. The following year saw him in private lodgings, where he took as a pupil William Blount, Lord Mountjoy, who was accompanied by a Fellow of Queens', Richard Whitford.[54] In 1499, Erasmus spent six months in England. He did not visit Cambridge, but observed that it was 'marvellous how widespread and how abundant is the harvest of ancient learning which is flourishing in this country'.[55]

He returned in 1505; in the following year, when Henry VII and Lady

---

[48] He did not live at the top of the turret known as 'Erasmus' tower', although this story was in circulation as early as the 17th century; his rooms were apparently below that, on the same staircase (the present-day 'I' staircase), see Searle, 153 – 6. Gray is emphatic that he occupied rooms just below the turret, but supplies no evidence for this, Gray, 44 – 5. Wordsworth reproduced this unattributed comment in his study of 18th century social life at Cambridge: 'When Erasmus was at Queens' his servitor's rooms were close above his own. He was wholly at his master's command, and sometimes at his mistress's', Wordsworth (1874), 105. The college still has 'Erasmus' chair', Porter and Thomson (1963), 36 n. 101.
[49] Chadwick (1972), 31 – 3.
[50] *ibid.*, 31.
[51] As raw, small and windy, Fuller, *History*, 131; Fuller noted that 'In my time [the early 17th century] . . . scholars continued Erasmus' complaint; whilst the brewers, (having, it seems, prescription on their side for long time) little amended it'.
[52] Chadwick (1972), 31.
[53] Caspari (1968), 46 – 50.
[54] Porter and Thomson (1963), 24; Emden ('Whitford').
[55] Caspari (1968), 46, 49.

Margaret visited Cambridge, Fisher seems to have invited him to be present at the event, and he may therefore have stayed in Queens' as Fisher's guest. He applied to the university for permission to 'commence'[56] doctor of divinity (he already had a bachelor's degree in divinity from the university of Paris), but before he could perform the necessary academic exercises, he was offered the opportunity to visit Italy, which he had wanted to do for a long time, and he remained there between 1506 and 1509.[57]

Erasmus was always looking for new and better opportunities for self-advancement, to which his many travels bear witness, and his subsequent long stay at Cambridge in the years 1511 – 14 should be seen in this context. He returned to England in 1509 in the hope of patronage from the new king, Henry VIII, whose learning and artistic accomplishments encouraged the hopes of humanists; moreover, William Warham, the archbishop of Canterbury had invited him to come, so that he could justifiably look forward to the future.[58] When he left England in 1514, it was because he had failed to secure the kind of patronage and position that he sought, and the letters from his years at Cambridge betray the frustration of his ambitions.[59]

Humanist learning lay at the heart of Erasmus' ideas for the spiritual regeneration of European civilisation, and he placed great stress on education as a teacher of reason and morality.[60] His appointment to lecture on Greek at Cambridge, which was almost certainly arranged by Fisher, marked an important advance, as the university had never before had a Greek lecturer. Yet it was also clear by that time (1511) that his other prospects were slow in being realised, and it is not surprising that his reflections on Cambridge should be subject to variable moods. He preferred London and returned there whenever he could: some of his closest friends, such as John Colet and Thomas More, lived in London.[61]

His early letters from Cambridge indicate a lack of enthusiasm for his changed circumstances. Things began badly: the journey from London was beset with various misfortunes and inconveniences, and Erasmus was gloomy about his poor financial position.[62] He was taken ill shortly after arriving, which delayed his opening lectures, and he took an

---

[56] i.e. to perform the necessary exercises or examinations; for the degree-taking procedure, see below, p. 98.
[57] Porter and Thomson (1963), 24 – 5; Allen (1906), i.590 – 1; Caspari (1968), 49.
[58] Caspari (1968), 49 – 50; Elton (1977), 17. Thomas More had introduced Erasmus to the future king when Henry was eight years old, and Erasmus had been much impressed by him, Scarisbrick (1971), 30.
[59] Caspari (1968), 50.
[60] ibid., 54 – 9; McConica (1968), 29 – 52.
[61] Porter and Thomson (1963), 8 – 9.
[62] ibid., 107.

instant dislike to the local ale and wines. He wrote that 'I expect I shall stay at this college for several days anyway', which does not suggest much enthusiasm for Queens'.[63] Other early letters from the autumn and winter of 1511 continue in this tone: Erasmus complained of poverty, and of the cold weather.[64] He planned to go to Rome in 1512, but the scheme came to nothing.[65] However, he did spend a good deal of time in London, and for a brief while in 1513 was exiled to Landbeach by an outbreak of 'plague' in Cambridge.[66] In December of that year he was back in the university, complaining that he could not leave: 'We're shut in by the plague and beset by highway robberies'.[67] The previous month had seen the collapse of another plan to go abroad, and he was bitter about broken promises of support.[68] He waxed indignant about the shortage of good copyists: 'What a University! No one can be found who will write even moderately well at any price'.[69] Nor did the townspeople escape his censure: 'Cambridge townsmen go beyond the inhospitable Britons, who have malice joined to their clownishness'.[70] It seems that he was discouraged even by his work. The only reference to his Greek lectures was in October 1511, shortly after he had begun teaching, and then he merely recorded that 'the audience is small'. The same letter noted that 'Perhaps also I will undertake lecturing in theology, for that's under discussion at present. The stipend is too small to tempt me' (in fact, he did lecture in theology).[71]

Erasmus' frequent references to his poverty whilst in Cambridge are something of an affectation, for it has been calculated that he was quite well rewarded at this time, with substantial stipends from his two lectureships, an annual pension from a Kent benefice (secured for him by Archbishop Warham), regular payments from patrons such as Warham and Erasmus' former pupil Lord Mountjoy, and irregular gifts from friends and supporters such as Fisher.[72] However, it seems that he usually managed to spend more than his income, whatever it might be.[73] Although in many of his letters there is a sense that his complaints are not wholly serious — a whimsical self-indulgence — underlying this is a real sense of dissatisfaction and disillusion.

His regular complaints about his health are more excusable. He was

---

[63] *ibid.*, 108.
[64] *ibid.*, 109, 121, 123, 126, 129.
[65] *ibid.*, 142.
[66] *ibid.*, 141, 143, 151 – 2, 159.
[67] *ibid.*, 174.
[68] *ibid.*, 166 – 7.
[69] *ibid.*, 136.
[70] Quoted by Fuller, *History*, 132.
[71] Porter and Thomson (1963), 38.
[72] *ibid.*, 69 – 71; Caspari (1968), 50.
[73] Porter and Thomson (1963), 68 – 9, 71.

seriously ill shortly after arriving in Cambridge, and he suffered badly from gallstones; fortunately the best treatment for this condition was to drink wine, 'and only selected wine'.[74] He used to ride about the town for exercise.[75] The austerity of college life and the cold of the English winter were not to his liking; his distaste for the former had been established long before he came to England.[76] It is possible that he may have moved out of Queens' into lodgings in the town for a time.[77]

His attitudes towards the university were not wholly negative. He made friends there, although not perhaps as many as in London; four of his closest Cambridge friends were Fellows of Queens'.[78] Fisher was particularly close, and a major reason for Erasmus' decision to come to Cambridge had been that he was inspired and encouraged by the reforms that Fisher and Lady Margaret were introducing at that time, especially the establishment of new colleges, 'in which the things to be taught are not those which fit men for sophistical contests, making them dull and witless in serious matters, but studies such that from them they may proceed forth well versed in true learning and sober discussion, men who can preach the word of God in a serious and evangelical spirit, commending it to the minds of learned men by well-nigh irresistible eloquence'.[79] This was written in 1529, and other observations on Cambridge made by him after his departure echo this spirit of optimism for the improved educational methods there. The university was flourishing; it was 'a changed place', and Erasmus was anxious to champion it in Europe.[80] He was equally enthusiastic in retrospect about the Cambridge colleges, 'in which there's so much religion and so marked a sobriety in living that you'd despise every form of religious regime in comparison if you saw it'.[81] All this is in marked contrast to the letters written during his stay there, and Mullinger's final, emotive impression of Erasmus during his last days in Cambridge is of 'a solitary, isolated scholar, prematurely old with anxiety and toil, weighed down by physical suffering, dejected by disappointment, and oppressed with debt'.[82] He made three more visits to England between 1515 and 1517, but did not return to Cambridge. In 1516 he planned to go there, but on hearing that Fisher was returning from Cambridge to London, he waited in the capital for him. His attachment to Cambridge

[74] ibid., 78, 108, 182.
[75] ibid., 27.
[76] ibid., 29 – 32.
[77] ibid., 29.
[78] ibid., 35 (John Fawne, John Vaughan, Humphrey Walkden, Henry Bullock; for these men, see also below, pp. 24, 26, 99 – 100).
[79] Porter and Thomson (1963), 189, and see 188.
[80] ibid., 195, 199.
[81] ibid., 183.
[82] Mullinger (1873 – 1911), i.506.

was almost exclusively to a small number of friends of humanist inclinations there: Queens' can have been no more than a *pied-à-terre* for him.[83]

Yet his personal influence on the intellectual development of members of the college was perhaps substantial. A particularly close friend was Henry Bullock, a Fellow of Queens', who helped Erasmus with some of his work there, and became a leading exponent of his religious thought and a prominent Erasmian humanist and philologist. He was involved with the establishment of a printing press at Cambridge in 1521, and owned a fine collection of humanist books which Queens' bought after his death.[84] The library of a later Fellow, William Framlingham (1530 – 7) has been said to show 'the humanist revival come of age at Cambridge', containing mostly books by foreign authors, and many classical works.[85] The humanist tradition lived on in Queens', therefore, and to some extent this was clearly Erasmus' doing; but it is difficult to define the exact links in any intellectual lineage, and the 'humanist revolution' was not the exclusive property of any one Cambridge college or group of scholars.[86] Moreover, it is easy to confuse cause and effect: there were humanists at Queens' before Erasmus, whose presence may have been a further encouragement to him to go there, and these men must also share the credit for transmitting humanist ideas to later generations; some of these are discussed elsewhere in this book.[87] The subsequent impact of the Reformation and the host of new theological notions carried in its train make the course of Cambridge humanism even less straightforward to chart.

[83] Caspari (1968), 50; Porter and Thomson (1963), 185 – 6. Erasmus retained a strong affection for Queens' in retrospect. His will, written in 1527, provided for a posthumous edition of his collected works of which there were to be twenty presentation sets, including one for Fisher and one for Queens'; but in later drafts of his will the idea of a collected edition was dropped for various reasons, Allen (1906), vi. 503 – 6 (appendix xix).
[84] Rose (1977), 53 – 4. Rose notes a strong humanist connection between Queens' and St John's, maintained into the next generation of humanists, *ibid.*, 57 – 8.
[85] Smith (1974), 20 – 2; see also Rose (1977), 54 n. 43.
[86] Smith (1974), 24.
[87] See below, pp. 99 – 100.

3

The Reformation (1520 – 1603)

Origins; background

A college is never immune to the events of the times in which it exists, but there are moments when these impinge upon its life with particular force and directness. For the medieval and early modern colleges, the events of the English Reformation were of great significance: beginning in the 1520s, and for well over a century thereafter, the changes which this Reformation set in train were the dominant influence on the history of the university, and this history is incomprehensible today without some wider knowledge of the period. It is possible to talk of a specifically 'English' Reformation: four Tudor monarchs — Henry VIII, Edward VI, Mary, and Elizabeth I — belong to this discussion, and the rule of each had a characteristic religious inclination which the university experienced and was forced to adapt to.

The Reformation was triggered by Martin Luther's rebellion against papal authority.[1] In the early 16th century there was a growing call in Europe for religious reform — though not for the revolution which ensued — in which the voices of the humanists, especially Erasmus, were prominent and influential.[2] The saying that 'Erasmus laid the egg and Luther hatched it', has been famous since the 16th century, but as the revolutionary implications of the latter's ideas became more apparent, many of the humanists were left behind. By the mid-1520s Erasmus was actively hostile to Luther;[3] so too were Fisher and More, who would later be martyred for their loyalty to the church of Rome.[4] Luther's rebellion began in 1517, when he fastened his 'Ninety-five Theses against Indulgences' to a church door in Wittenburg, and the movement thus begun developed and spread with great speed.[5] Luther's ideas were soon considered heretical — he was excommunicated in 1521 — and his writings were in great demand.[6]

In England, the earliest known Lutherans were a group which met in Cambridge from 1520 onwards at the White Horse Tavern, which was

[1]   For Luther, see Chadwick (1972), 40 – 75.
[2]   *ibid.*, 1 – 39.
[3]   *ibid.*, 62.
[4]   Elton (1977), 75 – 7, 96, 124, 193 – 5.
[5]   Chadwick (1972), 43.
[6]   *ibid.*, 49 – 55.

somewhere on the site of the newest buildings at St Catharine's; it was known as 'Little Germany', since it was from there that the new ideas came.[7] In June 1520 Pope Leo X condemned Luther's writings as heretical and ordered that his books should be burned; in December the university authorities at Cambridge burned texts which they had seized there, the first instance of this in England.[8] Lutheran works continued to be read nonetheless, imported through the East coast ports.[9] In 1528 a Cambridge bookseller was prosecuted for distributing these and William Tyndale's English New Testament. In the later 1520s there was alarm at Oxford over a Lutheran cell of former Cambridge men.[10]

Meetings at the White Horse were probably informal; most of those who went were young men of reformist sympathies, but it was not an exclusive gathering, and many others may have attended out of curiosity.[11] But the meetings were not approved of by the university authorities, and it was later suggested that the White Horse was chosen as a venue 'because many of them of St. John's, the King's college, and the Queen's college, came in on the back side.'[12]

The group was the earliest and arguably the most significant of the Lutheran groups in England, for most of the leaders of the first generation of English Protestants were Cambridge men, or had been in Cambridge, at the time of the White Horse discussions.[13] Although Erasmus had helped to prepare the ground for the Reformation by his criticism of church practices, and although his Greek and Latin New Testaments influenced several of the early Cambridge reformers, none of his known Cambridge associates was prominent in the movement.[14] His good friend Henry Bullock of Queens' was afterwards recorded by Thomas Fuller as one of the 'Opposers of the Protestant Religion'.[15] Bullock was happy to follow the Erasmian enthusiasms for plain preaching and lecturing 'without displaying any of the subtleties of men', and for more, and more careful reading of the Scriptures, but many humanists found the step from this to the Protestant enthusiasm for a Bible in English, and the idea of the revelation of grace through the reading of Scripture, a huge and impossible leap.[16]

Three Queensmen feature in the list of known early Cambridge

---

[7]   Dickens (1967), 101, 103; Porter (1958), 45.
[8]   Chadwick (1972), 54; Porter (1958), 45; Dickens (1967), 103.
[9]   Simon (1967), 141.
[10] Dickens (1967), 113 – 5. Vernacular scriptures were fundamental to Protestantism, and strongly opposed by the Catholic church, which sought to restrict access to the scriptures.
[11] Porter (1958), 45 – 6.
[12] Foxe, *Acts and Monuments*, quoted in Fowler and Fowler (1984), 39.
[13] Dickens (1967), 103.
[14] *ibid.*, 100 – 1.
[15] Fuller, *History*, 150.
[16] Porter (1958), 38 – 9.

reformers. Fuller noted of Thomas Forman (president, 1526 – 8) that he had 'concealed and kept Luther's books when sought for to be burnt'.[17] In 1528, as rector of Allhallows in London, Forman was less lucky, being suspended by the bishop of London for possessing such works.[18] Simon Heynes (president, 1529 – 37) was another member of the group.[19] The third was John Lambert, a Fellow briefly in 1521 – 2,[20] whose views were radical for his time, and who clashed with religious authorities more than once. He was burnt in 1538, ostensibly for having denied the doctrine of transubstantiation, but Henry VIII was at that time trying to gain the friendship of the Catholic powers in Europe and was keen to demonstrate his continuing religious orthodoxy; Lambert was tried before the king himself, and was manifestly offered up as a sacrifice for Henry's diplomatic aims.[21]

The Henrician Reformation (1529 – 47)

Lambert was one of 25 Cambridge men martyred for their Protestantism between 1531 and 1538.[22] Given the great speed at which new religious doctrines spread, and the vacillating state of Reformation politics during this period, it was inevitable that many should be out of step with the current official views; the highly-charged political and religious atmosphere was dangerous to those thus exposed. Though the state of the church was altered radically during Henry's reign, official religious doctrine did not develop at the same speed.

The first — dramatic — changes took place in the early 1530s and stemmed from Henry's desire for a divorce from Catharine of Aragon. Cardinal Wolsey, the dominant figure in church and state for over a decade, was dismissed in 1529, and a parliament was summoned whose members passed a series of bills over the next few years reforming the government of the church. The clergy were cowed into submission; in 1533 appeals from England to the pope were outlawed; and in the following year dues formerly paid by the English church to the papacy were transferred to the crown, together with all the pope's other legal

[17] Fuller, *History*, 150.
[18] Searle, 172.
[19] Porter (1958), 42 – 3. Searle notes that William Mey (president of Queens' 1537 – 53, 1559 – 60) was executor for another early reformer, Richard Smith of Trinity Hall, and suggests that Mey could have been involved in the White Horse group, Searle, 172. Mey was subsequently to show impressive reformist credentials, below, pp. 34 – 5, 38, 68.
[20] He appears in the college accounts for the first half of that financial year, but not thereafter, Book 2, f.38.
[21] Dickens (1967), 238 – 40.
[22] Porter (1958), 71.

rights and duties. Also in 1534, the Act of Supremacy declared the king to be the supreme head of the Church of England; John Fisher went to his death for his refusal to accept this.[23]

The universities were not threatened at first, but because of their special standing in the nation's religious life as seminaries for the clergy they could not expect to remain unaffected by the changes. In his youth, Henry VIII had received instruction from Cambridge tutors, recruited by Lady Margaret Beaufort,[24] but had shown no generosity subsequently towards her foundations there: Fisher struggled in vain to secure from the king the money she had set aside for St John's college after her death, and was forced to dissolve three small and nearly derelict monasteries to make up the shortfall in the college's revenue.[25] After Wolsey's fall in 1529, Henry was pettily vindictive towards the cardinal's educational foundations: his grammar school at Ipswich was suppressed, and Cardinal College at Oxford only saved after the duke of Norfolk had appealed on its behalf.[26]

At Cambridge the university prudently took Henry's side, though not without misgivings, when asked to pronounce on the validity of his marriage to Catharine of Aragon.[27] Simon Heynes, the president of Queens', was one of the syndics who supported the divorce, and three years later he attested to archbishop Cranmer's pronouncement that the marriage was null and void.[28] In the winter of 1533 – 4 Heynes was in London attending at court, from where he was sent back to Cambridge in 1534 to preach in support of the royal supremacy over the church; in the following year he was appointed to an embassy sent to entice the Protestant reformer Philip Melancthon to come to England.[29]

Two acts of 1534 brought the university further into contact with the new religious changes. The first concerned 'first fruits' (a year's income levied from every newly-beneficed person) and 'tenths' (a 10% income tax on every benefice) which had previously been paid to Rome and were now due to the king.[30] The alarm which the new legislation caused at Cambridge suggests that the custom had lapsed. Colleges were liable to pay tenths on their income — the income of Queens' was valued at £230 *per annum* — and newly elected Fellows had to pay first fruits. Queens' decided to reduce its fellowship by two, but does not seem to

23   Dickens (1967), 147 – 50, 161 – 175.
24   Scarisbrick (1971), 20 – 1.
25   *ibid.*, 664 – 5.
26   *ibid.*, 665 – 6; Simon (1967), 145.
27   Cooper, i.337 – 42; Mullinger (1873 – 1911), i.621 – 2.
28   Searle, 179 – 80.
29   *ibid.*, 180 – 1; see also *Letters and Papers of Henry VIII*, viii.425.
30   Elton (1977), 189 – 90; Elton (1972), 53 – 5.

have implemented this.[31] Two years later the universities were released from these obligations in return for each maintaining a lectureship in the king's name and promising to hold masses in his honour.[32] The reason for Henry's change of heart was given as his fear that many would give up their studies 'by reason of the tenuytie of lyvyng',[33] but he could afford to be generous, for he was now taxing his clerical subjects ten times more heavily than the papacy had done.[34]

The second act was the Act of Supremacy. By it, that power of 'visitation' of the universities formerly vested in the church was transferred to the crown, now given 'full power and authority from time to time to . . . amend all . . . errors, heresies, abuses, offences, contempts and enormities'.[35] Cambridge received five visitations during the next three decades, with each successive Tudor régime endeavouring to remould the university to its particular design.

Fisher was executed in 1535; he had been succeeded as chancellor by Thomas Cromwell, the king's chief minister and architect of the new ecclesiastical policy. The autumn of that year saw the compilation of the *Valor Ecclesiasticus*, a comprehensive survey of clerical wealth to ensure that the crown received its fair dues;[36] there were now widespread fears that the church would be stripped of its possessions. Little interest had been shown in doctrinal reform, but in 1535 the Scottish reformer Alexander Alane was sent to Cambridge by the king to lecture on the Scriptures. He lodged at Queens', where he found 'congenial companionship',[37] but left after a short while because of opposition to his lectures in the university at large.[38]

In the autumn of 1535 visitations of both universities were held and a series of injunctions was issued: an oath of obedience to the nation's new political and ecclesiastical arrangements was to be taken by university members;[39] old-fashioned scholastic lectures were to be replaced by those 'upon the Scriptures . . . according to the true sense thereof'; students were to read the Scriptures in their rooms; the teaching of canon law was abolished together with all 'ceremonies, constitutions, and observances, that hindered polite learning'; students

---

[31] Searle, 190 – 1; Book 2, f.203v; this was the number of Fellows in holy orders (cut from 12 to 10), but the number never came down so low: in 1534/5 it was 13; in the following year, 15, Book 2, f.204; Book 3, facing p. 1. The 'tenth' does seem to have been paid on one occasion under Mary, Searle, 191. Other colleges also had to reduce the number of their Fellows, Simon (1967), 200.

[32] Shadwell (1912), i.108 – 118.

[33] Cooper, i.379.

[34] Elton (1977), 190.

[35] Simon (1967), 147 – 8; Elton (1972), 353 – 6.

[36] Simon (1967), 148.

[37] Mullinger's translation of '*jucundissimum sodalitum*', (1873 – 1911), ii.15.

[38] Searle, 192; Cooper and Cooper (1858), i.238; Mullinger (1873 – 1911), ii.14 – 16.

[39] Cooper, i.375.

were to read original texts rather than scholastic glosses, and study certain humanist and reformist writings; each college was to have a daily public lecture in both Latin and Greek.[40] A second set of orders followed soon after, concerned mainly with the government of colleges: there were orders against bribery in college elections, and a demand 'that all factions between persons of particular counties, cities, or colleges should cease, and that college elections &c. be made freely from amongst the best learned and most meritorious' (in those days colleges restricted the numbered of Fellows from any one county who could be on the fellowship at the same time).[41]

The injunctions were wide-ranging, but many of the orders were vague. The visitation, by a single commissioner,[42] was hasty and superficial, because its purpose was essentially political and pragmatic: to secure the formal obedience of university men to the new constitution of church and state.[43] There were some genuine reforms the next year, with an act requiring the wealthier clergy to maintain scholars so that 'learned men may hereafter spring the more', and 'otherwise benefit the commonwealth with their counsel and wisdom'; and an act ordering beneficed men over forty still in residence at universities to return to their cures.[44] Both of these were slight reforms, and there is little sign that they or the broader reformist schemes came to much; more significant, and more in tune with the character of the Henrician Reformation, was the dissolution of the monasteries in 1536 – 40, brought about by the crown's acute financial problems.[45] After a study had been made of the *Valor Ecclesiasticus* returns, an act was passed in 1536 dissolving all religious houses with an annual income of less than £200.[46] From 1537 onwards, increasingly vigorous efforts were made to force the larger houses to surrender themselves to the crown; the last of them gave way in March 1540.[47] Many monastic lands were sold — the landed classes were eager to acquire them — and the crown's worsening financial position in the 1540s led to further sales.[48] The hopes of humanists that monastic wealth would be put to pious, especially educational uses, were largely unfulfilled.[49] At Cambridge, which petitioned in 1538 that the monasteries should be turned into 'colleges

[40] *ibid.*
[41] *ibid.*, i.376; Simon (1967), 201.
[42] Thomas Leigh, who was also active in the visitation of the monasteries, Cooper, i.376; Elton (1977), 233 – 4.
[43] The 1543 act of succession required anyone taking up an ecclesiastical post, or taking a degree to swear obedience to this, Shadwell (1912), i.138 – 141.
[44] Simon (1967), 173, 201 – 2.
[45] Dickens (1967), 199.
[46] *ibid.*, 202.
[47] *ibid.*, 203; Knowles (1959), iii.336 – 60.
[48] Half of the monastic wealth had been disposed of by 1547, Elton (1977), 245.
[49] e.g. Scarisbrick (1971), 658 – 9.

and places of good literature',[50] Henry created the Regius professorships in 1540, and the wealth of 26 dissolved houses went to endow Trinity College, founded in 1546. Emmanuel and Sidney Sussex were later to be founded on the sites of former monasteries, and several schools benefited elsewhere, but most of the monasteries' property was put to worldly uses.[51]

Queens' 'joined in the scramble' for the monastic pickings,[52] and petitioned successfully for the land and buildings of the adjoining Carmelite house, spared by the 1536 act.[53] Some houses sought to alienate their property after 1537, so that it would not fall into the hands of rapacious courtiers,[54] and the Carmelites were keen that theirs should go to Queens'. In August 1538 the house meekly surrendered itself to the college. No money changed hands; no reason was given, and the Carmelites promised to leave when asked.[55] Later that month the king authorised a commission consisting of the provost of King's and the president and two Fellows of Queens', to procure a surrender, take possession of the property for the crown and draw up an inventory of the house's goods. This royal ownership was a formality in practice, for Queens' was allowed to take possession of the site, and a complicated series of transactions in 1542 – 4 ensured that it became the true owner.[56] Building materials taken from the property were purchased from the crown in 1541 and resold by the college at a hefty profit; walls and buildings had already been pulled about and reordered.[57]

After Thomas Cromwell's sudden fall and execution in 1540, a conservative court faction led by the duke of Norfolk and Stephen Gardiner, bishop of Winchester, took control of government policy.[58] Gardiner succeeded Cromwell as chancellor of the university,[59] where he was already master of Trinity Hall, and demonstrated his conservatism in 1542 when he suppressed the 'new' (and more correct) Greek pronunciation which Erasmus had introduced. Gardiner's ban was opposed by Thomas Smith, a Fellow of Queens' and one of the country's foremost Greek scholars. Smith was one of a group of young Cambridge intellectuals continuing in the path of the Cromwellian reform movement, and had promoted the new pronunciation, but he

[50]   Simon (1967), 203.
[51]   Scarisbrick (1971), 667 – 8; Dickens (1967), 205, 211.
[52]   Scarisbrick (1971), 667.
[53]   Searle, 221, addenda to part I, vi – vii.
[54]   Knowles (1959), iii.353.
[55]   Searle, 222 – 3.
[56]   ibid., 223 – 232. See also Dewar (1964), 22 – 3.
[57]   Searle, 228 – 31; RCHM, 171, notes the presence of 15th century glass, said to come from the Carmelite friary, in the college's old library.
[58]   Elton (1977), 289 – 292.
[59]   Simon (1967), 209.

could not withstand the chancellor's authority.[60]

As its financial crisis worsened, the crown was forced to employ more ingenious methods to raise money,[61] and there were further seizures of religious property. The Chantries Act of 1545, which admitted freely to its financial purpose, permitted the king to appropriate all chantry foundations, and put virtually all college property at risk, since gifts of land to colleges were invariably made with some chantry motive.[62] The master of Corpus Christi, Matthew Parker, noted that there were many at court who were 'importunately suing . . . to have the lands and possessions of the universities surveyed, they meaning afterwards to enjoy the best of their lands and possessions'.[63]

There was some frantic lobbying at court by university *alumni* such as Thomas Smith, now Regius professor of civil law and clerk to the council of Henry's latest queen, Catherine Parr, and the queen brought her own influence to bear.[64] As a result, a three-man internal commission was set up to produce a detailed analysis of each college's accounts to be presented to the king. The three were Parker, John Redman (master of King's Hall, and subsequently the first master of Trinity) and the president of Queens', William Mey.[65] Their report showed that only five of the fourteen colleges — Queens' was one of the five — had incomes exceeding £200 *per annum*.[66] Only one of the colleges had an income greater than its expenditure.[67] Annual deficits ranged from under £2 to over £70.[68] When the king heard of the commission's findings, he 'in a certen admiration saide to certen of his Lords which stode by, that he thought he had not in his realme so many parsons so honestly mayntened in lyvyng bi so little lond and rent', but he was puzzled that the colleges 'shulde seame to expend yerly more than ther revenues amounted to'. The commissioners explained that the shortfall was made up by entry fines, charges for renewals of leases, and sales of timber from their estates. Henry was satisfied by this, and the lands were spared.[69] The commissioners' presentation of the accounts had however

---

[60] *ibid.*, 209; Elton (1977), 319, 320 (but c.f. Dewar (1964), 17 – 18); Allen (1965), 103 – 4; Allen (1968), 126 – 30. Gardiner's edict was repealed after Elizabeth I's accession, Allen (1965), *loc. cit.*

[61] Elton (1977), 304 – 12.

[62] Dickens (1967), 285; Simon (1967), 210.

[63] Quoted in Simon (1967), 211.

[64] *ibid.*, 211; Scarisbrick (1971), 669; Fowler and Fowler (1984), 20. Many bright young dons had entered royal service, Simon (1967), 209; Elton (1977), 318.

[65] Simon (1967), 211; Lamb (1838), 58 – 9.

[66] *ibid.*, 61 – 70. The five were: King's (£1011), St John's (£537), Christ's (£288), King's Hall (£215), and Queens' (£273). There is a manuscript copy of the survey in the Queens' archives, Book 68.

[67] Magdalene (founded in 1542); its income was only £44 *p.a.*, Lamb (1838), 63.

[68] *ibid.*, 61 – 70.

[69] *ibid.*, 60.

been somewhat disingenuous, for 'outside' — that is, irregular — receipts such as entry fines and the like could form a substantial part of a college's income.[70]

The Reformation under Edward VI (1547 – 53)

The reforming party at court had suffered a serious setback with Cromwell's fall and been forced to remain silent in the face of the conservative-Catholic reaction, but after Henry's marriage to Catherine Parr in 1543 Protestant opinions began to make headway again at court, cautiously favoured by the new queen.[71] By 1546, with the recognition that Henry would not live much longer, a fierce power struggle began among the court factions for control of his nine-year-old heir.[72] Henry died in January 1547; the reformist earl of Hertford became Protector (and shortly after, duke of Somerset) and replaced Gardiner as chancellor of Cambridge.[73] Catholic legislation was repealed and new injunctions facilitated Protestant forms of worship; in 1549 the first English prayer book was issued; after 1550, under the duke of Northumberland's protectorate, religious reforms proceeded apace.[74] Prominent reformers were invited from abroad. The Italian Peter Martyr Vermigli became Regius professor of divinity at Oxford and Martin Bucer was brought from Strasbourg to fill the same chair at Cambridge.[75] Bucer's stay was short: he was already ill on his arrival at the beginning of 1550, and he died in March 1551. He made a deep impression on many in the university, but also encountered fierce opposition to his teachings in many quarters; perhaps it was this that led to his complaint that Cambridge Fellows were 'either bitter papists or profligate epicureans'.[76]

Governments under Edward VI were sympathetic towards the universities. The 1547 Chantry Act, which reasserted the legislation of 1545, specifically exempted them from its provisions, and it was envisaged that chantry possessions would be used to benefit schools, universities, the parish clergy and the poor.[77] In 1548 plans were made for a new visitation of the universities, 'purposing to set some godlie direction and order there'.[78] The eight visitors, several of whom were

---

[70]   For an explanation of these terms see below, chapter 9.
[71]   Dickens (1967), 254 – 5.
[72]   Elton (1977), 328 – 32.
[73]   ibid., 333 – 4; Lamb (1838), lxvii.
[74]   For a brief summary, see Chadwick (1972), 117 – 8, 120; for a more detailed one, Dickens (1967), 273 – 354.
[75]   Chadwick (1972), 119; Dickens (1967), 319 – 21.
[76]   Porter (1958), 53 – 4, 62 – 7.
[77]   Shadwell (1912), i.151; Simon (1967), 216, 223 – 4.
[78]   Lamb (1838), 102.

prominent reformers, were all Cambridge men, and included Thomas Smith and William Mey.[79] Mey, Simon Heynes and John Taylor (a former Fellow of Queens' who had since become master of St John's) were also involved in the preparation of the 1549 prayer book.[80] The visitation took place in May – July 1549: its main provisions involved reform of the curriculum, but in addition there were some regulations for reforming college government and statutes in order to improve discipline and teaching there, and there was an impractical order that poor men were to be preferred in college elections.[81] For all its high aims, the visitation also had a political motive: university members had to renew their oath to the royal supremacy over the church.[82]

There were also changes in religious practice. In September 1548 Somerset commanded the university to follow the forms of service now being used in the king's chapel, until a new prayer book could be issued.[83] At Queens' religious images were removed from the chapel in 1547; the walls were whitewashed in May 1548, and a communion table was installed in that year or the next. The altars were not pulled down until July 1549 and there is no record of the new service books being used before 1551 – 2.[84] Willis and Clark regarded this as 'surprisingly gradual' reform, but the pattern is not dissimilar in other colleges: there seems to have been a second wave of reforms in 1549, probably inspired by the new prayer book.[85] In 1553 there were steps taken against religious dissent, with every university teacher or 'incepting' master of arts being required to subscribe to the new forty-two articles of religion,[86] but the young king died soon afterwards and was succeeded by his Catholic sister Mary.

The Marian reaction (1553 – 8)

The religious tone of Mary's reign was as doggedly Catholic as that of her brother had been Protestant. Soon after her accession the new queen

[79] Simon (1967), 252. See also Dewar (1964), 40.
[80] Searle, 239; Simon (1967), 263.
[81] *ibid.*, 252 – 4; Lamb (1838), 142 – 6.
[82] e.g. Lamb (1838), 109ff.
[83] *ibid.*, 103.
[84] *W&C*, ii.38.
[85] e.g. *ibid.*, ii.206 – 7 (Christ's). More traditional colleges might delay still longer, e.g. *ibid.*, i.59 (Peterhouse). At Jesus the altars were removed by the visitors in 1549, Lamb (1838), 111 – 12. At Queens' exequies were still being performed in 1550 – 1, but not thereafter, Book 3, fos.192, 201, 211. There was also a new form of service for commemoration of benefactors, introduced by the visitors, which Queens' seems to have adopted (that is to say, it was the form introduced into the new college statutes of 1559), Lamb (1838), 144 – 5.
[86] Simon (1967), 266. For 'incepting', see below, p. 98.

34

wrote to Cambridge to insist upon the restoration of old statutes and practices which had been 'muche altered broken and almost utterly subverted' by the Protestant Reformation.[87] The duke of Northumberland, chancellor of the university since 1550, was beheaded in 1553 for attempting to place Lady Jane Grey on the throne — one of five Cambridge chancellors to die on the block under the Tudors.[88] Stephen Gardiner was restored in his place, and sent his chaplain, Thomas Watson, to investigate the state of affairs in Cambridge. Watson is known to have visited Queens', but no record of his impressions has survived; however, the college was prompted to send two Fellows to London to ask the president, William Mey, about their 'ancient statutes'.[89]

Mey himself was brought before Mary's ecclesiastical commissioners and forced to resign, probably on the grounds that he was married. His successor, William Glynn, was a loyal Catholic who had been forced to resign the Lady Margaret chair of divinity in 1549, and he was made bishop of Bangor in 1555.[90] Glynn introduced Catholic forms of worship once again: prayers for the souls of the dead, formally abolished under Edward VI, were resumed; the chapel desks and the organ were repaired, and a gilt cross was purchased. The college now had to pay a quit-rent to the crown for the Carmelites' land.[91] Meanwhile, Catholic ceremonial was reintroduced throughout the university, which in 1555 was ordered to subscribe to new articles of religion. Nine Fellows of Queens' — a majority — did so; there had been a sharp fall in the number of the college's Fellows soon after Mary's accession, but the reason for this is not known.[92]

The ease with which the old order was restored demonstrates that Protestantism was not deep-rooted throughout the university, but there had been some support there for the Protestant pretender to the throne Lady Jane Grey, and at least 23 dons fled from Cambridge shortly after

---

[87] Lamb (1838), 165 – 6.

[88] Elton (1977), 374 – 7. The five were: John Fisher (executed 1535), Thomas Cromwell (1540), the duke of Somerset (1551), Northumberland, and the earl of Essex (1600), Lamb (1838), lxvii.

[89] 'antiqua statuta', Searle, 239 – 40.

[90] ibid., 240 – 8. Mey remained in England, possibly near Cambridge, and Searle argues that he may have had a room in Queens' in 1555 and 1558, ibid., 287.

[91] Book 3, fos. 216v, 218, 222v, 224v – 225v, 233v, 240v, 245v; W&C, ii.38. A communion book was purchased a month after Edward's death, but it is not clear what kind, Book 3, f.215.

[92] Porter (1958), 251 – 2; Searle, 252 – 3; Lamb (1838), 175 – 6. Searle only gives six subscribers; the other names are from Lamb (1838), cross-checked against AC. Another 7 Queensmen who moved to other colleges subscribed. There were 22 Fellows in 1553/4; 16 in 1554/5, Book 3, fos.217 – 217v, 223 – 223v. Two of the six who resigned became Fellows at other colleges under Mary; little is known about the others. Besides, it must be questioned how significant an indicator of beliefs such subscriptions are; they do not seem to have guaranteed loyalty, see below, pp. 36 – 8.

Mary's accession for fear of persecution.[93] In all, about ninety Cambridge *alumni* went into exile during the reign, including over forty dons and former Fellows; many were products of the Protestant university of the late 1540s and early 1550s, and some had been influential under Edward.[94] One was John Aylmer, a Queens' graduate who had embarked on a promising ecclesiastical career, and was Lady Jane Grey's tutor. One of the most distinguished was John Ponet, a former Fellow of Queens' and a bishop in Edward's reign; he was a notable scientist and linguist, and one of two Queens' graduates of the 1530s to take the advanced and enlightened view (for that time) that the North American Indians were more than mere savages.[95] John Pelham, who had come up to Queens' in 1549, left for Padua in the company of his tutor William Morley, a former Fellow. Anthony Mayhew, who had matriculated at Queens' but become a Fellow of Pembroke, concludes this list of Queens' exiles, a short one despite the college's prominence in the early reform movement.[96]

However, a visitation of the university in 1556 – 7 revealed conflicts with marked religious overtones within Queens'.[97] The visitors came to the college in January 1557 and were received 'with holywater and sensings in a cope and all the company in surplusses with crosses and candlestycks', but beneath this façade of orthodoxy they uncovered bitter quarrels and breaches of the statutes.[98] The allegations and counter-allegations which were put forward at the time have obscured some of the facts, but there were clearly breaches of the regulations governing fellowships: two Fellows were from the same county (the statutes permitted only one), another two had not been elected but were intruded by the visitors of 1549, and several had failed to take holy orders though obliged to do so.[99] Many did not attend services and arrived late for exequies and commemorations; such absences went unpunished, because no dean of chapel had been appointed. Academic exercises were avoided; Latin was no longer spoken at mealtimes; fellows did not take degrees at the statutorily specified times; and some did not study theology, as was required of them. Townsfolk and

[93]   Porter (1958), 75 – 8.
[94]   *ibid.*, 78 – 92.
[95]   *ibid.*, 82; Porter (1983), 12. More significant in this context is the fact that Ponet was the author of a justification of resistance to tyrannical monarchs, Skinner (1978), ii, 223 – 4, 234 – 5. Fuller recounts a tale of Aylmer hiding in a wine butt when escaping from England, Fuller, *Worthies*, ii. 447 – 8.
[96]   Porter (1958), 79, 95. St John's supplied a signficant proportion of the exiles, *ibid.*, 76, 82.
[97]   The visitation is recorded in Lamb (1838), 184 – 236. A manuscript copy of its survey of the college's finances is in the Queens' archives, Book 68.
[98]   Lamb (1838), 205. For the dispute in full, see Searle, 255 – 60.
[99]   The 1529 statutes required 14 out of 18 to be in orders, Book 79, f.14v. The complaint here was that only 6 out of the 11 who should have been in orders were.

tradesmen were to be found in the college at all hours, and there were often women within the precincts. Some Fellows stayed out late at night; others were over-fond of cards and dice. Long hair was prevalent. John Mey, bursar for the previous year, owed the college £40 and had not given a full account for his year in office; the vice-president was accused of failing to account for money he claimed to have spent on the chapel; the Fellow who held the keys to the college chest refused to surrender them to the vice-president. The college estates had not been visited during the previous year, and the president had been absent for the whole year without the Fellows' consent. Senior Fellows complained that juniors did not show them proper respect.

Whatever the accuracy of these accusations, the dispute clearly involved an attempt to at least stamp out slackness in religious performance, and quite possibly to rid the college of Fellows with Protestant leanings. The visitors' response is not known, but four Fellows took holy orders that year, two were ejected and another four went out of residence during 1557 – 8; six new Fellows were in place by the autumn of 1558, and the change of personnel may have restored the college to a more orderly state.[100] Late in 1557 Queens' also received a new president, Thomas Peacock, chaplain to the bishop of Ely, who had preached an anti-Protestant sermon before the visitors in January, 'inveying against heresies and heretyckes, as Bylney, Latamer, Cranmer, Rydley &c'.[101] Glynn may have been asked to step down, for Bangor was a long way away, and he had not even been present at the visitation; Peacock, at Ely, could watch over the college more easily.[102] The new order was short-lived, however, for Mary's death in November 1558 put an end to Catholic dominance of Cambridge.

Religion in the reign of Elizabeth I (1558 – 1603)

The reign of Elizabeth saw Protestantism firmly established as the state religion in England, but there was no putting the clock back to the reign

---

[100] Searle, 260. A MS note by Searle in the Queens' Library copy of his history (U.9.24) adds the name of George Alsop on this page to the three printed in the text as having taken orders. The four who went out of residence included Thomas Yale, one of the two Fellows from the same county; he may therefore have been ejected. For the changing numbers, see Book 3, f.246v. Each of the six who left was regarded as orthodox under Elizabeth, although three had subscribed to the 1555 articles, see n. 92 above. The college accounts for 1557/8 were not made up in the account book, but there was an audit, Book 3, fos.246v – 254; Book 10.

[101] Lamb (1838), 200.

[102] The details of Glynn's resignation and Peacock's election are unclear, Searle, 265. For Glynn's forewarning of the visitation and absence during it, see Searle, 252 – 3; Book 3, f.243; Lamb (1838), 221.

of Edward VI, and not all of the Protestant exiles who hurried home on learning of Mary's death found the new religious régime to their liking. Some prospered within the Elizabethan church, but others became nonconformists and rebels. Only twelve — none of them Queensmen — returned to Cambridge.[103] Religious disputes during Elizabeth's reign were quarrels between fellow Protestants — put crudely, between conservatives and radicals — about the government and practice of the Church of England. These disputes were frequent and often bitter, and Cambridge men were prominent in them.

Elizabeth's visit to Cambridge in 1564 was a grand demonstration of royal favour and interest in the condition of the university. Her vast entourage had to be housed in several colleges, including Queens'.[104] The visit set the seal on the reorganisation of Cambridge which had taken place from the beginning of the reign. In 1559, there had been a visitation of the university to put it in order, 'both for augmentation of good learning and for establishing of such uniformity in the cause of religion, touching common prayer and divine service, as by the laws of our realm is ordained'. The Edwardian statutes were restored.[105] One of the 1559 visitors was William Mey, who was restored as president of Queens'; Peacock wisely resigned following a dispute with the Fellows.[106] Only two Marian heads were removed from office in the university, although others resigned; nor was there a major purge of college Fellows.[107] The survival of so many dons who had conformed under Mary helps to explain the 'predominantly conservative age' which the universities now entered, kept in focus by the conservatism of the queen.[108]

Queens' adapted comfortably to the new order. Mey served on a commission to revise the prayer book (together with Thomas Smith) and was appointed archbishop of York in 1560, but died on the day of his election.[109] The college received new statutes in 1559 which were clearly infused with the new religious spirit. References to the 'high altar' were changed to 'the Lord's table', and the altars themselves were taken down in the chapel.[110] Prayers for the souls of founders and benefactors were replaced by a simple thanksgiving service, and there were several

[103] Porter (1958), 87 – 9.
[104] Searle, 299, 301, 387; Curtis (1959), 7; Cooper, ii.205.
[105] Searle, 294; Curtis (1959), 167; Book 3, f.261.
[106] Porter (1958), 101, 102, 104; Searle 268 – 283; see below, pp. 70, 116. Peacock continued to live privately in Cambridge, and the Fellows gave him a present as a token of goodwill; William Mey's brother John, also a Fellow of Queens', became master of St Catharine's in 1559.
[107] Curtis (1959), 168; Porter (1958), 104 – 7.
[108] Simon (1967), 291.
[109] Searle, 287 – 9.
[110] 'summum Altare' became 'mensam Domini', Book 79, fos.15v, 20; Statutes (1559), 5, 14; W&C, ii.38 – 39; see also Book 4, fos.75v,122.

other Protestant alterations to the performance of divine service.[111] The Fellows' oath included a clause of obedience to the state's new religious constitution.[112]

Elizabethan government pressed for little more than outward conformity in religion, but by the end of the 1560s serious differences began to emerge in Cambridge as more radical Protestants there complained of the conservatism of the university authorities, and there were disputes over religious practice.[113] Matters came to a head in 1570 when the new Lady Margaret professor of divinity, Thomas Cartwright of Trinity, delivered a series of lectures attacking the church establishment and advocating a Presbyterian system.[114] Cartwright had many followers in the university, including a Fellow of Queens', Robert Some, whose assertion that the laws of the realm 'did permit many detestable, devlish and damnable things' was a clear example of Puritan distrust of authority.[115] Orthodox Anglicans such as William Chaderton, Regius professor of divinity and president of Queens' at the time of Cartwright's lectures, equated Presbyterianism with anarchy: 'True it is suche seditions, contention, and disquietude, suche errors and schismes openlie taught and preached, boldlie and without warrant, are latelie growne amongst us, that the good estate, quietnes, and governance of Cambridge, and not of Cambridge alone but of the whole church and realme, are for great hasarde unles severlie by authoritie they be punished'.[116]

Puritans were particularly anxious to take control of schools and universities, fearing the continuance of corrupt, Catholic influences there. It was felt that the sons of the ruling classes were not receiving an adequate education; William Covel, a Fellow of Queens' in the 1590s, complained that many graduates were 'unmeet for the commonwealth'. Particularly urgent was the need for the universities to produce learned, preaching ministers to spread the word of God; it was to this end that Emmanuel (1584) and Sidney Sussex (1596) colleges were founded.[117]

---

[111] *Statutes (1559)*, 18, 21, 22, 31 – 3; Book 3, f.261; Book 4, f.2; Book 79, fos.22, 27v. A quit-rent for the Carmelite friary was paid in 1562, Book 4, f.14.

[112] *Statutes (1559)*, 15.

[113] Curtis (1959), 167; Porter (1958), 114 – 39.

[114] Porter (1958), 140, 174 – 8.

[115] *ibid.*, 141 – 3.

[116] Quoted in Morgan (unpublished thesis, 1984), 258; see also Porter (1958), 142. Chaderton had been first to complain about Cartwright and his followers (including Some) in 1570, Porter (1958), 174. He also noted that Some and a Fellow of Trinity, another supporter of Cartwright, had preached on similar themes: aiming 'to overturne and overthrow all ecclesiasticall and civill governance that now is, and to ordeyn and institute a new founde pollicie', quoted in Morgan (unpublished thesis, 1984), 258.

[117] Greaves (1981), 327 – 31, 334; Curtis (1959), 190; Edwards (1899), chapters 2 – 4; Shuckburgh (1904), 17 – 26.

Actions such as this were in no way subversive, and most Puritans could conform to the system without much difficulty. Only in extreme cases did the authorities bring pressure to bear: Cartwright was expelled from the university,[118] but his ideas survived. Both universities, but especially Cambridge, were focal centres for the national Presbyterian movement which emerged in the 1580s to compensate for the lack of reform in the state church; they provided leaders, recruits, and inspiration.[119] Presbyterian groups met secretly at Cambridge in the late 1580s; Thomas Brightman of Queens' was one of the small number of active Prebysterian dons.[120]

At a less radical level, seven out of nineteen Queens' Fellows signed the 1572 petition against the new university statutes of 1570, which had been designed by the authorities to curb indiscipline (and, by implication, Puritanism) by reducing the influence of young masters of arts in university government.[121] One of the seven was Edmund Rockrey, who had defied the authorities in 1570 by preaching against the statutes, and was expelled in 1571 for refusing to recant.[122] Restored by order of the university's chancellor, he was soon in trouble again for refusing to follow the rites of the church of England. William Chaderton was at a loss how to deal with him: 'Since his return I could never by any advice or charge bring him to receive the Communion in the College amongst us, neither yet to keep any order in apparel and ceremonies'.[123] He remained a thorn in Chaderton's flesh for several years thereafter, resigning at last in 1579, by which time Chaderton had already left to become bishop of Chester.[124] In 1586 John Smith of Queens' was brought before the university authorities to answer for an allegedly contentious sermon, although he was able to explain himself to their satisfaction.[125] Three Queens' Fellows signed a petition supporting a Puritan imprisoned and expelled by the university for outspokenness in 1589.[126] In 1595 William Covel delivered a sermon in the university church which aroused the displeasure of both the chancellor and the

---

[118] Porter (1958), 177 – 8.
[119] Curtis (1959), 199 – 204.
[120] Porter (1958), 190 – 5.
[121] ibid., 167 – 8, 209; Searle, 319. In 1569 Chaderton had doubted the ability of the vice-chancellor to curb this group: 'although he be minded to call them to accompt, yet, I think he will not or cannot minister sufficient punyshment to suppresse their errors: Satan will have the upper hande and we shall be all in a hurlye burlie and shameful broyle', quoted in Morgan (unpublished thesis, 1984), 255 – 6.
[122] Searle, 334 – 6.
[123] ibid., 338 – 41.
[124] ibid., 341 – 5; although Rockrey had held several college offices before 1570, he held none after his restoration, ibid., 338, 341. Book 14, 29, contains admonitions delivered to Rockrey; he also features in the university archives, CUA Collect. Admin. 13, fos.136v, 138, 141 – 3.
[125] Cooper, ii.415.
[126] Porter (1958), 209 – 12.

archbishop of Canterbury.[127] A Puritan sermon was recorded in London in 1602, delivered by 'a plaine plodding fellowe, sometimes of Queenes Colledge in Cambridge'.[128]

But Queens' was governed by impeccably orthodox presidents such as Chaderton (1568 – 79) and Humphrey Tyndall (1579 – 1614).[129] Apart from Rockrey's individual rebellion, there was no serious religious dispute within the college as there were at some others, nor was Queens' ever particularly associated with Puritanism.[130] Most Puritans were far from being extremists and had no desire to divide the church; Robert Some, who had supported Cartwright, became vice-president of Queens' before leaving to be master of Peterhouse in 1589, without shifting his theological ground.[131] Moreover, by the 1590s the first expansive, optimistic phase of Elizabethan Puritanism had ended and ecclesiastical discipline was tightened up during the last years of the reign; in 1587 William Harrison's *Description of England* had praised Cambridge's 'politic regiment'.[132]

Extremism was contained, but Puritanism as a broad movement had put down deep roots in Cambridge well before the turn of the century, and Puritanism as a cohesive national movement was created by university graduates, from Cambridge especially, who carried a sense of fellowship and common cause out into the parishes where they became ministers; one historian has even described Cambridge-educated preachers as 'the chief animating force for the spread of Puritanism among all classes of society'.[133] Several worked in parishes close to Cambridge; one such was Samuel Fairclough, who matriculated at Queens' in 1608, and served parishes in the area for nearly forty years; many Cambridge dons rode out to join the audiences which packed his church to hear him preach.[134] Such men, together with the great university preachers of that age, ensured that the Puritan spirit was maintained from one generation of graduates to the next well into the 17th century.[135]

[127] Searle, 389 – 90.
[128] Greaves (1981), 370, 450.
[129] Tyndall defended the university in the disturbances of 1589 — physically, on one occasion — and was active in enforcing orthodoxy against the anti-Calvinist movement of the 1590s, Porter (1958), 211 – 12, 314, 344ff; see also Searle, 360 – 1.
[130] For the serious troubles at St John's and Corpus Christi, see Porter (1958), 119 – 135, 146 – 54, 183 – 95.
[131] Curtis (1959), 189; Porter (1958), 315. For his theology, see Lake, 'Robert Some'.
[132] Curtis (1959), 194 – 5; Harrison (1968), 67.
[133] Collinson (1967), 122 – 30, 175; Porter (1958), 230ff; Haller (1938), 20.
[134] Porter (1958), 218 – 229.
[135] Curtis (1959), 204 – 5.

4

The early 17th century (1603 – 60)

The early Stuarts (1603 – 40)

In 1610 John Cotton, a Puritan Fellow of Emmanuel, returned to his
college rooms depressed after having preached a sermon which had
made no visible impact on his audience. At that moment, a visitor
arrived: it was John Preston, a young Fellow of Queens', who 'coming
in, acquainted him with his spiritual condition, and tells him how it had
pleased God to work effectually on his heart by that sermon'.[1] It was
turning-point in Preston's career; he had thought of abandoning
university life, but for the next 18 years until his death he was to be the
leading light of the Puritan movement in Cambridge. He was a
distinguished preacher in the university's great tradition, and enormously influential.[2] Whilst he was dean of Queens', his catechising was
so popular with members of other colleges and even townsfolk that the
college chapel was often full before the Fellows arrived, and the vice-
chancellor had to ban outsiders from attending services there.[3] Preston
also preached outside the college, where his sermons made a great
impression.[4] Preaching was important to Puritans, and the lectureship
at Holy Trinity Church in Cambridge, founded in 1610, was particularly
important as a platform for their religious ideas; in 1624 Preston turned
down the offer of a bishopric in order to become lecturer there. Three
years earlier he had refused a professorship at Trinity College, Dublin,
because his friends had persuaded him that he could do more good for
the cause by remaining at Cambridge.[5] In 1622 he was chosen master of
Emmanuel, by the influence of the duke of Buckingham, one of the most
powerful men in the land.[6]

Despite such promise, Preston's career did not progress as well as it
ought to have done. Admittedly, he turned down offers of preferment
outside Cambridge, and he died quite young, in 1628, but by that time
his star was falling. Although he was not an anti-establishment figure,

[1] Quoted in Porter (1958), 269.
[2] Ball (1885), 7, 13, 16; Porter (1958), 263 – 8.
[3] Ball (1885), 39 – 41.
[4] ibid., 78 – 9.
[5] Porter (1958), 260 – 2; Twigg (unpublished thesis, 1983), 10 – 11; Searle, 446.
[6] Ball (1885), 79 – 89.

he was never fully accepted by the establishment.[7] In January 1620 he preached a Sunday afternoon sermon at St Botolph's 'at which many disordered persons were present', in defiance of a royal ban on afternoon lectures in the town, which the authorities felt encouraged unruliness. The vice-chancellor's court, meeting the following month, banned Preston from preaching in Cambridge without express permission, and he was made to offer a formal apology for his action.[8] This probably did no long-term damage to his career; his problem was, as Thomas Fuller perceived, that he was a 'court-comet, blazing for a time, and fading soon afterwards'. Preston's patron Buckingham turned his back on his Puritan protégés in 1626 and put his support behind the rising high church 'Arminian' faction among the clergy, who were also favoured by the new king, Charles I.[9] From that time onwards Puritans, and indeed more moderate Protestants, were increasingly on the defensive against the new religious movement and what were believed to be its Catholic overtones. The strength of anti-Catholic feeling at this time can scarcely be overestimated: most Protestants regarded the pope as the Antichrist.[10]

Preston's story encapsulates many of the main features of the religious history of early Stuart England, and of Cambridge. In the 1590s, with extremism contained, the university had been relatively peaceful, dominated by orthodox Calvinist Protestants.[11] Queens' under Humphrey Tyndall was impeccably orthodox, and produced several future Puritan lecturers in the early 17th century.[12] Tyndall's successor as president was John Davenant, equally orthodox and more successful in his career: Lady Margaret professor of divinity in 1609, a representative at the Synod of Dort — a general council of the European Protestant churches — in 1618 – 19, and bishop of Salisbury in 1621.[13] But Davenant remained at Salisbury until his death in 1641, his traditional Calvinism no longer fashionable at court.

New, anti-Calvinist views had been expressed at Cambridge in the

---

[7] Curtis (1959), 208; see also Ball (1885), 52 – 9.
[8] Searle, 441 – 3; Ball (1885), 42 – 8; CUA VC Ct.I.9, fos.173v – 174. Such a ban on afternoon lectures was anti-Puritan by implication, the lecture being a particularly Puritan medium.
[9] Fuller, *Worthies*, ii.517. Buckingham's change of heart was revealed at the York House conference in February 1626, Coward (1980), 138.
[10] For Arminianism, see Tyacke (1975); for anti-Catholicism, see Clifton (1975); for the Pope as Antichrist, see Lake, 'Significance'; Lamont (1969), 67 – 8.
[11] Collinson (1982), 81; see also Morgan (unpublished thesis, 1984), 56 – 7.
[12] Seaver (1970), 184. If emigration to New England in the early 17th century can be taken as a reliable indicator of Puritan feelings, then Queens' may have been only moderately Puritan: five of its *alumni* are known to have emigrated before 1646; Magdalene (8), St Catharine's (8), St John's (10), Trinity (13), and especially Emmanuel (35), all provided more, Morison (1935), Appendix B. The Emmanuel figure is the most significant.
[13] Searle, 409 – 10, 413 – 4; Fuller (1897), 37, 59; OPR, f.9v.

1590s, and had caused some controversy, but under Elizabeth and James I (1603 – 25) such doctrines could only make slow headway.[14] James followed the Elizabethan policy of comprehension, though with a slightly higher level of interference in order to ensure good discipline.[15] A drastic change took place under Charles I, and its first sign came in 1626, when the duke of Buckingham was nominated for the vacant chancellorship of the university, even though he was under impeachment by the House of Commons. It was a controversial move, and the election was fiercely contested. Buckingham won, but by a mere six votes. Although college Fellows tended to follow their master's lead in voting on this occasion, at Queens' only one Fellow voted with the president, John Mansell, for Buckingham, and twelve against; it is not clear why, unless there was some other dispute within the college.[16]

It would be misleadingly simple to see the high church movement's advance in Cambridge as inexorable, but the university's religious complexion in 1640 was markedly different from that of 1625.[17] This was also true of Queens'. John Mansell, president from 1622 to 1631, was a capable college administrator rather than a notable churchman, and there is no evidence that he abandoned the Calvinist Protestant tradition of his predecessors.[18] The fellowship included Herbert Palmer, a leading Presbyterian in the Civil War; and in 1628 a former Queensman, Thomas Edwards, was accused of subversive (Puritan) preaching in Cambridge.[19] A decisive change took place in the early 1630s. In 1634 Samuel Ward, the Puritan master of Sidney Sussex, wrote that 'new heads [of houses] are brought in, and they are backed in maintaining novelties, and them which broach new opinions'.[20] These men thrived under the patronage of the new archbishop of Canterbury, William Laud, and formed a recognisable 'Laudian' faction.[21] One was Edward Martin,

[14]   Porter (1958), 277 – 413; Curtis (1959), 211 – 226.
[15]   Curtis (1959), 170 – 2. After the Hampton Court conference of 1604 a university grace was passed that any who, in word or deed, opposed 'the received doctrine and discipline' of the Church of England were to be suspended from their degrees, Fuller (1868), iii.218. In January 1605 Queens' sent in a certificate of its observance of the ecclesiastical order in holding services with the Book of Common Prayer, and wearing surplices and hoods, Searle, 361, 393.
[16]   Curtis (1959), 173; Twigg (unpublished thesis, 1983), 6 – 8; Morgan (unpublished thesis, 1984), 1 – 44. For the voting figures, see Mullinger (1873 – 1911), iii. Appendix A (but c.f. Twigg (unpublished thesis, 1983), 8 and notes 32, 33). Edward Martin voted against Buckingham, Twigg (unpublished thesis, 1983), 8 n. 34, but was a high churchman and royalist of note in his later career, this chapter below.
[17]   Twigg (unpublished thesis, 1983), chapter I; see also Hoffman (1984).
[18]   The college order and memorandum book, the Old Parchment Register, is used much more frequently to record decisions and other information after Mansell's election, OPR, f.134vff. and see also f.14.
[19]   Cooper, iii.199; Heywood and Wright (1854), ii.361 – 3. See Searle, 534, for Palmer's 1630 clash with new religious trends at Canterbury.
[20]   Parr (1686), 470 – 1.
[21]   Twigg (unpublished thesis, 1983), chapter I.

president of Queens' from 1631 to 1644. He had been Laud's chaplain when the latter was bishop of London, and had already gained some notoriety for his 'Arminian' views and actions.[22] One later 17th century historian commented on his being 'a zealous Man for the Church of England', and his 17th century biographer observed that 'he would never endure men to mince and mangle that in their practice, which they swallowed whole in their Subscriptions'.[23] During Martin's first year in office, an extraordinarily large sum of money was spent on repairing and cleaning up the chapel — the purity of worship was an important 'Laudian' theme. In January 1632 a tax formerly levied on the stipends of Fellows and scholars for paying the underbutler was now diverted to the use of the chapel. Religious discipline was tightened: an order of 1633 required all who were about to take a degree to first attend a service performed in strict accordance with the rites of the Church of England in the college chapel; this was designed to weed out Puritan conscientious objectors.[24]

By the mid-1630s the 'Laudian' heads and their followers were growing in confidence; controversial 'Laudian' sermons were delivered in the university.[25] One of the more notorious of these was given by Peter Hausted in Great St Mary's, the university church, in 1634. Hausted was a former student of Queens', where he had distinguished himself by writing and acting in plays.[26] In 1634 he was curate of Martin's living at Uppingham, and therefore clearly of the same religious stamp, Even Martin, who was notably partisan, was forced to admit that Hausted might have used 'some indiscretions of expression' in the sermon, in which he called out for 'reverence, alacrity, purity and order in God's service, for adoration in Churches, and bowing at the Blessed name, for the surplis and other Ceremonyes'. He also 'preached that himselfe had seene very grave men in that place neglect their dutyes and heard many in the Country excuse their profane [conduct] upon the practise of grave men in the University'. For good measure, he also slighted the Dutch (who were Calvinists) as 'naturally slovenly'. Hausted was seized as soon as he had finished preaching and taken before the university's consistory court, which tried religious offences; there he was 'arraign'd and sentenced' by the five heads of houses present, moderate Puritans who felt that it was time to take a stand against the encroachment of 'Laudianism'. The case did not end there: a subsequent meeting of the court, under a newly-elected 'Laudian' vice-chancellor, acquitted Hausted, and a deep split was exposed between

[22]   Searle, 467 – 8; Prynne (1646), 508.
[23]   Kennet (1728), 670; Lloyd (1668), 462.
[24]   Book 6, fos.46 – 49v (£93 13s 8d); OPR, fos.128v, 129v; Searle, 510.
[25]   Twigg (unpublished thesis, 1983), chapter I.
[26]   See Mills (1944); also below, pp. 107 – 8.

the two religious factions, with each side accusing the other of judicial irregularities.[27] In 1637 Anthony Sparrow, a young Fellow of Queens', preached in support of auricular confession and the priest's power of absolution — another overtly 'Laudian' enthusiasm — and had the sermon published in London; then, in the words of a Puritan critic, he 'returned in triumph to Cambridge, to the great griefe and discouragement of the Protestant but extraordinary encouragement of the Popish party there'.[28] In that year also, Martin drew attention to himself and caused much irritation by opposing vigorously a grace for Edward Lake, a former student of St Catharine's, to take his doctorate in law. We do not know why: Martin himself refused to give an explanation to the vice-chancellor.[29]

Several college chapels were now decorated and beautified in accordance with high church ideals. At Queens', curiously, there are no signs of chapel improvements between 1632 and 1637, when the old communion plate was replaced, there were repairs to the antechapel, and the organ was tuned and cleaned. In 1638 there was further alteration and renovation and, crucially, the altar was raised.[30] In 1636 a report on religious practice at Cambridge commissioned by Archbishop Laud had named Queens' as one of five 'Laudian' colleges where 'they endeavor for order and have brought it to some good passe'.[31] In 1641, amidst the parliamentary backlash against Charles I's rule and Laud's religious reforms, a committee of the House of Commons prepared a very different report on the university's religious worship. This noted that the chapel at Queens' and the ritual employed there 'have been much changed since Dr Martin came in to be Master there': the altar was not only raised but richly adorned; the rites were unambiguously high. Martin was said to be 'a great player at Cards, and that from Saturday night till one or two of the clock on Sunday morning', thereby profaning the Sabbath. The college cook reported him as saying that 'he would rather see his son in a whore house' than let him go to the Puritan lecture in Holy Trinity church. The committee also believed it had uncovered proof of covert Catholicism at Queens': one Fellow, Edward Kemp, was alleged to have preached a sermon upholding the doctrine of transubstantiation, and to have 'extenuated' Guy Fawkes and the other Catholic 'powder traitors' of 1605.[32]

---

[27] Searle, 512 – 13; CUA CUR 18, 6(7); CUA VC Ct.I.49, fos.232 – 3; CUA VC Ct.I.54, fos.1 – 14. See also Hoyle (1986).

[28] Sparrow (1637); *Hierurgia* (1902), iii.50 – 1; Prynne (1646), 186, 189 – 90. See also Hoyle (1986).

[29] CUL Add MS 22, fos.75 – v.

[30] Searle, 515; Book 6, fos.76v – 78.

[31] Cooper, iii.283; noted also in Hoffman (1984), 98.

[32] British Library Harl. MS 7019 (David Hoyle kindly lent me his notes on this manuscript, which I have used here).

This House of Commons investigation was far from impartial, but it is clear that by the end of the 1630s Martin had succeeded in remodelling the college to match his own religious ideals, and it is noteworthy that there was no opposition, considering the college's recent history. The extent to which 'Laudianism' had taken hold there was demonstrated in the troubled years that followed the summoning of the Long Parliament in 1640: the years of the Civil War and the English Revolution.

The English Revolution (1640 – 60)

In 1640 parliament met for the first time in over a decade and addressed itself enthusiastically to the task of redressing the excesses of Charles I's government during the 1630s, and to destroying the 'Laudian' religious innovations. It believed that both universities were in the hands of crypto-Catholics; the House of Commons issued orders against 'Laudian' religious ceremonies, and leading Cambridge 'Laudians' came under attack.[33] The rôle of Queensmen in the high church movement did not go unremarked: in November 1640 the names of Anthony Sparrow and Peter Hausted were mentioned in debate, in the context of 'audacious and libelling pamphlets against true religion'.[34] Both men, together with Edward Martin, came under the scrutiny of the Commons' subcommittee set up to examine the state of religion in Cambridge, and the committeemen were disturbed by what they found.[35] Moves in parliament to abolish episcopacy, deans and cathedral chapters threatened the career prospects of university graduates entering the church.[36]

There was more parliamentary bluster than action, but the threat remained, for all parliament's protestations of concern for the quality of university learning. The Grand Remonstrance of December 1641 pledged parliament to 'reform and purge the fountains of learning, the two universities'.[37] In September it had issued an order banning many

[33] Twigg (unpublished thesis, 1983), 19 – 21, 24 – 31. For the Long Parliament and the university in general before the outbreak of the civil war, see *ibid.*, chapter II; all unacknowledged general observations made here are derived from this chapter.

[34] *Parliamentary History* (1807), ii.670. It is not clear why Hausted was referred to as a pamphleteer, but on 22 November 1640 he had preached in the university church on the theme of obedience and the sinfulness of rebellion against the state. This was not published until 1647, but was clearly meant as a public warning to parliament, Hausted (1647).

[35] Twigg (unpublished thesis, 1983), 23ff; Hoyle (1986).

[36] Twigg (unpublished thesis, 1983), 37 – 39.

[37] *ibid.*, 20, 39 – 40; Kenyon (1966), 238. There are indications of some alarm at Queens': a gentleman who in 1637 had been promised a college lease to commence in 1645 'was to have enter'd upon the Estate at Michaelmas 1648 but the . . . Master and Fellows about the yeare 1640 being in danger of looseing their places in the College Mr Benchkin bought the then Tenant out at a deare rate and had a Lease seal'd him July 1641 paying then to the College £60 more', Book 80, f.44 (second pagination).

'Laudian' religious practices throughout the land. University and college authorities were to certify that parliament's instructions had been carried out, but most of the Cambridge colleges, including Queens', did not reply.[38] In January 1642 parliament ordered university members to take the 'Protestation', an oath to defend the church of England against 'Popish innovation'.[39] There were no difficulties: college heads, or their deputies, took the oath on behalf of their colleges; for Queens', this was performed by the senior Fellow, Robert Ward.[40] Martin's absence is unexplained; he was certainly in Queens' in April, when William Fane, fifth son of the earl of Westmorland, was admitted as his pupil.[41]

War broke out between king and parliament in the summer of 1642. Cambridge occupied an important strategic position, but was under the control of parliamentary forces. Nonetheless, parliament was concerned about royalism there.[42] The university was overtly royalist. In October 1641 Queens' had obeyed the vice-chancellor's order to light bonfires celebrating the king's return from Scotland, and the university made a great show of loyalty to Charles when he visited Cambridge in March 1642.[43]

Both sides badly needed money to finance the war. On 29 June, before the outbreak of hostilities, Charles wrote to the vice-chancellor of Cambridge asking for a loan 'for our necessary defence'. The response was lukewarm: the university gave nothing, and only a few colleges contributed. Queens' gave £185, of which £100 was given by Martin, and the remainder by ten of the Fellows.[44] The colleges were afraid of parliamentary retribution, which explains why the Fellows of Queens' took nothing from college funds: though they might be called to account personally, there could be no grounds for action against the college as a corporate body.[45] Charles wrote again on 24 July, inviting the colleges to send him their plate, ostensibly for safekeeping. Once again, the response was less than enthusiastic. Queens' however handed over 591oz. of gilt plate and 923 oz. of white plate to the crown's Cambridge

---

[38]   Twigg (unpublished thesis, 1983), 39. Only Corpus Christi and St Catharine's, both mildly Puritan colleges, replied.

[39]   Cooper, iii.317; Kenyon (1966), 223, 258; Twigg (unpublished thesis, 1983), 41.

[40]   CUA CUR 78, 62. *Historical Manuscripts Commission* (1878), 120; Twigg (unpublished thesis, 1983), 41. Ward was listed as senior Fellow in 1641/2, Book 6, f.99.

[41]   Registrum, f.14.

[42]   Twigg (unpublished thesis, 1983), 45 – 6, 48 – 9; for the civil war and the university in general in 1642 – 3, see *ibid.*, chapter III.

[43]   *ibid.*, 43; Book 6, f.101.

[44]   Twigg (unpublished thesis, 1983), 49 – 50. The donations are listed in Cooper (1851), 252, taken from MS 600; this evidence disproves Varley's claim that the remaining £85 was given by Sparrow alone, Varley (1935), 76.

[45]   Varley (1935), 77; Twigg (unpublished thesis, 1983), 50.

agent on 3 August.[46] Parliament was unaware of these plans, but swift action by two local commanders, Valentine Walton in Huntingdonshire and his brother-in-law Oliver Cromwell in Cambridgeshire, prevented most of the colleges' plate from leaving, although several colleges did not even consider sending any. Queens', Jesus, St John's and Peterhouse had already sent their plate; Magdalene's was seized en route.[47]

Parliament reacted on 17 August by empowering Cromwell and four Cambridge aldermen to take charge of the town, creating a state of martial law in effect, including the right to arrest on suspicion.[48] Soon afterwards, Cromwell took action against the heads of Queens', Jesus and St John's, which was described in royalist propaganda: 'before that month was expired, downe he comes again in a terrible manner with what forces he could draw together, and surrounds divers Colledges, while we were at our devotion in our several Chappels, taking away Prisoners . . . men of such eminent worth and abilities, as render them above the reach of our commendation, and these he carryes with him to London in triumph'.[49] It was also said that their colleges were searched, and plate and money taken; one broadsheet referred to armed volunteers from London having 'beset most of the Colledges'.[50] On arrival in London, the three heads were said by royalists to have been 'led captive through Bartholomew Faire, and so farre as Temple-Bar, and back through the City to prison . . . on purpose that they might be shouted at, or stoned by the rabble-rout', a story which is uncorroborated, and unlikely.[51] Another writer supplied an hysterically exaggerated account of their captivity aboard a prison ship, the *Prosperous Sarah*, moored at Wapping: 'and so that they might stifle one another, having no more breath than what they sucked from one another's mouths, most maliciously, and certainly to a murderous intent, they stopt up all the small auger-holes, and all other inlets which might relieve them with fresh air: an act of such horrid barbarism, that no age, nor story, nor rebellion can parallel'.[52] Even more ludicrous was the claim that an attempt was made to sell them into slavery.[53] In fact, after first being put in the Tower, the three heads spent several months under house arrest in the comfort of an aristocrat's town house, and only a week afloat,

---

[46] Cooper (1851); Book 75, 237 – 9; MS 600. For the plate episode in general, see Twigg (unpublished thesis, 1983), 51 – 8.
[47] *ibid.*, 52 – 7 and n. 49.
[48] See *ibid.*, 58ff, for these and subsequent events.
[49] *Querela* (1647), 5.
[50] *Thomason*, E115 (10); 669.f6 (75); and see E115 (14).
[51] *Querela* (1647), 5.
[52] Walker (1862), 73; also in Searle, 482 – 3.
[53] Barwick (1724), 42; Searle, 483 – 4.

when parliament had difficulty in housing all of its prisoners.[54]

The three petitioned the House of Lords for their release within a few days of their arrest, but the Lords showed little interest.[55] On 26 December, the Lords read a petition from their colleges, which tried to appease parliament by hoping for the 'happy Success and Accomplishment of your just Acts and Designs', but stressed the colleges' own 'urgent Necessities'. The presence of their heads was 'always most useful and beneficial for the Preservation of good Order and Unity amongst us', and was now particularly needed 'for the making up of our Audit Accompts now approaching, the choice of Scholars and Officers, the renewing of Leases, and many other Businesses most nearly concerning the Welfare of our . . . several Colleges'.[56] The Lords had no time for this petition either, nor — apart from changing their places of imprisonment — for the heads themselves. In August 1643 Martin was taken to the bishop of Ely's house in Holborn, where he remained until 1647, implacably opposed to the changes wrought on the college in his absence. In 1647 he drew up a mock petition to the House of Lords attacking parliament's actions in the past few years. He escaped in 1648, and subsequently went into exile before returning to Queens' as president in 1660.[57]

In Cambridge, the military position remained unstable for much of 1643.[58] The town was fortified; several bridges were pulled down, including two at Queens'.[59] There were sufficient disturbances by the parliamentary soldiers for the House of Lords to issue an order in March 1643 forbidding violence to university buildings, property and members, and commanding that divine service there 'be quietly performed and executed . . . without any trouble, let, or disturbance, until the pleasure of the Parliament be further signified'.[60] Nonetheless, several university events were disrupted; there was an outbreak of 'plague', and town-gown relations reached a low point as the townspeople used the prevailing instability to rebel against university dominance.[61] There is little evidence of direct disruption at Queens'. An account book entry for October 1642 refers to 'pewter in the kitchen taken by distresse' — in other words, seized — but it is not clear who took it. In 1644 the college discovered some buttery plate which seems to have been hidden during the war. Queens' was not one of the colleges which suffered from

[54] ibid., 474, 478 – 86; Twigg (unpublished thesis, 1983), 59.
[55] Searle, 475 – 7; MS 502; Twigg (unpublished thesis), 59.
[56] Searle, 477 – 8; Journals of the House of Lords, v.515 – 6.
[57] Twigg (unpublished thesis, 1983), 60; Searle, 486, 493 – 503; below, pp. 142 – 3.
[58] Twigg (unpublished thesis, 1983), 60ff.
[59] Cooper, iii.341; Searle, 522.
[60] Heywood and Wright (1854), ii.455 – 6. The earl of Essex, parliament's military commander, issued a similar order a few days later, ibid., ii.456 – 7.
[61] Twigg (unpublished thesis, 1983), 48 – 9, 61 – 4.

having soldiers billeted in them.[62] There is also circumstantial evidence: the monthly accounts for 1641 – 2 were not added up, and there are no monthly accounts at all between December 1642 and October 1647; the college audit books are blank between 1642 and 1660.[63]

There was a sharp fall in numbers throughout the university, with several colleges granting leaves of absence to their members. In February 1643 all the Fellows at Queens' were given leave until midsummer, and this leave was then renewed quarterly until January 1644, when it was extended until the following Michaelmas.[64] Figures for university matriculations and degree-taking show a slump in student numbers during the war years, followed by a recovery in the later 1640s.[65] No fellow-commoners were admitted to Queens' after April 1642, and only three pensioners and one sizar entered the college in 1643.[66] The case of Simon Patrick of Lincolnshire, who came up to Queens' in 1644, may not have been typical, but is instructive. The outbreak of war had delayed his going to university, his father's goods were sequestered by parliamentary troops, and 'all the country was so infested with soldiers that it was dangerous to travel. Notwithstanding which, my father adventured to carry me around from Boston to Lynn, and so to Cambridge; whereby we passed without any impediment'.[67]

In December 1643, when the House of Lords read a petition from Trinity College which complained of falling rents and sequestrations, the earl of Manchester expressed the hope that his fellow peers would 'think it better to endeavour the reforming of the University rather than to hazard the dissolving of it'.[68] Throughout the year there had been growing recognition that something should be done, both to protect the university from the ravages of war, and to rid it of royalists and high churchmen.[69] In August parliament passed an ordinance for 'the utter demolishing, removing and taking away of all Monuments of Super-stition or Idolatry', which ordered that all communion tables should be brought into the bodies of churches, altar rails be taken down, and tapers, candlesticks, basons, crucifixes and the like done away with.[70] William Dowsing, parliament's agent for implementing the ordinance in East Anglia, was in Cambridge from 21 December to 3 January 1644, during which time his journal records a flurry of licensed vandalism in destroying high church trappings. The entry for Queens', which he

---

[62] Book 6, f.106v; OPR, f.25; Twigg (unpublished thesis, 1983), 135.
[63] Searle, 521 – 2; Book 6, fos.99 – 109; Book 15, entry for 1647/8; Book 12.
[64] Twigg (unpublished thesis, 1983), 64; Searle, 521; OPR, f.131v.
[65] See appendix 1.
[66] Searle, 527; the terms refer to classes of student and are explained below, p. 89.
[67] Patrick (1839), 7 – 11; his father was clearly a royalist.
[68] *Journals of the House of Lords*, vi.327 – 8.
[69] Twigg (unpublished thesis, 1983), 65ff; Twigg (1983), 513 – 5.
[70] Firth and Rait (1911), i.265 – 6; Twigg (unpublished thesis, 1983), 44 – 5.

visited on 26 December, is typical of his work in the 'Laudian' colleges: 'We beat downe about a 110 Superstitious Pictures besides Cherubims & Ingravings, where none of the Fellows would put on their Hatts in all the time they were in the Chapell & we digged up the Steps for 3 hours and brake down 10 or 12 Apostles & Saints within the Hall'.[71]

At the beginning of 1644 parliament began to deal specifically with Cambridge affairs. On 3 January there was talk of an 'excise' to be set on the colleges, and on 6 January an ordinance concerning college rents from their estates.[72] Most significant was the ordinance of 22 January for 'Regulating the University of Cambridge' and removing 'Scandalous Ministers' in East Anglia. This empowered the parliamentary commander of East Anglia, the earl of Manchester, to set up committees to examine all university members, ministers and schoolmasters who were 'scandalous in their lives', 'ill-affected to the Parliament', 'fomenters of this unnatural war', refused to obey parliamentary ordinances, or deserted their places. They were also to administer a new oath, the Solemn League and Covenant, a subscription to the new Presbyterian system which parliament hoped to introduce to replace episcopacy and the existing church hierarchy. Those who refused the oath were to be expelled; Manchester was ordered to take special care to see it taken in the university.[73]

He arrived in Cambridge towards the end of February, anxious to finish his task there swiftly, before the start of the campaigning season. On 24 February he wrote to all college heads and ordered them to send him their college statutes and lists of members, indicating those who were absent, and the length of their absence. Two days later, the heads were ordered to inform the absentees that they must return to Cambridge by 10 March, when they would have to 'answer such things as may be demanded'.[74] This was a harsh deadline, given the general state of 17th century communications, and the disruption caused by the war, but Manchester was in haste. On 11 March he sent to the heads for information on all who had left or returned since his arrival, and for records of all college orders passed in the previous twelve years. On the same day he sent messages to George Huddleston of Magdalene and John Coldham of Queens' asking for their notes of their recent sermons in the university church. The outcome of this is not known: Coldham was later ejected, but for refusing the Covenant.[75]

The first ejections followed on 13 March, when five of the more

---

[71] Cooper, iii.365.
[72] Twigg (1983), 515.
[73] ibid., 515 – 6; the Covenant is printed in Kenyon (1966), 263 – 6.
[74] This implied that he might override the common law right to remain silent, Twigg (1983), 516 and n.4.
[75] ibid., 516 – 7

notoriously royalist and high church heads were put out, including Edward Martin.[76] There was then a lull until 3 April, when Manchester sent warrants to several colleges requiring absentees — five were named from Queens' — to appear before him in two days' time, when they would be ejected unless they could supply 'sufficient reasons' for their absence.[77] The first mass ejections began on 8 April, for non-residence and not appearing when summoned: 64 Fellows were put out, four of them from Queens'.[78] Four more Queens' Fellows were ejected the following day, for refusing to take the Covenant.[79] Fellows were given three days to leave the university, or face imprisonment and sequestration of their possessions. The profits of their fellowships were reserved for those to be appointed in their places, and colleges were to certify within one day that they had struck the names of ejected Fellows from their buttery lists.[80]

It is possible that rough justice was administered in some cases, but parliament clearly intended no more than summary treatment. The two standard reasons for ejection given in the ejection warrants were for refusing the Covenant, and for non-residence and non-appearance when summoned, but reasons for individual ejections are largely obscure.[81] A few university members avoided the oath-taking; Simon Patrick wrote that the Covenant 'was then so zealously pressed, that all scholars were summoned to take it at Trinity college. Thither I went, and had it tendered to me. But God so directed me, that I, telling them my age [he was seventeen, and all under eighteen seem to have been exempt] was dismissed, and never heard more of it — blessed be God'.[82] Edward Martin was later to write a harsh attack on the Covenant, declaring that he would 'embrace any extremity of torture or death', rather than subscribe to something 'so opposite to his Religion, Faith, and all his duties to God and man'.[83]

About half the total fellowship of the university was expelled, with some colleges suffering particularly.[84] Queens' seems to have been hardest hit: in the words of some of the ejected Fellows elsewhere in the university, 'the whole Corporation of Master & Fellows . . . were ejected, imprison'd, or banish'd thence'. Thomas Fuller noted 'a thorough reformation, neither Master, Fellow, nor Scholar being left', a

---

[76] ibid., 517
[77] ibid., 519 – 20; CUL Baker MSS xxxvii, 21 (Anthony Sparrow, Thomas Marley, Richard Bryan, Samuel Rogers and Heigham Hills).
[78] Twigg (1983), 520; CUL Baker MSS xxxvii, 24 (Sparrow, Bryan, Rogers and Hills).
[79] Searle, 530 (Ambrose Appleby, John Coldham, Edward Natley, Edward Kemp).
[80] Twigg (1983), 520.
[81] ibid., 518 – 21.
[82] Patrick (1839), 12.
[83] Searle, 496 – 503.
[84] See below, appendix 3.

view echoed by other royalists.[85] Simon Patrick arrived at Queens' in June 1644 to find himself in 'a solitary place', with 'about a dozen scholars, and almost half of the old fellows', but the latter, 'rarely appearing, were all turned out for refusing the covenant' during the next few months.[86] Meanwhile, new men were put in. The new president of Queens', Herbert Palmer, was one of five heads installed by Manchester on 11–12 April.[87] The installation ceremony took place in the college chapel, and was designed to resemble customary ritual. Manchester put Palmer in the master's stall, and handed him the college statutes 'in testimony of his actual investiture and possession of the said charge'. Martin was deemed to have been 'justly and lawfully ejected', and college members were commanded 'to acknowledge him the said Mr Herbert Palmer to be the actuall Master of this colledge, and sufficiently authorized to execute the said office, and accordingly to use unto him all such respects and obedience as the statutes of the said House doe require to be given unto him as Master thereof'. There was also mention of 'a necessity of reforming . . . the statutes themselves'.[88]

The introduction of new Fellows was a less urgent task, and Manchester recognised a need for conciliation and continuity: on 10 April he wrote to colleges inviting them to submit the names of any of their members who might qualify for fellowships 'in regard of degree, learning and piety'.[89] New Fellows had first to be approved by the Westminster Assembly of Divines, a consultative body set up by parliament to assist the remodelling of the church; some time could elapse before replacements were installed. New heads and Fellows had to swear to promote learning and piety, 'agreeable to the late solemn national league and Covenant, by me sworn and subscribed with respect to all the good and wholesome statutes of the said College, and of the university correspondent to the said Covenant', and also to 'endeavour to procure the good welfare and perfect reformation both of the College and the University, so far as to me appertaineth'.[90]

Once the first, major, stages of the purge were over, Manchester left most of the work to his local committee.[91] There was genuine concern that the university should resume normal life as soon as possible.

[85] Box 31; Fuller, *History*, 237; *Querela* (1647), 22–3.
[86] Patrick (1839), 12. The last ejections were in September, Box 31; see also Searle, 540, 547–50.
[87] Palmer was instituted on 11 April.
[88] Searle, 539–40; this was the standard formula used at all the colleges, Twigg (1983), 525.
[89] *ibid.*, 525; c.f. Searle, 530–1, who argues that this was not sent to Queens' — in view of the total reformation of the college, there would have been little point at that stage — and there is no record of such a letter in the college.
[90] Twigg (1983), 525; Searle, 548–9; Box 31; eight new Fellows took the oath on 19 June, one the following day, and two on 2 September.
[91] Twigg (1983), 526.

Manchester himself was anxious for its welfare: in November 1644 he advocated an increased maintenance allowance for heads of houses out of government funds, perhaps working on the principle he had espoused the previous year, that 'the University of Cambridge was a fountain of piety and learning, and, to afford countenance and relief to this University is to give encouragement to learning, and will make the University depend on it'. In May 1645 the university petitioned parliament for Manchester to remain in authority over it. But parliament's interest in Cambridge did not stretch far beyond the purge, and the university's welfare now lay in the hands of the intruded heads and Fellows.[92]

At Queens' there was a slow return to normality. Three students were admitted in May and June of 1644; then, on 11 June, nine new Fellows were admitted, and on 20 June eleven new students. The first college meeting was held the following day, and college officers were elected on 24 June.[93] The last intrusions of new Fellows were in January 1645; the first elections not until 1647.[94]

The new president, Herbert Palmer, had been a Fellow of Queens' in the 1620s. He had resigned in 1633, possibly because he did not care for Martin's religious reforms, but also because he had been presented to a living in Hertfordshire the previous year. His Puritan inclinations had long been in evidence, and in 1643 he was invited to sit in the Westminster Assembly of Divines.[95] A book published in 1643, *Scripture and Reason Pleaded for Defensive Arms*, which justified the use of force against the king, has been attributed to him, but the work appears uncharacteristically radical, and Palmer was a moderate man in life as well as beliefs.[96] Sermons which he preached before parliament during the 1640s show this. He was a firm believer in the Covenant and the Presbyterianism which it upheld, but he preferred to lead by example, and warned parliament against oppression; he was distressed by the continuance of the war.[97] Palmer valued the universities highly. In 1646 he stressed that a constant supply of 'Ministers and Builders' from Oxford and Cambridge was essential for the nation's well-being: it would 'make way for all the rest, and make all other things prosper'. He was concerned that so little had been accomplished since his plea to the House of Commons in June 1643 to 'Secure youth in the Universities, and Schools, with the utmost care; and even in Parents houses, what

---

[92]   *ibid.*, 527 – 8.
[93]   Searle, 540 – 1.
[94]   *ibid.*, 550.
[95]   *DNB*; Searle, 532 – 6.
[96]   ?Palmer (1643); Twigg (unpublished thesis, 1983), 91; Clarke (1677), 200.
[97]   Palmer (1644), 36 – 7, 41 – 2, 46, 50; Palmer (1643), 54 – 5; Palmer (1646), 10 – 13.

you can, specially the poorer sort. The young ones are the hopes or the bane of the Church and State in the next 20, 10, or 7 years'.[98] Certainly Palmer never considered changing the structure of the universities.[99]

All the intruded Cambridge heads were active in the Westminster Assembly, Palmer particularly so.[100] This work called him away from Cambridge for long periods of up to three months at a time, but he made careful provision for good government in the college. A college order was passed in January 1647 enabling the vice-president to summon the Fellows to discuss occasional, and not just essential business, if he was asked to do so by any two Fellows; and the president was at Queens' that month, when there was a flurry of college orders. Palmer always enquired into the progress of the students when he returned from London. The Puritan writer Samuel Clarke believed that he kept in touch whilst he was away, and returned the profits of his mastership to the college at these times, keeping only enough to cover travelling expenses.[101] He seems to have commanded the respect of the Fellows, and was a shrewd governor who worked hard for consensus. He insisted on the proper performance of academic exercises: 'commonplaces'[102] were now to be held throughout the year, not only in term time. Religious practices came under close scrutiny: full attendance was demanded at chapel and regulations against late-comers were tightened; Fellows were to gather their pupils together for prayers every night. Students — and even college servants — were to receive religious instruction. A new lectureship in ethics was created in 1645.[103]

Palmer's plans could not have succeeded without the support of the Fellows, and there are no signs of dissent. According to Clarke, Palmer was 'exceeding Circumspect . . . Cautious and wary in the choice of those who (as Fellows) were to joyn with him in the Government, that they might be learned, pious, and unanimous'. All new Fellows had to be approved by the Westminster Assembly, and had to take the Covenant; at Queens', in addition, Palmer insisted on full public examination of candidates to test their learning and abilities.[104] The new fellowship was young: of the first nine intrusions (in June 1644) only four were masters of arts; three were 'inceptors', and two bachelors of

---

[98] Palmer (1646), 44, 55; Palmer (1643), 54.
[99] Twigg (unpublished thesis, 1983), 98; for the remarks of the other other intruded heads, see *ibid.*, 93 – 100; their views on the universities are in J. D. Twigg (1984).
[100] Twigg (unpublished thesis, 1983), 105 – 6; he was one of the assembly's two assessors, and one of its six preachers.
[101] Patrick (1839), 13 – 14; OPR, f.133; Clarke (1677), 198.
[102] An academic exercise consisting of a discussion or debate on a set passage; the word has different meanings in other contexts.
[103] Patrick (1839), 13; Clarke (1677), 197 – 8; Searle, 554 – 5; OPR, fos.25v, 132v – 133.
[104] Clarke (1677), 197 – 8; Searle, 554; OPR, f.132; Box 31.

arts.[105] Six of the nine were recruited from the Puritan seminary of Emmanuel College, one came from Edinburgh (the Scots were Presbyterians), and the other two from Cambridge colleges with orthodox Protestant credentials.[106] Thomas Fuller (who was a royalist) believed the new men to be 'short of the former in learning and abilities', but they were no less distinguished than their predecessors.[107] Two of them, John Wallis and John Smith, were considerably more distinguished: both came from Emmanuel, where the restrictions on the number of Fellows who could come from any one county at a time had prevented their promotion. Wallis, who left after a year in order to marry, was an eminent mathematician, Savilian professor of Geometry at Oxford for over fifty years and a leading member of the Royal Society. Smith, who died in 1652, was a distinguished theologian at the forefront of the 'Cambridge Platonist' movement, and a superb prose stylist.[108]

The war continued, however; the legality of the parliamentary intrusions was open to question; and royalist elements survived within the university.[109] There was much sympathy for the ejected Fellows. Some colleges released them from their debts, paid up money they were still owed for their stipends, or gave them financial assistance. The Queens' accounts contain an entry from 1649 for 'a quarter stipend' owed still to Daniel Wicherly, an ejected Fellow. At some other colleges there was friction between old and new Fellows.[110]

Palmer died in September 1647. The college was permitted to hold a free election and it chose Thomas Horton, a former Fellow of Emmanuel who had since lived in London and worked there as a curate, as professor of divinity at Gresham College, and as preacher to Gray's Inn. His theological views were close to those of his predecessor; Simon Patrick thought him 'a good man', if not as good a governor as Palmer.[111] He was elected unanimously, and in January 1648 was granted all privileges formerly enjoyed by his predecessors (probably in case anyone should cast doubt upon his legal standing as president). It was understood that he too would have to spend a good deal of time in London.[112] The college remained peaceful under Horton's government,

---

[105] Of the 18 Fellows listed in 1647/8, only one had a BD degree, and only three were priests; six were only bachelors of arts, Book 15, entry for 1647/8. For inceptors, see below p. 98.

[106] Box 31; AC.

[107] Fuller, History, 237; AC.

[108] Feingold (1984), 53, 169; Scriba (1970), 31; Patrides (1980), 2, 33; DNB. For Cambridge Platonism, see below, pp. 147 – 8.

[109] Twigg (unpublished thesis, 1983), 106 – 123.

[110] ibid., 108 – 111; Twigg (1983), 527; Book 15, entry for 1648/9.

[111] Searle, 557 – 8; DNB; Patrick (1839), 14.

[112] OPR, fos.133v – 134. Book 28 has an entry in January 1648 for Fellows travelling to London to see the president.

and by 1647/8 there were eighteen Fellows entered in the books — a normal complement, more or less; student numbers also seem to have regained their pre-war levels by this time.[113]

Parliament was happy to leave Cambridge alone for the most part.[114] In November 1644 Manchester wrote to the House of Lords that 'there is an apparent change begun, for the advancing of learning and religion, especially in some colleges, where there are placed new Masters'. Stressing the heads' importance to the university, he argued that their stipends should be increased out of public funds; this would enhance their status and authority, enable them to give rewards to deserving students (which Palmer did anyway), and compensate them for the destruction of the old ecclesiastical career structure.[115] Parliament was sympathetic, but it was not until 1650 that a scheme of payment was worked out. The augmentations given varied from £40 to £100 a year. The previous value of the presidency of Queens' was stated as £68 3s 3d, but we do not know how this was calculated: it probably included estimates of 'dividend' returns, and perhaps of commons and other allowances.[116] The president was now to receive another £50 each year from the state, but in April 1654 Horton petitioned the Lord Protector, Oliver Cromwell, complaining that his stipend augmentation was one year in arrears; most of the other heads sent similar petitions at this time, and Horton petitioned again in 1656, probably for the same reason.[117]

Some colleges were hard-hit financially by the war.[118] Sixty-four heads and Fellows are known to have had property sequestered on account of their royalism; three — Edward Martin, John Coldham and Thomas Cox — were Queensmen. Both Coldham and Martin had their books taken. According to the notes of one of Martin's later 17th century successors, £250 of college money was in his hands 'till the Rebellion broke out, soe being driven from the College & his Right he made use of the mony as his owne in his great necessity. He did not live full two yeares after the King's return in the enjoyment of his owne & soe was not in a Condition

---

[113] Book 15, entry for 1647/8; Book 28, entry for 1647/8 (evidence from chamber rents, which were at the same level as in 1636/7, Book 27, entry for 1636/7). There is no record of any disputes under Horton.

[114] Twigg (unpublished thesis, 1983), 123 – 131; Twigg (1983), 528.

[115] Cooper, iii.382 – 3. Simon Patrick wrote of Palmer's generosity: 'those youths whom he heard well of, when he came back to college, he sent for to his lodgings, and commended them; giving books to those who were well maintained, and money to the poorer sort', Patrick (1839), 14. But note that Palmer came from a wealthy background, Searle, 532 – 3.

[116] For dividends, see below, p. 76.

[117] Cooper, iii.432; Twigg (unpublished thesis, 1983), 128 – 9; CSPD (1654), 71; CSPD (1655 – 6), 327.

[118] Twigg (unpublished thesis, 1983), 131 – 6, and Appendix C.

to repay the College.'[119] Despite parliamentary measures to protect college rents, many colleges lost rental income through disruption, damage and sequestration.[120] There was also a run of bad harvests between 1646 and 1651.[121] Gaps in the college archives make it impossible to discover how badly Queens' was affected by all this, but the college showed a small surplus in its annual account in 1648/9 and 1659/60, the only years for which figures are available.[122] In 1648 it was decided to prosecute the college tenant at Capel for felling college timber illegally on the property, and in 1651/2 the rights of tenants to fell trees were restricted, which may suggest that tenants were taking advantage of wartime disruption to cut down trees for their own use without permission.[123] But college leases were renewed in 1649 for the normal period of 21 years, and 'courts' were held on the estates regularly during the 1650s — both of these features suggest stability.[124] The war had brought an end to the traditional exemption of colleges from state taxes, and they were taxed sporadically throughout the 1640s and in particular the 1650s; Queens' paid out usually between about £12 and £25 a year, but sometimes more, in direct taxes and allowances to tenants for taxes levied on their lands.[125] The college was anxious about its financial position. In 1650 the university set a new poor rate on the colleges. Queens' contribution was set at £7 9s 4d a year, but it agreed to pay only 'so long as the Master and fellows shall judge the College able to pay the summe'. In January 1653 it was decided to reduce the number of Fellows to 17, keeping the profits of the others for college use; deferrals of college elections in 1648, 1652, 1653 and 1656 may also have been

---

[119]   CSPD (1625 – 49), 754 – 5; Twigg (unpublished thesis, 1983), 131 – 2; Searle, 480, 486, 523; OPR, fos.17v – 18; Book 80, f.6 (second pagination; two scholarships formerly paid out of the money were maintained out of chamber rents).

[120]   Twigg (unpublished thesis, 1983), 132 – 3; Twigg (1983), 515.

[121]   Howard (1935), 63; the other great periods of dearth in the century were 1658 – 61 and 1692 – 8.

[122]   Above, p. 51; Book 15, entries for 1648/9 and 1659/60; in 1647/8 there was a dividend of £290 to be split among the 19 Fellows, Book 28, entry for 1647/8. For college finances in general, see chapter 9.

[123]   OPR, fos. 135 – 6. In 1650 a college tenant applied for permission to fell timber on his land; this was granted, in view of the hard times which then prevailed, and the fact that he paid the taxes on the college's property. There are also some examples from 1652 of tenants being allowed to fell a little timber for repairs, Book 15, at back. Because of the gaps in the accounts, we do not know how many tenants defaulted on their rent payments during and after the war. In the last 17th century a legal action was brought to recover money owed to the college manor of Eversden, which 'was alwaies paid till 1641 and never since', Book 80, f.60v (second pagination). There are also two examples of defaulting tenants from 1648, Book 28, entry for 1647/8.

[124]   OPR, fos.169 – v; Book 15, passim, Book 49, fos.10 – 40; Book 28, entry for June 1648. College leases expired at different times. For courts, see below, p. 114.

[125]   Twigg (unpublished thesis, 1983), 135 – 6, 177 – 8; Book 15, entries for 1647/8 and 1659/60; Cooper, iii.433. See also below, chapter 9 for details of the college's normal annual income.

because of this.[126] However, there was no serious or long term damage to the college's financial position because of the war.[127]

The university was well on the way to recovery by the late 1640s, but the political situation worsened. Charles I was executed in January 1649, and England became a republic. The university was deeply shocked. In September parliament decided to hold another visitation, at which university members would have to take an oath known as the 'Engagement', to be loyal to the new republican constitution.[128] Fellows wrestled with their consciences. Henry Paman, a Fellow of St John's, commented in a letter on 'a report here, that the subscription was offered to Dr Horton, who promised readily that he would be true and faithful to them; by which he could not be any more than by telling them of their bloodshed and perjury, which he resolved to do to his utmost, the next time he had occasion to speak to any of them from the pulpit'. But Paman went on to say that 'I think this story is not like to be true', and Horton took the oath.[129] The visitation showed none of the urgency which had characterised Manchester's purge of 1644 – 5; even some of the staunch opponents of the oath were not expelled until the summer of 1651. About fifty men lost their places; six were from Queens', of whom two were students.[130] The earl of Manchester, chancellor of the university since 1649, was ejected in November 1651 and replaced by Oliver St John, a prominent parliamentary republican who had been a fellow-commoner at Queens' in the 1610s.[131] Most dons took the oath because they wished to avoid trouble, and university men tried to remain aloof from politics during the rest of the decade.[132]

Republican governments in their turn did not interfere in university matters, except when necessary, and then as guarantors of tradition.[133] One significant administrative reform at this time was that of the cycle of university proctors. Colleges took turns to nominate proctors, but the schedule of nomination then in use was out of date and a new cycle, instituted in 1650 after some years of debate, reflected the relative importance of the sixteen colleges in existence at that time: Queens' was

---

[126] Searle, 563, 566 – 7; OPR, fos.29v, 134v, 136 – 8.
[127] See also below, chapter 11, n. 13.
[128] Twigg (unpublished thesis), 138 – 9.
[129] D'Oyly (1821), 50 – 1. Horton certainly retained his job, which suggests that he must have taken the oath.
[130] Forty-seven definitely; possibly nine more, Twigg (unpublished thesis, 1983), 140 – 5; Searle, 573; CUL Baker MSS xxv.427 – 8; xxxiii.457; OPR, f.145 (c.f. fos.135v – 136, when, in 1650 and 1651, two Fellows, John Hoare and John Haddon, were granted leave, each having been 'called to a place for triall in order to his remooveall'). The ejected were: Michael Freer, John Haddon, John Hoare, John Jackson, John Fisher and Anthony St George; the two last were students.
[131] Twigg (unpublished thesis, 1983), 146; AC.
[132] Twigg (unpublished thesis, 1983), 142 – 4, 147 – 9.
[133] ibid., 148 – 151, chapter VI.

one of four colleges which now nominated approximately once every seven years; only three colleges nominated more frequently.[134] In 1653 there were anxious rumours that a newly-inaugurated, radical parliament was planning to close the universities down, but this came to nothing.[135] That parliament was short-lived, and the Cromwellian protectorate which succeeded it was conservative where the universities were concerned. Cromwell was a staunch supporter of the university system — he had been a student at Sidney Sussex — and in 1656 he told parliament that 'I believe God hath for the ministry a very great seed in the youth of the universities'.[136] Government propaganda portrayed Cambridge as both prosperous and loyal: a newspaper, the *Publick Intelligencer*, observed in 1656 that 'The Colledges are well stored with Scollars both pious and studious, and who (for the time) have made such progress in solid literature, that they never were excelled in times of the greatest encouragement'.[137] Thomas Horton was well thought of by the protectorate. He was one of twelve Cambridge heads appointed visitors for the university in 1654, and one of four made a 'Trier' to ordain prospective clergymen.[138]

Cromwell is known to have interfered in one or two college elections at Cambridge, but this was slight compared with that under Elizabeth and the early Stuarts, and slighter still compared with that under Charles II to come; only rarely was pressure brought to bear. In January 1657 Queens' voted to resist an order (or 'mandate') to elect John Lawson, a former pensioner there, to a fellowship 'for as much as they are not satisfyed in the condition mentioned in the sayd mandate'. The 'condition' was not specified, but Lawson was not admitted.[139] The protectorate government was also responsive to requests from colleges: there is almost certainly a link between the testimony of Thomas Horton and eleven Fellows of Queens' to the good conduct of Martin Pindar, bachelor of arts of the college, in October 1657, and Richard Cromwell's

---

[134] *ibid.*, 151; Cooper, ii.39; iii.434.
[135] Twigg (unpublished thesis, 1983), 158 – 9.
[136] *ibid.*, 159 – 60; Firth (1953), 349.
[137] *Thomason*, E494 (11), 688.
[138] Twigg (unpublished thesis, 1983), 166; Neal (1754), ii.447. Thirty visitors were appointed for the university, but the bulk of their work was probably done by the heads. A curious contemporary passage describes the university's commencement ceremony of c. 1651, and contains references to some of the intruded masters, including this of Horton: 'Next appears in a Vision of the young Husband of Queens [Horton married in 1651, Searle, 558]; when he looks upon his Sweeting, he lifts up the eyes of his minde, and blesseth all his Fellows. Who observed his Syllogismes? they were all corrected: and indeed the common Example which Logicians give to the Rule, may be applied to him; though so careful a Man of his Wife, that when he goes forth, he locks up the Chamber-door, (I wish he would lock up her mouth too) and carries the Key in his Pocket with him; so it is not for us to lodge here', printed in Wordsworth (1874), 673.
[139] Twigg (unpublished thesis, 1983), 162 – 5; Searle, 568 – 9; OPR, f.137v.

order of November 1658 to elect Pindar to the fellowship recently vacated by Simon Patrick.[140]

Although both Palmer and Horton would have followed the Presbyterian system of worship, based on a new prayer book, there is almost no information surviving on religious practice at Queens' under their rule.[141] Not all conformed happily. Simon Patrick was ordained by 'a classis of presbyters who then sat; and was examined by them, and afterward received the imposition of their hands', but he began to have doubts about the validity of such a form of ordination, and was won over to belief in the old episcopal form. Since episcopacy had been abolished, he sought out the former bishop of Norwich and, with two other Fellows of Queens', was examined and ordained by him in 1654.[142] In 1657 Patrick was offered a vicarage at Battersea, and was afraid of being 'examined and rejected by the triers', who had to approve all new incumbents; but he was admitted after an undemanding examination.[143]

Horton, on the other hand, was demonstrably orthodox, and his sermons from the 1650s illustrate well the mood of the university in that decade. In 1646 he had preached before the House of Lords on the theme of 'Sinne's Discovery and Revenge', an appropriate subject for such a period of turmoil.[144] In 1653 he preached to the City of London a simply homily on the dangers of relying too much on earthly wisdom rather than faith and humility. He was content with the nation's religious settlement: men were to 'do that which is our Duty, and to leave the event of things to God'.[145] Three years later he preached before the City again, on the happy state of the land, and the need to maintain it; he was prepared to tolerate differences of opinion among Christians if these did not disturb 'the common peace of the Church'.[146] Horton's theme was echoed by a Fellow of Queens', Samuel Jacombe. In a sermon delivered in December 1656 Jacombe urged the values of candour and moderation: 'The heat of the heart purifies the blood, yet if good air be not sucked in by the lungs to cool it, it will ruine the body by hectick feavers'.[147] Jacombe's friend Simon Patrick praised his 'prudent, courteous, obliging behaviour', and one of Patrick's own jottings from

---

[140] *CSPD* (1657 – 8), 135; (1658 – 9), 171; *AC*. It is not clear if Pindar became a Fellow; see the lists of Fellows in Book 15.
[141] See Twigg (unpublished thesis, 1983), 123 – 5, 169 – 175, for religious changes in the university during this period.
[142] Patrick (1839), 23 – 4; his companions are not named.
[143] *ibid.*, 30 – 1.
[144] Horton (1646).
[145] Horton (1653), 61, and see *ibid.*, 1 – 22, 40 – 2, 46, 67 – 8. Horton also contributed to a volume of verses issued by the university in 1660 to celebrate the restoration of the monarchy, Cooper, iii.480.
[146] Horton (1656), 23, and see *ibid.*, 6 – 9, 14, 16.
[147] Jacombe (1657), 43 and *passim*. Jacombe was no longer a Fellow at the time of this sermon; see Patrick (1839), 27, and c.f. *AC*.

this time expressed the similarly moderate view of one influenced by the Cambridge Platonists (John Smith had been Patrick's tutor): 'Embrace that which is good in any man, and look not strangely upon him because he differs from thee in some opinions'.[148] These were the authentic voices of Interregnum Cambridge, which had suffered enough from overzealousness, and now sought only peace, stability and undisturbed scholarship.[149]

---

[148] Patrick (1839), 25, 27; it was written in c. 1654. Patrick and Jacombe were described by a university member as being among 'divers young preachers . . . in those times, who were of a freer temper and genius', Gascoigne, 'Barrow'.

[149] Twigg (unpublished thesis, 1983), 175.

5

The early presidents (1448 – 1644)

'Grievous, therefore, is their offence who infect Colleges, the fountains of learning and religion; and it concerneth the church and state, that the Heads of such Houses be rightly qualified'. (Thomas Fuller, 'The Good Master of a College'.)[1]

Between its foundation and the outbreak of the Civil War, Queens' was governed by 17 presidents. Each held the office for just under eleven years on average, but this figure is distorted by long-serving presidents such as Andrew Doket and Humphrey Tyndall: ten of the 17 were in office for less than ten years, five for less than five.[2] Their places of origin, and especially their social backgrounds, are often obscure.[3] Their careers are better documented: the mastership of a Cambridge college was often just one step along the road of an ecclesiastical career. Four were bishops, many held other ecclesiastical positions of importance, and all held parish livings at some time.[4] Fifteen had been fellows of colleges, ten at Queens'.[5] Thirteen followed the clerical-academic course of studies as far as the degree of doctor of divinity; two others trained as lawyers.[6] Ten held university offices.[7]

---

[1] Fuller (1841), 93.

[2] See appendix 4; the averages are calculated from dates given in Searle, Emden and *AC*. William Mey served two times as president, and this has been counted as two periods of office-holding for the average; if Mey is counted twice, then six presidents held office for less than five years.

[3] We know the places of origin of ten of them: Yorkshire (Fisher), the diocese of Coventry and Lichfield (Bekynsaw); Buckinghamshire (Franklyn), Suffolk (Mey), Anglesey (Glynn), Lancashire (Chaderton), Norfolk (Tyndall), London (Davenant), Lincolnshire (Mansell), Cambridgeshire (Martin). We know the social origins of three: Fisher was the son of a Yorkshire mercer; Davenant the son of a London merchant taylor; Tyndall the son of a Norfolk knight.

[4] The four bishops were: Fisher (who was already a bishop when elected), Glynn, Chaderton, and Davenant; Mey was elected archbishop of York, but died on the very day of his election, see above, p. 38. Queens' presidents also held 18 prebend's stalls, 5 archdeaconries, 8 deaneries, 7 canon's places, and 14 other ecclesiastical positions (other than parish livings); they held 46 (perhaps 47) parish cures. Pluralism was not uncommon, therefore.

[5] Seven at Queens' throughout; three at Queens' and other colleges.

[6] Wilkinson was only a master of arts; Doket was probably a master of arts also, to judge from the 1475 statutes.

[7] It was not usual for the vice-chancellor to be a head of house before the mid-16th century.

Before 1475, when the first statutes were issued, the college must have been governed by presidential whim.[8] While there were only four Fellows, as at the foundation, this may not have caused any great problems; but by the 1470s, when the number had risen threefold, and Doket no longer spent so much of his time in Cambridge, there was need of more formal regulation.[9] The 1475 statutes directed that there should be one '*Superior*', elected for life and responsible for the college's government, discipline and religious observance.[10] The qualities required of him included honesty, discretion and sound business sense; more specifically, he had to be a graduate and a priest, and to have a private income of at least £20 a year. His stipend was a mere five marks (£3 6s 8d) — half that of a Fellow — wth an extra allowance for each week spent in college.[11]

Such stipulations allowed the president to be an absentee with a comfortable church living. Elsewhere, the statutes expected him to reside for only one month in each term, later changed to one month in each quarter; the fellowship could authorise longer absences.[12] The early presidents were often absent, holding parish livings or other ecclesiastical preferments, with some in higher positions. Robert Bekynsaw (1508 – 19), an assiduous collector of church offices, was active at court, and was dispensed from all residence restrictions by the university when he was attending Lady Margaret Beaufort; by 1509 he was Catherine of Aragon's chaplain.[13] Fisher used Queens' as a lodging house when he visited Cambridge on Lady Margaret's business.[14] Simon Heynes and William Mey, both active in the reform movement of the 1530s and 1540s, were often employed by the state.[15]

One exception to this rule, at least for part of his career, was Andrew Doket, who remained rector of St Botolph's well into the 1460s and had

[8] Riley-Smith comments on this that either the Fellows 'were all remarkably flexible and tolerant, or the first President exercised an overpowering domination over them', and is inclined to believe the latter, Riley-Smith in *Record* (1975). It does seem likely.
[9] See above, pp. 1, 9; below, p. 66.
[10] Book 79, fos.2v – 4.
[11] *ibid*. The 1559 statutes were to require the president to be a doctor in divinity, or at least a bachelor in divinity '*ordinem cooptatus*', *Statutes (1559)*, 5. His stipend was the same in both the 1529 and 1559 revisions of the statutes, Book 79, f.36; *Statutes (1559)*, 43 – 5; he was also allowed a servant's expenses, Book 79, fos.11 – 11v. By the end of the 16th century, he received a stipend of £5, Book 5, *passim*; see also Searle, 143; *Documents* (1852), i.212.
[12] Book 79, fos.9v – 10, 17; *Statutes (1559)*, 8. There is an example of extra leave being granted in 1615, OPR, f.5v. Considerable activity elsewhere was compatible with a fair amount of residence.
[13] Emden, 51 – 2, 639 – 40; Searle, 104 – 5, 144 – 145, 161 – 8, 171 – 2, 175 – 6, 179 – 81, 213 – 5, 316, 409; Ball (1885), 12. Martin held several livings and is known to have employed a curate (Peter Hausted) at Uppingham, Searle, 468, 470, Mills (1944), 42 – 3. For Lady Margaret's patronage of Bekynsaw, see Underwood (1982), 74.
[14] Above, p. 18.
[15] Searle, 179 – 81, 213 – 5; above, pp. 28, 34; below, p. 68.

no need to seek lucrative preferments elsewhere, being already a man of some means.[16] But from 1466 onwards he succeeded to a series of more important church offices in other parts of the country. His obvious piety — he refused to become a pluralist — suggests that he would have been absent from Queens' more frequently in performance of these other duties, but there is no way of judging precisely how long such absences were.[17]

Absentee presidents were not thought to handicap the college in any way — if they achieved positions of importance elsewhere, it might even benefit the college. After 1529 they were required to be present at Michaelmas, but this was the only such stipulation; they seem to have attended elections and audits, where their presence was also necessary, but most business could be entrusted to the vice-president and Fellows.[18] Nonetheless, it was sometimes necessary to send messengers to consult presidents on matters of college business, a costly and time-consuming procedure.[19] William Glynn's prolonged absence as bishop of Bangor in the 1550s allowed a major factional dispute to break out among the Fellows; his successor, Thomas Peacock, was a man with a local base.[20] William Chaderton (1568 – 79) and John Davenant (1614 – 22), later presidents who also became bishops, left Queens' on their promotion. Presidents may have spent more time in college towards the end of the period, but after 1569 the residence requirements seem to have slackened, since a college order of that year allowed the president to remain away from Queens' at his pleasure.[21]

Presidents were chosen by the Fellows, and none of the early elections were contested.[22] Doket recommended his successor in his will — such was the measure of his influence — and the fellowship complied dutifully. Thomas Wilkinson (1484 – 1505) was in turn invited by the

[16] Above, pp. 5 – 6.
[17] Emden, 190, for details of these posts; his refusal is shown in his resigning each post to take up the next.
[18] The Fellows did not recognise Fisher's absences as a handicap, above, p. 18. Wilkinson and Bekynsaw were firmly non-resident, Searle, 104 – 5, 144 – 45. For the statutory requirements, see Book 79, f.17. Mullinger's criticism of Tyndall for non-residence is probably an example of a 19th century writer applying the values of his own time to the 16th century, Mullinger (1873 – 1911), ii.478.
[19] Searle, 104 – 5, 142 – 3, 144 – 5, 171 – 2, 179; Book 3, f.270; Book 4, fos.54v, 118v, 132. The election of John Jennyn in 1519 seems to be a clear example of the college moving towards the notion of having an internal candidate, with knowledge of college business, as president, but there was no change in the attitude towards absenteeism, Searle, 161; Emden, 331 – 2.
[20] Above, pp. 36 – 7.
[21] Above, pp. 40, 43; below, pp. 68 – 9. Davenant, though promoted in 1621, only resigned as president in 1622, and then reluctantly, Searle, 414, 417; Morgan (unpublished thesis, 1984), 315. The 1569 order is in Book 62, 103.
[22] Book 79, fos.2v – 4, 15 – 17; Statutes (1559), 4 – 7. None are known to have been contested before the late Tudor period.

Fellows to nominate his replacement, in deference to Lady Margaret, who sought Fisher's election, and had persuaded Wilkinson to stand down to this end. Robert Bekynsaw, the third Michaelhouse man in succession to be president, was similarly nominated by Fisher at the Fellows' request, for they hoped to secure Lady Margaret's patronage thereby. John Jennyn (1519 – 26) was probably chosen on account of his considerable experience of college business acquired under previous absentees, although he maintained the non-resident tradition.[23] Most presidents thereafter were former fellows; Simon Heynes (1529 – 37) was active in the Fellows' campaign to depose Jennyn in 1524 – 6.[24] Heynes' successor, William Mey, shared his advanced religious views, but it is not known if this helped his election. Both William Glynn and Thomas Peacock may have been elected under pressure from the Marian régime.[25]

In Elizabeth's reign court influence became a significant factor in college elections, for several reasons. During the 16th century, as colleges became more important within the university, the status and power of their heads also grew, not only inside the colleges, but in the university at large; the Elizabethan statutes of 1570 made the heads the dominant force in university government.[26] Their power within colleges — of influencing elections, issuing leases and allocating pupils to tutors — was desirable, increased the competition for masterships, and led to bitter divisions at election time, with rival factions turning increasingly to influential patrons for support; these patrons, mostly courtiers, seized this opportunity to extend their sphere of influence, and by the end of the century almost every election was accompanied by faction-fighting.[27] Court involvement was not wholly self-interested: the religious upheavals of the century and the social changes within the universities gave Oxford and Cambridge immense national significance. At a time of revolutionary change, the nation's élite youth had particular need of a disciplined, orthodox education. The skills of college government became more important than distinguished scholarship (although Queens' had two good theologians — Chaderton and Davenant — as presidents). In Fuller's words, 'Sometimes ordinary scholars make extraordinary good masters. Every one who can play well on Apollo's harp, cannot skilfully drive his chariot; there being a peculiar mystery of government'. Central government maintained its

[23] Searle, 56, 104, 125 – 6, 139 – 44, 161 – 2; Emden, 331 – 2.
[24] Searle, 168, 171 – 2, 175 – 9; below, pp. 69 – 70.
[25] Searle, 213, 246, 265; above, pp. 35, 37.
[26] Morgan (unpublished thesis, 1984), 295 – 303; Heywood and Wright (1854), i.44 – 5; Curtis (1959), 35 – 7; Twigg (unpublished thesis, 1983), iv.
[27] Morgan (unpublished thesis, 1984), 295 – 303, 387 – 412, 572 – 635, discusses these questions in detail.

control over the universities through such men.[28]

For the heads in return, there were new opportunities for advancement in the service of the state, as well as the church. Both Heynes and Mey were sent abroad on government missions, the latter having been recommended as 'a man of the most honest sort, wise, discrete, and well lernyd, and one that shall be very mete to sarve his Majestie many wayes'.[29] The successful defence of university property in the 1540s demonstrated the strength of the university's influence at court; there was a significant 'Cambridge connection' at the Elizabethan religious settlement of 1558 – 60, and sixteen Cambridge heads became bishops between 1558 and 1640.[30] William Chaderton was bishop of Chester and subsequently of Lincoln after leaving Queens'. Orthodox in religion, and a disciplinarian, Chaderton was ideal material for court patronage, and his career was advanced by the distinguished Elizabethan statesman William Cecil (Lord Burghley): in 1567 he was elected Lady Margaret professor of divinity; three years later be became Regius professor. Court influence probably secured his election to Queens' in 1568, and he was ever-hopeful of further promotion. He was chaplain to another influential courtier, the earl of Leicester, to whose patronage he may have owed his promotion to be bishop of Chester.[31] Burghley and Leicester also secured the election of Humphrey Tyndall, another of Leicester's chaplains, to succeed Chaderton in 1579; a solitary Fellow protested that Tyndall was too young and inexperienced, and petitioned in vain for a free election.[32] Tyndall defended religious orthodoxy when controversies broke out in the university, and collected several church offices, but he did not secure a bishopric and remained president of Queens' until his death in 1614.[33] Well before this date, there were manoeuvrings by those who wished to succeed him. In 1608, when he fell ill, one of the Fellows, George Montaigne, wrote to the university's chancellor, the earl of Salisbury, asking for a free election, and confident of his own victory. In 1611, when Tyndall's death was rumoured, a former Fellow, George Meriton, secured a royal mandate to be elected president. In 1614 Montaigne, who was embarked on a promising ecclesiastical career in London (where he was dean of Westminster) was

---

[28] Above, chapter 3; below, chapter 7; Morgan (unpublished thesis, 1984), 253 – 4; Porter (1958), 112, 170 – 1; Fuller (1841), 93.
[29] Searle, 181, 213 – 4; Morgan (unpublished thesis, 1984), 183, citing *DNB*.
[30] Morgan (unpublished thesis, 1984), 184 – 7; Collinson (1982), 60 – 1; Parker (1721), 161 – 176.
[31] Searle, 303, 305 – 12, 315; above, pp. 39 – 41; Le Neve (1854), iii.654 – 6. Leicester was High Steward of Cambridge: for his patronage in general see MacCaffrey (1981), 440 – 4. Cecil is known to have been unhappy about the calibre of the Cambridge heads in 1562, Porter (1958), 112.
[32] Searle, 332, 351 – 8. Tyndall may have been only 30 years old, *AC*.
[33] Porter (1958), 211 – 12, 314, 344ff; Searle, 358, 361.

still keen to succeed Tyndall. He was defeated by John Davenant, a current Fellow, with the aid of subterfuge: by the time that Montaigne learned of Tyndall's death, Davenant's supporters had already sent an embassy to court and secured the support of the influential earl of Rochester, on whom Montaigne had been counting for help.[34] Davenant had previously enjoyed the patronage of the earl of Salisbury, he was to be a representative at the Synod of Dort, and his promotion to be bishop of Salisbury in 1621 showed that he was still well thought of at court.[35] His successor John Mansell was freely elected by the college, but only after widespread rumours that an outsider would be imposed, and indeed the duke of Lennox wrote to the college urging them to elect another of the Fellows, Lewis Wemis. Lennox was a relation of the king's, but James does not appear to have taken any interest in the business. Mansell was an able college administrator, and 'a very moderate goodnatured man'. In 1631 the Fellows sent an obsequious letter of thanks to Charles I for allowing them to elect Edward Martin freely.[36]

* * * * *

'He not only keeps the statutes (in his study), but observes them. — For, the maintaining of them will maintain him, if he be questioned. He gives them their true dimensions; not racking them for one, nor shrinking them for another, but making his conscience his daily visitor'. (Thomas Fuller, 'The Good Master of a College'.)[37]

Only six presidents died in office during the period; most of the others resigned following promotion in the church, but some were forced out, especially at times of religious and political upheaval.[38] Most college statutes contained a provision for removal of unsuitable masters; the president of Queens' could be removed if he neglected college business, was incapacitated by illness, or was a criminal.[39] Removal was not so easily achieved in practice: in 1525 an argument broke out between the Fellows and John Jennyn over the latter's excessive claims for expenses whilst on college business; the dispute went before the queen's council,

[34] Morgan (unpublished thesis, 1984), 629 – 34, 639 – 41; Searle, 361, 411 – 12; Ball (1885), 36 – 8. Montaigne was associated with the rising high church movement.
[35] Fuller (1897), 37; above, p. 43; Searle, 414. A dinner was held in honour of his promotion at his departure, Book 6, f.5.
[36] Searle, 445, 449 – 50; Ball (1885), 71; above, p. 44 and chapter 4, n. 18; Box 31.
[37] Fuller (1841), 93.
[38] Jennyn, Mey, Peacock, Martin, and possibly Glynn and Wilkinson were/may have been forced out.
[39] Cobban (1975), 155 – 6; Book 79, fos.10 – 10v, 37v – 38v; *Statutes (1559)*, 36 – 8.

and it was nearly two years before Jennyn was removed.[40] In 1529 an agreement between Simon Heynes and the fellowship regulated the president's perquisites in detail, and made him more accountable to the college; the new statutes of that year defined his authority and office more clearly: he was enjoined to compel observance to statutes, and empowered to allocate rooms, and examine and approve accounts, as well as being permitted to delegate college business outside Cambridge to Fellows.[41]

Yet disputes between presidents and Fellows continued. The 1557 visitation discovered violation of statutes by senior members from the president down.[42] Two years later chancellor Cecil was called in to resolve a major row between two rival factions, one led by the president, Thomas Peacock. There were religious overtones here, for Peacock was trying to install Catholic Fellows after Elizabeth's accession. The dissident minority faction accused him of having kept fellowships vacant in order to keep his faction in a majority, and to divide their stipends among the rest; his supporters were accused of illegal absences from college and disreputable behaviour. Although Peacock's opponents clearly exaggerated the 'brechys of the statutes by our master and his evyll regiment', there was scope for widely different opinions over interpretation and observance of statutes, which could only be resolved by a higher authority. With characteristic judiciousness, Cecil put the matter before a committee of senior dons, and took further advice from William Mey and Thomas Smith concerning the statutes themselves. As a result, the crown ordered the admission of Fellows elected by Peacock's faction, but Peacock resigned, almost certainly under court pressure. Cecil was afraid of a protracted war between the factions; by removing Peacock, he hoped to 'avoide all suche inconveniences as was supposed wold have insued, and they all together henceforth lyve in more quiet than hitherto they have don'.[43]

A single rebel Fellow, such as the Puritan dissident Edmund Rockrey in the 1570s, could sometimes defy the president's authority. With the chancellor unwilling to support the president, William Chaderton — much to the latter's annoyance — Rockrey outlasted Chaderton's rule at Queens'. Differences here over interpretation of statutes may have been genuine, but as in most other cases could be just a medium for expression of personal or religious hostilities.[44] Chaderton received little more support from Cecil in his campaign to be rid of another Fellow, William Middleton, in 1575. With the support of a majority of the

[40] Searle, 168 – 9.
[41] *ibid.*, 182 – 4; Book 79, fos.17v – 19; *Statutes (1559)*, 8 – 13.
[42] Above, pp. 36 – 7.
[43] Searle, 268 – 283; Mullinger (1873 – 1911), ii.175.
[44] Above, p. 40; Searle, 334 – 45.

Fellows, he refused permission for Middleton to take his MA degree, knowing that the statutes insisted on the degree being taken within a certain time if Middleton was to keep his fellowship. Middleton promptly took his MA at Oxford, but his enemies alleged that this was invalid, and a fierce row over the meaning of the relevant statutes ensued. Cecil ordered Queens' to restore Middleton to his fellowship, but not to his seniority. Middleton does not seem to have welcomed discipline: he was only readmitted after a 'submyssyon and promes to lyve orderlie and quietlie hereafter', having been admonished the previous year for 'sowing discord'. In 1585 he quarrelled with Tyndall over the allocation of Fellows' rooms.[45] Though Cecil might not care for Middleton's character, he could not uphold the twisting of the statutes practised in order to remove him.[46]

* * * * *

'He counts it lawful to enrich himself, but in subordination to the College-good'. (Thomas Fuller, 'The Good Master of a College'.)[47]

The status of college heads was considerably enhanced during the 16th century: their lifestyles became grander, their separation from the Fellows greater.[48] At Queens' there was a widening range of visible, material distinctions. From an early date the president was allowed two servants; in the early 17th century these had their own liveries. In 1623 the accounts referred to 'the Master's men Coques and butlers'.[49] In 1532 he was given a garden-orchard for his sole use; by the 1580s he had his own gardener. The garden had a dovecot by the 1540s and a summer house by 1617.[50] The president also had his own woodhouse, pump, kitchen and cellar.[51] In the chapel he was made more comfortable by the purchase of 'a squaire cushion and a long one' for his personal use.[52] Three horses were provided for him, with their food, stabling and

[45] Searle, 324 – 31; Book 14, 126 – 7, 129; for the statutory requirements, see below, p. 77.
[46] See Searle, 330.
[47] Fuller (1841), 94.
[48] Morgan (unpublished thesis, 1984), chapter VI.
[49] Book 79, f.14v; Statutes (1559), 3; Book 5, f.121; Book 6, f.13. See also Searle, 182 – 3; Morgan (unpublished thesis, 1984), 310.
[50] Searle, 184; Book 3, fos.81, 91; Book 4, fos.132v, 145; Book 5, fos.165 – 165v; Book 6, fos.13v, 17v – 18. See below, p. 133 and chapter 10, n. 85. The Fellows seem to have had their own gardener, at least for some of the Tudor period, Book 4, fos. 107, 113 – 113v, and c.f. chapter 10, n. 8.
[51] Book 5, fos.12v, 13v, 152v; Book 6, f.13.
[52] Book 5, f.59.

shoeing (but not their saddles and bridles) paid for the college; keeping horses was a costly business.[53]

The president's changed status was most strikingly demonstrated by his improved lodgings. During the 16th century, particularly in the latter half, college masters moved into separate lodges and ceased to dine with the Fellows.[54] The new fashion reached its final stage with the addition of galleries to these lodges, where the master could walk and entertain in private; the great extension at Queens', which includes the long gallery, was built in the Elizabethan period. Lodges were also embellished internally, especially with panelling and wainscoting; sometimes the decoration was ostentatiously lavish. A college order of 1563 at Queens' directed that 'the Masters lodginge shalbe furnyshed with all manner of Implements and furniture, decent and mete for the same as he shulde thinke most convenyent in his conscience at the colledge cost'. New furniture was put in on Chaderton's installation in 1568.[55] Humphrey Tyndall installed a great deal of panelling, and the overall level of comfort was raised by carpets, cushions and wall hangings. In 1624 and 1664 the college bought 'Russian leather chaires' for the lodge.[56]

Masters thus came to resemble heads of well-to-do households, a resemblance increased by their freedom to marry brought about by the Reformation. Priests in England were formally permitted to marry in 1549, although conservative opposition to the practice continued for some time. Elizabeth I certainly disapproved, and though it was by then too late to reverse the trend with regard to the clergy in general or to heads of colleges, she ensured that Fellows were forbidden to marry.[57] Some priests, among them Simon Heynes, had married before 1549; Heynes' widow married his successor as president, William Mey. Marriage was usual among Elizabethan masters: Chaderton married, as did Tyndall, who was criticised by Fuller for paying too much attention to his wife and not enough to the college, a common complaint of conservatives at that time; Jane Tyndall is the first president's wife known to have visited Queens'.[58] The combined effects of marriage and

[53] Searle, 183; Morgan (unpublished thesis, 1984), 310, citing Book 5, *passim*. Examples of purchase of hay, straw, etc. are in Book 2, fos.43 – 43v, 60v; Book 4, f.88v. In 1595 a half-year's allowance for the president's horses came to £6 13s 4d, Book 5, f.46.
[54] Morgan (unpublished thesis, 1984), 358 – 60.
[55] Book 62, 103; Book 4, fos.63v – 64. For improvements to lodges in general, see Morgan (unpublished thesis, 1984), 363ff. For the long gallery at Queens', see below, pp. 131 – 2.
[56] *RCHM*, 174; Book 4, f.144; Book 5, fos.43, 146, 150 – 150v; Book 6, f.121; Searle, 462. Such embellishment had begun in the 1530s, *W&C*, ii.31; Searle, 197.
[57] Morgan (unpublished thesis, 1984), 253, 349 – 52; Dickens (1967), 336 – 9; Heywood and Wright (1854), i.43; Brooke (1985), 68 – 9.
[58] Morgan (unpublished thesis, 1984), 314, 316, 348 – 51; Searle, 306, 365.

separate lodgings increased the distance between masters and Fellows generally, but we cannot be sure how much this increased the likelihood of conflict between them.[59]

---

[59] Morgan (unpublished thesis, 1984), 354.

6

College Fellows (1448 – c. 1640)

Queens' was the recipient of a spate of benefactions in its early days. In the 15th century, endowments specifically for the purpose of maintaining fellowships were received from thirteen different people, who came from several walks of life: duke Richard of Gloucester, noble ladies, gentry, London traders, clergymen, and one former Fellow.[1] Their gifts were of land, or of money to purchase land and supply a regular income, and in almost every case the holders of the fellowships were required to offer prayers for the souls of their benefactors and others. A few had other duties, such as preaching in parish churches away from Cambridge or (in one case) serving a parish cure. Endowments went to pay the stipend fixed by college statute; on one occasion where the source of income became insufficient, the benefaction was joined with another to make up the difference.[2]

In the 16th and 17th centuries benefactions were less frequent and usually went to endow scholarships.[3] Nevertheless, the number of Fellows grew. The statutes of 1475 provided for twelve Fellows in holy orders, with permission to employ 'more or less' according to the needs and capacity of the college.[4] In 1529 the number permitted was 18; in 1559, 19.[5] In practice, the number fluctuated above and below the statutory limit.[6]

To be eligible for a fellowship under the 1475 statutes, one had to be at least a 'questionist' in arts or a scholar in theology; obedient; proficient in the schools; healthy; and sufficiently poor to need a Fellow's stipend.[7] Men previously expelled from another community were barred. These requirements were maintained in essence by later editions of the statutes,[8] the only significant change being in the number of

---

[1] Searle, 72, 79 – 81, 88 – 94, 112, 119 – 24; Williams (1933), 1; MS 30, fos.14v – 16v; Book 77, fos.5, 8, 10, 12, 16, 21, 28, 30.

[2] As n. 1; see also chapter 9, pp. 111, 117 – 20.

[3] See below, pp. 117 – 20.

[4] Book 79, fos.2 – 2v ('*aut plures aut pauciores secundum quantitatem honorem dicto Collegio pertinentium*').

[5] *ibid.*, fos.14 – 14v; Statutes (1559), 3 – 4.

[6] Books 2 – 6, *passim*; Searle, 119; below, appendix 2.

[7] Book 79, f.4 ('*non habentem unde sufficienter vivere valeat*'). See below, p. 98 for terminology relating to degrees.

[8] Book 79, fos.19v – 21; Statutes (1559), 13 – 15.

Fellows required to be in holy orders: 14 in 1529; 12 in 1559.[9]

In 1475 a Fellow's stipend was ten marks (£6 13s 4d) a year, with 'commons' (daily meals) and other necessities supplied by the college; in Elizabeth's reign a Fellow in holy orders could expect a stipend of £9, and the four senior bachelors in divinity on the fellowship £10 (a day labourer's wage in the 16th century, by comparison, would be anything up to a shilling a day).[10] Fellows also received money from other sources. Before the Reformation there were fees for performing exequies, although these were rarely more than a few pence at each service. The feasting which took place afterwards was probably more significant: Lady Margery Roos (1506) provided for an 'honest repast' for the Fellows; Lady Joan Ingaldesthorpe (1491) ensured that they should 'have at there dyner amonges them iii galons of wyne'.[11]

College offices brought more substantial pecuniary benefits; there were also paid sermons and lectures. The Fellow endowed by Dame Alice Wyche in c. 1472 received half a mark (6s 8d) for an annual sermon, and forty shillings for lecturing in divinity.[12] A century later Sir Thomas Smith endowed lectureships in arithmetic and geometry, whose holders received £3 and £4 respectively for daily reading.[13] In about 1580 another former Fellow, John Josselin, endowed a lectureship in Hebrew worth £5.[14] The returns of 1546 showed the college lecturer in theology receiving £2 for thirteen lectures and the rhetoric and philosophy lecturers £1 each; the Greek lecturer received £2. The dean of chapel received only 6s 8d (raised to 13s 4d in 1559).[15] By the end of John Davenant's presidency college lecturers and officers received stipends of between £2 and £5.[16] In the early 17th century, if not before, the senior bursar received quarterly payments from students to augment his

[9] Book 79, f.14v; *Statutes (1559)*, 41 – 2. An interpretation of the statutes made in 1679 confirmed the 1559 regulations for the number of Fellows in orders, OPR, f.108v. There is a 16th century example of a Fellow being expelled for offences which included not taking holy orders at the specified time, Book 51, f.1. Two Fellows were exempt from this requirement: one a Fellow in civil law; the other a Fellow in medicine; see below, p. 77. In 1653 the Fellow in civil law was allowed to choose if he wished to take holy orders or not; if he chose not to, this was not to affect his seniority, OPR, f.136v. A similar allowance seems to have been made for the Fellow in medicine, OPR, f.133.

[10] Book 79, fos.11 – 11v, 36v; *Statutes (1559)*, 43 – 5.

[11] Searle, 72, 119 – 20; MS 30, fos.1, 14v; Book 79, f.134v; Book 77, fos.21, 25, 28; Bach (1981), 19.

[12] Half a mark if a bachelor in divinity; twice that if a doctor in divinity, Searle, 80 – 1; Book 77, f.12; MS 30, fos.14v – 15.

[13] Searle, 320 – 1.

[14] *ibid.*, 374; OPR, f.8; see also Book 80, f.42v (second pagination).

[15] *Documents* (1852), i.213; Lamb (1838), 70 (these two sources contradict each other); *Statutes (1559)*, 46 – 9.

[16] The censors in theology and philosophy, dean, examiner, and Greek lecturer received £2 each; the arithmetic lecturer, £3; the geometry lecturer, £4; the Hebrew lecturer, £5, Book 6, f.2v.

stipend.[17] Fellows also received fees for occasional sermons preached outside Cambridge.[18]

Other, significant, sources of income were not part of the conventional accounting system, and our knowledge of them is more fragmentary. Dividends (college profits from entry fines and wood sales and the money from corn rents,[19] which were divided among the Fellows) could be very remunerative in times of prosperity — in 1624/5 each Fellow received a dividend payment of £18 18s 6d; in 1636/7 the dividend was £19 7s 6d — although the returns varied greatly. The fees of graduating students were also divided, and there were tutorial fees.[20] In the 17th century new Fellows were expected to give five marks (£3 6s 8d) to the library and 13s 4d for a silver spoon, in addition to feasting the other Fellows shortly after their admission, which suggests a comfortable standard of living, and this is one explanation for the growing competition for fellowships after the mid-16th century.[21]

The particularly fortunate or talented might find wealthy patrons willing to underwrite their academic careers. Thomas Smith was said to have come close to leaving Cambridge in 1532, after only two years as a Fellow of Queens', because he was nearly destitute. He was saved by outside support, although his poverty may have been merely relative to his ambitions.[22] In James I's reign, Sir Fulke Greville was so impressed with John Preston's performance in an academic 'disputation' before the king that he settled some £50 a year on him. This, together with his success in attracting well-to-do pupils, made Preston a wealthy man, for in 1617 he purchased £400 worth of new joint stock in the East India Company, secretly, so that his colleagues would not realise how rich he was.[23] Yet when Davenant became bishop of Salisbury, Preston's thoughts also turned to leaving Queens', in the realisation that 'the fellows for the most parte were not his friends, envyed his numbers [of

---

[17] A shilling from each fellow-commoner, 6d from pensioners, 3d from poor scholars, OPR, f.5 (entry of 1615). In the late 17th century, a wider levy was made on Fellows and students for the bursar, catechist, theology censor and head lecturer, Book 78. In 1546 the bursar received £1 6s 8d as his stipend; in the 1660s, he received £3 6s 8d, Lamb (1838), 70; Book 14, 132ff.

[18] Searle, 379, OPR, f.13v.

[19] For entry fines and corn rents, see below, pp. 112 – 13.

[20] For dividends, see Howard (1935), 36 – 40; Morgan (unpublished thesis, 1984), 321ff; Aylmer (1986); Duncan (two articles, 1986). The Queens' dividends given in the examples here are from Book 26, entry for 1624/5; Book 27, entry for 1636/7; for other examples, see OPR, fos.5v, 6v, 14v, 16, 134.

[21] OPR, fos.8, 132v. A rising standard of living, or at least rising expectations, is suggested in the 17th century by references to a Fellows' bowling green, W&C, ii.54; Book 6, f.84. From at least 1611 Queens' lent plate to Fellows for their personal use, OPR, fos.2, 31v, 32v, 34.

[22] Dewar (1964), 13.

[23] Ball (1885), 27; Hill (1965), 240 and n. 3. For disputations see below, p. 98.

pupils], & great relations, & there was no man like so to befriend him.'[24]

The first statutes provided for a small number of college offices: two treasurers (who functioned as senior and junior bursar), a cantor (who ran the chapel), two deans (who oversaw lectures and disputations), and a vice-president.[25] Apart from the vice-president, these officers seem to have been elected annually and from 1484 — the first date from which we have any evidence — a system of irregular rotation prevailed, in common with the methods of other colleges.[26] It was usual for the junior bursar in one year to become senior bursar the next, and those who remained Fellows for long could expect to occupy both bursarships and the cantor's place — we know very little about the deans — although few returned to the same college office for a second spell.

Under the 1529 statutes, the duties and powers of these officials were defined more closely, and some of the titles were changed: the cantor became dean, and the deans became censors.[27] The statutes also contained, for the first time, provisions for reading lectures and holding academic exercises in college, with fines for non-performance. The two censors had to read three daily lectures between them, together with others on special occasions; other lectureships were subsequently endowed.[28] The 1475 insistence that only two Fellows could read subjects other than theology after taking the MA degree remained in force, despite the increased number of Fellows, and strict timetables were set for taking higher degrees, with expulsion the penalty for not qualifying within the statutory time.[29] The college could grant permission for Fellows to delay their degrees, and to delay taking holy orders, and this may have been something of a formality.[30]

There were also university appointments to be secured. Queens' Fellows of the 15th century filled the following university positions: preacher, mathematics lecturer, auditor/keeper of a university chest, junior and senior proctor, and vice-chancellor; three Fellows were employed by the university to write letters.[31] As yet there is no

[24] Ball (1885), 71.
[25] Book 79, fos. 6 – 7. The vice-president's office was not formally established in the statutes, but there are frequent references to persons acting in that capacity for absentee presidents; nothing is known of the appointment or tenure of the post: the vice-president may have been nominated by the president, or may have been the senior Fellow.
[26] This is derived from the details of the pre-1500 Fellows supplied in Emden. For colleges in general, see Cobban (1975), 137 – 8.
[27] 'Decanus' and 'Censores', Book 79, fos.23 – 24v.
[28] Book 79, fos.24v – 26; above, p. 75.
[29] Book 79, fos.26v – 27; c.f. ibid., fos.5v – 6 for the 1475 arrangements. See also Statutes (1559), 40 – 2, for later modifications. Richard III's Fellows had been obliged to study theology, Searle, 88 – 9.
[30] OPR, fos.4 – 4v, 13v.
[31] From Emden. It was not necessary for the vice-chancellor to be a head of house until the Elizabethan period, Cooper, ii.428 – 9.

comparable analysis of Fellows in the 16th and 17th centuries; there were doubtless similar opportunities, but these would have been reduced by the increase in the number and size of colleges during the period. In 1534 St Bernard's hostel was sold, and so Queens' Fellows lost the opportunity to serve as outside principal of the hostel, a post nominated by the college.[32] There were also benefices to which the college had the right of appointment, and Fellows might hope to be promoted to these.[33]

Few Fellows anticipated remaining in the university for life. The evidence of college office-holding in the 15th century demonstrates fluidity within the academic profession. Further evidence of the mobility of Fellows is given by examining the 67 (?69) Queens' Fellows listed in Emden's *Biographical Register*, 55 of whom took up their fellowships before 1500 and all of whom began at Cambridge in the 15th century.[34] On average, each of the 55 held his fellowship for 6¾ years; the range was from a few weeks to 25 years. When the other twelve are added, the range is increased to 43 years, and the average rises to 7⅔. Over half were Fellows for less than ten years — 16 for one year or less — and only three for more than 20. Fellowships were but a first step in the careers of most of these men, but in fewer than one half of these cases do we know why they left: 21 left to take up other ecclesiastical positions (another two probably did so), and it is likely that there were many more. Four left to become Fellows at other colleges; another two are found later as Fellows elsewhere. Two (probably three) died in office; another was forced to resign because of blindness. Two became principals of Cambridge hostels, and two were chosen presidents of Queens'.

Crude calculations suggest that Queens' fellowships were held on average for between six and seven years in the period 1500 – 1640, with signs of a rising average.[35] A fellowship therefore remained a starting-point in a young man's career. The church was still the principal vocation: the demand for educated clergymen grew during the period so that clergy without a university education were at a disadvantage.[36]

---

[32] Stokes (1924), 34, 37; below, p. 111.

[33] This would mean resigning their fellowship in most cases. For college livings, see below, pp. 165 – 70.

[34] Searle, addenda to part I, i. refers to a John Crowland as a Fellow of Queens', but this seems to have been discounted by Emden, and I have left Crowland out of this list.

[35] My figures, compiled from *AC*, part I, names A – C; the numerical base for these calculations is relatively small. The average at Trinity in the 17th century was just over 14 years, but these were perhaps better posts, my figures, compiled from Innes (1941). It remains clear nonetheless that fellowships represented the first stage of a career.

[36] O'Day (1979), 132 – 142. An act of 1571 ordered that nobody was to serve a benefice worth more than £30 *per annum* unless they were at least a bachelor of divinity or licensed by a bishop or university, Shadwell (1912), i.177 – 8. Twenty Queensmen are known to have become bishops before the end of the 17th century, Carter (1753), 178 – 9.

There was also a need for chaplains in the houses of the nobility, and with merchants and ambassadors abroad.[37] By the late 17th century, graduates made up a large proportion of grammar school masters, but these posts were not well paid and less likely to attract former Fellows.[38] The ban on marriage probably shortened many an academic life; most of those who left the university married.[39]

Elections to fellowships were made by a majority vote among the Fellows; the 1529 statutes stated that a fellowship could not be kept vacant for more than six months.[40] The crown interfered in elections from an early date. In 1483 or 1484 Richard III recommended William Ustwayt for a fellowship; the college paid little heed, although it had apparently accepted earlier recommendations from Richard.[41] A fragment of a similar recommendation by Elizabeth of York, wife of Henry VII, is the only record of that queen's interest in the college.[42] Queens' resisted Catherine of Aragon's mandate for John Lambert in 1521, for the college could not elect anyone 'but suche as they knowe vertuus & well lernyd', and Lambert refused to be publicly examined, which was required by statute.[43] He was admitted, but was only at Queens' for a few months; ironically, in view of Catherine's patronage, he became a notable Protestant reformer.[44]

These were isolated examples, but during the second half of the 16th century such interference became increasingly common. As with court interference in mastership elections, the causes were complex. The growing prestige of colleges made academic life more attractive for some; there were more places available; colleges sought to encourage promising students to stay by pre-electing them to fellowships. Fellowships were more sought after during the Elizabethan period, partly because they were better paid.[45] Factional disputes became more common at elections, which led to more soliciting for testimonials at court.[46] Royal interference, which took several forms, was sometimes

---

[37] Twigg (unpublished thesis, 1983), vii. In 1655 Samuel Jacombe of Queens' received a London benefice, and was subsequently asked to recommend someone for a vacant household chaplaincy. He suggested his friend Simon Patrick, another Fellow of Queens'. The post was worth £70 a year, Patrick (1839), 27 – 8.

[38] Vincent (1969), 112, 120 – 1; Orpen (1977), 183 – 94; Feyerharm (1976); Greaves (1981), 348.

[39] Morgan (unpublished thesis, 1984), 357.

[40] Except in emergencies, Book 79, fos.4, 19v.

[41] Searle, 118; Emden.

[42] Searle, 124; the recommendation may have been for a fellowship or a scholarship — the fragment is not clear.

[43] ibid., 164 – 6; Book 79, f.4.

[44] Searle, 164 – 6; above, p. 27.

[45] Morgan (unpublished thesis, 1984), 242 – 5, 321 – 2; Charlton (1965), 132. There are some examples of pre-election at Queens' from the late Tudor and early Stuart periods through into the 18th century, Book 80, fos.89 – 90 (second pagination).

[46] Morgan (unpublished thesis, 1984), 392 – 400.

welcome — for example, dispensations which overrode statutory restrictions such as those of county, to enable the election of candidates of real merit from whatever county — and the crown was responsive to initiatives from within the colleges, although its responses were often ill-informed.[47] One of the most common forms of royal letter was the dispensation from any college statute which might otherwise hinder a person's election; this kind was sent on behalf of Gregory Isham, who wished to become a Fellow of Queens', in 1628. There was no royal pressure behind such intervention; Isham was not elected.[48] More sinister were resignations in favour of a named successor (often a court nominee), which probably carried some financial inducement. There are two examples of this at Queens' from the 1620s and 1630s: in 1624 James I supported Edward Davenant's resignation in favour of Robert Townson (Davenant was nephew of John Davenant, the former president who had since become bishop of Salisbury; Townson's father was married to John Davenant's sister), reminding the college that 'you cannot doe a thing more acceptable unto us' than to support this expression of the crown's 'princely care of the Children of such worthy ornaments of our Church' as the bishop of Salisbury; Townson was admitted.[49] In 1630 the university's chancellor, the earl of Holland, promised the college his favour in future in return for its acquiescence in a similar deal.[50] In 1585 a royal mandate of this kind had provoked a quarrel between the president, Humphrey Tyndall, who hoped to placate court interests, and the Fellows, who had their own candidate. Matters were complicated still further by the arrival of a mandate from the queen in favour of a third person. The two court candidates were successful; the Fellows' nominee was not.[51] There had been a similar muddle in 1576 when Sir Thomas Smith pressed Queens' to admit his nephew to a vacant fellowship without realising that the queen had her own candidate for the post; Elizabeth was indignant in response.[52]

There were other absurdities: in 1574 Garret Wallis arrived from Eton to begin his undergraduate course bearing a royal recommendation for his election to a fellowship as soon as possible; when he took his BA degree in 1577/8 there was no fellowship vacant and so he applied to the crown for a fresh mandate for some other preferment.[53] There were many kinds of dispensation: in 1580 the earl of Leicester asked for royal

---

ibid., 420–36, 475, for this in general; for examples of dispensations at Queens', see Box 31; OPR, f.141v.
[48] Morgan (unpublished thesis, 1984), 437; Searle, 456; AC; Book 6, f.28v.
[49] Box 31.
[50] ibid.
[51] Morgan (unpublished thesis, 1984), 384–5, 459 and n. 39; Searle, 375–6. Both of the court candidates were from other colleges.
[52] Dewar (1964), 189; Searle, 331–2; in fact, both received fellowships.
[53] Searle, 332.

dispensation for his chaplain Robert Some, a Fellow of Queens', to be excused certain academic requirements for his doctorate in divinity.[54] In 1579 the university complained to Burghley about the frequency and abuse of mandates, and was promised that more care would be taken in future, but it was also made clear that mandates were part of the crown's prerogative power and should not be resisted.[55] In 1611 the university protested against James I's excessive issue of mandates in favour of Scotsmen, his fellow-countrymen, but in 1618 Lewis Wemis from Fife was elected a Fellow of Queens' by royal mandate.[56] In 1623, when James sent a mandate for Herbert Palmer to be elected Fellow, there were some who voted against him, although elections in such cases were often mere formalities.[57]

For these and other reasons, college elections were brought into disrepute in the late 16th century. They were regarded as corrupt: in 1588/9 parliament passed an act against electoral abuses, noting that such elections were 'manye tymes wrought and brought to passe with Monye Guyftes and Rewardes, whereby the fyttest persons to be presented elected or nominated, wanting Money or Friendes are sildome or not at all preferred'.[58] The act's penalties were insufficient deterrent, for parliaments in the early Stuart period continued to debate corruption in college elections.[59] By the end of the 16th century there were complaints that it was difficult for poor men's sons to obtain fellowships — though they had originally been intended for such men[60] — and of packing of elections and outside interference. William Harrison noticed that many Fellows, after taking their doctorates, did 'give over their wonted diligence and live like drone bees on the fat of colleges', occupying places which ought to go to more deserving younger men.[61] John Davenant's father, a London merchant taylor, would not allow his son to accept a fellowship, 'as conceiving it a bending of those places from the direct intent of the Founders, when they are bestowed on such as have plenty'. Davenant was admitted to a fellowshp after his father's

[54] Curtis (1959), 26 – 7.
[55] Searle, 332 – 3; Curtis (1959), 27 – 8.
[56] Searle, 399; AC; see also Box 31; Wemis was a candidate for the presidency in 1622, see above, p. 69.
[57] Searle, 533; it would be interesting to know on what grounds Palmer was opposed.
[58] Shadwell (1912), i.209 – 11; Morgan (unpublished thesis, 1984), 385 – 6; Curtis (1959), 53.
[59] Twigg (unpublished thesis, 1983), 6; Russell (1979), 198, 234, 406.
[60] Hence the 1588/9 act. An act of 1536 had tried to compel residence at benefices to prevent pluralism among Fellows over 40, and to ensure that those under 40 were genuinely reading for higher degrees, but it is not clear how much effect the act had, Shadwell (1912), i.121 – 22. There is an example at Queens' of talent enabling a young man of relatively poor means to rise: Robert Townson, son of the college's subcook, was admitted a sizar at 12, became a scholar, and (in 1597) a Fellow, and married John Davenant's sister; one of his sons also became a Fellow of the college, Searle, 415 – 6.
[61] Harrison (1968), 70 – 1.

death, although when he became president he opposed the election of John Gore to a fellowship on the grounds that 'you have worth, but not want, enough to be one of our society'.[62] After leaving to become bishop of Salisbury Davenant pressed hard to secure a fellowship for his nephew Thomas Fuller. The new president, John Mansell, dragged his feet for over two years in the face of Davenant's repeated efforts, until it became clear that Fuller would not be elected; Davenant therefore decided to remove his nephew from the college, 'where he shall see many of his punies stept before him in preferment'.[63]

In theory the lives of Fellows were strictly controlled. The 1475 statutes had newly-elected Fellows take several oaths: to behave well, be loyal and diligent on the college's behalf; study hard and perform all required exercises and religious duties.[64] There was an oath against heresy, naming specifically the beliefs of John Wyclif, inspirer of the Lollards, and Reginald Peacock, a bishop condemned in the mid-15th century.[65] Conversation at table was to be in Latin.[66] Fellows were not to be outside the college gates after 8 p.m. (9 p.m. in summer) and were not to be away from Cambridge for more than two months a year.[67] It is clear from the accounts that Fellows were often absent for long periods.[68] Permission for leave of absence was granted frequently in the 17th century, for periods ranging from a few weeks to a year, and occasionally longer than this.[69] Herbert Palmer, a Fellow from 1623 – 33, was granted three separate leaves of one year each in 1626/7, 1628/9 and 1631/2.[70] Such absences might be for business, or health.[71] In 1519 John Craforth was granted permission to go away for three years, either to court, or to any other place of learning.[72] This grant must have been intended to facilitate foreign travel, and from an early date leaves were readily granted to travel and study abroad. Richard Whitford was given five years' leave in the 1490s to take his aristocratic pupil Lord Mountjoy on what may have been something like a continental grand

---

[62] Fuller, quoted in Searle, 408; Fuller, *Worthies*, ii.359 – 60.
[63] Fuller (1897), 254 – 64; see also Searle, 415 – 6; Fuller (1868), iii.330; Aubrey, *Brief Lives*, 174 – 6. Other examples of outsiders trying to interfere in fellowship elections are contained in Box 31.
[64] Book 79, fos.4v – 5v.
[65] Peacock had discussed theological ideas in English, rather than in Latin, McFarlane (1972), 132; Riley-Smith states that he was condemned 'for his rationalist thought', Riley-Smith in *Record* (1975). For Wyclif, see above, p. 4.
[66] Book 79, f.8v; c.f. *ibid.*, f.27v; *Statutes (1559)*, 21 – 2.
[67] Book 79, fos.9 – 9v; c.f. *Statutes (1559)*, 24. In 1561 a Fellow was ejected for remaining absent longer than was allowed by statute, Book 51, f.1v.
[68] See e.g. the payments to Fellows in Books 5 and 6.
[69] OPR, fos.1 – 2, and *passim*. There is no evidence from the period before this.
[70] He was a lecturer at Canterbury, Searle, 534 – 5; Clarke (1677), 185. In January 1631 Edward Martin was given leave of absence for one year, OPR, f.161v; Searle, 466.
[71] e.g. OPR, f.136 (and c.f. f.138); Book 5, f.151; below, p. 138.
[72] Searle, 158.

tour.[73] In 1508 Thomas Austyn and Richard Stanbanke were each given three years' leave to study theology, presumably abroad; Henry Bullock was absent between 1513 and 1515.[74] Lawyers benefited particularly from study at continental universities: Roger Collyngwood was allowed a year off to study canon law in Paris in 1502/3 and another four years abroad in 1507.[75] The Reformation put an end to Englishmen studying theology at foreign universities, but doctors and civil lawyers still found study abroad valuable.[76] In 1540 Thomas Smith was given a year off to go abroad 'for the further yncrese of his learnyng', the year to count as part of the requirement for his doctorate in civil law.[77] There are also 17th century examples of Fellows travelling. In 1615 John Towers was given leave for three years, although in 1617 he took a parish living in Northamptonshire and resigned his fellowship; in 1648 John Pypard was given leave to go abroad for two years. Edward Davenant was allowed to accompany his uncle the college president to the Synod of Dort in 1618 – 19.[78] John Preston made a secret visit to the Netherlands in 1621, possibly on unofficial diplomatic business for his patron, the duke of Buckingham.[79]

The 1475 statutes directed that any Fellow found guilty of a criminal offence was to be expelled.[80] New Fellows forswore speaking and writing in such a way as to cause anger; they were to converse 'peacefully'.[81] The 1529 statutes refined this further, making the Fellows' oaths more wide-ranging: in addition to swearing obedience to college statutes and customs (1475), a Fellow now had to swear not to seek any abrogation of the statutes and to obey any statutes made in the future. If expelled by the college, he would not appeal or seek any remedy at law; he promised not to reveal college secrets, and to resign if he received an annual income for life worth £5 above his college stipend.[82] The oaths demanded by the 1559 statutes were almost identical, but there was a new oath of obedience to Elizabeth's ecclesiastical settlement, and a new statute against heresy, with

---

[73] Emden; Book 76, f.20; above, p. 20.

[74] Emden; Book 76, fos.24 – 24v, 27; Stanbanke had to promise to live 'lyke an honest preeste'. He was a protégé of Lady Margaret, Underwood (1982), 80.

[75] Emden; Book 76, f.23.

[76] John Caius is one of the best known examples of a doctor travelling, Brooke (1985), 56 – 9; there are no known examples from Queens'. The Elizabethan writer William Harrison thought Italy, where Caius had gone, a dangerously corrupting place, Harrison (1968), 74.

[77] Book 3, f.58; Dewar (1964), 20 – 3.

[78] OPR, fos.5v, 134v; AC ('Towers'); Searle, 413; see also OPR, f.140.

[79] Ball (1885), 73 – 6 (and see ibid., 7 – 8); Smith (1968), 18 – 21; DNB.

[80] Book 79, fos.10v – 11; see ibid., fos.38v – 39 for the 1529 version, which added to the list any crime or scandal which might damage the college's reputation.

[81] 'pacifice', Book 79, fos.4v – 5v, 8.

[82] ibid., fos.20v – 21. In 1625 Charles I dispensed a Fellow, William Roberts, from the wealth limitation for four years; Roberts was royal subalmoner, Box 31.

Anabaptism regarded as a particular threat.[83]

During the 15th century, at least, there is no sign of discord within the college, but the rules of conduct contained in later editions of the statutes were obviously born of experience, and the content of the 1529 oaths is therefore significant. In 1511 a debate arose over the statute limiting the number of Fellows who could come from any one diocese (two only) or county (one only) designed to prevent regional bias in college elections:[84] an attempt was made to modify this rule with regard to the college fellowship endowed by Hugh Trotter, a former Fellow, although the college felt that it would be 'agayns the quyette lyvyng in our coledge as we knowe by many occasyons of debate that war lyke to falle thereuppon and as of late we have had experience'.[85] A dispute which broke out between two Fellows, Anthony Maxwell and Simon Heynes in 1524 had to be put before an outside authority for arbitration, the college promising to 'suffer the ward, arbitrement, ordinance and jugement' and to 'take effect accordyng to the same in every poynt; withowt ony maner let or disturbance of the seyd president and felaws'.[86] The 1529 statutes included penalities for Fellows who stayed out of college overnight, or spent their time in taverns: there were fines for first offences, leading to expulsion if the offence was repeated too often.[87] Any member of college, Fellow or scholar, who struck another, was fined 3s 4d (if there was bleeding) or 2s (if not).[88] There were graded punishments, leading to expulsion, for those who spread discord; disputes were to be heard before the president and the rest of the Fellows whose judgement was final.[89]

Evidence of Fellows' quarrels and misdemeanours is not abundant. There are some known 16th century disputes: the cases involving Rockrey and Middleton, and the disputes of 1557 and 1559, described above.[90] In 1559, although the crux of the dispute was religious, there

[83] Statutes (1559), 26 – 7.
[84] Book 79, fos.4 – 4v. The diocese of Lincoln was allowed three, from any county, because of its vast size. Such restrictions were in force until 1838, Searle, 149. For the 1529 and 1559 restrictions, see Book 79, fos.21 – 21v; Statutes (1559), 17 – 18 (this added a new proviso that an extra Fellow was allowed from each diocese or county in which the college had lands, provided that the rents from such lands were sufficient to maintain a fellowship). London was apparently always (or at least since 1537, perhaps) allowed two Fellows, Book 80, f.89 (second pagination). Wales was considered to be a county, and the college had a small but significant number of Welsh Fellows between 1530 and 1642; there was a definite Welsh connection, Griffith (unpublished thesis, 1982), 376 – 7, 383, 539 – 40, and personal communication. See also chapter 7, n. 10.
[85] In the end the college appears to have compromised but only with regard to the Trotter fellowship, Searle, 147 – 9.
[86] ibid., 167.
[87] Book 79, fos.29, 35v – 36; see also Statutes (1559), 24 – 5, 34 – 5.
[88] Book 79, f.39 (which toned down the harsher penalties of the 1475 statutes).
[89] ibid., fos. 35 – 35v; c.f. Statutes (1559), 33 – 34.
[90] Above, pp. 36 – 7, 70 – 1.

were some savage attacks on Fellows' conduct (as there had been two years earlier): the rebel minority described the president's faction as 'unlerned and unthriftye', and the usual complaints were voiced against card-playing, outstanding debts, staying out of college, and frequenting 'unsemelye places'. One Fellow was described as 'a comon talecarier and a shamefull sclaunderer and evell reporter of men, verye unquiet to lyve withall when he ys in the colledge', and another said to be 'a verye stubborne unquyet quarrellinge and chydinge fellowe'.[91] It is impossible to separate truth from fiction at this distance in time, but in general it may be inferred that the statutory restrictions of a Fellow's life represented an ideal only, that in practice his life could be much more relaxed if he chose, and that such breaches of the statutes were often ignored, except when quarrels broke out over other issues. Even so, one should still make great allowances for exaggeration; polemic in this period was quite uninhibited.

There were always Fellows who did not conform.[92] Ralph Jones was admonished by the president in 1568 for sowing discord between two other Fellows and further admonished in 1574 for quarrelling; in 1575 he was expelled for retaining nearly £45 due to the college after the audit of his year's accounts as senior bursar, but he was restored by Burghley after paying the debt and promising to behave himself in future. He signed letters on behalf of another rebel, William Middleton, later in the year.[93] In May 1645 John Pypard received an admonition for having been 'found disorderlie at a taverne in disorderlie company at eleven of the clocke of the night'.[94] It is not clear if Pypard was in fact a Fellow at this time — if he was not, then he became one soon afterwards, so that the offence cannot have been held against him. In August 1644 Gamaliel Capel had been less fortunate, but his misdemeanour was more serious: the college expelled him when it learnt of 'A stillborne child of Doctor Capells buried in Allhallowes parish March 12'.[95] Yet such examples are infrequent in the college's history, and with such limited evidence available, it cannot be said that the Fellows of Queens' were particularly badly behaved.[96]

---

[91] Searle, 271 – 6.

[92] Such as Rockrey and Middleton, n. 90.

[93] Searle, 321 – 2; Book 14, 128; CUA Collect. Admin. 13, fos.131, 234v. In 1620 it was decided that William Cox's debts to the college should be taken out of his commons allowance, OPR, f.11v. An action for debt was brought against John Fawne in 1527 – 31, but it is not clear when and how the debts had been incurred, Searle, 189.

[94] OPR, f.132; Searle, 550.

[95] OPR, f.25; Searle, 549; he had been recommended for a fellowship by Charles I in 1629, Box 31.

[96] It is odd that there should be no evidence of disputes over seniority. In 1572, though, the seniority of those who were then Fellows was formally fixed, perhaps to forestall or resolve a dispute, Searle, 320.

7

Students and student life (15th – 17th centuries)

The growing importance of the universities during the late medieval and early modern periods was reflected in new foundations and endowments, and in the growth of their populations. Numbers at Cambridge seem to have increased slightly during the second half of the 15th century. Vitality was shown in the new collegiate foundations, and the completion of new university buildings: schools of theology (1400), canon law (by 1458), philosophy and civil law (1458 – 71). There were great annual fluctuations in numbers, however, with a small stable core bound strictly to the degree course. The university had no 'admissions policy'; it was composed of those who chose to study there.[1]

The 16th and 17th centuries were a period of spectacular expansion, as shown in appendix 6.[2] By the end of the 17th century, the universities were in decline, and numbers did not revive until the time of the Napoleonic wars.[3] Precise figures for the number of students at Queens' are unobtainable at present; the number in receipt of scholarships can be discovered from the account books, but the bulk of the expanding university comprised a new class of fee-paying students, and records of these are much less formal and complete.[4]

In the medieval period and afterwards most Cambridge students came from the north and east of the country, rather than the more populous south and west.[5] In the 15th century, the best represented dioceses were those of Ely and York; others with above-average representation were Durham, Carlisle, and Coventry and Lichfield.[6] Some colleges had regional preferences embodied in their statutes; others, such as Queens', limited the number of Fellows and scholars permitted from any one diocese.[7] Northern dioceses became increasingly well repre-

---

[1] Aston *et al.* (1980), 19 – 28, 86. In the mid-15th century the population of the university was about 1,300, but accurate figures are not available before the second half of the 16th century.

[2] See also Stone (1975), 92; below, appendix 5.

[3] Stone (1975), 92. Venn, *Matriculations*.

[4] See also below, n. 9.

[5] Aston *et al.* (1980), 28 – 36; O'Day (1982), 103. The diocese of origin is known for only 19% of all pre-1500 students; recruitment was based on distance and ease of communications.

[6] Aston *et al.* (1980), 28 – 36 (and *ibid.* for all general comments here on the 15th century).

[7] Book 79, fos.4 – 4v, 8 – 8v. Gonville and Caius, for example, had a preference for Norfolk men, Brooke (1985), 10, 15 – 17, 39 – 40.

sented in the university during the 15th century, and only in a tiny proportion of students came from outside England. The dominance of northern and eastern dioceses is almost equally true for Queens', where the diocese of origin is known for 23 out of 87 recorded Queensmen before 1500: York supplied five; Coventry and Lichfield, Durham, and Norwich three each; Ely and London two each. Canterbury also supplied three; Chichester and Lincoln one each.[8]

There is much more information concerning 16th and 17th century *alumni*. A university statute of 1544 required all new members to matriculate, and colleges also began to keep admissions registers, although the amount of information contained in these varies greatly from college to college.[9] The details of Queensmen reproduced in appendix 7, with county rather than diocese of origin now recorded, affirm the continuance of the previous regional bias; the proportion of students from Essex and Suffolk is particularly striking.

Colleges enjoyed close links with particular localities within counties, where they owned land, or from where they received benefactions. College *alumni*, clerical and lay, renewed and strengthened these contacts on returning to the localities.[10] The early modern period witnessed the development of family connections with individual colleges; there are several examples of fathers and sons at Queens',[11] and some connections (such as the examples reproduced in appendix 8) spanned more than two generations. Much detailed local research would be required to establish less direct and obvious family links, but the frequency with which certain surnames recur among Queensmen from certain counties suggests a more extensive network. Most freshmen received advance information on colleges from relatives, friends, local clergymen or schoolmasters.[12]

Relatively little information is available on the social origins of medieval students. They were mostly poor, and their surviving correspondence consists largely of begging letters.[13] The student

---

[8] All the pre-1500 data concerning Queens' is compiled from Emden; there is no telling how many Queensmen were not recorded by the college and university sources.

[9] Cooper, i.413 – 5; *AC*, preface to part I, vol. i.

[10] Morgan (unpublished thesis, 1984), especially chapter III; Morgan (1975). Note also that there was a small but significant number of Welsh students attending Queens' in the 16th and 17th centuries: 65 between 1544 and 1642; only St John's (130) is known to have had more during this period, Griffith, personal communication, and see Griffith (unpublished thesis, 1982), 376 – 7, 383, 539 – 40 for aspects of the Welsh links (noted in chapter 6, n. 84). Other regional studies of this kind would be valuable.

[11] For example, William Barnes (matriculated 1596) and William Barnes (matriculated 1634), from Cambridgeshire/Norfolk; Edward Bigland (matriculated c. 1591) and Edward Bigland (matriculated 1637), of Nottinghamshire; William Buckby (matriculated 1610) and William Buckby (matriculated 1651), of Bedfordshire. *AC* contains numerous other examples.

[12] O'Day (1979), 258, n. 20; Harrison (1958), 35.

[13] Haskins (1929), 7 – 19; Jacob (1953), 209.

archetypes portrayed by Chaucer — the Oxford cleric whose 'only care was study', the womaniser 'Nicholas the Gallant', and the two 'headstrong' Cambridge students 'eager for a joke' — were united in their poverty.[14] Books were expensive in the days before the invention of printing, and degree fees were high; after the fourth year of study, most students needed either to secure a fellowship or scholarship, or take holy orders, find a benefice and obtain a dispensation to return to the university.[15] Thomas Chapman of Queens' secured a Huntingdonshire living even before taking his BA, in 1480, and went out of residence for a while, returning in 1492; others might go down and return later for a higher degree, or just for further study.[16] Family support was the most important element in maintaining students, most of whom were of 'intermediate social status'. Very few came from noble families, although the universities provided a useful channel for putting superfluous younger sons into the church.[17]

In the 16th century the universities underwent a social revolution. The medieval colleges had been few in number and (with a few exceptions, such as King's College and King's Hall) generally small, their members mostly postgraduate Fellows reading for higher degrees. By Elizabeth I's reign they had become primarily institutions for educating under-graduates, and there had been a vast influx of fee-paying students from the wealthier groups in society.[18] The ruling classes were won over to humanist ideals of the need for civilised learning to instill wisdom and virtue; boys from this élite flooded into the universities, where such courtly virtues were to be learned relatively cheaply.[19] The Tudor state required trained men in its government.[20] John Preston, whilst still an undergraduate, 'looked high & grew acquainted with those that were Gentile, & fancied State affairs, and Courtship, & that had desires or dispositions to be secretaries or agents in Princes' Courtes'.[21] By the second half of the 16th century, a university education sufficed for one to be able to call oneself a 'gentleman' — an important badge of status.[22] The extent of this influx at Queens' is shown by appendix 5, in which

---

[14] Chaucer (1960), 27, 105, 127.
[15] Haskins (1929), 23 – 7; Jacob (1953), 213 – 6; c.f. Trio (1984). One of the reasons for the growing popularity of colleges was the scholarships and fellowships that they offered, especially desirable becuse the real value of benefices was declining at the time.
[16] Aston *et al.* (1980), 41 – 2.
[17] *ibid.*, 42, 44 – 51; Jacob (1953), 220; Rosenthal (1969), 432 – 4. There was only a limited amount of patronage available: MAs could teach freelance, and there were also university loan chests, but few students benefited from these.
[18] Curtis (1959), 38, 125; but for this, and the following remarks on the influx of the upper classes and the shift towards the college system, c.f. Russell (1977).
[19] Curtis (1959), 56 – 64, 70 – 2; Simon (1967), 246 – 7; Kearney (1970), 25 – 8.
[20] Curtis (1959), 74 – 7; c.f. Simon (1967), 247; Kearney (1970), 25, 37.
[21] Ball (1885), 7; he still hoped for this after becoming a Fellow, *ibid.*, 13.
[22] Kearney (1970), 26 – 7; Curtis (1959), 270; Stone (1965), 49; Laslett (1971), 33.

three categories of student are recorded: sizars were poor scholars who augmented their scholarships by sizing — performing a few menial tasks, such as waiting at table; pensioners were fee-paying students; fellow-commoners, the aristocratic élite, also paid fees, but enjoyed greater privileges, such as better accommodation and the right to dine with the fellows.[23] During the 16th century these two fee-paying categories, and the social classes which they represented, especially the gentry, became predominant.[24] The trend had begun in the 1540s, when several noblemen and courtiers sent their sons to Cambridge. The earls of Huntingdon, Arundel and Surrey sent their heirs to Queens'; Arundel's son Henry Fitzalan was only twelve when he went up in 1549.[25]

The arrival of the upper classes brought financial benefits to colleges, but was not welcomed universally. There were complaints that the sons of the poor were being squeezed out by the sons of the rich; modern research, whilst not going quite so far, has confirmed the growing dominance of the latter group.[26] The dress and behaviour of wealthy students were condemned as unscholarly.[27] A foreign visitor to Cambridge at the end of Elizabeth's reign suspected that the students 'perhaps keep more dogs and greyhounds, that are so often seen in the streets, than they do books'. Roger Ascham had complained half a century earlier that such students sought 'superficial knowledge', not 'perfection of learning'. William Harrison argued in 1587 that 'most of them study little other than histories, tables, dice and trifles'. Few remained at university long enough to take a degree; they had no need of such qualifications.[28]

For intelligent boys from poor backgrounds, university education afforded a unique opportunity for advancement, principally through the church. In medieval times a significant proportion of higher ecclesiasti-

---

[23] Fellow-commoners were required to donate plate, or to give money to buy plate, to the college, Morgan (unpublished thesis, 1984), 142 – 3; for Queens' examples, see OPR, f.27v; Cooper (1851); Fuller (1897), 260; Book 62, 102. In 1647 they were required to pay 10s each towards the college gardens; OPR, f.137v.

[24] Simon (1963); Charlton (1965), 135 – 6; O'Day (1982), 93; Anderson and Schnaper (1952), 2; Cressy (1970). For Queens', see below, appendix 5. Charlton gives these figures for the increase in fee-paying students at Queens': 1531: 14; 1565: 20; 1581: 70; 1612: 184, Charlton (1965), 136. Students in general were grouped into two classes — 'amateur' (fee-paying), and 'professional' (working hard for their degrees in order to secure a good ecclesiastical position), and the two classes probably had little to do with each other, Venn (1913), 191 – 2.

[25] But Fitzalan was in the company of a slightly older relation, Simon (1967), 246, n. 1.

[26] Harrison (1968), 70 – 1; Curtis (1959), 69; Charlton (1965), 137; Simon (1967), 250; Cressy (1976); Wrightson (1982), 187 – 9.

[27] Curtis (1959), 54 – 5, 65; Charlton (1965), 139 – 40.

[28] Stettin-Pomerania (1892), 35; Simon (1967), 249; Charlton (1965), 138 – 9, 144; O'Day (1982), 95.

cal offices were held by university men.[29] Many Cambridge men gained lesser preferments, especially in the local dioceses of Norwich and Ely; elsewhere, the appointment of a Cambridge man as bishop might herald an increase in the number of Cambridge graduates appointed to benefices in his diocese.[30] By the end of the 15th century, the university-trained intelligentsia was highly valued at the upper levels of lay society, as well as forming a dominant proportion of the ecclesiastical hierarchy, almost monopolising cathedral positions and becoming ever more numerous in the parishes. During the 16th and 17th centuries the demand for a graduate clergy became much greater.[31] The importance of church careers is shown in appendix 9.

Although poor scholars declined as a proportion of students at Queens' in this period, their numbers rose.[32] The 1475 statutes stipulated that there should be three scholars of the foundation; by 1559 the number specified was eight, but the total number listed in the accounts was considerably larger, thanks to benefactions.[33] The scholars were to be 'clever and indigent, of good morals, sophisters or at least sufficiently instructed in grammar', and were chosen from different counties, like the Fellows.[34]

By 1559 scholars received 1s per week each.[35] In return for their keep and scholarships, certain services were required: reading aloud from the Bible at the main meal of the day, waiting on the Fellows at table, serving in chapel and singing in the choir, among other duties.[36] There are examples from the 15th century of poor students helping with repairs, and cooking.[37] In 1571, when 13 new scholarships were endowed, it was decided that one of the scholars should serve as the

---

[29] This proportion rose during the 15th century; the proportion of Cambridge men to Oxford men also rose, Aston et al. (1980), 67 – 76.

[30] ibid., 77 – 80; see also below, appendix 9.

[31] Aston et al. (1980), 80 – 81, 84 – 85; O'Day (1979), 2, 24, 28, 55 – 6, 77 – 8, 128, 132 – 4, 138 – 43, 156, 161, 233.

[32] Below, appendix 5 (for proportions): appendix 10 (for numbers).

[33] Book 79, fos.8 – 8v; Statutes (1559), 20 – 1; below, appendix 10.

[34] 'ingeniosi et indigentes morum bonorum sophistae vel saltem in grammatica sufficienter instructi', Book 79, fos.8 – 8v, 22v – 23; Statutes (1559), 20 – 1; for sophisters, see p. 98.

[35] Statutes (1559), 45.

[36] Book 79, fos.22v – 23; The terms 'scholar' and 'bible-clerk' are sometimes used as distinct appellations, at other times seemingly without discrimination, and the distinction is not clear. Ivory's chart of university numbers in 1672 draws a distinction between the two groups, but the distinction is not defined, Ivory (1672). In 1648 a student was admitted to be a bible-clerk instead of (as previously) a Montaigne scholar, OPR, f.134. Yet the college account books do not always make the distinction. See also Bach (1981). The duties of different scholarships might vary according to the terms of the benefaction.

[37] Searle, 127; early 16th century examples in ibid., 159 – 60. In 1532 there is a reference to an Austin friar being paid for painting work in the college, and it has been suggested that he was a poor scholar earning money for his studies, Salzman (1967), 169, citing reference from W&C, ii.65.

college librarian, another as its scribe or registrary, with weekly stipends of 10d. In the 1650s one of Simon Patrick's sizars was responsible for keeping the college clock wound, and scholars also served as gate-keepers.[38] In 1679 a student was given a 'smaller Schollarship . . . in regard of his extream poverty & service in the Chappell'. Sizars sometimes received small extra payments from the college dividend, together with other servants, and their rights were protected: an order in the early 17th century decreed that 'He that sizeth more then his allowance to be out of sizing the next week'; and in 1648 the number of bedmakers was restricted to ten, and they were forbidden to size.[39]

Because scholarships were meant only for the truly deserving, their holders were obliged to take the BA degree at the earliest possible opportunity — four years after admission — or else forfeit their scholarships. Payments ceased automatically three years after the BA, or immediately after taking holy orders, at which stage it was felt that scholars should secure either a fellowship or a parish living.[40]

The development of the collegiate system went hand in hand with the extension of the tutor's rôle. At first, tutors were guarantors that students paid their college for board and lodging, but it was subsequently accepted that all students should have tutors to act *in loco parentis*, with whom they lived, and who had an extensive advisory and teaching rôle. The university statutes of 1570 ordered that 'tutors shall teach their pupils diligently, shall correct them in proportion to their faults, and shall not allow them to wander idly in the town'. The tutor's job was a demanding one if undertaken conscientiously, and tutors could exercise considerable spiritual and intellectual influence on their charges. The character and reputation of a tutor was the primary concern of parents seeking to admit their sons: they chose tutors, rather than colleges.[41]

Those qualities thought to be desirable in a tutor are given in contemporary descriptions. Herbert Palmer was said to be 'more than ordinarily carefull' with his students, 'being very diligent both in praying with them in his Chamber, and instructing them in the grounds of Religion; as also keeping them to their studies, and the performance of disputations, and other exercises of learning, privately in his Chamber, beside the more publique exercises required of them by the Colledge, to the great benefit of those that were his pupils'.[42] Simon

---

[38]   Searle, 319; Book 15, entry for 1656; W&C, ii.37; below, pp. 139 – 40; in 1566, 4d was paid 'to a scholler for his paynes in goynge to Mr Gardiner our Stuarde for knowledge of keepinge the curtes [courts]', Book 4, f.54v; this must refer to the manor courts held on the college estates, see p. 114.
[39]   OPR, fos.1, 127v, 134v – 135; Book 4, f.93v. For bedmakers see below, p. 124.
[40]   Book 79, fos.22v – 23.
[41]   Curtis (1959), 78 – 91, 107 – 122; Stone (1965), 689.
[42]   Clarke (1677), 185.

Patrick took care 'to bring up my pupils not only in human, but in divine knowledge. For I not only read lectures to them in philosophy, but constantly had them to my chamber at night, and examined what they had read, and prayed with them before I dismissed them'.[43] Of his own first tutor at Queens', John Wells, Patrick recorded with gratitude that he 'loved me very well, insomuch that he left me the key of his chamber, and of his study, when he was out of town'. His subsequent tutor, the Cambridge Platonist John Smith, had a considerable influence on Patrick's intellectual development; in Patrick's words, he was 'a living library', for 'I never got so much good among all my books by a whole day's plodding in a study, as by an hour's discourse I have got with him. For he was not a library locked up, nor a book clasped, but he stood open for any to converse withal that had a mind to learn'.[44] When John Jegon, vice-president of Queens', was elected master of Corpus Christi in 1590, he took his pupils with him; John Preston did the same when he was chosen to be master of Emmanuel in 1622. As a student, Preston had moved from King's to Queens' when his tutor at King's left the university.[45]

Preston was described by Thomas Fuller as 'the greatest pupil-monger in England'.[46] Almost one quarter of the students entered at Queens' whilst he was a Fellow there were his pupils. It was said that 'every time when Master Preston plucked off his hat to Doctor Davenant the college master, he gained a chamber or study for one of his pupils'.[47] A remarkably high proportion of these were fellow-commoners: between April 1618 and April 1619, 20 pupils were entered under him, of whom 13 were fellow-commoners, five pensioners, and only two sizars.[48] This redounded to his fame: one of his students was reminded that 'By the multitude of your Tutor's pupils you maie well perceave their is some matter of worth in him'.[49] Preston was said to accept only students who met two conditions: they were of 'stayd sober carriage', and eldest sons.

[43] Patrick (1839), 26; clearly, Patrick did not sleep in the same room as his pupils; nor, it seems, did Wells, see p. 94.

[44] Patrick (1839), 16; Patrick (1673), 505 – 7; above, p. 63. Smith shaped Patrick's views on predestination, Patrick (1839), 18 – 19; Gascoigne, 'Barrow'.

[45] Searle, 378; Porter (1958), 237; Ball (1885), 5 – 6. Jegon was a royal nominee, and this may have been the result of connections made through his aristocratic pupils, Morgan (unpublished thesis, 1984), 572 – 3.

[46] Fuller, *Worthies*, ii.517.

[47] Searle, 439; Fuller, *Worthies*, ii.517. Ball noted Preston's declining influence after Davenant's promotion: 'A great tutor hath much occasion to use the Master's influence, for accommodation and advancement of his pupils', Ball (1885), 76. See Morgan (unpublished thesis, 1984), 299 – 301, for this feature in general.

[48] Searle, 434 – 5. Fuller noted that he had 16 fellow-commoners, 'most heirs to fair estate', admitted in one year, *Worthies*, ii.517. Forty of his pupils are listed in the Registrum, of whom 15 were fellow-commoners or sons of nobles, and 17 pensioners, Registrum, fos.1 – 15v.

[49] Smith (1968), 16.

The former condition was reasonable enough; the latter was not adhered to in practice, but the stated intention, and the high proportion of fellow-commoners among his pupils, betoken considerable ambition, either for self-advancement, or for promoting Puritan ideals among influential quarters of society.[50] Parents knew that Preston could be relied upon to protect their sons from Catholic influences whilst at university.[51]

A relatively small number of Queens' Fellows were assiduous collectors of pupils.[52] Families might send several members to the same tutor; Preston, for example, taught five of the Capel family listed in appendix 8.[53] There were also regional connections. Richard Bryan (Fellow 1632 – 44, 1660 – 70) was from Leicestershire, which supplied a moderate proportion of Queensmen in the period, but eight of his 21 pupils recorded in the college *Registrum* were from that county. Six of the eight pupils admitted under Herbert Palmer between 1623 and 1625 were from his native county of Kent.[54] In other cases there is no discernable regional bias, and the nature of recruitment was probably more complex. Simon Patrick, who had originally sought admission to Emmanuel, was recommended on arrival to try his luck at Queens', where many of the Fellows were newly promoted from Emmanuel. Two of Humphrey Tyndall's nephews went to Queens' while he was president there.[55]

Tutors' duties included handling their pupils' money, for which they were responsible to parents, as well as being held responsible by the college for payment of students' bills.[56] The way in which individual

---

[50] Searle, 435; Registrum, fos.1 – 15v; Hill (1965), 240. Religious education for undergraduates came not from the academic course, but from hearing and discussing sermons, commonplaces and other religious topics, for which there was great enthusiasm, Curtis (1959), 184 – 7. The rôle of college tutors in affirming and promoting Puritanism is discussed in Morgan (1986), 282 – 92, which includes references to Palmer and Preston.

[51] Ball (1885), 30 – 31.

[52] Registrum, fos.1 – 15v.

[53] Roger, Gamaliel (1616), Arthur, James, Moses.

[54] Registrum, fos.1 – 15v; Searle, 533.

[55] Patrick (1839), 11 – 12; Searle, 366 – 7; Tyndall's niece married William Hitch, who had been a sizar at Queens'.

[56] Venn (1913), 193, 222 – 3. In 1529 Queens' ordered that no tutor could accept pupils without first promising to be answerable for them to the college; in 1620 there were further moves to ensure that students paid their bills, for apparently tutors were suffering financially from students not paying (this was renewed in 1676, which suggests that the problem could not be surmounted entirely), Book 62, 102, 107 – 8. A tutor's account book of 1644 lists the charges, regular and otherwise, which some fee-paying students paid at Queens': to the bursar, cook, laundress, bedmaker, barber, shoemaker, tailor, apothecary and physician, sizar and carrier; for tuition, books, repairs and improvements to the room, chamber rent, coal, candles, commons, admission and degree fees, and expenses of the final journey home. The tutor kept a careful account of each pupil, Book 27A. For student expenses elsewhere, see Harrison (1958), chapter IV.

students were educated owed much to parental wishes. The father of Henry Slingsby, one of Preston's pupils, wrote to his son: 'Some tell me that you are sadde and melancholly. It is much against my will that you shoulde be soe and my desire is you shoulde have all fitting recreation that you be as merrie as you like in honest and civill compaynie. And if your Tutor be a little too reserved in granting you tymes of recreation . . . soe I will, upon your just complaynte, enjoyne him to amende it'.[57] Henry Slingsby was a fellow-commoner, and the lifestyle of this class could be costly as they asserted their status by ostentation.[58] Slingsby's father, noting the expense of the special gown worn by fellow-commoners, reminded his son that 'this difference of garment for Fellow Commoners is not for their own meritt but for the dignitie of the Fellows into whose societie they are admitted'.[59] There were complaints that wealthy students encouraged their poorer colleagues to overspend in trying to imitate their expensive fashions — not wilfully, but by example.[60]

Fellow-commoners also enjoyed better — that is to say, less crowded — rooms. Chambers were normally assigned to Fellows, who let them out; students provided their own furniture and paid for repairs, with contents sold by one occupant to his successor.[61] Sharing was usual; college rooms in Queens' and elsewhere consisted of one main sleeping chamber, with a main bed and truckle beds — the former for a Fellow, the latter for the students. Each inhabitant had his own private study partitioned off from the main chamber along the wall. The number of inhabitants of a room varied according to size, status of the students concerned, and the pressure of numbers — this pressure was particularly intense in the late Tudor and early Stuart periods, which at Queens' saw two new ranges built and attics brought into use to provide further accommodation. It was not usual for dons anywhere to have a room to themselves before the end of the 17th century, but this was sometimes possible.[62] Henry Slingsby shared with one other fellow-

[57] Smith (1968), 15 – 16.
[58] Venn (1913), 208 – 227.
[59] Smith (1968), 12 – 13.
[60] Curtis (1959), 54 – 6.
[61] Harrison (1958), 5 – 14; c.f. Book 15, entry for July 1649, which records 5s given to Simon Patrick 'that hee layed out in his foundation chamber'.
[62] In general, before the extension of college buildings in the 17th century, buildings in most colleges were of only two floors, with between four and six rooms to each staircase, Jackson-Stops (1979), 183 – 4; Brooke (1985), 21 – 2; RCHM, lxxxii – iii, lxxxv; Drinkwater (1934 – 5), 157; Pevsner (1970), 23; OPR, f.169. MS 30, fos.23v – 27v, has a late 16th century inventory of rooms and their fittings: at that time there were 32 chambers (and many more studies) in Old Court.

commoner, with whom he squabbled over furniture. Once again, his father provided sage counsel: 'Care the less so you hold your chamber, for though the beddesteade may be his, I am sure the bed is your own, and you maie in reasonable tyme get a beddesteade'.[63]

Tutors were also responsible for moral welfare and discipline; they could even inflict corporal punishment.[64] The age of students at their admission has been the subject of some debate amongst historians.[65] By the 17th century, it seems that most students came up between the ages of 15 and 18, especially at 16 or 17. In the late medieval period the average may have been lower, though this is not clear.[66] Youthful exuberance was a perennial problem. The 17th century writer John Aubrey noted that 'The stage of adolescence, seventeen, eighteen, nineteen and twenty, is an ungovernable age: lust does then pullulate, and they do grow *in venerem*. They have the strength of men, with boys' heads'.[67] It was for this reason that caution money — effectively a bond for good behaviour — was charged on students, a practice which endures to the present day.[68] Medieval student society, allowed little or no recreation, was often volatile, unrestrained and violent.[69] In 1470 the chancellor of the university was authorised to imprison undergraduates who disturbed the peace, and to expel those who rebelled against his authority.[70] Fee-paying students of the early modern period were indulged in a variety of recreations, including music and dancing, fencing, football, bowls, and acting, as well as the less reputable cards and dice. Henry Slingsby rode, and played the viol; his father suggested that he should take singing lessons.[71]

Students continued to get themselves into trouble, however. Evidence

[63] Smith (1968), 13.
[64] Stone (1965), 35.
[65] DeMolen (1976); Stone (1977); Stone (1980); Cressy (1979); Charlton (1976).
[66] Stone (1977), 9; Stone (1980), 97 – 9; Charlton (1965), 131; Charlton (1976), 225 – 6; Cressy (1979), 167 – 8, 173 – 6; Cobban (1975), 208 – 9. Queens' probably conformed to this pattern; where ages are known from the early modern period, these tend to fall into the 17 – 18 age group, e.g. from appendix 8: Theophilus Aylmer (1583): 17/18; Edward Aylmer (1625): c. 18; William Bramston (1639): ?17; Anthony Bramston (1658): 18. Henry Slingsby went up at 16, Smith (1968), 12. I see no evidence for Stone's assertion that there were significant variations in age between different colleges, nor any reason why this should be so, Stone (1980), 97.
[67] Aubrey, *Education*, 29; c.f. Simon Patrick, who went up to Queens' 'when I was between seventeen and eighteen years old, and had some discretion to govern myself', Patrick (1839), 11. See Morgan (unpublished thesis, 1984), 226 – 235, for dress, and disorder in general.
[68] OPR, fos.8, 15v, 150v – 151v.
[69] Cobban (1975), 212 – 13.
[70] Cooper, i.218.
[71] Harrison (1958), 48 – 50; Smith (1968), 14; for acting, see below, pp. 106 – 9.

of indiscipline comes from 'official' sources; students were hardly likely to write home about the wild side of life.[72] Warnings and punishments could be administered informally by tutors, so that many minor misdeamours went unrecorded, but all the evidence points to an unending battle by colleges to maintain order.[73] Tutors were expected to prevent their well-born pupils from contracting marriages with girls of lower social rank, but were not always successful: in 1577 a Cambridge minister was imprisoned by the university for performing a secret, irregular marriage between Anthony Byron, a fellow-commoner at Queens', and a Miss Beaumont from Leicestershire, who was staying in the town. Byron then went into the country, so that the vice-chancellor could not 'take ordre for the restoringe of him to his Tutor untill his father's pleasure be knowen'. To add to the difficulty, there was a 'common report' that Byron had precontracted to marry 'another yonge gentlewoman of the town'.[74] John Preston was more alert when one of his fellow-commoners, Capel Bedle, became friendly with the daughter of a local lawyer. To avoid the risk of an engagement, Preston took all his fellow-commoner pupils away from Cambridge for a while, and wrote to Bedle's guardian, who promptly removed the youth and sent him abroad to conclude his education.[75]

At Queens', repeated misbehaviour resulted in formal, public warnings, and in expulsion if these were disregarded. There was provision for immediate expulsion in the case of 'any crime of particularly evil report, which brings infamy upon the college'.[76] A few public admonitions have survived: there were several in the late 17th century for 'unseasonable drinking parties, notable arrogance and insolence, together with lies and other disgraceful actions', and there are other, similar standard formulae.[77] Under Edward Martin's presidency a sizar, Thomas Agar, was admonished for 'pernoctation and other crimes'.[78] In 1659 William Cummins was admonished for being found 'in a Booth of ill-fame at Sturbridge Fair'; he promised to mend his ways, but was expelled for 'contumacy' (insubordination) the

---

[72] Haskins (1929), 32, for medieval student letters.
[73] Twigg (unpublished thesis, 1983), vii – viii.
[74] Cooper, ii.347 – 9.
[75] Ball (1885), 48 – 52; Searle, 435.
[76] 'ullo Crimine notabili diffamari, unde Collegio nascatur Infamia', Book 79, fos.22v – 23; Statutes (1559), 20 – 21.
[77] 'intempestiori compotationibus, insigni arrogantia et contumatia cum mendaciis divis caeterisque flagitiis conjuncta', Book 3, f.275v. See also OPR, f.150; Book 14, 129 – 30, for other 16th and 17th century examples.
[78] 'pernoctatione et aliis criminibus', OPR, f.150.

following year.[79]

Two other Queensmen are known to have fallen foul of the university authorities. In 1596 Matthew Wellbore, a fellow-commoner, was forced to make a public promise to mend his ways after being summoned to answer for insulting behaviour towards the mayor of Cambridge.[80] In 1609 Thomas Pestell, a sizar, was brought before the vice-chancellor's court to answer for 'his publike offence by him given openly in the last Commencement'.[81] The commencement was the university's major degree ceremony in July each year, an important social event thronged with family and friends.[82] Pestell had acted as 'praevaricator' — a student chosen to make a witty speech at the ceremony — and whilst irreverance was customary on these occasions, praevaricators often overstepped the mark.[83]

[79] Book 51, f.lv. Sturbridge fair, held on the outskirts of Cambridge every September, was said in 1589 to have 'far surpassed the greatest and most celebrated fairs of all England'; in the 16th century it lasted for over a month. Virtually everything that could be purchased was on sale there, and there were numerous entertainments and sideshows — even theatrical performances — for the fair was as much a social as an economic event. Queens' purchased utensils at Sturbridge fair for the most part although it also bought fish there sometimes, reflecting the fair's origins as a fishmarket: nails were bought, and also iron, timber, colanders, ladles, knives, bellows, pails, kettles, lanterns, baskets and dishes; worn utensils could be part exchanged for new ones, Everitt (1967), 535 – 6; Cam (1959), 92 – 5; Gunning (1854), i.162 – 173; Book 3, 16; Book 4, fos.63, 74, 85v, 127v, 148, 155; Book 5, fos.7, 28v, 50, 54; Book 14, 130; Searle, 400.
[80] CUA CUR 7, 11 (1) – (6).
[81] CUA VC Ct.I.38, f.60.
[82] Harrison (1968), 69; Wall (1828), 119 – 128.
[83] Costello (1958), 27 – 9.

8

Studies and degrees (15th – 17th centuries)

Written sources have not, in general, reflected the central importance of study in university life. The awarding of degrees was well documented, but study was a personal business, not much written about. It was almost taken for granted: at Oxford and Cambridge, according to the Elizabeth visitor William Harrison, 'the use of tongues, philosophy, and the liberal sciences, besides the profound studies of the civil law, physic, and theology, are daily taught and had'.[1]

Almost all students in hostels and colleges in the 15th century had to follow the same course for the arts degree, the prerequisite for higher study; this course altered little in essence during the next two centuries.[2] The degree of bachelor of arts required four years of study, centred on the *trivium*, which, as its name suggests, consisted of three subjects: (Latin) grammar, rhetoric and logic. Standard texts by classical authors were prescribed authorities; the works of Aristotle were of great importance. In his second year, the student was allowed to attend some of the academic debates ('disputations') which took place in the university schools; as a 'sophister' in his third and fourth years he took part in these debates. In these last two years moral, natural and metaphysical philosophy were studied, with Aristotle as the undisputed authority and guide. The aspiring bachelor of arts was then allowed to 'commence', or take his examination: this took the form of participating in public disputations, and if adjudged successful in his performances, he was admitted to the degree.

To become a master of arts, three further years of study were necessary. These included the subjects of the *quadrivium* (arithmetic, geometry, music and astronony), yet more Aristotle, some public disputing and a little lecturing. The student was then allowed to 'incept' (participate in a further series of public disputations) for the master's degree. Higher degrees were attained by extension of similar formulae over many years; a further ten years were necessary to become a doctor of divinity (including the taking of the bachelor of divinity degree). There were some attempts to modify the curriculum in the 16th century,

[1] Harrison (1968), 65.
[2] Porter (1958), 4 – 5, and Charlton (1965), 143, are the sources of the following general
information.

but for the most part it remained fundamentally conservative and scholastic.[3] The continuing strong commitment to the Aristotelian philosophical system was the primary manifestation of this: John Preston's 17th century biographer observer that Preston had 'waded far in Aristotle' and regarded Aristotle as a kind of 'tutelary saint'.[4] Lawrence Bretton, a contemporary of Preston's at Queens', wrote in his notes: *'vera et sana philosophia est vera Aristotelica'*.[5]

But in many ways university education was undergoing considerable change.[6] Lectures, once the central element in the teaching system, were undermined in the 16th century by the new availability of printed books, the development of college teaching and the tutorial system.[7] In addition, a wide range of extra-curricular studies became available to those who sought to be cultured rather than qualified: such as history, geography and modern languages.[8] From relatively modest beginnings, humanist ideas rapidly permeated areas of the arts course.[9] Queens' established Greek and Hebrew lectureships in the 16th century, and an ethics lectureship in the 17th.[10] Queensmen were prominent in the first humanist developments in Cambridge: three lectureships in the humanities (or at least providing a humanist slant to traditional studies) were created in the university in 1488. Fisher was one of the early lecturers while still a don at Michaelhouse in the 1490s; John Fawne, a Fellow of Queens', may have been one also at the turn of the century. Another Queens' Fellow, John Philippe, held one of the lectureships from 1505 to 1507; he had been composing Latin texts for the university since 1500. Erasmus' description of another Queens' Fellow of this period, John Vaughan, as 'a learned man', indicates that he also was an early humanist.[11]

---

3 Simon (1967), 252 – 3, 358; Charlton (1965), 141, 150 – 2; Curtis (1959), 85 – 92; Kearney (1970), chapter V; Costello (1958), *passim*; c.f. Feingold (1984), 24 – 32; see also Leader, 'Philosophy'.
4 Ball (1885), 9, 13.
5 Kearney (1970), 84.
6 Only the arts degree is referred to here; for the higher faculties, see Curtis (1959), 150 – 62.
7 Charlton (1965), 143 – 50; Curtis (1959), 98 – 106; O'Day (1982), 112 – 115. For the debate on the decline of attendance at lectures, see Curtis (1959), 96 – 7; Feingold (1984), 46 – 7.
8 Curtis (1959), 127 – 144.
9 Jardine (1974); Jardine (1975); Simon (1967), 358; Curtis (1959), 94 – 6; c.f. Charlton (1965), 145 – 8. O'Day (1982), 130, argues that the 'tone' of the arts course became more humanist. A letter from Robert Aldrich of King's to Erasmus in 1526 illustrates these informal beginnings: he reminds Erasmus of 'the time when I personally read with you some books by Seneca and Jerome at Queens' College', Porter and Thomson (1963), 208.
10 *Statutes (1559)*, 49; above, pp. 56, 75; Searle, 554.
11 Leader (1983), 216 – 221. For a discussion of 15th century college lectures at Queens', see Leader, 'Teaching', 114 – 15, which demonstrates that the college was educationally progressive in this regard too; see also Book 79, f.9v; Mills (unpublished thesis, 1977), 6 – 7.

Interest in scientific matters grew, largely informally.[12] At the beginning of the 16th century, the study of mathematics underwent a revival at Cambridge as part of the general revival of the liberal arts there by humanist scholars. In about 1500 a new lectureship in mathematics was created in the university; the first known lecturer was Roger Collyngwood of Queens', who began lecturing in 1500/1, and then went to Paris to study canon law before returning to lecture again between 1503 and 1507. In 1507 he set off for another four years abroad, but was lecturing in mathematics again at Cambridge between 1514 and 1517. Collyngwood was interested in mathematical research as well as being a teacher; he left a treatise on the subject of *'Arithmetica Experimentalis'*. Between 1507 and 1514 the mathematics lecturership was held successively by three Queensmen: William Peyton, Henry Bullock, and Humphrey Walkden, and the college library seems to have gained books on astronomy and geometry at about this time. Although the lectureship was no longer monopolised by Queensmen after 1517, interest in mathematics was maintained by the next generation of Queens' humanists, principally by Thomas Smith, one of the foremost scholars of his age, and a Fellow at Queens' in the 1503s.[13] Even after he had left Queens' for a distinguished career in the service of the Tudor state, Smith retained his interest in the college's mathematical tradition. In 1573, now Sir Thomas Smith, he endowed lectureships in mathematics and geometry at Queens', insisting that these were 'not to be redd of the reader as of a preacher out of a pulpit, but "per radium et eruditem pulverem", as it is said, that is with a penn on paper or tables, or a sticke or compasse in sand or duste to make demonstracon that his schollers maie both understand the reader and also do it themselves and so profit'.[14] The college statutes of 1559 had already ordered the reading of mathematics lectures.[15] Edward Martin was geometry lecturer during his first few years as a Fellow, and it was said of him that 'his parts, as his nature, inclining to Solidity, rather than Politeness; he was for the exact Sciences, Logick and Mathematics in his Study, as he was for strick Rules in his Conversation'.[16] The Cambridge Platonist John Smith became college mathematics lecturer in 1644, the year of his arrival from Emmanuel, and university mathematics lecturer in 1647; a large proportion of the vast library he bequeathed to the college in 1652 consisted of books on mathematics and astronomy. The eminent 17th century mathematician John Wallis arrived with Smith from Emmanuel,

---

[12] Feingold (1984), *passim*.
[13] Rose (1977), 47 – 57.
[14] Searle, 320.
[15] Feingold (1984), 35; *Statutes (1559)*, 47.
[16] Feingold (1984), 60 – 61.

but was only a Fellow for a short time.[17] Edward Davenant (Fellow, 1615 – 25) was later described by Christopher Wren as the best mathematician in the world. He held strong views on the publication of work that was not original, claiming that he 'would have a man knock't in the head that should write anything in mathematiques that had been written of before'. Both his daughters became algebraists.[18] In 1706 algebra lectureships were endowed in nine colleges, including Queens'.[19] The college also produced some astronomers. John Ponet gave Henry VIII a dial of his own invention which showed the hour of the day, day of the month, planetary hour, change of the moon and 'divers other things no less strange'.[20] Andrew Perne had left Queens' to become master of Peterhouse, and on his death in 1589 bequeathed globes and astronomical instruments to the latter college. Robert Some, another Queens's Fellow, who succeeded Perne as master of Peterhouse, is known to have taught mathematics and cosmography.[21] John Mansell, president of Queens' during the 1620s, bravely defended Copernicus at his master of arts disputation in 1601.[22]

Some Queensmen took an interest in medicine, although only a very small proportion of students took degrees in that subject; Queens' was one of the least medically-inclined colleges in the university.[23] Richard Eden, a pupil of Thomas Smith and a Fellow from 1525 till 1544, updated an anatomical work, although his main writings were on navigation and geography.[24] John Wallis, although primarily a mathematician, was among the early supporters of Harvey's theory of the circulation of the blood.[25] John Preston learned about medicine just in case he should ever have to fall back on it for a living.[26] Walter Needham (Fellow, 1655 – 60) researched into embryology, and Robert Boyle thought this work sufficiently valuable to persuade Needham to publish it.[27] Thomas Lorkins (Fellow, 1551 – 3, subsequently Fellow of Peterhouse) became the university's fourth Regius professor of physick in 1564.[28]

Astrology was a reputable scientific subject at that time, and a

---

[17] *ibid.*, 53. Smith was said to be knowledgeable about ancient languages, natural philosophy, music, medicine, and mathematics, Worthington (1673), ix – x. For Wallis see also above, p. 57.
[18] Feingold (1984), 80, 154 – 55; Gunther (1969), 39; Frank (1973), 250.
[19] Frank (1973), 202 – 3.
[20] Gunther (1969), 141 – 42; c.f. Rose (1977), 54; Searle, 241.
[21] Gunther (1969), 142; Feingold (1984), 100.
[22] Feingold (1984), 102.
[23] See below, appendix 11. Queens' provided a small proportion of the university's total output of medical students and practitioners between 1501 and 1600 (3.5%, only 12 names in all, making it 11th in the list of colleges), Robb-Smith (1971), 21.
[24] Rose (1977), 54; Gunther (1969), 207.
[25] Wordsworth (1968), 172, n. 7.
[26] Ball (1885), 13 – 14.
[27] Webster (1975), 138.
[28] Gunther (1969), 251; Rolleston (1932), 133 – 7.

traditional don's interest, though less fashionable from the late Tudor period onwards.[29] Preston studied it.[30] Edward Davenant 'thank't God his father did not know the houre of his birth; for that it would have tempted him to have studyed astrologie, for which he had no esteeme at all'.[31] John Maplet (Fellow 1560; subsequently Fellow of St Catharine's and of Caius), who was both naturalist and astrologer, published an astrological treatise, *The Diall of Destiny*, in 1581.[32] Robert Watson matriculated at Queens' in 1581 and later practised as a physician; he also published several astrological almanacks.[33] John Harvey, a Fellow in the 1580s, was one of three brothers — the other two were Fellows of Pembroke — with strong astrological enthusiasms, often involved in controversy; Harvey also became a physician after leaving the university.[34]

In the late 17th century, when new scientific ideas flourished in England, new philosophical theories such as those of Descartes were said to be 'much in all people's discourse' at Cambridge, although the Lucasian chair in mathematics had only been founded in 1663, and the age of Newton was still to come.[35] The university's first professor of chemistry was John Francis Vigani of Newark, who had begun teaching privately at Cambridge in the 1680s; he was a practical rather than a theoretical chemist, published only one book, and clearly preferred teaching. Some of his public lectures were said to have been given 'in Queens' College Cloysters', and he is thought to have had a laboratory in the college, but he taught and experimented in several other colleges besides, before leaving Cambridge in 1708. A Cambridge student of the 1690s described him as 'a very learned chemist, and a great traveller, but a drunken fellow', and also complained that 'by reason of the abstruceness of the art, I got little or no good thereby', but this is the only personal memory of Vigani that has survived. The extensive collection of drugs, or *materia medica*, which he assembled in 1704, was paid for by Queens' and has remained in the college's possession to this day.[36]

Both in science and in the main arts course we know that certain studies were pursued by committed individuals, but not if they were

[29]   Thomas (1971), 353 – 4.
[30]   Ball (1885), 15 – 16.
[31]   Gunther (1969), 154.
[32]   *ibid.*, 151, 338.
[33]   *ibid.*, 152; AC.
[34]   Feingold (1984), 77 – 8.
[35]   Hunter (1981), 141 – 42, and chapter 6.
[36]   Gunther (1969), 222 – 24, 472 – 81; Frank (1973), 240, 257; Coleby (1952), 46 – 60; Peck (1932 – 3), 37 – 9; de la Pryme (1869), 24 – 25, 247; Winstanley (1935), 143 – 44; see also Gascoigne (1985), 404. The library at Queens' has a student notebook containing notes made from Vigani's lectures in 1707 (unclassified MS).

taken up widely or enthusiastically by students. Some students studied hard: Preston, when he finally made his mind up to pursue an academic career, worked so hard that he 'seldome or never could be seene abroad'.[37] Simon Patrick claimed to have been 'so studious as to fill whole books with observations out of various ancient authors, with some of my own which I made upon them. For I find one book begun in the year 1646, wherein I have noted many useful things, and another more large in the year 1647, having the word *aeternitas*, at the top of many pages, by the thought of which I perceive I was quickened to spend my time well'. It was also, he wrote, 'usual with me to sit up till one or two o'clock in the morning, even in winter time; and yet I rose to go to chapel constantly'.[38] But these men became Fellows, and were clearly the exception rather than the rule. Elsewhere, little is known; though there is sometimes evidence of enforcement of rules for performing college academic exercises and disputations, this need not mean that students were particularly lax.[39] The course of study was long and demanding, even for the basic arts degrees. In effect, there was total continuous assessment: complex exercises and oral examinations which required great intellectual discipline and considerable knowledge and understanding of the texts. Scholasticism was slighted by the humanists, and has been criticised in that light ever since, but for all its restrictiveness and rigidity it met many of the needs of the age; it would not have been tolerated had it merely turned out useless dialecticians.[40]

Degrees

Many students took no degree at all: even in the 14th and 15th centuries perhaps as many as two thirds may have left university without graduating, and few remained to read for higher degrees.[41] Some 10 – 15% of those 'secular' clerical students (those who were not members of monastic orders) who came to Cambridge stayed on to study theology, a graduate faculty for masters of arts.[42] But in those later

[37] Ball (1885), 10.
[38] Patrick (1839), 14 – 15, 28.
[39] e.g. OPR, f.129v.
[40] Cobban (1975), 164 – 67, 209 – 10, 218 – 34; c.f. Costello (1958), *passim*, for 17th century scholasticism in the curriculum and its failings.
[41] Aston *et al.* (1980), 24 – 5; Rosenthal (1969), 419, n. 14. There is little evidence before the mid-16th century.
[42] The proportion studying theology was much higher amongst the 'regulars' (members of monastic orders): almost all of the friars who attended Cambridge went on to do so. About one half of the seculars took the basic arts course, and one third to two fifths took law, for which no prior training in arts was needed, Aston *et al.* (1980), 57 – 9 (figures for 1340 – 1499).

medieval colleges which were intended for graduate students, theologians were predominant. Late 15th century foundations such as Queens', St Catharine's and Jesus, which were intended to encourage theological studies, became centres for the subject. Queens' produced only two lawyers in the last twenty years of the 15th century: 97% of its output between the year of its foundation and 1499 were theologians.[43]

In the centuries that followed, the proportion of students who failed to graduate varied according to their social class. In the late 16th and early 17th centuries as many as three quarters of the fellow-commoners may not have taken a degree, and over half of the pensioners; nearly a quarter of the sizars may also have failed to graduate, probably for financial reasons.[44] Some suggestion of the situation at Queens' is given below.[45] Those incepting for degrees (and new Fellows, too), were expected to feast their colleagues; the feasts were taken seriously and there were fines for those who failed to do their duty, but from the early 17th century at latest steps were taken by the college authorities at Queens' to ensure that students were not forced by custom into overspending, and price limits were set.[46]

The library

Queens' is fortunate in having a library catalogue which was drawn up as early as 1472.[47] This lists almost 200 volumes, a reasonable stock for that time, when books were still handwritten and expensive, and lectures remained the most important means of communicating ideas.[48] These books were working copies, probably pawned when they deteriorated or were no longer useful. By 1538, when a second catalogue was drawn up, only twelve of the volumes listed in 1472 had survived; none of the books in either of these catalogues was in the college's possession by the middle of the 19th century.[49]

The invention of printing, which made books cheaper (though not cheap) and more accessible, brought about a rapid increase in the size and importance of college libraries between the 1530s and the beginning

---

[43] Cobban (1980), 2–11; see below, appendix 11.

[44] O'Day (1982), 95.

[45] See appendix 11.

[46] Searle, 435–6, 440, 510, 583; OPR, fos.8, 11v; see also Brooke (1985), 30. There are some examples of commencement expenses in Book 17 and Book 26.

[47] MS 30, fos.1v–8, printed in Searle (1864), 165–193.

[48] c.f. Pembroke (140 volumes in the 14th–15th centuries), and St Catharine's (137 in 1475), Mullinger (1873–1911), i.324–5. Gonville Hall had c. 300 by 1500, Brooke (1985), 33–5. Very few individuals owned books at this time, Aston et al. (1980), 63–6.

[49] Searle (1864), 167; Gaskell (1980), 7, 20, n. 2. There is a fragmentary list of early 17th century books at Queens', Book 26.

of Elizabeth's reign.[50] There was another major increase from the 1580s, thanks to donations and an increasing reluctance to throw old books away; many 16th century books survive at Queens'. Book-cases began to replace the older lecterns, which could not hold a sufficiently large number of volumes; Queens' was the only college in either university where the medieval lecterns were not destroyed, but were adapted to form part of the new book-cases; this was done in the Jacobean period.[51]

The library was intended for the use of Fellows rather than students. It was unsupervised at first, and keys were issued to Fellows. The books were chained to their shelves to prevent theft.[52] Sir Thomas Smith's Latin and Greek books were left to the college 'upon condition that they chain them up in the library or do distribute them amongst the fellows such as will best occupy them'.[53] It was not until 1571 that a scholar was appointed librarian. In 1616 a student was given ten shillings 'for writeing the names of the bookes in the librarie'.[54] When borrowing was permitted, it was thought necessary to restrict it. In 1647 the college ordered that the president might borrow books, but Fellows could not do so for more than three days without the permission of the remainder of the fellowship; even then they had to give notice to the librarian, and subscribe their names for each day the book was kept out. A fine was subsequently levied on those who failed to subscribe.[55] There were other fines and fees levied on Fellows which went to support the library.[56]

The library relied heavily on benefactions of books for its stock; there are several examples of these from an early date, some of them complete libraries.[57] John Davenant gave £100 for the library in 1626, which was used to buy 130 volumes.[58] Among the more significant benefactions is that of Sir Thomas Smith, whose Latin and Greek books amounted to some 300 volumes; only about 60 remained by the late 17th century. He left them to Queens', he declared, 'because I see that none of those which shall succeed me of long time are learned' — Smith was not famous for his modesty — and he instructed his executors that if Queens' did not collect his books within ten days of receiving notice, they were to go to Peterhouse instead.[59] By the time of his death in 1652 at the age of 34, the Queens' Fellow John Smith had collected about 600

---

[50] O'Day (1982), 121 – 22; Gaskell (1980), 7; see Bennet (1970), 228, for prices of books.
[51] Gaskell (1980), 10 – 18. Gaskell claims that this happened at Queens' in 1614, *ibid.*, 14; but in fact the work was done in 1612 – 13, Book 5, fos.146 – 146v.
[52] Gaskell (1980), 6; Book 4, fos. 102, 129; Book 5, fos.3v, 15v, 33v.
[53] Dewar (1964), 203.
[54] Searle, 319; Book 5, f.161.
[55] OPR, fos.132v, 133v; Clarke (1677), 197 – 8.
[56] Searle, 510, 554; Book 25 (for examples from the 1630s).
[57] Searle, 30, 74, 85, 313, 363, 389, 545, 577; OPR, fos.138, 160.
[58] Searle, 422; Book 25; Book 43, fos.124v – 125v.
[59] Dewar (1964), 203.

books on a wide range of subjects, including history, geography and travel, medicine, philosophy, theology and Rabbinical writings, but especially mathematics and astronomy; most of this 'noble company of books' (in Simon Patrick's words) came from continental presses.[60] It was presumably thanks to bequests such as this that a visitor in Queen Anne's reign could note that the library at Queens', 'though small, has yet many good books'.[61]

The college theatre

During much of the 16th and 17th centuries the performance of plays was, in effect, part of the course of college studies. There was very little play-acting before 1500, save of a crude kind. Festivities at holiday times were of a quasi-theatrical nature: colleges appointed 'lords of misrule', mock dignitaries who held sway temporarily over the student body and sometimes paid visits to other colleges. The Queens' accounts for 1548 show the purchase of refreshments for the visit of two of these lords, the 'king' of King's and the 'emperor' of Trinity. The university visitors of 1549 tried to abolish these practices, fearing that they encouraged indiscipline, but their orders were ineffectual.[62]

In the early 16th century, mumming and the performance of morality plays became more common, and true drama (in the modern sense) evolved from this; by the middle of the century, several Cambridge colleges mounted plays annually or even more often. This development was inspired by humanism, which saw theatre as a potent educational influence. The statutes of Trinity, St John's and Queens' required the performance of plays in their colleges. At Queens' two plays (comedies or tragedies) were to be performed between 20 December and Ash Wednesday each year, and college officers were ordered to ensure that this was done. The Queens' statutes stated explicitly that the plays were meant to teach civility of bearing and speech, qualities which the upper classes now clearly required of a university education. College plays were performed, and in many cases written, by members of the colleges concerned.[63]

[60] Saveson (1958), 215 – 6; Saveson (1955), appendix 2, 2 – 4; Patrick (1839), 20; Patrick (1839), 20; Patrick (1673), 508 – 9. In 1634 the vice-chancellor's court heard a dispute over books left by a fellow of Queens' the previous year: it was alleged that they had been promised to another Fellow, CUA VC Ct. II.25, fos.38 – 38v.

[61] The library was also said to contain few manuscripts worthy of note, Mayor (1911), 144 – 5.

[62] Boas (1914), 1 – 10; Smith (1923), 19.

[63] Boas (1914), 11 – 16; Smith (1923), 11, 20 – 22; Nelson (unpublished paper). Plays were referred to in the college statutes in an interpretation of 1546. They were first embodied properly in the revision of 1559, Statutes (1559), 53 n. The words of the statute outlining the purpose of the theatre were: 'Et ne Juventus nostra, exercitata forsan ad alia, pronunciando ac gestu rudis et inurbana maneat', ibid., 53 – 4.

Classical drama was the first to be performed, but subsequently there were neo-classical plays, some written by Cambridge men, such as the comedy *Strylius* performed at Queens' in 1552/3, which was written by Nicholas Robinson, a Fellow of the college who was to become a bishop of Elizabeth's reign. In the 1560s and 1570s Roman and humanist dramas were the most popular forms, but from the 1570s onwards newer styles, such as history plays and Italian-style comedies became fashionable.[64]

Most plays were performed in college halls. This was certainly true of Queens', which possessed a dismountable stage of sophisticated design; it was built in the 1540s and remained in use, with modifications, well into the 17th century.[65] Plays were often long and refreshments were provided after the performance for players and audience.[66] Before Elizabeth's reign, colleges usually held performances in private before their own members. Excluded members of other colleges might cause trouble outside, and windows were often broken; there were more serious disturbances on occasion. Performances by professional companies were reckoned to be even more disruptive, and were therefore firmly opposed by the university authorities.[67]

During Elizabeth's reign and afterwards, plays were also provided as an entertainment for distinguished visitors; sometimes these were presented by the university, at other times by colleges. At Elizabeth's visit to Cambridge in 1564, four plays were prepared by the university, with participants from several colleges; one of the Queensmen involved was Nicholas Robinson.[68] In 1595 an Italian comedy, *Laelia*, was performed before the earl of Essex and other nobles at Queens' as part of the commencement celebrations. Essex was said to have been so impressed by two of the actors that he secured them to perform before the queen on a later occasion; the two, George Meriton and George Montaigne, were both Fellows and subsequently distinguished clergymen (Meriton became archbishop of York) and it has been suggested that they may have written *Laelia*.[69] In the 17th century Queens' plays were performed before both James I and Charles I, but at Trinity and Newmarket, rather than in Queens' itself. *The Rival Friends*, by Peter

---

[64] Boas (1914), 17 – 23, 109, 111 – 132, 134ff, 288; c.f. Smith (1923), 6 – 7, who argues that romantic comedy in Queens' may go back to the 1540s. For Robinson, see *DNB*.

[65] Boas (1914), 23 – 24; Nelson (unpublished paper); Smith (1923), 28 – 29, and see *ibid.*, 23, 28, 31 – 32. The earliest reference to a stage is in 1522/3, *ibid.*, 28, 32; Nelson (unpublished paper), citing Book 2, f.51v. See also Wright (1986) — the most recent published work on the college stage, which summarises all the latest research.

[66] Smith (1923), 33 – 34, 42 – 44.

[67] Boas (1914), 110 – 11, 220 – 26; Smith (1923), 45 – 8, and see *ibid.*, 21 – 22.

[68] Boas (1914), 89 – 91; Smith (1923), 23. The government provided financial assistance for such royal performances, Boas (1914), 89.

[69] Boas (1914), 289 – 90; c.f. Smith (1923), 6 – 7, and see *ibid.*, 33.

Hausted of Queens', and *The Jealous Lovers*, by Thomas Randolph of Trinity, were both acted before the king and queen at Trinity in 1632. Hausted and Randolph were the most prominent Cambridge playwrights of their day, and there was also much rivalry between their colleges, both of which had a fine reputation for theatrical productions; Trinity men are said to have heckled Hausted's play on this occasion.[70]

Fashions in college theatre continued to change. Humanist interest in classical plays was supplanted by enthusiasm for Italian romantic comedy, and tragedy also declined in popularity. Morality plays, in which the characters represented abstract concepts, were revived in the early 17th century, but romantic comedy remained popular, a good example being Peter Hausted's *Senile Odium* of c. 1628/9. Several Queens' plays of this period attacked Puritanism and Puritan hostility towards the theatre: Robert Ward's *Fucus Histriomastix* of 1622/3 (which also satirised the common lawyers), Hausted's *Senile Odium*, and William Johnson's *Valetudinarium* of 1637//8.[71] Puritan opposition to the theatre, which they saw as immoral and licentious, was apparent by the end of the 16th century, and increased in the 17th. Perhaps this was one reason for the decline of college drama at this time; certainly it was recognised that the younger generations of university men were not as enthusiastic as their predecessors had been. It may also have been felt that plays were too expensive and time-consuming.[72]

Plays continued to be performed in some colleges until the end of the 1630s, but others had already abandoned the practice; St John's, once famous for its plays, did not perform any after 1620, and at other colleges where there had been only sporadic performance the custom also lapsed. Trinity and Queens' were the only colleges where plays continued to be performed with distinction.[73] The building of a 'stage house' at Queens'in the late 1630s to store the stage and its equipment suggests that here too the decline had set in, though it may have been thought only temporary.[74] The English Revolution put an end to college plays, and although Trinity attempted to revive the tradition after the Restoration, it had died out before the end of the century.[75] The last known performances at Queens' were in 1638, bringing to an end a series of regular theatrical productions in the college which had begun in the early 1540s and had been an important part of college life, involving students and Fellows alike in writing, acting and production. Nearly

---

[70] Smith (1923), 9, 10; Mills (1944), 17 – 20, 21 – 24, 24 – 37. The heckling may also have been due to the content of the play, which satirised clerical failings such as pluralism.
[71] Smith (1923), 8 – 9, 11; Boas (1914), 249 – 50; Mills (1944), 13.
[72] Smith (1923), 11 – 13, 13, n. 1.
[73] *ibid.*, 10; Mills (1944), 21.
[74] Smith (1923), 10, 24, refers to the building, but the best study is Nelson (unpublished paper), which disproves the ideas put forward in McKenzie (1970).
[75] Smith (1923), 14 – 16.

fifty performances are recorded from this period, many of the plays written by Fellows or graduate students, although few have survived. College theatre did not recommence in Queens' until relatively recent times.[76]

---

[76] *ibid.*, 50 – 72, 85 – 88, 109 – 110.

9

College estates, c. 1500 – c. 1640; benefactions; college charity

In the early modern period a college's prosperity depended almost entirely on income from lands.[1] Despite the confiscation of Richard III's great benefactions, Queens' was well endowed with land at the end of the 15th century, owning properties in seven counties.[2] By 1506 twenty benefactors had given land, or the means to acquire it; during the rest of the period there was some buying and selling of land, but few significant benefactions.[3] The audits for the years of Elizabeth's reign comprise estate revenues entered under 25 different headings, in nine counties: eleven in Cambridgeshire, seven in Essex, and one each in Bedfordshire, Hertfordshire, Huntingdonshire, Kent, Northamptonshire, Suffolk and Surrey.[4] Such local concentration was convenient administratively, and in part deliberate.[5] In 1502 money given by Hugh Trotter enabled Queens' to extend the possessions it had held at Fulbourn since 1479.[6] In 1530 an estate at Guilden Morden given in 1474 was sold for £80 and the money used to buy more land at Eversden, where a manor had been given to Queens' in 1491; more Eversden land was purchased in the 1550s.[7] Remote Lincolnshire properties which the college had received in the 1470s were sold in 1534.[8]

Profitability and not mere consolidation was the reason for buying and selling of estates; in the late 1550s, Queens' was looking at property in Northamptonshire for possible purchase.[9] After spending £60 on legal proceedings against an Essex tenant who would not pay his rent, the

---

[1] For an explanation of college economics and finances in general during the early modern period see Aylmer (1986); although this discusses the Oxford colleges only, colleges at both universities exhibit the same characteristics in this regard.

[2] Cambridgeshire, Essex, Huntingdonshire, Lincolnshire, Suffolk, Surrey, and Kent.

[3] The later benefactions are in Searle, 299, 320, 395, 412, 422.

[4] A single heading in the audit may cover more than one property, and more than one tenant, although the properties were grouped together; nor were individual properties always entered under the same heading, Book 11, *passim*.

[5] For administration of estates, see below, pp. 114 – 15.

[6] Searle, 93, 124; Book 76, f.21v; Book 77, f.8.

[7] Searle, 119, 188, 295.

[8] *ibid.*, 80 – 81, 188.

[9] Although it settled instead for the manor of Oakington, for which it paid £770 in 1560, Searle, 295 – 6.

college sold him the property in 1529 for £120 — the rent was only £5 *per annum*.[10] In the same year two Cambridge hostels were sold because of the expense of keeping them in good repair. St Bernard's hostel was sold to Corpus Christi in 1534 and a fourth hostel was sold in 1548; with the rise of colleges, it may have been felt that hostels were no longer a good investment.[11] Money received from such sales was earmarked for purchase of other property — the college could not hope to buy lands otherwise — although the £200 received from some 80 acres at Babraham in 1598 lay unused for nearly twenty years, when it was put towards the building in Walnut Tree Court.[12]

Most, if not all of the income from benefactions was assigned for specific purposes by the donors.[13] The £24 annual income from property at Abbotsley, Pampisford and Haslingfield given by John Drewell in 1494 was divided to endow two fellowships and a bible-clerk's place.[14] The £12 7s 4d which came annually from Sir Thomas Smith's gift at Overston went to pay for two lectureships (£4 and £3 each), two scholarships (£2 3s 8d each) and an annual dinner for the Fellows (£1).[15] In 1571 thirteen new scholarships were endowed out of the revenues of the manor of Oakington (purchased in 1560).[16] The number of fellowships and scholarships could only be increased through new benefactions, or more profitable exploitation of existing property; this number rose during the period, but there were occasions when benefactions could no longer sustain their original purpose: in 1470 – 1 a London haberdasher had given the college property in Southwark to found a fellowship; but by 1529 these houses were in such a poor state of repair that their rents and other charges could no longer be kept high enough to maintain the fellowship, which was therefore amalgamated with another.[17]

The Tudor and early Stuart period was a prosperous one for most landowners.[18] Rents rose, although since most leases were for long periods it was difficult to adjust rents to keep place with the considerable inflation of that time, and some colleges did not increase rents when leases were renewed, in the mistaken belief that inflation

[10] *ibid.*, 93 – 94, 187.
[11] *ibid.*, 186, 188 (the library copy of Searle (U.9.24) has a manuscript correction by the author altering 1535 to 1534), 238 – 39; Goodman (1922), 31.
[12] Searle, 391.
[13] See below, pp. 117 – 20.
[14] Searle, 122.
[15] *ibid.*, 320 – 1. The feast is still held, but costs rather more.
[16] *ibid.*, 319; the scholarships were 10d per week each; the fixed annual value of the estate was £46, Book 11, f.69v and ff.
[17] Searle, 79, 187.
[18] Bowden (1967), 674 – 95.

was only short-term.[19] It is often difficult to gain a clear picture of a college's prosperity, even where accounts have survived;[20] the evidence from Queens' suggests a steady growth in receipts — though not necessarily in net receipts — during the period, particularly marked in the middle decades of the 16th century, with another substantial increase from the middle of the century onwards; colleges elsewhere exhibit a similar pattern.[21] Direct income from estates remained steady: a group of properties in Eversden, for example, which yielded almost £81 in 1563/4 produced £83 a decade later, £70 in 1583/4, £83 in 1593/4 and £76 in 1603/4.[22]

In general there was a tendency towards shorter leases, partly as a result of Tudor legislation: acts limiting the length of ecclesiastical and college leases were passed in 1571, 1572 and 1576.[23] Despite this protection, colleges were happy to ignore the law when it suited them: in 1598 Queens' circumvented the ban on alienation of property by selling an estate at Babraham in all but name: a rent was charged, but was not to be collected, and the tenant was to run the property 'as if the same were absolutely his owne'.[24]

The most significant legislation to affect college rents was the 1576 act 'for the Maintenaunce of the Colledges in the Universities', otherwise known as the Corn Rent Act, which protected rental income against inflation by insisting that in all future leases one third of the rent was to be paid in corn or its current market rate in cash.[25] This third was to be used solely for 'the Relief of Commons and Diett' in the colleges, and the act gave a welcome boost to college incomes.[26] It was probably drawn up by Sir Thomas Smith, possibly with the help of his friend Andrew Perne, master of Peterhouse and a former Fellow of Queens'; Smith was certainly responsible for steering the bill through the House of Commons.[27] Payment in kind was not new, and had long been

---

[19] ibid., 593 – 616, 674 – 75, 690 – 93; Aylmer (1986), 524 – 5; Duncan, 'Balliol', 565.
[20] Aylmer (1986), 524 – 9, 532, 545. My own researches into colleges at both Oxford and Cambridge in the 17th century confirm this view.
[21] See below, appendix 12; c.f. Aylmer (1986), passim.
[22] Book 11, fos.30, 86v, 138, 177v, 215. Other estates show similar patterns.
[23] Bowden (1967), 686 – 87; Shadwell (1912), i.176 – 77, 188 – 89, 192 – 95; Duncan, 'Balliol', 566 – 7; Aylmer (1986), 534 – 5.
[24] Searle, 391, from Book 42, 216 – 20; Stone (1956), 273. Stone suggests that Palavicino, an ambitious courtier, put pressure upon the college to sell, but he does not substantiate this; Searle believed the price to be a fair one, but his account is rather defensive. For dodging of regulations in general, see Duncan, 'Balliol'; Howard (1935), 28 – 29; Aylmer (1986), 535.
[25] Shadwell (1912), i.190 – 92; Aylmer (1986), 535 – 43.
[26] Duncan, 'Balliol', 564; Duncan, 'Corpus Christi', 580, 583; Aylmer (1986), 536; Morgan (unpublished thesis, 1984), 321 – 22. For details of the act's operations at Queens', see OPR, fos.126v – 127v, 129, 164v – 166; Book 78; Book 80, fos.9 – 9v; Book 17; Book 24.
[27] Aylmer (1986), 541 – 3; Dewar (1964), 185 – 86.

practised by Queens'. In 1496 the college leased out land at Stambourne in Essex for an annual rent of £7 plus two loads of straw; pasture land close by was leased for 30s and a pound of pepper *per annum*.[28]

Landlords throughout the country also increased their revenues in this period by making tenants responsible for repairs to their property, and by raising entry fines, which were lump sums charged on tenants when they entered upon or renewed leases, calculated at several times the annual rent of the property. The sums raised by these fines varied greatly from one year to the next, but they were often lucrative, and overall they comprised a very important part of the landlords' income. But we do not know the extent to which collegiate landlords in general were raising entry fines during this period, and there are some signs that they were not taking full advantage of this facility.[29] Certainly these matters are unclear at Queens', although a few details of fines have survived: some of them were indeed substantial.[30] The college also paid for repairs on some of its estates during the Tudor period at least.[31] Sales of timber, though an irregular source of income because of the time wood takes to mature, could be lucrative too: the accounts presented to Henry VIII by the university in 1546 deliberately excluded 'wood salys', together with fines, lest they should give too rosy a picture of college finances.[32] The Queens' accounts contain many references to surveying college woods in order to select trees for felling, and for transporting timber.[33] Colleges had to keep a watchful eye on their woods to prevent illegal felling and theft of timber by their tenants.[34] In a college order of 1635 Queens' commented that it had suffered 'much injury' from such practices; in 1648 a tenant was prosecuted for illegal felling; and further restrictions were introduced in 1651–2. There are many detailed memoranda from the late 17th and 18th centuries granting and regulating permission to tenants to fell trees and specifying the amount

---

[28] Williams, (1933), 7, 8. For payments in kind generally, see Bowden (1967), 682–83; Howard (1935), 34.

[29] In general, Bowden (1967), 680–81, 684–86; Batho (1967), 293; Aylmer (1986), 527–8, 534; Duncan, 'Corpus Christi', 577–9; Howard (1935), 40–44, 64, 69–70; Dunbabin (1986), 276–7.

[30] e.g. OPR, fos.6v, 8v; Book 80, fos.6, 13v; Book 24; Book 25; Book 26; Book 27.

[31] e.g. Book 2, f.24; Book 4, fos.99v, 132v. In 1666 a college property in London was destroyed 'in the dreadfull fire', and the tenant was given a rent abatement for 40 years in return for rebuilding the property, Book 80, f.10. There is also a late 17th century memorandum (undated) that 'Heretofore the College us'd to be at all charge for reparations except for thack-Clay [clay for thatching] &c', *ibid.*, f.2 (second pagination).

[32] Williams, (1933), 8; *Documents* (1852), i.216–26; Lamb (1838), 60; above, pp. 32–3; OPR, f.125v; Book 80, f.10 (second pagination). In general, see Bowden (1967), 605–7, 677; Duncan, 'Corpus Christi', 577–80; Aylmer (1986), 528–9.

[33] e.g. Book 4, fos.100v, 102, 108, 111v, 134v, 166; Book 6, f.171; there are other examples throughout the college accounts.

[34] For Oxford examples see Duncan, 'Balliol', 570; Eland (1935), 86–87, 91.

of timber allowed to them for their own repairs.[35]

Wood sales were only one of a variety of items entered in the accounts as 'outside receipts', which also included, as well as fines, miscellaneous sales, manorial court dues, chamber rents, and any other irregular payment.[36] Variations in these receipts explain the great annual fluctuations in college income overall: in 1550/1, when receipts totalled £648, outside receipts accounted for nearly £300; in 1578/9, when the total was low at £392, outside receipts fell short of £30.[37] The underlying steadiness of rental income protected the college's long-term prosperity.[38]

The main method of supervising college estates was by means of the 'progress' — a visitation of properties held usually during the summer months when travel was more pleasant and the university less busy.[39] The statutes of 1529 directed annual visits to each property — although the accounts suggest that this was not observed — and the 1559 statutes provided more detailed explanation of the kind of enquiries that should be made of tenants.[40] The account books for 1579 – 80 demonstrate the routine of progresses: five separate estates were examined in two progresses in June 1579, and six estates were visited the following summer between June and September, with manorial courts held at two other estates in September and October; the courts settled disputes and regulated most aspects of local life.[41]

The account books illustrate the frequency, though not usually the exact nature, of contacts between the college and its tenants, as this illustration from the financial year 1566/7 shows:[42] in September 1566 a college servant was sent to Abbotsley on unspecified business. In October the senior bursar visited Bumpsted Helion; two shillings were paid for hiring his horses (expenses were strictly controlled by statute).[43] In January 1567 there was a trip to Eversden to gather rent; a Fellow rode

---

[35] OPR, fos.129v, 135, 136; Book 39, entry at back; Book 40. Henry James (president, 1675 – 1717) took a characteristically dim view of the arrangements for felling timber, recording in about the 1680s that the college should take care that 'we be not wrong'd in the measure as I am afraid we are and have been for these forty [years] last', Book 80, f.9 (second pagination), and see *ibid.*, f.7v (second pagination).

[36] See e.g. Duncan, 'Corpus Christi'. External or outside receipts at Queens' for the 1650s are recorded in some detail in Book 15, entries at back. For chamber rents, see *ibid.*; Book 27, 137; Book 28; these could be a considerable proportion of outside receipts at this time.

[37] Book 11, fos.17v, 115; see below, appendix 12.

[38] See above, pp. 111 – 12; below, appendix 12.

[39] e.g. Duncan, 'Corpus Christi', 574 – 5; Eland (1935), *passim*.

[40] Book 79, f.18v; *Statutes (1559)*, 11. Visitations must have been held from the start on some basis, regular or irregular.

[41] Book 4, fos.134v, 135, 143v, 144, 148v; Book 80, f.10 (second pagination). For manorial courts see Everitt (1967), 459.

[42] Book 4, fos.56v – 60.

[43] Book 79, fos.18v – 19; *Statutes (1559)*, 12 – 13.

out to Furneaux Pelham; and the bursar and president visited Haslingfield and Eversden. In February the bursar took a carpenter to Bumpsted Helion to select timber for felling, to be used for repairs in the college; some had already been cut down in January, and more was felled, sawn up and squared ready for use in March and April; in April, the president rode to Abbotsley to choose further timber for repairs. In May there was a visit to Holmsted Hall to supervise repairs on the estate there; in June the president and bursar went to Capel; in July two Fellows were sent to Furneaux Pelham; in August the rent was collected at Eversden once more, and there were courts at Bumpsted Helion and Haverhill. Great savings of time and money could be made by visiting several estates at once, and it is likely that hospitality was provided by the tenants. Farmers who visited Queens' to bring in rents or for other reasons were fed at the college's expense, and supper (with wine and beer) was supplied for college representatives at their return from visiting property.[44] In the 17th century — and probably well before this — there is evidence of these progresses being supplemented by the appointment of regular college bailiffs for the different estates, and stewards to manage the courts.[45]

Even strict visitation could not prevent problems arising from landowning; there was always a risk of disputes and litigation, and all landowners were often involved in legal action. There are several examples of this in the Queens' accounts.[46] In the 1570s the college was at odds with the dean and chapter of Canterbury over rents due to the latter from college property on the Isle of Thanet. The case was resolved by Archbishop Grindal in 1579, who fixed the rents which Queens' had to pay, and ordered the admission to the college of two bible clerks who were to be nominated by the dean and chapter, in lieu of rent arrears.[47] Although the threat to collegiate property posed by rapacious courtiers in the 1540s was averted, colleges were always vulnerable to the greed of powerful secular interests.[48] In 1530 Queens' was forced to sell a property to its tenant, an influential protégé of Cardinal Wolsey, because he refused to pay his rent, and it is possible that pressure was brought to bear on the college to part with Babraham in 1598.[49] Demands

---

[44] Book 4, fos.81, 94 – 94v, 108 – 108v, 135; Book 5, f.59v; see also Book 5, f.3, and *Statutes (1559)*, 28.

[45] OPR, fos.13v, 34v, 131, 135v, 136 – 38, 157 – 157v, 164; there is an example from 1566 in Book 4, f.57v.

[46] Book 2, fos.25 – 25v, 36; Book 4, f.58; Book 5, fos.15v, 18, 23, 26v, 35v, 43, 152v; Book 6, fos.66, 156. See also Book 5, f.160; OPR, f.13v; Book 80, fos.25v – 26v (second pagination). See Aylmer (1986), 547 – 8 for a very lengthy lawsuit involving an Oxford college.

[47] Searle, 333, from Book 42, 316.

[48] Above, pp. 31 – 2; Howard (1935), 28.

[49] Above, pp. 110 – 12.

from courtiers for favourable leases became widespread from the 1580s onwards, and it was difficult for colleges to deny them. By the 1620s these depredations were so great that the university complained that 'our goods are but few our household stuffe little'.[50] The crown was one of the chief offenders. In 1595 the queen's tailor demanded a lease in reversion of a Queens' property for forty years, and produced a royal letter in support of his demand, even though it was contrary to the legislation of 1571–6.[51]

Most business matters concerning the college's estates were in the president's hands, although the signing of leases required the approval of the fellowship.[52] The dispute between Thomas Peacock and the Fellows in 1559 involved abuse of these extensive powers: Queens' had recently bought land at Eversden from one Thomas Leete, who was clearly a friend of the president, and the Fellows complained that Leete had been given £10 more 'then his lande was worthe by our estimation which was appoyntid to vewe the landes he solde to the colleadge', and that the president had allowed him to keep a further £6 of college money. Leete had also been given 'certayn of the colleadge woode under pretence, that it is a custome to geve allways the colleadge woode to all copiholders to buylde what they would therwith'.[53] There were no objections, however, when Humphrey Tyndall's family benefited from his office at Queens': his brother Francis leased estates from the college in the 1580s and 1590s, and was one of its auditors in 1611; his other brother and his son were appointed stewards; and his sister and her husband leased college land at Coton in 1608.[54]

Queens' was reckoned to be well endowed in the 16th century. The *Valor Ecclesiasticus* of 1535 placed it third among the Cambridge colleges in terms of income, behind King's and St John's; the 1546 visitors placed it fourth, behind King's, St John's and Christ's.[55] In some years, annual expenditure exceeded receipts, but this was relatively infrequent.[56] In 1580, when the college was slightly in debt on its annual account for the past financial year, it complained that 'the yearly rent or revenues of their lands will not discharge the ordinary and yearly charges of the college', although this was deliberate exaggeration to defend the college

[50] Morgan (unpublished thesis, 1984), 332–39; the quotation is from p. 336.
[51] *ibid.*, 335–57, 385; Searle, 387–88. A lease in reversion was a lease sold well before the current lease had expired, see Morgan (unpublished thesis, 1984), 326. The laws governing renewals of leases were strict, but often avoided, Aylmer (1986), 534–5; above, p. 112.
[52] At least, the 1529 agreement between Simon Heynes and the Fellows made this proviso, although the statutes are not clear about leases, Book 2, f.107v; Searle, 185–86; Book 79, fos.17v–18v; *Statutes (1559)*, 9–10.
[53] Searle, 276; there is a similar example from St John's, Howard (1935), 30–32.
[54] Searle, 366–67.
[55] Below, appendix 13.
[56] Fourteen times between 1534/5 and 1608/9, Books 9–11, *passim*.

COLLEGE ESTATES, c. 1500 - c. 1640

against the charge of unwarranted felling of trees.[57] The overall picture remained one of prosperity.

Benefactions

Gifts to universities and colleges require a study to themselves. The description of such gifts was an integral part of the traditional college history: a commemoration of the benefactors in print, without considering the nature of benefactions in general.[58] A detailed investigation, though desirable, is beyond the scope of this history, but a few significant features should be noted.

Although it has been suggested that educational benefactions formed a small part of medieval charitable donations (the bulk of them being for religious purposes), education and religion cannot be separated in this way; this is shown clearly in the cases of the various 15th century college foundations, and Fisher's early 16th century reforms.[59] In the late middle ages the concept of purgatory became particularly significant, which made priestly intercession more important and led to the chantry becoming the most popular and widely endowed institution; the offering of prayers for the dead was an accepted priestly duty. The donor decided what sort of prayers should be offered, and for whom, but mostly these followed orthodox patterns: prayers for the donor, his wife, parents and ancestors, and sometimes for the royal family.[60] The nobility showed little interest in university endowment, although the episcopate were generous; there were also gifts from merchants and country clergy with property.[61] Such gifts were not extorted by religious terror, but often given with a genuine consideration for the people who were to benefit from them. There was a strong desire to be remembered: each beneficiary knew whom to thank, and all the gifts that the colleges received were clearly identified with their donors.[62]

Benefactions to Queens' in the late medieval period can be divided into three broad categories. The simplest were objects which would be of use to the college. These included books: the college library was reasonably well stocked in the early 1470s.[63] The chapel received

[57] Searle, 374. There was a slight deficit for two consecutive years, Book 11, fos.115 – 115v, 120 – 120v.
[58] Feingold (1981), 207.
[59] Jordan (1961), 25, 92 – 93, 219; c.f. Feingold (1979). Evidence for benefactions, especially in the medieval period, is often scarce.
[60] Rosenthal (1972), 11 – 37; Book 62, 1 – 5.
[61] Rosenthal (1972), 56; Rosenthal (1973), 117 – 125; Venn (1913), 36 – 38.
[62] Venn (1913), 34 – 38; Morgan (unpublished thesis, 1984), 137 – 43, citing Searle, 333, 349, among other sources.
[63] Above, p. 104.

missals, plate and vestments and by the 1470s it too seems to have been reasonably well endowed; there were also many gifts of plate and linen to the buttery.[64] In many cases, these gifts were in addition to more substantial endowments, but those of fewer means provided objects alone. Thomas Duffield, a former Fellow of Peterhouse, gave money for a lamp to go before the altar in the chapel, but expected the same rights as any other benefactor: the college was to name him as such, and to pray for him and his family.[65]

The second category consists of gifts of money. These ranged from £10 to over £200, and there may have been many smaller donations. Money was usually given for a particular purpose, often to purchase land; the income from these lands went to support fellowships, or other aspects of the college's work.[66] Some gifts were to fund building work. Henry VI gave £200 in 1449 'for as much as the seid president and felowes have not wherwith to edifie the seid College in housing and other necessaries'. Thomas Barry, a citizen of London, gave £100 on similar grounds five years later. A Boston merchant, Thomas Parys, gave £10 'for building a room above the library'. Elizabeth Woodville is reported to have 'appropriated a part of her income to the completion of this college', but there is no record of this.[67] Other money was given to provide materials for celebrating mass in chapel, or simply in order to be recognised as a benefactor.[68]

The third category consists of gifts of land. Queens' received town property, pasture, arable and even marshland during the late medieval period, in several counties.[69] As well as for maintaining fellowships, lands were given for scholarships, to pay for preaching in the college, and for remembrance services and prayers.[70] The value of the land lay in its annual income, which is sometimes noted in the terms of the benefaction: in the 15th century such incomes ranged from just over £3 a year to nearly £20; Richard III's benefactions were far more substantial, but only short-lived.[71] The donors included members of the nobility and gentry, clergymen, a former Fellow, a mercer and a haberdasher from London. Richard Andrew, a Cambridge spicer, granted two tenements in Cambridge and two properties outside the town; a few years later his

64 Searle, 72, 74, 81, 94 – 95, 101, 122 – 23, 125; Book 77, f.7; MS 30, fos.8v – 12v.
65 Searle, 94 – 95; Book 77, f.7.
66 Searle, 72, 92 – 93, 122, 124; Book 77, fos.5, 16, 28; MS 30, fos.14v – 15v.
67 Searle, 62, 63, 65; Cooper (1860 – 6), i.280.
68 Searle, 65, 83 – 84; Book 77, f.9; MS 30, f.18. Thomas Wilkinson, the college's second president, left each Fellow 13s 4d on his death in 1511, and to the college he also left two linen tablecloths and two linen towels, Emden; Searle, 125.
69 Before 1500: Cambridgeshire, London, Essex, Huntingdonshire, Lincolnshire, Suffolk, Northamptonshire, and Berkshire; see above, p. 110 and chapter 9 n. 2.
70 Searle, 65 – 66, 73, 77, 84 – 85, 133; Book 77, fos.4, 6, 19, 27; MS 30, fos.16 – 18.
71 Searle, 66, 72, 80 – 83, 93 – 94, 107 – 8, 122; Book 77, fos.8, 12, 19, 28, 29; MS 30, fos.14v – 17v.

benefaction was said to consist of a hostel and four tenements in the town, the college having consolidated its property. Another Cambridge tenement, given by the local physician William Syday in 1470, was sold for £80 in 1529 and the money used to buy land elsewhere.[72]

Charity towards educational foundations increased significantly as a proportion of charitable giving overall during and after the Reformation, among many classes of society.[73] With the demise of prayers for the dead under the pressure of Protestant beliefs, college benefactions were mostly directed towards founding fellowships and scholarships. At Queens' there was a steady increase in landed wealth; in the 17th century Thomas Fuller claimed boldly that 'no House, for the quantity, is endowed with better land of manors and farms'.[74] Many of the 16th and 17th century benefactions followed the customary forms already described — there were gifts of lands, church livings, rent charges and money, often from former Fellows and presidents; donations of books and items of silver continued.[75] Humphrey Tyndall gave 'all the seeling and waynscoting' of his chamber, panelling worth more than £250, in his estimation. In 1661 Henry Coke, a former fellow-commoner, and friend of Edward Martin, gave wood to panel the chapel.[76] Tyndall's brother Francis, a former college auditor, gave £40 to purchase silver, and £5 to be distributed amongst poor scholars; in 1666 the college baker Samuel Bryan (brother of the vice-president, John Bryan) gave £20.[77] There were several gifts to the chapel. One former Fellow left £300 to buy lands to maintain it, specifying that the income was not to be alienated to any other use. In 1673 a former Fellow gave a velvet covering for the altar. Benefactions were not always put to their proper use. Herbert Palmer's bequest of £53 to be spent on poor scholars was in fact spent on repairs to the chapel by Edward Martin in 1661. The Josselin bequest to found a Hebrew lectureship went to pay for the building in Walnut Tree Court, although the lecturer was paid out of room rents from the building. In the 1630s Queens' was involved in negotiations with a benefactor's executors, in trying to secure money instead of the lands which they had been left; the college succeeded, but

[72] Searle, 66, 77, 186; Book 77, fos.6, 19; MS 30, fos.16 – 17v.
[73] Jordan (1961), 25 – 26, 93 – 94, 220 – 222; Jordan (1959), 48 – 50, 236 – 238, 280 – 2, 292 – 96, 343 – 55, 363, 373; c.f. Feingold (1979). For the wider implications of benefactions with regard to college-country relationships, see Morgan (unpublished thesis, 1984), 107ff.
[74] Fuller, *History*, 122; above, pp. 110 – 11.
[75] Searle, 291 – 3, 299, 319 – 21, 333, 366, 374, 377, 378, 394 – 5, 412, 422 – 3, 429; Fuller (1897), 533 – 9; OPR, fos.5 – 5v, 17v – 18, 112, 153v, 168v, 255; Book 80, f.6 (second pagination); Cooper (1851).
[76] Was Tyndall's a high estimate? Searle, 363 – 4; OPR, f.160. In 1686 part of the cost of panelling the combination room was defrayed by a donation of £100 from a former president, Anthony Sparrow, *W&C*, ii.49.
[77] Searle, 366; OPR, f.171.

the money was spent by Martin during the civil war.[78] For the most part, though, it seems that the college honoured the intentions of its benefactors — it had to if the gifts were to continue.

College charity

In addition to receiving charitable benefactions, the college made its own donations to a wide variety of worthy causes. The sums given ranged from a few shillings to several pounds; ten guineas was generally the maximum, but more was found in one or two cases.[79] Donations were given mostly in response to direct requests.[80] Gifts to charity feature regularly in the account books, continuing even through the troubled years of the English Revolution, although in 1650, when called on to contribute to the university's collection for the poor of the town, Queens' agreed to pay only so long as its finances could bear the strain — the sum involved was less than £8 a year.[81] These regular university payments to the town's poor appear to have begun in the 1590s, and continued without interruption thereafter.[82] Different rates were fixed for each college: Queens' contribution was the sixth largest among the colleges in the 17th century.[83] The poor of St Botolph's parish occasionally received gifts in addition to this, and in the late 18th century such giving was extended to paupers in villages where the college owned lands.[84] There were also some donations to individual paupers.[85] In some cases the cause of impoverishment is known: there was a donation in 1752 to 'the Sufferers by loss of Cattle at Newnham', and in 1786 a tenant farmer at Haddenham was given money 'on Account of several failures of Crops'.[86] Also in the 18th century there were gifts to prisoners in the town gaol, and sometimes to those in the county gaol.[87] Another aspect of community spirit was demonstrated in

[78] OPR, fos.111v, 160; Searle, 545; Clarke (1677), 198 (c.f. Book 28, for the Palmer bequest); below, p. 113; above, pp. 58 – 9.
[79] Books 4 – 8, *passim*, Books 16 and 17.
[80] e.g. Book 16.
[81] OPR, f.29v; Searle, 566, 569. For charitable payments by the college during the English Revolution, see Books 15 and 28.
[82] Books 5 – 8, *passim*.
[83] Cooper, iii.613.
[84] Book 5, f.7; Book 8, fos.13, 47v, 90, 99v, 114v, 130v, 133v, 136v. See Howard (1935), 145 – 6 for similar examples of charity by St John's.
[85] Book 5, f.42; Book 8, f.120v; Books 16 and 17.
[86] Book 7, fos.250, 251v; Book 8, f.106v; in 1632/3 Queens' gave money to a woman whose husband had been captured by the Turks, to another who had lost her husband in a tempest, and to a 'decayed Tradesman', Book 16.
[87] Book 8, fos.6v, 9v, and *passim*; *ibid.*, fos.93, 123v. There is a reference in 1597 to a payment to 'prisoners', Book 5, f.63.

1766, when Queens' gave three guineas towards repairing the road from Cambridge to Barton.[88]

The college owned almshouses, and was responsible for their repair; Andrew Doket had bequeathed three small tenements in Smallbridges St (now Silver St), occupied by three poor women, whose successors were to be nominated by the president and Fellows.[89] Many, but not all, were widows, and the criteria for selection shown in this 1644 example may have been typical: 'Goodwife Rose was chosen one of the Almeswomen, with this proviso, that if her husband be not dead but returne to her she shall leave the place immediately; Widow Thatcher a blind woman was also at the same time chosen'.[90] The women were sometimes given food in return for weeding the college courtyards.[91]

Elsewhere, college charity consisted mostly of single payments to those who had experienced particular hardships. Victims of fire formed a significant proportion of these; sometimes the payments were merely to 'a Sufferer by fire', but the accounts contain more specific entries, especially for victims in the surrounding villages, and also in cases of more serious conflagrations further away.[92] Victims of 'plague' were another important group of sufferers, and the account entries — 'a pore Woman infected', 'the poor visited with the plage', 'the visited' — probably refer to local outbreaks.[93]

Donations for specifically religious purposes were also especially significant. Queens' was principally concerned with maintenance of its own livings, but in 1632/3 it gave 6s 8d towards 'reedifyinge a Church in Essex', and in 1633 over £33 towards repairing St Paul's cathedral.[94] Protestants persecuted abroad and converts from Judaism or Catholicism were favoured charitable causes from the 17th century onwards.[95] In 1689 a double scholarship was awarded to Charles Daubuz, a Huguenot refugee, 'in regard he is a poor Orphan the son of a Protestant Minister in France'.[96] In 1706 Queens' gave money to relieve

[88] Book 8, f.45v.

[89] Searle, 57, 68; Book 4, fos.53v, 134; Book 5, f.47v; Book 16.

[90] OPR, fos.3v, 6, 13. The almshouses were in Silver Street until 1836, when the women were moved to houses in Queens' Lane; these houses were in turn pulled down in 1911 to make way for the Doket building, Goodman (1922), 47.

[91] Book 4, fos.108v, 152v.

[92] Cooper, iii.570; Searle, 571; Book 6, f.173v; Book 7, fos.111, 154, 165, 166v, 182, 198; Book 8, fos.3v, 87, 89v, 99v, 103, 112v, 133v, 139.

[93] Book 4, fos.132v, 176; Book 5, f.106, and *passim*.

[94] OPR, fos.128v – 129; Searle, 510 – 11; Book 16; see also Book 7, f.149v. The payment to the Essex church may well have been a donation inspired by 'Laudian' religious ideals; see above, chapter 4.

[95] Searle, 403, 569; OPR, f.139; Book 6, f.120; Book 7, fos.68v, 172v; Book 17. All Souls College Oxford made similar donations, and it is likely that many other colleges did so, Burrows (1874), 155 – 6.

[96] Book 80, f.42 (second pagination); *AC*; there were also plans to take Irish student refugees at this time, Book 80, fos.42 – 42v (second pagination); see also Book 17 for other payments arising out of the troubles in that year.

episcopal clergy in Scotland, and for building an Anglican church in Rotterdam, and in 1738 it gave three guineas to 'a Clergyman from New England'; six years later it contributed towards the cost of printing Bibles in Welsh.[97] These, and all the other college donations, were straightforward demonstrations of conventional piety.

[97] Book 7, fos.64v, 195, 224v.

10

Miscellany, 15th – 17th centuries
(servants and tradesmen; the college and the town;
college buildings; visits; health and disease)

It has been seen that some menial duties were performed by poor
students, but most essential services were carried out by largely
anonymous college servants.[1] There were perhaps only a few full-time
servants: the two cooks, butler, porter and gardener, although others
received regular payments for services.[2] In addition to their college pay
some of these also received shares from the college dividends, and by
the late 17th century there was a levy on Fellows and students to
augment their wages.[3] One of the earliest cooks whom we know by
name was William Grimston, chosen sub-cook in 1637 after giving a
bond of £40 for the utensils and plate in his care, and on condition that
he remained unmarried; a senior cook appointed four years later was
also required to remain single. This practice died out in the 18th century;
in 1762, when the cook Thomas Eate died, his widow was chosen in his
place.[4] By that time the bond required from new cooks and from butlers
had risen to £100, which indicates that these were responsible positions,
and their status in society was rising during the period; during
Humphrey Tyndall's presidency, Queens' leased property to one of its
cooks, and there is a late 17th century record of a college lease to a cook
at Christ's.[5] There are references to two butlers in the 17th century, one
for bread and one for beer; in 1636 it was decided that the latter should
always be a poor scholar.[6] Robert Roberts, appointed principal butler in

[1] Above, pp. 90 – 1; see also Harrison (1958), chapter III.
[2] For examples of the quarterly stipends, see Book 4, f.93v; Book 5, fos.20, 22. In 1613
    there is a reference to a college woodman, OPR, f.2v.
[3] OPR, f.168v; Book 78.
[4] Searle, 515; OPR, fos.19, 131; Registrum, entry at front. We know the names of two
    college cooks in Edward VI's reign from a court case: in July 1548 William Stokedall
    and William Lammas 'were in the kitchen of Queens' College there preparing supper
    for their masters and because Lammas found fault with Stokedall for not doing his
    duty, the latter assaulted him with a basting styke [stick], and when he had fled and
    the kitchen wall prevented his fleeing further, and Stokedall drew blood upon him
    and would kill him, he, in self defence, with a stick . . . struck Stokedall on the left
    side of the head, a fatal wound an inch wide, of which the said Stokedall died'.
    Lammas was pardoned, Dial, (Lent 1932), 3, citing Calendar of the Patent Rolls, entry of
    30.1.1549/50.
[5] Registrum, entry at front; Book 80, fos.25, 26v (second pagination).
[6] OPR, fos.25v, 26v, 130, 168v.

1701, had been admitted a sizar of the college four years previously; he remained butler until 1738.[7]

Some gardening work, such as hedging and cutting back undergrowth, was done by day-labourers from outside the college, but by Elizabeth's reign there was a college gardener, who also performed other occasional duties in return for extra money.[8] The choice of a new gardener for a probationary year in 1671 was made by the combined fellowship.[9] The existence of a college porter is likewise only apparent in the late Tudor period; if his duties at that time included gatekeeping, then this was shared with some of the poor scholars.[10] In the late 17th and 18th centuries, he was called on to perform other occasional tasks: making up a bonfire, cutting down a tree at a college almshouse, street-cleaning, keeping the clock wound, 'blowing the Organs', and court-keeping.[11] From the 1590s ownards, he was supplied with liveries for winter and summer wear.[12]

For other services, the college hired help whenever necessary. Its auditors attended in January each year, and their fees and entertainment were costly.[13] Musicians — principally trumpeters — were paid for playing on special occasions, such as Christmas or the anniversary of a king's coronation.[14] A laundress was paid regularly by the college.[15] The services of ratcatchers and molecatchers were sometimes required, and payments are occasionally recorded for catching buzzards; in 1569 it was necessary to remove rooks from the college storehouse.[16] There were always repairs of one kind or another to be done, and the accounts record payments to blacksmiths, masons, coopers, plumbers, pump-menders, goldsmiths and pewterers, bricklayers, glaziers, clock-menders, tinkers, chimney-sweeps and carpenters.[17] Women were employed as bedmakers, and also sometimes for scouring vessels or making tablecloths.[18] Scavengers were paid to clean the streets about the

[7]   Registrum, entry at front.
[8]   Book 2, f.80; Book 3, f.225v; Book 4, fos.58, 94, 107 – 8, 113v, 149v, 156; Book 5, fos.47v, 58v. By the 1590s at latest one gardener was responsible for both the president's and the Fellows' garden, c.f. above, chapter 5, n. 50.
[9]   OPR, f.3v.
[10] Book 5, passim; above, pp. 90 – 1; below, pp. 139 – 40.
[11] Book 6, fos.220, 235; Book 7, fos.52v, 75v, 102v, 119, 150.
[12] Book 5, fos.20v, 22v, and passim; Book 7, f.54v; Searle, 401 – 3.
[13] Books 4 – 7, passim; and see Book 2, f.60v; Book 4, fos.50v, 92, 100v. There are some recorded payments to legal assistants; for example, to a scrivener for drawing up an indenture, Book 5, f.42v; and to a tipstaff (sheriff's officer), Book 4, f.106v.
[14] Searle, 401 – 4, 443 – 4, 461 – 3; Book 4, fos.132v, 163; Book 6, f.42v.
[15] e.g., Book 4, f.92; Book 5, fos.21v – 22.
[16] Searle, 242, 401; Book 4, fos.74, 75v, 83, 132 – 132v, 133v; Book 6, fos.57v, 215.
[17] Book 2, f.68; Book 4, fos.94v, 112v, 127v; Book 5, fos.2, 3, 5, 7, 8, 22, 26v, 28, 32, 33 – 33v, 38v, 40v, 53v; Book 6, fos.135v, 136 – 137, 149, 155v, 173v.
[18] Above, p. 91; Book 4, f.111v; see also ibid., f.25v.

college.[19] Day-labourers were hired for such unskilled jobs as cleaning out ('purging') the ditches surrounding the island site on the west bank of the river; certain men could expect to be hired repeatedly for these jobs.[20] The college preferred to deal with known, trustworthy workers; in 1645 it ordered that 'all Idle Persons that hang about the Colledge be discharged & put away'.[21] Workmen were also hired to help with emergencies. When the president's woodshed caught fire in 1690, two men were paid one shilling each for sitting up through the night to watch over it.[22] In 1594 there was flooding, and six men were paid sixpence each 'to get the beere out of the sellar'.[23]

Sometimes members of the same family served the college in different capacities. John Starre was the college gardener in the 1560s, while his mother was paid for sweeping out the hall, and there are instances of husbands and wives working for the college.[24] The accounts for the late 17th and early 18th centuries show that several members of the Moore family worked for Queens' and that the college took an active interest in the welfare of its servants at that time.[25] In 1700 it spent 11s 5d on Robert Moore's apothecary's bill, and 9s on expenses associated with his subsequent funeral; Moore was clearly a servant of some kind, but his duties are not recorded. In 1702 £5 was given to 'Thomas Moore Gardener in consideration of much work done and his poverty', and another £1 14s was spent on apothecary's fees for Goody Moore, his wife. Two years later there is an entry for 5s paid to a Mr Punt for curing one Betty Moore, perhaps a daughter of Thomas and Goody. In 1704 Thomas again received £5 from the college 'as a charity, having many children'. He died in 1713 and Queens' gave his widow £4 for the funeral. In 1745 there is a reference to a 'Widow Moore' who washed the college linen and swept out the library; her daughter Henrietta was employed in the same tasks in 1753, having occupied the college almshouse made vacant by her mother's death in 1748.[26] Similar help was given by the college to the family of the porter William Peachy. In

---

[19] Book 4, f.112; Book 5, fos.93v, 96v, 98.

[20] Book 2, fos.39, 53; Book 5, f.33. Book 5 contains frequent references to one 'Morris' and his men, who were called in for various (usually unspecified) tasks; Morris may have been a supplier of labour. It is not clear if he was connected with the Morris family which had been prominent in Cambridge since the 13th century, and was closely associated with St Botolph's church and parish, Goodman (1922), 26, 28; one of its members had been a colleague of Andrew Doket in the establishment of Queens', above, p. 6.

[21] Searle, 554; OPR, f.25v.

[22] Book 6, f.251; similar examples are noted by Searle, 349, 528.

[23] Book 5, fos.42v – 43.

[24] Book 4, *passim* among entries for 1560s; *ibid.*, fos.48, 86v, 143, 174v; Searle, 417 – 8 refers to John Rosse, a college servant for more than 20 years at the end of the 16th and beginning of the 17th centuries.

[25] Such an interest is not revealed in the account books before this time.

[26] Book 7, fos.37, 41v, 51, 57, 93v, 221, 251; CB (1734 – 87), f.44.

1702 it paid an apothecary's bill for his wife and son, and it paid for Peachy's funeral in the following year. In 1708 his widow was given a small cash present.[27] In 1733 Queens' gave two guineas to help clear the debts of its pewterer and silver repairer, a Mr Urlin.[28] As a smaller example of generosity, Christmas boxes were given to workmen such as the college carpenter, mason, painter, smith and bricklayer.[29]

The college and the town

The story of town-gown relations in the early modern period has been characterised as one of 'endemic border warfare, with recurrent crises', caused by and expressed in many different ways.[30] Visitors to Cambridge who left written accounts of their journeys tended to take the university's side; they had come to see the colleges rather than the town. Zacharias von Uffenbach, who came at the beginning of the 18th century, dismissed the town as 'no better than a village'. A Hungarian noble observed in 1787: 'Cambridge is not big, its streets are narrow and muddy and its houses are generally miserably built and kept'. He also commented that 'The citizens of Cambridge live mostly on the students', a view which had been expressed more forcefully two hundred years before by William Harrison: the townsmen, Harrison wrote, were 'glad when they may match and annoy the students by encroaching on their liberties, and keep them bare by extreme sale of their wares'.[31] Daniel Defoe in the early 18th century was more sympathetic to the town, arguing that the university had an economic hold over it which kept it in submission and that 'the tradesmen may justly be said to get their bread by the colleges'.[32] These sources tend to overemphasize the hostility between the two societies; in fact, the town-gown relationship was a complex, shifting mixture of co-operation and conflict.[33]

A similar pattern, although on a smaller and sometimes trivial scale, can be seen in the relationship between Queens' and the town. There are several examples of co-operation: townsmen had helped Doket to acquire the site for the college; local labour was employed there; and the college was obviously dependent on the town for supplies, even though

[27] ibid., fos.46v, 50v, 73v.
[28] ibid., f.174v.
[29] ibid., fos.71v, 75v, 79v, 121v; the practice went back to the 16th century, e.g. Book 4, f.93.
[30] Cam (1959), 76 – 86. The most recent survey of the question is Parker (1983).
[31] Mayor (1911), 123; Széchenyi (1929), 213; Harrison (1968), 68.
[32] Defoe (1974), 86.
[33] See Cam (1959).

price levels were controlled by the university.[34] Queens' was responsible for paving and cleaning the streets which ran alongside it, and seems to have performed this duty conscientiously for the most part.[35] A college memorandum of 1663 recorded that 'the college hath layd some rubbidg along the wall side at the bridg, that so foote passengers might not be forced in winter time to come through our College (as of late yeers they have been) yet what was so done was onely out of common charity; the cart-way there not belonging to us to repaire, but to those who maintaine the bridg'.[36] Money was levied on certain college lands for repairing and rebuilding the town's main bridge.[37] In 1575 the town ordered colleges to be prepared against fire, and specified the equipment which each was to hold in readiness.[38] In 1623 Queens' contributed towards the town's celebrations at Prince Charles' return from Spain; in 1699 it bought two bottles of wine to 'treat the Mayor and Town-Clark'.[39]

But it is in the nature of historical evidence that conflicts should be more prominent that co-operation. The first known examples of this at Queens' date from the Reformation, when both universities were particularly vulnerable; at times of national upheaval the town of Cambridge invariably tried to escape the university's economic and judicial powers.[40] In 1534 Simon Heynes, then serving as vice-chancellor, urged the university to defend its privileges vigorously against town encroachments.[41] In 1547 the university applied to Edward VI for additional protection, suggesting that seven university men should be made justices of the peace: the vice-chancellor and the heads of six colleges (including Queens').[42] Two years later the town complained that colleges were enclosing common ground; Queens' was said to have 'taken in a pece of common ground commonlye called Goslinge grene withowte recompense', together with 'a nother pece lying withowt their pales and within the ryver that owght to be common'.[43] In 1629, when it was learned that Queens' had 'often digged

---

[34]   Above, p. 6; Cam (1959), 83 – 4. The Puritan lectureship at Holy Trinity church which John Preston held in the early 17th century was a town appointment, above, p. 42.

[35]   Book 5, *passim*, and fos.4v, 40v, 45; see also Book 6, f.110, and Book 8, f.38, for examples of fines on the college for not mending the highways; see also Parker (1983), 80.

[36]   OPR, f.171.

[37]   Cooper, i.251 – 2; iv.26; Book 5, fos.52 – 52v; Book 8, fos.3 – 4.

[38]   Cooper, ii.336 – 7.

[39]   Book 6, f.13; Book 7, f.36v (concerns the case involving Miller, see below, p. 128).

[40]   Storey (unpublished paper, 1981/forthcoming); Twigg (unpublished thesis, 1983), 46 – 8, 136 – 7; Parker (1983), 76 – 88.

[41]   Searle, 181; Book 3, f.99v contains college expenses in a case against the town in 1542/3, but it is not clear what the case was about.

[42]   Cooper, ii.7.

[43]   *ibid.*, ii.39; Parker (1983), 86.

up sods in the Green by Newnham, for the repairing of their [archery] butts', the town corporation voted to enquire if the college was acting 'in their own right or in presuming the favour of the Town'.[44] At the end of the 17th century there was a dispute — amicably resolved — when Queens' discovered that the town was about to let 'that peice of wastground without our back-gate to Miller who kept hogs there & cattle to the annoyance of the College'.[45] In 1780 the college had to pay £50 to prevent the corporation from felling trees at the north end of Queens' Green.[46] There are other, isolated incidents. In 1709 a butcher, William Wendy, was made to sign an undertaking 'not to desire or expect, that the College should pay any thing more than, what is spent for the Commons of Fellows & Scholars', but this probably owed more to the meticulous, pedantic business mind of the then president, Henry James, than to any major quarrel.[47] An incident in 1596 when a student abused the mayor in public was another individual action, set in the context of poor town-gown relations.[48]

Theft of college property is a recurrent theme, however. In 1593 it was decided to put bars in college windows which faced the streets. In 1613, 2s 6d was spent on 'a bill of inditment against Nixon that stole the college peuter [and] for a poor labourer that was stopped a whole day for a witnesse'. In July 1634 the college gave a reward of 6s to 'a man that brought the stoale plate backe'. In November 1737, 2s was given to 'Meers who went after the Thieves that stole the Plate', and in the following month an identical sum rewarded 'the Clerk & Constable who took up the Woman who Stole the Plate'. In March 1738, 19s was given to 'the Men at Royston who recovered the Plate'.[49] In the late 1790s several colleges were relieved of plate by a series of skillful and audacious robberies, which reduced the university to 'the greatest state of alarm . . . The most absurd reports were in circulation. Some persons insisted that the robberies must have been committed by college-servants; others suggested that some members of the societies must have been concerned; and some Fellow-commoners, whose connections were not apparent, were also among the suspected'. It was some years before the thief, Richard Kidman, a local clock-repairer and silversmith, and his associates were apprehended; by then they had robbed six colleges, some more than once.[50] Oral tradition in the later 19th century

---

[44] Searle, 458. The butts were set up in the garden on the opposite side of Queens' Lane, W&C, ii.54; archery was still practised in 1663, Book 6, f.117v.
[45] Book 80, f.33 (second pagination); Book 7, f.36v.
[46] Cooper, iv.389.
[47] Book 80, 9 (third pagination).
[48] Above, p. 97.
[49] Book 5, f.39v; Book 6, f.57; Book 7, fos.193 – 194; Searle, 403. In 1635, 6s was given to a man for bringing back 'lost' plate, Book 6, f.60v.
[50] Gunning (1854), ii.45, 103, 125 – 31, 268 – 72; Brooke (1985), 188 – 9.

had it that Kidman had also intended to rob Queens', but on attempting to enter the long gallery from the garden stair, saw from a light in the gallery that the president, Isaac Milner, was sitting up late reading, and that therefore he abandoned the attempt.[51] It seems unlikely, however, that so accomplished a burglar as Kidman would have been thus deterred from making a further attempt had he seriously intended to rob the college.

The college buildings (15th – 17th centuries)

'Queens College is old but a stately and lofty building' (Celia Fiennes, 1697)
'an old, mean building' (Z. C. von Uffenbach, 1707)
'two courts beside a pile of buildings near the gardens' (mid-18th century guide book).[52]

College buildings, including those of Queens', have been the subject of extensive and detailed studies, and this history can do no more than summarise these. To a great extent, the history of the college's fabric can be treated as a parallel study to the history of its society, and there is a need for a new, specialist monograph on the subject, able to examine the buildings in detail, and including the most recent research.[53] Yet some outline history of the site and buildings is necessary for understanding the evolution of the college's society.

The present site of Queens' was not that originally chosen by Doket; this was a narrow piece of land on the present site of St Catharine's, running from Trumpington Street, in front of St Bernard's hostel, to Milne Street (the present-day Queens' Lane), which was secured in 1446. In the following year a new site was purchased, bounded by Milne Street to the east, Smallbridges Street (today's Silver Street) to the south, the river to the west, and a Carmelite monastery to the north.[54] The new site was larger and squarer — a more convenient place on which to build and with a valuable riverside location.[55] Such a place cannot have been easy to come by. It was in a crowded, populous district of houses and tenements. Milne Street was a busy thoroughfare

---

51 W&C, ii.22, n. 1.
52 Fiennes (1949), 66; Mayor (1911), 144; Wordsworth (1874), 393.
53 Dr R. D. H. Walker, the junior bursar of Queens', hopes to do this one day.
54 Searle, 4 – 6, 9. There was a house on the corner of Silver Street, which the college bought at some later date. Silver Street was first known by that name in 1615, but the old name was in regular use until the 18th century, Goodman (1922), 19, n. 2, 106.
55 Searle, 10; in the words of the 1447 foundation charter, 'pro placabiliori situ ac elargatione edificiorum et habitationis hujusmodi collegii.'

from which lanes led down to riverside wharves; here there was a thriving commercial quarter based on river traffic.[56]

The earliest buildings at Queens' are those of Old Court.[57] These were erected in two instalments, the first starting in April 1448 and continuing through the summer, the second beginning in March 1449. Henry VI contributed £200 to the 1449 work.[58] The buildings were probably designed by the master mason Reginald Ely, one of Doket's parishioners at St Botolph's. Ely had been chief mason at King's and his master carpenter there, Thomas Sturgeon of Elsenham, was also employed with him at Queens'. There are similarities of style in some features of the earliest buildings of the two colleges.[59]

Ely followed the standard collegiate plan of an enclosed courtyard which had already emerged in the 14th century, but was now fully developed to include all the principal college buildings: kitchen, chapel, hall, library and living accommodation for the president and Fellows.[60] The impressive gate tower was in a slightly newer Cambridge tradition: the first had been at King's Hall, begun in 1428, and the style reached its peak in the early 16th century at Christ's and St John's; the great gate at Trinity is its most monumental expression. This, together with the positioning of the hall opposite the main entrance, was derived from domestic architecture.[61] Because there was no good stone available locally, Old Court was built of clunch (a chalk) with a brick facing. Brick was in common use by this time, but Queens' is the first Cambridge college known to have used exposed brick extensively, an example followed by other colleges such as Jesus and St John's.[62]

Shortly after the completion of Old Court — just when is not certain — another range was built alongside the river in the same style and of the

---

[56] Goodman (1922), 18 – 19; Darby (1977), 38 – 9; for river traffic, see also below, p. 134.
[57] For a detailed description, see *RCHM*, 168 – 174. For the college buildings in general, see the relevant passages in *W&C* and *RCHM*.
[58] Searle, 38 – 40, 62; *W&C*, ii.7 – 11; above, p. 118.
[59] Oswald (1949), 16 – 18, 20, 23 – 4; Searle, 38 – 40; *W&C*, ii.7 – 11; *RCHM*, lxxvii. For the origins of the master mason in general, see Salzman (1967), 22; for contracting labour in general, see *RCHM*, ciii – civ. Ely had also worked on a staircase at Peterhouse in 1438, Oswald (1949), 16. For Ely's career, see Harvey (1984), 94 – 9; for Sturgeon see *ibid.*, 289 – 90.
[60] *RCHM*, lxxvii, 168; Oswald (1949), 23; Pevsner (1970), 25.
[61] *RCHM*, lxxvii – viii; Pevsner (1970), 23, 25.
[62] *RCHM*, xcviii, c; Oswald (1949), 20 – 21; Drinkwater (1934 – 5), 156 – 7; Pevsner (1970), 23 – 4. The roof was of slate, Salzman (1967), 238. For the development of brick building, see *ibid.*, 143; Hoskins (1977), 136, but especially Wright (1972), 30 – 52; Brunskill and Clifton-Taylor (1977), 13 – 20. William Waynflete, bishop of Winchester, who may have had some connection with the founding of Queens' (see chapter 1, n. 20), was a great builder, and his later building projects, after the building of Queens', made extensive use of brick. Waynflete had no influence on the design of the college, but knowledge of Ely's work may have influenced him in making greater use of brick elsewhere, although he was familiar with a number of other brick building; see Davis (unpublished thesis, 1985), 350 – 69.

same construction. It was unusual among Cambridge college buildings of this period in that it was freestanding; covered walkways linking it to Old Court were added in the 1490s.[63] The building must originally have been intended to provide accommodation. It was appropriated for the president's use in the 1530s — until then he had lived above the parlour next to the hall — probably to mark his enhanced status. There was also a large reception room for visiting dignitaries.[64]

In 1475 Queens' purchased an island site west of the river from the town corporation for 40 marks (£26 13s 4d); this forms the bulk of the college's present holdings on the west bank of the Cam.[65] The river was not the carefully trained watercourse of today: a host of lesser streams ran through the fenland on its western side; the present ditches along the 'Backs' are remnants of these former streams, which marked parish boundaries.[66]

The 16th century was, as has been shown, a period of unprecedented expansion for the university and its colleges, including Queens'.[67] The acquisition of the lands of the neighbouring Carmelite monastery at the Reformation made a large and welcome increase to the college's site, but with the exception of the building in Walnut Tree Court (1617 – 19) the ground was used for gardens and orchards until the 19th century.[68] A new building was added between the southern cloister of Cloister Court and Smallbridges Street in 1564 – 5 to cater for the growth in student numbers. It was pulled down, together with part of the earlier riverside range, in the 18th century to make way for the Essex building.[69]

The date of the construction of the long gallery on the north side of Cloister Court has been the subject of some debate.[70] References to a gallery go back to the early 16th century, and some sort of walkway seems to have been in existence from that time onwards, but it may have been of a very simple kind; it was perhaps altered or replaced at some time during this period.[71] The present long gallery — one of only three which survive in Cambridge — is clearly Elizabethan in style; such galleries are a feature of later 16th century domestic architecture, when

[63] *RCHM*, lxxv, 168, 174 – 7; *W&C*, ii.14; Oswald (1949), 25; Walker in *Record* (1984), 7.
[64] *W&C*, ii.23 – 6; below, pp. 134 – 6.
[65] Searle, 85 – 7; *W&C*, ii.6.
[66] Gray (1894 – 5), 71, 74 – 5; Darby (1977), 38 – 9; *W&C*, ii.5; Hall and Ravensdale (1976), 80 – 7.
[67] Above, chapters 3 and 7.
[68] Above, p. 31; *W&C*, ii.5, facing 10; Browne and Seltman (1951), plates 14 – 17.
[69] *RCHM*, 168; *W&C*, ii.18; Book 4, fos.39ff; MS 30, fos.26v – 27; below, p. 312.
[70] The principal arguments are in *RCHM*, lxxxv – vi, 174; *W&C*, ii.30 – 6; there is a good summary and explanation by Walker in *Record* (1984), 6.
[71] *W&C*, ii.30 – 6, for the evidence, although some of their conclusions are challenged here.

the style was reaching the peak of its development.[72] College architecture adopted the fashion, imitating the splendour of the great homes of the period just as masters of colleges imitated the rôle of heads of household.[73] It has been established for some while that the long gallery was built after the 1560s;[74] the most recent attempt to discover its date, using tree-ring dating techniques (the gallery is timber-framed) suggests that it could not have been begun before 1595; the date of 1604 inscribed on one of the door panels may mark the completion of its internal fittings.[75] The college archives are of little assistance here: no distinction is made between different kinds of gallery before or during the Elizabethan period, and the expression 'Long Gallery' does not appear until the reign of Charles II.[76] But the college accounts for October 1569 refer to the purchase of bricks, lead and sand for 'the new great randg', which can only refer to some structure on the site of the long gallery; the only other contemporary building, that of 1564 – 5, was always called the 'new building'. Contemporary illustrations show a structure of some sort, but are unclear.[77] Perhaps a building was put up at this time, replacing an earlier walkway, to be replaced in its turn at the very end of the century, but many questions on the subject remain unresolved.

The next major building, the range in Walnut Tree Court, is much better documented. The reasons for its construction were clearly stated by John Preston's pupil and biographer Thomas Ball, who matriculated shortly afterwards: 'the college for the most part was well assayd, & grew in Reputation very much, and, because they wanted roome to enterteyne the numbers that flocked to them, they built that goodly fabrick that conteyns so many faire lodgings, both for fellows & scholars, towards King's College'.[78] Such single ranges extending from earlier courts, and even free-standing ranges, were a feature of college architecture in this period of expansion.[79] The Walnut Tree Court building was put up between 1617 and 1619; one of the two architects, Gilbert Wigge, had been employed on the second court at St John's in 1602.[80] It was a functional, two and a half-storeyed brick construction with attics; the third storey was added in 1778 – 82. In 1823 it was

[72] Girouard (1978), 100 – 102; Summerson (1963), 29. The other two are at St John's and Emmanuel, RCHM, 64, 66, 187. Galleries were built at other colleges in the mid-16th century, but have not survived, W&C, i.224, 270.
[73] Summerson (1963), 20, 99; Morgan (unpublished thesis, 1984), 251 – 3.
[74] RCHM, 174.
[75] Carter, Switsur, and Ward (unpublished report, 1984).
[76] Book 6, f.160.
[77] Book 4, f.74; above, n. 69; W&C, ii.5; Fowler and Fowler (1984), 3; Browne and Seltman (1951), plates 14, 15.
[78] Ball (1885), 39. It was probably at about this time that the attic rooms in Old Court were built, also to house the growing student population, Drinkwater (1934 – 5), 157.
[79] RCHM, lxxxiii.
[80] W&C, ii.19 – 20; Searle, 436 – 8.

reroofed, and the present battlemented parapet added.[81] The building was financed from several sources: £200 received from the sale of college property at Babraham in 1598 and £100 given to establish a Hebrew lectureship in the college were appropriated; proceeds from sales of timber, and from entry fines, were also put into the building account; the sale of 'ould plate' realised over £90, and smaller amounts were gathered here and there. Over £663 was raised in this way, but even so the president, John Davenant, had to lend the college £172 of his own money to complete the project.[82]

In addition to these major buildings, the college put up a number of lesser structures; the accounts contain references to a coalhouse, limehouse, bakehouse, woodhouse, millhouse, stables, and other 'houses' of inspecified purpose; we know almost nothing about these temporary structures.[83] The first college brewhouse, where it produced its own ale for internal consumption, was built on the island in 1533/4; it was replaced by another in 1580, and there was a brewhouse on the site into the present century.[84] There was also a real tennis court in the garden opposite the main gate, a site now belonging to St Catharine's College. In 1532 the garden had been assigned to the president's use; it is not clear when he first gained another garden beside the river, next to the lodge.[85] The island contained a garden and orchard; walks were laid out there in 1539 and in the 17th century ash and elm trees were planted. The ditch on the south side was deepened in 1547 to make the site more completely into an island.[86] The accounts contain several references to bridges, and for much of the 16th century there seem to have been three of these, one from Cloister Court to the island, one from the Fellows' garden on the Carmelite land across to what is now the Grove, and a third from the island over the ditch to the Newnham road.[87]

This riverside situation made Queens' vulnerable to flooding. On several occasions beer had to be rescued from flooded cellars; workmen were regularly employed to mend the banks of the river and streams, or

---

[81] W&C, ii.19 – 20; RCHM, lxxxiv, 168, 177. Its original form is seen in Loggan's view of 1685.

[82] OPR, fos.8, 169v (and c.f. Book 43, f.123v); above, pp. 111, 119.

[83] Book 4, fos. 133, 134, 141v, 174v; Book 5, fos. 2 – 2v, 45, 47, 52, 120. There is a reference to building new stables in 1714, Book 7, f.98; they were still there in the 1860s, Searle, 85.

[84] RCHM, 178; Searle, 85, 371.

[85] W&C, ii.34, 52 – 4; Searle, 184; Book 15, entry for April 1648; Morgan (unpublished thesis, 1984), 311; Book 4, fos.151v, 175v. For the layout of the gardnes, see W&C, ii. facing 10, 11; Browne and Seltman (1951), plate 17.

[86] W&C, ii.56 – 8. Colleges grew many of their own vegetables; in 1877 Wordsworth commented that 'To this day Queens' has its own kitchen garden', Wordsworth (1968), 203, n. 1.

[87] W&C, ii.5 (fig. 2), 53, 55; Book 4, fos. 130, 165, 175; Book 5, fos.2, 47, 70, 81v, 109, 115, 136, 151v; Book 6, fos.42v, 78; Searle, 263, 400 – 1. The second bridge was taken down in 1793.

to clear mud from the ditches.[88] In 1774 the college gave one shilling to 'A Man, for bringing back, the Garden Bench after the flood'.[89] The floods of 1795 were particularly severe: furniture which had floated away from a house in Newnham was found in Silver Street, and a student at Queens', who had been at a ball until four in the morning, and was 'utterly unconscious of what had taken place, sprang from the top of the steps on the left of the cloisters, and was surprised to find himself up to his waist in water'.[90]

The river was important to the college as a means of supply. From Roman times waterways had played an important part in the East Anglian economy, and there were close commercial links between Cambridgeshire and King's Lynn. Heavy items were normally transported by water, even over short distances; timber, coal and building materials were brought to Cambridge by boat.[91] The Queens' accounts support this general picture, and we find tiles, slates, bricks, lime, timber, and sea coal arriving in this way.[92] It was sometimes necessary to clean out the river bed and remove obstructions; hence in 1625 the college paid 3s for 'a boate and fowre men to draw trees out of the river that boats might passe'.[93] The river's importance as a supply route explains the frequent petitioning by both university and town in the 17th century against plans to drain the fens, which, it was felt, would lower the water level of the major waterways, and thereby imperil river traffic on the Cam. In response, provisions were made to protect this, most notably an act of 1703 for making the Cam more navigable, which appointed conservators over a stretch of river from Queens' to Clayhithe, some seven miles downstream.[94] The river was still of commercial importance in Victorian times.

Visits

One way in which the college maintained its links with patrons and the outside world was by playing host to visiting dignitaries; sometimes,

[88] Searle, 386 – 7; Walker in *Record* (1984), 7; Book 5, fos.42v, 43, 45v, 57, 59, 62v, 70v, 87v, 135, 161; Book 6, fos.26, 117, 117v, 123; Book 8, fos.7, 35v, 48v, 131, 139, 242.
[89] Book 8, f.68v.
[90] Gunning (1854), ii.1 – 2.
[91] Darby (1977), 31 – 2; Everitt (1967), 492; Bowden (1967), 611; Harrison (1968), 67; *RCHM*, cii.
[92] Book 4, fos.155 – 155v; Book 5, fos.2, 45, 47, 51v; Book 6, f.30v; *RCHM*, 171. In 1700 there is an entry for 'bringing up the Pots for the Master's Garden from the Great Bridge', Book 7, f.37.
[93] Book 6, fos.21, 25v, 31.
[94] Darby (1940), 52 – 3, 68, 103 (and *ibid.*, chapter 2 for 17th century drainage schemes), Shadwell (1912), i.324 – 30.

only for an hour or so; sometimes for a few days. Such visits brought material benefits to the college, or enhanced its status, according to the interest or quality of the guest. Only a few visitors lodged at Queens'; a greater number were entertained there, or visited it as part of a tour of the university.[95] It was customary to make a present to distinguished guests; a pair of gloves was the usual gift.[96] Colleges might also be called upon to contribute towards the costs of university entertainment of visiting royalty or nobles.[97] We do not know the purpose of all of these visits; some had no obvious connection with the college's affairs. In 1594 it presented a pair of gloves to the bishop of Lincoln, who had come to Cambridge to conduct a visitation of King's college; in the 18th century, Queens' played host to circuit judges.[98] In other cases, the link with the college is apparent. Former Fellows were entertained.[99] The earl of Huntingdon was entertained in 1607; his grandson had entered Queens' as a fellow-commoner in 1601.[100] In 1671 the college bought 'two bottles of Clarret' and one of 'Rynnish wine' to entertain Sir John Bankes of Kent; the purpose of Bankes' visit is not known, but his son Caleb was admitted as a fellow-commoner four years later.[101] In 1685 the countess of Aylesbury was given a Bible 'at her sonns leaving the College'.[102]

Members of the royal family and great figures of state bestowed great prestige on colleges at which they stayed. Chancellors of the university seem not to have lodged at Queens' — Fisher of course was an exception — although the earl of Essex may well have done so in 1598 shortly after his election; there is still an 'Essex room' in the president's lodge, the windows of which contain representations of his coat of arms in stained glass.[103] In its early days the college was the regular resting place for members of the royal family. Henry VII and his wife were entertained at Queens' in 1497.[104] Lady Margaret Beaufort came in 1505; her son and grandson (the future Henry VIII) stayed there in the same year, and all

---

95 It is not always clear from a source if a guest stayed overnight or not.
96 Searle, 386; Book 4, f.98v; Book 5, fos.42v, 156 – 156v; Book 6, f.9v. There are some gifts recorded of unknown nature, Book 4, f.95v; Book 5, f.47.
97 Book 5, fos.131v, 152, 156 – 156v; Book 6, fos.10, 14v, 22, 25v, 29v, 33v, 35, 58v, 93v, 97; Book 7, f.61.
98 Searle, 386; Cooper, ii.525; Book 7, fos.60, 154, 166v.
99 Book 3, f.216 (Thomas Smith); Book 5, f.156 (George Montaigne).
100 Searle, 395; Book 5, f.115, and see f.156v.
101 Book 6, f.149v; AC.
102 Book 6, f.220v; see also f.189v; AC; Searle, 318, for the entertaining of Samuel and James Fortrey in 1689; James was admitted a fellow-commoner two years later, having been in the service of James II.
103 The room was clearly named after the earl's visit: he must have rested there, Cooper, ii.592; Searle, 390; RCHM, cxiv, 175; W&C, ii.30, n. 1; c.f. the alternative but less plausible view of the origins of the room's name in Morgan (unpublished thesis, 1984), 146.
104 Book 6, f.256; Book 80, f.51v (second pagination).

three seem to have returned in 1506.[105] Catherine of Aragon had previously called off two intended visits, in 1517/18 and 1519, before staying at Queens' in 1521; Henry VIII was there for two days the following year.[106] From an early date there was a reception room, known as the 'queen's chamber', in the range next to the river; the title was probably adopted after the visit of 1497.[107]

Royal servants followed this example. In 1518/19 Cuthbert Tunstall, the master of the rolls, was entertained at Queens', and Cardinal Wolsey stayed there in 1520.[108] Queens' subsequently lost its favoured status to Trinity, but still received brief visits. In 1564 Elizabeth I returned from Peterhouse to King's 'by the Queen's College, and . . . S. Katherine's Hall; only perusing the houses: because it was almost one a clock'[109] In 1681 Charles II and his queen 'did us the Honour to visit this College where they staid about an houre', but the cost of their reception, which included presents for the royal couple and the purchase of a looking-glass for the 'queen's chamber', came to over £26.[110] Queen Anne also entered the college briefly during her grand visit of the university in 1705, after attending prayers in King's College chapel, and before moving on to Newmarket.[111]

Health and disease

In 1679 Thomas Edwards, a Fellow of Queens', 'who has been depriv'd of his sight a longe time, & is much in yeares, & is very infirm', was given permission to go out of residence, retaining his Fellow's stipend and other allowances.[112] Loss of sight may have been a regular consequence of an academic career. Erasmus' friend Henry Bullock reflected sombrely on 'that merest shadow of learning to which I have attained, scarcely able to use more than a single eye, by means of those

[105] Reynolds (1972), 34 – 5; Searle, 133 – 4, 136 – 7, 143.
[106] Searle, 163 – 4, 167; below, p. 139.
[107] W&C, ii.216; Searle, 128. It was known by that name in the late 17th century, Book 6, fos.200v, 253.
[108] Searle, 162 – 3, 169.
[109] Cooper, ii.191 – 4; iii.71, 85, 156, 170, 250; Nichols (1788), i. entry for 1564, p.19.
[110] Book 6, fos.200v, 203v; Book 80, f.18 (second pagination); Cooper, iii.590 – 2, reprints a contemporary account of the visit in general which does not mention a visit to Queens'. It must have been this visit which was referred to by William Sedgwick, an 18th century president, in a letter of 1736; the queen, he wrote, had wanted to use a chamber pot when she was in the lodge, and the president, Henry James, 'not being provided of one Handsome enough made her wait till he sent to King's College to borrow a Silver one for her use. She retired into the Room now my Study . . . and Dr James afterwards Christened it . . . in perpetuam rei memoriam the Queens Chamber, which Name it still retains', unclassified MS, Queens' library.
[111] Cooper, iv.72.
[112] OPR, f.108v; he died in 1683, AC.

tiny Greek letters and at the expense of losing my health', and in 1536/7 Robert Garret, a Fellow of Queens' for over 30 years, was excused from taking part in university processions because of his failing eyesight.[113] Scholarship brought other inconveniences too: in the early 17th century John Preston suffered from insomnia as the result of overwork; tobacco was prescribed, which effected a successful cure.[114] Simon Patrick 'conflicted with a sore distemper, which I brought upon myself by hard and unseasonable study; it being usual with me to sit up till one or two o'clock in the morning . . . This brought upon (me) a sore disease, the hoemaroides, with which I was so afflicted, that I was forced to lay aside my books, and wholly mind my health. For being obliged to be let blood by leeches, they were so carelessly administered, that I bled all night in my bed; and was brought so weak on a sudden, that I could scarce crawl about my chamber'.[115] Roger Ascham, a distinguished Tudor education-alist, believed that 'pastimes for the mind only, be nothing fit for students because the body which is most hurt by study, should take away no profit at all thereat. This knew Erasmus very well, when he was here in Cambridge: which when he had been sore at his book . . . for lack of better exercise, would take his horse, and ride about the Market Hill'.[116]

In addition, Cambridge men were believed to suffer as a result of the town's unhealthy atmosphere, unlike Oxford, which was praised in the 17th century for its 'healthy air'.[117] The poet George Herbert, whilst a student at Trinity in the early 17th century, would sometimes 'ride to Newmarket, and there lie a day or two for fresh Air'.[118] A Caius student in the 1630s described Cambridge as 'a very sickly place, for there dy many every weeke of agues and other diseases'.[119] In 1577 William Harrison observed that it stood 'somewhat low and near unto the fens, whereby the wholesomeness of the air there is somewhat corrupted', and John Evelyn's description of 1654 went even further: 'the whole town is situate in a low dirty unpleasant place, the streets ill-paved, the air thick and infected by the fens'.[120] The part of the town that lay along the river was not neatly laid out as it is today, but was a 'belt of

---

[113] Porter and Thomson (1963), 198 – 9 (Bullock maybe exaggerating, in imitation of Erasmus's epistolary style); Emden, 252 (Garret lived another 20 years).

[114] Ball (1885), 34 – 6.

[115] Patrick (1839), 28 – 9. A Fellow of New College Oxford wrote in a letter of 1632: 'I am much troubled with the swellings of my inward haemarroids and I thinke that causeth a weaknes in my backe . . . If I knew how to order those inward haemarrhoids it would bee a greate meanes of health'. New College Archives NCA 11,704. An occupational hazard of the academic profession, perhaps?

[116] Porter and Thomson (1963), 27.

[117] Frank (1973), 194.

[118] Fowler and Fowler (1984), 70.

[119] Venn (1913), 208.

[120] Harrison, quoted in Cressy (1975), 115; Evelyn (1966), i.307.

commercial quarters, of sheds and warehouses as well as colleges, along narrow lanes leading to hithes at the river-side on the margins of alluvial marshes'; the surviving ditches along the 'Backs' are the last trace of former islands and marshland.[121] There were many other drains and ditches, particularly the King's Ditch which bounded the eastern side of the town, and these were more or less open sewers.[122] Repeated efforts were made to improve the level of sanitation here and in other parts of the town during the medieval and early modern periods.[123] The 16th century statutes of Caius College, devised by a leading physician of the day, forbade any buildings which would close the south side of Caius Court, 'lest the air, being prevented from free movement, should be corrupted, and so do harm to us . . . and bring on sickness and death'.[124]

Given this environment, it is not surprising that there were frequent outbreaks of disease in Cambridge. The most common illness was the 'ague', a kind of fever which was almost certainly malaria.[125] The presence of tuberculosis is not well documented, but it must have been relatively common. In 1671 Queens' granted leave of absence to one of its Fellows, Richard King, who was 'very far gone in a consumption'; King died two weeks later.[126] There are other examples of college members being permitted to leave for the sake of their health, although the nature of their afflictions is not revealed.[127] Henry Bullock was struck down by a mysterious disease in 1517 which 'attacked me so cruelly that I gave up hope of life, and for several days it was rather the physician than I that judged me likely to live'.[128] Also mysterious is the 'sweating sickness', common in those days and still not identified. It was this which afflicted Erasmus shortly before his arrival in Cambridge in 1511 and there was an outbreak there in 1551.[129] Typhus is known to have broken out in 1556, and in 1683 bible-clerks at Queens' were reported

[121] Darby (1977), 38-9.
[122] ibid.; Williamson (1957), 53.
[123] Williamson (1953), 53-6.
[124] Brooke (1985), 67.
[125] Venn (1913), 207, 208, 231; Fowler and Fowler (1984), 72; the word may have been used to describe many kinds of fever.
[126] OPR, f.139v; AC. Simon Patrick described the disease which killed John Smith: at first he had 'a husking cough, and frequently spit up stones. So I call them, for they resembled a cherry stone, and were of that bigness'; Smith subsequently 'fell into a looseness, which brought him very low', and a remedy which he tried against his doctor's advice was disastrous, for immediately 'the humour flew up into his head, and never could be got out; but he dosed perpetually, and rarely spoke anything of sense'; he died soon afterwards, Patrick (1839), 19-21; Patrides (1980), xxix, claims that Smith died of consumption (tuberculosis), and the symptoms described by Patrick do suggest that, although it is odd that he should not have referred to it by name; consumption was a familiar enough disease in those times.
[127] OPR, fos.132, 157v. In 1661 two Fellows who were 'both by sicknes fastned to their beds' were granted leave of absence, ibid., f.138v; and see f.92.
[128] Porter and Thomson (1963), 197, and see 199.
[129] ibid., 78-80, 108; Shrewsbury (1971), 185.

'absent upon the small pox'.[130] One Fellow, Edmund Smith, had died of smallpox during an outbreak seven years previously, and two Fellows are known to have died of it during the 1740s, before the more widespread use of inoculations curbed its threat.[131]

The greatest terror was produced by the 'plague', although the word was used loosely to describe a wide range of diseases, by no means necessarily the disease now known as bubonic plague.[132] 'Plague' broke out in Cambridge in over twenty different years between 1510 and 1667, sometimes with great severity.[133] The threat of it deterred Henry VI from coming to Cambridge in 1444; in 1519 Catherine of Aragon planned to pass through the town on her pilgrimage to Walsingham, but enquired first 'whether Cambrigge stood cler from eny contageous sykkenesse or no'.[134]

A standard procedure was employed whenever 'plague' broke out or threatened, which altered little over the years save in detail: trade and commerce were restricted, to prevent the disease from spreading; the university closed down; and the members of colleges either locked themselves in with provisions, or fled into the countryside.[135] The Queens' statutes of the 16th century contained regulations for dealing with such outbreaks, which tried to maintain some academic routine even when the college was forced to disperse.[136] Students and college lecturers were to reassemble elsewhere and continue their academic exercises and disputations; no particular place was specified, although there were several college livings and other properties nearby.[137] The president, three Fellows, the butler and two scholars were to remain to look after the college until it was deemed safe for the others to return.[138] In 1529, though, Robert Nunne, a bible-clerk, was awarded five shilllings 'because he was alone during the outbreak of plague'.[139] There are several illustrations in the archives of the college breaking up after the outbreak of an epidemic, with financial allowances made to absentee

---

[130]   Shrewsbury (1971), 194 – 5; Book 6, f.210; Venn (1913), 213.

[131]   Book 80, fos.85v, 87, 90v (second pagination); f.26v (third pagination). Inoculation was introduced in the 1720s, and became widely used after the middle of the 18th century, Speck (1977), 65.

[132]   G. I. Twigg (1984) overturns much of the conventional wisdom concerning so-called 'plague'.

[133]   Shrewsbury (1971), 160, 163, 167, 169, 172, 181, 201, 219, 232, 237, 246, 271, 282, 299, 307, 354, 356 – 7, 395 – 6, 404, 422, 423 – 4, 514 – 6.

[134]   Above, p. 1; Searle, 163.

[135]   Williamson (1957), 57 – 61; Cooper, iii.222 – 3; Porter and Thomson (1963), 207; see also the sources cited in Twigg (unpublished thesis, 1983), appendix A, n. 3. See also above, n. 133.

[136]   Book 79, fos.34 – 34v; *Statutes (1559)*, 28 – 30.

[137]   See for example above, p. 22.

[138]   President or vice-president, the president being often away; the three Fellows were the two bursars and the dean of chapel.

[139]   *'pro regardo quoniam solus erat tempore pestis'*, Searle, 188, from Book 2, f.118.

Fellows and scholars, and there are several entries throughout the period of payments to servants 'for keepinge the gates' — in other words, barring them against outsiders — when disease was about. The college also made donations of money to victims of epidemics in the town.[140]

As far as we know, 'plague' only entered the college once. A letter to Lord Burghley in October 1578 commented on a recent outbreak in Cambridge: 'the plague began in Queen's College, the infection being taken by the company of a Londoner in Stourbridge fair. There died only two scholars, whose death, although it caused a dissolution of the college, yet the danger was not found to be general, till it was further known that they were visited by divers scholars coming out of other colleges, suspecting not any contagious disease. This fear conceived, moved many to depart for a time.'[141]

---

[140] Searle, 349, 394, 396, 460, 461; OPR, fos.1v, 16, 118v, 130; Book 4, fos.111v, 113v, 129v, 176; Book 5, f.106v; Book 6, fos.18, 21, 43, 210. For relief in general, see Williamson (1957), 61 – 3; Cooper, iii.223 – 7.

[141] Historical Manuscripts Commission (1888), ii.215. The reference to the burning of boards in Book 4, f.132v, in December 1578 may refer to this, although it took place some time after the deaths.

11

The Restoration and the reigns of Charles II and James II (1660 – 88)

Despite the acquiescence of most Cambridge dons under the various revolutionary republican régimes of the 1650s, the university's response to the restoration of the monarchy in 1660 was jubilant, and there were widespread celebrations.[1] The president of Queens', Thomas Horton, together with two of the Fellows, contributed to a book of verses published by the university press to celebrate the king's return,[2] and in another volume of a different kind a third Fellow, Daniel Nichols, published a poem maintaining that some Cambridge men had always been

> 'Joynt haters of the Tyrant [Cromwell] and his train,
> And faithfull subjects to our Sovereign'.

Clergymen and academics, wrote Nichols, were in their own way 'fellow-soldiers', who fought with 'prayers and tears', instead of more conventional weaponry, and who had

> '. . . with many a sigh and groan
> Pray'd and believ'd Him [Charles II] to his Crown and Throne'.[3]

Nichols was perhaps excessive in his profession of royalist sentiments, but there was nothing essentially insincere or hypocritical about either his poem, or the contributions of Horton and the two other Fellows to the royal welcome.[4] In the 1650s dons had sought peace and stability above all else, and to a large extent they had found this under the Cromwellian protectorate. When, after 1658, the republican government began to disintegrate, the restoration of the monarchy in the person of

---

[1] Twigg (unpublished thesis, 1983), 197; Searle, 571. For acquiescence in the 1650s, see above, pp. 62 – 3.

[2] *Academiae* (1660), noted in Bowes (1894), 39. The names of the other Queens' contributors are also given in Gray, 173.

[3] Godman (1660), preface; the poem is reproduced in full below, appendix 14.

[4] c.f. the harsh comments by Gray on Horton, Gray, 173; Gray's view was clouded by the prejudices of Victorian historical scholarship.

Charles II appeared the only practical alternative to chaos and anarchy, and was thus generally supported.[5]

Yet many in the university had good reason for disquiet at the turn of events, especially those who had been appointed to positions in place of expelled royalists. In June 1660 the House of Lords commanded that all university and college members who had been 'unjustly put out' by the purges of the 1640s and 1650s were to be restored; the earl of Manchester, reinstated as chancellor of the university, began to restore ejected Fellows during the summer.[6] Fifty are known to have returned, eight of them to Queens', including the former president, Edward Martin.[7] The first to be restored was Michael Freer on 27 June, who was back at Queens' in early July. The warrant for Martin's restoration was issued on 2 August. Martin immediately informed Horton of the fact, and Horton quietly gave up his place, having doubtless expected to be removed.[8] It is ironic indeed that Manchester, who had ejected Martin and the Queens' Fellows in 1644, was now restoring them to their places. The warrant issued by him for Martin's reinstatement began: 'Whereas I am informed that Edward Martin . . . hath been wrongfully putt out of his Mastershipp', and a similar formula appears in the other restoration warrants.[9]

The Fellows who had been admitted to Queens' since the 1644 purge were all allowed to remain. Manchester had ordered that nobody should be ejected in any college to make way for ejected Fellows who were returning unless there were no empty places, and he insisted that the appointments and admissions of the intruded Fellows were legally valid. Nevertheless, Martin had the Queens' Fellows re-elected and readmitted to make their titles doubly secure (and perhaps also because he could not himself accept the validity of their appointments otherwise).[10] When his had been done, Martin noted that the college had been rescued from its 'Babylonian captivity', and properly

---

[5] For a detailed account of national proceedings at the end of the Interregnum see Hutton (1985), parts one and two; noted briefly in Coward (1980), 234 – 6.

[6] Twigg (unpublished thesis, 1983), 197.

[7] ibid.; Searle, 573 – 5; Gray 177 – 8; Book 6, fos.108, 113; Book 73, f.49.

[8] Searle, 572 – 6.

[9] ibid., 572 – 3.

[10] ibid., 576. Manchester's order required Queens' to 'take care not to remove any from being fellowes or schollers . . . that are in places vacant by death or other incapacities and likewise that none be removed from being fellowes or schollers till those places be filled which are allready void, or may be immediately made void by voluntary resignations and if such vacant places shall not be enough for the reception of all who are to be restored then to make roome for the rest by the removall only of so many of the juniors as shall be necessary', ibid., 574 (original in Box 31). For the restoration of Fellows in general, see Twigg (unpublished thesis, 1983), 197 – 8. Hutton notes that 'By this process, generally an amicable one, some colleges were left with a majority of former royalists, while others retained all of their intruded fellows', Hutton (1985), 130 – 1.

reconstituted.[11]

Martin's experiences between his arrest in 1642 and his return to Cambridge in 1660 had not softened his temper or his beliefs. He had suffered several years' imprisonment, escaping in 1648 but being rearrested two years later; shortly afterwards he was released, and spent most of the 1650s in France among other exiled royalists and high churchmen. He described those eighteen years as full of 'nothing but Prisons, Ships, wandrings, and solitude', when he was 'very well satisfied with one Meal a day, and at night a Crust of Bread, and a Cup of any Drink'.[12]

Together with re-establishing the constitution and government of the college, Martin's other principal concern was to restore the religious practices which he had introduced in the 1630s.[13] This was achieved swiftly and without fuss: hoods and surplices were purchased in September 1660; the college accounts for October mention altar rails, and there are further references to work in the chapel the following month. An organ was reintroduced; in 1661 the east end was wainscoted with cedar.[14] The Anglican Book of Common Prayer must have been brought back into use immediately upon Martin's return.

These moves paralleled the return of Anglicanism throughout the university, and in the country as a whole there was a marked Anglican reaction.[15] Although Charles II's Worcester House declaration in October 1660 permitted freedom of choice nationally in many non-essential religious practices, this freedom did not extend to the universities, whose members were required to stick rigidly to the pre-war form of worship.[16] During the next few years the Anglican reaction grew irresistibly, and a series of acts of parliament was issued imposing harsh penalties on those who would not conform to the restored state church; foremost among this legislation was the Uniformity Act of 1662 which required all ministers and university dons to swear oaths of

[11] 'captivitate quadam Babylonica', Searle, 576; OPR, fos.102, 147 – v.
[12] For Martin, see above, pp. 44 – 50; for his experiences 1642 – 60, see Searle, 504 – 7, from where this quotation comes.
[13] Martin also drafted a petition to parliament when it was debating a bill for confirming leases made by colleges since the 1644 purge, in which he alleged that the college's property had been severely damaged by the intruded Fellows, with timber being felled, leases altered, rents lost and royalties alienated, 'and the College itselfe so ruinated in edifices and otherwise, that we are no wayes able to maintaine it, together with the Composition of the Founders and Allowances of Fellowes and Schollars'. This picture was not so much exaggerated as downright dishonest; the petition does not seem to have been presented to parliament, Searle, 582 – 3; Book 4, f.119v. The act confirming leases and fellowship elections were the fellowship had fallen vacant by normal processes was passed in December 1660, Shadwell (1912), i.264 – 71.
[14] Searle, 582, 584; Gray, 179; W&C, ii.39 – 40; Book 6, f.109; OPR, f.160.
[15] Below, n.17, for the national settlement; for the universities, see Twigg (unpublished thesis, 1983), 198 – 9; Gascoigne (unpublished thesis, 1980), 1 – 30.
[16] Twigg (unpublished thesis, 1983), 198.

allegiance to the crown and Book of Common Prayer, and to repudiate the Solemn League and Covenant. About one tenth of the clergy of England and Wales were expelled from their places for refusing these oaths. At Cambridge only about fifty dons and students were removed for failing to conform between 1660 and 1662; apart from Horton, who had withdrawn peacefully, nobody was expelled from Queens' at this time.[17] This shows clearly the university's desire for peace and quiet.[18]

The restored Anglicanism was high church in its ritual, and intolerant of even the slightest dissent: criticism of any kind was deemed to be subversive. These views were enforced at Cambridge by the heads of houses, some of whom were restored 'Laudian' heads of the 1630s and 1640s such as Edward Martin. This group was not influential for long, its members either retiring, or, in most cases, receiving promotion in the church as a reward for past loyalty. Martin was appointed dean of Ely in 1662, but died three days after his installation.[19]

More significant were the heads appointed during the 1660s, many of whom had been expelled from fellowships in the parliamentary purges, and several of whom later became bishops; this group included Anthony Sparrow, ejected from a fellowship at Queens' in 1644, and a zealous royalist and high churchman, who succeeded Martin as president.[20] Once established in positions of authority within the university, these men naturally advanced their own kind, and almost all of the masters of Cambridge colleges during the remainder of Charles II's reign were high churchmen; this ensured the continuance of the mood of Anglican reaction.[21] As early as 1663 a visitor to Cambridge was able to write that Sparrow and some of the other heads 'carried things so high that I saw latitude and moderation were odious to the greater part even there'.[22]

The crown had traditionally seen heads of houses as agents for maintaining orthodoxy in the universities. This was especially important to the state when it came to quietening down the turmoil produced by

[17] The Uniformity Act is printed in Kenyon (1966), 378 – 82. For the religious settlement in general, see Green (1978); Hutton (1985); for a brief summary of Anglican legislation, Hutton (1985), 172 – 80. The figure for numbers of clergy expelled nationally is given in *ibid.*, 176 – 7. For expulsions in the university, see Matthews (1934), xiii – xiv. Hutton (1985), 131, n.7, argues that Matthews' figure is too low, but it is impossible to arrive at precise figures.
[18] Although there was some resistance to the restoration of Anglican ritual, Gascoigne (unpublished thesis, 1980), 1 – 4.
[19] *ibid.*, 7, n. 3; Searle, 577.
[20] Gascoigne (unpublished thesis, 1980), 7; for Sparrow, see above, pp. 46 – 7; below, pp. 145 – 8.
[21] Gascoigne (unpublished thesis, 1980), 7.
[22] Burnet (1902), 464. Sparrow was seriously concerned at the spread of religious heterodoxy in the university, including Socinianism at Queens', Gascoigne, *Holy Alliance* (forthcoming), chapter ii.

1   Detail of centre panel of triptych in new Chapel. Attributed to the 'Master of St Gudule', Brussels, 1480s.

2 Margaret of Anjou, with her husband, Henry VI, receiving presentation by
John Talbot, Earl of Shrewsbury, of his book of *Poems and Romances*, 1445
[British Library, Royal MS II 15 E VI, fo. 2b].

3 Carved keystone over old Main Gate of College, 1450, traditionally thought to be Andrew Doket holding the College's foundation charter.

4 Elisabeth Woodville, queen of Edward IV. The best surviving panel portrait
of her, traditionally thought to be the original from which the other portraits
derive.

5A Sir Thomas Smith, contemporary portrait panel.

5B Isaac Milner, by G. H. Harlow, 1798.

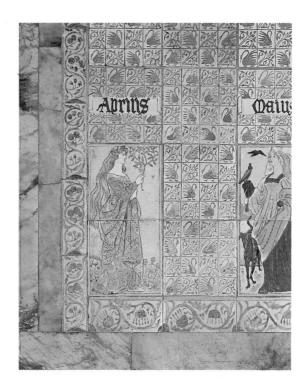

6 Fireplace Tiles from Old Hall, 'April' and 'June' by William Morris, 1862.

7A Arthur Wright, by G. Henry, 1915.

7B Sir Harold Bailey, by Ronald Way, 1972.

8   Final phase of Cripps Court. Model of winning design by Bland and Brown.

the revolutionary years. For this reason, the king issued several mandates to colleges during the 1660s to ensure the election of proven royalists as masters; thereafter, with orthodoxy successfully restored, there was less need to intervene.[23] The most blatant example of royal interference was at the election of Edward Martin's successor at Queens' in 1662. There were two candidates: one was Anthony Sparrow; the other was Simon Patrick, who had been a Fellow in the 1640s and 1650s. Patrick's unease within the religious establishment of the 1650s had led him to seek episcopal (i.e., Anglican) ordination in secret while he was a Fellow, and shortly before leaving Cambridge for London later in the decade he had preached in the university church against the continued persecution of royalists — ' a vehement discourse against the hypocrisy of fasting and prayer, when we continue to be unjust, and oppress our neighbours'.[24] Nevertheless, he was a man of relatively liberal religious views, which were not in favour with the restored establishment of church or state.[25] At Queens', though, he was popular with the junior Fellows, who, like him, were products of the more liberal intellectual atmosphere of the Cromwellian period. Sparrow was the nominee of the restored senior Fellows, and the election contest represented a genuine ideological clash.[26]

Patrick's supporters invited him to come to Cambridge at the time of the election; presumably, they wished to admit him as president as soon as possible, and they were clearly confident of victory because they had a definite numerical advantage. When Patrick reached Trumpington, just outside Cambridge, word was brought him 'that I was legally chosen by the majority of the fellows, but another [Sparrow] admitted, contrary to the statutes'.[27] Patrick's supporters, fearing royal intervention, had petitioned the king to be allowed to hold a free election, expressing their desire to choose someone of 'of unquestionable loyalty during the late times of Rebellion', and refuting the claim of the senior Fellows that 'if the society should be left to the Liberty of their votes some nonconformist might be pitched upon; who wou'd destroy all that good order and discipline which at present obtained amongst them'.[28]

The crown had in fact decided that the job should go to Sparrow, but a formal election had to take place, under the direction of the senior Fellow, Richard Bryan, one of Sparrow's supporters and another victim of the 1644 purge. Accounts of what happened at the election were

---

[23] Gascoigne (unpublished thesis, 1980), 8 – 9, 11 – 12.
[24] Above, p. 62; Patrick (1839), 34 – 5.
[25] Below, pp. 147 – 8.
[26] Ray (1928), 29; Gascoigne (unpublished thesis, 1980), 11.
[27] Patrick (1839), 41 – 2; see also CUL Add MS 20, fos.23 – v. The election was on 5 May 1662, Patrick (1839), 42; Kennet (1728), 675.
[28] CUL Add MS 20, f.23, quoted in Gascoigne (unpublished thesis, 1980), 9 – 10.

issued subsequently by both camps, and although these differ in some details, the essential story of the proceedings is clear enough. In the early stages of the election, Bryan read a letter from the king *recommending* Sparrow; then, when another vote was taken and the result again looked certain to go in Patrick's favour, he produced a royal mandate *ordering* Sparrow's election. Patrick's supporters protested that the mandate was too late, for the election had already begun, but Bryan pronounced Sparrow to be president, and he was admitted forthwith.[29]

Whatever Bryan's reasons for delay in producing the mandate, he had committed a tactical blunder, and his subsequent pronouncement and admission of Sparrow as president were most irregular. But the history of Cambridge college elections during the 16th and 17th centuries is full of similar muddles, and it was generally appreciated that when the crown was determined to see someone elected, it would have its way, whatever the proprieties.

Patrick refused to give up the fight. The election at Queens' was held on 5 May 1662; four days later, he presented his case before the court of King's Bench in London. His petition was rejected, but accepted when it was submitted again on 12 May.[30] Already on 8 May, the king had written to the vice-chancellor ordering him to confirm Sparrow as president, and to suspend Patrick's supporters from the privileges attached to their fellowships until they submitted to the royal will.[31] It was not until the end of October that Patrick and the recalcitrant Fellows appeared before a special royal commission established to hear the case, and not until November that he was allowed to plead his cause; on the latter occasion, his defence counsel was not present, having been summoned to attend the king at precisely the time of the hearing.

Patrick and his supporters made it 'so evidently appear that I was duly chosen, that the counsel on the other side had nothing to reply, but that they were fellows only by the King's grace and favour, who sent a mandamus that all should keep their fellowships who were not in sequestered places'. This referred to the regulations of 1660 which had permitted many of the intruded Fellows of the 1640s and 1650s to retain their places. However, in the case of Queens' the argument carried no weight, because Martin had had all the Fellows readmitted according to the statutory forms, to guarantee their positions. The lord chancellor, who presided over the royal commission, was compelled to admit that Patrick had been 'legally chosen', and could only ask 'will he yield nothing to the King?' On Patrick's refusal to surrender his legal

---

[29] The two accounts are in Patrick (1839), 42 – 3, and Book 73, f.53 (part of the latter is reproduced in Gray, 185). The recommendation and mandate are in Box 31; the mandate is briefly paraphrased in *CSPD* (1661 – 2), 359.

[30] Patrick (1839), 43 – 4.

[31] *ibid.*, 44; *CSPD* (1661 – 2), 365; Cooper, iii.496 – 7; Box 31.

entitlement, the lord chancellor 'bade all our names be taken and set down in writing, that we might be noted as a company of factious fellows', but the commission did not resolve the dispute. A few days later, Patrick's legal counsel withdrew from the case, having 'received instructions to meddle no more in my business'. The case was returned to King's Bench, and then lost in the maze of the legal process; after two years, with no solution in sight, Patrick decided to 'let it fall'.[32] Sparrow was in any case securely in possession of the presidency; shortly after the election, he had put pressure on Patrick's supporters to acknowledge their fault in opposing the royal mandate and promise obedience in future.[33]

In the words of the botanist John Ray, a Fellow of Trinity, the dispute over the Queens' election was a sign that the 'old and new University will never kindly mingle, or make one piece'.[34] Yet under the direction of its heads of houses, Cambridge soon became a bastion of high churchmanship.[35] Nor, although Sparrow's relations with his Fellows must have been severely strained, are there any indications of continued conflict at Queens'.[36]

In this strict atmosphere there was no room for the spirit of compromise and toleration which Simon Patrick represented. As an undergraduate at Queens', Patrick had been strongly influenced by his tutor, John Smith, who, despite his early death, had already made his mark as a leading figure in the so-called 'Cambridge Platonist' movement, which stemmed from a small group of Cambridge intellectuals who were active and prominent from the late 1640s and especially during the 1650s.[37] By returning to the inspiration and authority of the early Greek philosophers instead of the early Christian ones, as well as by their dethroning of Aristotle as the king of philosophers, the Cambridge Platonists made a radical break with English intellectual tradition — perhaps even a 'rejection of the entire Western theological tradition from St Augustine'.[38]

Their thinking was characterised by an emphasis on the rational aspects of Christianity, a rejection of much religious dogma and the many minor distinctions which divided the Christian community, and a

---

[32] Patrick (1839), 44 – 5; Gascoigne (unpublished thesis, 1980), 10 – 11. The case features in several collections of law reports: Siderfin (1683), i.346; Raymond (1696), 101 – 113; Levinz (1702), i.65 – 7.

[33] MS 73, 34, cited in Gascoigne (unpublished thesis, 1980), 10.

[34] Ray (1928), 29; Gascoigne (unpublished thesis, 1980), 11.

[35] Gascoigne (unpublished thesis, 1980), chapter 1.

[36] But see below, ns.41, 44.

[37] For Patrick and Smith, above, p. 92, chapter 7, n. 44; for the Cambridge Platonists, see Patrides (1980), 1 – 41. For Smith, *ibid.*; Powicke (1926), 87 – 109; Tulloch (1872), 117 – 191. Tulloch also writes briefly about Patrick, *ibid.*, 440 – 1.

[38] Patrides (1980), 4.

tolerant, irenical spirit in religion. In the long run this was to have a great influence on English theology, but in the early 1660s such notions were out of fashion. Cambridge Platonists were as loyal as anyone to the crown and state church, but many people believed them to be subversive, and they received fierce criticism within the university.[39] In 1662 Simon Patrick was driven to publish a defence of the 'latitudinarian' movement with which he was associated and which favoured a broad, tolerant church comprehending many shades of opinion, and of the 'New Philosophy' (Cambridge Platonism) which inspired it. In this, he observed that 'Latitude-men' at Cambridge in the 1640s and 1650s had been considered subversive by many Presbyterians 'because they were generally ordained by Bishops; and in opposition to that hidebound, strait-laced spirit that did then prevail', and he was upset that they should now be considered equally subversive by the high churchmen. Although he maintained diplomatically that 'I do not find that the grave heads, or other prudent persons of the University give any countenance to this peevish talk of some few, who for distinction sake . . . will not I hope be offended to be called Narrow-men', he must have recognised the strength and inflexibility of the high church movement in Cambridge.[40] The latitudinarian movement was more successful outside the universities — Patrick was to become a bishop — especially after the overthrow of James II in 1688, but Cambridge remained a bastion of the high church for many years.

Anthony Sparrow's reward for his services in promoting uniformity in the university was promotion to be bishop of Exeter in 1667. It was said that the king allowed him to nominate his successor at Queens'; certainly the new president, William Wells, was elected by royal mandate — the crown may not have trusted the Fellows to elect a suitable president after the troubles of 1662.[41] Wells was a former Fellow and a victim of Manchester's purge of 1644; he died in office in 1675 without, apparently, having left much of a mark upon the college.[42] His successor, Henry James, was also elected by royal mandate — the only such mandate at a mastership election in Cambridge between 1670 and the end of the reign in 1685.[43]

James was already a Fellow of Queens', and a royal chaplain, and was nominated apparently 'as a particular mark of Our grace and favour

---

[39] Twigg (unpublished thesis, 1983), 200. For Cambridge Platonism, latitudinarianism and the university, see Gascoigne (unpublished thesis, 1980), chapter 2.

[40] Patrick (1662), 5 – 6 and *passim*.

[41] Kennet (1728), 596; Book 79, f.95v. It was said that some of the Fellows still wished to elect Patrick on this occasion, Book 73, f.57, repeated in Gray, 194.

[42] *AC*. He was suspended from his living in the diocese of Ely for not appearing there at the archdeacon of Ely's visitation in 1673; his excuse was that he was sitting in Convocation at the time, Cooper, iii.556 – 7.

[43] Gascoigne (unpublished thesis, 1980), 8.

towards our said Chaplaines'. He was a precise, fussy man in business affairs; more importantly from the crown's point of view, he was a vigorous defender of religious orthodoxy.[44] The year before his election as president, he preached before the king at Newmarket in defence of the state church. Although his sermon stressed the values of the *via media*, simple piety, and avoidance of extremes, it also emphasised the importance of worship (and, by implication, of not quibbling over the particular ritual forms instituted by the Church of England), and argued that people should 'rest very much pleas'd with God's Dispensations towards them, though they may be contrary to what they could have wish'd to themselves' — the *status quo* was not to be challenged. The message is straightforward, commonsensical, and rather bland, avoiding any religious passion, but it is typical of the orthodoxy of the time, and Charles enjoyed it sufficiently to order that the sermon should be printed.[45] James, who was only thirty-three when elected president, remained at Queens' until his death in 1717, longer than any president since the foundation.[46]

The crown's employment of mandates in elections to masterships was deliberate and political. In addition, it issued a whole range of recommendations, dispensations and mandates at fellowship elections, directly or through courtiers.[47] The purpose behind these was less sinister: as in the past, many were issued as an automatic response to lobbying at court by university members, although some loyal sufferers for the royalist cause during the English Revolution were also rewarded in this way. Many were simply dispensations to ensure that promising young men were not presented from staying on in the university by restrictive college statutes. Not all mandates were promoted with equal vigour, and the right of colleges to resist mandates for genuinely

---

[44] Box 31. It was said that some of the Fellows wished to elect Patrick on this occasion also, which seems unlikely, Book 79, f.95v; Book 73, f.58, repeated in Gray, 198 – 9. James was an able theologian who became Regius professor of divinity; *AC*. See Gascoigne (unpublished thesis, 1980), 7, n. 5 for a later illustration of his defence of orthodoxy. James could not guarantee the orthodoxy of all the Fellows of Queens': Joseph Wasse, who became a Fellow in 1698, published a book in 1719, two years after James' death, containing unorthodox Arian views on the doctrine of the holy Trinity, Gascoigne, *Holy Alliance* (forthcoming), chapter v. This may have represented a swift conversion, or Wasse may have felt that it was safe to express his views in the more liberal theological atmosphere of the Hanoverian period.

[45] James (1674), 5 and *passim*. For the similar quality of much of Restoration theology, see Cragg (1950), 10; Green (1969), 43. Another Queensman to defend the reestablished church was Edward Kemp, who had been restored to his fellowship in 1660. Kemp preached in the university church in September 1668 in defence of Anglican orthodoxy and priesthood, warning preachers against making personal statements based on their own interpretations of Scripture when these clashed with the official doctrines of the church, Kemp (1668), *passim* (20 pp.).

[46] Book 73, f.60; Gray, 207; below, appendix 4.

[47] For these mandates in general, see Twigg (unpublished thesis, 1983), 207 – 8, 227.

unsuitable men was respected; but the right to issue mandates was part of the royal prerogative, and could not be challenged. The crown was too liberal in this regard: nearly 200 mandates were issued during Charles II's reign, an unprecedented and remarkably high number. Queens' received 22 of them — only two colleges received more — despite Charles' assertion when recommending John Cawley in 1662 that 'for the future Wee shalbe tender of making use of Our authority in that kind'.[48]

In many cases, the college was given freedom to elect, the crown merely dispensing with any college statutes which might stand in the way. But the granting of such freedom was seen by the crown more as an illustration of its own generosity than as a recognition of the college's right to choose. In 1676 the university's chancellor, the duke of Monmouth, in forwarding a recommendation for Francis Master(s) to be chosen Fellow, reminded Queens' that 'it is an effect of his Majestyes goodnesse towards you that hee is onely recommended', and that he had 'prevail'd with the King to leave it to your ingenuityes that Mr Masters may owne the obligation of his Fellowship to your choice rather than to any other means'. After this, Monmouth's further claim that he was 'studious to preserve the liberty of your Election' was unconvincing.

The college complied dutifully for the most part with the royal will. The only occasion on which it is known to have resisted during Charles' reign came in 1672. In February 1671 it had received a mandate to elect Ferdinand Smythes (or Smythies), a scholar of the college. In April 1672 it received an angry missive sent on behalf of the king explaining that four others had been pre-elected to fellowships instead of Smythes, although they were all junior to him. Queens' was ordered to pre-elect the royal nominee too, and to admit him to the next fellowship to fall vacant. We do not know why Smythes' nomination was resisted, but the college now bowed to royal pressure, and he was a Fellow from 1673 to 1725.[49]

There was occasional resistance in the university at large to Charles' promiscuous issuing of mandates because it infringed upon university and college liberties, but in general Cambridge remained staunchly royalist: loyal addresses and sermons were delivered, and celebrations held, on every appropriate occasion.[50] At Queens', the customary

---

[48]   *ibid.*, 227. The Queens' mandates are in Box 31, from which the following examples are taken; see also OPR, fos.110v – 111, 149 – v. In 1684 it was decided that a Fellow chosen by royal dispensation was not subject to the statutes of county, and was therefore not to be considered of any county, CB (1734 – 87), f.124.

[49]   Smythes' mandate was issued on 25 February 1671; the four others were pre-elected on 18 January 1672, Box 31. For Smythes, see *AC*.

[50]   Twigg (unpublished thesis, 1983), 201 – 8.

bonfires were lit to mark the anniversaries of the king's return from exile and his coronation, and in 1683 the college celebrated a day of thanksgiving for Charles' escape from the Rye House plot.[51] Such demonstrations of loyalty continued under Charles' successor, James II, despite misgivings in the university and the country at large about James' religious views: he was a Catholic, and anti-Catholic feeling remained widespread and intense.[52]

Quite indifferent to such sentiments, James set himself to the task of re-establishing Catholicism in England, and in this context he recognised the need for a Catholic foothold in the universities. In 1686 the powers of the new ecclesiastical commission extended to amending university and college statutes, which was clearly aimed at facilitating the admission of Catholics.[53] In the following year a Catholic was elected master of Sidney Sussex by royal mandate, but the university opposed an attempt to force it to award an MA degree to a Benedictine monk in the following year. A nine-man university deputation which included a Fellow of Queens', James Smith, argued its case before the ecclesiastical commission; this led only to the dismissal of the vice-chancellor, but the university continued to resist the king's demand, and amidst the growing political crisis of 1688, which culminated in James' overthrow and exile, the crown was not able to press its claims further.[54]

This relaxation of royal authority in 1688 probably explains why Queens' was able to resist a royal mandate for the election of George Gerey, a student of the college, to a fellowship there. James had followed his brother's practice of sending numerous mandates and recommendations for fellowships, but almost all of these were of the traditional kind, with no hidden (Catholic) intent.[55] Five of these were sent to Queens', of which two were merely dispensations.[56] Gerey's mandate was the only one to have been resisted, although we do not know why.[57]

The university's opposition to James' Catholic policies showed that here, as well as in the rest of the nation, loyalty to the Church of England was in the last resort stronger than loyalty to the crown.[58]

---

[51] Book 6, fos.110, 132v, 149, 210v.
[52] Queens' expressions of loyalty in Book 6, fos.219 – 220, 230 – 1; the university's loyalty and misgivings in Twigg (unpublished thesis, 1983), 209 – 10; Gascoigne (unpublished thesis, 1980), 19.
[53] For this and James' interference in the university described here, Gascoigne (unpublished thesis, 1980), 19 – 21; Twigg (unpublished thesis, 1983), 210 – 13.
[54] For the case and its aftermath see the references in n. 53; Cooper, iii.620 – 34.
[55] Twigg (unpublished thesis, 1983), 211. James' mandates to Queens' are in Box 31.
[56] Gray, 199, 202, only mentions two, but cannot have seen the mandates now in Box 31.
[57] The earl of Huntingdon, who had secured Gerey's mandate, warned the college in March 1688 not to oppose the royal prerogative in this matter, Box 31. According to Gray, 202, Gerey was elected, but not admitted (pre-elected perhaps?).
[58] Beddard (1979), 158; Gascoigne (unpublished thesis, 1980), 18 – 30.

Queens', in common with the rest of the university, celebrated the accession to the throne of James' triumphant rivals, William and Mary, in 1689.[59] About forty Cambridge men were forced to leave for refusing to swear oaths of allegiance to the new sovereigns, over half of them from St John's. Only one Queensman, Ephraim Howard, left over this issue; he had been elected a Fellow by royal mandate in 1686.[60] But the president, Henry James, must have been alarmed at the report given to the House of Commons in June 1689 that copies of a declaration by the exiled James II had been sent to Cambridge 'by Carriers in Boxes, directed to the Master of Queen's College, and Master of St John's Colleage'; the boxes were seized by the vice-chancellor, and it is not clear who sent them, nor for whom they were intended.[61]

The so-called 'Glorious Revolution' of 1688 brought to an end a period of intense political and religious upheaval which had persisted for over one hundred and fifity years, and wrought great changes in the university and at Queens'. The century which followed seems static and lifeless in comparison. The universities were in a state of relative decline in the 18th century, it is true, but our picture of them is still clouded by the views of Victorian reformers who tended to emphasise the achievements of their age and undervalue those of their predecessors. The history of Queens', and of the university, in the 18th century is less exciting than in the 17th, but it is not without interest.

[59] Twigg (unpublished thesis, 1983), 214; Book 6, f.241.
[60] Wordsworth (1874), 14 – 19, 23 – 4, 603 – 5. Howard took his MA in 1690, but seems to have left soon after, Book 6, f.249; Book 7, f.2; see also Book 80, f.42 (second pagination). The other name given in Wordsworth (1874), 603 – 4, as a non-juring Queens' Fellow does not correspond with any Fellow of that time. Palin (1851), 408 records only one Fellow of Queens' as a non-juror — presumably Howard, although no names are given.
[61] Cooper, iv.5 – 6.

12

The eighteenth century:
introduction, politics and religion

Introduction

It has become usual to think of the university world of the 18th century as one of sloth, torpor, self-indulgence and indiscipline, when the universities sank into a deep decline, not to recover until the era of the great Victorian parliamentary reforms. Although it has for some time been suggested that 18th century Cambridge has had a bad press, historians have only recently begun to reappraise many of the judgements of older generations, and to supply a more balanced interpretation; much more work still needs to be done in this field.[1]

The numerical decline of the university was not exclusively the product of the 18th century. It may have begun long before, perhaps even before the outbreak of the Civil War. Evidence from the 1630s suggests, if not a decline proper, then at least a tailing off of the vast expansion of the late Tudor and early Stuart period. This expansion could not have continued indefinitely at such a rate; nevertheless, student numbers and the level of new endowments were less in the 1630s than in the previous decade, although it may be that the 1620s were years of particularly good fortune.[2]

The decline proper is deemed to have set in not during the English Revolution, but after the restoration of the monarchy in 1660.[3] There had been many schemes for university reform earlier in the century, and especially during the revolutionary decades, but they had come to nothing, because the need for reform was not widely recognised; the reformers had no new conception of the university-in-society to challenge that which was already in place and to which the universities owed their success.[4] But after 1660 the perception of the universities'

---

[1] Winstanley (1922), 2, notes the need for re-evaluation of 18th century Cambridge. Winstanley and Wordsworth wrote several valuable books on the subject, but these are now quite old.

[2] For student numbers, see below, appendix 6; Twigg (unpublished thesis, 1983), appendix A. Searle, 438 – 9, attributes the very high numbers at Queens' in the 1620s to John Preston. For endowments, see Jordan (1959), 373; Feingold (1979), 272.

[3] Student numbers recovered to a large degree in the Revolution, see below, appendix 6. For the state of the university in the later 1640s and 1650s see above, chapter 4; Twigg (unpublished thesis, 1983), chapters V – VI.

[4] J. D. Twigg (1984).

153

social rôle and usefulness began to alter: fewer people were convinced of the value of a university education, and in consequence there was a steep decline in student numbers from the later 17th century until the middle of the 18th.[5]

Among the reasons that have been advanced to explain the post-Restoration disenchantment with the universities has been the suggestion that the university curriculum could not meet the demands of an increasingly commercially-minded age, and that by the beginning of the 18th century the traditional concept of the professions in England as 'learned' occupations requiring university training was undergoing substantial modification; there was a more utilitarian spirit about.[6] For wealthy young men, a private tutor and the grand tour were often felt to provide a more valuable, liberal, education.[7] For the less well off, the costs of residence at a university might be thought too high.[8]

Oxford and Cambridge were no longer the sole centres of intellectual life. They were challenged by London with its Royal Society, and also by new rivals in the field of higher education: the dissenting academies, founded by religious nonconformists who had been excluded from the universities by regulations introduced during the Anglican reaction of the 1660s.[9] It has often been argued that the academies deprived the universities of many men of talent, and stole a march on them by offering more up to date and useful courses of study, with greater emphasis on scientific subjects, in contrast to the universities' academic conservatism.[10] Far from being national institutions, as at the time of their greatest expansion and vitality, the universities shrank to little more than seminaries for the church, with religious intolerance and the falling status and appeal of the clerical profession all contributing to the decline.[11]

Each of these factors has its significance, no doubt, but the work of assessing their rôles in the decline of the English universities has scarcely begun; much more work on 18th century Cambridge is needed.

[5] For the fall in numbers, see below, p. 192; appendix 6.
[6] Kearney (1970), 144 – 5, 159 – 62; Holmes (1982), 7 – 8, 17, 118, 147 – 9. The university found it difficult to adapt its 16th century statutes for its own modern needs, Winstanley (1935), 4 – 5.
[7] Hill (1961), 294. See Rothblatt (1976), 75 – 100, for an important discussion of the universities and liberal education.
[8] e.g. Green (1969), 45 – 6; Holmes (1982), 209 – 10. More research on expenses would be useful.
[9] For the significance of the Royal Society see Hunter (1981), chapter 2; for the Anglican reaction see above, chapter 11.
[10] Hill (1961), 293; Green (1969), 44 – 5; Kearney (1970), 147 – 50, 158 – 9; Porter, *English Society*, 179. For the dissenting academies in particular, see Parker (1914), chapter 2; McLachlan (1931), chapter 2; Griffiths (1935), chapters II – III. The dissenting academies only began to flourish after 1688, when they were allowed to function openly.
[11] Simon (1974), 27; Kearney (1970), 143. Conversely, Cambridge may have suffered in conservative eyes from its association with the Cambridge Platonists.

The task of setting the condition of Queens' at this time into its university context is therefore more difficult than it has been for the earlier centuries, and the survey which follows is to some extent a case study.

Politics

Cambridge, and Queens', celebrated the success of William and Mary in 1689, and although there were perhaps a few Queensmen with Jacobite sympathies, the college as a whole was loyal to the new monarchy.[12] The accession of Queen Anne in 1702 was celebrated likewise, together with her anniversaries, and there were thanksgiving days for English victories over the French in battle at Blenheim and Ramilles in 1704 and 1706; the union of England and Scotland in 1707 was also deemed to be a cause for thanksgiving.[13] When Anne visited Cambridge in 1705 she was received at Queens' by the president, Henry James, with 'expressions of Duty and Loyalty'; James also contributed to a volume of verses published by the university in condolence for the death of the queen's consort, George, prince of Denmark, in 1708.[14]

Demonstrations of loyalty to the controversial Hanoverian succession of 1714 were just as prominent, and as before, Fellows were obliged to swear oaths of loyalty upon admission to their fellowships.[15] In 1747 the college celebrated the first anniversary of the defeat of the Young Pretender and his Jacobite cause at Culloden.[16] The readiness with which the Fellows of Queens' celebrated the anniversaries of royal accession days, coronations and birthdays during this period is a mark of their pleasure in holding celebrations as much as their loyalty to the crown, but the loyalty was doubtless sincere. There were a few Jacobites elsewhere in the university in the early 18th century, but in general the same enthusiasm and loyalty were evident there too.[17]

Other forms of political affiliation were more complicated. The pattern of British politics in the 18th century appears by no means as clear-cut as in the 17th or the 19th. It was the first age of party politics, in which the nation was divided in its allegiances to Whig and Tory, and the universities were equally caught up in this world.[18] It is difficult to define what the labels 'Whig' and 'Tory' meant in a university context.

[12] See above, pp. 151 – 2; Wordsworth (1874), 37.
[13] Book 7, fos.46, 50v, 56v, 65, 68 – 68v, 72, 76, 85.
[14] Wordsworth (1874), 37; Cooper, iv.72, 85; above, p. 136.
[15] Book 7, fos.100v, 103, 109v, 111 – 111v, 113v, 114v – 115, 119v, 121v, 122v, and *passim* Book 86 (register of oaths, 1715 – 1826); and see Shadwell (1912), ii.1 – 5.
[16] Book 7, f.229v.
[17] Wordsworth (1874), 40 – 9; Cooper, iv.108 – 113, 122 – 123, 139, 145. But c.f. Gascoigne, *Holy Alliance* (forthcoming), chapter IV.
[18] See e.g. Wordsworth (1874), 24 – 6.

In the early 18th century, Tory ideology tended to be high church, and uneasy over the Hanoverian succession; it was often tainted with Jacobitism. The Whigs were more latitudinarian, and enthusiastic supporters of George I and his successors. There was great hostility between supporters of the two factions. Eighteenth century parties were not rigidly defined and organised in the modern fashion, there was a good deal of tactical, power-politics, and both the Whigs and the Tories represented a complex, shifting mixture of personal alliance, tradition and ideals.[19] Party politics was all-pervasive, nonetheless, in church as well as state, a fact which caused Cambridge Fellows to look carefully to their political allegiances if they wished to progress to good ecclesiastical livings.[20]

Oxford remained strongly Tory; Cambridge acquired a reputation for Whiggism in the 18th century which persisted well into the 19th century, long after it had ceased to be deserved; the Tory party faded from the scene after the 1750s, not to re-emerge until the 19th century, but there was a wide range of views among those who saw themselves as Whigs during the interim.[21] The Cambridge Whigs did not have everything their own way, for party strife persisted there for some time after the Revolution of 1688, and party struggles attended several vice-chancellorship elections in the 1720s and 1730s, with the Tories victorious until the beginning of the reign of George II.[22] But by the middle of the century the university had fallen under the influence of the Whig duke of Newcastle, who was elected high steward in 1737 and chancellor in 1748. Newcastle fell from power at court in 1762, although he remained influential at Cambridge; after his death in 1768 a more conservative movement began to gather pace in the university and for the remainder of the 18th century both universities were assimilated to this new tendency, a successor to the old Tory movement which had become reconciled to the Hanoverians by the time of George III's accession.[23]

[19] Brooke (1985), 162 – 3, has a good summary of this; for many of the general remarks, I have used Speck (1977), and have also benefited from Christopher Brooke's advice, but the generalisations here are my own.
[20] Hence Byron's jibe about
'Fellows who dream on lawn or stalls,
The price of venal votes to pay', Byron (1963), 17, and see *ibid.*, 33.
[21] Wordsworth (1874), 41 – 5, 61 – 3, 80; Green (1969), 251 – 6. In the middle of the nineteenth century a German traveller in England observed that Cambridge was distinguished from Oxford by its Whiggism and emphasis on mathematics in the curriculum, Fontane (1979), i.605. I have employed rather crude labels in an attempt to differentiate between different types of Whig in these chapters.
[22] Roach (1959), iii.213, 220; Wordsworth (1874), 59 – 60. See Gascoigne, *Holy Alliance* (forthcoming), chapter IV, for the great strength of Toryism in early 18th century Cambridge.
[23] Green (1969), 256; Roach (1959), iii.220 – 1; Wordsworth (1874), 59 – 80; see Gascoigne, *Holy Alliance* (forthcoming), chapter VII.

Queens' appears to have been predominantly Whig throughout most of the century. Voting figures recorded at some of the general elections of the period — in those days, the universities each returned two MPs — demonstrate the strength of the allegiance: in 1727, 1734 and 1741 the college was firmly behind the court-Whig party; in 1784, when the political pattern had altered, the mood at Queens' also shifted, but there remained a strong body of traditional Whig support.[24]

The involvement of Queensmen in university politics also demonstrates this strong Whig sentiment. In 1706 Henry Plumptre, a Fellow of Queens', was prominent in securing the expulsion of the university's professor of music, Thomas Tudway, who was a staunch Tory, 'for scandalous and Toriacall [Tory] reflections on the Queen'.[25] The president of Queens' at that time was Henry James, who does not appear to have had any strong political allegiances.[26]

James' successor, John Davies (1717 – 31) was very clearly a Whig. He was elected president through the influence of Thomas Parker, earl of Macclesfield, a prominent Whig politician and supporter of the Hanoverian succession, and was created doctor of divinity by royal mandate at George I's visit to the university in 1717.[27] In 1719 he stood against the Tory master of Caius, Thomas Gooch, in the election for vice-chancellor, but was heavily defeated.[28] He was also a close friend and ally of Richard Bentley, the autocratic master of Trinity, who was a prominent university Whig. Davies was active in Bentley's campaign to succeed Henry James as Regius professor of divinity, and the only head of house to support Bentley in 1718 when a university grace was passed depriving him of his degrees.[29]

Davies was succeeded as president by William Sedgwick, a Whig although not apparently a very active one.[30] But during the presidency of Robert Plumptre (1760 – 88), the college had a reputation for

[24] Cooper, iv.194 and n. 6, 412; Book 80, f.23v.
[25] Gunther (1969), 281. Tudway was reinstated after making an apology in 1707, *DNB*.
[26] For James' religious views see above, chapter 11. Gascoigne (unpublished thesis, 1980), 7, n. 5, comments that he was one of the few Cambridge men to seek ecclesiastical advance under James II. He owed the presidency of Queens' to Charles II, and became Regius professor of divinity after the revolution of 1688, so that it seems he could adapt to every political climate.
[27] Davies had also been chaplain to John Moore, the latitudinarian bishop of Ely, Gascoigne, *Holy Alliance* (forthcoming), chapter IV; *DNB*.
[28] Cooper, iv.160; for Gooch, see Brooke (1985), 163 – 70.
[29] Monk (1833), 8 – 15; *Account* (1719), 5; White (1965), 160 and n. 1, 161.
[30] Sedgwick was a protégé of the Hardwicke family, who were prominent Whigs, see below, p. 180. An instance of the pettiness of party strife in Cambridge dates from Sedgwick's time: in 1748 the university was presented with a statue of Queen Anne, which was welcomed by Tories because she was considered to have been a supporter of the high church. The statue was placed in the senate house, but Daniel Wray, a former fellow-commoner of Queens', discovered that it was not of Anne at all, and led a Whig call for its expulsion, Nichols (1817), i.64 – 70.

attachment to Whig and reformist principles. Plumptre enjoyed the patronage of Lord Chancellor Hardwicke, a leading and influential Whig; he contributed to university collections of congratulatory verses on the occasion of George III's marriage in 1761, the birth of the Prince of Wales in 1762, and the end of the Seven Years' War in 1763.[31] In 1761 he provided 'a very fine entertainment' at Queens' for the duke of Newcastle, who was a close political ally of Hardwicke.[32] More importantly, he promoted his patron's cause actively within the university when required. Eighteenth century politicians were keen to extend their powers of patronage everywhere, including the universities, although the prizes there were not great. This was particularly evident during the period of Newcastle's influence, for Newcastle was an almost compulsive politician, an active university chancellor, and a diligent promoter of Whig ideals.[33] There are no signs though of external influence at Plumptre's election as president in 1760: Newcastle was quickly informed that 'a major part of the society . . . are determined in favour of Dr Plumptre', and he would have been delighted at the choice of a protégé of his political ally. It is moreover unlikely that the Fellows would have been put under pressure to please the chancellor: although the full extent of Newcastle's interference in the internal affairs of colleges has not yet been uncovered, it does seem that he exerted little influence over most mastership elections.[34]

The election of a new high steward of the university in 1764 gave Plumptre an excellent opportunity to demonstrate his loyalty and political skills. The two candidates for the post, which was commonly regarded as a stepping stone to the chancellorship, were the earl of Sandwich, secretary of state in Grenville's ministry, and Lord Hardwicke, son of Plumptre's patron and identified with the Whig opposition. Newcastle had fallen from power two years previously, and the election represented a trial of strength between the government Whigs and those still loyal to the university's chancellor.[35]

There was a fierce contest. Plumptre was a leading — perhaps the leading — campaigner for the Hardwicke-Newcastle cause, and Queens' was one of six colleges firmly on Hardwicke's side; Newcastle described David Hughes, a Fellow of Queens', as his 'honest friend'.[36] Various kinds of political skullduggery by both sides and an extremely close

[31] Cooper, iv.311 – 12; *DNB*. For the Plumptrees, see below, pp. 180 – 1.
[32] Newcastle's words, quoted in Winstanley (1922), 150; examples of the Hardwicke-Newcastle alliance can be found in Speck (1977), 229, 237, 240, 259.
[33] Winstanley (1922), 34 – 6, 48 – 9, 53 – 5.
[34] *ibid.*, 234 – 7. Plumptre was opposed by another Fellow, Owen Manning, Bowdler (1821), 49. But see also Gascoigne, *Holy Alliance* (forthcoming), chapter IV.
[35] The events are described in Winstanley (1922), 55 – 139 (revised and expanded from Winstanley (1910), appendix II).
[36] Winstanley (1922), 61, 104, 61 – 139.

contest led to a chaotic election which was resolved only by legal proceedings in the court of King's Bench. Hardwicke was the victor, but the election had shown that Newcastle's influence in the university was on the wane, and after his death in 1768 discreet enquiries undertaken by Plumptre on behalf of Hardwicke showed clearly that the high steward had no hope of succeeding Newcastle as chancellor.[37]

Liberal and reformist Whigs continued to be numerous and influential in Cambridge for some while after this, despite being increasingly outgunned in political battles within the university.[38] Their continuing strength was most apparent in the near defeat in the senate of a proposal to present a loyal address from the university to the king condemning the American rebels in 1775.[39] But the liberals lost much of their ground throughout the country and in the university after the outbreak of the French Revolution in 1789, which brought reformist ideals into great disfavour. Henry Gunning, the university's esquire bedell, who sympathised with the radicals, observed that 'in a very short time scarcely a Whig was to be found among the resident members of the University'. Even those who were initially enthusiastic about the Revolution became disgusted by the bloodshed which followed.[40] At Queens' they lost ground still further with the election of the reactionary Isaac Milner to be president following Plumptre's death in 1788. It is a curious and inexplicable phenomenon that a society with such a strong reforming tradition should have elected such a man, even allowing for the signs of more conservative sentiment among the Fellows in the 1780s. Milner was to be president for 32 years.[41]

The university gave financial and moral support to the wars against the French which followed the Revolution. It was exempted from some, but not all of the taxes introduced to pay for the wars.[42] The Queens'

---

[37] *ibid.*, 137 – 44.
[38] See Schneider (1957), chapter V.
[39] *ibid.*, 117, 119. Schneider claims that Queens' voted unanimously against the loyal address, but the references which are cited in this context make no mention of the matter. In fact Queens' was strangely divided over the address, with Plumptre, acting under the influence of his patron Hardwicke, abandoning his liberal principles to support it, to the outrage of some of his former allies; other senior Queensmen such as Russell Plumptre and David Hughes were opposed to the address; see Gascoigne, *Holy Alliance* (forthcoming), chapter VII. I am grateful to John Gascoigne for showing me his notes on Plumptre and the voting pattern in Queens'.
[40] Gunning (1854), i.189 – 90, 290 – 1; Gunning tends to employ the term 'Whig' to denote the more liberal faction with which he identified, and the anachronistic 'Tory' for the conservative Whig elements. See also Schneider (1957), chapter V, for the continuance of a liberal, reformist movement in the university. See Gascoigne, *Holy Alliance* (forthcoming), chapter VII, for political and religious developments in Cambridge after the outbreak of the French Revolution.
[41] For Milner's influence on the college's political and religious outlook see below, pp. 161 – 2, 170ff.
[42] Shadwell (1912), ii.232, 236 – 9, 241 – 7, 261, 269, 273, 295, 300.

accounts contain several entries for payments of government and university levies, together with voluntary donations, for such purposes as raising militia, and hiring seamen; in 1798 it gave £200 — a considerable sum for a college — to the Bank of England as 'a Voluntary Subscription for the Defence of the Country'.[43] The college also made charitable donations to victims of the Revolution and the wars: French émigrés, and widows and orphans of seamen killed in their country's service.[44] In September 1803, amidst widespread fear of Napoleon's projected invasion, the university formed a volunteer corps from its own members. About 180 men took part, from 15 colleges, including 10 from Queens'. The colleges allowed their men to drill for one hour each day under the direction of a professional soldier, but would not permit the creation of a more regular armed force.[45]

Cambridge men were of course steadfastly loyal to the crown and constitution during the many years of war — lasting peace was not achieved until Napoleon's final defeat in 1815 — but at a time of such great tension and extreme feeling those of liberal or reformist sympathies were in danger of being labelled republicans by reactionary and conservative elements. Feelings grew stronger as the Revolution degenerated into a series of bloody purges.[46] In the spring of 1793 William Frend, a Fellow of Jesus, published a pamphlet advocating peace between republicans and anti-republicans, and attacking conservative attitudes.[47] Frend was soon ejected from his fellowship, and a case was brought against him in the vice-chancellor's court; the vice-chancellor for that year was Isaac Milner, an implacable opponent of Frend's ideals. Gunning, who was sympathetic towards Frend, was critical of Milner's method of proceeding: he alleged that Frend was not allowed to see a copy of the case against him, and that in the vice-chancellor's court itself,

'it was apparent from the first, that the Vice-Chancellor was determined to convict, otherwise the blunders of the Promoter were so gross and so palpable, that he must have been defeated. In the examination of witnesses, the forms established in courts of justice

---

[43] Book 8, fos.130, 132v, 133v, 136v, 139 – 139v, 142v (and see Gunning (1854), i.317); CB (1787 – 1832), 12.4.1794; there are similar examples at St John's, Howard (1935), 145 – 6.

[44] CB (1787 – 1832), 26.3.1796, 11.1.1798; Book 8, fos.124v, 126v, 135v, 139v.

[45] Gunning (1854), ii.187 – 8; CR (17.5.1900), 317. Perhaps the authorities felt a regular force would cause problems of discipline.

[46] Gunning (1854), i.276 – 9.

[47] Gunning (1854), i.280; Schneider (1957), 207. For Frend's political and religious outlook, see Schneider (1957), 98 – 9, 119, 131, 137 – 9, 145, 149, 155, 185 – 6. Knight (1971) is a biography of Frend, but is unreliable. The case is discussed in Gascoigne, *Holy Alliance* (forthcoming), chapter VII.

were constantly violated, and every objection brought forward by Frend, whether founded on the statutes of the University, or on the maxims of the civil law, were [sic] overruled by Dr. Milner'.[48]

Although the undergraduates were largely on Frend's side, he had scarcely any support among the senior members, and was expelled from the university; his appeal against the sentence, to a committee dominated by Milner's friends, was doomed to failure.[49]

For Milner, Frend's expulsion had achieved 'the ruin of the Jacobinical party' in the university, but Gunning suspected that the president of Queens' was deliberately blowing the affair out of proportion.[50] It seems that Milner hoped thereby to bring his own actions to wider public notice, and perhaps to advance his career: the prime minister, William Pitt, was one of the MPs for the university at this time.[51] There were also rumours in circulation that five university men, including Frend, were involved in treasonable correspondence with the French revolutionary government; this seems to have been another story dreamed up by overexcited imaginations. The supposed conspirators included a Fellow of Queens', Martin Naylor, whom Gunning described as 'a man of coarse and rough manners', and 'in the habit of using violent language when talking on political subjects'. Milner was said to enjoy drawing Naylor out on such topics, laughing at the vehemence with which he criticised conservative views. Such behaviour shows that Milner for one cannot have believed Naylor to have been involved in any underhand political acts, and he was nominated by the college to serve as senior proctor in 1797 – 8.[52]

But another Fellow of Queens', Thomas Fyshe Palmer, was expelled from the college in January 1794 'on account of his seditious Conduct'.[53] Palmer was a non-resident Fellow who had become a Unitarian minister in Scotland, and was active in the movement for political reform. In 1793 he had been involved in the publication of a handbill complaining against excessive war taxation, and calling for short parliaments and universal suffrage. The government over-reacted: Palmer was tried for treason and sentenced to seven years' transportation to Botany Bay, despite attempts in parliament to have the sentence reversed.[54] Like William Frend, Palmer seems to have been a victim of political hysteria.

---

[48] Gunning (1854), i.291 – 8.
[49] ibid., i.291 – 307, for the details of the case; see also Schneider (1957), 207 – 9.
[50] Gunning (1854), i.308 – 11.
[51] See ibid., i.323 – 6, ii.105 – 6. For further illustrations of Milner's feelings, see Milner (1842), 83, 106 – 8, 113, 126 – 7, 161 – 2. Milner was not just cynically presenting himself as a conservative: he was genuinely opposed to reform.
[52] Gunning (1854), i.309 – 11.
[53] CB (1787 – 1832), 16.1.1794, partly reprinted in AC (Palmer).
[54] DNB. For non-resident Fellows see below, pp. 185 – 6.

Milner and 12 of the Fellows of Queens' voted for his expulsion in January 1794, but another 3 (including Martin Naylor), wished to postpone a decision, and a fourth would not vote.[55] Palmer survived the term of his sentence, but died on the journey home.[56]

Politics, and Milner, also took a hand in an election to a fellowship at Trinity Hall in 1793. To the great astonishment of many in the university, a talented internal candidate, Francis Wrangham, was rejected in favour of John Vickers, a Fellow of Queens' and protégé of Milner. Wrangham's failure was political: he was known to be a liberal and he had supported William Frend, and a rumour was put about that he was a republican. The tutor of Trinity Hall was known to be deeply under Milner's influence, and a third Fellow of Queens', Thomas Bourdillon, migrated there in 1795; junior Fellows of Trinity Hall were said to speak of their college as the 'Fief of Queens' '.[57] Queens' itself was to reflect Milner's politically conservative and low church outlook well into the 19th century.

Religion

The religious life of late 17th and 18th century Cambridge lacked the passion which had been characteristic of the century and a half between the Reformation and the collapse of the English Revolution.[58] At the Restoration, it has been argued, the Church of England 'had taken on its celebrated rôle as the vehicle for social and political conservatism in the life of the nation'; the alliance between parson and country squire had been forged.[59] It has been shown how Cambridge became a bastion of conservative high churchmanship, excluded dissenters and discouraged liberal or reformist notions. Anglicans believed that such actions protected the integrity and purity of their church against those who wished to corrupt or subvert it, but the wave of reaction left religious life and thought in the university considerably less dynamic than it had

---

[55] Above, n. 53.

[56] DNB; Gentleman's Magazine (1803), ii.1254; Dyer (1814), ii.159 – 60. Two other notable political radicals of the period had been students at Queens' in its reforming phase under Plumptre: Hamilton Rowan, the United Irishman; and Christopher Wyvill, founder of the Yorkshire Association; see Gascoigne, Holy Alliance (forthcoming), chapter VII; DNB for further details of both of these men. Robert Plumptre's daughter, Anna, also held radical views at this time and was a staunch supporter of Napoleon, DNB.

[57] CB (1787 – 1832), 14.1.1794, 11.1.1798; Pryme (1870), 246; Gunning (1854), ii.17 – 38; Crawley (1976), 137 – 9.

[58] See above, chapter 11. The 18th century was not without some intense theological debate, though; see Gascoigne, Holy Alliance (forthcoming), chapter V.

[59] Beddard (1979), 156 – 9, 166.

been before.[60] Ten years after Charles II's return from exile the future master of St Catharine's, John Eachard, a staunch Anglican, complained that the universities were producing dull, inadequate clergymen, thereby undermining many of the benefits of the church settlement of the 1660s; but even this constructive criticism brought down a torrent of protest.[61] In such an atmosphere, it was inevitable that religious life should lose its vigour, and even atrophy.

Fierce religious conflicts were therefore largely absent from the 18th century university. Attempts at religious reform were effectively stifled by the academic-ecclesiastical establishment, but towards the end of the century a new and different expression of frustration with the existing order broke out successfully in Cambridge in the shape of the evangelical movement, which was spectacularly successful in Queens'.

Henry Gunning observed that during Robert Plumptre's presidency, Queens' was 'distinguished for its attachment to Civil and Religious liberty'.[62] This was apparent in a campaign in the early 1770s to free university members from the obligation to subscribe to the Church of England's 39 articles. Opposition to such subscriptions had been mounting in clerical circles for some time, and in 1771 a group of clergymen formed a committee to organise a petition to parliament calling for their abolition. There was much sympathy at Cambridge for their aims, and according to a historian in the early 19th century, George Dyer, 'Queen's-men were then foremost among the petitioning clergy, who met at Archbishop Tenison's library, for ameliorating the subscription to articles'.[63] All the resident Fellows of Queens' were said to have signed the petition, and virtually all the students.[64]

An attempt within the university to abolish subscriptions there having failed,[65] a petition from some 50 undergraduates was sent to the vice-chancellor in December 1771; it was presented by Charles Crawford, a fellow-commoner at Queens'. Crawford was something of a trouble-maker,[66] and it is possible that his involvement in this dispute was from love of mischief, although the other petitioners were quite sincere: they claimed that the burden of their other academic work gave them no time to study sufficient theology to understand the 39 articles fully, and called for release from the obligation to subscribe, or at least help in satisfying their consciences over the contents of the articles.[67] The

[60] See chapter 11.
[61] Eachard (1670) and (1671), criticised by Shelton (1671) and Standish (1672).
[62] Gunning (1854), i.262 – 3.
[63] Winstanley (1935), 304 – 5; Dyer (1814), ii.145.
[64] Winstanley (1935), 304 – 5; Milner (1842), 7; Dyer (1814), ii.158 – 9. See Gascoigne, *Holy Alliance* (forthcoming), chapter VII.
[65] Winstanley (1935), 305.
[66] See below, pp. 200 – 1.
[67] Cooper, iv.363.

petition was rejected, and the parliamentary campaign failed also, but in 1773 the university introduced a measure of reform by limiting the subscriptions of students taking degrees to a declaration that they were *bona fide* members of the Church of England.[68]

Some of the reformers were suspected of Unitarianism, and some did later become Unitarians. Two Fellows of Queens' did so: one was Thomas Fyshe Palmer, in Dyer's opinion, 'a man of an acute mind and ardent disposition'. Palmer had leaned towards Methodism before becoming a Unitarian, when no longer a resident Fellow.[69] The other was John Hammond, who became a Unitarian after leaving the college in 1785.[70]

Other useful evidence of religious life at Queens' is in very short supply.[71] Large sums of money were spent on the chapel at different times, which may indicate extravagance rather than piety. In 1710 the college installed a new organ, costing over £164.[72] In 1744 a new organ loft was added.[73] Between 1773 and 1775 the interior of the chapel was refurbished by the local architect James Essex; a room above the buttery was used as a temporary chapel during the refit.[74] The college had to borrow £300, and sequester the salary from a vacant fellowship, to pay for the work.[75]

As well as receiving benefactions for the purchase of college livings — some of which were considerable — Queens' also received a few donations specifically for the chapel.[76] A former Fellow, Edward Kemp, gave £300 in 1671 '*in usum sacelli*', which was put towards the purchase of a rent charge two years later; £16 which accrued from this annually

[68] *ibid.*, iv.363, 366; Winstanley (1935), 306 – 14.
[69] Winstanley (1935), 305 – 6; Dyer (1814), ii.159. The prosecutor at Palmer's trial warned the jury that the accused was 'a clergyman of that description whose principles are as hostile to the religion of this country, as to the established government of it', Gascoigne (1986), 30 – 1.
[70] *AC*. Knight (1971), 105 – 6, mistakenly asserts that Hammond was driven out in Milner's purge of nonconformists: in fact his fellowship was declared to be vacant, on account of his having married, in 1785 – three years before Milner became president, CB (1734 – 87), f.128v.
[71] Queensmen do not seem to have reached the highest offices in the church with the same frequency as in previous centuries. Two presidents — Henry James and Robert Plumptre — held university chairs in divinity, but neither was a major theologian.
[72] Book 12, entry for 1709/10; Book 80, f.10v (first pagination), p. 9 (third pagination); Book 7, fos.81v, 82v.
[73] CB (1734 – 87), f.36v.
[74] W&C ii.40 – 2, iii.543; RCHM, 169, 170, 173; CB (1734 – 87), fos.90v, 91v, 96v – 97; Book 8, f.66v; Book 73, f.73. But Loggan's 1685 print shows garret windows above the chapel, which suggests that the false ceiling, generally thought to have been put in by Essex, may date from much earlier; I owe this observation to Robin Walker. For Essex's other work at Queens' see below, pp. 311 – 13.
[75] CB (1734 – 87), fos.98v – 99.
[76] For livings, see below, pp. 165 – 70.

was paid to the dean of chapel.[77] Another Fellow, Thomas Edwards, gave £20 in 1678 towards the purchase of a rent charge, intending it to yield £1 *per annum* for providing the chapel with 'waxlights'.[78]

The records which survive do not enable us to draw any conclusions about the nature of worship in the college chapel. With a large proportion of the fellowship now non-resident, and many Fellows' places left vacant on financial grounds, the duty of conducting services devolved upon a small number of active Fellows.[79] The dean was paid by the college for reading in place of absent Fellows at services, and in 1768 it was ordered that Fellows who did not preach commemoration sermons when it was their turn to do so had to pay an additional amount to their substitutes over and above that already allowed by the college.[80] In 1766 the college regulations against coming late to chapel were redefined more carefully, but it is not clear how great a problem this had become: such regulations were always tightened up from time to time, and there is no other evidence of slackness in religious performance.[81]

The chapel was also used to perform wedding services. Until 1753 marriages held in college chapels were just as valid legally as those held in parish and other churches, and there are 140 recorded marriages in the chapel at Queens' between 1723 and 1753.[82] These were mostly of local people of humble backgrounds, and the services were led by Fellows of the college. Four college servants were married there between 1742 and 1752, three of them by the president, William Sedgwick.[83] Essex's refit of the chapel in the 1770s also included digging a burial vault beneath the chapel, although this was little used.[84]

All colleges owned advowsons, which they had acquired through benefactions and by purchase; some of the wealthier and better endowed colleges possessed a large number of these, which had always been a feature of the collegiate system. It was customary to present college Fellows to these livings. The value of livings — and hence the incumbents' salaries — varied greatly.[85]

---

[77] Book 80, f.3 (second pagination).

[78] *ibid.*, f.18 (second pagination).

[79] For non-residence, see below, pp. 185 – 6.

[80] CB (1734 – 87), fos.57v, 80, 101. In 1758, the dean received half a guinea per week for reading for absent Fellows; in 1777, he received 14s per week for this duty.

[81] CB (1734 – 87), f.75v.

[82] Weddings may well have been performed there before this time, but there are no records of them before the 18th century.

[83] Williams (1939 – 42), 13 – 20, prints the register, with comments; the original is in Box 101. Williams suggests that the services were for parishioners of parishes which had Fellows of the college as incumbents.

[84] It contains the coffins of two presidents (Isaac Milner and Henry Godfrey), and an eighteenth century Fellow, David Hughes, *Dial* (1948), 31.

[85] See *Clergyman's Intelligencer* (1745).

Although the church in the 18th century is thought to have declined in popularity, and though it was certainly no longer held in such high esteem by the laity, the clerical profession does seem to have remained attractive, and as the century wore on there was a growing surplus of clergymen. There was also an increasing tendency for incumbents to serve for long periods in the same livings, and patronage became more important than ever in securing well endowed appointments. In the early part of the century many Oxford and Cambridge colleges began to buy up livings in order to place their Fellows in good positions, and to ensure a steady turnover among their fellowships. For young scholars without family connections or other backing, college livings were the best chance of a well paid ecclesiastical position.[86]

Queens' also increased the number of livings in its possession at this time. Thomas Fuller recorded four livings belonging to the college in his survey of 1655, three in Cambridgeshire and one in Wiltshire.[87] Almost a century after Fuller, Edmund Carter listed eight Queens' livings, with new acquisitions in Norfolk, Nottinghamshire, and Essex.[88] This was a relatively modest number for a Cambridge college.[89] The three local livings were St Botolph's in Cambridge, Oakington and Little Eversden. The right to present to St Botolph's had been acquired from Corpus Christi in 1460; Oakington and Eversden were acquired in Elizabeth's reign.[90] The college began to acquire livings further afield immediately before the civil war with the two Wiltshire benefices of Newton-Toney and Great Cheverell, bequeathed by a former president, John Davenant, in 1641; but it did not present to them until some time after. They were in the diocese of Salisbury, where Davenant was bishop from 1621 until his death. Certain conditions, typical of such benefactions, were attached to his bequest: only Fellows of Queens' were to be presented to the livings, and they were to reside there — in the case of Great Cheverell, for at least nine months of the year.[91]

At some time during the 1670s the college received the rectory of Hickling in Nottinghamshire, also as a benefaction, from Sarah Bardsey, widow of George Bardsey, a former Fellow who had been ejected in

---

[86] Holmes (1982), 83 – 108; Gascoigne, 'Mathematics', 562 – 3. In the early 1730s there was a good deal of lay opposition to the buying up of advowsons by colleges, Best (1964), 102 – 3.

[87] Fuller, *History*, 121. The 19th century editor mistakes the Wiltshire living for one in Essex, acquired in the 18th century.

[88] Carter (1753), 184 (including a second Wiltshire living, not recorded by Fuller though acquired at the same time as the first).

[89] Ten owned more — some of them a great deal more — and only five owned less, *Clergyman's Intelligencer* (1745).

[90] Searle, 66 – 8, 75 – 7, 295, 319 – 20, 377; Goodman (1922), 99 – 102.

[91] Book 80, f.31 (second pagination); *VCH Wiltshire* x.49.

1644 and died before the Restoration.[92] Two Norfolk livings (which because of their low value were joined together as one preferment), and a rectory at Sandon in Essex, were acquired in the early 1730s.[93] These acquisitions were made possible by large-scale benefactions.[94] At about the same time the college also received the living of Trimden in Durham, which was not recorded in a list of college and university livings published in 1745, nor in Carter's account of 1753.[95] Perhaps there was some ambiguity about the college's right of presentation, for in 1781 its nominee was resisted by a local family which thought Queens' had given up all interest in the living and believed it had bought the advowson. The college decided to contest this, but without much enthusiasm, for it decided in 1782 that any expenses incurred in litigation should not be borne by Queens' but by its nominee to the living. The result of the dispute is not clear, but the living does not feature again in the college records, which suggests that the case was lost.[96] In 1762 Queens' had been similarly fearful of a dispute, or even a lawsuit, over its right to present to Sandon, and decided that the Fellow who accepted the living might give it up at any time during his 'year of grace' and retain his fellowship if he did not think it worth having.[97]

In 1767 the college agreed to exchange Great Cheverell with the earl of Radnor for 'a Living of rather superior value, in a healthfull Country within a hundred miles of Cambridge'. Radnor was to find and suggest suitable livings for Queens' to choose. In 1769 the college agreed to take a living in Hampshire in exchange, but the proposal must have fallen through, for in 1772 it approved the rectory of Seagrave in Leicestershire, apparently worth much more than Great Cheverell. An act of parliament was required to complete the deal, since colleges were forbidden by law to alienate property: this was passed in 1774.[98]

College livings were filled by Fellows until recent times: the custom only began to decline after the university reforms in the second half of the 19th century and did not die out until the 20th.[99] It was the custom in

---

[92] OPR, f.152v; Book 80, fos.65 – 7 (second pagination); see also Book 6, f.195. A dispute with Sarah Bardsey's heirs meant that Queens' had to wait until 1686 before receiving the title deeds.
[93] CB (1734 – 87), f.7v (c.f. Carter (1753), 184); Book 29; Gray, 224; Book 80, fos.14, 18v, 41 (second pagination).
[94] Above, n. 93, and also Book 80, fos.29, 58, 84, 88 (second pagination); Book 79, f.96.
[95] CB (1734 – 87), f.2v; Clergyman's Intelligencer (1745) (but this omits other Queens' livings); Carter (1753), 184.
[96] CB (1734 – 87), fos.113v – 114, 117.
[97] CB (1734 – 87), fos.66, 68v. The 'year of grace' was the first year from presentation to a living, during which the Fellow was permitted to keep his fellowship, but at the end of which he had to resign; see Winstanley (1935), 377, n. 131.
[98] CB (1734 – 87), fos.76, 81, 90, 94 – 94v; VCH Wiltshire x.49; there is a printed copy of the act in Box 102.
[99] Formal presentations to livings from the 17th and 18th centuries can be found in OPR and CB (1734 – 87).

most colleges to offer vacancies to the senior Fellow in holy orders.[100] In the 17th century, Queens' did not follow this practice invariably, although seniors were given preference *ceteris paribus*. Henry Walters lost the opportunity to be the first Fellow of Queens' to be presented to Great Cheverell to a junior 'both in standing and as a Fellow and less deserveing', because he 'was in Kent at that time and had been lame for severall yeares'. In 1680 Nathaniel Shute was preferred to Michael Belk for the same living, because although Belk was the senior by several years and 'earnestly desir'd' the place, 'he livid soe very irregularly'.[101] Charles Farish failed to secure nomination to the vacancy at Newton Toney in 1809, apparently as the result of some misdemeanour, although he had asked that credit might be given him that he would live in future 'according to the usual tenor of my life, rather than according to the worst part of it'. He added that he was already 42 years old, 'a time of life of which Cowley says, that if a man wishes to settle in the world he has no time to lose'.[102]

Elections to livings, like those to masterships and fellowships, could be subjected to the influence of powerful outsiders, although we have only one example of this: in 1640 Edward Martin was put under such pressure to present George Bardsey to the vacant living of Little Eversden; Bardsey and Martin had quarrelled over the presentation the previous year, and the place had already been allocated to another. Martin was now forced to halt the appointment 'though with great hazard of the Colledge peace', and tried to secure agreement among the other Fellows for Bardsey to receive the place instead, but abandoned the effort because it had reopened old disputes between Bardsey and several of the other Fellows.[103]

In practice Fellows were obliged to resign from the college in order to take up college benefices, except at local livings, where performance of priestly duties does not appear to have been incompatible with college residence, and the stipends were low enough to permit Fellows to hold them concurrently with their fellowships in accordance with the

---

[100] Chadwick (1970 – 2), ii.208; Gascoigne, 'Mathematics', 563. Henry James, who left over £600 for the purchase of a benefice, directed that the living should be at the disposal of the president alone, instead of the usual choice by the Fellows, and that it could be bestowed upon any of the eight senior Fellows in holy orders, see Book 80, f.84 (second pagination); CB (1734 – 87), f.32. In 1737 the college ordered that no Fellow (apart from the law and physic Fellows) was to be allowed to claim any college living by virtue of his seniority unless he had been in holy orders for at least 6 months before the living became vacant, or unless the other Fellows in orders relinquished their claim, CB (1734 – 87), f.18v.

[101] Book 80, f.31 (second pagination).

[102] Box 16/10.ii.

[103] This is a rather complicated story, however, and there may be more to it than our source, Martin's account, suggests, MS 502; see also OPR, fos.131, 150.

regulations in the college statutes.[104] John Davies noted in 1731 that incumbents of college livings were expected to spend at least nine months of the year in their parishes, but that it was college practice to allow non-residence during the 'year of grace'. This practice permitted Walter Post to be nominated a proctor by Queens' in 1731 – 2, his first year at the living of Great Cheverell, although there was opposition to this within the college, and Davies' successor, William Sedgwick, was sure the action was 'not reasonable'; Sedgwick was also unhappy that Post, who had not yet taken his BD degree, should have secured one of the best college livings.[105]

It was important that Fellows should move into college livings at regular intervals, to ensure a steady turnover in the profession and thereby encourage young men of talent to come to Queens' to study. In 1797 Queens' took legal advice concerning its living at Eversden. The living was by tradition tenable with a fellowship, on account of its low income, and this privilege had been protected by the college.[106] By the end of the 18th century, however, the value of the living had increased to the extent that it was no longer desirable to the college that it should be held with a fellowship. The college's legal counsel saw no legal obstacle to a change in the regulations, and fully agreed that the college's well being depended to a large extent upon 'promoting the succession of the fellows, and speedily rewarding persons of merit and distinction'.[107] At about the same time Queens' was seeking to augment the income of one of its smaller livings 'so as to take off a Fellow', and it was alleged then that between 1776 and the beginning of 1797 not one Fellow of the college had left his fellowship for a college living. Queens' was in no doubt that, as a result, it was losing good students and potential students to other colleges which could offer better opportunities.[108]

The college was concerned therefore to provide for the future ecclesiastical careers of its Fellows, but not everyone supported this aim. In 1759 a former Fellow, Richard Davies, complained that Fellows in colleges should not be made to take holy orders, for they were forced thereby to commit themselves to the church too soon, before they could

---

[104] For example, Doket and Milner were both rectors of St Botolph's while serving as president, above, pp. 66 – 7; Milner (1842), 13. For the statutory regulations see above, pp. 74, 83. Incomes of college livings are listed in Fuller, *History*, 121; *Clergyman's Intelligencer* (1745); Carter (1753), 184.

[105] Book 80, f.30v (second pagination); *AC* (Post).

[106] Book 62, 104; Box 15/15; CB (1734 – 87), f.69v. For the living's income, see Fuller, *History*, 121; *Clergyman's Intelligencer* (1745), 173; Carter (1753), 184.

[107] Box 95 (Serjeant le Blanc's opinion). An act of 1736 restricting the number of advowsons a college could own to no more than half the number of its Fellows was repealed in 1805 because it had been found to harm colleges 'by rendering the Succession [of Fellows] too slow', Shadwell (1912), ii.25 – 6, 279 – 80.

[108] Box 95 (Hughes bequest).

be sure of their true inclinations. 'I need not remark', Davies continued, 'with how violent a biass necessity may hereafter draw him; not to quit hold of his only subsistence: And thus the Soldier of Christ, instead of coming in as a Volunteer, is entered a pressed man into the Service'.[109]

Almost nothing is known about the performance of divine service and the general quality of religious life at these parishes. There was no question of the college visiting its benefices as it did its estates, and it had no business to do so; strictly speaking, this was the concern of the ecclesiastical authorities of the dioceses in which the livings were situated. There was a closer relationship with the three local parishes of St Botolph's, Oakington, and Little Eversden, and the college regularly paid for repairs to the fabric of the churches there.[110] But it did not exercise any closer controls. A visitation by the archdeacon of Ely in 1685 noted that whilst the church of St Botolph's was in adequate condition, that at Oakington was 'in great neglect like a Barn or Dovehouse', and there was little evidence of any religious zeal.[111] In the late 18th century many parishes close to Cambridge were served by Fellows of colleges who merely rode out on Sundays and often disappeared during the vacations; these were livings with poor stipends, which could not support a full-time minister.[112]

The evangelical movement

Towards the end of the 18th century there arose in Cambridge in the form of the evangelical movement a strong reaction to the lukewarm quality of much of the university's religious life. During the 1770s and 1780s the movement consisted of a small, shifting group of undergraduates who were partly inspired by local clergymen. Slowly, it infiltrated the college establishments, principally Magdalene at first, but subsequently it was strongest at Queens'.[113] Its spiritual leader in Cambridge was Charles Simeon, a Fellow of King's, but its position in the university was greatly improved by the more worldly activities of Isaac Milner, the president of Queens'.[114]

[109]   Davies (1759), 20 – 1.
[110]   e.g. Book 4, fos.57v, 165, 182v; Book 5, fos.5, 39v, 57, 59, 185 – 185v; Book 6, f.26v; Book 8, f.205v, 208, 253v; CB (1734 – 87), f.12.
[111]   But one reason for the lack of zeal seems to have been the large number of nonconformists in the parish; this could hardly be blamed on the college, Bradshaw (1874 – 5), 352, 356 – 7.
[112]   Owen (1967/8), 375. Some colleges were slow to make repairs even when pressed by the bishop, ibid., 378.
[113]   Green (1964), 224 – 238. The evangelical movement in Cambridge is also discussed in detail in Gascoigne, Holy Alliance (forthcoming), chapters VII – VIII.
[114]   For some brief accounts of Simeon and his significance, see Elliot-Binns (1953), 363 – 5; Green (1964), 241 – 5, 251; Brown (1961), 292 – 5.

Milner arrived in Queens' as a student in 1770 and became a Fellow six years later. When Robert Plumptre died in 1788 he was elected president, at the age of 38.[115] As has been noticed earlier, the reasons for his election remain unclear, since even at that stage it was apparent that his political and religious views were very different from those of his predecessor. It may be that he was chosen as a 'strong man' who would improve the college's discipline,[116] but this can only be speculation.

Milner was not the first evangelical to come from Queens'. One of the early evangelical influences on Cambridge undergraduates was Henry Venn, who from 1771 to 1797 was rector of Yelling in Huntingdonshire, only 12 miles from Cambridge. Many students and young ministers journeyed there to hear him preach, just as Puritans had ridden out to hear Samuel Fairclough and other preachers in the early 17th century. Venn was a former Fellow of Queens' who had subsequently been won over to evangelical ideals in the early 1750s. During the period of his incumbency at Yelling he made several trips to Cambridge to promote the cause there, and observed the growing influence of Simeon's preaching on the undergraduates.[117]

Evangelical doctrine contained nothing that was new theologically: it was in essence reactionary — a reaction against the rationalist theology of the age, and its corrupt, decadent spirit.[118] In 1793 Milner measured the level of religious enthusiasm at the time of the Reformation against that of the late 18th century, finding the latter woefully deficient: 'Then, persons of rank and eminence, some of them at least, attended to the Gospel; now, in general, the lower orders only regard such things, and the great and the high have, all over Europe, forgotten that they have souls'; in 1800 he spoke of the 'lamentable truth, that the bishops of our country do not understand the real state of religion'.[119] Evangelicals promoted the idea of justification through faith alone characteristic of the early Protestant reformers, and in consequence stressed the need for regular reading of scriptures for personal guidance. William Mandell, an evangelical Fellow of Queens' under Milner, described the doctrine of 'election' in a sermon as 'one of those deep and mysterious topics, whose consideration, for the most part, is not profitable, and which, in consequence, it is in general better to avoid', and he advised his audience 'not to perplex your minds with unavailing and dangerous speculations respecting the inscrutable counsels of Jehovah. They are

---

[115]   For biographical details, see *DNB*.
[116]   See below, p. 201. He was opposed by Thomas Jordan, Fellow and vicar of Oakington, Bowdler (1821), 49.
[117]   Venn (1834), 14 – 15, 18 – 22, 29, 50 – 1, 187, 193, 258, 352, 375, 408, 423. For Fairclough, see above, p. 41.
[118]   The general remarks on evangelical character and ideas are from Dyer (1814), ii.145 – 6; Green (1964), 222 – 4.
[119]   Milner (1842), 100, 219, and see *ibid.*, 173.

not proper subjects for inquiry'. In 1798 Milner complained of the *'rational* way of preaching' adopted by many of the clergy.[120]

The movement tended towards austerity; social worldliness was deprecated. Hence Thomas Thomason, another evangelical Fellow of Queens', warned of the corrupting aspects of college life: 'Here is every thing that can contribute to the ease and comfort of life. Whatever pampers the appetite and administers fuel to sloth and indolence is to be found in abundance. Nothing is left to want or desire'.[121] Evangelicals were expected to show a high standard of personal conduct. They were staunch supporters of missionary work.[122] In addition, they were zealously anti-Catholic, and conservative, even reactionary, in their political outlook. Milner, for example, opposed fiercely the slightest sign of anything which he deemed to hint of Jacobinism, and resisted to the utmost moves by reformers to allow non-conformists and Roman Catholics to study at the university.[123] The movement was characterised by its intolerence of other points of view. As one historian has commented:

'Their forthright condemnation of those with whom they disagreed was on occasions lacking in Christian charity. Their genuine holiness and faith had for more worldly Christians a saccharine quality which made them turn with relief from high-minded prayer meetings and good causes to more secular pursuits. Even their jocularity could possess a rebarbative brightness, and their charm appear synthetic'.[124]

Their smug spiritual pride was satirised in a poem by Byron, who was

---

[120] Mandell (1819), 16; Milner (1842), 172.
[121] Quoted in Sargent (1823), 85. In this context might perhaps be noted the decision of the college in 1794 to melt down various items of plate, including five tankards, three pint pots, a punch bowl and ladle, and to replace them with items including 'a Silver Tea Urn and Teapot and a Silver Coffee Urn for the use of the Lodge', CB (1787 – 1832), 8.3.1794. A description of Cambridge in 1827 noted of Queens' that 'The Simeonitish [evangelical] members are as famous for abstinence from wine, as for excessive bouts of tea-drinking', Wright (1827), ii.181.
[122] See below, pp. 267 – 8.
[123] Green (1964), 240 – 1; Milner (1842), 344; Furneaux (1974), 210. In 1818 there was a controversy over the appointment of Sir J. E. Smith, who was neither a member of the university, nor of the Church of England, to lecture as deputy for the professor of botany: 14 college tutors, including William Mandell of Queens', refused to allow their pupils to attend his lectures, despite the bishop of Carlisle urging Milner to put Smith's scientific skills above other considerations, Gunther (1969), 396 – 7; Wordsworth (1968), 212 and n. Cooper, iv.521, n. 1. In 1806 Milner opposed a candidate to be the university's MP in place of Pitt because, although he was opposed to the slave trade, he was a supporter of Catholic emancipation, 'so replete with dangers' in Milner's view, Milner (1842), 316 – 18.
[124] Green (1964), 224.

an undergraduate at Trinity during the evangelical heyday in Cambridge.[125]

Evangelicalism did not make much headway in Queens' while Plumptre was president. Milner was apparently the only student to refuse to sign the petition against subscription to the 39 articles, but he was not regarded as an evangelical before the early 1780s, when he was already a Fellow.[126] Milner's close friend William Wilberforce, the campaigner against the slave trade, believed that his evangelical views did not come out into the open until a serious illness in 1789;[127] but he had nailed his colours to the mast three years earlier, when he had kept his act for the degree of BD on the theme of justification by faith alone. Henry Venn recorded that the schools were crowded with those who had come to hear him.[128]

Simeon's preaching inspired several generations of evangelicals, but it was Milner who created an enduring evangelical party within the university. The movement was widely unpopular: many people associated it with Methodism, against which there was strong and widespread prejudice[129] — a tag which obscured the distinction between evangelicals within the Church of England and those in the dissenting bodies outside it. Perhaps the Fellows, when they elected Milner president, had underestimated him; perhaps the alarm generated by the French Revolution gave him more freedom to promote his cause; for by the early 19th century he had turned Queens' into an evangelical stronghold. Gunning observed that the college 'entirely changed its character', and now became known for 'its opposition to liberal opinions'.[130] Another contemporary, George Dyer, wrote that it had 'returned to the doctrine of justification by faith alone, and of the co-equality of the Son and Holy Ghost with God the Father; the doctrines taught by Luther, with some of the other first reformers, and by the modern Calvinists. Such is human opinion: thus it circulates round colleges, and round the world'.[131]

---

[125]   'Not so the methodistic [i.e. evangelical] crew,
Who plans of reformation lay:
In the humble attitude they sue,
And for the sins of others pray:

Forgetting that their pride of spirit,
Their exultation in their trial,
Detracts most largely from the merit
Of all their boasted self-denial', Byron (1963), 18 – 19.
[126]   Milner (1842), 7, 20 – 1; above, pp. 163 – 4.
[127]   Elliot-Binns (1953), 363; Milner was largely instrumental in converting Wilberforce to evangelicalism, see Furneaux (1974), 32 – 7.
[128]   Venn (1834), 423; Knight (1971), 57; see also below, chapter 15, n. 46.
[129]   Elliot-Binns (1953), 361; Gunning (1854), i.263; Green (1964), 244 – 5.
[130]   Gunning (1854), i.262 – 3.
[131]   Dyer (1814), ii.145 – 6.

The transformation in Queens' was Milner's work, not merely the result of the fickleness of intellectual fashions. He was explicit about his aims and methods:

'At Queen's we happened unfortunately to have several clever fellows, some time ago, who should have filled our offices of trust, as tutors etc., but were disqualified on account of their principles [i.e., they were evangelicals]. I was positively determined to have nothing to do with Jacobins or infidels, and custom has placed in my power the appointment of the tutors, provided they be Fellows of our own College. Our own being very unfit, we went out of college sorely against the wish of several; however, by determining to make no jobs of such things, but to take the very best men I could find, I carried the matter through, in no less than three instances'.[132]

The result of such changes was to give Milner 'such entire ascendancy over the Fellows, that, after a few years, no one thought of offering the slightest opposition to his will'. Those who tried to oppose him were forced into resignation, or pushed out into college livings.[133] It is hard to see how this came about: Milner was a man of great determination and obstinacy, who would have done his very best to make life unpleasant for Fellows who were out of sympathy with his views, but a concerted effort by these Fellows would surely have had some effect in at least slowing down the evangelical takeover of the college. Milner's account reveals that there was some opposition to his methods, but not how it was overcome.[134] The most likely explanation is that there were three principal reasons for Milner's success: his own determination and utter ruthlessness; the hysterical atmosphere caused by the French Revolution in which he could represent his own brands of religious and political opinion as the safest bulwark against revolutionary atheism; and the fact that college Fellows, who expected anyway to move on to other positions within a few years, were not disposed to remain and fight.

One of those who moved on was Robert Ingram, presented by the college to the rectory of Seagrave in 1802. Although Ingram voted for Thomas Palmer's expulsion in 1794, he was an advocate for the teaching of political economy in the university — a subject with some radical political overtones at that time — and he was no friend of evangelicalism: in 1807 he published a pamphlet, *The Causes of the Increase of*

---

[132] Milner (1842), 243, also cited in Green (1964), 241; see also Milner (1842), 136. For the significance of the tutor's office, see below, p. 189.
[133] Gunning (1854), i.263 – 4, quoted also in Balleine (1908), 127 – 8; and in Brown (1961), 291.
[134] See also Thomas Palmer's expulsion, above, pp. 161 – 2.

Methodism and Dissension, and of the Popularity of what is called Evangelical Preaching, and the Means of Obviating them.[135]

Milner was unable to drive out George Hewitt, a Fellow since 1783, but he did summon him into residence from the college living at Eversden, according to Gunning, 'as a lenient punishment for his *irregularities* in the country, of which the President said he "was in possession of the *strongest proofs*" '. Hewitt was rector of St Botolph's from 1799 until 1834, when he was finally moved out to the college living at Sandon. The difficulty with him, from Milner's point of view, was not that his principles were in opposition to those of the president; rather it was that Hewitt does not appear to have been a man of high principles. He was a fine example of all that the evangelicals found distasteful about the 18th century church. His successor at St Botolph's completely filled a hitherto virtually empty church in six months with his preaching, though Hewitt was unimpressed: 'what of that?' he was quoted as saying, 'I could preach it empty again in a fortnight'.[136]

The creation of an evangelical party among the Fellows led in turn to Queens' becoming the natural choice of evangelical parents for their sons. According to Milner's niece and biographer, the college 'became remarkable for the number of religious young men who studied there, and of whom many are still, in various places, serving God and their generation, as able and faithful clergymen of the establishment, or in other influential stations'.[137] The number of students rose dramatically; this was part of a general increase in numbers at about this time, but the rise at Queens' was ahead of the average, and the college now became one of the largest within the university.[138]

Queens' was an evangelical seminary, whose products were intended to spread out across the country and promote the cause. Academic learning came second to these spiritual concerns. In the words of one evangelical Fellow, study should be 'subservient to the spiritual life', although he believed students should also 'seek to excell' in their studies.[139] Milner chose tutors solely on the grounds of religious

---

[135] *DNB*; above, pp. 161 – 2; Ingram (1807); and see also Ingram (1792), viii, 19 – 21, 23, 30, 46ff, 119. For his views on political economy, below, p. 218.

[136] Gunning (1854), i.263 – 4; *AC*; Romilly (1967), 57 – 8. At the end of the century J. H. Gray noted: 'That there were proofs of Mr Hewitt's irregularities will unhappily appear only too probable to those who have heard the stories still current of the conduct of that eccentric gentleman', but, sadly, he did not relate any of these stories, Gray, 242. One, not very scandalous at all, is told in Joseph Romilly's diary: Romilly dined at Queens' in May 1832 with one of the Fellows, William Mandell, to celebrate the king's birthday. An American was present at the dinner, and Mandell gave the toast 'Prosperity to the United States'; Hewitt proposed an emendation 'May they be united to the Mother Country', Romilly (1967), 14.

[137] Green (1964), 243; Milner (1842), 46.

[138] Gunning (1854), i.263; Brown (1961), 291; Venn, *Statistical Chart*, 10, n.

[139] Venn (1828), 29, and see *ibid.*, 16.

character,[140] and although academic matters were by no means neglected, there was a trace of philistinism in the evangelicals' attitude towards learning.[141] On one occasion, Milner made the ambiguous observation that 'a man with some learning may possibly be very mischievous in the pulpit, though a tolerable classical scholar'.[142] His plan for theological study for students was relatively superficial, reflecting the standard anti-rationalist bias of the evangelicals, for he feared that students who were given too long a course in biblical criticism would become 'less solicitous to understand and remember the well-tried established arguments for the authority of the Sacred Writings', and more inclined to 'give too great a weight to minute and trivial objections and difficulties'.[143]

Milner's efforts were in large measure responsible for the secure establishment of evangelicalism in the university by the beginning of the 19th century.[144] In 1792 he was appointed dean of Carlisle, the first evangelical to attain such a high office in the church, but there were to be no more for over 20 years. Milner owed the post at Carlisle in part to the influence of Wilberforce, but was unable to progress any further in the church.[145] His attempts to expose 'Jacobinism' in the university were, as we have seen, designed at least in part to impress the prime minister, William Pitt, who was one of the university's MPs, but Pitt was no friend of the evangelicals, and Milner could not secure patronage at a sufficiently influential level to win him a bishopric.[146]

High churchmen had not been slow to perceive the threat which

---

[140] Milner (1842), 294. Solomon Atkinson left Queens' for Trinity in 1818 (where he came top of the mathematical tripos in 1820) because his county was already represented on the fellowship at Queens' and he was told that the college would not apply for any more royal dispensations. But he observed that it had subsequently secured a dispensation for an individual of no exceptional talents, and suggested that religious reasons might have prevailed: 'For the profession of certain theoretical opinions, attendance at a certain place of worship, a thorough conceit of their own goodness, and a due contempt and pity for the rest of mankind . . . is a surer recommendation than talents and learning, however adorned by beauty of moral demeanour', Atkinson (1825), 509. In 1827 J. M. F. Wright wrote of Queens' that 'In a *ceteris paribus* case, a Fellowship would be conferred, perhaps, upon a Simeonite [evangelical]. But even that is not a certainty', Wright (1827), ii.179.

[141] For science at Queens' in the evangelical period, see below, pp. 208ff.

[142] Milner (1842), 135.

[143] Baker (1869), 844 – 8; Milner (1813), 229 – 30, and see *ibid.*, 224, 227. This view is contained in Milner's attack on Herbert Marsh, the Lady Margaret professor of divinity, who had criticised the Auxiliary Bible Society in Cambridge with which Milner was connected, and was not friendly to the evangelicals, Marsh (1813), 131 – 40, also quoted in Baker (1869), 849 – 58.

[144] Note also his influence over Trinity Hall and his use of the vice-chancellor's powers, above, pp. 160 – 2.

[145] For Wilberforce's influence, Brown (1961), 291 – 2; and see Gunning (1854), i.266. See also Gascoigne, *Holy Alliance* (forthcoming), chapter VII, citing Milner (1842), 71, for his appointment to Carlisle.

[146] For Pitt's view of the evangelicals, see Gunning (1854), ii.280.

evangelicalism posed, and opposition to it persisted strongly in the university, where the movement was forced onto the defensive by the appointment of the hostile Thomas Dampier as bishop of Ely in 1808. Dampier attempted to suppress Simeon's evening lectures at Holy Trinity church through the vice-chancellor and heads of houses, and Milner had to exert himself to prevent any action being taken. But in 1811 the evangelicals achieved a major success in securing the election of a sympathetic chancellor, the duke of Gloucester.[147]

A serious threat to the movement emerged in the same year as Gloucester's election, with a proposal to establish a branch of the Bible Society in Cambridge.[148] Evangelicals were of course not hostile to Bible study *per se*, but were suspicious of the Bible Society because it was interdenominational. The move to establish the Cambridge branch came from undergraduates, but was opposed by senior members, 'who considered that if the young men assumed the character of a deliberating body, it would be productive of great mischief to the university';[149] freedom of debate was regarded as dangerous in the aftermath of the French Revolution. The branch needed the support of senior members to appear respectable, and inevitably Milner was asked for his, but the students' request placed him in a dilemma: if he refused, 'he ran the risk of offending the whole of that party of whom Wilberforce was the head, and on whose influence he calculated for promotion to the higher preferments of the Church'; if he accepted, he would offend many senior members of the university, whose suspicions of the new body he shared.[150] Milner sat on the fence for as long as he could, but when finally forced to choose, attended the inaugural meeting, and according to Simeon, 'spoke nobly and manfully, and took shame to himself for being so long in making up his mind'.[151]

The meeting was a great success, and helped to consolidate the evangelicals' position in Cambridge still further. This may have been the high water mark of the movement there.[152] Milner died in 1820 and by the middle of the 1820s Wilberforce, who had been a great ally of the evangelicals and whom Milner had converted, was moving back towards the mainstream of the established church. There were other

---

[147] Brown (1961), 298 – 303. There were 468 votes cast for Gloucester in the election, and 351 for his opponent; in Queens', the figures were 23 and 8 respectively, Cooper, vi.495, n. 3.
[148] For the events which follow, see Milner (1842), 463 – 71, 518; Gunning (1854), ii.278 – 80; Winstanley (1940), 19 – 25; Brown (1961), 296 – 7, 301 – 8; Green (1964), 245 – 7.
[149] Gunning (1854), ii.278 – 9.
[150] *ibid.*, ii.279 – 80; Green (1964), 241.
[151] Quoted in Brown (1961), 307.
[152] Though there remained a good deal of opposition to them, Brown (1961), 307 – 11; above, n. 143.

leaders — Simeon was at his peak, and did not die until 1836[153] — and Cambridge continued to produce many prominent evangelicals, but perhaps the movement was beginning gradually to alter in character and even decline; this was a long term process, however.[154] Many years were also to pass before Queens' shook off Milner's legacy.[155]

---

[153] Simeon's funeral sermon was delivered by William Mandell of Queens', Mandell (1836).

[154] Brown (1961), 445 – 6, 500 – 2, 518. There was a national revival in the 1850s.

[155] See below, chapter 18.

13

Presidents and Fellows
(18th and early 19th centuries)

Presidents

Between 1660 and 1820 Queens' had only eight presidents. This suggests stability in the college, and in the university world, a suggestion which is enhanced when it is considered that three of the eight presidents served between 1660 and 1675: only one of the remaining five was in office for less than twenty years.[1] Anthony Sparrow (1662 – 7) was the only one of the eight to resign his place on receiving promotion: the others died in office. All of this is in marked contrast to the pattern of the 16th and 17th centuries. Every one of the eight presidents had been a Fellow of the college; after Henry James' appointment in 1675, there was no royal interference in elections. In addition to the impression of stability, then, a picture can also be built up of a somewhat parochial, self-sufficient and introspective college society, at its upper levels.[2]

This picture is reinforced by studying the five men who held the office during the 18th century.[3] Each in his own way to some degree embodies some feature generally thought to be characteristic of the 18th century head of house. Henry James (1675 – 1717) was described by one of his 18th century successors as 'very attentive to the business and Interest of the College'.[4] His memorandum book survives, and shows him to have taken a detailed, meticulous interest in financial matters; he was precise and fair, but fussy, a stickler for the rules.[5] In a small society, there must have been times when this led to tensions, although there is little evidence of this from James' time.[6] In 1708 he opposed Bentley's scheme to alter the operations of the Corn Rent Act of 1576, but with many of the

---

[1] See below, appendix 4.
[2] The picture should be viewed in relation to what had gone before, not in relation to the 19th century reforms.
[3] The information is derived from *AC* and *DNB*, where appropriate, and other sources. as cited below. The three other late 17th century presidents (Martin, Wells, and Sparrow) are discussed in chapters 4 and 11.
[4] By Robert Plumptre, Book 73, f.59.
[5] Book 80. For his fairness, see *ibid.*, f.15v (second pagination), where he complains that the college has set too high a fine on one of its tenants. As a university moderator (chief examiner), he could be witty and humorous, Mayor (1911), 333 – 4.
[6] But see below, pp. 184, 190.

Fellows being 'taken with the Novelty' of Bentley's proposals, he decided to 'leave them to follow their own fancy because some seem to say I am against the good of the College'.[7] Perhaps this sentiment among the fellowship was partly a reaction to James' character and methods; perhaps he could seem overbearing at times.[8] But there can be no doubting his dedication to the welfare of the college, to which he devoted his life; James never married.[9]

His successor, John Davies (1717 – 32), was a former Fellow, a prebendary of Ely and chaplain to the bishop. He married, but had no children. Nothing much is known about him, apart from his abilities as a classicist, nor about his government at Queens'.[10] Davies was followed by William Sedgwick (1732 – 60), about whom very little is known either. Like Davies, he was a Whig — he enjoyed the patronage of Lord Chancellor Hardwicke, who presented him to a London living — and like Henry James, he died unmarried.[11] We know most about his health, which was poor: his successor as president, Robert Plumptre, described him as 'a man of weak nerves, and an infirm constitution, which he probably render'd still more so by too much indulgence, instead of using proper methods and exertions to strengthen it. For the last 15 years of his life he very rarely went out of the Lodge'.[12] Both Davies and Sedgwick must have been elected as conscientious administrators and good college men, although a large-scale building project undertaken during the latter's presidency nearly bankrupted the college.[13]

These early 18th century presidents were much of a type: able and conscientious, no doubt, but without much ambition. The college came nearest to breaking the mould in its last two presidents of the century. Robert Plumptre (1760 – 88) was a member of a remarkable dynasty which sent seven generations to Cambridge, where eleven Plumptres were senior members in the 18th and early 19th centuries.[14] The family

---

[7] Book 80, f.9v.

[8] He may have been regarded as too staid, and conservative: of Bentley's scheme he noted that 'I wish it end well, but am not for unsetling thinges in such a body', ibid., f.9v.

[9] Book 73, f.59.

[10] ibid., f.59; DNB.

[11] AC; Book 73, fos.62, 64. Sedgwick did not have a BD degree at the time of his election, although this was required by the 1559 statutes (see chapter 5, n. 11); and a royal mandate had to be procured for his admission to the degree, Book 79, f.96; Book 80, f.88v (second pagination).

[12] Book 73, f.64. One of the town's MPs commented on his poor health in 1748, Winstanley (1922), 45. There is a reference to Sedgwick as tutor in Cannon (1984), 58, when the earl of Bristol wrote to him concerning his son Charles, who was at Queens' under Sedgwick's care, and complained about the bad habits which his son had fallen into, suggesting that the tutor was partly to blame. We have no way of knowing if the accusation was justified; in any case, aristocratic students were not easy to discipline at this time, see below, chapter 14.

[13] See below, p. 313.

[14] See below, appendix 15. For Robert Plumptre and the other Plumptres, see AC; DNB.

had strong links with Queens': Robert Plumptre's father and two of his uncles had been students there; his uncle Henry, a distinguished physician, had been a Fellow in the first decade of the century. One of his brothers preceded him as a Fellow, and his cousin Russell, also a Queensman, was Regius professor of physick for over 50 years. Two of his sons, and a nephew, were Fellows of Queens' during his presidency; a third son, and another nephew, became Fellows of other colleges.[15] Some of the family enjoyed the patronage of the great Whig patron the earl of Hardwicke,[16] and their good fortune in this respect was mocked by the poet Thomas Gray when he wilfully mistranslated Robert Plumptre's motto '*Non magna loquimur, sed vivimus*' as 'We don't say much, but we hold good livings'.[17] But the Plumptres were a talented family, whatever assistance may have been given to them by outsiders, and by them to each other.[18] Robert Plumptre was an active proponent of political, religious and university reform, an important figure within the university.[19] Queens' was inspired by his ideals, although there are hints that he was not the firmest of governors with regard to college discipline and financial arrangements.[20]

In Isaac Milner, too, Queens' had a president who played on a larger stage: as we have seen, he was active in the political and religious life of the university, and he left a deep impression upon the society of the college.[21] He was an unappealing character, described by one who met him as 'a rough loud and rather coarse man', who 'used to say all he thought and ask for all he wanted'.[22] He was a glutton, who had to have a specially large chair made to accommodate his vast bulk.[23] He could be awkward, arrogant and contemptuous.[24] He is known to have stolen a

---

[15] Robert was one of ten children, and was father to ten, Book 73, fos.66–7.

[16] *DNB*; Nichols (1814), viii.389; Yorke (1913), ii.486, 563 and n. 4; and see above, p. 158.

[17] Gray (1935), 646.

[18] There is no evidence of any nepotism or undue influence in the election of Plumptres to academic positions, although this was strongly hinted at in the case of Queens' in Reginald Bligh's unreliable account of 1780; see below, pp. 190–1. See *AC*; *DNB* for the achievements of the family's members. Robert Plumptre's daughters Anna and Annabella were well known writers of their time (novels, travel writings, and translations from French and German); his son James, a Fellow of Clare, was a dramatist, *DNB*.

[19] See above, pp. 158, 163 for political and religious reform; see below, p. 217; Plumptre (1802) for his views on university reform.

[20] See below, pp. 200, 301, n. 14. He also took an interest in the history of the college, and compiled a manuscript history (Book 73), which contains much useful information on Queens' in the 18th century.

[21] See above, chapter 12.

[22] Quoted in Furneaux (1974), 167.

[23] *ibid.*, 167; Gunning (1854), i.262, 270–1. Another contemporary described him as 'the most enormous man it was ever my fate to see in a drawing room', Furneaux (1974), 32. The chair is still in the college.

[24] Wordsworth (1968), 365; Gunning (1854), i.90–1.

manuscript which belonged to the university.[25] He does seem to have been dogged by ill health, although it is not always easy to distinguish this from hypochondria, and he could appear healthy enough in public.[26] In addition, it was suggested (by Gunning) that he employed his allegedly poor health as an excuse to save himself from effort: when chosen vice-chancellor, a post he tried to avoid, he sought medical certificates to justify his being exempted from some of the more onerous tasks of the office, and persuaded other heads of houses to take them on.[27]

He was indolent in all affairs which did not interest him: in 1785, according to Gunning, he went on a tour of the continent while serving as one of the university's moderators (chief examiner), provoking complaints from the other moderator for that year that he had been left to do all the work on his own, without being consulted.[28] Even his niece and biographer Mary Milner, who was quite uncritical in her admiration for her uncle, admitted that Milner quarrelled in 1803 with some of his Fellows, who complained of his self-indulgence and indolence; and her account of the dispute is a badly disguised cover-up.[29] In 1814 he went on his customary summer visit to Carlisle, where he was dean in the cathedral, and was detained there supposedly by ill health for nearly

---

[25] On 11 December 1835 the university registrary, Joseph Romilly, recorded in his dairy: 'Today received from the President of Queens' 2 magnificent [16th century] MS volumes . . . these had been stolen by Milner and kept in his Study', Romilly (1967), 95.

[26] Gunning (1854), i.261, 267 – 8; much of the evidence we have concerning Milner's character and habits comes from Gunning's account, but he was not generally sympathetic. In 1799 Milner wrote to Wilberforce that he had to take 'almost twenty grains of opium daily', Furneaux (1974), 79. Shortly after his election he was said to have been so ill that the college summoned its Fellows to elect another president, contemporary letter reprinted in QC (1950 – 1), 24 (source not given).

[27] Gunning (1854), i.262, 265 – 6, 269 – 70. In November 1802 a college order was passed that the college seal should be brought from the treasury, where it normally remained for safekeeping, to the president's lodge 'on account of the Master's indifferent state [of] health', CB (1787 – 1832), 13.11.1802. In 1778 Milner was presented to St Botolph's; according to his niece, he was rarely able to officiate in person because of his ill health, but this did not prevent him from keeping the living until he was made dean of Carlisle in 1792, Milner (1842), 13. It was said after his death that it had been 'generally understood by the Fellows that the said I. Milner for several years held the living of St. Botolph's in Cambridge, (which was tenable with his Fellowship) for the express purpose of possessing the income necessary to make him eligible to the . . . Office of President', Bowdler (1821), 48, 50.

[28] Gunning (1854), i.257 – 8.

[29] Milner (1842), 265 – 70. An evangelical Fellow of Queens' had later, after Milner's death, to refute the charge 'that persons distinguished by strictness in religion, neglect the duties of this place [the university], and make their religion a cloak for idleness'; this may well have been in response to an attack on Milner's reputation, Venn (1828), 12. Mary Milner refers to him supporting Wilberforce's campaign against the slave trade with 'solid and well-directed advice', but makes no mention of his doing anything active in the cause, which she would surely have mentioned had he done so, Milner (1842), 75. But c.f. Gascoigne, Holy Alliance (forthcoming), chapter VII.

two years. In the later 19th century the story was told that some undergraduates at Queens' tore down the brass knocker from the door of the president's lodge, and sent it to Carlisle 'with a message that perhaps it might be of some use to the Dean of Carlisle, for it was of no use in Cambridge'.[30] Yet when he did choose to apply himself to college business, he could be thorough and efficient, and he was fully aware of the responsibilities of his office.[31]

Fellows

Eighteenth century Fellows have generally been given an unfavourable character: they have been described as pedantic, melancholic, drunken, gluttonous, boorish, servile and materialistic.[32] Lack of evidence renders it difficult to say if these were characteristics of Queens' Fellows in general. We know of two certain gluttons: Milner and Ferdinand Smythies (elected 1673); perhaps significantly, both were senior members of the college for over forty years.[33]

In the decoration of their senior combination rooms, and their interest in fashionable objects, foods and drinks, 18th century Fellows were attempting to imitate the style of smart London society, and there are some signs of this at Queens'.[34] But it was a superficial affectation: in most important respects, the don of the period, who was often humble in his background, was characterised as blunt and provincial in his manners, with little chance therefore of cutting a dash in society.[35] John Venn, who was a Fellow of Caius in the second half of the 19th and early part of the 20th centuries, was the son of Henry Venn, an evangelical Fellow of Queens' between 1819 and 1829, and received from him the

---

[30] Milner (1842), 598, 605 – 6; Gray, 238; see also CB (1787 – 1832), which contains only two entries between May 1814 and May 1816, neither signed by Milner; his absence must have disrupted much college business.

[31] For his awareness of the responsibilities, see Milner (1842), 41 – 2, 103. His many notes and memoranda show his efficiency and thoroughness; and see below, chapter 20.

[32] Wordsworth (1874), 96 – 9; Winstanley (1922), 3 – 16; Winstanley (1935), 256 – 61; Green (1969), 287 – 91; Rothblatt (1976), 91 – 5; Porter, *English Society*, 178; see also Holmes (1982), 35 – 42.

[33] Smythies from 1673 until 1725; Milner from 1776 until 1820. The story is told of Smythies that when he saw 'a woman with her child in her arms, a fine boy, fresh and white-haired . . . [he] could not help crying out to his companion in the hearing of the mother, "Good God, how nicely that boy would eat, boiled with collyflowers" ', Winstanley (1935), 258.

[34] In general, see Rothblatt (1976), 95, 97. For Queens' purchases of pipes and tobacco, coffee and chocolate, chestnuts and cherries, glasses and decanters, oysters and oyster knives, a barometer, maps of London and north America, a card table, and Wedgwood plate, see Book 6, f.236v; Book 7, fos.36v, 51, 69v, 76, 98, 204v, 208v, 210v, 212v, 216v, 217v, 220v, 221 – 221v, 233; Book 8, fos.17, 53v, 92v, 131.

[35] See above, n. 32.

impression that the bulk of the college's resident Fellows in the early 19th century were 'of a very rough and uncultivated character. I never heard my father, with all his charity and his keen appreciation of humorous character, refer to any one of them as either willing or able to sympathise with the students or influence them for good'.[36]

There are a few examples of indisciplined behaviour. In the early 19th century it was said that two Fellows had fought each other in front of students.[37] In 1718 Thomas Read 'was sent from College for his Irregularities', but 'as he was upon a Journey to have the Sentence revoked He hanged himself at an Inn in Surrey'.[38] The most striking example comes from the beginning of the period, under the presidency of Henry James. In 1677, the year of his admission to the fellowship, Francis Master was publicly admonished 'for sowing discord' ('*pro seminatione discordiarum*'). In March 1678 he was privately admonished by the president for 'pernoctation' — that is, staying out of college overnight without permission, and he later received a further such admonition for his 'loose liveing'. In October 1678 he was admonished in public, and made to apologise, for two offences: the first was having said that 'the last Congregation was a pack'd Congregation';[39] the second was being 'one of those that broke into the Master's Orchard and destroyed the Fruit-trees in August 1677'. His behaviour worsened thereafter: in January 1679 he came to chapel one evening 'much disorder'd with drink', and for much of that year it seems that he lived out of college 'at houses of noe good note', despite repeated orders to return. Yet it was not until April 1680 that he was punished for pernoctation, and then he was merely fined £1 and sent into the country 'at his owne request', not to return without leave. He was allowed to return in October, but immediately reverted to his old habits, and received yet another public admonition in November. For reasons which remain unclear, Master was not expelled, although in view of his repeated misdemeanours he must have been fortunate; and he remained a Fellow, without further incident, until 1684.[40]

In order to explain some of these features, it is necessary to understand the ways in which the career pattern of the academic

---

[36] Venn (1904), 153. Henry Venn was an evangelical; here he describes a predominantly evangelical college society.

[37] *ibid.*, 153, n. 1; and see below, pp. 220 – 3.

[38] Book 80, fos.86v – 88v (second pagination).

[39] A congregation was an assembly of senior members of the university, called to vote on university business.

[40] Book 80, 45, 47 (third pagination), some of which is cited in Gray, 210 – 11; Book 5, f.188v; OPR, f.92. It was not a good time for Henry James: in November 1678 another Fellow, Charles Allington, had to apologise before the society for the public uttering of 'unworthy false upon mistake and injurious reflexions upon the Master', Book 80, f.12v (second pagination).

profession in the 18th century had changed from that which had become established between the mid-16th century and the English Revolution. First, it was now customary for Fellows to retain their fellowship for much longer than had been the case before 1640.[41] The average length of tenure of fellowships at Queens' in the period 1660 – 1778 was just under twelve years, compared with between six and seven between 1500 and 1640.[42] The number of fellowships remained more or less constant at a slightly lower level than previously.[43] In consequence of these factors, opportunity and mobility in the academic profession were seriously restricted. Richard Davies, a Fellow of Queens' in the 1730s, was one of the few dons to suggest that the tendency towards longer tenure should be curbed: in his book *The General State of Education in the Universities*, published in 1759, he proposed that no Fellow should be allowed to continue beyond ten years after taking his BA; this was 'a sufficient time to finish any course of Study; and men will then, if ever, be fitted to enter into the world'; they would also be more likely to concentrate on producing good academic work in the limited time available to them.[44]

In one respect the statistics for length of tenure of fellowships are misleading, for in the 18th century it became increasingly common for many Fellows to be non-resident, attending at parish cures or in other situations. It was a practice which must have developed partly for good, practical reasons: with the fall in student numbers, it was unlikely that a full complement of Fellows would be kept sufficiently busy or well remunerated, and non-resident Fellows were less costly for the foundation to maintain. But it brought problems, too. William Sedgwick expressed concern about it, and its effects on the state of the profession and the college: non-resident Fellows did not acquire a sound working knowledge of college business which they might one day have to conduct, and Sedgwick feared that in addition, the practice might lead

[41] At Trinity Hall, on average for 18½ years in the period 1688 – 1767; at St John's, on average for 15 years in the late 18th century, Gascoigne, 'Mathematics', 562; see also Holmes (1982), 35 – 6.

[42] Above, p. 78, for 1500 – 1640. Figures for 1660 – 1778 are from 111 Fellows listed in Book 80, fos.86v – 91 (second pagination), pp. 26 – 31 (third pagination), whose dates can be checked against *AC*.

[43] See below, appendix 2. Numbers of Fellows are as follows: in 1754: 19; 1764: 16; 1774: 21; 1784: 19; 1794: 17; 1804: 13; 1814: 13; 1824: 14; 1834: 18; Book 8, *passim*. There was only one new fellowship endowment: in 1690 the college created a new kind of fellowship out of the income of an estate in Carmarthen recently given it, but the profits of the estate were to be for the Fellow's commons and room rent only, he was to have no stipend, and no share in the college's government, Book 73, f.90v. This curious benefaction is the original of the present-day Bye-fellowships. Large scale benefactions, which at other times would have gone to endow fellowships, were more likely in this period to be given for the purchase of livings.

[44] Davies (1759), 30 – 2; he also complained of the restrictions on election imposed by the statutes of county, *ibid.*, 23.

one day to 'a want of that affection for the common good of the college which arises from living together in the Society'. It was also a purpose of fellowships to make their holders 'more fit to go out into the World by the advantages of a learned Conversation', which Fellows who left for curacies immediately after election did not possess to the same degree as those who remained, and because of their example, 'the credit of the College in particular and the University in general very much suffer' in the outside world.[45]

Non-residence on this scale was, according to Sedgwick, a recent problem, which had only arisen since he first came to the college as a student in 1716.[46] Another recent practice was that of choosing Fellows from those men who had just taken their BA degrees; the custom previously had been to wait until they were rather older, a tradition which Sedgwick felt should be preserved.[47] In the early years of Sedgwick's presidency, some attempt was made to restrict non-residence: in 1735 the college ordered that the five junior Fellows were not to be allowed to reside away from Queens' except on condition that they attended the annual audit; in 1736 it was further ordered that no Fellow was to be allowed absence of more than six months in a year until at least one year after he had taken his MA, unless we was ill, or wished to travel overseas, or was tutor to a nobleman's son or a chaplain to a peer of the realm.[48] The college conclusion books, which record the formal decisions of the society, show large numbers of non-resident Fellows returning each January for the audit, and for the election of new Fellows, which also took place at this time of year.[49] The career of Henry Venn may be typical: elected in 1749, he remained in residence until 1751, when he was granted leave of absence for that year; this grant was renewed annually until 1757, when he married and resigned his fellowship.[50]

Formal payments to Fellows did not alter, but they had traditionally received most of their income from dividends, and continued to do so in the 18th century; there was also the possibility of private tuition, which

---

[45] Box 102, undated MS entitled 'Reasons for the Residence of the Fellows'.

[46] ibid.

[47] ibid. He felt that they would be unlikely to remain in their fellowships for so long if they had to wait longer for them, but his argument for making them wait is not very clear, and he expected friends of students to maintain them if they had the promise of a fellowship in a few years' time. It is not clear why Fellows were elected younger, unless it were felt that they would not wait — the fear which Sedgwick was trying to allay.

[48] CB (1734 – 87), fos.7, 10v; see also CB (1787 – 1832), 26.4.1796, for a further attempt to tighten up.

[49] CB (1734 – 87), passim. In March 1745 Sedgwick planned to hold an election for vacant fellowships, but it had to be deferred because of 'the Snow lying so deep and the Roads being so bad that the absent fellows cannot come to College without great danger', CB (1734 – 87), f.37v.

[50] Venn (1904), 69 – 70.

became increasingly common with the growing importance of the mathematical tripos.[51] It has been suggested that the 18th century agricultural revolution boosted the income from college estates, and thereby increased dividends substantially: they may have been 11 times higher in 1810 than they had been in 1690, although the cost of living had only increased threefold.[52] But Charles Farish, a Fellow of Queens' at the end of the century, believed that fellowships were still poorly paid, and that this was a depressing influence on the profession, and he urged that greater provision should be made for Fellows; this may have been special pleading,[53] but we do not know the financial condition of the Fellows of Queens'.[54]

Though they remained longer in their fellowships, Fellows' career expectations remained the same: to secure a good ecclesiastical living. A list, apparently compiled in the late 18th century, of 170 Fellows of Queens' who left their fellowships between 1660 and 1778 also contains the reasons for each individual's going: it shows that 60 left because they had received promotion outside — usually in the form of presentation to benefices, although this is not always specified — and another 26 left on being presented to livings in the college's gift. Thirty-three were said to have resigned in order to marry, but most of these would also have gone into the church. Twenty-eight died as Fellows; nine received an estate of sufficient value to compel them to resign their fellowships.[55] In the later 18th century it became usual to admit resigning Fellows to fellow-commonerships, presumably to encourage them to maintain their contacts with the college.[56]

A royal commission into the state of the university in 1852 was in no doubt that enforced celibacy 'has tended to prevent many men of ability and eminence from continuing their residence in the university as long as might have been desirable', and a speaker on the Cambridge university reform bill in the House of Commons two years later presented a picture of the elderly don waiting for the distant paradise of a college living 'with perhaps a veritable Eve waiting for him in the

---

[51] For stipends, see Book 8, *passim.*; for private tutors, see below, p. 201.

[52] Gascoigne, 'Mathematics', 562 – 3; c.f. below, pp. 300 – 4.

[53] Farish (undated), 2 – 9; the argument was employed as part of his attack on the enforced celibacy of Fellows. Farish felt that poverty was more likely to make Fellows remain until they could secure a living good enough to support a family, rather than to make them move on. Solomon Atkinson in the early 19th century reckoned that many Fellows were very comfortably off thanks to the income from private teaching, and that this led them to become indolent and forsake academic work, Atkinson (1825), 502 – 3.

[54] There is one example known of a Fellow running into debt: in 1696 Gervase Needham was given £50 by the college 'to get him out into the World' and a further £20 'to pay poor people'; he resigned his fellowship, the salary of which was sequestered to pay off the money given him, Book 80, f.18v (second pagination).

[55] Book 80, fos.86v – 91 (second pagination), pp. 26 – 31 (third pagination).

[56] CB (1734 – 87), f.98v and ff.

Garden'.[57] Celibacy had long been unpopular: voices were raised against it in the 18th century, especially in the years after 1760.[58] One of its active opponents was Charles Farish. 'What God puts upon a man he must bear', he wrote in a pamphlet on this subject, 'but let not this unnecessary restraint be rashly imposed by the hand of man'. He argued that celibacy had been imposed on the universities by 'a foreign force' — the Roman Catholic church, before the Reformation — and deprived dons of man's 'natural and spontaneous right' to marriage. It seemed obvious to Farish that Fellows ought to enjoy those social and domestic comforts which obtained in other walks of life: learning would not be advanced by men who were unhappy, and Farish called for a general improvement in Fellows' standards of living. Marriage would give tutors 'new motives for industry' — presumably, the need to support their families — would by no means loosen their attachment to their colleges, and would leave the appearance of the colleges and the number of students unchanged. The residence of married Fellows in the town would promote order and respectability there; the town's society would gain from its learned inhabitants; and married tutors would be more likely to remain in Cambridge to attend to college business during the long vacation, when most Fellows were absent.[59]

These views may appear amusing to us now, in an age when the right of Fellows to marry is taken for granted, but in Farish's time every possible argument had to be employed against the many university men who were opposed to the idea. The campaign against celibacy failed in the 18th century, partly, no doubt, because of the university's innate conservatism, but conservatives were not alone in defending the *status quo*: Robert Plumptre, a reformer in many other matters, thought the proposal to allow Fellows to marry 'so very absurd that I have been, and still am, much in doubt whether it was ever seriously intended'. If all Fellows were permitted to marry, Plumptre argued, 'the ruin of the University as a place of education would infallibly and speedily ensue: if restrained to non-resident Fellows, the ruin would perhaps be not quite so expeditious but no less certain'.[60] Celibacy was seen by many as a means of keeping college societies fluid and dynamic by encouraging Fellows to move on.[61] Opponents and supporters of celibacy argued from mutually incomprehensible viewpoints, and the modern idea of the academic life as a profession was still a long way from winning widespread acceptance.

[57] Wordsworth (1874), 361; Stone (1977), 48 – 50.
[58] Wordsworth (1874), 353 – 7; Wordsworth (1968), 264; Winstanley (1935), 300 – 1; c.f. Rothblatt (1976), 90 – 1.
[59] Farish (undated), 1 – 24.
[60] Winstanley (1935), 300.
[61] *ibid.*, 301.

One significant change in college societies was the decline in the number of college tutors: in the 18th century, most small colleges had only one tutor, although some of the larger ones might have two.[62] This was probably because of the fall in the number of students. With the decline of the tutorial system as a means of instruction, for reasons which are still not entirely clear, a tutorship became a more formal, institutional post within the college: it was lucrative and therefore much sought after, and was often a stepping stone to a mastership.[63] College offices tended to be monopolised by a small number of active residents.[64]

Fellowships remained much sought after. A student who achieved distinction in the mathematics tripos (which after the middle of the century assumed great significance in the university)[65] could expect to be elected to a fellowship: the practice was more or less fixed before the middle of the 19th century. But some colleges, such as Queens', had statutory restrictions on the number of Fellows permitted from any one county at a time, and there might not be a vacancy at the right moment. There was relatively little movement between colleges, although Henry Venn of Jesus was elected to a fellowship at Queens' in 1749 on the recommendation of the Queens' tutor, Owen Manning.[66] Milner's move to bring in outsiders to be tutors was unpopular within the college, and it produced a further unwelcome consequence in that the belief spread in the university that Queens' would continue to welcome outside candidates for fellowships: Milner wrote that he had received 'applications without end to this purpose; and not only so, but admonitions, sometimes anonymous'.[67]

Royal interference in elections had vanished with the overthrow of James II, but outside influences continued to be felt: it was one of Richard Davies' complaints in his 1759 critique of university teaching.[68] In 1749 the poet Thomas Gray sought assistance in securing a fellowship for a friend, and observed that the master of Peterhouse had promised to try to bring this about 'either at Queen's or Christ's, where he has

---

[62] Queens' had 3 in 1796, which was unusually high, Gascoigne, 'Mathematics', n. 42. It may have been due to the increase in student numbers in the college at this time.

[63] Winstanley (1935), 269 – 76; Gascoigne, 'Mathematics', 554.

[64] CB (1734 – 87), and CB (1787 – 1832), *passim*, annual elections to offices; see also Book 79, fos.126 – 126v for the bursar's office.

[65] Below, pp. 208 – 10.

[66] Gascoigne, 'Mathematics', 561 – 2; Venn (1904), 69, 155. One of the grounds for Milner's dispute with the Fellows in 1803 was his attitude towards the statute of county, Milner (1842), 265 – 70.

[67] Milner (1842), 243; see above, p. 174. It had been alleged that 'not infrequently *no proper candidates* for fellowships present themselves', Box 95, documents on Hughes bequest.

[68] Davies (1759), 24 – 5.

interest'.[69] Isaac Milner wrote in 1812 that 'I would not advise the dearest friend I had in the world, to go to College, (unless he had a fortune,) except he had considerable abilities to push his way; and after all, there is an amazing deal of accident in the getting of Fellowships and such like'.[70]

Inevitably, there were disputed elections. In 1715 seven Fellows appealed to the university's chancellor against the conduct of the president, Henry James, who had refused to admit William Ayerst to a fellowship after an election in May 1714 at which he had, it was alleged, been legally chosen by the Fellows. James' irregular action was said to be 'on account of his Godson, whom he could no otherwise hope to make Fellow'. Ayerst was only admitted after James' death, in 1717.[71] In 1721 it was decided to keep a recently vacated fellowship vacant for the time being, 'a sufficient number of Fellows not consenting to Dominus Cranfield's Election'. If, as seems likely, this 'Cranfield' was Henry Crownfield, a student of the college, then a second attempt secured his election, for he was a Fellow from 1722 until 1744.[72]

In the late 1760s Robert Plumptre was accused by a former Fellow, William Lloyd, of having 'exerted some undue influence' over the fellowship to prevent the election of Lloyd's brother John. William Lloyd's loyalty to his family seems to have blinded him to his brother's manifest unsuitability for a fellowship: Plumptre spoke of his 'unmeasurable Self-conceit, pride, Arrogance, caprice, imperiousness, and assuming airs', qualities 'which it was feared would operate very fatally on the peace and good order of the Society if he was elected into it', a view borne out by Lloyd's behaviour as a student; and the president clearly enjoyed the support of the fellowship in the business — yet William Lloyd's vigorous opposition culminated in a legal action in the court of chancery.[73]

Just over a decade later Plumptre was subjected to another energetic campaign by Reginald Bligh, who was rejected as a candidate for a fellowship in 1780. Bligh blamed his defeat on the influence of Milner, who was then tutor and did not want anyone elected to a fellowship who might stand up to him and oppose his ambitions. Bligh reckoned himself to be sufficiently qualified intellectually for a fellowship, and much more so than Plumptre's son Joseph, who was successful in the

---

[69] Gray (1935), 324. It is not known what influence the master of Peterhouse had; the friend became a Fellow of Peterhouse.
[70] Milner (1842), 497.
[71] Box 95, document entitled 'A State of the Case of Queen's College 1715'; Book 80, f.88v (second pagination).
[72] Book 80, 48 (third pagination).
[73] Box 95, documents on case of John Lloyd; for Lloyd's behaviour as a student see below, pp. 198–200.

same election at which he was rejected.[74] Bligh's account may contain some valuable insights into the state of the college at this time, and in particular to Milner's rise to power — he alleged that Milner already had his eye on the presidency — but his observations cannot be trusted, since the general tone of the account is wild, even hysterical, full of crude personal attacks. He aimed to bully Plumptre into securing his election by threatening to stir up a public scandal: several frantic, blustering letters written by him to the president survive as testimony to his highly emotional and confused state of mind, but the college was unmoved by his threats, and in December 1780 he was expelled for his 'most false, Scurrilous, defamatory, and malicious Libel'.[75]

The vigour with which William Lloyd and Reginald Bligh pursued their campaigns, and the shrill recklessness of their accusations, all so characteristic of the fierce disputes of the Tudor and Stuart periods, are sufficient proof of the continuing attractiveness of college fellowships at this time, not as an end in themselves, but as a means to promotion elsewhere — in Bligh's words, 'the only Chance I stood of obtaining a genteel Livelihood'.[76] It was not until the middle of the 19th century that such traditional views began to alter, and a more recognisably modern don began to appear.[77]

---

[74] Bligh (?1780), *passim*; see also Bligh (1781).
[75] See n. 74; Box 95, documents concerning Bligh; CB (1734 – 87), f.113.
[76] Box 95, Bligh documents.
[77] This is described below, chapter 16.

14

Eighteenth century students

Although in many respects student life in the 18th century was little different from that of the 17th, there were changes too. First, there was a serious and prolonged fall in numbers, beginning in the later 17th century and continuing until early in the 19th; the lowest point was reached in the years around 1760. The average number of matriculations in the university in the decade 1630–9 was 373; by the decade after 1700, this had fallen to 204; and in the decade 1760–9 the figure was as low as 112. There seems to have been a proportionate decrease at Queens' also, where the number of students matriculating was usually well below ten each year between 1740 and 1770.[1]

There may well have been an increase in the average age of students at admission, with more coming up to the university at 18 or 19.[2] Changes in the social composition of the student body also took place: there was apparently a gradual increase in the proportion who came from the gentry class, and a decline in the number of low social origins.[3]

The categories of student remained unchanged. The sizars remained at the bottom of the student pecking order thoughout the period, but by the 19th century their position had improved greatly. The 17th century had seen them often acting in effect as servants to Fellows and fellow-commoners, a practice which persisted in the early part of the 18th century. Originally there had been no social stigma attached to this, but as the century wore on opposition mounted to the sizars having to perform such menial tasks, and they began to receive more generous treatment: they ceased to act as gyps, were allowed commons instead of high table leftovers, and by the end of the century no longer served at high table. In the early 19th century Cambridge men argued that the

---

[1] Stone (1975), 92; Venn, *Statistical Chart*; Venn, *Matriculations*; below, appendix 6; see also Carter (1753), 184; CUA CUR 82,3.

[2] Wordsworth (1874), 94–5; Winstanley (1935), 203.

[3] The proportion of students at Cambridge from the gentry rose from 25% in 1700 to 35% in 1800; the proportion from the lower social classes fell from 30% to 18% in the same period, Hans (1951), 44. A growing proportion of the aristocracy were educated at the universities in the 18th century, and the nobility grew as a proportion of the student body at Oxford and Cambridge, but it remained a tiny proportion of the whole (only 1.84% of total matriculations in 1780–99), Cannon (1984), 46–54.

distinction between pensioners and sizars had grown slight.[4]

Although Mary Milner claimed that at Queens', sizars' duties were 'undoubtedly finally abolished' by her uncle while president, the process of reform had begun a long time before.[5] In 1734 they were allowed to dine in hall — we do not know where they had taken their meals hitherto — and in 1773 they were excused from waiting at table in hall at dinner and supper time, but were still allowed to take high table leftovers if they chose; the duty of waiting at table was now to be shared between the president's gardener and the porter, and one of the college exhibitions was to be divided between them as remuneration.[6] Earlier in 1773 it had been decided that these two servants should also share 'the Gatekeeper's place and the Chapel Clerk's place . . . till a Sizar comes who shall be willing to accept the latter place'.[7] This suggests that one reason for transferring sizars' duties to others was that there were no longer enough sizars to carry them out properly, which is quite likely in view of the very low number of students at the time. But we should not discount genuine humanitarian motives for the abolition of the sizars' tasks. Richard Davies, a Fellow at the time of the 1734 reform, later commented on a dangerous psychological consequence of sizarship, in that poor scholars who acted as menial servants to Fellows often made a sudden transition to becoming Fellows themselves on graduation, and 'A man bred a Slave is educated to become a Tyrant; when power devolves to him'.[8]

The pensioners do not appear as a distinct body in the 18th century with the clarity or prominence which they show in the 17th. Their numbers had fallen, too, and they are often hidden by the fellow-commoners' display.[9] Fellow-commoners were also less numerous in absolute terms, but they were more prominent. They formed only a small proportion of the student body as a whole, and their style of living was by no means typical of student life in that period, but it was often

---

[4] Wordsworth (1874), 107 – 110; Winstanley (1935), 201 – 2; Farish (undated), 27. But there was probably still often a very great difference between the two groups in material terms. For an illustration of the expenses and hardships of a poor student in the early 19th century, see Atkinson (1825), 506 – 8.

[5] Milner (1842), 6 – 7, 103 – 4; see also Atkinson (1825), 497.

[6] CB (1734 – 87), fos.6v, 92v.

[7] CB (1734 – 87), f.92, and see f.117v.

[8] Davies (1759), 25 – 6.

[9] Wordsworth claimed that in the 18th century and until the mid-19th, pensioners were scarcely distinguishable from scholars, and that in the 18th century both pensioners and scholars were from lower social grades than in the mid-19th, Wordsworth (1874), 98.

public, and has been well recorded.[10] Their outlook and actions were linked to those of the 18th century aristocracy. It seems to have been an age of display: the great landowners attended the winter season in London and the summer season in Bath, sent their sons to university after providing them with private tuition at home, and often completed their education with the grand tour; lesser landowners imitated this pattern according to their means.[11] The universities had lost their former pre-eminence in the schemes of these wealthy men for the education of their sons; it was more than ever likely that the sons would emphasise the social aspect of their university lives to the detriment of the civilized learning which they were also meant to acquire.

One striking feature of this change of outlook was a new interest in life and events outside the university, especially in London, which began in the late 17th century. Improved means of communication made the capital seem much closer than before. The first coach service between Cambridge and London began in 1653; in the 1670s, the journey took approximately 12 hours. It was only in the late 18th century that this time was reduced significantly, and not until the early 19th that the journey was possible regularly in 7 hours.[12] Nevertheless, from the middle of the 17th century Cambridge was brought into much closer contact with the capital. News from London travelled more swiftly and regularly, and the development of newspapers assisted its spread. From the Restoration period onwards, Cambridge students became avid for news. At the same time, the new fashion for coffee houses was beginning to find support in Cambridge, so that by the early 18th century 'it is become a custom, after chapel, to repair to one or other of the coffee-houses . . . where hours are spent in talking; and less profitable reading of newspapers, of which swarms are continually supplied from London. And the scholars are so greedy after news . . . that they neglect all for it'.[13] Daniel Wray, a former fellow-commoner of Queens' who continued to live in Cambridge after graduation, pointed to the sterility and superficiality of coffee-house society when he wrote in a letter of 1739: 'Our Coffee-house has not experienced any change,

[10] Fellow-commoners made up 11% of the Cambridge student population between 1678 and 1800, pensioners 49%, and scholars and sizars 39%, Hans (1951), 43, 46 – 7. Solomon Atkinson, a student in Milner's time, felt that pensioners then were 'altogether superior to the Fellow Commoners in point of respectability, and perhaps of wealth', the latter having been 'very far from possessing that superiority in station and wealth which their gown indicates', Atkinson (1825), 497.

[11] Speck (1977), 39; Porter, *English Society*, 177 – 9.

[12] Cooper, iii.454; Wordsworth (1874), 405 – 8.

[13] Wordsworth (1874), 126 – 7; and see also *ibid.*, 140 – 4; Fowler and Fowler (1984), 101; Mayor (1911), 132. For some general remarks on coffee-house culture and the cosmopolitan stances of students, see Rothblatt (1975), 250 – 1; this stimulating essay contains valuable observations on 18th and early 19th century students.

either as to *company*, or *way* of thinking, since last year'.[14]

Leisure time and recreational pursuits were important to fellow-commoners, An early 18th century account referred scathingly to idle 'Lowngers', students who were 'content to carry their speculations . . . no farther than bowling-greens, billiard-tables, and such like places'.[15] There was a wide range of recreations to be enjoyed. Many were traditional, such as riding, tennis, football, bowls and cards, but there were newer pastimes too: walking and swimming became more popular in the 18th century, as did billiards; music was also of greater importance as concert-going became fashionable. There are references to cock-fighting and bull-baiting in the 17th and 18th centuries, and also to the more refined and cerebral chess.[16] Shooting became very popular, for there were plenty of wildfowl in the fens around Cambridge, and student shooting parties were a considerable nuisance to local farmers.[17] It must have been because of such sporting interests that Queens' ordered in 1795 'that no person whatever be allowed to keep a Dog in College'.[18]

It has been claimed that there was relatively little gambling in the university in the 18th century, but Newmarket was close to Cambridge and the races there were said to be a temptation to many.[19] The guardian of Philip Yorke, an undergraduate at Queens' in the 1770s, was alarmed to hear of his ward's visit to the races, and warned him that 'As you have satisfied your curiosity about Newmarket, I presume you will not be in haste to make another excursion there. The mischief done by gaming at that place is more than a ballance for the service it is in the breed of horses'. He worried unnecessarily, for Yorke wrote that the races 'gave me very little pleasure indeed'.[20] But Yorke was a serious-minded young man; his free time was spent in more respectable pursuits such as fishing, walking, riding, fencing, and playing bowls.[21] Others took a different view: in the later 19th century a former student wrote that 'When I was an undergraduate at Queens' (about 1808 – 11) it would have been counted a disgrace to the college if any man had been

[14] Nichols (1817), i.78. For Wray, see *DNB*.
[15] Wordsworth (1874), 372 – 8.
[16] *ibid.*, 162 – 84, 201 – 3, 443. Solomon Atkinson believed that physical exercise was necessary for sustained mental effort, and therefore 'read hard for two or three hours in the morning, and the like again in the evening, and the rest of the day I ranged about the town, or rambled four or five miles into the country, alternately conning over some proposition mentally, or picking up an adventure, as accident or inclination served', Atkinson (1825), 508.
[17] Wordsworth (1874), 176 – 7; Cooper, iv.423; Gunning (1854), i.40 – 2. Shooting declined in popularity even before the 19th century as the fens were drained, removing the birds' natural habitat.
[18] CB (1787 – 1832), 25.4.1795.
[19] Wordsworth (1874), 183.
[20] Winstanley (1935), 225 – 6.
[21] *ibid.*, 208.

present in hall on a Newmarket day'.[22]

Life was ostentatious and expensive for many fellow-commoners. They had to keep up with the latest fashions, and had anyway always been criticised for excessive spending on fine clothes.[23] The wearing of expensive modern clothes was a way of demonstrating status. Fellow-commoners' academic dress was different from that of other under-graduates by tradition, and for the same reason, and was one aspect of their self-display, satirised by Daniel Wray:

> 'Gold were my tufts, and velvet was my cap;
> In state my dinner I *cum Sociis* eat,
> And loll'd on Sundays in the rev'rend pit;
> Thus plac'd, who saw me well might judge my Sire
> Some Bank Director, or wide-acred Squire'.[24]

The expenses of fashionable show rose during the period. In 1715 it was calculated that a fellow-commoner needed about £120 for his annual maintenance at the university, an increase of 50% during the past 40 years or so; a pensioner's expenses were reckoned to be only half those of a fellow-commoner.[25] Robert Plumptre, asked in 1774 how much Philip Yorke would require to live as a fellow-commoner in Cambridge, estimated that he would need about £300, 'keeping a servant and horse, clothes and pocket money included'.[26] The horse and servant were important badges of status, but the college's permission was required to keep them there, and such permission was granted only with parental approval, as a safeguard against boys overspending in imitation of their wealthier friends.[27]

The lifestyle and outlook of many fellow-commoners surely encour-aged indiscipline. There are many examples of student disorder in 18th century Cambridge, and the problem troubled the university authorities greatly on several occasions.[28] It is important that this should be seen in context: student indiscipline was not new, and the largely subjective evidence available offers little opportunity for discovering if it was any worse in the 18th century than at other times. But contemporaries seem to have believed that matters were getting worse. In 1749 the

---

[22] Bradley (1922), 47 – 8, cited in Fowler and Fowler (1984), 173. Note that Queens' was in its evangelical phase at the time described.

[23] Wordsworth (1874), 469 – 76, 484ff; above, p. 94.

[24] Nichols (1817), i.28 – 9; for gowns, see e.g. Wordsworth (1874), 693.

[25] Wordsworth (1874), 557.

[26] Winstanley (1922), 23, n. 2.

[27] Winstanley (1935), 208, n. 56; CB (1734 – 87), fos.82v – 83, 95, 116, 127v, 131 – 131v; CB (1787 – 1832), 5.12.1787.

[28] e.g. Wordsworth (1874), 72, 96, 147 – 9, 156 – 7, 428, 436 – 7; Winstanley (1922), 16 – 23, 51.

university's public orator put the blame on 'the licentiousness of the age in general', and new regulations covering behaviour and discipline were issued the following year.[29] It has been argued that the rising age of students may have contributed to this growing problem.[30]

The foremost manifestations of student indiscipline were summed up concisely by Isaac Milner in 1810:

'Breaking of lamps and windows, shouting and roaring, blowing of horns, galloping up and down the streets on horseback or in carriages, fighting and mobbing in the town and neighbouring villages; in the day-time breaking down fences and riding over corn-fields, then eating, drinking, and becoming intoxicated at taverns or ale-houses; and, lastly, in the night frequenting houses of ill-fame, resisting the lawful authorities, and often putting the peaceable inhabitants of the town into great alarm'.[31]

Disorder and assaults in the streets, smashing lamps and heavy drinking were apparently endemic.[32] In the early 19th century there was much alarm among university officers over the collapse of order and discipline, fears which may have been related in part to the impressions made by the recent revolutionary anarchy in France.[33]

As Milner observed, most undergraduates showed 'a laudable disposition to be attentive to the studies, and obedient to the laws of the University', and it was only a small number who gave the rest a bad name.[34] This group came largely from the wealthy elements in student society; only they could afford to misbehave. Gunning felt that the authorities were lenient towards fellow-commoners because they were afraid of litigation.[35] Colleges may have been unwilling to discourage them by too strict an observance of rules, for they were a valuable source of income.[36]

There is little evidence of indiscipline at Queens', but many

---

[29] Winstanley (1922), 51; Cooper, iv.278 – 80; Wordsworth (1874), 72, 428.
[30] Wordsworth (1874), 94 – 5.
[31] Milner (1842), 399.
[32] Wordsworth (1874), 147 – 8; Gunning (1854), i.95 – 6, 321 – 2; Winstanley (1922), 211 – 17.
[33] Winstanley (1922), 214 – 5. Gunning suggested that certain expressions of hostility by junior members towards the university authorities may have had political and religious undertones, Gunning (1854), i.94 – 5.
[34] Milner (1842), 397 – 8.
[35] Gunning (1854), i.60 – 1, and see *ibid.*, i.57.
[36] On a loose sheet of paper at the front of CB (1734 – 87) are the signatures of students to a promise to 'submit to the Rules and Discipline of the College, of which I am about to be admitted a Member; and will be obedient to the Master or his Locum-tenens in all lawful Commands'. The signatures are those of fellow-commoners admitted between the 1750s and 1790s; I know of no such subscription required from the other categories of student.

misdemeanours took place outside colleges, and are unlikely to have found their way into college archives; and it may be that only the most serious occurrences within the college were recorded. Sexual offences, as in previous centuries, are conspicuous by their absence from the college records, although prostitution was a serious problem for the university authorities in the 18th century.[37] In 1676 eight Cambridge taverns were put out of bounds to university members because they were 'infamous for harbouring lewd women'; many scholars were said to visit these places, which included 'the saracen's head upon the causeway to Queen's College'.[38]

One practice of fellow-commoners which attracted criticism was the giving of private dinners rather than attending college hall.[39] These dinners demonstrated that fellow-commoner society was independent of collegiate social practice and routine, and weakened the bond between wealthy undergraduates and their colleges. In 1762 Queens' decided to put an end to the dinners, on the grounds that they were 'attended with so much expence, and with such ill-consequences in various ways both to the College in general, and to its particular members'. The cook was ordered not to prepare any private dinners or suppers for students unless they were entertaining guests from outside the university, and then only with tutorial permission.[40]

The remaining evidence concerns individual misdemeanours. It is not always explicit. We know that in November 1761 Thomas Leach, a sizar, was made to apologise 'for his behaviour to the Dean and indecent manner of giving up his place', but it is not quite clear what he had done.[41] Drunkenness was a major problem. In the late 1770s Younge Gilson, a pensioner, was rusticated 'for coming to chapel intoxicated'.[42] Gilson was a heavy drinker: a contemporary recorded that 'He kept in a room above me one whole term, in which term, I rarely, tho' I saw him often, saw him sober. And in what company did he get drunk? in no company at all, except bottles of rum and brandy'.[43]

One night in December 1768 John Lloyd, a scholar, having just learnt that he would almost certainly not be elected to a fellowship at the annual election the following January, 'violently intoxicated himself

[37] e.g. Green (1964), 235; Winstanley (1935), 210 – 11. Again, it is hard to tell if the situation was worse than previously.
[38] Cooper, iii.571. Stone argues for increased tolerance of sex at the universities in the late 17th and 18th centuries, Stone (1977), 540; but more research is required to demonstrate this.
[39] Wordsworth (1874), 149.
[40] CB (1734 – 87), fos.66v – 67; and see also f.80.
[41] *ibid.*, f.63v; AC. He was restored to his half share of the chapel clerk's place after making an apology.
[42] Bligh (?1780), 11; it is not clear exactly when Gilson was expelled.
[43] Box 95, letter from Thomas Willis to Bligh, dated 27.6.1780.

with liquor, and in that state did come out into one of the Courts of the College, did there make a great riot and disturbance, and did grossly abuse and violently threaten some of the Fellows of the College whom he supposed not favourably dispos'd towards him, and did strike his Tutor who came to quiet him several blows'.[44] Lloyd was treated with exceptional leniency, for the college decided to overlook the whole business, recognising his deep disappointment at not receiving a fellowship.

Lloyd was fourth wrangler in the 1768 tripos and in normal circumstances would have been elected a Fellow without any difficulties, but this drunken outburst was not his only offence since coming up to Queens'. In 1767 he had left college without permission, apparently intending never to return, 'and his friends search'd some days in London for him before they could find him to send him back'. He had gone unpunished on this occasion, too: the president, Robert Plumptre, did not learn of the incident for some while, 'and that being the case, in hopes it was a sally of youth which would have no farther consequences, no notice was taken of it'.[45] In the same year Lloyd 'did in order to obstruct the discipline of the College enter into an association to miss Chapel a greater number of times than was commonly allow'd them in a week, and then if any [academic] exercise was set them [as punishment] to refuse one and all to comply with it'. The students duly missed chapel, but their plan was discovered and they were warned of the 'ill consequence' of refusing to perform their exercises; they submitted therefore to the college authorities.[46]

Once again, Lloyd does not seem to have been punished, and perhaps it was the college's repeated leniency which encouraged him to further misbehaviour in February 1769, when a chair bottom was thrown from a college window late one night at a post-chaise in Silver Street, terrifying the horses. A servant sent back by the occupants of the chaise to make a note of the room from which the object had been thrown was met by the students gathered there, including Lloyd, who climbed down from the window to the street, assaulted the servant, 'and threw him over the rails into a muddy place adjoining to the river'. The driver of the chaise, who followed in search of the servant, was also beaten up, and the chaise's occupants, together with those of an accompanying post-chaise, who were all respectable townspeople, were subjected to 'indecent and abusive language'.

One of the townspeople knew Lloyd, and the affair was settled between them afterwards without the college authorities getting wind of it. When Plumptre finally found out, about a month later, a college

[44] Box 95, documents concerning John Lloyd.
[45] ibid.
[46] ibid.

meeting was held immediately to determine punishments. Another Queens' scholar who had taken part in the affray — the remaining participants were from other colleges — was rusticated; he had a reputation for disorderly behaviour. But Lloyd, despite his history of misconduct, was spared: he was ordered to make a public apology, and to learn and recite by heart in hall one of Cicero's orations, until which time he was confined to college. The reason given for his light treatment was that rustication would mean the loss of his exhibition from his school, his college scholarship, and his private pupil, which would place an excessively heavy financial burden on Lloyd's father, who wished to keep his son at Queens' a while longer. Surprisingly, both Lloyd and his father protested at the terms of his punishment, although he did submit.[47]

Lloyd must have received special treatment, but we do not know why, and the fact that incidents involving him could be kept secret from the president for such a long time says little for Plumptre's awareness of what was going on in his college. A few years later, Queens' was forced to act more decisely against a particularly awkward fellow-commoner, Charles Crawford, who had arrived in 1768, and soon acquired a reputation for drunkenness and acts of violence, including an unprovoked attack on a postillion, and threatening to throw the senior Fellow of Pembroke through a window. Crawford was also a champion of free thought, and published a pamphlet anonymously in 1772 attacking certain tenets of Christian belief. The college considered expelling him for this on the grounds of blasphemy, but abandoned the idea because his authorship could not be proved.[48]

He was finally expelled in August 1773 'for having been drunk, and for assaulting and beating a waterman in the town, and for making a riot', but he would not leave. The order for his expulsion was repeated in September, but he challenged its legality; when the college attempted to bar his rooms against him, he hired a blacksmith to break the door open. In November he left, but locked his rooms, and threatened legal action against anyone who occupied them. The door was broken down by the college, which in anticipation of a court case had already decided that any lawsuit arising from Crawford's expulsion was to be paid for out of college funds.[49]

---

[47] ibid.

[48] Winstanley (1935), 218; AC; see also above, p. 163. The tone of Crawford's pamphlet suggests that he was more motivated by love of mischief than by ideological conviction, but he does seem to have been a rationalist in his interpretation of Scripture, Crawford (1772), passim.

[49] Winstanley (1935), 218 – 224; Cooper, iv.378 and n.3; CB (1734 – 87), fos.92v – 93v, 95v. There is plenty of correspondence about and from Crawford in Box 95 (4 bundles, which I have marked and numbered); since these do not alter Winstanley's account, I have used that version here for ease of reference.

He returned at the beginning of January, claiming that his expulsion was invalid because it had not been ordered by a majority of the governing body; this was true, but at a college meeting on 13 January a majority of the Fellows confirmed the order. Crawford was an aggressively determined man, and in the summer of 1774 he came back to Cambridge, took lodgings in the town, and made several visits to Queens' in order to provoke the college authorities. He was thrown out twice by the porter, and immediately sued him for assault; he had almost certainly sought ejection so that he could go to court. But less than a week after this second ejection he came into college armed with a pistol, and was bound over for breach of the peace. Both his action against the porter, and that now brought against him for breach of the peace were heard before the court of King's Bench in January 1775, which found in favour of the porter, who was protected by the college's order of expulsion.[50] Though Crawford grumbled on for a while, he did not seriously challenge the college's authority again.[51]

Crawford's story is a highly unusual one, but a good illustration of the power of the fellow-commoner to defy and obstruct the college authorities. The evidence which survives, admittedly limited, does not suggest that discipline at Queens' was enforced particularly firmly at this time, but it may have been no worse than in many other colleges. In the 1780s an attempt was made to improve standards of behaviour by instituting an annual prize in 'morals': the president was to award five guineas (or the same value in books) to the undergraduate whom he felt to be most deserving 'by regularity in attendance on Chapel, Hall, and Lectures, frugality in his Expences, and general Propriety of Conduct'.[52]

Fellow-commoners were unlikely to have been tempted by such a prize, which must have been designed to encourage the poor students, and we do not know what effect it had. Such measures stood less chance of success than the suggestion of Isaac Milner in 1810 that 'both in our domestic and our public discipline, a more strict attention to the infliction of the lesser censures for the lesser faults, and these censures gradually increasing in severity according to circumstances, would lead to the improvement of our Academical regulations', although he recognised that the best way to deal with persistent troublemakers was to have their parents remove them before they could do too much mischief.[53] It is possible that Milner's election to be president of Queens' in 1788 may have owned something to the belief that he would be a firm disciplinarian.

It must be stressed, however, that many students, including the

---

[50] Above, n. 49; Cowper (1783), 315–22; Howell (1814), xx.402–3.
[51] See his letters in Box 95, Crawford correspondence/4.
[52] Box 102 (the money was paid out of the Hughes bequest).
[53] Milner (1842), 396–8, and see also *ibid.*, 340.

wealthier ones, were studious and hard-working, although their activities were largely private and have therefore been less well recorded. Cambridge was far from dormant intellectually during the 18th century, and one of the most significant changes in its curriculum, the creation of the mathematics tripos, was a product of these years, as the following chapter seeks to explain.

15

Study and the curriculum in the 18th century

Teaching

Intellectual life in 18th century Cambridge was far from moribund, though at first sight it seems to lack the vigour of previous centuries. If it produced few great names after Newton and Bentley, there were many there who were good scholars in their day, but have since been forgotten.[1] One such was David Hughes, a long-serving Fellow of Queens' (1727 – 77), who 'was not known as a writer, except by some piece known only to his friends, without a name; but he was a judicious scholar'.[2] Hughes bequeathed a library of over 2,000 books to the college.[3] Henry James, president from 1675 – 1717, although he was Regius professor of divinity, published only one work, and that an unremarkable sermon,[4] but he did act as a moderator (a chief examiner in the schools), and this duty was regarded as being of great importance at that time: the reputation of a professor was made by his performance on such occasions, and the 'determination' (summing up and adjudication) which he delivered at the end of a disputation which he was judging was usually lengthy and used to display the full extent of his learning. A contemporary claimed to have 'seen the late Professor James so ready and fluent at the work on publick occasions, that strangers have been greatly surprised at it, and could hardly be convinced that there had not been some management and private correspondence beforehand between Professor and respondent'. James' fame endured long after his death.[5]

A foreign visitor to the university in Queen Anne's reign was surprised at the apparent lack of enthusiasm for learning there, and at how few lectures were given.[6] It became increasingly unusual for professors to lecture: when the chair of casuistical divinity became vacant in 1769, it attracted Robert Plumptre, who commented that 'though small in value . . . [it] has the recommendations of having

---

[1] Winstanley (1922), 4 – 5.
[2] Dyer (1814), ii.159.
[3] Book 73, f.100; this was the number received by the library after duplicates had been removed.
[4] Above, p. 149.
[5] Winstanley (1935), 104 – 6; Wordsworth (1968), 140.
[6] Mayor (1911), 134.

nothing to do for it, of interfering with no other preferment, and bringing with it no new residence or old house'.[7] A means of reforming this practice was suggested by Richard Davies in 1759: he wanted the creation of a large, separate, and professional lecturing corps, whose members would be allowed to marry and live in the town, and who would make their profits by levying fees on their audiences — thus the most popular lecturers would make the most money.[8] The notion was too radical to be taken up: ideas were expected to travel through informal, personal teaching, rather than university lectures, making the college the main forum for instruction.[9]

For a prospective student, the choice of tutor was all-important, determining the choice of college in most cases.[10] The procedure for admissions remained informal, depending largely on personal recommendations and introductions. In 1714 Ralph Thoresby of Leeds came to Cambridge to find a suitable college for his son. He visited the master of Trinity and a Fellow of Clare, to whom he had been recommended by the bishop of Ely, 'and after at Queens' College with the ingenious Mr Langwith (a native of York) recommended by Mr Baker of St John's, and preferred rather than any of his own College'. Thoresby had come to look for a suitable tutor above all else, and although Langwith's Yorkshire connections must have counted for something in his eyes, he did not find it easy to come to a decision: 'The Lord direct me in this matter of so great concern to the temporal and eternal interest of my son Ralph. Whether Clare Hall or Queens' College I cannot determine'.[11]

Initial personal contact might be with the master of a college rather than a tutor. The benefactor who sent Claudius Buchanan to Queens' in 1791 was acquainted with Milner and believed that this would help Buchanan's Cambridge career.[12] Milner's reputation was of great influence in raising the number of admissions to Queens' from the end of the 18th century.[13] Some parents were importunate: in 1708 Henry James recorded a visit he had received from a clergyman who 'came hither to enquire whether Archbishop Mountain did not found two Scholarships and whether his son who is now a boy of ten years old might not have one of them when he came to the University. I told him I did not doubt but he might, but that in probability I should not live soe

[7]   Winstanley (1935), 137 – 141; Wordsworth (1968), 133.
[8]   Davies (1759), 33 – 6.
[9]   Wordsworth (1874), 83 – 4; Wordsworth (1968), 11 – 12; Winstanley (1922), 5 – 7.
[10] Milner, for example, did not think there was much difference between colleges as such, Milner, (1842), 136.
[11] Wordsworth (1874), 113; he went to Queens', AC.
[12] Milner (1842), 104; AC.
[13] Above, p. 175. Milner had been sent to Queens' by his brother, a schoolmaster, former student at St Catharine's, Milner (1842), 4 – 6.

long'.[14]

The lack of a formal entrance procedure was to be regarded by 19th century reformers as a major failing, and a hindrance to further academic improvement. A university entrance examination would have remedied this, but colleges were jealous of their autonomy and blocked any schemes for a common entrance policy.[15] There is a story of Milner secretly examining two schoolboys who were pupils of a former Fellow of Queens' on a visit to the lodge:

'On the second or third day of our visit, he placed us in a bed-chamber, and said that he had a curiosity to know how we should translate certain passages from some classic authors, and do a problem or two in mathematics; that we should oblige him.

We got into a state of extravagant laughter while closeted together, and had not the slightest suspicion that we were undergoing an examination. We found afterwards, that each of us was admitted to his College on the ground of what we then did'.[16]

Although the number of tutors declined, and there was in consequence a greater emphasis on formal teaching, principally through college lectures, this did not necessarily mean that academic work was taken any less seriously. At some time in the late 17th century Queens' decided to hold an annual examination at the start of the Michaelmas term for students who were about to 'commence' for the degree of bachelor of arts in that academic year, and this practice continued throughout the 18th century.[17] Towards the end of the century some colleges introduced annual examinations for all students, and by the 1830s these had been adopted throughout the university.[18]

Such examinations were in addition to the traditional form of college exercise. At Queens' these continued to be taken seriously, but there are signs of change and even decay, caused largely by the fall in student numbers. In 1761 it was decided that the head lecturer in college should no longer charge fellow-commoners and absent Fellows for not performing disputations in chapel, 'they having been omitted for some years past', and some of the lesser lectureships were combined.[19]

---

[14] Book 80, f.10.
[15] Winstanley (1940), 167 – 8.
[16] Milner (1842), 288. Solomon Atkinson, a native of Cumbria, travelled to Carlisle on his own initiative to seek Milner's aid in gaining admission to Cambridge; Milner examined him on the spot, and recommended him to the college, Atkinson (1825), 495 – 6.
[17] OPR, f.157; Bligh (?1780), 19 – 20, (and see ibid., 15 – 19).
[18] Wordsworth (1874), 99 – 100; Wordsworth (1968), 14; Winstanley (1935), 316 – 8; Gascoigne, 'Mathematics', 556 – 7.
[19] CB (1734 – 87), f.63.

The exercises were also reformed and modernised: scholars were expected to compose verses in Greek or Latin once a week, but in 1761 this practice was abolished and instead they were instructed to prepare English themes on subjects to be set by the theological censor.[20] In 1768 the obligation laid on scholars to produce further verses twice a year on set subjects was replaced with a biannual essay in Latin prose or verse on some set topic 'relating to the British History or Constitution'; those who failed to do so were no longer to be fined, the traditional practice, but to be set to perform a declamation, or to learn some passage from a classical author by heart.[21] Such changes well reflect the reformist spirit in the college in its Whig-liberal heyday.

College scholarships and prizes were another spur to academic endeavour. In the late 17th century Queens' offered 40 scholarships and exhibitions, most of them worth about one shiling per week to their holders.[22] The number and value of scholarships had to be altered subsequently to compensate for their waning attractiveness. By the 1760s it was said that election to a scholarship at Queens' 'is by the alteration of times become no Mark of favour or distinction', for the number of students had fallen so low that the college had 'no choice ' in awarding them: 'They give them in course to those Students who will accept them, and they are often refus'd when offered'; the problem was apparently widespread in the university.[23] In 1779 several scholarships endowed in the 16th century were combined into a much smaller number, because they had been 'out of use for many years past on account of their trifling value'. A poor student at Queens' in the early 19th century recorded that 'my tutor had given me the benefit of some half dozen small scholarships'.[24]

The low number of students in the college meant also that there was seldom much competition for college prizes; by the 1760s these too were said to be often given to students who did not deserve them, for it was felt that the withholding of prizes would discourage other students from studying.[25] Efforts to raise academic standards at Queens' included the instutition of Hughes prizes in 1780, endowed out of the benefaction of David Hughes. Five annual prizes were to be awarded. Two, worth five guineas each, were for the students best at declaiming during the year,

[20] ibid.
[21] ibid., fos.79v – 80.
[22] Book 80, f.48 (second pagination); there were 22 at 10d per week each, 10 at 1s, four at 2s, two at 2s 6d, and two at 4s.
[23] Box 95, documents on John Lloyd.
[24] CB (1734 – 87), f.105v; Atkinson (1825), 506.
[25] Box 95, documents concerning the Hughes benefaction. In 1783 and 1784 the chapel clerk's place, which was usually shared between two students, was granted to a single student until another could be found to share it with him, CB (1734 – 87), f.123; and see above, p. 193.

'regard being had to the Composition and Manner of Delivery'. Two more prizes of the same value were for the students who did best in the college examinations, which were said to be held by the tutors biannually.[26] The final prize, of ten guineas, was for the bachelor of arts 'as shall make the best Discourse in English on a subject out of the New Testament to be given by the Master'; in practice, it was common to give extra, smaller prizes to runners-up for this award, although there were some years when it was not awarded at all.[27]

Fellow-commoners were encouraged to compete for some of these Hughes prizes. They were generally exempted from the regular academic obligations, such as college lectures and many of the college exercises. At most colleges they had only to declaim their own compositions in the later 18th century, and at Queens' they were spared even that: it was said that no fellow-commoner declaimed in the chapel there before 1782.[28] In the university overall, slightly fewer than a third of them graduated in the 18th century (although the proportion increased towards the end), compared with 70% of pensioners and well over 80% of scholars and sizars.[29]

Some fellow-commoners were serious-minded and hard-working — one such was Philip Yorke, who came up to Queens' in 1774. Yorke's self-imposed timetable reveals his conscientiousness, and is an important illustration of the academic routine of the college. He rose at 7.00; he was at chapel from 7.30 till 8.00, and breakfasted and studied Demosthenes from 8.00 till 9.00, before his tutorial on that author (with his private tutor, which only the wealthier students could afford). Between 10.00 and 11.00 there was a college lecture on classics; from 11.00 till 12.00, another on Euclid. Between 12.00 and 1.00 Yorke walked and dressed for dinner; 1.00 till 2.00 was spent at dinner and in the combination room (for fellow-commoners dined with the Fellows). From 2.00 till 3.00 he visited friends in their rooms, and between 3.00 and 5.00 he read and wrote letters. He attended chapel from 5.30 till 6.00; between 6.00 and 7.00 he visited friends and drank tea, and from 7.00 until 9.00 was back in his own rooms studying classics and mathematics. From 9.00 till 11.00 he again visited friends in their rooms, or recieved them in his own.[30]

The lectures in classics and mathematics which Yorke attended were daily ones, and these remained a central part of college instruction. But

[26] See above, p. 205, for the introduction of college exams.
[27] CB (1734 – 87), fos. 109 – 109v; Book 83. In 1811 the BA prize went to G. C. Gorham, a college Fellow, MS 80/2; Gorham was later to be involved in a celebrated theological dispute, see below, p. 268.
[28] Winstanley (1935), 198 – 9.
[29] Hans (1951), 45.
[30] Winstanley (1935), 225 – 6; see also Winstanley (1922), 24 – 5.

with so many Fellows non-resident there was sometimes a shortage of willing lecturers, and during the second half of the century several of the lectureships were combined.[31] The small number of official college tutors, and the growing importance of the mathematics tripos, encouraged the use of private tutors by those who could afford them, and these became a prominent feature of teaching in the university in the later years of the century. Many Fellows were grateful for this extra source of income, and any MA with a reputation as a good scholar and a competent teacher could secure almost as many pupils as he wished. Officially, private tutors were not approved of, for the colleges did not control them. It was customary to hire one for the last undergraduate year only, which to Robert Plumptre's reckoning 'on the one hand encouraged idleness in the foregoing years, and on the other occasioned expence to parents and [has] been heavily complained of by them'.[32] Isaac Milner admitted to disliking them 'as a general system, but . . . if a good private tutor can be provided, who will live a good deal with the young man, and watch him, I think *that* the likeliest method of insuring success; that is, freedom from the corruption of numbers of youths let loose'. But he also warned that 'if you send a lad to any college, and write to his public tutor, requesting a good private tutor, the object often is, rather to gratify some poor Bachelor of Arts than anything else'. Solomon Atkinson, a harsh critic of private tuition, reckoned it was the result of inadequate lecturing.[33]

Attempts made by the university in the late 18th and early 19th centuries to restrict the activities of private tutors were unsuccessful: as long as there was no reform of university and collegiate teaching, they remained a necessary evil.[34] The teaching system was probably in need of improvement by this time, although vigorous and widespread reform remained a long way off.

Studies

The most significant aspect of the university's intellectual history in the 18th century — and one of the most important features of its intellectual history as a whole — was the emergence and dominance of the mathematical tripos. By the end of the 17th century the scholastic curriculum was beginning to decay, and the value of the traditional academic disputation came increasingly into question during the

---

[31] Sargent (1833), 78 – 9; Box 102; CB (1734 – 87), f.95v; CB (1787 – 1832), 26.4.1796. See also above, p. 205.
[32] Winstanley (1935), 331 – 4.
[33] Milner (1842), 136; Atkinson (1825), 501 – 2.
[34] See above, n. 32.

century which followed. Hence a hitherto relatively minor regulation — that a candidate after fulfilling all the necessary requirements for the degree could be questioned publicly in the schools by any MA — was used increasingly as a means of evaluation.

This process was well under way by the 1730s. Tripos lists were first published in the late 1740s, and from 1753 these were divided into wranglers and senior and junior optimes, a sign of the attention now paid to the results of the examination. The disputation degenerated still further into a preliminary classification only; the examination became dominant, and there was intense competition for high positions in the tripos list — although for most undergraduates, who sought a pass degree only, the examination was a perfunctory business, and the competition was solely for those who sought it. At the same time, the philosophical content of the examination declined, and it became predominantly mathematical.[35]

The reasons for this transformation are complex, but the new emphasis on mathematics is significant. It may have been favoured because, as a supposedly closed and unchanging system, it was uncontroversial, and unlikely to lead to challenges of the authority of church and state. But more significantly, it was seen as a vigorous mental discipline, a modern substitute for the logic which had been studied since medieval times and virtually died out in Cambridge in the 18th century.[36]

There was opposition for the changes: complaints against mathematical abilities being the sole criterion for election to fellowships (which were made on the basis of tripos results) led finally to the creation of the classics tripos in 1824. Robert Ingram, a Fellow of Queens' in the 1790s, was among those who complained: he wanted more emphasis placed on the study of divinity. Another was Thomas Thomason, a Fellow at about the same time, who spoke of 'the "mathematical religion" which so prevails'. Solomon Atkinson, who migrated from Queens' to Trinity, where he came top of the mathematical tripos in 1820, was subsequently a bitter critic of the system:

'The period which should have been employed in acquiring information that might have rendered me a useful and enlightened member of society, was wasted in marshalling mathematical symbols, which in the process did not discipline the mind, and which in the acquirement did not prepare it for any useful and active

---

[35] Gascoigne, 'Mathematics', 547–553; Wordsworth (1968), chapters II–VII.
[36] Gascoigne, 'Mathematics', 554–76.

occupation'.[37]

But the subject had come to dominate the undergraduate curriculum, and academic life in the colleges altered radically as a result.

With the notable exceptions of Isaac Barrow and Isaac Newton in the late 17th century, Cambridge did not produce any great mathematicians during the period. During the Restoration many dons were interested, but there was little new research.[38] In the 18th century, Cambridge mathematics was totally dominated by the ideas of Isaac Newton, and this inspiration must have been one cause of the growth of the mathematical tripos.[39] The unfortunate result of this was that Newton's theories acquired the status of holy writ, and almost all English mathematicians in the 18th century were impervious to new mathematical ideas emerging on the continent.[40]

Towards the end of the century an 'analytical school' rose up to oppose this.[41] Its case was argued forcefully by a Fellow of Queens', John Toplis. In an influential article published in 1805, the year after he had taken his MA, Toplis lamented the fact that 'this island, after having astonished Europe by the most glorious display of talents in mathematics and the sciences dependent upon them, should suddenly suffer its ardour to cool, and almost entirely to neglect those studies in which it infinitely excelled all other nations'.[42] Two years later he wrote an article in the *Edinburgh Review* alleging that scarcely a dozen men in England had read one of the most important mathematical works published in Europe, La Place's *Traité de Mécanique Céleste*; still less had anyone added to its conclusions. Toplis translated parts of the work himself, with notes.[43]

On a more personal note, perhaps, Toplis had also complained in 1805 of the lack of patronage afforded to mathematics and science in general; he felt that 'The sciences are so abstruse that, to excel in them, a student must give up his whole time, and that without any prospect of recompense; and should his talents and application enable him to

---

[37] Wordsworth (1968), 214; Ingram (1792), 46ff; Sargent (1833), 85; Atkinson (1825), 492. As early as 1739 Daniel Wray was amused by a fierce mathematical dispute in the university because its passion was as intense as any theological or political quarrel, Nichols (1817), i.79. Another difficulty caused by the new emphasis was that mathematical teaching in schools did not develop at the same rate, so that few boys were sufficiently prepared for the Cambridge course, see e.g. Winstanley (1935), 53 – 4, for Philip Yorke. This was surely a major reason for the rise of the private tutor or coach.

[38] Gascoigne (1985), 413 – 9; and see above, p. 101.

[39] Wordsworth (1968), 65 – 71; Ball (1889), 74 – 116; see also Gascoigne, 'Newtonianism'.

[40] Ball (1889), 117.

[41] *ibid.*, 117; Dubbey (1978), 10 – 22.

[42] Dubbey (1978), 11.

[43] *ibid.*

compose a work of the highest merit, he must never expect, by publishing it, to clear one-half of the expense of printing', and he contrasted this with the much more favourable conditions which then prevailed in France.[44] Toplis was a non-resident Fellow for much of his career at Queens'; for many years he was headmaster of a school in Nottingham, and it seems likely that he gave encouragement — and quite possibly private tuition — to the young George Green, who was to become one of the most eminent 19th century mathematicians, although when Green went to Cambridge it was to Caius rather than to Queens'.[45]

Toplis is the only mathematician at Queens' known to have taken an interest in new mathematical ideas, although Isaac Milner, who was president when Toplis was elected a Fellow, held the Lucasian professorship in mathematics which had once been Newton's. Milner had been a brilliant undergraduate mathematician. He was senior wrangler in 1774, and his examiners were so overwhelmed by his performance that they wrote the word '*Incomparabilis*' against his name.[46] He did not produce any original work thereafter, and he never lectured, but certainly until his election as Lucasian professor in 1798 he often examined in the senate house, 'and was frequently called upon to settle the places of men in the higher brackets'. His strong will and strong opinions made him oblivious to the complaints of praelectors who disputed the positions he had given their men in the tripos.[47] He is also said to have been a successful mathematics tutor whilst a Fellow at Queens', the practice papers which he made out for his pupils being so highly prized that on one occasion a bedmaker was bribed by a student at another college to obtain some for him.[48]

Another president of Queens', Joshua King (1832 – 57), became Lucasian professor in 1839; he too had been senior wrangler, in 1819, but he did not make any significant contribution to mathematical studies. According to Solomon Atkinson in 1825:

'He *might* have been one of the first mathematicians of Europe: he *is* the tutor of a college. His extraordinary powers of acquisition, the energy of his mind, and the vigour of his temperament, are wholly

[44] *ibid.*, 20 – 1.

[45] AC; D. M. Cannell, pers. comm.; for Green, see Brooke (1985), 195 – 6.

[46] *DNB*; Milner (1842), 707 – 8. Milner's gifts were not confined to mathematics: his act for the BD degree in 1786 was described by one moderator as 'the best act . . . that I ever presided at', and an 'intellectual feast', Watson (1818), i.35 – 6; see also Gunning (1854), ii.47.

[47] He was quite impartial, Gunning (1854), i.90 – 3. For Milner's lecturing and examining in general, see Wordsworth (1968), 71, 78; Ball (1889), 102 – 3; Tanner (1917), 83 and n. 6; Baker (1869), 849.

[48] Milner (1842), 11.

employed in making up college bills, arranging college squabbles, and looking after the morals of Freshmen . . . The man that might have rescued the name of English science from contempt is fast approaching the honours of a three-bottle man in a tippling college, and of the best whist player in a gambling University. The resident fellow who in his youth spends his afternoons over bad port, and his nights in cardplaying, in the decline of life becomes, as a matter of course, a silly and besotted old woman in a Doctor's gown'.[49]

There may be an element of poetical licence in this description, but both Milner and King are typical of that conventional attitude of the 18th and early 19th century university which saw teaching, and not research, as a Fellow's main duty, and which regarded professorships as rewards for ability, and not as positions with major academic obligations.

It is not true, as has sometimes been suggested, that for scientific studies in general Restoration Cambridge was something of an intellectual wasteland. Students continued to learn much outside the traditional curriculum, new philosophical and scientific ideas, especially those of Descartes, were a major topic of discussion, and traditional scholasticism was gradually losing its central rôle in the undergraduate course.[50] Science was not separate from other academic interests: not only did many university men work in different fields of science, but it was still normal for dons to research into both arts and sciences.[51] Vigani's friends in Cambridge, who included Newton, were men who shared his interest in a wide range of scientific subjects.[52] Richard Davies was interested in medicine principally, but a 'Pneumatick Engin' was to be found in his rooms in 1735. William Sedgwick is not remembered for any great academic excellence, but in 1752 it was reported that the president's lodge contained several musical and mathematical instruments, and that there was a printing press in a room on the ground floor on which he was printing his astronomical works.[53]

There was a respectable scientific tradition in the college in the 18th century. Vigani was the university's first professor of chemistry, but this was a personal title only, without stipends or duties.[54] In the middle of the century, after the chair had been formally established and endowed, it was occupied by John Hadley, a Fellow of Queens' and a friend of the poet Thomas Gray. In 1758, two years after becoming professor, Hadley was granted leave by the college 'to divert to the Study of Physick and to

[49] Ball (1889), 132; Atkinson (1825), 504.
[50] Gascoigne (1985), 391 – 411.
[51] ibid., 420 – 3.
[52] ibid., 404, 418 – 9.
[53] Gunther (1969), 79.
[54] See above, p. 102.

have the Physick Fellowship', and he subsequently became a physician.[55]

We know that Hadley lectured, because a plan of his lectures was printed in 1758,[56] but one of his successors, Isaac Pennington, enlisted Milner, then only a Fellow of Queens', to substitute for him.[57] Milner printed plans of some of these lectures; nobody has suggested that they were brilliantly original, but the publication of the plans, and Milner's willingness to lecture, point to his enthusiasm for the subject.[58] This must have made him an obvious candidate for the new Jacksonian professorship of natural and experimental philosophy endowed in 1783, and which he held for nine years: the terms of the benefaction specified that the professor was to lecture and give public demonstrations of experiments frequently.[59] Milner was a popular lecturer, and apparently a good one: in Gunning's words, 'He did not treat the subjects under discussion very profoundly, but he continued to amuse us, and we generally returned laughing heartily at something that had occurred during the lecture'.[60]

He was also a keen experimenter. In 1782 he was given permission to build a chemistry laboratory in the college's stable yard, but he developed a lung complaint 'by incautiously inhaling some noxious gas', from which it was said he never fully recovered.[61] In addition, Milner was interested in practical mechanics, and he had a workshop fitted up in Queens' — in the lodge, according to his niece — complete with lathes, furnace, work-benches, grind-stones, bellows and all kinds of apparatus.[62] This had to be paid for out of his own pocket, but in 1794 he persuaded the college to provide substantial financial assistance for a new air pump and 'pneumatical apparatus', which, though it was to be kept in the lodge and intended principally for Milner's own use, was to be available to the college tutors 'for the purpose of instructing their Pupils in their public Lectures',[63] so that it seems there was some

[55] Tanner (1917), 86; CB (1734 – 87), f.58; *DNB*. Hadley's work is discussed in Gascoigne, *Holy Alliance* (forthcoming), chapter VI.
[56] Wordsworth (1968), 188.
[57] *ibid.*, 172 – 3.
[58] *ibid.*, 190, n. 3; Milner (?1780), and (1784); Coleby (1954), 237. There is a fair copy of some of his lecture notes in the college library, MS 77.
[59] Thirty-six lectures and thirty experiments per year, Coleby (1954), 235 – 6.
[60] Coleby (1954), 241 – 57; Gunning (1854), i.259 – 60; see also Winstanley (1935), 177 – 8. Gunning, who did not like Milner, remarked of him that 'The University, perhaps, never produced a man of more eminent abilities', Gunning (1854), i.257.
[61] Milner (1842), 14; Coleby (1954), 237; CB (1734 – 87), f.118. But note his suspected hypochondria, above, p. 182.
[62] Milner (1842), 51; Coleby (1954), 237. Milner also designed a new kind of reading lamp, Box 102; Milner (1842), 364 – 5. Perhaps Milner's enthusiasm for practical science is shown in the donation by the college of 10s 6d in 1794 to 'J. Bowles the Improver of the Churn', Book 8, f.130.
[63] Gunther (1969), 94; Book 8, fos.131, 135v, 136v, 142v; CB (1787 – 1832), 2.6.1794.

interest in natural science at Queens' at this time.[64]

There had been some rudimentary study of geology at Cambridge in the 17th century, and the Woodwardian chair of geology was established in 1727. The third Woodwardian professor was the brilliant Queens' scientist John Michell. He held the post for only two years, from 1762–4, when he resigned in order to marry and take up a benefice; he is not known to have lectured. His scientific distinction was mainly in the field of astronomy, where he was the first person to make a realistic estimate of the distance to the stars, and to discover the existence of double stars,[65] but he read a paper on earthquakes to the Royal Society in 1760, which was highly regarded, and this may have been one of the reasons for his election to the Woodwardian professorship.[66]

In 1818 another Queensman, George Gorham, sought election to the chair, but he was heavily defeated by Adam Sedgwick of Trinity, who knew nothing of geology, but promised to apply himself to its study after his election. Although Gorham had not published on geology, he had worked in the field, and Sedgwick's much-publicised remark about him that 'I knew absolutely nothing of geology, whereas he knew a good deal — but it was all wrong' was just a cheap joke.[67] British geology remained an 'essentially amateur' affair until the middle of the 19th century;[68] and Sedgwick was to become a notable geologist, but his election in 1818 owed much to the formidable canvassing machine at Trinity, which provided more than one third of his votes, and more than Gorham could muster in total. The large colleges could exert great influence in such elections; Gorham saw this one as a contest between qualifications and influence, 'To say nothing of the prejudices against a small College, and a methodistical [evangelical] one — and my having little acquaintance in the University'.[69] The anti-evangelical feeling which Gorham cited may have been a significant factor in his defeat.

---

[64] Milner and another Queensman, Joseph Carlyle (who was to become professor of Arabic), were among the founder members of a society for the promotion of philosophy and general literature in 1784, but this collapsed two years later for want of support. In 1819 Milner was one of the signatories to a notice calling the meeting at which the Cambridge Philosophical Society was founded, Cooper, iv.410; Coleby (1954), 238.

[65] DSB; Michell had a wide range of other scientific interests; see also Gascoigne, Holy Alliance (forthcoming), chapter VI. The study of astronomy was in a healthy condition in both universities in the 18th century, Wordsworth (1968), chapter XXI.

[66] Clark and Hughes (1890), i.191–2; Winstanley (1935), 169; Wordsworth (1968), 196–7; Gunther (1969), 84, 439. He also constructed an apparatus for measuring the relative density of the earth, Gunther (1969), 84.

[67] Clark and Hughes (1890), i.155–161; Gunther (1969), 435; Wordsworth (1968), 198.

[68] Porter, 'Natural Sciences', 194.

[69] Clark and Hughes (1890), i.155–61; the quotation is from p. 157. Queens' was much larger than before, thanks to the evangelicals, but Trinity and St John's were much larger still and very influential.

The standard of medical teaching in the English universities in the 18th century was not regarded nearly as highly as that given by Scottish and continental universities,[70] and they did not make a significant contribution to the development of medical science.[71] Although medicine had been in the university curriculum since the earliest times, the number of students taking medical degrees had never been large, and the subject continued to be of little significance numerically.[72] Nonetheless, there was a core of students and Fellows sufficiently interested to undertake scientific enquiry.[73]

The number of medical students at Queens' increased in the 18th century as a proportion of the university's total, although not enough to make it one of the foremost medical colleges in this respect.[74] Medical teaching was primarily a college activity, and a college which had one or more physicians of repute was sure to attract students.[75] The peak period for several colleges in terms of the number of students was in the late 17th century, and the standard was by no means poor. After 1730 there was something of a decline in university medicine, and it did not revive again until the 1820s.[76] Richard Davies (Fellow of Queens' 1730 – 40; Fellow of the Royal Society in 1738), was one of the most articulate and important critics of the quality of medical teaching given at the university. In a book which he published in 1759 Davies called for greater statutory freedoms to allow Fellows, instead of being compelled to read for holy orders, to study subjects such as medicine; and for far greater expenditure on scientific instruments and equipment. He pointed to a general decay in standards, a 'universal Rust' which had 'spread over the Institutions of both ancient and modern times'.[77]

Several medical Fellows of note were at Queens' during the period. In the 1650s there had been a flourishing group of young Fellows at Cambridge interested in medicine and related subjects such as zoology, botany and chemistry, which had included Walter Needham of Queens', and interest in medicine continued there after the Restoration.[78] The boundaries between scientific subjects were loosely drawn: Vigani, though he was a chemist principally, lectured on *materia medica*,

---

[70] Speck (1977), 50. The expenses of a medical education increased from the late 17th century onwards, Holmes (1982), 209 – 10.
[71] Wordsworth (1968), 171 – 2.
[72] Above, p. 101; Rook (1969), 111 – 14.
[73] Gascoigne (1985), 396.
[74] Thirty-four out of 678 who received all or a substantial part of their medical education at Cambridge between 1660 and 1759; Queens' was equal eighth in the list of Cambridge colleges, Rook (1969), 111.
[75] *ibid.*, 116 – 7, 119 – 20.
[76] *ibid.*, 111, 120 – 1.
[77] Davies (1759), 1 – 59; the quotation is from p. 16. For Davies, see *DNB*; Rook (1969), 114.
[78] Gascoigne (1985), 397 – 400; see Rook (1969), 117; For Needham, see also above, p. 101.

and may have lectured in anatomy, as well as prescribing medicines to students.[79] Russell Plumptre, a medical graduate of Queens', though not a Fellow of any college, was one of the university's three 18th century Regius professors of medicine. Nothing is known of his abilities: he does not seem to have lectured or published, according to the fashion of the time, although he was professor from 1741, when he was 32, until 1793. The Plumptre family included several physicians: Russell's father Henry was a Fellow of Queens', a Fellow of the Royal Society and president of the Royal College of Physicians; his great-grandfather was also a successful physician.[80]

Several other noted physicians of the early 18th century were products of Queens': Cambridge, if it did not produce any great medical scientists, did produce a number of successful and respected physicians, including several of the period's most important medical investigators.[81]

Philip Yorke's timetable reveals the continuing importance of classics in the undergraduate curriculum, and eighteenth century Cambridge possessed some eminent classicists.[82] Richard Bentley, the irascible master of Trinity, was of course the *nonpareil*, and it is all too easy to overlook the other lesser, but gifted classicists in the university.[83]

There were some distinguished classical scholars at Queens' in Bentley's time. Joseph Wasse, who became a Fellow in 1698, produced critical editions of Sallust and Thucydides which were widely praised. He was a friend of Bentley, who is said to have observed: 'When I am dead, Wasse will be the most learned figure in England'. In fact Bentley survived him by four years.[84] While a student, Wasse had studied under John Davies (president, 1717 – 31), another close friend, and ally of Bentley. Davies edited texts by several classical authors, but was particularly known for his commentaries on Cicero's philosophical works. Bentley contributed an appendix to one of these editions; and another work which Davies left unfinished on his death was destroyed shortly afterwards in a fire at the house of Bentley's nephew, who was preparing it for the press.[85] A foreign visitor to the college in Queen Anne's reign recorded in his diary that 'we visited at Queens' college

[79] Gascoigne (1985), 401 – 4; Rook (1969), 117 – 8.
[80] Wordsworth (1968), 172; Rook (1969), 116; Rolleston (1932), 161 – 2; below, appendix 15. Plumptre attended patients at Addenbrookes hospital in the first year after it was opened (1766 – 7), but not thereafter.
[81] Rook (1969), 115. Such men as Thomas Pellett, Poley Clopton, and Thomas Fuller, *DNB*; *AC*; Rook (1969), 114; Gray, 215 – 6.
[82] Winstanley (1922), 4.
[83] For Bentley, see Pfeiffer (1976), 143 – 159.
[84] Sandys (1908), ii.412, 447; *DNB*; Nichols (1812), i.706 – 7. Wasse also wrote scientific articles. The most recent historian of classical studies in England has described Wasse as 'massively learned, but lacking in discrimination', Brink (1986), 85.
[85] Nichols (1812), i.706; Mayor (1911), 450 – 6; Sandys (1908), ii.412; *DNB*; White (1965), 160 – 1; Brink (1986), 35, 36, 85, 96.

Mr. John Davis, who is *socius* there, and has made himself famous by the editing of some *autorum classicorum*'.[86] Wasse and Davies did not bring about any major advance in classical studies — that had to wait for Porson — but they were energetic scholars with much of interest to say.[87] There were no classicists of their stature at Queens' during the rest of the century.

Latin remained the formal university language.[88] The story that Robert Plumptre was ridiculed for making several errors in a Latin speech he delivered as vice-chancellor in 1777 need not be proof that his grasp of the language was poor, but it does appear that facility in classical tongues generally declined in the period.[89] At Queens' in the late 17th century all students were expected to speak Latin at table, except on a few special days when English was permitted. But by the late 18th century fines were imposed on anyone who spoke three consecutive words of Latin in hall. J. H. Gray wrote in the 1890s that there were still Fellows alive who could remember being fined a bottle of wine for the offence.[90] It is a strange transformation, not easily explained.

With the exception of the mathematics tripos, there were no great academic reforms university-wide in the 18th century, although there were several proposals for reform. The proposal by John Jebb of Peterhouse in the early 1770s to introduce annual university examinations was the most substantial of these. In 1774 a university committee was set up to consider reforms in the light of Jebb's proposals. Its members included Robert Plumptre, who was known to be a supporter of Jebb, and its report came out in favour of annual university examinations for sons of the nobility and fellow-commoners, who had not had to sit any before, and additional examinations for pensioners and sizars. But, as Plumptre predicted, the committee's labours would 'be rendered vain by the Senate', with its 'disinclination to innovation and reformation', coupled with prejudice against some of the reformers.[91] It was the last major attempt at reform before the 19th century.

Plumptre was also a critic of the lax regulations for degrees in law, which made their acquisition a scandalously easy matter: in 1766 he complained that the practice had 'got to such a height that it most

---

[86]   Mayor (1911), 145 – 6. Dyer called Davies 'one of the most correct critics of his age', Dyer (1814), i.158; Brink states that he had 'more sense' than Wasse, and that 'his interests have something of that seventeenth-century range which was fast disappearing in his time', Brink (1986), 85.

[87]   Brink (1986), 84 – 5, 96.

[88]   Wordsworth (1968), 90 – 1.

[89]   DNB; Wordsworth (1968), 99 – 106; Gascoigne, 'Mathematics', 549.

[90]   Wordsworth (1968), 90; Gray, 209 – 10; OPR, f.157v; and see above, p. 206.

[91]   Winstanley (1935), 323 – 6. For the broader context of these reforms, see Gascoigne, *Holy Alliance* (forthcoming), chapter VII.

undoubtedly requires some stop to be put to it. It is the refuge of idleness and ignorance, and yet gives advantage over those who employ their time and pains in taking a degree in arts'. But such criticisms had little effect at that time.[92]

Throughout its Whig phase, Queens' was a home of sympathisers with academic reform, as with other reforms. Richard Davies wrote in 1759 despairing at 'the Custom, which has of late years prevailed, of sending many of our youth to foreign Universities for their Education'.[93] Regulations and discipline had been 'too much permitted to creep on in the same lazy channel, which was marked out for them in the days of Gothic ignorance and superstition: While nothing is wanting but a power to give their waters new directions, in order to fertilize every quarter of useful knowledge'. He also brought a complaint against a fundamental failing in academic method: disputations, he felt, were 'very apt to give a polemic turn of thought; in common life to raise every discourse into a debate, thereby stamping the Scholar with the unfashionable name of Pedant'.[94] He was an opponent of the statutes which compelled Fellows to take holy orders, arguing that this forced many gifted intellectuals out of the university.[95]

Another Queens' reformer, at the end of the century, was Robert Ingram, whose opposition to evangelicalism has already been noted.[96] Ingram was interested in political economy, which though a popular interest of the British educated classes in the early 19th century, was slow to gain a foothold in Cambridge, thanks to innate conservatism, apathy, and a dislike of anything to do with politics intruding into academic life.[97] Ingram published several works on the subject, including an attack on Malthus, and a pamphlet urging the university to establish a course of public lectures.[98] The call attracted little interest. Political economy was at that time associated by many with the radical doctrines of the French Revolution, and Ingram's claim that it would teach the poor the proper limits of their aspirations was doubted.[99]

As with so many 18th century reform proposals, Ingram's was ahead of its time: it was not until 1863 that a salaried chair in political economy was endowed. It would be wrong of course to judge the century as a whole by the standards of the later Victorian era, with which it has so often been unfavourably compared, but the changes — in all aspects of academic life — which the university experienced in the 18th century are

[92] Winstanley (1935), 57 – 60.
[93] Davies (1759), 7.
[94] ibid., 9, 12 – 13.
[95] ibid., 21 – 2.
[96] Above, pp. 174 – 5.
[97] All these general details are from Rashid (1980), 282 – 90.
[98] ibid., 283; DNB; Dyer (1814), ii.160.
[99] Rashid (1980), 287.

dwarfed by the massive and far-reaching innovations of the 19th, which transformed the university more radically than at any time since the period of the Renaissance and Reformation.

16

College Fellows in the nineteenth century

In the 19th century, and especially with the enhanced moral righteousness of the Victorian period, college Fellows began to attract increasing criticism from the outside world. The conventional characterisation of donnish types had rarely been complimentary: they were typically regarded as isolated, pedantic, formal, authoritarian, humourless, indolent, and as great feasters and drinkers. These were stereotyped pictures, but like all such stereotypes they were not without foundation, and they were significant in setting the ideological framework for the Victorian university reforms.[1]

It is by no means clear if the period of the evangelicals' domination of Queens' led to any significant improvement in the standard of behaviour and conscientiousness of the fellowship. Milner's strong rule may have suppressed deep divisions within the society, for a series of bitter disputes broke out after his death, perhaps all the more bitter for having been suppressed for so long.

The first signs of trouble appeared at the election of Milner's successor, Henry Godfrey. It was usual for mastership elections to be contested: Godfrey, a Fellow since 1803, was opposed by William Mandell, who had become a Fellow in the same year, and by George Barnes, elected in 1799, and now rector of the college living at Grimston in Norfolk.[3] Mandell's was the more serious challenge, and he commanded a fair measure of support among the fellowship on account of his great experience of college business and his solid evangelicalism; one of the Fellows, Joseph Jee, claimed that he was Milner's favourite to succeed him as president.[3] J. H. Gray, evidently relying upon some oral tradition which has not survived, alleged that the reason for Mandell's failure to win sufficient votes 'is to be found in the unhappy mental

---

[1] Rothblatt (1981), 190–3; Winstanley (1940), 397–403. There was a new interest in drink in the early 19th century: heavy drinking was not new, but college societies now began to consume a wider and more sophisticated range of drinks, Rothblatt (1975), 270–1. At Queens', sherry, port and madeira appear in the 1820s instead of just red or white wine as previously, Book 8, fos.213v, 214–214v, 233v, 235v, 236v, 244v. The university registrary, Joseph Romilly, dined at Queens' on the audit day in 1835: 'A very hospitable entertainment with kitchen wines and kitchen candles: the last I thought objectionable. — I left at 7.30 before Cards began', Romilly (1967), 67.

[2] Bowdler (1821), 3; AC.

[3] Bowdler (1821), 63; Joseph Jee's letter book, letter of 11.5.1820.

aberration of which he was afterwards the victim', but we do not know what this was, and it is surely unlikely that Fellows would have voted for him had there been doubts concerning his mental stability. Mandell was active for a good many years to come — he preached Charles Simeon's funeral sermon in 1836 — and he remained a Fellow until his death in 1843.[4]

Godfrey was elected in April 1820, but a quarrel then broke out about the validity of the election: it was alleged that the procedure followed at his admission had been irregular, and, more substantially, that he was not eligible to stand for the presidency. The case was heard early in 1821 by the lord chancellor, acting on behalf of the crown as visitor of the college; and although a great number of accusations were bandied about at this time, in March 1821 he found in favour of Godfrey and ruled that the result of the election should stand. He further decreed that the costs of all the contending parties, which were not insubstantial, should be paid out of college funds.[5]

The dispute generated much ill-feeling in the college, expressed in a series of quarrels over the next four years. The first which we know of came to a head in 1821: in October of that year Godfrey summoned the Fellows 'for the purpose of taking into consideration frequent interruptions of Harmony and open Violations of Decency which had been stated by a Majority of the Fellows as having prevailed for some time past, in one instance unhappily productive of Personal Violence'. They met on six days, four of them consecutively, and as a result, several Fellows were censured. William Mandell expressed the 'deepest contrition' but was nonetheless 'very severely reprimanded' by the president for 'repeated Insults in the Hall and Combination Room . . . open Acts of Provocation . . . Attacks on Private Character . . . a want of Delicate Regard to the feelings of several Members of the Society'. He promised to 'be more circumspect in the whole of my conduct and behaviour'. George Hewitt was found guilty of 'violating order and Decorum in the Combination Room . . . by striking Mr. Mandell the first Blow and using terms of Reproach to him under the Irritation of great provocation'; Hewitt also tendered his profound apologies.

Two censures passed at one of the meetings were, for some reason, not recorded in the college conclusion book: Hewitt, in addition to his other offence, was censured 'for accusing the President of Partiality'; and John Hubbersty was found guilty of 'Violating Order and Decorum in the Combination Room', but was not censured further because 'he acted under the influence of Passion having been irritated by Gross Provocation'. The meetings were evidently heated: at one of them

---

[4]   Gray, 249; AC; above, chapter 12, n. 153.
[5]   Bowdler (1821); Box 95; Book 8, fos.211, 216v; Gray, 247 – 9.

Edward Anderson was censured for 'tending to asperse most grossly' the characters of three other Fellows present; he quickly apologised, claiming that his remarks were uttered in the 'heat of Debate'.[6]

Conflict was renewed in 1822 when the society held judgment in a quarrel between Hubbersty and the senior bursar, Joseph Jee. Jee admitted to having cast unfair aspersions upon Hubbersty's character, and offered a full apology. The Fellows decided that no further action was necessary: Jee's words, they felt, had been uttered 'under the influence of peculiar circumstances which might lead him to entertain a mistaken notion of his duty but which by no means afford any justification of his Conduct'. But they also rejected Hubbersty's counter-accusation that Jee had brought a 'conspiracy' against him; and whilst Jee had 'manifested some neglect and betrayed confusion in managing the pecuniary concerns of the College', it was felt that 'his integrity and zeal for the best interests of the College have been altogether unimpeached and . . . his incapacity to conduct its affairs has not been established'. The hearing of these accusations and counter-accusations occupied six days.[7]

One can only speculate about the causes of this and the other quarrels. Jee claimed in April 1822 that in 1819 Milner had asked him to enquire into Hubbersty's character, and that rumours were in circulation that Hubbersty had kept a woman in the town; these matters were doubtless raised at the hearing.[8] The quarrels of 1821 and 1822 were probably connected; they were only the visible features of a deeper undercurrent of discontent. In September 1821 Jee was in dispute with Mandell over the latter's failure to settle the tutorial account, and had to submit the case to the president's arbitration; Jee had supported Mandell in the election of 1820.[9] In July 1821 Jee commented in a private letter on the hostility between himself and some of the other Fellows; and in 1825 he was admonished and fined by the governing body for absenting himself from the college without leave and refusing to explain his action, as well as for having 'denied and resisted the Authority of the President in manner and language most contemptuous and insulting'.[10]

The bitterness generated by the disputes of 1820 – 1 was perhaps still felt in 1827, when there was a row between Godfrey and the Fellows over the election of a senior bursar. Godfrey's nominee was rejected by a majority of the Fellows, but he would not permit the nomination of anyone else, arguing that the president's concurrence was necessary in the election; the Fellows doubted this, and did not believe that he was

---

[6] CB (1787 – 1832), 17.10.1821, 18.10.1821, 19.10.1821; Box 102.
[7] Box 102. Note the difficult financial situation at the time, below, pp. 304 – 5.
[8] Joseph Jee's letter book, entry of 2.4.1822.
[9] *Dial* (Lent 1950), 12 – 13; Bowdler (1821), 6.
[10] *Dial* (Lent 1950), 11; CB (1787 – 1832), 14.1.1825.

entitled to reject a reasonable motion supported by a majority. The matter was heard by the lord chancellor, and he decided in January 1828 in Godfrey's favour, ruling that the costs of both sides were to be borne by the college.[11]

We do not know how unpopular Godfrey may have been, nor why; but it is noteworthy that upon his death in 1832 the Fellows elected Joshua King, who had led the case against him in 1827 – 8. King was not in holy orders, and a special royal dispensation was secured to override the college statutes. He had been a Fellow since 1820, and in the first year of his fellowship had been active in the dispute over Milner's successor, calling rather precociously for a fresh election.[12] Under King's presidency (1832 – 57) stability appears to have been restored to the college society.

'The Revolution of the Dons'

Partly as a result of the parliamentary reforms of the university in the 1850s and 1880s, and partly owing to the social and ideological forces which had shaped those reforms, the second half of the 19th century witnessed a radical transformation in the senior membership of the university and colleges. The archetypal Fellow of the 18th century was clerical, and saw his fellowship as a reward for achievement in the tripos and as a short stage in his ecclesiastical career; in contrast, the new don of the late 19th century was increasingly likely to be a layman dedicating himself to the academic life, with a strong sense of the vocation and duties of his chosen career. This change has been described as 'The Revolution of the Dons', and it was indeed revolutionary, laying the foundations of the modern university.[13]

The revolution began in the middle years of the century. In part, it was the result of a series of parliamentary reforms; but there were also internal pressures for change. By the mid-19th century there was a great gap between the expectations of the serious students reading for high places in the tripos, and the ability or inclination of the dons to supply these needs. The reforms in the public schools which Thomas Arnold had inspired a little earlier in the century had emphasised the significance of the teacher as educator and moral guide, and university students came to expect the same dedication from college Fellows. The first generations of students to be aware of this were up at university in the 1850s, and by the following decade many had become dons themselves and had the opportunity to implement their new collegiate

---

[11] Box 95; Cooper, iv.558.
[12] Gray, 254; Venn (1904), 192 – 3; Cooper, iv.558; Bowdler (1821), 1 – 5.
[13] Rothblatt (1981); similar work has been done on the changes at Oxford by Engel (1983).

ideal, stressing educational aims and community values: a familial view of college life, with the aim of reviving close personal relations between Fellows and students, and stressing the importance of character development in university education.[14] There were several phases of reform throughout the later 19th century, inspired by each new generation of Fellows, and colleges responded to the changing social and cultural perceptions and values of the times.

The changes at Queens' were also radical. There was some tinkering with the statutes in 1838, when the restriction on the number of Fellows permitted from any one county was removed, but at the beginning of the 1850s the statutory regulations governing the fellowship had altered relatively little since the 16th century.[15] The main features of college statutes in general on which the reformers focussed their attention concerned Fellows: the insistence that most Fellows be in holy orders (at Queens', only two were permitted not to take orders), the ban on marriage, and the widespread practice of non-residence. Many senior members of the university were content with matters as they stood and fearful of change. J. N. Peill, tutor of Queens', maintained that to keep Fellows in college would need 'a more radical change in the University and College system than it is possible in my opinion to carry out at the present time'.[16] The impracticability of change has always been one of the foremost arguments of those who oppose it on principle, and it is probably no coincidence that Peill left Queens' for a college living in 1853, the year after the publication of a royal commission's report advocating university and college reforms.[17]

The college's statutes were altered in 1860, in consequence of the parliamentary legislation which had followed upon the recommendations of the royal commission;[18] many Fellows elected under the old statutes volunteered to be governed by the new.[19] The principal changes in the terms and conditions of fellowships were outlined by W. M. Campion, tutor of Queens', before a parliamentary select committee in 1867.[20] Fellowships were now held until ten years after the Fellow had taken his MA degree, without any formal restrictions on marriage during that time. After these ten years, any Fellow not holding major

---

[14] Rothblatt (1981), 193 – 6, 227 – 40.
[15] Searle, 149; *Documents* (1852), iii.65 – 71; the situation prior to the changes is described in *Report* (1852), 354 – 5.
[16] *Report* (1852), 178 – 9.
[17] AC.
[18] A college committee was established to consider the implications of the new parliamentary legislation for the university in 1856, CB (1832 – 88), 11.10.1856.
[19] ibid., 4.10.1860, 5.11.1860, 11.1.1861, 8.10.1861, 9.1.1862, 13.10.1862.
[20] One feature not mentioned by Campion was that the number of foundation Fellows was reduced to eleven. The average number of Fellows during the first three quarters of the century is as follows: 1800 – 9, 14.3; 1810 – 19, 14.2; 1820 – 9, 15.9; 1830 – 9, 16.7; 1840 – 9, 14.5; 1850 – 9, 14.3; 1860 – 9, 10.6; 1870 – 9, 12.5, *CU Cal*.

college office (as lecturer or tutor), or who was not in holy orders, had to leave; Fellows in holy orders might remain only if, and for as long as, they were unmarried. It also seems that only Fellows who were single could hold major college office, and years spent in such office did not count as part of the ten years. Therefore, a Fellow who vacated college office through marriage or some other reason would remain until his term expired — the point of this being to induce good men to stay with the college and involve themselves in teaching. Campion saw 'no reason to be dissatisfied' with the new system.[21] The reforms may seem at first sight to be a rather crude compromise between modern and traditional values, but in the context of their time they were genuinely radical, especially the abolition of Fellows' celibacy: Trinity Hall and Christ's also gave restricted permission to marry at this time, and Caius abolished all restrictions, but the other colleges waited until the second wave of parliamentary reforms in the early 1880s.[22]

There was one point on which Campion was not prepared to countenance reform: he was strongly opposed to any attempt to compel colleges to open their fellowships formally to outsiders. Most colleges had open fellowships anyway in theory, and it was not uncommon for the smaller ones to recruit men from outside when qualified internal candidates were in short supply. Campion argued that a formal enactment on this issue would require the institution of a special examination, 'and the multiplication of such examinations is an evil', which would favour rich men who were better able to prepare for them; Queens' had abolished fellowship examinations in 1834.[23] In common with the other colleges, Queens' took its Fellows from students who had been placed among the first fifteen wranglers or the first fifteen places in the classical tripos. This ensured a high standard, and stimulated students — and their teachers — to perform well in tripos. Campion did not believe that good men were lost to the university, for on the whole, 'men who take high places in the triposes are provided for by fellowships, and they get their fellowships at their own colleges'.[24] This

21 *Select Committee* (1867), 229; the new arrangements are also in *Student's Guide* (1862), 304. There is a brief summary in Gray, 259; but he gives the limit of tenure as twelve years after the MA, contrary to the other sources.

22 Brooke (1985), 224 and n. 4; Peile (1900), 286.

23 *Select Committee* (1867), 230; CB (1832 – 88), 14.1.1834. Fellowship examinations were in general a late 18th century and early 19th century innovation, though it is not clear just when they were introduced at Queens'. In 1824 the college decided that candidates for fellowships might present themselves twice in the examination, CB (1787 – 1832), 16.1.1824.

24 *Select Committee* (1867), 237 – 8. The procedure for electing Fellows of Queens' at this time was described in uncomplimentary terms in 1910 (perhaps by Arthur Wright?): the tutor announced that anyone achieving a place in the first fifteen of the mathematics or classical tripos would be admitted to a fellowship, 'and so little were the rights of the Fellows to elect respected, that the candidate was told by the Tutor to come up for the day of the meeting to be admitted', *Dial* (Easter 1910), 358.

was probably true, but Campion was also expressing the widespread fear amongst dons that college autonomy might be eroded by the new reforms.

The new measures transformed college fellowships. The removal of the clerical qualification enabled a new breed of lay Fellows to emerge; although many still chose to take holy orders, changing views of theology and the rôle of the church in society led to a growing reluctance among dons to follow a religious career, and to the development of the modern academic profession.[25] Many Fellows took advantage of the opportunity to marry. Colleges were anxious lest there should be a conflict of demands between Fellows' families and their college work, but this did not happen. It did not cause any known difficulties at Queens', which abandoned its opposition to married Fellows holding major college offices in the early 1880s, if not before.[26] Non-residence did not die out entirely but it was less significant in the context of the new collegiate environment.[27] The new dons placed more emphasis on their tutorial rôle and showed more concern for their pastoral duties, holding social functions at which senior and junior members could mix, promoting college clubs and activities and generally trying to create a full college community of Fellows and students.[28]

These changes began after the 1850s, but were particularly noticeable in the succeeding decades, and especially after the renewed government intervention of the late 1870s which culminated in further statutory reforms in 1882. The statutes of Queens' were revised in that year and there were further minor alterations in the 1890s, which continued the work of the 1860 reform.[29] Under the new statutes, all Fellows were permitted to marry, and none were obliged to take orders; they were to be chosen 'from among the graduate members of the College who have distinguished themselves in the examinations of the College or of the University, and whom the Governing Body, having regard to the interests of education, religion, learning, and research, shall think fit', or from anyone outside the college with similar qualifications; the emphasis on research was a significant innovation. Fellows were to vacate their positions after six years, unless they held major college office; if they held such office for more than seven and less than 25 years, they were permitted to retain their fellowships after leaving office for a period of time equal to that by which their term in office exceeded seven years; if they held office for more than 25 years, they were awarded fellowships for life. There was now a very strong incentive

---

[25] Haig (1984), chapter 2; Haig (1986).
[26] Rothblatt (1981), 242–3; *Statutes* (1882); CB (1889–1937), 8.6.1892.
[27] e.g. MS 79, 27; and examples below, pp. 227–8.
[28] Rothblatt (1981), 196–210, 227–9, 236–40.
[29] *Statutes* (1882), contains the 1891, 1893, and 1897 revisions.

therefore for Fellows to take an active part in the college's teaching activities.[30]

But the best insight into the changed character of the fellowship is to look at the Fellows themselves. There was no clear-cut transition from the old type of don to the new. One enduring legacy of the old order was the presence of John Clark, who had arrived in Cambridge in 1832 and remained there until his death in 1900, when he was said to be the oldest resident member of the university. He was not a distinguished academic, but had a good reputation as an examination coach.[31] William Gibson, elected in 1869, the year of his graduation, also epitomised certain aspects of the old type: he never resided after taking his degree, though he came to Queens' three times a year for college meetings. The college magazine, the *Dial*, asserted loyally that he took an 'active' part in college government, but it is hard to imagine how he could have done so. Gibson was a layman — he practised as a solicitor — and married, and his three sons were sent to Queens'.[32]

Arthur Wright, who was elected to his fellowship two years before Gibson, was the first prominent representative of the new order of the late Victorian and Edwardian eras. At first, he had to go out of residence, having been told that there was 'no opening' for him in the college, and he worked as a parish priest in London for five years before returning as dean and college lecturer in 1872. He owed his return to the influence of George Pirie, assistant tutor to Campion, who had been appointed at the urging of the junior Fellows, and who persuaded the fellowship that Wright should be invited back.[33] In his own account of these events, written many years later, Wright appears to have been very sure of himself even at this time: he refused to return unless the college conceded the rights to tenure of fellowships permitted by the new statutes. To this Campion replied

'that I must on no account insist on that, for it would never be granted me. Moreover, it would be useless, for in three or four years a college living would fall vacant and I would be provided for. Now I had no intention of rusticating in a country living. If I came to Cambridge, it would be to stay, and after five or six letters had passed

[30] *ibid.*, 14, 20 – 21; as in 1860, major offices were tutorships and lectureships. University professors and public orators were entitled to remain Fellows for as long as they held these posts; any new lectureships created by the governing body were to carry the same privilege.

[31] *AC*; *Dial* (Easter 1938), 6. J. F. Williams wrote down the story that Clark had arrived in 1832 from a remote Welsh village on the top of a coach, MS 79, 41; in fact, he came from Yorkshire.

[32] *Dial* (Michaelmas 1917), 4; *AC*.

[33] *Dial* (Easter 1916), 10; for Pirie, see *AC*.

my terms were granted. So unwilling were the seniors of that day to admit any reform'.[34]

Wright and Pirie seem to have worked together in reforming college teaching, and when Pirie went to Aberdeen to become professor of mathematics in 1878, Wright became assistant tutor; but with Campion now devoting most of his time to parochial work at St Botolph's, he took up most of the tutorial duties, and was clearly given a free hand.[35] He was enormously influential in the reshaping of the college. An undergraduate who came up in 1897, wrote that 'in his curious way he was virtually the ruler of Queens'', and devoted to the college, although he was a 'shy and retiring man, spare of speech and somewhat morose and alarming in his manner'. Another undergraduate said of him in 1922 that 'I would not give sixpence for all the clothes he had on in K.P. [King's Parade] one day when he stopped me; he always stopped any Queens' lad he met for a chat'.[36] Wright was a Fellow until his death in 1924, and gave his life to the college; this was characteristic of the new type of don, and in marked contrast to the old.[37]

Other new Fellows followed these new paths. Ernest Temperley (Fellow, 1871 – 89) intended originally to go the bar, 'but as he secured popularity as a private tutor he changed his line, married at an early age, and settled down to a life in Cambridge'.[38] J. H. Gray (1879 – 1932) served as classical lecturer, dean, tutor and vice-president at various stages of his long college career. Like Wright, he was ordained, and had at first had to go out of residence, working as a schoolmaster for a year before being brought back to help Wright with his pastoral work. Gray was active in university sports clubs, a justice of the peace, and a prominent freemason.[39] His successor as vice-president was Andrew Munro (1893 – 1935), who at the time of that appointment had been a Fellow of the college for 39 years, 'all of which have been spent in active

[34] *Dial* (Easter 1916), 10.
[35] *ibid.*, 10 – 11.
[36] MS 79, 29; diary of H. C. Alexander (recording the remarks of a friend).
[37] But Wright was a great traveller, visiting Europe, the Holy Land, South Africa, North and South America, Australia and New Zealand, CR (2.5.1924), 307; *Dial* (Lent 1909), 249 – 50. There was more interest in foreign travel at this time; other Fellows who are known to have travelled abroad are A. B. Cook (to Italy, Greece, Asia minor); and Andrew Munro (who in his early days ventured no further than Scotland, but later visited Europe and the middle east), Seltman (1952), 297; *Dial* (Michaelmas 1935), 9. G. B. Harrison recalls of Munro that 'In term time he was a celibate bachelor, but in the vacations he had lady friends in Paris', G. B. Harrison: letter. (An undergraduate rumour, perhaps?).
[38] CR (24.1.1889), 150. Arthur Wright portrayed Temperley as an active, even hyperactive worker for the college, Wright (1889), *passim*.
[39] *Dial* (Lent 1915), 3; (Easter 1916), 13; (Easter 1932), 9 – 11; CR (24.11.1915), 112; below, pp. 257 – 9.

work within its walls'.[40] W. M. Coates (1887 – 1912) was active in the university and served on committees in the town; a married Fellow, Coates often entertained undergraduates at his home.[41] The *Dial's* obituary notice of R. H. Kennett (1888 – 1932) referred to the many generations of Queensmen with 'delightful memories of the warm welcome' given by him and his wife; Kennett was a serious scholar of semitic languages, who became Regius professor of Hebrew in 1903, and he would often hold discussions with students in his rooms on religious and Biblical matters late into the night. The *Dial* recorded of him in 1910 that

'From the greenest Freshmen to the greyest old maid of his acquaintance, he would offer you Hebrew lectures, invite you to tea-parties where only Syriac was spoken, or recite you the sixth chapter of Micah . . . If your sympathies were not Semitic, you had no need to fear; he would quote you poems from *Punch*, and talk with equal ease on Art or Politics, on country life or cooking'.[42]

The same tendencies are visible in the college's presidents. The *Cambridge Review's* obituary of George Phillips (president, 1857 – 1892), referred to the 'genial hospitality' which he and his wife offered to undergraduates; such an observation could never have been made of any previous president, for in the past they had kept their distance.[43] Phillips' successor, from 1892 to 1896, was W. M. Campion, who had stood against him in the election of 1857. The *Cambridge Review* remarked of him that 'Without being exactly a prominent man in the history of his time, he was for several years conspicuous in the annals of the University and the Town'; moreover, 'His was one of those lives, of which we have many examples here, which are closely bound up with the history of the College to which they belonged and to which they gave their life's work'.[44]

The three presidents who followed, H. E. Ryle (1896 – 1901), F. H. Chase (1901 – 5), and T. C. Fitzpatrick (1906 – 31), were all elected from outside the college but clearly they were chosen to fit in with this new tradition of involvement in all aspects of college life. Arthur Wright, observing that George Phillips had described the president's office as a 'sinecure' and 'a luxury which we could not afford', felt that this had all

[40] *Dial* (Easter 1932), 5.
[41] CR (25.1.1912), 209; *Dial* (Lent 1912), 8.
[42] *Dial* (Michaelmas 1910), 4; (Lent 1932), 5 – 8; (Michaelmas 1937), 15. After moving to Ely in 1903 when he became a canon there, Kennett would often show Queensmen round the cathedral, *ibid.* (Lent 1932), 5 – 8.
[43] CR (11.2.1892), 192.
[44] Gray, 259; CR (29.10.1896), 38; Campion had been tutor for nearly 40 years before becoming president, and was popular in the college, CR (25.2.1892), 221, 231.

been changed by Ryle: 'From the time that Dr. Ryle turned the Parisian drawing room into the President's study and opened the old spiral staircase, that undergraduates might have free access to the President, the head has become as necessary as the body'.[45] A friend of the president's family observed that 'In University entertaining the Ryles made it their special delight to break down the last remnants of the old traditional etiquette which built up walls of division between seniors and juniors'.[46] In his letter thanking the undergraduates' debating society, the St Bernard Society, for their good wishes on his promotion to be bishop of Exeter in 1901, Ryle wrote: 'I feel the approaching severance from the College will be to me one of the great sorrows of my life; and the fact of its being so arises from the happiness and the intimacy of the relations in which I have been privileged to live with all members of the College'.[47] Mrs Ryle sang in the college's May Week concert in 1898.[48] Chase continued Ryle's practice of having under-graduates in to talk in his study; his wife was said to be 'ready at times even to nurse the sick in the Lodge itself . . . [she] welcomed every member of the College with a hospitality that was as charming as it was simple and kindly'.[49]

The intention was to create a familial atmosphere. The *Cambridge Review* noted that Fitzpatrick 'was Head of the House, and . . . every member of the Household was reckoned a member of his family'. He was said to know 'every man belonging to the College — not merely his name, but his work, his parents, and to a large extent his habits and character. He was even at pains to memorize the names on each staircase, that he might get some idea of the men's *entourage*'.[50] It must have been under Ryle or one of his two successors that the custom originated of opening the long gallery to undergraduates on Sunday evenings, after chapel and hall. The earliest reference to this is from Fitzpatrick's time: 'There can be few of those who came under his influence as Head of the College who have not joined on a Sunday evening the throng in the Long Gallery . . . Here many an under-graduate has sought and received kindly advice from a "Head" who knows well how to give it'.[51] Although C. T. Wood (Fellow, 1900–53) noted that 'In some moods, particularly when he was tired, he did not find ordinary small talk with Undergraduates easy', Fitzpatrick was

[45] *Dial* (Easter 1916), 14.
[46] Fitzgerald (1928), 113, and see *ibid.*, 111–114 for Ryle's cultivation of good relations with students at Queens'. As a Fellow of King's between 1881 and 1886, Ryle had already shown himself a typical representative of the new breed of dons, *ibid.*, 43–52.
[47] SBSM, 24.1.1901.
[48] CR (16.6.1898), 415; see below, p. 248.
[49] *Courier* (15.3.1906), 7.
[50] Rackham (1937), 10–11, and see *ibid.*, 21–2; Harding (1950), 38.
[51] Rackham (1937), 26.

popular with the students, who responded to his kindness and sincerity.[52] Other Fellows adopted the practice of opening their rooms to undergraduates on Sunday evenings, and this became part of the college's social routine.[53]

Dons became involved in other ways, by their interest in college sports, for example; and from 1908 at latest they took part in an annual dons' debate in the St Bernard Society.[54] But the extent of their familiarity with students is prone to exaggeration. They were friendly, but ultimately paternalistic; their relationship with the students was founded on mutual awareness of their differences in status. This was quite natural in the context of contemporary attitudes, and was desired by both sides. The undergraduates welcomed the friendliness and encouragement of the dons, but were increasingly conscious of themselves as members of a separate estate, and sought to organise their own activities and demonstrate their own maturity.[55] The dons were glad of this, because self-reliance was one of the principal ends of the new spirit they wished to promote in higher education. In addition, they had to adopt a more formal position when dealing with undergraduate pranks and exuberance, a stance which too much familiarity would have undermined. Dons were always portrayed as something akin to a separate species in undergraduate magazines; and it should also be remembered that for the first time a large proportion of Fellows were choosing to grow old in the service of their colleges, and therefore had in some respects less in common with students than Fellows of earlier generations, who were closer to them in age.

Tutors' books, containing brief details of the academic performance, personal characteristics and family situations of the undergraduates,

[52]   *ibid.*, 21 – 2; diary of H. C. Alexander. Gilbert Harding, a student at Queens' in the 1920s, observed that he had hardly any conversation, and his wife was also very nervous, Harding (1950), 38 – 9. G. B. Harrison remembers him as 'very quiet and withdrawn', and his wife as being much liked and respected in the college, Harrison (1985), 55. Fitzpatrick was active on various administrative bodies in the university and outside; and sometimes allowed the long gallery to be used for meetings of charitable societies; he had also been an enthusiastic mountaineer and was a keen traveller, Rackham (1937), 2, 9, 35 – 53.

[53]   For example, G. B. Harrison: letter; diary of H. C. Alexander. Students were not discouraged from calling on Fellows at other times, too. The concept of the college as a family was summed up by A. B. Cook, who wrote: 'It is not a small thing, as life goes on, to find ourselves still members of a family, dwelling together in the ancestral home. Outside we might be ploughing a lonely furrow. Here brother-man is working at our side. And the crop that we raise is seed-corn for the world', Cook (1927), 14.

[54]   For sports, see chapter 17; for the dons' debates, CR (27.2.1908), 272; (17.2.1910), 283; (9.3.1911), 362; (4.3.1914), 349 (on this occasion they debated whether modern undergraduates were degenerate). C. T. Wood and A. B. Cook had participated in debates for some years, but the 1908 debate was the first with a don on each side of the house; it was first called the 'dons' debate' in 1909, SBSM, 2.11.1901, 1.11.1902, 21.2.1903, 31.10.1903, 29.10.1904, 11.11.1905, 22.2.1908, 6.3.1909.

[55]   See below, chapter 17.

appear at Queens' for the first time in the late 1870s, and are witness to the new interest which Fellows took in the welfare of their students; but their terse comments sometimes seem patronising.[56] J. H. Gray, though known affectionately as 'Joey' by many generations of undergraduates who passed through Queens', and an enthusiast for sports and games, was also reputed to have been firm with undergraduates when required.[57] Arthur Wright was known for his 'prodigious walks into the country during the summer . . . and as often as not he would be followed by an undergraduate whom he had commandeered as an escort. Conversation with him was always of the briefest nature, and very staccato'.[58] One of the principal reasons for the history don R. G. D. Laffan's relative lack of popularity with students in the 1920s was that, as one of them, H. C. Alexander, observed at the time, 'He is always trying schemes to make himself an influence and liked . . . by undergraduates. But they never come off'.[59] In trying too hard to be one of the boys, Laffan broke wth the conventions of student-Fellow relationships; this made undergraduates uneasy and caused them to hold aloof.

The dons were thoroughly conservative in their political outlook. The French Revolution and the Napoleonic wars had left the university firmly Tory, which it seems to have remained until the 1840s at least.[60] It may be supposed that Queens' conformed; certainly Joshua King, its president from 1832 to 1857, was vigorously Tory.[61] It has been argued that in subsequent decades, before the 1880s, the 'intellectual and literary society of London and the Universities' was 'mainly Liberal', but during the 1880s it became mainly conservative and Unionist once more, in reaction to the awesome pace of contemporary change and reform, and in fear of mass democracy.[62] In the election of 1882 the Fellows of Queens' voted to a man for the conservative candidate.[63] W. M. Coates was reported to be an active conservative in university politics, and a man of strong views; J. H. Gray was described as 'an honest, straightforward Englishman of the Victorian age', which may have been a way of describing his 'vigorous Conservative politics'; Andrew Munro was 'a Conservative of the right Cambridge breed', who 'used to admit, half in jest but also half in earnest, that he always voted against any

---

[56] See especially, TB (1878 – 87); TB (1885 – 91).
[57] Diary of H. C. Alexander; *Dial* (Easter 1932), 9 – 12.
[58] MS 79, 29. A good tale of one of these walks is told in G. B. Harrison: letter. Harrison also describes him as 'alarmingly reticent' in general, Harrison (1985), 55.
[59] Diary of H. C. Alexander.
[60] Winstanley (1940), 97 – 121; Green (1969), 256 – 9.
[61] For example, Winstanley (1940), 110 – 111.
[62] Roach (1957), 58 – 81 (quotation on p. 80).
[63] CR (29.11.1892), 130; (18.4.1883), 303.

change'.[64]

These then were some of the leading members of the new generation of dons which transformed the college almost out of recognition from its early Victorian state. That transformation was intended for the benefit of the students, and it was accompanied by an equally radical alteration of the character of the undergraduate body, which the following chapter seeks to illustrate.

[64] *CR* (8.11.1906), 62; (25.1.1912), 209; *Dial* (Easter 1932), 9 – 12; (Michaelmas 1935), 8 – 9. c.f. the meeting in F. G. Plaistowe's rooms in 1890, to hear about Toynbee Hall, *CR* (6.2.1890), 184.

17

Students in the late 19th and early 20th centuries

Those social and institutional forces which transformed so many aspects of university life in the Victorian period had an equally great impact on the student body. The typical undergraduate of 1900, if we may imagine such a creature, was very different from his predecessor of 1800. Both were products of their time: the student of 1800 bore the traits of his 18th century inheritance, and his ancestry could be traced, without too much difficulty, to the students of the centuries before. The student of 1900 seems to have been of an altogether different breed, and is a recognizable progenitor of the modern undergraduate.

The growth of the student population

In terms of student numbers, the 19th and early 20th centuries were a period of rapid, though uneven, expansion. This began from the beginning of the century, especially after the end of the Napoleonic wars; it tailed off slightly between the 1840s and 1870s, but resumed again from the 1880s onwards until the outbreak of the first world war.[1] The increase in numbers at Queens' at the beginning of the 20th century was spectacular: in 1883 there were 84 students; in 1903, there were 100; in 1913 there were 212.[2] The college's undergraduate population was reckoned to have increased threefold in the 30 years from 1879.[3] Nonetheless, Queens' was one of the smaller colleges in the university.[4]

In general, the expansion of the student population from the late 19th century can perhaps be ascribed to the effects wrought by that host of reforms introduced by internal and external authorities since the 1850s, which were thought to have made the universities more useful and valuable to society, and more genuinely 'national' institutions once again.[5] The 'Revolution of the Dons' had been rewarded. J. H. Gray

---

[1] See below, appendix 16.

[2] CR (31.10.1883), 41; (29.10.1903), 100; (30.10.1913), 56. The numbers include some BAs, but these were only a small proportion.

[3] Dial (Michaelmas 1909), 299.

[4] Thirteenth in 1870, 15th in 1871, 13th in 1883, CU Reporter (19.10.1870), 28; (26.10.1870), 51; (25.10.1871), 36; CR (31.10.1883), 41.

[5] But the problem is probably more complicated than this. The early 19th century expansion cannot be explained in this way.

suggested a 'personal equation' to explain to a large degree the expansion at Queens': 'Happily the men whose influence and work have done most in increasing the numbers and raising the tone of the College are still with us and working amongst us', he wrote in 1909, and he also praised the efforts of presidents Ryle and Chase, who had 'contributed very largely to the success of the College in comparatively short periods of time'.[6]

Prospective students were better informed about individual colleges in the second half of the century, as the publication of a number of quite sophisticated and detailed student guides testifies;[7] colleges were much more evidently in competition with each other for students, and had to present themselves as attractively as possible in every respect. Apart from the general improvements brought about in Queens' by the new generation of Fellows, Gray cited two other major causes of the college's enhanced attractiveness: the so-called 'New System' of 1883, and the opening of the Friars building in 1886.

The 'New System' was a simple administrative measure concerning students' charges. Hitherto, undergraduates had paid caution money to the college on coming up, university fees as they fell due, and college charges for each term before coming into residence the following term. Under the new system, caution money was no longer levied as such, and all university and college charges apart from room rents and degree fees were compounded for by a sum paid in advance at the beginning of each term, which covered fees, commons, hall dinner, coal, laundry and shoecleaning.[8] This was more convenient for the college, and was very popular with the students, who seem to have benefited financially as well as administratively.[9] Another consequence of the 'New System' was that the college now took over responsibility for furnishing students' rooms and supplying other 'requisites', the charges for which were included in the rent; this also saved the students from extra expense, and ensured that the rooms were kept to a reasonable standard. Gray felt that it did 'a great deal to make the rooms more uniformly sightly and comfortable', and Arthur Wright, who first proposed the arrangement, observed that 'Most of the old bedding had

---

6   *Dial* (Michaelmas 1909), 299 – 303. Gray also cited the generally improved efficiency of the college as a reason for its success. The sudden increase in numbers in the Edwardian period surely requires further explanation.

7   For example, *Student's Guide* (1862); Dickens (1884); *Student's Handbook* (1902). Writing in one of these, in 1862, J. R. Seeley listed the wide range of features which prospective students should investigate in choosing a college, *Student's Guide* (1862), 67 – 81.

8   CB (1832 – 88), 6.10.1882, 9.1.1883, 6.10.1883; 17.1.1884; *Dial* (Michaelmas 1909), 301; Dickens (1884), 89; *Student's Handbook* (1902), 75.

9   *Dial* (Michaelmas 1909), 301; Gray, 263 – 4. Student life in Cambridge was generally costly, but the expenses remained relatively stable in the 19th century, Rothblatt (1981), 65 – 71.

to be burnt and other things were no better'.[10]

The opening of the Friars building meant that Queens' could now accommodate a high proportion of its students in college, rather than in lodgings. It had always been desirable for a college to be able to house as many of its students as possible within its walls, and after the decline of the hostels in the 16th century virtually all students were accommodated in their colleges. Exceptions were made in the case of fellow-commoners who were married: these lived in the town with their wives and families.[11] This may have been a 19th century phenomenon; certainly, the only examples known at Queens' are from this period: Charles Laing (who was a pensioner) lived in the town with his sister in the 1830s,[12] and in 1834 Robert Alston, a fellow-commoner, and his wife, who lived in Silver Street, were brought before the local magistrates 'for cruelty to their child, a little boy of 3 years old'.[13]

In the early 19th century, pressure of numbers made it necessary for some students to take lodgings in the town. There was no new building in Queens' between the 1750s and the 1880s, and students would no longer tolerate the cramped living conditions which had been considered acceptable by their late 16th and early 17th century forbears, for their social expectations had changed. As early as 1822 Joseph Jee noted that the university was full, and that rooms in college were becoming hard to find.[14] Though the use of licensed lodgings became usual from this time, W. M. Campion recorded in 1867 that Queens' had experienced 'the greatest difficulty' in securing accommodation for students in the previous two years.[15] In Joseph Jee's day, lodgings were reckoned to be more expensive than college rooms — perhaps because they were still meant for the wealthier students — but in the second half of the century students could save a little money by living out.[16]

Reformers outside the universities were afraid that students who lived in lodgings were less subject to college discipline. Campion did not agree. When giving evidence before parliament's select committee in

[10] *Dial* (Michalemas 1909), 301; (Easter 1916), 12; Gray, 263 – 4. Arthur Wright recorded that the idea arose out of the realisation that the students in the Friars building would not pay out the large sums required to furnish their rooms from scratch, and was extended from there, *Dial* (Easter 1916), 12; but the system was certainly in operation by 1884, Dickens (1884), 89. The college had undertaken 'the papering and painting of the rooms' in 1873, CB (1832 – 88), 17.5.1873. In the 1920s there are instances of students decorating their own rooms, which does not seem to have been considered unusual, diary of H. C. Alexander.

[11] *Report* (1852), 356. For 19th century lodging houses in general, see Winstanley (1940), 59 – 60.

[12] Romilly (1967), 132, 133, 139, 144, 148, 214 – 5.

[13] Romilly recorded that the child was beaten, and on one occasion 'his Mother put him into a tub of cold water for an hour for being naughty', *ibid.*, 49, 236n; AC.

[14] *Dial* (Lent 1950), 14.

[15] *Select Committee* (1867), 238 – 9.

[16] *Dial* (Lent 1950), 14; *Select Committee* (1867), 228 – 9; Dickens (1884), 89.

1867 he explained that all possible precautions were taken when licensing lodging houses to ensure their good reputation: many were kept by college servants, and most lodging house keepers reported men who came in after 10 p.m., the hour at which the gates of Queens' were shut. When asked if students were exposed to great temptations by maidservants in lodging houses, Campion replied: 'Considering the specimens of servants . . . that I have seen, I should say that they are not'; nor did he believe Cambridge to be a particularly immoral town.[17] The moral dangers of lodging houses being greatly exaggerated, in Campion's view, their only real drawback was that the students who lived in them 'cannot so thoroughly realise the collegiate system'.[18] The new generation of dons in the later 19th century were acutely aware of this problem, and the new building of 1886 was a response to it.

In the short term, it solved the problem effectively enough. Slightly over half of Queens' students lived in lodgings in the early 1880s, more or less the same proportion as in the university as a whole; the proportion of first year men living out was rather higher. But by 1894 only 16% of Queens' students had to live out, compared with 45% in the university overall; although increased numbers eroded this advantage thereafter, Queens' continued to house a higher proportion of its students in college than most of the other colleges.[19] But the sudden expansion of the undergraduate population in the Edwardian period compelled Queens' to provide more residential accommodation in 1912 — the Doket building — and the problem of housing the steadily growing number of its students has bedevilled the college ever since.[20]

The social composition of the student body

These physical changes are apparent enough, and their explanation is relatively straightforward, but the social changes which accompanied them were more complex. In the 18th century, there had been a slight narrowing of the university's social base.[21] In the 19th, the picture is

---

[17] *Select Committee* (1867), 231, 236.

[18] *ibid.*, 231. The point was also made by J. R. Seeley in *Student's Guide* (1862), 7–8.

[19] In 1883 50% of Queensmen were in lodgings, and 50% of university students as a whole; in 1885 the figures were 55% and 49% respectively; in 1886, before the opening of the Friars building, 57% and 51%; in 1902 only 31% of Queensmen lived out of college, and only four colleges had a lower percentage than this, *CR* (31.10.1883), 41; (21.10.1885), 39; (10.11.1886), 65; (28.11.1894), 83; (6.2.1902), 169. The proportion of first years who lived out varied: in 1881, only eight out of 20 had rooms in college; in 1882, only three out of 15, *CR* (19.10.1881), 11; (11.10.1882), 8. The lodgings were scattered over the town, *ibid.*, (15.10.1879), 7; (13.10.1880), 7; (19.10.1881), 11.

[20] For the Doket building, see below, pp. 315–16.

[21] Above, chapter 14, n. 3.

unclear, and there does not seem to be any general consensus amongst historians on the nature and extent of social change. It does appear that the proportion of students from the landowning classes dropped substantially, and that the proportion from business and industrial backgrounds rose, but it is possible that the general social composition of the student body remained relatively stable before the 20th century.[22] A predominant, and growing, proportion of students were from the public schools, which became more prestigious and exclusive, as well as more numerous, in the 19th century, but these too are an unreliable guide to social class.[23] The question of the influence of the 19th century reforms on the university's social base must therefore remain an open one, and there is as yet no evidence to suggest internal social change as a causal explanation of university reform.[24] As in the past, it may be that most undergraduates were still of moderate means, who had to make their own way in the world,[25] but by modern standards, the university population remained 'highly selected and narrowly restricted'.[26]

The social composition of Queens' in this period is no more susceptible to analysis than that of the university. From appendix 16 it can be seen that the proportion of pensioner students increased until it comprised nearly all of the student body, whilst the proportion of fellow-commoners and sizars diminished into insignificance, but the old distinctions in status among undergraduates were no longer so significant, and the pensioner group included students from a relatively broad range of backgrounds within those social classes who made up the student body in general.

There were certainly students from poor backgrounds among the pensioners, who depended to a greater or lesser extent on college scholarship and prizes.[27] In the 18th century Queens' had often given these awards to the undeserving for want of competition,[28] but the increased number of students in the 19th century soon put a stop to this. In 1801 the college was said to offer 45 scholarships each worth £8 *per annum* and eight exhibitions 'inconsiderable as to value'; in the early 1820s this number had been consolidated, because of inflation, to a total of 26 awards with values ranging from £9 to £25 *per annum*, and it was

[22] For interpretations of this problem, see Jenkins and Jones (1950), 99 – 100; Anderson and Schnaper (1952), 7; Rothblatt (1981), 87; see also below, appendix 16.
[23] Jenkins and Jones (1950), 30 – 3, 57 – 62, 102 – 3; Rothblatt (1981), chapters 1 – 2. Students at Queens' at the end of the century came from a wide range of public schools, TB (1896); President's Records (1907 – 8).
[24] See Rothblatt (1981), 87.
[25] Winstanley (1940), 416.
[26] Jenkins and Jones (1950), 102.
[27] For general observations on scholarships, see Rothblatt (1981), 75 – 86.
[28] Above, p. 206.

further consolidated in 1839.[29] Two new awards were established from benefactions in the early 1840s, and the value of awards in general was increased again in 1860.[30] It was of course vital to maintain the value of scholarships and prizes in order to attract students. By the early 1880s Queens' was reckoned ninth among the colleges in terms of the total amount given in scholarships and exhibitions.[31]

The establishment of entrance scholarships in 1864 was a significant move to attract entries. Initially there were two, one in classics and one in mathematics, open to any prospective student under twenty, and awarded on the results of a competitive examination taken before coming up; but the number of entrance scholarships grew subsequently, the range of subjects was widened and the age limit lowered to nineteen.[32] These awards were made simply on the basis of academic merit, but Queens' also introduced a small number of exhibitions for poor students: in 1903 it offered five of these, one of which was for the sons of clergymen.[33]

This was well-meaning, of course, but the numbers involved were relatively tiny. At the very end of the 19th century and the beginining of the 20th, local authorities began to help students financially for the first time, but this too was on a very small scale, and nothing serious was done to benefit students from poor backgrounds until the introduction of state scholarships in the 1920s.[34] In the 19th century the prospects for those who had no private funding from family or friends, and who were unable to win one of the relatively few scholarships on offer, were bleak indeed. A clergyman in Gravesend wrote to Queens' in August 1840 that someone claiming to be Henry Dixon, a student of the college, had come asking for money to support him there; the clergyman wanted to know if such a person existed 'and if his character etc. merits the aid of the Clergy here . . . We have so many Imposters'. Dixon had been admitted to Queens' in May 1840, but he did not take a degree, almost certainly since he could not afford to.[35]

There were other ways in which the college could help. Queens' had the facility to create supernumerary scholarships if and when its

[29] CU Cal. (1801), 63; (1840), 220; CB (1787 – 1832), 17.1.1823; CB (1832 – 88), 25.2.1837, 14.3.1839.
[30] CU Cal. (1841), 221 and n.; (1842), 232; (1860), 284; Student's Guide (1862), 305 – 6.
[31] CR (21.2.1883), 229.
[32] CU Cal. (1864), 306 – 7; CR (14.2.1872), 166; (28.1.1873), 55; (27.4.1881), 279; (24.1.1883), 164; (1.12.1886), 122; Student's Handbook (1902), 107; see below, p. 292. Queens' was one of eight colleges offering an entrance scholarship examination by 1902, Student's Handbook (1902), 108.
[33] ibid., 81, 107; Queens' was one of 9 colleges offering exhibitions to poor students at this time, and one of four which had some reserved for sons of poor clergymen, ibid., 81.
[34] Rothblatt (1981), 78 – 80, 84 – 6.
[35] Box 16/10. iii; AC.

financial circumstances permitted, and it also had funds set aside for deserving individuals. In 1854 the president had £75 *per annum* at his disposal to assist 'poor and deserving' students; five years later, the sum had risen to £120, and it was £130 in 1862.[36] These benefactions were usually based on the tutor's recommendations, and in allocating the money the college also took into account 'the merit and good conduct of the Student as well as his poverty, without measuring such merit by his ability and attainments'.[37] The college has records from the late 19th century of applications for money from the president's fund, and of the donations made. The sums involved were not insubstantial, but they were not maintenance grants: they were intended to provide extra help for those whose support from other sources was not quite adequate.[38]

The tutors' books sometimes contain references to students' financial problems and backgrounds. We learn, for example, that H. J. Parsons, awarded an entrance scholarship in mathematics worth £35 in 1896, had turned down a scholarship at Trinity Hall because it was 'too expensive a College'. For some even a scholarship was insufficient to counter their poverty: in the same year, J. E. Metcalfe, an 'Orphan son of [a] cleric' was offered a classical exhibition of £30, but 'Cannot afford to come'; nor could T. C. Buchanan, 'doubly orphan', who had been offered an exhibition of £20.[39] Others came to Queens' for a while, but could not afford to remain: one student was said to be 'diligent; not stupid. Too poor to reside longer. Took a [school]mastership'. Of another it was recorded: 'Father failed. Wants help'; of another: 'Engagement broken off: funds gone. Withdrawn'. One student was described by his tutor as 'bumptious' one term, and a 'pauper' the next.[40] There are genuine human tragedies in these terse comments, and there is no reason to doubt that the tutors were deeply sympathetic, but according to the standards of the time there was little more that could be done to help students struck by poverty.

Whatever the precise social composition of the late 19th century student body, its social ethos remained that of the traditional ruling élite. It has been argued that one of the aims of the university reforms was to ensure that Cambridge did not lose its traditional connections, and to exclude the rising non-professional middle classes unless they were prepared to accept Cambridge values and style.[41] Speaking to the royal commissioners in the early 1850s, J. N. Peill argued that college expenses could not be cut any further to meet the needs of poorer

[36] *CU Cal.* (1840), 220; (1854), 265; (1859), 282; (1860), 284; *Student's Guide* (1862), 305.
[37] *Select Committee* (1867), 238; *Report* (1852), 178.
[38] See for example TB (1889 – 1916); Scholarships, Exhibitions and Grants (1895 – 1908).
[39] TB (1896), (*passim* for other similar examples).
[40] TB (1885 – 91), 13, 36, 61, 70.
[41] Rothblatt (1981), 87 – 92.

students unless board, lodging and tuition were made largely gratuitous; nor could he conceive 'that such a gratuitous system of education
would be attended with any beneficial results to the community,
inasmuch as it would necessarily introduce a pauper class of Students
who might not duly appreciate the advantages thus extended to them'.[42]

The point was re-emphasised by Campion before the parliamentary
select committee in 1867, when he claimed that it was not possible for
the university to take in more students from the new middle classes,
because 'I do not see what is to become of them after their University
course'. Cambridge already took in the élite members of this group —
'all who can make their University course profitable; and I believe that
with the present great pressure in the country you will not get persons
who are going into commerce, or who are going into trade, or what I
might call the lower professions, to come and spend two years at the
University'. He denied the charge that openings for the middle classes
were limited by the small number of scholarships available; they were
limited, he said, by 'the number of openings that there are likely to be in
the professions that they mean to follow . . . no man, I conceive,
however distinguished he was in a middle-class [local] examination, and
however sure of getting a scholarship, would come up to Cambridge if
he intended, after coming to Cambridge, to go into a merchant's office
in Liverpool; for the merchant would tell him that it would serve his
purpose much better to go into the office at once'.[43]

Campion's argument was disingenuous, for there was widespread
interest in university education among the middle classes — this, after
all, was one of the forces behind the parliamentary reforms. The dons
were willing to cut their embarrassing 18th century associations with the
landed gentry and to identify with the old professions, seeing the
academic life itself as a profession too, but that was as far as they were
prepared to go.[44] The relatively small number of students from the
newer middle classes were accepted on the understanding that they
would adopt the values of the older élite. Campion observed that 'the
great advantage which the men get in coming to Cambridge is by
rubbing against each other, and a man gets to learn what he is properly
worth; in fact, as we say, the conceit gets taken out of him',[45] but in fact
the aim was to promote class solidarity by the incorporation of
outsiders, not by some general process of levelling. Campion expressed
this more directly in the remark that a Cambridge BA degree 'represents
not only a certain amount of general education (and in the future it will

[42] *Report* (1852), 178.
[43] *Select Committee* (1867), 239; his remark about the merchant's office in Liverpool is
mentioned in Rothblatt (1981), 89.
[44] Rothblatt (1981), 90–2.
[45] *Select Committee* (1867), 239.

represent a certain amount of special education), but it also represents the social training which may be given during three years' residence'.[46]

The tutors' books at Queens' refer vaguely to the social ideal, in phrases such as 'gentlemanly', 'most respectable man', 'good style of man', and 'a gentleman, good manners, good style, bright and eager'.[47] They give some clues also to the characteristics of those who did not match the ideal: 'vulgar: provincial accent: aspirates'; or 'This man omitted all aspirates: coached him, till he cured himself'.[48]

T. C. Fitzpatrick, in a university sermon in 1915, spoke of the changes which the university had experienced in recent times. There was now, he believed, a greater variety of character among the students, and though the problem of maintaining poor men remained, he argued that Oxford and Cambridge had never been exclusively for the wealthy. It was beneficial, he felt, for students from different social groups, and with different views, to rub shoulders together.[49] These remarks hint at a slightly more egalitarian social outlook than that of Campion nearly half a century before, but they are vague, and rather self-congratulatory. If the university's social ethos did alter in the years leading up to the first world war, this has not yet been demonstrated.

Clubs and societies

The students' beliefs and attitudes are expressed in the activities of their clubs and societies. Perhaps the most significant of these was the St Bernard Society, founded in 1862 'for the promotion of debates and the reading of original papers'. The new society was supported by Campion, but there was some opposition among the Fellows to its establishment.[50] We know little about its early years: its minute books were given to the college library in 1928, but the first of these, covering the years 1862 – 83, can no longer be found.[51] In addition to its originally stated aims, the society later began to organise light musical entertainments, and to function, in effect, as an embryonic junior combination room. In 1866 the college lecture room began to be used as the society's reading room, and newspapers and magazines were taken.[52] It became,

[46] ibid., 232, and see 233.
[47] TB (1885 – 91), 95, 112, 118, 131, 134.
[48] ibid., 18; TB (1878 – 87), 31.
[49] CR (20.1.1915), 147.
[50] Dial (Easter 1916), 22.
[51] Five of the six surviving minute books are now in the college's tutorial office; the other is in the president's study. This characteristic lack of system in the keeping of documents may explain the loss of the earliest minute book.
[52] Dial (Easter 1916), 24; MS 79, 51 – 3. In 1877 the governing body voted £15 towards furnishing a lecture room for 'a reading room to be used by the undergraduates', CB (1832 – 88), 2.1.1877. This entry makes it seem as if the reading room was an innovation at this time.

therefore, a society for the whole college, and in a primitive way a form of gentleman's club.

Debates were held often, and on a wide range of subjects. In the society's earlier years, historical subjects were popular in addition to the more usual topical themes, but this does not seem to have lasted for long, and students soon began to show an overriding interest in the affairs of their own times.[53] Some of these themes are discussed elsewhere in this book:[54] the topics were sometimes serious, sometimes light-hearted, and favourite subjects were often repeated. The evils of tobacco and alcohol were debated more than once, with different results.[55] Capital punishment, vivisection, the justification of suicide, and the desirability of a channel tunnel were other recurring themes.[56] Other topical and serious subjects which arose included vegetarianism and cremation (at the time when cremation was technically illegal), the introduction of old age pensions, and the extension of municipal trading.[57] There was some discussion of university matters, such as the tendency towards specialisation in university education, the value of classical studies, and the examination system, although such subjects were not always very popular.[58] There were also many light-hearted meetings, principally in the form of 'impromptu' debates (at which a number of humourous topics were debated briefly in the same evening), and mock trials.[59]

---

[53] For example, whether Elizabeth I was justified in consenting to the execution of Mary Queen of Scots, *Dial* (Easter 1916), 23. All the debates recorded in the society's minutes up until the outbreak of war are listed below in appendix 18.

[54] See below, pp. 256, 278 – 9, 434.

[55] CR (2.3.1881), 200; (26.11.1891), 107; (18.2.1892), 214; (19.11.1896), 98; *Dial* (Easter 1916), 23; SBSM, 20.11.1886, 21.11.1891, 13.2.1892, 14.11.1896, 29.1.1898. The society took a higher moral tone in voting for the suppression of the Indian opium trade in 1892 and in 1910, CR (3.11.1910), 58; SBSM, 29.10.1892.

[56] CR (12.11.1884), 70; (13.2.1890), 200; (16.11.1893), 96; (30.11.1899), 127; (4.12.1902), 125; (7.2.1907), 229; (30.1.1908), 202; (4.2.1909), 229; (14.11.1910), 86; (23.10.1913), 43; (30.10.1913), 66; SBSM, 8.2.1890, 11.11.1893, 9.11.1895, 25.11.1899, 29.11.1902, 26.1.1907, 25.1.1908, 30.1.1909, 25.10.1913.

[57] CR (28.2.1883), 252; (18.11.1888), 65; (13.12.1908), 145; *Dial* (Easter 1908), 205; SBSM, 11.2.1888, 17.11.1888, 19.10.1889, 8.2.1908, 28.11.1908.

[58] *Dial* (Michaelmas 1907), 168 – 9; (Michaelmas 1909), 333; CR (7.2.1889), 190; (12.11.1891), 77; (7.11.1901), 62; (23.11.1911), 138; SBSM, 7.11.1891, 2.11.1901, 1.11.1902, 25.1.1907, 6.3.1909, 18.11.1911.

[59] SBSM, 14.2.1891, 16.11.1895, 28.11.1896, 6.11.1897, 27.1.1900, 7.2.1903, 13.2.1904, 25.2.1905, 3.11.1906. The motions at the impromptu debate of 25 February 1905 were: 'That the College Dons are inadequate'; 'That a new University Church be raised and that the bedmakers be used as gargoyles'; 'That the association [football] team should go into strict training'; 'That the hair on the outside of a cocoanut accounts for the milk on the inside'; 'That rowing should succeed the treadmill as a method of condign punishment'; and 'That it is better to be a happy pig than an unhappy man'. These are typical examples of the humour of the period. See also below, appendix 18 for other light-hearted or semi-serious debates — all debates were meant anyway to provide an opportunity for the speakers to demonstrate wit.

The students were fascinated by modernity and its appurtenances, and some of them at least were anxious to demonstrate their intellectually and aesthetically progressive ideas. The St Bernard Society debated 'modern' literature on several occasions;[60] it discussed the development of advertising, the introduction of aeroplanes, and the extension of state control over the individual.[61] In 1881 it soundly rejected the idea that 'change of fashion in dress is neither conducive to true art nor beneficial to trade'; in 1888 there was little opposition to the motion that 'Philistinism is the prevailing characteristic of life and sentiment in this University'; in 1903 it decided that the present age was 'essentially inartistic'; and five years later it addressed itself to the question that 'conventionality was not opposed to true progress'.[62] The suggestion that society had deteriorated, or that the present race — especially that of undergraduates — had degenerated was raised frequently.[63]

The society was far from progressive in its thinking on social matters. In 1880 it passed the motion 'That the tendency of the present age is to over-educate the lower classes' by a majority of four to one, despite the motion having been opposed by 'a large majority of speakers'; in 1888 it agreed that 'any system of Free Education would be disastrous for the best interests of the nation'; and in 1890 it decided 'that no limit but an economic one should be put on the education of the lower classes'. In 1894 it rejected a motion that an eight hours bill should be passed; in 1897 it supported the view that trades unions were 'producing a harmful effect upon the National peace and prosperity'. In 1910 the motion that the house should be 'disgusted at the squalor of the middle classes' was defeated only by the chairman's casting vote; in the following year the house deplored 'the increasing power of the industrial classes'; and in 1913 it affirmed that class distinctions were 'always necessary to national existence'.[64] The students would have repudiated any charges of social snobbery levelled against them, but a sense of their social, as well as intellectual and cultural, superiority was implicit in much of their debating.

The students' political attitudes were utterly conservative; in this they

[60] CR (28.11.1889), 102; (5.3.1896), 254; (19.11.1903), 94; SBSM, 23.11.1889, 29.2.1896, 14.11.1903. They also debated modern journalism, and the influence of drama on the nation, CR (15.3.1882), 234; (9.11.1905), 73; SBSM, 18.2.1888, 16.2.1901.

[61] CR (2.12.1909), 165; (2.2.1911), 248; (4.12.1913), 183; SBSM, 27.11.1909, 29.11.1913; see also CR (28.2.1907), 293.

[62] CR (16.2.1881), 168; (1.2.1888), 166; (26.2.1903), 221; (5.11.1908), 70; SBSM, 28.1.1888, 31.10.1888; see also SBSM, 1.11.1890, 5.12.1896, 29.10.1898, 14.2.1903, 21.2.1903, 27.10.1906, 24.11.1906, 31.10.1908, 13.11.1909, 12.11.1910, 1.2.1913.

[63] CR (29.1.1891), 168; (3.3.1898), 267; (16.11.1905), 93; (4.3.1914), 349; SBSM, 20.10.1888, 24.1.1891, 7.3.1898, 11.11.1905, 14.2.1914.

[64] CR (27.10.1880), 39; (6.3.1890), 248; (8.2.1894), 214; (10.3.1910), 352; SBSM, 3.11.1888, 1.3.1890, 3.2.1894, 20.11.1897, 12.3.1910, 4.11.1911, 15.2.1913.

were at one with the dons. Their conservatism was expressed repeatedly and forcefully in the St Bernard Society's debates. In 1882 the society condemned the policies of Gladstone's Liberal government after a 'desultory' discussion, but two years later it passed a vote of censure against the same administration by forty votes to none. In the same year the house rejected a motion supporting the Liberals' franchise bill (the Third Reform Bill), having already 'speedily proceeded to show its disapproval of the motion by the most noisy and incessant interruptions, which all the tact of the worthy president seemed powerless to control'; and in 1887, 'after a very lively debate', it also rejected the motion that the 'present policy of the Unionists is fatal to the best interests of the country'. From then until the outbreak of war in 1914 the society regularly condemned Liberal administrations emphatically, and maintained its staunch support for the Conservatives.[65] A similar tone is evident in its expressed views on such matters as free trade and reform of the House of Lords.[66]

The society may have been a little more forward-looking regarding the British empire. Although it denied the assertion 'that England's glory was on the wane' in 1882, two years later the motion that the people of India should be allowed some share in their own government was carried by a single vote; and in 1886 and 1896 there was a majority in favour of the introduction of some scheme of imperial federation.[67] The governing body at this time was undeniably patriotic: in 1899 it cancelled the annual Thomas Smith feast 'in view of the present War in South Africa', and in 1909 agreed to allow college servants who were members of the territorial army extra leave on full pay to attend their annual training camps.[68] At about the same time an OTC unit was set up in the college; in 1910 about one third of the undergraduates were members, and the unit remained active until the outbreak of war.[69] A student's description of an OTC camp at Aldershot in 1912 is a

[65] CR (22.11.1882), 105; (27.2.1884), 216; (29.10.1884), 38; (23.11.1887), 104; (29.10.1891), 42; (11.3.1897), 297; (20.11.1902), 93; (8.2.1906), 224; (7.11.1912), 86; SBSM, 19.11.1887, 24.10.1891, 26.11.1892, 26.10.1895, 6.3.1897, 11.2.1899, 15.11.1902, 3.2.1906, 2.11.1912; see also CR (20.2.1884), 200.

[66] SBSM, 5.11.1887, 2.3.1889, 12.11.1892, 25.11.1893, 11.3.1899, 9.2.1907; CR (7.3.1889), 256 ('The St. Bernard kept up its character of being a strong Tory assembly'); (17.11.1892), 90; (30.11.1893), 134; (16.3.1899), 280; Dial (Michaelmas 1907), 168 – 9; and see also SBSM, 3.11.1900, 31.10.1903.

[67] CR (15.2.1882), 169; (3.12.1884), 118; (27.10.1886), 37; (6.2.1896), 190; SBSM, 23.10.1886, 1.2.1896; but c.f. SBSM, 18.10.1890. Another college society, the Quaerists, heard a paper on the subject of imperial federation in 1910, (8.12.1910), 185.

[68] CB (1889 – 1937), 11.11.1899, 14.1.1909; see also CR (2.11.1899), 58; (7.12.1899), 130; (18.1.1900), 146; (1.2.1900), 177; (22.2.1900), 219. In 1882 the governing body gave £10 to the Unionist Property Defence Association in Ireland, CB (1833 – 88), 3.1.1882. The St Bernard Society rejected home rule decisively in 1903, SBSM, 31.1.1903.

[69] Dial (Michaelmas 1910), 26 – 31; (Lent 1911), 67; (Michaelmas 1912), 153 – 4; CR (9.12.1909), 188; (8.5.1913), 434; (22.5.1913), 478.

youthful mixture of exuberance and earnestness:

'It's a pleasant business, this playing at soldiers . . . We don't pretend to overmuch usefulness, but we do give ourselves the chance of getting a glimpse at the harder side of the game, and it pays now, in health and enjoyment, and it will pay, in case we have to adopt compulsory service or if at the worst we have a large war, and there is need, as there will be, of volunteers, trained or untrained, to take the places of men killed in battle'.[70]

The St Bernard Society supported compulsory military training on several occasions, not always with excessive enthusiasm. Although it rejected calls for war in 1893 and 1905, it was generally unsympathetic to schemes for disarmament and compulsory arbitration of international disputes. In 1906 it refused, narrowly, to deplore the growth of militarism; and in 1911 defended 'modern warfare' as a remedy for disputes between nations.[71]

It is evident then that students were becoming only too aware of the growing threat of war in Europe, and there are other signs of change in the political atmosphere in the years immediately preceding the first world war. Socialism had traditionally been beyond the pale, but in 1904 the St Bernard Society approved 'the spread of Socialistic ideas in England'; three years later a motion welcoming the 'rise of Socialism' was defeated by only two votes; and in 1912 the house refused by a narrow majority to condemn recent strikes.[72] In 1910 we learn that one of the college's resident BAs, T. H. Cleworth, who had formerly been a Unionist, was now regarded as almost a Liberal, with a tendency towards socialism. J. W. C. Turner, an undergraduate, was reported in the same year as being quite unequivocal in his political allegiances: he was a socialist and a Fabian, and college secretary for the Cambridge

[70] *Dial* (Michaelmas (1912), 153. There are references to a college volunteer contingent in the mid-1890s, which had apparently been in existence for some while, *CR* (9.5.1895), 315. It was not, in those days, taken so seriously by some other members of the college: in May 1893 it was reported to be 'in a state of great efficiency at present; they were assaulted by the college in general on Monday night, but owing to the great gallantry of Pte. Wood the disrespectful movement was repulsed', (11.5.1893), 332. In 1910 the *Cambridge Review* carried a reference to Old Court as a parade ground for boy scouts, probably a humourous description of the O.T.C., (2.6.1910), 458.

[71] *CR* (2.11.1893), 62; (5.11.1896), 62; (16.11.1899), 95; (3.3.1904), 238 – 9; (3.11.1910), 79; (30.11.1911), 159; (20.11.1913), 134; (13.12.1913), 275; SBSM, 28.10.1893, 30.11.1895, 12.11.1898, 11.11.1899, 27.2.1904, 29.11.1905, 14.2.1906, 29.10.1910, 25.11.1911; see also SBSM, 31.10.1896, 24.1.1900.

[72] *CR* (10.11.1886), 70; (8.3.1894), 276; (21.2.1895), 217; (3.11.1904), 46; (28.11.1907), 127; SBSM, 6.11.1886, 3.3.1894, 16.2.1895, 29.10.1904, 16.11.1907, 16.11.1912. The society had also rejected republicanism and decided that the effects of the French Revolution were 'adverse to progress', *CR* (16.2.1887), 211; (7.3.1888), 250; (4.2.1892), 181; SBSM, 12.2.1887, 3.3.1888, 30.1.1892.

branch of the suffragettes.[73] Such men were still regarded as oddities, and the political complexion of the undergraduate body overall did not shift dramatically — they continued to support the Conservative party with enthusiasm, and to reject schemes for political reform[74] — but their appearance and recognition does signify a broader range of views within the college.[75]

The St Bernard Society was not necessarily representative of the whole body of undergraduates, and attendance at debates was often low; the standard of speaking also varied greatly.[76] The debates were not always taken seriously, and were sometimes disorderly. In December 1884 the society's president 'called attention to the disorderly nature of the debates and entertainments of the Society, and expressed a hope that members would assist himself and the other officers in raising the tone of their meetings'. The standard of behaviour was said to have improved in the Edwardian period, and there are some hints perhaps of a more orderly and serious tone, but this is difficult to assess: in 1909 the *Cambridge Review*'s correspondent in Queens' expressed the hope that 'the serious side of debating will usurp the hitherto prevailing tendency to "rag" '; and at a debate in 1911 'an interlude of disorder was caused by the second year mistaking beer for brilliantine'.[77] But the debates must be taken seriously. The topics chosen are often of more significance than the number of votes cast for and against a particular motion, and show the students to have been well aware of the main issues of their day, and keen to express themselves upon them. They believed that they had something of value to say, perhaps conscious of their destiny as members of the nation's leading class: most Queensmen, it was assumed, would be 'men of affairs' in later life.[78]

Complaints about low attendance at the society's debates were based in part on the assumption that students should participate as much as

---

[73] *Dial* (Easter 1910), 353; (Michaelmas 1910), 15.

[74] See above, notes 65 and 66.

[75] In debates it seems that the students were not interested in complex or technical political subjects: in 1911 a planned debate on tariff reform was cancelled; in 1912 the Quaerists heard a paper on home rule for Ireland, but there was a small audience even for a subject as contentious as this. In 1914, in contrast, a debate on the daylight saving bill was popular, but then this was a subject on which everyone could express an opinion, *CR* (16.2.1911), 294; (1.2.1912), 236; (4.3.1914), 349; (10.6.1914), 517; SBSM, 28.2.1914. Daylight saving had previously been debated in 1909, SBSM, 20.10.1909.

[76] *CR* (28.11.1889), 102; (20.10.1892), 26; (26.1.1911), 229; (2.2.1911), 248; (9.2.1911), 274; (26.10.1911), 57; (8.2.1912), 257 – 8; (21.11.1912), 127; *Courier* (15.3.1906), 36 – 7; *Dial* (March 1907), 131 – 2, 138 – 9. According to one late-19th century student, the standard of debating was not very high, MS 79, 51.

[77] *Dial* (Easter 1916), 24 – 6; *CR* (4.2.1909), 229; (9.11.1911), 98; SBSM, December 1884.

[78] The expression was used in the *Dial* (March 1907), 138 – 9. See also, for example, the arrogant assumption in the 1891 motion for debate 'That the abolition of compulsory Greek in the Examinations for the Arts degree at the University would be detrimental to the best interests of the nation', SBSM, 7.11.1891.

possible in college activities, and that the society represented, in a way, the undergraduate community at Queens'. Its common room, the Bernard Room, was said to be the one place in the college 'where men of all sorts and conditions may meet to their mutual advantage, for the interchange, formation and modification of ideas, and for the acquisition of a modest hope of future sanity', and where there was 'that chance of rubbing shoulders with all the world for the sake of which — for Triposes are merely means — schools and colleges are founded'.[79]

Debates were held on Saturday nights, alternating with smoking concerts consisting of a number of light musical items performed by students; these events were generally well supported and formed an important part of the college's social life.[80] In 1898 permission was given by the governing body to hold a smoking concert in the college hall, which was described in the *Cambridge Review* as 'a new and welcome departure';[81] by this time the custom of a more formal May Week concert in the hall was also established.[82] College musical societies were founded, notably the St Margaret Society in 1884, which is still flourishing.[83] The first May ball held in Queens' was in 1913, and was so successful that another was arranged the following year.[84]

The students organised their own literary and intellectual societies, of which four are recorded in this period (this excludes bodies which were more directly connected with the university curriculum, such as the classical society). One, the Poets, was seemingly short-lived, for only two of its meetings are recorded, in 1900 and 1901, when it heard papers on Tennyson and 'Poets, otherwise than serious'. In the year before the first world war a society for philosophical discussion was created, but we know nothing of its activities.[85] The other two, both established in the 1890s, lasted longer. The Erasmus Society, first recorded in 1896, was principally concerned with theological subjects, but in 1907 it is known to have heard a paper on the geography of Belgium, perhaps in a desperate attempt to drum up support, for it was said to have been in decline in the previous year, and it folded up shortly afterwards.[86]

The Quaerists, also a theological society in the beginning, first appear

[79] *Dial* (March 1907), 138 – 9.
[80] *ibid.* (March 1907), 131 – 2; (Easter 1916), 24 – 6; *Courier* (15.3.1906), 36 – 7; MS 79, 51. Behaviour at these events was not always immaculate, *CR* (26.10.1911), 79.
[81] *CR* (10.2.1898), 218.
[82] For example, *ibid.* (11.6.1896), 382; (13.6.1900), 371.
[83] *Record* (1985), 20. The Queens' College Musical Society was founded in 1914, *Dial* (Lent 1914), 324.
[84] *Dial* (Easter 1913), 213; (Michaelmas 1913), 269 – 70; (Michaelmas 1914), 4.
[85] *CR* (29.11.1900), 111; (28.2.1901), 218; (19.2.1913), 302. The Poets are mentioned in Ryle's dairy in December 1901, Fitzgerald (1928), 139. In 1890 there is a reference to a club called the 'Shakespeareans', possibly some form of literary society, SBSM, 1.12.1890.
[86] *CR* (7.11.1907), 71; *Dial* (March 1907), 135 – 6; (Easter 1910), 371.

in 1895, and may have been in existence for some time already.[87] The society broadened its range to include philosophical and literary subjects, especially in the Edwardian period, under the strong challenge of the Christian Union: in 1906 it declared itself distinct from the latter body, in that it was not intended for 'devotional purposes', but for the discussion of 'theological and philosophical questions in their general relation to modern thought'.[88] In the years which followed it heard papers on several different authors,[89] the art of biography, 'what is beauty', and the Greek view of life (these last two given by one of the Fellows, A. B. Cook).[90] In 1911 – 12, following a suggestion that a college play-reading society should be formed, the Quaerists are known to have held two play readings, but the experiment was not apparently continued.[91] In 1914, the society's last recorded meeting, it heard a paper on 'Mysticism and Logic' given by a Fellow of Trinity, Bertrand Russell, who 'showed (by example) that it is possible even for philosophers to be intelligible to the outside-the-palers. We hope that even those who disagreed with his conclusions will not lose heart but do their best to stimulate the interests of men in philosophy — the most garrulised and least understood of sciences'.[92]

Although it saw the failure of the Erasmus Society, the Edwardian period was the heyday of the college's literary and intellectual societies. In 1907 Queens' was said to be 'in a whirl of literary activity'; in 1911 it was reported, somewhat facetiously, that 'A certain section of the third year are appalling the more frivolous members by their sudden intellectuality'; in 1912 it was observed that 'societies, official and unofficial, have been busy'; and there was a similarly high level of activity early in the following year.[93] The college Classical Society, revived in 1912, flourished up until the first world war.[94] This trend,

---

[87] CR (24.10.1895), 35. See also below, p. 278.

[88] The formal shift to a theological and philosophical society came in 1906, but it was said to have been discussing philosophical subjects for some while already, and it is known to have discussed literary matters since the late 1890s, although this became more significant in the years after 1906, *Courier* (15.3.1906), 36; *Dial* (March 1907), 133 – 4; (Easter 1910), 371. See also above, n. 89.

[89] Ibsen, Crabbe, Spenser, George Meredith, R. L. Stevenson, Chaucer, and Tolstoy. In 1897 and 1901 it had heard papers on Browning (read by the president, F. H. Chase), and Dante respectively, *CR* (25.11.1897), 113; (7.2.1901), 171; (30.1.1908), 203; (4.2.1909), 229; (11.11.1909), 101; (17.2.1910), 283; (24.2.1910), 303; (16.2.1911), 294; (23.11.1911), 138.

[90] ibid. (7.11.1907), 71; (3.12.1908), 145; (15.12.1912), 78. Cook was a keen lecturer to college societies. In 1901 he gave a talk on Greek vase paintings, with slides, to some college group — it is not clear which, *ibid*. (7.3.1901), 237.

[91] ibid (23.11.1911), 138; (7.12.1911), 179; (1.2.1912), 236; (8.2.1912), 257. The plays were *The Winter's Tale* and *The School for Scandal*.

[92] ibid. (29.1.1914), 237.

[93] ibid. (7.11.1907), 71; (16.11.1911), 117; (7.11.1912), 86; (30.1.1913), 233.

[94] *Dial* (Lent 1914), 332.

taken with the developments in the students' political consciousness, suggests a growing awareness of and interest in the world outside the university, and in the movements and ideas of their times; in this, it was a genuine precursor of the student culture of the 1920s and 1930s.

There were several other societies with a primarily social aim, which, for want of a better term, may be called dining clubs, although their activities did not necessarily take that form. These originated at the same time as the literary and intellectual societies. The first references to these societies occur in October 1895, when there were already two: the Kangaroos and the Mahatmas. We know very little about the Mahatmas at this time, save that they were noisy. The Kangaroos' weekly meetings, at which various light-hearted and trivial motions were discussed and passed with mock formality, sometimes included games, and usually ended with some of the members entertaining the rest with song.[95] The clubs were apparently a new phenomenon, and soon became all the rage, for in February 1896 the *Cambridge Review* reported that 'This week has been chiefly characterised by an almost mushroom growth of clubs and societies'; and, later in the month, that 'We understand that the few remaining members of the College who have not hitherto succumbed to the recent attack of Club fever, have at last fallen victims, and have assumed the somewhat appropriate title of "The Pariahs" '.[96]

The clubs' activities do not feature much thereafter in the under-graduate press.[97] Some were only ephemeral, and the social distinctions between them are not clear.[98] Yet they did form distinct social units, with recognised rivalries. The St Bernard Society, which administered the Bernard Room, tried to act as a focal point for the whole college, transcending the divisions of cliques and clubs, but without much success. In 1907 a plea for greater attendance at debates argued that the

---

[95] CR (24.10.1895), 35; (7.11.1895), 70. The first surviving minutes book of the Kangaroo Club begins in October 1895, but there is a reference to the club having been in existence in 1891, Kangaroo Club Minutes, 29.10.1895. For the nature of their meetings, see *ibid., passim.*; the tone changed during the Edwardian period, however, see below, n. 101.

[96] CR (6.2.1896), 190; (20.2.1896), 221.

[97] The Kangaroos are known to have held an annual dinner in 1907, *ibid.* (9.5.1907), 388. In 1906 one man was described as a Quaerist, a Kangaroo, and a Friar, *Courier* (November 1906), 74; this is the only reference to the Friars that I have found.

[98] J. F. Williams wrote that the Kangaroos were mostly public school men and sportsmen, MS 79, 53. Their formal association with sports did not occur until after the first world war, but a greater emphasis on sports may have occurred during the pre-war period: in 1920, when the club's rules were redrawn, its originally defined purpose of holding social meetings once a week was rejected as no longer reflecting the club's true aim, which was now defined as 'to maintain and further the best sporting traditions of the College', Kangaroo Club Minutes, 28.2.1920. The *Dial* observed of R. H. E. H. Somerset in 1908 that 'Socially, he is a Kangaroo', (Easter 1908), 196, and Somerset was not particularly sporty.

clubs were only transient, that behind them all lay a greater institution — the college — which affected every clique and every individual in a deeper way, so that first and foremost one was a member of Queens' and not of a particular society.[99] This was without doubt an attempt to resurrect an ideal united college community, which had in practice fragmented thanks to the clubs and their rivalries. As early as the 1890s there was friction between two of the leading clubs, the Kangaroos and a club called the Pi-Posse, which was a religious group of some kind, and the antagonism was shown in fiercely contested elections to the committee of the St Bernard Society, which thus became prey to factions.[100] This problem was clearly present in 1907, and the dangers of factionalism were expressed forcefully by the dean, C. T. Wood, in 1916. Writing in the *Dial*, he noticed that the two principal clubs, the Kangaroos and the Cherubs, 'have often contained some of the nicest men in the college'. Nevertheless, he continued, 'the existence of these clubs has again and again caused bad feeling and created cabals', with club loyalty dominating elections to the committees of athletic and other societies. Wood continued:

'I shall be told that this is the abuse, not the use of clubs: but the danger is always latent and often active. On the other hand, I cannot see that their existence has ever been of use to the College as a whole . . . I hoped that the war would bring our clubs to an end. Instead of this, I understand that there is danger of their numbers being increased. I hope that I shall not be regarded as interfering in matters beyond my province, if I appeal to members of the clubs and others to join in ending what is a standing menace to the unity of our college life'.[101]

One reason for this fragmentation was the rapid increase in the college's size, which was bound to lead to the formation of subcultures within the larger group as the bonds between individual students and the college as a whole became slightly more attenuated.[102] Perhaps this had been

---

[99] *ibid.* (March 1907), 137 – 9.

[100] MS 79, 53 – 5; for Pi-Posse, see below, pp. 279 – 80.

[101] *Dial* (Easter 1916), 30. The Kangaroos and Cherubs are still thriving. The minutes of the Kangaroos show their meetings becoming more chaotic and disorderly and vulgar in the Edwardian period. This continued into the 1920s, when members were amused by the relatively subdued character of the club in its late Victorian years as revealed by its minutes, Kangaroo Club Minutes, 21.1.1922. It is perhaps another sign of the decadence of the age.

[102] J. F. Williams believed it to be one of the advantages of a small college that all of its members could dine together at the same time, MS 79, 47 (presumably because this would enhance the feeling of being part of a single college community). A. H. Noble (1905 – 9) recounted that the custom of breakfast parties given by the dons died out as student numbers increased, Noble, MS Autobiography. It should be noted that none of the clubs was very large; the Kangaroos had usually 10 – 12 members before the war, and only a slightly larger number afterwards.

one of the reasons for Wood's promotion of a college magazine, the *Courier*, in 1906, which hoped 'to supply, successfully, both the serious and the comic element so desired by a college citizen in a record of college life' — in other words, it was meant to appeal to the whole college, and to be a focus for college sentiment. After the magazine became the *Dial* in the following year an editorial announced the intention of changing its style in order to render it 'more in unison with College spirit'. Perhaps this too was at the instigation of the dons, for there was always one Fellow on the magazine's editorial committee.[103]

Athleticism

Closely bound up with the radical changes in student life and culture, and with the 'Revolution of the Dons', was what may legitimately be termed a 'sporting revolution'. Organised sports and games are now deeply ingrained in the British educational system, but they have been prominent only for about a century and a half, and their rise was achieved in a relatively short period in the early years of Victoria's reign.

There was really no organised sport in the modern sense in the universities before this time, although students had always participated in a wide range of sporting recreations, most of which were associated with the leisured, moneyed classes.[104] Poorer undergraduates seeking exercise had to take it by walking. In addition, sporting recreations were often morally suspect: at their worst, they were associated with gambling; at their best, with self-indulgence and excessive high spirits. The early evangelical Henry Venn, before migrating from Jesus to Queens' to become a Fellow there in 1749, had been a keen and distinguished cricketer, one of the best players in the university. In 1747, one week before his ordination, he played for Surrey in an important match against All-England, and after the game was finished offered to give his cricket bat away. When his surprised friends asked why he wished to do this, he replied 'Because I am to be ordained on Sunday, and I will never have it said of me, "Well struck, Parson!" '. Venn never played cricket again.[105]

Such puritanical views of sport were typical of their time, but by the middle of the 19th century a complete transformation in attitudes had been effected: sports and the church had become allies, not enemies, and 'muscular Christianity' had arrived. Sport was now seen to be

---

[103] *Courier* (15.2.1906), 1; *Dial* (Michaelmas 1907), 146. The proposed introduction of the magazine, at Wood's instigation, is mentioned in SBSM, 18.10.1905.
[104] Above, pp. 95, 195.
[105] Quoted in Venn (1904), 70 – 1.

character-building by encouraging self-displine, self-reliance and deter-mined endeavour. The origins of this remarkable shift in outlook, which was so important in the social history of modern Britain, can be traced to the reforms in the public schools, where a sporting mania spread like wildfire in the 1830s and 1840s.[106]

Organised games were seen as a civilising infuence, therefore, curbing immorality and indiscipline; and for this reason they were as welcome to university and college authorities as they were to schoolmasters. A historian brought up in the late Victorian era wrote of 18th century student behaviour that 'though riotous and disorderly conduct was far too common, it is important to bear in mind that the offenders belonged to the comparatively small class of wealthy young men who came up to the university to amuse themselves and lacked the outlet of athletics for the dissipation of their energy'.[107]

This change in the university seems to have begun in the middle years of the 19th century, picking its inspiration up from the movement sweeping the public schools.[108] Sports were certainly well established by the early 1860s, when a contributor to the *Student's Guide to the University of Cambridge* observed that:

'few men study between 2 p.m. and the dinner hour; this time is given by the most industrious to open-air exercise and recreation. The students are English youths, and a large proportion of them have grown up in the great public schools. Athletic sports accordingly are pursued with ardour. There is a boat-club in every College, and the science of rowing is studied by as many men with as much ambition, and perhaps even with as much seriousness, as either Classics or Mathematics'.[109]

Queens' was probably abreast of the fashion, although lack of evidence prevents precise dating of the arrival of organised games there. The first college sporting club was the Boat Club, which was in existence by 1831, when it had 45 members.[110] But it went into decline at the end of the decade, and came close to breaking up in 1841 for want of support,

---

[106] The reforms were inspired by the work of Thomas Arnold at Rugby, but Arnold was not responsible for the games cult, which was a later accretion. For the nature and development of athleticism in the public schools, see Mangan (1981). There was a reciprocal relationship between schools and universities, for the latter sent back schoolmasters who were enthusiasts for the games cult.

[107] Winstanley (1922), 23.

[108] Mangan (1981), chapter 6. Tony Mangan is currently engaged upon research for a book on athleticism at Oxford and Cambridge in the Victorian and Edwardian periods.

[109] *Student's Guide* (1862), 47 – 8; the entry was by J. R. Seeley.

[110] Queens' had 17 fellow-commoners, 96 pensioners and 30 sizars in 1831, *CU Cal.* The club's minute books survive from 1831.

remaining in a precarious position for much of the 1840s. In 1857 the boat was taken off the river because a crew could not be raised.[111] The club survived, however, and began to thrive. It probably remained the only college sports club into the early 1870s, although students often played croquet, quoits and tennis on ground alongside the Fellows' garden on the west bank of the Cam.[112]

The sporting revolution was in full swing at Queens' by the end of the 1870s. In 1873 a governing body committee recommended 'That a lawn for out of door games should be prepared in the paddock', and in 1874 the governing body voted to build a fives court.[113] By 1879 there was a college rugby team, and almost certainly a cricket XI too.[114] New cinder tennis courts were built in the grove in 1880 to replace the existing grass ones, and cricket nets were prepared there shortly afterwards.[115] In 1881 the governing body set up a committee with St Catharine's to acquire a sports field jointly. A field was purchased, and was in use by the end of the year, when plans for 'a dressing shed' were under discussion.[116] Also in 1881 the tennis, cricket and rugby clubs were united to form the Amalgamated Clubs.[117]

The college played its first soccer match in 1884, when it was observed that 'Talent was conspicuous by its absence; those who had any knowledge of the rules were very rusty, besides being in the minority', but a second game played a week later was more successful, and it was

[111]   *Dial* (Lent 1911), 113 – 6; (Easter 1912), 100 – 3; QCBC minutes, 11.11.1841, 19.11.1841, 11.2.1857, 12.2.1857, 13.2.1857, 19.10.1858, and see *ibid*. (1842 – 53), *passim*.
[112]   QCBC minutes (1853 – 63), (1863 – 77), *passim; Dial* (Michaelmas 1935), 17 – 19. Skating was a popular undergraduate outdoor activity. In 1895 several university students skated from Cambridge to Ely; two Queensmen who started out on the journey gave up before the end because the ice was unsafe, and some undergraduates went in, but others completed the trip, *ibid* (Lent 1929), 4. In February 1909 the Queens' correspondent of the *Cambridge Review* reported that 'Football [i.e., rugby] has been put on one side for skating' (the ground would have been too hard for rugby), *CR* (4.2.1909), 229.
[113]   CB (1832 – 88), 17.5.1873, 8.1.1874. The paddock was also on the west side of the river, alongside the outbuildings.
[114]   *CR* (15.10.1879), 8; (3.3.1880), 75. There is a reference to members of the boat club participating in a cricket march in 1863, quite probably for a college team, QCBC minutes, 27.5.1863. See also below, p. 259.
[115]   *CR* (12.11.1879), 72; (21.4.1880), 23. The courts were replaced again in 1882, *ibid.*, (1.11.1882), 54.
[116]   *ibid*. (2.3.1881), 200; (4.5.1881), 296; (9.11.1881), 56. There are further references to extending and levelling the ground in *ibid*. (6.12.1882), 150; (21.2.1883), 233; (31.10.1883), 39. The ground was said to be on the corner of Barton and Newnham roads, *Dial* (Michaelmas 1947), 8 – 10. Hitherto college sport had been played on Parker's Piece in the town, *CR* (15.10.1879), 8; (3.3.1880), 75.
[117]   The clubs were combined under one management, *CR* (4.5.1881), 296; Dickens (1884), 89. The arrival of the new sports challenged the pre-eminence of the boat club, which complained in the autumn of 1891 of the difficulty of getting boats out for trials with the rugby and soccer men withdrawing their support, QCBC minutes, 16.11.1891. But the boat club demanded a very high level of loyalty.

decided to continue the experiment.[118] For a while, soccer had to take its place as a lesser game behind the senior sports of rugby, rowing, cricket and tennis, and in March 1885 Queens' was unable to raise a soccer XI because of the difficulty of finding a practice ground: the college ground was already reserved for preparation for the next term's cricket.[119] The situation altered subsequently, for in the years preceding the first world war the college had a fine reputation for soccer, and its soccer pitch had to be roped off, 'so keen was the town attendance at College matches'.[120] Hockey arrived in 1898,[121] and in 1910 the college moved to a new sports ground on the present site at Barton Road, purchased from King's.[122]

Other evidence reveals the extent of the hold which sports acquired on college life.[123] They brought about a radical change in dining habits. Traditionally the main, formal, meal of the day was dinner. In the mid-17th century colleges dined in the late morning; by the middle of the 18th century, all of the colleges at Cambridge dined at midday; and towards the end of the century the dinner hour shifted towards the early afternoon.[124] In 1781 dinner at Queens' was taken at 1.00 during term and 2.00 outside term; two years later it was put back to 2.00 for the whole year except during examination periods. There was an informal supper in the evenings; at Queens' in the 1780s this was between 8.30 and 9.00 in summer, and half an hour earlier in winter. During the 19th century college dinner hours were put back progressively later in the afternoons to allow more time for games. Queens' changed its dinner hour from 3.00 to 4.00 in 1831, and in 1837 suppers in hall were discontinued.[125] In 1887 there were two halls, at 5.00 and 6.00; in 1898 dinner was between 6.00 and 7.00 on weekdays, and by the 1920s it was at 6.30.[126] G. B. Harrison, who came up to Queens' shortly before the first world war, recalls that 'The morning was the time for work and

[118] CR (13.2.1884), 182; (20.2.1884), 200.
[119] ibid. (11.3.1885), 261.
[120] Dial (Michaelmas 1937), 14; (Michaelmas 1947), 8 – 10.
[121] CR (20.1.1898), 166; (27.1.1898), 186. There was also a chess club by 1889, and, apparently a 'Ping-Pong' club by 1913, ibid. (5.12.1889), 117; (20.11.1913), 134. There is a reference to a college whist team in 1896, ibid., (5.3.1896), 254.
[122] ibid. (28.4.1910), 370; CB (1889 – 1937), 21.9.1907, 28.9.1907; see also Dial (Michaelmas 1935), 3.
[123] University and college magazines, themselves a product of the late Victorian and Edwardian periods, are full of sporting notes and comments. This is why the Cambridge Review and the Dial are cited here so extensively.
[124] Wordsworth (1874), 123 – 5, 129 – 30. At this time students dressed for dinner, but the custom had died out by the middle of the 19th century, Winstanley (1940), 387.
[125] CB (1734 – 87), fos.66v – 67, 111v, 115, 121v; Bradley (1922), 42 – 3; CB (1787 – 1832), 13.1.1831; CB (1832 – 88), 11.10.1837; Winstanley (1940), 386 – 7; Gray, 252.
[126] CR (26.1.1887), 160; CB (1889 – 1937), 16.11.1897 (and see also ibid., 10.10.1901); diary of H. C. Alexander. The introduction of two halls must have been due to the increase in student numbers: although when J. F. Williams came up in 1897 there was only one, at 7.00, two halls were again introduced early in the 20th century, the first at 6.00, the second at 7.00, MS 79, 47, 49; CB (1889 – 1937), 10.10.1905, 11.3.1907.

reading, the afternoon was for exercise, games if one belonged to a team, or what you would, but it was contrary to custom to work or read in the afternoon. The time 4 – 6 was the social period, then dinner in hall with the rest of the college'.[127]

Sporting matters provided a regular subject of debate at the St Bernard Society. In 1881 it rejected the motion that 'Horse-racing merits the support given it by the country', perhaps giving expression to a high Victorian moral tone concerning the evils associated with it, such as gambling.[128] Gambling was formally condemned at debates in 1895 and 1900, but in 1890 the society had been persuaded to accept the view that horse-racing was compatible with the character of a gentleman, and in 1913 the *Cambridge Review*'s correspondent in Queens' maintained that there was 'no truth in the rumour that a special train was chartered by the College for Newmarket'.[129] Predictably, the St Bernard Society also condemned attempts to revive prize-fighting in 1890, and opposed professionalism in rugby in 1893.[130] The society subscribed to several sporting periodicals.[131] It is not surprising to find that the first paper read to the college's newly-revived classical society in 1912 was on 'Greek Games'.[132]

The sporting revolution could not have occurred without the permission of the university's senior members. Many of the dons welcomed games for promoting discipline and morals, and as the mania for sports grew and spread, the quality of a college's sporting facilities and the standard of its sporting achievements might come to affect its attractiveness to potential students. The most notable example of this was at Jesus, which in the 1850s lay in the doldrums in terms of numbers and reputation, but revived in the 1870s to become the third largest college in the university chiefly because of the fame of its oarsmen; and it established a reputation as the 'hearty' college *par excellence*.[133]

Other colleges did not go so far, but no tutor could fail to take account

---

[127]   Harrison (1985), 56.
[128]   *CR* (23.3.1881), 249; the voting was said to have been 'less uneven than might have been expected', but I am not sure which way. In 1889 the society voted that 'the abolition of the so-called sports of Coursing and Horse-racing would be of permanent benefit to the community', SBSM, 16.2.1889. But there was apparently betting on a scratch fives tournament in the college in 1884 — or so I interpret the report: 'We wonder that those interested in the vast stakes do not stir up those in authority', *CR* (20.2.1884), 200. Two members of the Kangaroos were rebuked at a meeting in 1897 'for indulging in betting and gambling contrary to the rules of the Club', Kangaroo Club Minutes, 14.2.1897.
[129]   *CR* (27.11.1890), 120; (7.2.1895), 182; (15.2.1900), 213; (8.5.1913), 434; SBSM, 22.11.1890, 2.2.1895, 10.2.1900.
[130]   *CR* (30.1.1890), 168; (9.2.1893), 194; SBSM, 25.1.1890. In 1898 the society debated the relative merits of rugby and association football, *ibid.*, 26.11.1898.
[131]   SBSM, *passim*.
[132]   *CR* (7.11.1912), 86.
[133]   Mangan (1984).

of the significance of sports and games in university life. It was certainly appreciated at Queens'. The proposal to prepare a lawn for outdoor games within the college grounds in 1873 was one of many substantial and wide-ranging recommendations put forward by an influential governing body committee consisting of the president, tutor, and three Fellows, which had been formed earlier that year to enquire into 'the causes which result in the present low state of the College and to suggest measures for removing them and increasing the general usefulness of the College'.[134]

Perhaps the later improvements in sporting facilities at Queens' should also be seen in this light. The undergraduates were full of gratitude for the governing body's assistance. The creation of cinder tennis courts in 1880 was acknowledged as being 'by the kind liberality of the Fellows'. When the joint committee was formed by Queens' and St Catharine's to purchase a sports field, it was reported that 'the Fellows of both Colleges are entering into the matter heartily', and the field was obtained 'chiefly through the kind assistance of the Fellows'.[135] When the sports clubs were amalgamated in 1881, the president of the new body was one of the Fellows, J. H. Gray, who may have drawn up the scheme.[136] It was Gray who, in his capacity as president of the clubs, supervised the levelling in 1883 of a piece of land adjoining the sports field purchased the previous year.[137] The boat club's finances were managed by the bursar at this time, and when a new financial committee for all the college clubs was formed in 1886, it included two Fellows.[138]

Such involvement of the Fellows was official and paternalistic, taking care of administrative and financial arrangements which students were thought to be too inexperienced to handle by themselves. Individual Fellows were genuinely enthusiastic about sports, too, being products of the same educational system as their undergraduates. In the 1870s Queens' owned a six-oar boat known as 'Noah's Ark' in which dons used to exercise.[139] W. M. Campion had been involved in the running of the boat club as a student in the 1840s. Ernest Temperley was an active

---

[134] CB (1832 – 88), 7.1.1873. The decision to build a fives court the following year probably owed something to this recommendation. Sporting causes were explicitly rejected by J. H. Gray as a causal explanation of the rapid increase in student numbers at Queens' at the end of the 19th century, although the fact that the equation between sports and success in attracting students was thought worthy of repudiation is in itself significant, *Dial* (Michaelmas 1909), 302.

[135] CR (21.4.1880), 23; (2.3.1881), 200; (4.5.1881), 296.

[136] *ibid* (4.5.1881), 296; (6.12.1882), 150. The *Dial* (Michaelmas 1923), 2, is the source for Gray drawing up the scheme, but it gives the wrong date (1898, perhaps that of a reorganisation). There are still strong signs that Gray was active in its establishment.

[137] CR (6.12.1882), 150; (21.2.1883), 233.

[138] *ibid*. (21.10.1885), 20; (27.10.1886), 37. The bursar was probably Ernest Temperley, then junior bursar.

[139] *Dial* (Michaelmas 1935), 17 – 19.

257

oarsman as an undergraduate there in 1867 – 71; and after his election to a fellowship, when 'his duties compelled him to cease rowing', he became auditor and then president of the boat club.[140] His successor as bursar, W. M. Coates had played rugby for the college, and was said to have devoted much of his time to ordering the financial affairs of the college clubs.[141] C. T. Wood had rowed at Shrewsbury, and run for the university when an undergraduate at Pembroke.[142] According to the *Cambridge Review* in 1915, J. H. Gray might 'almost be called the father of Cambridge Athletics'. He was treasurer of the university athletics club for 25 years, and president of the rugby club for even longer; he was also treasurer of the town's Rob Roy boat club in its early days, and in the memory of an undergraduate of the Edwardian period, 'a typical specimen of the mid-Victorian sporting parson'.[143] R. G. D. Laffan, who came to Queens' as a Fellow from Oxford in 1913, was said soon after his arrival to be 'now one of the strongest players in the Rugger side'.[144]

The enthusiasm extended to presidents. When F. H. Chase left Queens' in 1905 to become bishop of Ely, the Queens' *Courier* remembered his wife for, among other things, being 'always ready to dispense tea and coffee to individuals, to societies, or to crews in training, from morning to night'.[145] Of T. C. Fitzpatrick, it was recorded that 'College games in general meant much to him, and he was eager that every man, by the formation of Third Teams or otherwise, should be given a chance to play them'.[146]

The students were glad of such encouragement, and came to expect it. The *Dial*'s obituary notice for Andrew Munro in 1935 noted his care for the college both as an academic and as a sporting institution.[147] J. F. Williams, who came up in 1897, wrote warmly of Arthur Wright that 'Though with no pretensions whatever of being a "sportsman", he certainly maintained an underground interest in the doings of the

---

[140] QCBC minutes, 2.11.1846 and ff.; *CR* (24.1.1889), 150. One of the tutors, George Pirie, coached the college boat in 1872, QCBC minutes, 13.3.1872; and several dons subscribed to relieve the boat club's debts in 1879 and 1889, *ibid.*, 25.4.1879, 6.6.1889.

[141] *CR* (25.1.1912), 209; *Dial* (Lent 1912), 6.

[142] *CR* (18.10.1900), 4; *AC*; *QC* (1960 – 1), 6 – 7. Wood coached the 'Getting-on' boat in the Lent term of 1901, QCBC minutes, 12.2.1901.

[143] *CR* (17.10.1895), 15; (16.10.1902), 5; (24.11.1915), 112; (28.4.1922), 294; (26.5.1922), 363; *Dial* (Michaelmas 1919), 4; (Easter 1932), 9 – 12; Harrison (1985), 56. Gray had been active in the boat club as an undergraduate, QCBC minutes, 14.3.1877 and ff. In 1922 the university rugby club gave him £1,000 in appreciation of his long presidency: this he employed to endow a series of annual classical lectures, which are still given (Gray was himself a classicist), *Dial* (Michaelmas 1926), 3.

[144] *Dial* (Michaelmas 1913), 257; see also *CR* (23.10.1913), 42. Laffan also played in Michaelmas 1920, *ibid.* (Michaelmas 1920), 23.

[145] *Queens' Courier* (15.3.1906), 7. Mrs Ryle had embroidered a new flag for the college boat in 1897, Fitzgerald (1928), 112.

[146] Rackham (1937), 10; Fitzpatrick was particularly interested in the boat club.

[147] *Dial* (Michaelmas 1935), 10.

various teams and crews'.[148] A Fellow's popularity might depend to no small extent on the degree of commitment he showed to college games. Williams felt that J. H. Gray was far less popular in Queens' than in the rest of the university, where he was heavily involved in university sports.[149] Laffan's performances on the rugby field had apparently been forgotten in some quarters by 1922, when an undergraduate was recorded as being willing to 'turn him out because he can't coach any game'.[150]

The social pressures placed on students to play sport were considerable. In 1867 a parliamentary select committee put questions about the state of the university to many prominent university men including W. M. Campion, then tutor of Queens'. At Campion's interview, a discussion of the costs of student life at Cambridge led to a question of subscriptions to college sports clubs. When asked 'A person could hardly be attached to a college without subscribing to a cricket and boat club could he?' Campion replied 'No'. When asked further if he knew of any instances of college men refusing to subscribe to such clubs, he replied: 'I have no doubt there are instances, but then they are rare instances of men of iron determination, and you cannot expect that every man would do so'.[151] At a special meeting of the Amalgamated Clubs in 1887, 'several members spoke on the urgent necessity of all the men in the college taking an active part in the various branches of sport'; the *Cambridge Review*'s correspondent in Queens' hoped the meeting would 'waken up some of our languishing members'.[152]

Although there were some who managed to combine athletic and intellectual pursuits, most colleges were clearly divided into those who played games and those who could not.[153] In 1881 the St Bernard Society rejected the motion that 'this house views with disapproval the undue prominence given to athletics at Cambridge' by a comfortable majority, but only after 'a long and acrimonious debate'; in 1904 a motion that 'the existing devotion to Sport is excessive and deplorable' was only narrowly defeated.[154] There was a wide gulf of incomprehension between the two groups, with the games players usually adopting a superior tone. In 1912 a former captain of boats appealed in the *Dial* for oarsmen:

[148]   MS 79, 31.
[149]   *ibid*, 33 – 5.
[150]   Diary of H. C. Alexander; the remark was by one of his friends.
[151]   *Select Committee* (1867), 234 – 5.
[152]   CR (23.11.1887), 104. At a meeting of the St Bernard Society in November 1887, the society's president observed that 'a great number of the members of the College did not belong to the Clubs', SBSM, 28. 11.1887.
[153]   Mangan (1984), 248 – 51.
[154]   CR (30.11.1881), 104; SBSM, 30.1.1904.

'If these men only realised how important it is to the College that it should strive for a decent reputation in sports, if they only knew the difficulty a conscientious and painstaking Boat Captain has in making up his Lent Boats and if, above all, they only knew the keen pleasure there is in rowing, the feeling of fitness of strength and of *capability* it gives, I feel sure they would not mind the undoubted grind of learning to manage an oar . . . It is most saddening for those who have done their best in the past for the dark green and white, to hear reports of lack of men at the beginning of each October term'.[155]

The description given here of the pleasure of rowing, with its implied sense of the manliness of sporting achievements, coupled with the suggestion that those who would not row were lacking in college patriotism, was characteristic of the superior outlook of the contemporary sporting crusader.

The sportsmen's sense of their own importance was taken to more extreme lengths by a contributor to the *Dial* in 1922. Observing that scholars were granted the privilege of rooms in college for the whole of their three undergraduate years, he argued that captains and secretaries of college sports clubs should also be allowed college rooms during their terms of office, on the grounds that 'If room can always be found for a Scholar, whose work is, after all, for his own immediate benefit, surely it can be found for a man who is giving up his time to the College, thus incidentally facilitating the efficient running of the College clubs'.[156]

It was all too easy for the sporting enthusiasm to become fanatical. The purpose of athleticism, to Victorian minds, was as much moral as physical: sport was meant to be character-forming. Formation of the intellect was distinctly secondary.[157] The ideal sportsman in late Victorian times was the all-rounder, not just in the variety of his sporting interests, but in his civilised and Christian way of life.[158] The *Dial* ran a series of humorous pen pictures of prominent college members entitled 'Men of Mark'; most of these were sportsmen. The ideal of this type would have been someone like E. L. Guilford, a 'Man of Mark' in 1911: hockey blue, captain of the Queens' soccer team,

---

[155] *Dial* (Lent 1912), 53. In 1891 the resigning May Boat Captain 'remarked that he thought it essential to the welfare of the College that Boating should be well supported', QCBC minutes, 16.11.1891; no justification of this notion was thought necessary. In 1924 the first boat captain stated that 'it behoved all members to take interest not only in the Boat Club but in all College sports', *ibid*, 14.10.1924.

[156] *Dial* (Michaelmas 1922), 38 – 9.

[157] This has been demonstrated with regard to the public schools, Mangan (1981), 103 – 10; and it seems to hold true for the universities also. Tony Mangan's forthcoming book on the subject will resolve the matter more clearly.

[158] In 1947 the *Dial* commented that there had been more all-roundedness in games in the late 19th century, (Michaelmas 1947), 8 – 10.

tennis player for the college, and president of the Queens' College Christian Union. Or someone like H. D. Hooper, described in 1912: he was captain of hockey, a rugby player, and likely to row for the college in the summer term; Hooper was also president of the college Christian Union, and hoped to go to Africa as a missionary.[159] In 1892 a university student magazine, the *Granta*, in a piece on C. B. Nicholl of Queens', who was captain of the university's rugby team and had played rugby for Wales in 1891, pointed to features meant to exemplify the character-building quality of sports: Nicholl was competitive — 'There has been no harder player at Cambridge for many years' — but was also 'very good tempered and deservedly popular with all who know him'.[160]

In the same article, the magazine hinted at another, less respectable sporting archetype when it wrote that in the course of his rugby-playing forays, Nicholl 'has, on occasions, found great difficulty in locating his hotel'.[161] The hard-drinking sportsman is not readily identifiable in Queens' at this period, but it is apparent that sports — or rather, sports clubs — instead of suppressing students' energies through exhaustion on the games fields and on the river, often promoted high-spiritedness. This was particularly associated with boat clubs at that time, and the association persists to this day with no sign of diminishing. In the Lent races of 1898, for example, the college first VIII won their oars, and celebrated their success with a bonfire in Walnut Tree Court 'on which many loose articles of College property perished'.[162] In 1909 the earth closets around the college 'were stripped of their woodwork' for another bonfire after the Lent races.[163] In 1912 the *Dial* suggested 'in all courtesy . . . that it would be wiser *not* to entertain ladies in College on Bump Supper nights'.[164]

Perhaps the spirit of athleticism was beginning to grow decadent. The *Dial*, in an editorial of 1911, feared that the ideal balance of intellectual, cultural and athletic interests and capacities had been eroded by unavoidable specialisation.[165] This was probably a belated recognition of a trend which had been marked for some time, and which had anyway

---

[159] *ibid.* (Lent 1911), 57; (Lent 1912), 17.
[160] *Granta* (29.10.1892), 44 – 5.
[161] *ibid.*
[162] MS 79, 67.
[163] Autobiography of A. H. Noble (MS), 3. This event was said to have led to the installation of water closets. Noble was a member of the boat; he also rowed in the summer races that year and noted that 'Unfortunately my geology exams clashed with the river event and I had to cut short one practical to get down to the river in time', *ibid.*, 4.
[164] *Dial* (Lent 1912), 4. The club had to pay for damage by its members after a Bump supper in 1909, QCBC minutes, June 1909. Perhaps these growing signs of rowdy behaviour by the club's members were also in keeping with the decadent spirit of the times, see n. 101.
[165] *Dial* (Michaelmas 1911), 152.

often represented an ideal rather than reality. Earlier in the year the college dean, C. T. Wood, had complained to the magazine about the excessive amount of time devoted to cricket. Until recently, he alleged, there had never been more than three or four college matches per week, lasting from 1.30 till 6.30, but the past two seasons had seen a game nearly every day, and players were 'often too sleepy to do any work after Hall'. Wood's recommended solution was to play matches over two days, from 2.15 till 4.30, to allow students time for play and study; he clearly wished them to have plenty of opportunity to do both.[166]

In 1916 Wood spoke out again, this time against the athletic bias exhibited by the college's two principal dining clubs: 'We have even seen the clubs joining in a scramble to secure some athletic freshman while he was still at school'; and the other side of the coin was that 'Elections for athletic and other offices have at times turned on the question, not who was the fittest man for the job, but to what club someone belonged or did not belong'.[167] It seems therefore that the sporting mania may if anything have been intensifying; and though the pre-eminence of sports was to be challenged in the new cultural and intellectual atmosphere of the post-war years, they remained an important and vital part of college life.[168]

Order and revolt

The more spectacular excesses of the wealthy fellow-commoners in the 18th century died away with the decline of that class, and perhaps also under the pressure of Victorian morality. The revolution in the public schools which Thomas Arnold had inspired had been particularly successful in restoring them to good order and discipline, and their pupils now came up to university at a more advanced age than hitherto, an age no different from that of the present-day student in most cases.[169] But this, as the royal commission of 1852 noted in its report, was 'an age, when they cannot be subjected to the minute surveillance and rigid constraint exercised in a school, and when, on the other hand they are not fit to be intrusted with absolute liberty and independence in acting for themselves'.[170]

There was, in consequence, a good deal of high-spirited behaviour, much of it communal, rather than individual as it had tended to be in the past; and most of it relatively trival and good-natured in comparison

---

166   *ibid.* (Lent 1911), 100 – 1.
167   *ibid.* (Easter 1916), 30.
168   Below, chapter 23.
169   Rothblatt (1981), 210 – 11, 248 – 9; Winstanley (1940), 416.
170   Quoted in Rothblatt (1981), 210 – 11.

with former times. The simplest expressions of this were keeping late hours, often noisily. On the night of 9 November 1888, for example, the college was said to have been 'decidedly lively. The ardour, however, of certain members, who thought that a concert on the top of the gate-tower at one o'clock in the morning was very delightful, was considerably damped by the appearance of the Dean upon the scene'; and in 1912 the *Cambridge Review* noticed 'that sharp warnings, in the shape of spikes and cheveaux-de-frise, have just been issued to would-be breakers of bounds. Also ultimata to unofficial musical societies and athletic contests'. The Kangaroos' musical *soirées* were sometimes suppressed by the Dean.[171]

Hall dinner was often rowdy, as the *Dial* reflected in 1907: at dinner, 'Men of the most simple and refined habits outside are affected by a strange spirit of levity . . . They exhibit a strange proclivity to the inane, and pelt each other with bucolic *badinage* and bread rolls'. In 1912 there was a complaint that 'even before the last words of grace have died away we are struck violently about the head by sodden discoloured globules of bread . . .The bombardment continues throughout the meal'.[172] Another college custom, which seems to have persisted in the face of official disapproval, occurred on the day when the first year students, gathered in Old Court in order to be led off to the schools to sign their names in the university matriculations register, were bombarded with assorted rubbish from the windows of the rooms overlooking the court.[173] Unofficial firework displays on 5 November were also illegal, but customary, and generally tolerated by the Fellows; more serious were the traditional town/gown riots which took place on that night, and in which some Queensmen of the period were involved.[174]

In many cases, the fun was relatively harmless, or humourous.[175] In some, however, it may have been less so: in 1911 the *Cambridge Review* cautioned inhabitants of Old Court 'not to leave their windows open on

[171]   CR (15.11.1888), 86; (21.11.1912), 127; Kangaroo Club Minutes, February 1896, 21.2.1896, 20.1.1899, 4.11.1899, and *passim*. It seems that no music was allowed after 11 p.m., *ibid.*, 18.1.1913. In March 1905 it was reported that 'There has been a epidemic of 'Smokers' [i.e., smoking concerts?] this week, and the Porter has been kept busy at his favourite occupation', CR (16.3.1905), 271. In 1912 it was observed that 'Some residents . . . have lately been expressing their approval of existing society in heartfelt tones during the late hours of the night', *ibid.* (8.2.1912), 258.
[172]   *Dial* (Michaelmas 1907), 159; (Easter 1913), 248.
[173]   CR (27.10.1910), 59; (26.10.1911), 57; (31.10.1912), 65; *Dial* (Michaelmas 1911), 199.
[174]   CR (7.11.1883), 54; (12.11.1908), 87; (11.11.1909), 101; (10.11.1910), 99; TB (1885 – 91), 77, 92, 110; below, pp. 339 – 40.
[175]   Many, though by no means all, 'rags' (hoaxes, practical jokes, mock pageants) were; there is a reference to Queensmen participating in a 'Mock Funeral' in 1912, CR (7.3.1912), 342. So was graffiti, *ibid.* (13.2.1913), 275; (6.3.1913), 358. In 1905 there was 'a rumour that a poultry farm was being started in College, but an extensive search by the authorities has proved abortive', *ibid.* (16.2.1905), 207.

Sunday nights'; in 1913 the same journal referred to a meeting of the otherwise unrecorded Walnut Tree Club, when 'Less friendly relations with neighbouring colleges were successfully promoted'.[176] The tutors' records are also revealing: there are students caught wandering about in the town after 10 p.m., practical jokers, and indulgers in rowdy behaviour.[177] Drinking to excess, one of the oldest problems of all, may not have been so serious by this time, and was no longer such a threat to good order, but it had by no means gone away. For example, the tutorial records report one who was 'Gated [confined to college] for "Taverning" ', and another who was 'seldom sober'.[178]

Certainly the tutors kept a close watch on misbehaviour, and 'gating' was not uncommon. H. E. Ryle seems to have attempted to take a hard line on this: five students were deprived of their scholarships and exhibitions following the bonfire in college to celebrate the success of its boat in 1898, and N. C. Fletcher, a rugby blue, was sent down for a year following a disturbance in January 1899. Neither action was popular with the undergraduates: a petition protesting about the treatment of the five who had taken part in the bonfire celebrations was said to have been signed by 'almost every member of the College *in statu pupillari*'; and there was a large demonstration in support of Fletcher when he left Cambridge. The *Cantab*, an ephemeral student newspaper, was most indignant about the severity of these punishments, regarding the offences as relatively trivial, and alleging that 'the Tutorial Body of Queens' is attempting a return to the Inquisitorial barbarities of medievalism', although it did argue that Fletcher had been made a scapegoat for other people's misdemeanours. The vice-chancellor took an interest in the case, and it seems that Fletcher's sentence was reduced, since he won a further blue for rugby in 1899.[179] But after the *Cantab*'s fierce condemnation of Ryle's actions and behaviour, the college rushed to its president's defence: the captains of the sports clubs and the president of the St Bernard Society, some of whom were alleged to have participated in the demonstration in support of Fletcher, wrote a letter to the *Cambridge Review* repudiating 'all connection with the article or with the sentiments expressed therein'; and a meeting of the whole college was called to condemn it.[180]

Another of the oldest, and most serious, disciplinary problems concerning students has never featured much in college records.

[176] *ibid*. (7.2.1911), 179; (22.5.1913), 478. There may have been a general worsening of behaviour in the Edwardian period; see above, n. 101
[177] TB (1885 – 91), 77, 92, 97, 139, 145, 164, 172, 205; TB (1878 – 87), 33.
[178] TB (1885 – 91), 57, 199; c.f. this comment of the university registrary in 1846: 'To-day a Queens' man . . . paid me his fees: he was very drunk (reeling and stammering), and offered me sixpence', Winstanley (1940), 417.
[179] *Cantab* (23.2.1899), 205 – 6; AC.
[180] *Cantab* (9.3.1899), 240; CR (2.3.1899), 247; (16.3.1899), 270.

Prostitution, which had alarmed the university authorities so much in the 18th century, had declined by the 1860s to the extent that Campion claimed Cambridge was not a particularly immoral town.[181] But tutors remained anxious that students should not let their hearts get the better of their sense of social position. In 1913 J. H. Gray had to make enquiries about a relationship involving a student at Queens', and received this reply from an informant:

'I . . . find that he has only known the girl a short time and has been out for walks on a few occasions, but I am convinced that nothing serious has taken place. His parents do not know anything: the girl's parents seem respectable, but I am making enquiries . . . from what I gathered I should think there might be a danger that he would fall in love with the girl, but I pointed out to him that his conduct was not fair to the girl, besides being very foolish'.[182]

Gray, in his capacity as dean, was also involved with precautions against misdemeanours of a different kind. In 1876 he drew up a set of regulations concerning the college's choristers, who were young boys from the town, and there is no doubt what these regulations were designed to prevent: the choristers were forbidden 'To go to the rooms or lodgings of members of the University. To walk with them. To receive presents from them directly or indirectly. To correspond with them. To associate with them'. Gray recommended that the parents of each chorister should have to read and sign a copy of the regulations, but he added that they were 'Not recommended to be made public'.[183]

The many changes in student life, especially the new emphasis on group activities, and the numerous clubs and societies, led to growing self-awareness among them, and to recognition of themselves as a distinct group with its own ideals and values. This had been encouraged by the dons insofar as it promoted more mature attitudes among the undergraduates, but it also made them more assertive as a group, a completely new development which in the long run would lead to the dissident student movements of the 1960s. The first expression of this was in 1907, when the *Cambridge Review* reported that 'As a result of long and continued agitation it is now possible to obtain cider from the buttery'.[184] This was trivial enough, but there was more significant student agitation concerning the kitchens and gate hours; both questions, in various forms, would continue to dominate student concerns into the present day.

[181] See above, p. 237.
[182] Letter inside TB (1910 – 14).
[183] Dean's Chapel Book (1854 – 1944).
[184] *CR* (2.5.1907), 371.

In 1910 a meeting of the students was called in order to form a kitchen committee; there was no doubt among them that improvements were needed. The committee was still in existence in 1911, but we do not know its terms of reference, nor what was decided or achieved; and equally important, there is no record of the attitude of the Fellows to these activities.[185]

Agitation on gate regulations was more significant. In 1913 the *Cambridge Review*'s Queens' correspondent remarked cheerfully that 'Last trains from town are being missed this season',[186] but gate hours were a serious matter. Colleges had always closed their gates at set times, and fined their members who returned late. This was a necessary and important disciplinary measure, and applied to Fellows as well as to students in pre-Victorian days. The hour of closing had become progressively later over the centuries: at Queens' in the late 19th century it was at 10 p.m. This time had been fixed in 1854, when Fellows were also exempted from gate fines for the first time.[187] In 1870 fines were set at 3d for those arriving between 10 and 11 p.m., 6d for the hour following, and 2s 6d for anyone coming in after midnight.[188]

In 1909 the college's BAs petitioned successfully to be exempted from gate fines, and to be allowed to sign out of hall dinners,[189] and this must have inspired the undergraduates to make their own protest. In 1912 the *Dial* called for the abolition of the 10 p.m. rule, arguing rather pompously that 'the spirit of conservatism is rampant, and nowhere more so than among the Cambridge authorities'.[190] By 1913 a more moderate view prevailed, and a petition, signed 'by every member of the College who could be found', was sent to the Fellows asking that gate fines be reduced. The governing body responded at the beginning of 1914 by abolishing the fine for latecoming between 10 and 11 p.m., but maintaining the same fines for those returning at later hours. The students' gratitude was expressed in the *Dial*.[191] To modern eyes this may not amount to much, but in the context of its time it was radical enough, and a significant pointer to future trends.

---

[185] *ibid.*, (3.2.1910), 240; (10.2.1910), 261; (16.11.1911), 117; (30.11.1911), 159.
[186] *ibid.* (6.2.1913), 255. See also CB (1889 – 1937), 21.11.1913.
[187] CB (1832 – 88), 15.11.1854.
[188] *ibid.*, 5.1.1870; Harrison (1985), 54.
[189] *Dial* (Michaelmas 1909), 298.
[190] Students were allowed 'to break three tens a week', *ibid.* (Lent 1912), 1 – 3. They could, of course, also climb into college secretly, if they came back very late, see e.g. G. B. Harrison: letter.
[191] *Dial* (Michaelmas 1913), 258 – 9; (Lent 1914), 310; CB (1889 – 1937), 13.1.1914.

18

Religion in the nineteenth and early twentieth centuries

The evangelical tradition

The college which Milner left on his death in 1820 was staunchly evangelical, and appears to have remained so for some time thereafter, although the evangelical movement in general suffered its ups and downs. By the 1840s students at evangelical colleges such as Queens' were increasingly ridiculed for their views by the rest of the university, and despite a national revival in the 1850s, the movement declined further in popularity in the following decade.[1]

Queens' continued to uphold the tradition. In the 1820s, under the presidency of Henry Godfrey, it was inevitably still imbued with Milner's spirit. One of its most notable evangelicals from that period was Henry Venn, a Fellow from 1819 – 20: he was to become a prominent and active evangelical, especially as secretary of the Church Missionary Society, visiting Oxford and Cambridge regularly to raise missionary recruits.[2] There was a strong and enduring link between evangelicalism and missionary work at Queens', which preceded Venn's activities by some years. Claudius Buchanan, who graduated from the college in 1796, was an active missionary and lecturer in Bengal for a decade; he returned to Britain in 1808 and became a leading advocate of missionary work in India. Buchanan's often quoted justification for introducing Christianity to the sub-continent was that 'it attaches the governed to their governors'.[3] Thomas Thomason, an evangelical Fellow under Milner, was a chaplain to the East India Company, also in Bengal, for twenty years, and helped to direct the Church Missionary Society's missions there.[4] Samuel Lee, the noted Queens' orientalist, taught languages to CMS missionaries preparing for their work abroad; he had been brought to the CMS committee's notice by Buchanan, and the society hoped he too would go out to

---

[1] Garland (1980), 83; above, chapter 12, n. 154; Chadwick (1970 – 2), i.440 – 55.
[2] AC; Hennell (1979), chapter 5; Piggin (1984), 204. See Yates (1978) for his work. He was a grandson of Henry Venn the Fellow of Queens' in the 1750s and an early evangelical, above, pp. 171, 186, 252.
[3] Piggin (1984), 19, 138; AC; DNB.
[4] Piggin (1984), 19 – 20, 24, n. 32.

India, but he remained in Cambridge.[5]

The missionary tradition continued even into the period when Queens' was overtly abandoning its former low church image. Thomas Skelton, (Fellow, 1858 – 9), was sent by the Society for the Propagation of the Gospel to restore its mission in Delhi after the massacre of missionaries in the Indian Mutiny, and spent nearly ten years working in India.[6]

The evangelical tradition continued at Queens' into the 1840s, however. Henry Godfrey's successor as president, in 1832, Joshua King, had come to the college from Trinity in 1816, probably on account of its evangelicalism. Robert Bickersteth, admitted to Queens' in 1837, was a well known evangelical preacher who became bishop of Ripon in 1857.[7] He was presumably attracted to the college by its continuing evangelical reputation under King. In 1847 George Gorham, a former Fellow (from 1810 to 1827), now a minister in Cornwall, was examined over the soundness of his beliefs by the bishop of Exeter, the bishop concluding that his views on baptismal regeneration were unsound and refusing in consequence to institute him to a living in his diocese. Gorham fought the verdict until it was overturned by the Privy Council in 1850, and the case aroused great interest nationally. Although he was not a typical evangelical, Gorham's case and the great publicity it received can only have maintained the public identification of Queens' with evangelicalism.[8]

One of the continuing links with both the evangelical and missionary traditions is demonstrated by the story of Alexander Crummell, a black clergyman from the U.S.A. Crummell was born, free, in New York City (slavery was practised in the southern states of the U.S.A. until much later) in 1819, and educated at institutions run by black clergymen and abolitionists. After graduating from Oneida Institute in 1839, he spent several years fighting against racial prejudice in his efforts to become an ordained minister of the Episcopalian Church — he succeeded in 1844 — and then in trying to secure equal recognition within the church establishment. In 1847, on the advice of influential friends, he sailed to England to raise funds to build a church for his poor black congregation

---

[5]   Lee's published works include 'Rules for the guidance of persons who have to fix a language', a translation of the Old Testament into Persian, a revised translation of the New Testament into Hindustani, and the translation of various tracts, *ibid.*, 196, 240 – 1. For his theology and his academic work, see below, pp. 273, 297, chapter 18, n. 22.

[6]   Piggin (1984), 278; *AC.*

[7]   *AC.*

[8]   He had been in conflict with Thomas Dampier, bishop of Ely, over the same question in 1811, when he was a Fellow of Queens'. Nias (1951) is a study of the Gorham case. Many of Gorham's papers are in the college library, and contain many sermons from his time at Queens', MS 80-82.

in New York.[9]

He arrived in England, in his own words, 'full of earnest purpose and bright hopes'. Introductions from his American friends brought him into contact with politicians, churchmen and literary figures; he was received everywhere 'with favor and courtesy', was invited to preach in several places, and raised the equivalent of over $8,000 for his new church. However, his efforts were interrupted by 'fits of illness', so that friends suggested 'that I should retire for a season from over-work, and become a student in the University of Cambridge'; he enrolled at Queens'.[10]

After graduating in 1853, he spent many years in Liberia, a nation newly created especially for former slaves. There he worked as schoolmaster, lecturer, priest and missionary, and, although not politically active himself, as a 'public Teacher' and 'censor' of the nation's faults when called upon, as he often was, to give his opinions 'concerning national life' and to make public addresses. He returned to the United States in 1873 and was a minister in Washington, D.C., for over 20 years at St Luke's Episcopal Church, now a U.S. national monument. In 1897, the year before his death, he helped to found the American Negro Academy.[11]

His considerable influence as a writer, teacher of moral ideals, and opponent of racial persecution is well recognised today in the United States. Over forty publications by him are listed; one of his pamphlets is said to have sold over half a million copies. He was a tireless worker for black rights and, despite many reverses, constantly optimistic. His inspiration was deeply Christian, and strongly moralistic in a typically British mid-Victorian way, rather than political. He worked for a moral revolution based on philanthropy, honesty, self-restraint and hard work: industry and education were the principal means by which black people were to conquer racial injustice, raising their own self-respect and giving the lie to notions of white superiority.[12]

Very little is known about Crummell's Cambridge career. According to his own account, he was entered at Queens' in 1851, but this is clearly

---

[9]   The biographical information on Crummell from which this account is taken is contained in Brawley (1970), 229 – 301; Du Bois (1953), 215 – 227; Scruggs (1972); Crummell (1894), 5 – 22. I am deeply grateful for the considerable assistance given me by Dr D. Nicol of Sierra Leone, honorary Fellow of Christ's College, who first drew my attention to Crummell and supplied me with a great deal of information on his life and work.

[10]   Crummell (1894), 16 – 17.

[11]   See above, n. 9; the quotations are from Crummell (1894), 20.

[12]   See above, n. 9. His writings are listed in Moorland (1970); and discussed by Loggins (1931), 199 – 209; and by Moses (undated), 27, 31, 51, 61, 66, 81 – 99, 102 – 3, 129 – 32, 138 – 9. There is no telling how much his literary works owed to his Cambridge education; like two thirds of his student contemporaries there, he read for a pass degree, but he was a conscientious man and would not have wasted his time.

a mistake: J. A. Venn's register of Cambridge *alumni* claims that he was admitted on 22 June 1849, and although the college's admissions register from which Venn took this information has since been lost, the university archives show that he matriculated in the Michaelmas term of 1849. There is no further reference to him in the college archives until he took his BA in 1853.[13] W. Wells Brown, a fellow-countryman and escaped slave who visited England at about the same time, wrote in September 1851 that he had visited Crummell at Cambridge 'a few months since', but gave no further details. Crummell's own account is scarcely more forthcoming: he stated merely that 'I was often in the hands of doctors. Not seldom I fell into a state of discouragement and despair, on account of my health. Now and then my studies were interrupted'.[14]

But there is an anecdote from the very end of his time there. Crummell may have been the first black recipient of a Cambridge degree — he was certainly one of the first — and at the degree ceremony in the senate house 'A boisterous individual in the gallery called out, "Three groans for the Queens' nigger" . . . A pale slim undergraduate shouted in a voice which re-echoed through the building, "Shame, shame! Three groans for you, Sir!" and immediately afterwards, "Three cheers for Crummell!" This was taken up in all directions . . . and the original offender had to stoop down to hide himself from the storm of groans and hisses that broke out all around him'.[15]

Why did Crummell choose to go to Queens'? It is here that the evangelical connection becomes apparent. Personal contacts were all-important, and Crummell referred to 'a personal interest' which arose on his behalf, 'unsolicited, nay, unthought of by myself'.[16] He did not reveal who these particular individuals were, but we know that in general he was well connected.[17] Several of his friends and patrons were evangelicals; the evangelical movement had long been associated with campaigns against slavery. One of the friends listed by Crummell was Henry Venn, the secretary of the Church Missionary Society; another was the Methodist and distinguished antiquarian Thomas Horne, who had compiled a catalogue of the college library in 1821 when Venn was a

---

[13]   Crummell (1894), 16; *AC*; *Matriculations* (1902), 149; CUA Matr. 17, 13.11.1849; CB (1832 – 88), 13.1.1853. The loss of the admissions register, which covered more than forty years, is a serious one. Sadly, it is not the only valuable document from the college's archives to have gone missing in recent times.

[14]   Brown (1852), 233; Crummell (1894), 16.

[15]   Crummell's champion was E. W. Benson, later archbishop of Canterbury, Fowler and Fowler (1984), 209 – 10, taken from A. C. Benson's life of E. W. Benson.

[16]   Crummell (1894), 16; somebody must have paid for him to study at Cambridge, for he certainly could not afford to do so himself.

[17]   His friends and contacts are listed in *ibid.*, 16 – 18; the list is misinterpreted in Du Bois (1953), 224, and by *AC*.

Fellow.[18] These men may not have introduced Crummell to Queens' themselves, but they were part of a widespread network of personal contacts which embraced both him and the college.[19]

The high church revival

From the 1830s onwards the religious order was challenged by reform movements, old and new. Once the Whigs emerged from the shadow of the French Revolution, traditional reformist notions began to circulate publicly once again, and were further encouraged by a series of reforming acts passed by parliament in the late 1820s and early 1830s, and by the return to power of the Whigs at the election of 1831.[20]

Reformers in the university now pressed ahead for the admission of non-conformists there, and in 1833 and 1834 put forward proposals for the abolition of religious tests and subscriptions for university members, but on each occasion these were vetoed in the *caput senatus* before they could reach the senate to be voted upon. Under the university statutes of 1570 all motions for debate in the senate had first to go before the *caput*, which was a steering committee dominated by the vice-chancellor, each member having the power to veto any proposals; the procedure had been designed to discourage radicalism in the university.[21] The proposals of 1833 and 1834 were vetoed by Joshua King, who was then serving as vice-chancellor, and this led the reformers to petition parliament; the conservative party counterpetitioned, setting up their petition in the hall at Queens'.[22] In 1835 King was one of seven Tory heads active in securing the election of a Tory vice-chancellor, instead of a Whig who supported the admission of non-conformists.[23] Moves in parliament to legislate for their admission petered out in 1834,

---

[18] For Horne, see *AC*.

[19] Venn, through his work with the Church Missionary Society, was involved in the missionary movement to W. Africa, Ayandale (1966), 180 – 3, 185 – 6, 197, 206 – 32; perhaps this link influenced Crummell's decision to go to Liberia.

[20] Specifically, the repeal of the Test and Corporation Acts against non-conformists in 1828, Catholic emancipation in 1829, and the Reform Act of 1832, Winstanley (1940), 85 – 6.

[21] Curtis (1959), 42 – 3; Porter (1958), 164 – 6; Mullinger (1873 – 1911), ii.223 – 4, 233; Wall (1828), 28 – 33.

[22] Winstanley (1940), 86 – 92; Romilly (1967), 55 – 7. Samuel Lee, recently of Queens', joined in the debate with publications asserting that non-conformity was 'Unscriptural and Unjustifiable', Lee, *Dissent*; Lee (1835). Curiously, he favoured their admission to the university, on the grounds that: 'to give Dissent its fairest trial, would be to submit it to the habit of severe investigation which is usually acquired at the Universities. In that case, I feel assured it must fall, and with it all the evils so invariably brought along with it', Lee, *Some Remarks*, 22.

[23] Romilly (1967), 93.

but parliament had acquired a taste for university reform which in the long run would transform both universities radically.[24]

In the 1830s the publication of a series of *Tracts for the Times* heralded the birth of the high church Oxford Movement. The authors of the *Tracts* were Oxford dons, and the movement was powerful there, far more so than in Cambridge, although it was not without influence in the sister university.[25] Needless to say, the Queens' evangelicals opposed the message which the *Tracts* contained. In January 1839 Thomas Webster, rector of St Botolph's and former Fellow of Queens', was recorded as having preached 'for near an hour' in his church, delivering a 'stout attack on the Oxford "Tracts for the Times" and on their shameful declaration that the Reformation was a doubtful good'.[26]

In Cambridge the growing tendency towards higher churchmanship was not expressed so much through tractarian doctrines, but partly transmuted into an enthusiasm for the Gothic revival in church architecture. There had been signs of such a revival in grand domestic English architecture in the late 18th century, but many old Gothic churches remained in a state of neglect and decay into the 1830s, and in the early decade of the 19th century innovation in church building was chiefly on classical — especially Grecian — lines. But during the 1830s there was a renewed interest in England's past, and in particular, thanks to the influence of romanticism in the early 19th century, in the middle ages. The object of this growing number of ecclesiologists — the term 'ecclesiology' being employed by them to mean specifically the study of church building and decoration — was to restore churches to their medieval purity of design. Interest in ecclesiology at Cambridge, mostly among undergraduates who were more affected by the new currents of romanticism and tractarianism, led in 1839 to the formation of the Cambridge Camden Society, with the object of promoting the new architectural enthusiasms; its membership rose rapidly in the early 1840s.[27]

The society's aims were avowedly aesthetic, but its affiliations were with the high church movement and tractarianism; however, it did not admit to this. In 1845 it split over the question of its covert religious aims: slightly under one sixth of its membership, who sought to confine it more strictly to architectural matters, resigned; and the society later changed its name to the Ecclesiological Society, and moved to London. Some of the dissidents joined the new Cambridge Architectural Society, which maintained the old interest in church architecture without such strong theological convictions, although the two were too closely

[24] Winstanley (1940), 94 – 5.
[25] Chadwick (1970 – 2), i.64ff, chapter iii; Winstanley (1940), 405.
[26] Romilly (1967), 161 – 2.
[27] White (1962), chapters 1 – 4.

enmeshed ever to be wholly separated.[28]

One of those to leave in 1845 was Samuel Lee, now at Trinity since becoming the university's Regius professor of Hebrew, but a product of Milner's dominance at Queens', where he had resided from 1814 to 1831.[29] Lee criticised the Cambridge Camden Society's religious tendencies vigorously, if without theological subtlety. In 1845 he complained that the Society's leanings would lead to 'great and violent political commotion, and, it may be, to distress and bloodshed'; Lee believed that the church had 'enemies enough already, what with Romanism without, and something like Romanism within, to say nothing of dissent'. Later in the year he complained that both the Oxford and Cambridge movements aimed at the 'development of Jesuitism' and accused the Cambridge Camden Society of secretly promoting 'the interests of the schismatic Church of Rome'.[30]

Most of the society's younger members took no notice of Lee's views; they were of a different generation, fired by different ideals. Several Queensmen are known to have belonged to the society in its early years. Most were students;[31] but two were Fellows: George Phillips, one of the college tutors, and William Walker. Another of the students who joined at this time, Thomas Staley, became a Fellow later in the decade.[32] Walker was rector of St Botolph's, where in 1842 a subscription was opened to raise money for its restoration. The Cambridge Camden Society's journal, the *Ecclesiologist*, described the church as having 'much room for improvement both in internal appearance and interior arrangements; and we heartily wish well to this as to every new evidence of the spirit of church-building and church-restoration at present so prevalent in Cambridge'.[33] Sufficient money was not apparently forthcoming on this occasion, and the church was not restored until some afterwards.[34]

In 1845 the *Ecclesiologist* observed that 'college chapels generally in Cambridge fall very far short of the dignity they once possessed, and . . . a distressing apathy on the subject continues to exist', but it also reported that at Queens' restoration of the chapel was planned: the flat ceiling was to be removed, and 'a new east window filled with stain [*sic*] glass is also contemplated'.[35] This seems to have been achieved in

---

[28] *ibid.*, 144 – 5, 198 – 9.
[29] *DNB; AC;* below, p. 297.
[30] White (1962), 34 – 5, 77 – 8, 121 and n., 150 – 3; see also Lee (1896), 154 – 60. Lee had previously engaged in a public dispute with one of the leaders of the high church movement, Lee (1896), chapters IX – XI.
[31] *Ecclesiologist*, i. (1842), 6 – 7, 22 – 4, 53, 119, 135 – 6; ii. (1842), 38 – 9; iii. (1843), 44 – 5; iii. (1844), 114 – 5.
[32] *ibid.*, ii. (1842), 38 – 9; iii. (1844), 114 – 5.
[33] *ibid.*, i. (1842), 142 – 3.
[34] Under W. M. Campion (rector, 1862 – 92), Goodman (1922), 70.
[35] *Ecclesiologist*, iv. (1845), 142.

1846 – 7, the restoration of the window under the direction of Phillips together with the senior bursar, J. N. Peill, and the dean, W. H. Edwards.[36] A stained glass window was donated by another Fellow, Thomas Beevor, soon afterwards, and further windows were given by other college members.[37]

Phillips, Peill and Edwards had all become Fellows in the 1830s, although Beevor had been elected in 1810, at the heart of the evangelical era at Queens';[38] it may be that, like Lee, his interest in church restoration was essentially aesthetic, but the introduction of stained glass had distinctly high church connotations. Henceforth in Queens' it was the younger men who called the tune. Joshua King was still president, but in 1843 he had suffered a stroke, and thereafter much of the college's business may have been left to its other officers.[39] In the 1850s, the more active Fellows included S. T. Gibson, W. G. Searle, W. M. Campion and Richard Watson, all elected in the late 1840s and early 1850s, and all members of the Cambridge Architectural Society; the resident fellowship in general consisted of recently elected men.[40]

Under the direction of these Fellows, moves towards architectural restoration and higher churchmanship proceeded apace. In 1854 Queens' reintroduced choral services in the chapel,[41] and decided to set up a chapel restoration fund with annual contributions out of the college rents.[42] No further steps were taken until after King's death in 1857, when the Fellows became free to act as they wished; King was succeeded as president by George Phillips. In January 1858 a committee consisting of the new president, Campion, Gibson, and G. C. Pollard the senior bursar and a Fellow since 1851, was created to restore the chapel, although no changes were made immediately.[43] One of the Fellows, J. N. Goren, offered to present new stained glass; the glass

[36] CB (1832 – 88), 7.5.1846, 14.1.1847, 12.1.1848; Ecclesiologist, ix. (1849), 147; xii. (1851), 325 – 6; Gray, 256. The work is described in W&C, ii.42 – 3.
[37] CB (1832 – 88), 10.1.1850 (and see 15.1.1851); Gray, 257; W&C, ii. 43.
[38] AC.
[39] Gray, 255, remarks on King's stroke, but is mistaken about the date. It is clear from his signature in the conclusion books that the stroke occurred in late 1843. Although he continued to attend governing body meetings, and cannot have been wholly incapacitated, the burdens of routine administration are likely to have fallen more onto the shoulders of the other college officers.
[40] AC; Ecclesiologist, xii. (1851), 140; xiv. (1853), 201; xv. (1854), 130; xviii. (1857), 52. Edwards also remained influential at this time. Campion was apparently an active member of the Cambridge Architectural Society, Ecclesiologist, xvi. (1855), 128; xx. (1859), 130. For the college offices held by these men, see CB (1832 – 88), entries for the relevant years (officers were appointed in October of each year); for tutors, see C.U. Cal., which also contains lists of Fellows.
[41] CB (1832 – 88), 10.1.1854, and passim. There were choral services in the college in the late 17th century: they had been resumed at the Restoration. It is not known when they were discontinued.
[42] ibid., 12.1.1854, 11.1.1855, 10.1.1856, 15.1.1857, 7.1.1858.
[43] ibid., 7.1.1858, 6.1.1859.

inserted in the previous decade had not been well received, for the *Ecclesiologist* described it as 'very inferior' and had 'seldom seen money more thrown away'.[44]

The architect chosen by the committee to restore the chapel was G. F. Bodley. He was young and near the beginning of his career, but was not unknown in ecclesiological circles: he was a member of the Ecclesiological Society, which had inspected many of his designs.[45] Those Fellows of Queens' who were associated with the Cambridge Architectural Society would certainly have been aware of his work and his reputation. The *Ecclesiologist* expressed itself 'very glad' when it learnt that Bodley had been chosen, and was confident that he would perform the task 'in a very satisfactory manner'; the Ecclesiological Society was similarly delighted.[46] Bodley also had a more direct link with the Fellows of Queens': two elder brothers had been students there in the 1840s.[47]

The work on the chapel was completed in 1860. The Cambridge Architectural Society thought it 'a most valuable specimen of modern art', and was pleased also 'that the fellows are not content with this good beginning, but are endeavouring to make the music of their services worthy of their architecture'; two years later the college appointed a choral scholar.[48] The *Ecclesiologist* was more critical. It felt that Bodley had disobeyed a cardinal rule of restoration: that one should restore in the style of the period at which the building was put up; whereas he had employed a mixture of styles from various periods.[49] Bodley's own view was that architects should 'Be not afraid of beauty and richness when you can get it', and his restoration has recently been described as 'an unusually rich example of high Victorian construction'.[50] The Fellows of Queens' were apparently quite content, and Bodley's restoration of the chapel marked the beginning of a long professional association with the college.[51] At the same time it laid the ghost of the evangelical tradition there for some while.

Religious life in the later nineteenth century

After the middle of the century, the university's religious life underwent new and radical transformations as the result of changes to its rules and

---

[44] *ibid.*, 6.1.1859; Gray, 257; W&C, ii. 43; *Ecclesiologist*, xii. (1851), 325 – 6.
[45] *Ecclesiologist*, xv. (1854), 191; xvii. (1856), 297; xviii, (1857), 186; xix. (1858), 259. See also Bodley's obituary in the *Builder* (26.10.1907), 447.
[46] *Ecclesiologist*, xx. (1859), 212, 266.
[47] AC; I owe this point to Robin Walker. G. F. Bodley was not university-educated.
[48] *Ecclesiologist*, xxi. (1860), 383; CB (1832 – 88), 9.1.1862.
[49] *Ecclesiologist*, xxiii. (1862), 17 – 19.
[50] Robinson and Wildman (1980), 21. 27.
[51] See below, pp. 277 – 8, 313 – 14.

statutes and in response to new ideological forces which created a 'crisis of faith'.

The movement to allow non-conformists to study in the universities, which had been defeated by Joshua King and men of like mind in the 1830s, continued to press for reform, and its efforts were partially rewarded by the Cambridge University Act of 1856, which allowed students to take their degrees without making any declaration of faith. This privilege did not yet extend to senior members, but with the passing of the University Tests Act by Gladstone's Liberal government in 1871, after eight years of public agitation and parliamentary debate, all religious barriers were removed.[52] As has been shown already, the restriction of fellowships to men in holy orders was abolished at roughly the same time.[53]

These reforms no longer aimed simply at the inclusion of traditional religious dissenters, for they came in an age when Christianity itself was increasingly called into doubt, and when many people no longer wished to pledge themselves to any particular form of religious belief.[54] The challenge of new scientific ideas and enquiries, Darwinism prominent among them, together with new methods of Scriptural criticism, combined to undermine customary belief in the literal truth of the Biblical accounts, and compelled a re-evaluation of Christian faith.

One effect of these challenges was to reduce sharply the proportion of university students at Cambridge seeking ordination, especially among the most academically distinguished; there was a rise simultaneously in the proportion of those who turned to teaching (at all levels) for a career. A similar pattern may be seen in college fellowships. This change began before the relaxation of the university's religious restrictions, and the blossoming of the academic profession thus owes a great deal to the 'crisis of faith'.[55] Orthodox religion lost its dominance in the university, which in the late 19th century came to encompass a wide variety of religious views.[56] But if scepticism and agnosticism were on the increase, Christianity remained strong in Cambridge: many observers believed that the universities were more religious in the 1880s than they had been during the period prior to the 1870s, when Darwinism and associated ideas were first making their impact.[57]

---

[52] Chadwick (1970 – 2), ii.443; Garland (1980), 70 – 89; Winstanley (1947), 36 – 90.
[53] Above, pp. 224 – 6.
[54] Winstanley (1947), 40.
[55] Haig (1984), 27 – 60; Haig (1986), *passim*. The number of ordinands did not begin to fall in absolute terms until the end of the century, Chadwick (1970 – 2), ii.448. A. H. Noble, who came up in 1905, described Queens' at that time as 'essentially a breeding ground for parsons', Noble (MS), 2; G. B. Harrison, who came up in 1913, notes that it had a large number of ordinands, Harrison (1985), 53.
[56] Haig (1984), 51; Haig (1986), 193.
[57] Chadwick (1970 – 2), ii.448.

Religious life in Queens'

One of the aims of the alterations made to the college's statutes in 1860 was to encourage Fellows to remain at Queens' and involve themselves in college life, rather than to regard their fellowships merely as pathways to a college living. In 1861 it was proposed that regulations governing nomination to livings be altered, with priority to go to Fellows who had taken holy orders within two years of their MA degrees, and had remained unmarried during the tenure of their fellowship; the college petitioned the Queen for the necessary changes to the statutes in the following year.[58] It is clear that it soon became difficult to find Fellows to fill the livings, and in the early 1880s Queens' sold three of its advowsons;[59] this trend led in the 20th century to incumbents being chosen from among the ordained old members of the college and not merely from among the Fellows.

Religious life within Queens' remained vigorous. The most obvious sign of this was the building of the new chapel in 1889 – 91. It was designed by Bodley, who had been employed by the college on various tasks since his successful restoration of the old chapel in 1858 – 60; his work had included repairs and redecoration of the chapel's East end in 1871 – 2.[60] According to Arthur Wright, the idea of building a new chapel came from a walk in the country which he took with Campion: Wright suggested enlarging the existing chapel, and although Campion thought this an impractical idea, he offered to subscribe £1,000 towards the cost of a new chapel if Wright would take the responsibility for arranging its construction.[61] Bodley was invited to draw up plans in January 1887, and a formal decision to build the chapel was made in January 1888.[62] The necessary funds were raised by subscription, with several Fellows giving generously,[63] and the chapel was consecrated in

---

[58] CB (1832 – 88), 11.10.1860, 10.1.1861, 13.5.1862.

[59] *ibid.*, 1.1.1880, 12.1.1883, 26.4.1884, 7.10.1884. In 1852 Queens' had repealed an 18th century order that no Fellow could be presented to a college living who had been in orders for less than six months before the vacancy, *ibid.*, 16.1.1852; does this indicate the first signs of difficulty in filling livings? In 1892 the Fellows of Corpus Christi debated whether to open negotiations with Queens' 'for the removal of St Botolph's Church with a view to the enlargement of this College', but the matter was never raised, Bury (1952), 111.

[60] CB (1832 – 88), 9.1.1868, 16.5.1871, 11.10.1872. The chapel is usually thought to have been designed by Bodley and Garner, but an article on Bodley in the *Builder* in 1899 stated that the work was carried out by him alone, *Builder* (1.7.1899), 15.

[61] *Dial* (Easter (1916), 12.

[62] CB (1832 – 88), 5.1.1887, 14.1.1888. At first it was intended that the chapel should be on the north side of the Fellows' bowling green, but this was changed to the site in Walnut Tree court, *ibid.*, 16.6.1888.

[63] *Dial* (Easter 1916), 12; CR (11.2.1892), 192; (2.5.1924), 307; CB (1832 – 88), 14.1.1888, 16.6.1888; Gray, 265 – 8; Wright (1889), 7. Many of the internal fittings were given by the Fellows, CB (1889 – 1937), 8.6.1892, 20.6.1893; Gray, 266 – 8.

1891.[64] The old chapel was put to a variety of uses before finally becoming an undergraduate library after the second world war.[65]

Even as the new chapel was being raised, the *Cambridge Review*'s correspondent in Queens' commented that 'The need for increased accommodation has been plainly demonstrated at the Sunday services'.[66] We cannot say if this was the result of increased religious enthusiasm among the undergraduates, or merely of the growth in the student population, for evidence of chapel-going at this time is somewhat ambiguous. In 1871, probably in response to the Tests Act, Queens' abolished all fines for non-attendance at chapel services, but the St Bernard Society debated the question of compulsory chapel in 1885 and 1893, which implies that attendance was still required. J. F. Williams recorded that services were 'more or less compulsory' at the very end of the century, with attendance recorded by one of the porters.[67]

More reliable evidence for the strength of religious sentiment comes from the activities of various undergraduate societies. The Quaerists are known to have heard papers on a wide range of religious subjects — not necessarily Christian — from the mid-1890s, some delivered by Fellows of the college.[68] The Erasmus Society also listened to some papers on religious matters.[69] Religious topics cropped up occasionally on the agenda of the St Bernard Society. In its early years, the society followed a traditional, narrow orthodoxy: in 1866 there were no votes cast in support of a motion proposing that non-conformists should be admitted to fellowships in the university; even the proposer of the motion voted

---

[64] CR (15.10.1891), 16. For descriptions of the chapel, see *ibid.* (19.11.1891), 86; (12.10.1893), 4; *Builder* (1.7.1899), 14 – 15; Robinson and Wildman (1980), 25.

[65] CB (1889 – 1937), 11.12.1926; Gray, 257; CB (1937 – 63), 2.5.1947, 31.7.1947; MS 79, 21. The stalls were given to the college's living at Little Eversden; the reredos to St Mark's in Cambridge, CB (1889 – 1937), 11.3.1892; Robinson and Wildman (1980), 27; see also CB (1889 – 1937), 2.3.1925, 18.5.1925, 9.11.1925.

[66] CR (24.10.1889), 21.

[67] CB (1832 – 88), 5.1.1871; CR (18.2.1885), 218; (2.3.1893), 252; SBSM, 25.2.1893; MS 79, 33. By the revised college statutes of 1838, fines and other penalties for non-attendance at chapel were to be imposed at the discretion of the president, *Documents* (1852), iii.69. In a sermon in the university church in 1915 T. C. Fitzpatrick observed that whereas there had formerly been much discussion of the question of compulsory chapel, now there was none: chapel services had changed for the better, and were associated with worship rather than discpline; but attendances had fallen, and there was much scope for religious expression outside the chapel. He felt that chapels must work out 'how their services may be modified so as best to meet the spiritual needs of the whole body', CR (20.1.1915), 148.

[68] CR (23.1.1896), 154; (21.5.1896), 334; (5.11.1896), 62; (3.12.1896), 139; (4.2.1897), 210; (6.12.1900), 125; (19.11.1903), 94; (5.11.1908), 70; (4.3.1909), 313; (2.12.1909), 165; (10.3.1910), 352; (19.5.1910), 422; (3.11.1910), 79; (24.11.1910), 141; (1.12.1910), 162A; (2.12.1911), 248. See also above, pp. 248 – 9.

[69] *ibid.* (6.2.1902), 177; (24.11.1904), 93; (26.10.1905), 36. See also above, p. 248.

against it.[70] A more liberal mood became apparent thereafter: in 1880 a motion condemning the French government's expulsion of the religious orders was defeated by the chairman's casting vote; and though in 1892 the society rejected a proposal to disestablish and disendow the Church of England, by 1898 disestablishment commanded a small majority.[71] In 1903, though, there was opposition to opening the Bernard Room on Sundays.[72]

The religious and theological societies were a new form of expression of interest in religion, perhaps reflecting the increasing thoughtfulness and maturity of students' attitudes towards religious questions. They arose at the same time as a number of other literary and intellectual societies, and their presence, though it does demonstrate a high level of interest in religious questions, does not necessarily denote any new religious fervour. This is better observed in the activities of more strictly devotional religious groups, of which the most notable was the Cambridge Intercollegiate Christian Union (CICCU), a student society which emerged in the mid-1870s out of the remnants of the old evangelical movement that had been kept going by various prayer and missionary groups between the 1840s and 1860s, although the movement as a whole had rather lost its way after the spectacular successes earlier in the century.[73] By the 1870s it seems that the undergraduates at Queens' were no longer particularly influenced by evangelicalism in comparison with students in some other colleges.[74]

The CICCU began to take off in the 1880s, and henceforth was to be a significant element in the university's religious life.[75] It was composed of a federation of Christian unions in the separate colleges. At Queens' a Wednesday evening prayer meeting was instituted at some time during the 1870s; this was later united with a younger society, the 'Pie Posse'

---

[70] *Dial* (Easter 1916), 23.
[71] *CR* (1.12.1880), 119; (10.3.1892), 259; (17.2.1898), 233; SBSM, 5.3.1892, 12.2.1898. The debate of 1892 was described in the *Cambridge Review* as 'rather poor'; and it reckoned the result of the 1898 debate was due to a dull speech by one of the opponents of disestablishment. The St Bernard Society's rules of 1897 included: 'That debates be on any subject not Theological and that no arguments on a Theological or religious basis be permitted', SBSM, Lent 1897. Disestablishment of the church was presumably reckoned to fall outside the scope of this rule.
[72] SBSM, 9.3.1903; there had been opposition on previous occasions also. Sabbath day observance even affected the Kangaroos, whose minutes record in 1896: 'The absent members having scruples regarding the Sabbath as a day of rest were, it seems, occupied in refreshing their weary souls and frames with soft sleep, but the present members, not approving of their action, proceeded to unanimously pass on them a vote of censure', Kangaroo Club Minutes, 18.10.1896.
[73] Pollock (1953), 13 – 27; Haig (1986), 193.
[74] Pollock (1953), 28 and n.
[75] *ibid.*, chapter VI and *passim*.

(or Pi-Posse, about which almost nothing is known) and reorganised again in 1893 under the title of the Queens' College Christian Union, with the declared aim of uniting all Christians in the college.[76] Apart from the prayer meetings and Bible readings which were at the heart of this form of evangelical revival, the QCCU also listened to speakers and held religious discussions.[77] Queens' did not possess a markedly evangelical character in the 1890s, but in 1909 the *Cambridge Review* reported that the QCCU was 'still as popular as ever', with seldom less than 30 members present at its weekly meetings, as many as would gather in the college in the late 1940s for its weekly Bible readings, when both the QCCU and the CICCU were thriving organisations.[78] Yet this was a relatively small proportion of the college in the early 1900s: the history of the CICCU and its affiliates has been recorded, but we still know relatively little about the religious life of the great majority of undergraduates.

Missionary work was an important part of the evangelical revival — although it was no by means an exclusively evangelical concern — and there was renewed enthusiasm for it among undergraduates from the 1880s; there are isolated instances of Queensmen becoming missionaries from this time.[79] But it was also recognised that there was a need for missionary work nearer home; missionary societies and philanthropists had been much criticised during the century for failing to recognise the problems of the poor in Britain. In the 1880s and subsequent decades several colleges established boys' clubs and missions in the London slums, run by local clergy or by full-time missioners, where students would go down to help out during vacations and other free time.[80] This was quite unconnected with the CICCU, which had reservations about

---

[76] *Courier* (15.3.1906), 31. c.f. the declared aims of the CICCU in 1894 – 5: 'To unite men whose definite aim in University life is to extend Christ's Kingdom, whether in seeking the conversion or spiritual help of men around them, or in promoting work for Home or Foreign Missions, or the like', Pollock (1953), 141. Its aims appear to be the same today; the emphasis on seeking conversion remains a controversial aspect of the CICCU's work. For the only other known reference to the Pi-Posse see above, p. 251.

[77] e.g. CR (7.11.1907), 71; (2.12.1909), 165; (9.12.1909), 188; (27.1.1910), 225; (3.2.1910), 240; *Courier* (15.3.1906), 31 – 2.

[78] Pollock (1953), 132, n. 257 – 8; CR (11.11.1909), 101. But note that the *Cambridge Review*'s representative at Queens' in 1909 was a devoted and loyal evangelical.

[79] Pollock (1953), 88, 167, 190, 213, chapter VI *passim*. The Quaerists heard a talk on the Delhi Mission in 1896; there was a talk on the work of the Society for the Propagation of the Gospel in the college in 1897; H. E. Ryle, a keen supporter of the SPG, chaired an annual meeting of the Universities Mission to Central Africa in the same year; W. M. Coates was said to be keen on university men becoming involved in foreign missions, CR (28.11.1895), 110 – 111; (26.11.1896), 120; (3.12.1896), 139; (11.3.1897), 297; (11.9.1897), 67; (10.2.1898), 206; (1.11.1900), 45.

[80] Chadwick (1970 – 2), ii.450; *Cambridge in South London* (1910).

the aims of these clubs and missions[81] — almost certainly because they were thought to place insufficient emphasis on religious conversion — and it betokens a broader religious revival in the university.

At Queens' there are signs of interest in 1889, when a meeting chaired by the dean, J. H. Gray, heard a talk by a former student of the college now working as a minister in the East end of London. In 1897 a meeting was held in the college to raise support there for Cambridge House, the university's London mission which had been launched in the previous year, and a college secretary was elected. Two years later a meeting of representatives of the various college missions and Cambridge House was held in the president's lodge; and in 1901 the bishop of Rochester addressed what was said to be a 'very representative meeting' of the college on the subject of Cambridge House.[82] In 1901 the college adopted a boys' club in Peckham, inaugurated in October of that year. Sunday Bible classes were the main feature of the mission's work, and by 1909 – 10 the average attendance at these was 60 or 70 boys; but it was stressed that there was no compulsion to attend.[83] In view of the influence of muscular Christianity and athleticism among students in general, it is no surprise to learn that physical exercise was encouraged at the mission: in 1907 the *Dial* reported that 'One of the recent improvements is the acquisition of horizontal and parallel bars which have been fixed up in the Club-room and form a great source of amusement'.[84] There were also mission camps.[85] Because most of the boys came from bad homes — some had none at all — one of the mission's prime concerns was to find work for them; in this, help was solicited from old Queensmen living in London. In 1909 the *Dial* reported that 'In view of the great distress prevalent in S.E. London, the Missioner would gladly welcome gifts of cast off clothing and boots, for distribution among the boys'.[86] These missions and clubs were a

---

[81] According to the historian of the CICCU, the college missions of the 1890s 'not only left scope for further effort, but were varied in aim and therefore drew an uncertain loyalty from Christian Union men', Pollock (1953), 153. The CICCU presumably wished them to place greater emphasis on religious conversion. Christopher Brooke tells me that high church elements were very strong in some London missions.

[82] CR (14.11.1889), 70; (25.11.1897), 113; (2.12.1897), 134; (22.2.1899), 223; (14.2.1901), 190. In 1896, shortly after his appointment as president of Queens', Ryle was one of the speakers at the launching of Cambridge House, Fitzgerald (1928), 114.

[83] *Cambridge in South London* (1910); *Dial* (Michaelmas 1909), 326; (Lent 1911), 61 – 4; CR (24.10.1901), 30. In 1903 some 200 people were present at a concert to raise money for the Queens' College Mission to South London, CR (21.5.1903), 320.

[84] *Dial* (March 1907), 132 – 3.

[85] *ibid.* (Michalemas 1909), 334 – 7. The work of the mission, and the camps, are also described in G. B. Harrison: letter.

[86] *Cambridge in South London* (1910); *Dial* (Michaelmas 1909), 326. In 1910, following a dispute with the missioner, who was the parish curate, the college withdrew from its mission and set up a new club which was not under any parish control at Rotherhithe, College Reports (1914 – 37), 204 – 5.

significant new departure in the university's religious life, and a sign of real religious enthusiasm which was welcomed by H. E. Ryle, who wrote that 'the future historian of the Church will find few more remarkable features of healthy and hopeful life than that series of School and College Missions and University Settlements, in which men of all schools of thought have sought to link the fortunes and the happiness of the students of the land with the barren monotony and heathen hopelessness of thousands in East and South London'.[87]

Students and dons united in their support for these London missions. If more and more Fellows were coming to reject dogmatic Christianity in the late 19th century, they had by no means abandoned Christian morality.[88] Moreover, many of them developed a more modern, liberal faith which was able to reconcile Christianity with new intellectual advances. There is no sign of any diminished religious commitment among the Fellows of Queens'. Many of the leading figures among the fellowship were ordained ministers and many of those who were not ordained are known to have been sincere Christians. There were several noted religious scholars, and two presidents, Ryle and Chase, left Queens' upon promotion to the episcopal bench — the first time that a president of Queens' had become a bishop since Anthony Sparrow in 1667.[89]

The Fellows endeavoured to maintain the importance of chapel worship in the college's devotional life. An order of 1855 required resident Fellows to take turns to preach a short sermon every Sunday morning during full term. Arthur Wright, dean from 1872 to 1882, tried to make the chapel services 'real occasions of worship';[90] and both the restoration of the chapel in 1858 – 60, and the building of the new chapel in 1880 – 91 were clearly genuine acts of piety. A college chaplain was

---

[87] Ryle, *Church of England*, 11.
[88] Rothblatt (1981), 244.
[89] Campion, Arthur Wright, Gray, Wood, and Kennett were all ordained. For Ryle and Chase, see *DNB*. Fitzpatrick was also in orders, and said after his death to have been in the old evangelical tradition, but generally moderate and tolerant in his religious views, Rackham (1937), 11, and see 3 – 4, 23. For religious scholars, see the following pages of this chapter. Those who were not ordained but are known to have been sincere Christians include W. M. Coates, below, p. 283; and A. B. Cook, described by J. F. Williams as a 'very perfect Christian gentleman', MS 79, 39. G. B. Harrison recalls that Cook and his wife were 'strict Plymouth Brethren', G. B. Harrison: letter. Cook was described after his death by C. T. Wood as an old-fashioned evangelical — not a fundamentalist — who later shifted his theological position, apparently away from orthodox Christianity towards more deistic views, though Wood is not specific, QC (1951 – 2), 5 – 6. T. B. Howarth also describes Cook as having moved towards a deistic position in later life, having become an evangelical and Sunday school teacher in middle age, Howarth (1978), 133 – 4. Arthur Wright wrote of Ernest Temperley that 'his consideration for the feelings of others marked him for a true, Christian, gentleman', Wright (1889), 8.
[90] CB (1832 – 88), 2.11.1855; *Dial* (Lent 1909), 246 – 9.

also appointed, perhaps in response to the growing number of students: the first known holder of this post from outside the college fellowship was C. H. W. Johns (1893–1901), a distinguished Assyriologist who became master of St Catharine's in 1909.[91]

Several of the dons were also involved in college and other religious activities in a personal capacity. Arthur Wright, C. T. Wood, A. B. Cook, and R. H. Kennett are known to have given talks to religious societies such as the Quaerists and the QCCU.[92] Kennett held informal religious discussions with students in his rooms, often well into the night;[93] Arthur Wright inaugurated a voluntary series of Sunday evening lectures on the Greek Testaments for men entering the ministry;[94] and W. M. Coates ran a Bible class on Sundays for St Mark's parish in Newnham.[95] Presidents Ryle, Chase and Fitzpatrick were encouragers of the CICCU, as were Kennett and Coates.[96]

Many of the Fellows of Queens' in the late 19th and early 20th centuries — certainly the prominent clergymen amongst them — were members of that more advanced theological wing of the church which was prepared to reinterpret its faith in the light of new and more searching methods of Biblical studies: the so-called 'higher criticism' emanating from the continent and especially from Germany, which overturned traditional beliefs in the literal and historical authenticity of many of the Biblical narratives. This issue, which had first arisen in the middle years of the century, lay at the heart of the 'crisis of faith'.

Where their views are known, the clerical Fellows of Queens' seem to have been largely of one mind on this issue. R. H. Kennett, who became Regius professor of Hebrew in 1903, was an original and fearless Old Testament critic, who believed that the Bible should be subjected to 'honest investigation', and who around the turn of the century 'shocked many of the old-fashioned by his ruthless frankness about some

---

[91] AC; *Dial* (Michaelmas 1909), 305. The provision of a college chaplain in addition to the dean was required by the statutes of 1883, but the chaplain could be one of the Fellows, *Statutes* (1883), 30, 33–4.
[92] CR (5.11.1908), 70; (2.12.1909), 165; (3.2.1910), 240; (10.2.1910), 261; (10.3.1910), 352; (19.5.1910), 422; (24.11.1910), 141.
[93] *Dial* (Lent 1932), 5–8. See above, p. 229.
[94] *Dial* (Lent 1909), 246–9; CR (2.5.1924), 307.
[95] *Dial* (Lent 1912), 8. The *Cambridge Review* described Coates as strongly religious in 1912, CR (25.1.1912), 209. J. F. Williams thought that he was a member of the Plymouth Brethren, MS 79, 35, but he may have confused Coates with Cook, above, n. 89.
[96] *Dial* (Lent 1909), 284; CR (28.1.1897), 184; (12.5.1898), 319; Pollock (1953), 117, 144, 163, 168, 184, 230. Fitzpatrick was treasurer of the University Mission to Central Africa in 1921, CR (14.11.1921), 56. Coates was said to be the only don working actively for the CICCU mission to the university in 1911, Pollock (1953), 184. Support for the CICCU by senior members may have been rather limited.

problems of the Bible'.[97] Kennett's view was that much of the Old Testament could not be true in any precise historical sense, but that it was not written as history in the way that the term was understood in the 19th century, and that its authors were interested in the edifying qualities of their stories rather than in their literal accuracy.[98]

Similar points were made by H. E. Ryle, like Kennett a prominent figure in the challenge to the old orthodoxies. Ryle returned to Cambridge as Hulsean professor of divinity in 1888, when the 'higher criticism' was still in its infancy in England. His letter of application for the post, outlining the work he would do if elected, emphasised that 'The great problems raised by recent criticism seem to make a special claim upon the enthusiasm and courage of the younger generation of students', and from the first he was an outspoken advocate, attracting criticism from some traditionalist quarters.[99] His religious views would have been well known to the Fellows of Queens' when they elected him president.

Ryle recognised that 'The theology of no generation exactly resembles that of its predecessors . . . It too sifts tradition . . . rearranges ideas, states old truths in new lights, casts aside crudities, and sooner or later drops superstitions'.[100] Neither the history of the church nor the study of the Bible could ever again be exempt 'from the searching and faithful scrutiny which the methods of this new age of historical science have made necessary', and Ryle warned Christians 'against an attitude of acquiescence for themselves and for their children in a standard of ignorance upon the history of their communion and their Bible, upon the fundamental facts of their faith, and upon the origin and growth of their sacraments, their liturgy, their service books, and their institutions'.[101]

Ryle's views on the early chapters of Genesis are a good example of his thinking: he argued that these chapters taught 'neither accurate science nor literal history', but they did contain 'under the form of a symbolism for which a phase of rudimentary and erroneous science in Palestine was the chosen vehicle, spiritual truths which belong to the very foundation of our faith'.[102] He therefore rejected the notion that modern scholarship had damaged the value of the appeal to Scriptural

[97] *Dial* (Michaelmas 1910), 4 – 6; (Lent 1932), 5 – 8. Pollock maintains that Kennett 'combined an advanced higher critical position with an evangelical message', Pollock (1953), 163. Much the same might be said of Ryle. The support of such men for the CICCU indicates that it was identified with a broader range of religious outlooks than the term 'evangelical' might suggest to many at the present day.

[98] Kennett (1910), 23, 27 – 9.

[99] Fitzgerald (1928), 84 – 101, chapter VI *passim*. Fitzgerald describes Ryle as a moderate, or liberal evangelical, a man of strong views but not partisan, *ibid.*, 121 – 7.

[100] Ryle (1896), 8.

[101] Ryle (1913), 3, 6.

[102] Ryle, *Holy Scripture*, 50 – 1, and *passim*; Ryle (1896), 10 – 11, and *passim*.

authority, and saw no reason for the disturbance of a Christian faith which rested 'not upon opinions, new or old, right or wrong, respecting the literary structure of the Bible — but on the Lord Jesus Christ, to whom the Scriptures testify'.[103]

F. H. Chase, Ryle's successor as president of Queens', was also a prominent university theologian of the day, being elected Norrisian professor of divinity in 1901.[104] Kennett and Ryle had concentrated their studies upon the Old Testament; Chase was among those who now applied the 'higher criticism' to the New Testament, in which the question of historical authenticity was even more pertinent and thorny for Christians. Although in his analysis of the Acts of the Apostles, Chase appreciated that there were 'problems, historical, psychological, and religious', he argued the need 'to stand in the attitude of suspended judgment' and to 'wait for further evidence and for fuller light, assured that there speaks to us in that Book an honest and well-informed Christian man, the companion and friend of St. Paul — St. Luke'.[105] Similarly, in the case of the Gospels, Chase believed strongly that 'Criticism even of the Gospel records of the Lord's earthly life must among thoughtful Christians be allowed reasonable freedom'. But as he noted in discussing the historical evidence for the Resurrection (which he felt to be sufficient): 'no historical evidence can compel men to believe in an event of the past . . . it can only demonstrate its probability. If the event belongs to the sphere of religion, when historical religion, when historical criticism has done its work, its results become the material with which faith deals. Faith in the living God alone enables us to discern the congruity of the Resurrection, to realize it, to know in our lives its power'.[106]

The views of Ryle, Kennett and Chase echo those of an earlier, though less well known, generation of clerical Fellows at Queens'. In 1896 Arthur Wright published a *Synopsis of the Gospels* 'to facilitate the Historical Criticism of the Gospels by the comparative method', and two years later he published a book entitled *Some New Testament Problems*. 'It is impossible', Wright wrote in his preface to the latter work, 'that "the higher criticism" . . . should so rapidly gain ground in the domain of the Old Testament, and yet the New Testament remain in the grasp of medieval harmonists . . . We must keep pace with the age, if we would hand down the truth to future generations'. Historical criticism was 'essential' to Scriptural exegesis, for without it 'the commentator is at

---

[103] Ryle, *Holy Scripture*, 8.
[104] AC.
[105] Chase (1902), 301–2. Chase believed in Christ's miracles because he believed that Christ was God manifest; but he thought that the miracles described in the Acts of the Apostles might have been supernatural interpretations of natural events, *ibid.*, 299–301.
[106] Chase (1903), 14, 23.

fault and the apologist loses his most effective weapons. Destructive it may be — like every other weapon — if unfairly used; but as it is a true science, it must in the long run prove the supporter of the truth'.[107]

Campion took a similar line, in 1892 advocating the use of modern critical methods in Old Testament study, and maintaining that 'The questions raised, though involving matters which affect Christian doctrine, must be discussed as literary questions. They cannot be decided by mere ecclesiastical authority'. Campion was confident of the results of such critical enquiry: Christian life, being based on Christ's sacrifice, 'cannot be affected by any conclusions drawn by any critics respecting the origin of any Scriptures of the Old Testament'.[108]

For all its controversial qualities, the 'higher criticism' was a liberal theology, and its proponents had a horror of factions within the church. Campion lamented 300 years of disputes among Anglicans 'respecting some of the accessories of public worship . . . Predilections for such things indifferent and prejudices against them have broken the unity of the Church'.[109] Himself of high church leanings, Campion favoured freedom of choice in non-essential rites and practices.[110] Ryle, whose churchmanship was rather lower than Campion's, also believed in freedom of choice in non-essential articles of worship. He wrote of the dangers of trying to impose uniformity, and recognised the beneficial influence on the 19th century church of groups as diverse as the evangelicals and the Oxford Movement.[111]

It is clear from the evidence above that although scepticism may have been on the increase, religious life at Queens' was vigorous, confident and wide-ranging, both in its devotional and theological aspects. How far this was representative of the college as a whole it is impossible to say, but it was certainly a significant feature of its society in the years leading up to the first world war.

---

[107] Wright (1906), v; Wright (1898), vii – viii.

[108] Campion (1892), 8 – 10. George Phillips, Campion's predecessor as president, was cautious about the claims of the new Old Testament criticism, CR (11.2.1892), 192.

[109] CR (30.3.1881), lxv – lxvi.

[110] ibid., lxvi – lxvii. He defended the beautifying of churches, Campion (1892), 10 – 11. See also above, pp. 274, 277. It is not clear how much high church influence there was on the undergraduates. J. F. Williams recalled that in his day one student with high church tendencies sometimes had his room smoked out with incense by other undergraduates, MS 79, 63.

[111] Ryle felt that there were few inessential articles of worship left, though, Ryle, Church of England, 6 – 7, 9 – 11, chapter xxii passim. 'We have to think of the Church as of a State, and not as of an army. Military metaphors, however inspiring, are perilously misleading', ibid., 6. Apparently on a similar theme, Arthur Wright argued that 'Most of the perversions of Christianity have arisen from taking some one or more ideal principles as though they were literal guides, while the others have been treated differently or ignored', Wright (1891), 7.

19

The educational revolution

The changes in the university's education system in the second half of the 19th century were extensive and rapid. Some were the result of internal reforms; some the work of parliament. They came piecemeal, sometimes in the face of strong opposition.[1] Eighteenth century Cambridge had not been changeless in this respect, but it had often been resistant to reform: the failure of Jebb's proposals in the 1770s, which had received strong support from reformers at Queens', is a prominent illustration of this.[2] Left to itself, the university did introduce some measure of educational reform during the first half of the 19th century, but its apparent resistance to any substantial changes led to mounting pressure upon it from outside, and subsequently it was external agencies which forced the pace.

This pressure for reform built up because the old universities had failed to keep up with changes in English society. An educational system cannot exist in isolation: it must remain attuned to the wider organisation of culture and society,[3] and in Victorian Britain this was changing quickly. From Jebb's time onwards, but especially in the 19th century, criticism of the education given at Oxford and Cambridge persisted and mounted as the universities became increasingly aloof and remote from the leading elements in society and their values. The middle classes had become a powerful economic, social and political force by the middle of the century, and had increasingly denounced what they perceived to be the old-fashioned aristocratic pretensions and exclusiveness of the country's higher education system. They wanted a system which was more responsive to the needs of the new middle class élite.[4] In response to this pressure, parliament began to take an interest in university reform, and compelled the universities to change. Parliamentary legislation in the 1850s and 1870s effected radical reforms at Cambridge and stimulated the reform movement inside the

---

[1] The educational reforms described in this chapter are separated from other contemporary reforms for convenience of discussion, but the reform movement in general was more closely integrated; this chapter should be read in conjunction with chapters 16 and 17.

[2] Above, p. 217.

[3] For a discussion of this question, see Williams (1961), 125 – 7.

[4] Roach, 'Victorian Universities', 131 – 6; Simon, *Two Nations*, 73 – 93, 280 – 99; Green (1969), 54 – 63; Heyck (1982), 64 – 74; Winstanley (1940), 148ff.

university.

At the heart of these reforms were changes to the university's teaching structure and curriculum. The alterations to the statutes governing the tenure of college fellowships in 1860 and 1882 which have been discussed elsewhere in this book were aimed at facilitating these changes.[5] The effects were dramatic: before the 1840s an honours student could read only for the mathematical or classical triposes, but by 1914 a wide range of subjects was on offer, both in the sciences and in the humanities.[6] University teaching had been revitalised by the endowment of numerous new professorships and lectureships and by the provision of new buildings and facilities; and greater emphasis was placed on academic research. Together with Oxford, which experienced similar changes at this time, Cambridge was generally recognised once more as a centre of education and scholarship, with a high reputation. No longer aloof and remote from society and its wishes, the universities supplied its need for qualified men for the professions; and the intellectual class which emerged for the first time in England in the late Victorian period was university-centred, professional in status, and highly specialised in its thoughts and studies — a direct product of the university reforms.[7] Students took their studies more seriously: there was a slow but steady increase in the number of men reading for honours instead of the pass degree.[8]

The progress of reform was an uneven one, however, and it was not uniformly successful in all areas. As has been demonstrated, there was little expansion in the social base of the student population.[9] There was also fierce resistance to many of the reforms from conservative elements within the university. The proposal to expand the curriculum and to make the university a place of more specialised study struck at the roots of the university's accepted educational ideology: the concept of the 'liberal education', which, in the words of one of its most important

[5] Above, chapter 16. Statutes were altered at all the colleges in those years.
[6] There were new triposes in moral sciences, natural sciences, theology, law, history, oriental languages, medieval and modern languages, mechanical sciences, and economics, Tanner (1917), 703 – 986. The expansion of science was particularly noticeable, and the royal commission of 1919 was so carried away in its enthusiasm for this that it reported : 'The growth of science at Cambridge since the era of the Royal Commissioners [the early 1850s] has been perhaps the greatest fact in the University since its foundation', Green (1969), 238.
[7] Roach, 'Victorian Universities', 131 – 150; Green (1969), 73; Rothblatt (1981), 184 – 5, 248 – 257; Winstanley (1947), 185 – 193; Heyck (1982), chapter 8.
[8] Between 1851 and 1906 one third of students at Cambridge took pass degrees, and over a quarter left without any degree. By 1902, though, about 53% took honours, and this figure had risen to about 62% by 1913 – 14, Rothblatt (1981), 184 – 5. But there are signs of increasing seriousness about examinations throughout the 19th century, Heyck (1982), 70; Rothblatt (1982), 6 – 20.
[9] Above, pp. 237 – 40.

advocates, J. H. Newman, aimed at creating an 'intellectual culture' rather than merely conveying knowledge, educating the intellect 'to reason well in all matters, to reach out towards truth, and to grasp it', and supplying 'a faculty of entering with comparative ease into any subject of thought, and of taking up with aptitude any science or profession'.[10] According to this school of thought, character was more important than proficiency; self-reliance, hard work, thrift and moral uprightness were more valuable qualities for achieving success than specialised skills or training.[11] The intellectual underpinning of the 'liberal education' — the belief in a 'unitary world of truth' — crumbled during the second half of the century under the pressure of new scientific ideas and advances, and society's growing need for specialists,[12] but many dons remained committed to the older ideal. They gave little thought to their students' careers, and so were of little help in finding them jobs after graduation.[13]

But there was sometimes a rather blurred distinction between admiration for the 'liberal education' as an intellectual ideal, and the contempt for professional skills and 'business values' which could lead from it — a thinly disguised form of social snobbery which is hinted at strongly in Campion's remarks on the 'merchant's office in Liverpool' made during his interview with the parliamentary select committee in 1867.[14] This was an attitude shared by many dons, and is reflected in the small number of Cambridge graduates going into business in the 1880s and 1890s; even students from business backgrounds tended to use their university qualifications to enter more prestigious careers. This attitude persisted well into the 20th century.[15]

---

[10] Newman (1976), 114 and *passim*, especially Discourses V – VI.

[11] Rothblatt (1982), 1 – 6.

[12] Garland (1980), 113, chapters 6 and 7.

[13] No official action was taken to help students find work until the formation of the Cambridge Appointments Association in 1899, given formal university status as the Cambridge Appointments Board in 1902, and intended to open up links with the business world. Between 1899 and 1914 it found jobs for about 20% of graduates, and by 1908 all the colleges made financial contributions to its work, Rothblatt (1981), 257 – 264. Dons were most helpful at getting their students into teaching, *ibid*. One undergraduate of the 1920s, dismissed from a post at a preparatory school in 1932, wrote to R. G. D. Laffan 'in case his influence can manage one of the better public schools', and became a master at Stowe, but whether through Laffan's influence or not it is impossible to say, White (1984), 28.

[14] Above, p. 241. For Campion, therefore, the Cambridge BA represented not merely 'intellectual attainments' but also 'academical training', explained as 'The social influences of the place; the association with their fellow students, and coming into contact with the tutors and fellows of their colleges, and so forth', *Select Committee* (1867), 233.

[15] Rothblatt (1981), 267 – 73; below, appendix 16. The relationship of Oxford and Cambridge to British industry in this period is discussed in more detail in Sanderson (1972), chapter 2, and reinforces these conclusions.

Changes at Queens'

It is no easy task to assess the academic standard of a college at any time in its history: its gifted scholars are easily pinpointed, but the academic achievements and calibre of its students are at least as important, and for this there is hardly any evidence until a great majority began to sit tripos examinations in the present century. For the state of Queens' in the middle of the 19th century, we have to rely principally upon subjective accounts.[16] In 1827 J. M. F. Wright had described it as 'a goodly college enough, for real and substantial learning'.[17] By 1867, however, William Everett could write that 'of late, though it has produced some splendid mathematicians, [Queens'] has for some unexplained reason been greatly lowered in general estimation'.[18] A writer in the 1920s observed that it 'dropped right to the bottom' in the second half of the century.[19] The present-day historian is no more able than Everett to explain the alleged low esteem in which Queens' was held at this time, but it is possible to outline some of the changes in teaching there, and to show how the college reacted to the parliamentary reforms.

Queens' was not wholly unresponsive to calls for reform, but it was not equally enthusiastic about every kind of reform. Dons who might disagree over the nature and extent of the changes that were needed tended to unite in their opposition to external interference in their college affairs, especially if this came from outside the university. There is an illustration of this at Queens' from the 1830s: in 1837 the college petitioned the queen to be allowed to make changes to its statutes, which was granted in the following year. These changes were not really concerned with educational reform, but with removing the encumbrances of obsolete regulations, and they did not introduce any radical changes.[20] But they were the work of an internal movement for reform. In the same year as petitioning to change its statutes, Queens' also decided to petition against a proposed bill in parliament for the establishment of royal commissions to look at college statutes in Oxford and Cambridge.[21]

With the appointment of a royal commission for the university of

---

[16] The evidence of tripos lists is ambiguous, owing to fluctuations in the number of students.

[17] Wright (1827), ii.179.

[18] Everett (1867), 162.

[19] Bradley (?1922), 46. Gray argued that the college was academically successful around 1850; perhaps his judgement was influenced by college patriotism, Gray, 260. J. F. Williams alleged that Queens' had a poor reputation in the university in the 1890s, MS 79, 9.

[20] CB (1832 – 88), 22.4.1837, 30.12.1837, 5.7.1838, 17.11.1838; Winstanley (1940), 189; the alterations are given in *Documents* (1852), iii.65 – 71.

[21] CB (1832 – 88), 10.4.1837.

Cambridge in 1850, reform from outside was seen to be irresistible.[22] Queens' duly returned its replies to the wide-ranging and detailed questions of the commissioners in 1851.[23] Their report was published in the following year, and in 1853 the college established a committee to examine the report and 'suggest such alterations as they may deem necessary so as to render the college more efficient and in accordance with the changes introduced into the University course', although nothing seems to have been done at that time.[24] After the passing of the Cambridge University Act in 1856, which set up a statutory commission to reform college statutes, another college committee was appointed to consider its implications; and this led in turn to the new statutes of 1860, which were an important step forward in the creation of a more stable and permanent academic profession which the royal commission had called for.[25]

Queens' was more hesitant in other respects. The expansion of the university curriculum had begun before the intervention of the royal commission, with the creation of the natural and moral sciences triposes in 1848. Few students took these courses at first, for they were relatively superficial, and until 1861 nobody could take them who had not taken a BA in one of the other triposes first.[26] This lukewarm enthusiasm for the new subjects was echoed at Queens'. The first instance of a student there taking the natural sciences tripos was in 1853, and over a decade elapsed before there was another. The first to take the moral sciences tripos was in 1855, and the next not until 1867.[27] In 1867 Campion claimed that the smaller colleges were not electing Fellows on the basis of good performances in these triposes, as they had traditionally done for the older triposes, because they were waiting for the larger colleges to give a lead, and thereby to establish some recognised level of achievement for election to fellowships. He did, however, recognise an improvement in the standards of the new triposes since their inauguration.[28] In 1870, though, the college voted to award a three-year studentship to the value of £50 a year to Robert Watson who had just

---

[22] Winstanley (1940), 198 – 232, 263 – 286.

[23] CB (1832 – 88), 20.11.1851, 11.12.1851.

[24] ibid., 13.1.1853; and see 12.1.1854.

[25] ibid., 11.10.1856; above, pp. 224 – 5. The commissioners urged the creation of more public lectureships and of a 'definite and permanent' career for university teachers, Report (1852), 80 – 1. The colleges had no choice but to amend their own statutes, or have these amended for them by statutory commissioners, perhaps to an even greater extent, Winstanley (1940), 286.

[26] Winstanley (1947), 185 – 8.

[27] The first examinations in these triposes were not of course until three years after their establishment, in 1851, Tanner (1917), 704, 707, 737, 741.

[28] Select Committee (1867), 230. Campion was an examiner for the moral sciences tripos in 1861, 1862, and 1867, Tanner (1917), 706, 707.

come top of the natural sciences tripos.[29] In 1877 the governing body agreed 'to prepare the Senior Fellow's stable for the purpose of making experiments in Elementary Physics'.[30] In 1890 an external director of studies in natural sciences was appointed, and in 1891 it was agreed to offer entrance scholarships in natural sciences and in Hebrew, as well as the traditional mathematics and classics.[31] T. C. Fitzpatrick was the first director of studies in natural sciences to be appointed from within the college: he took up the office shortly after his election as president, in 1906.[32] Fitzpatrick was a university demonstrator in physics, and the first senior member of Queens' to be an examiner for the natural sciences tripos, in 1909.[33]

Other new subjects arrived in the college as the university curriculum grew. By the first world war, Queens' also had directors of studies in law, history, and modern languages. These were appointed from outside the college, although with the arrival of R. G. D. Laffan as a Fellow in 1913 Queens' had an internal director of studies in history for the first time.[34] But the college could not hope to offer teaching in every subject that was now on offer, and its fellowship continued to be dominated by classicists, mathematicians, theologians and orientalists.

One major area of controversy was the relationship between university and college teaching. The supremacy of the former was necessary in order to support an expanded and more highly specialised curriculum, and was stoutly resisted by the colleges, which were fearful of what they perceived to be assaults on their autonomy.[35] When in 1865 a university committee complained of 'the scanty and imperfect training of a large number of our students, and their want of adequate elementary knowledge on entering the University', and urged the institution of a general university entrance examination, there was fierce resistance: Campion denounced the plan as 'an undue interference with the colleges', and it was rejected by the senate.[36]

In an attempt to ward off moves to expand university teaching, J. N.

[29]   CB (1832 – 88), 28.1.1870; CU Cal. (1870), 356.
[30]   CB (1832 – 88), 2.1.1877.
[31]   CB (1889 – 1937), 23.9,1890, 8.10.1891. These are the first instances of these, as far as I know. The older subjects still dominated, however: in 1908 there were three entrance scholarships and three entrance exhibitions in mathematics, and in classics, but only one scholarship and two exhibitions in natural sciences, CB (1889 – 1937), 17.3.1908.
[32]   ibid., 10.10.1906.
[33]   CR (18.10.1906), 2; Dial (March 1907), 105; Rackham (1937), 1, 28 – 34; Tanner (1917), 797.
[34]   CB (1889 – 1937), 11.10.1897, 10.10.1906, 14.6.1907; CR (23.10.1913), 42; Dial (Michaelmas 1913), 257. Queens' offered entrance scholarships in history in 1913, CB (1889 – 1937), 8.3.1913. At the beginning of the century, the college's history lectures were given by a classicist, J. H. Gray, Student's Handbook (1902), 10.
[35]   Rothblatt (1981), 198 – 210, 230 – 35, contains some general remarks on this; there are numerous illustrations in the literature.
[36]   Winstanley (1947), 156 – 7.

Peill claimed to the royal commissioners in 1851 that

'Our College staff of Lecturers is sufficiently complete to prepare the Students for the different College and University Examinations excepting some provisions of the new triposes: hitherto we have not had any Student reading a subject beyond the usual subjects for the B.A. degree, and so soon as the necessity arises we shall provide ourselves with efficient Lecturers in the newly introduced subjects'.[37]

Similarly, the argument put forward by George Phillips in 1877 against the creation of more university professorships was that 'Every college is able to provide adequate instruction for its pupils, not only in the old subjects of study . . . but also in the new'.[38] Peill and Phillips were probably bluffing to a large extent. Even with only classics and mathematics on the curriculum, the full BA course had to be taught in college lectures.[39] These were more what we today would call 'classes' rather than 'lectures', with students being asked questions and expected to solve problems. According to Campion, the combination of lectures of this kind and college examinations kept the students 'under a continual state of catechetical examination'.[40] Campion was prepared to admit that the smaller colleges would not be able to offer teaching in all the new subjects, and felt that they would have to pool their resources by sending their students to other colleges for lectures in subjects they could not teach themselves,[41] but there is no indication that this practice was taken up at Queens' at that time.

The lectures in the college in those days were said to have been 'almost useless' as preparation for the tripos examinations, and were 'regarded rather as part of the machinery of college discipline than as possessing much practical utility'; most serious teaching was in the hands of private tutors.[42] Lectures were nominally compulsory, although the vice-president reported to the 1851 commission that lecturers were allowed some discretion in enforcing this on those who were not sufficiently advanced in their studies and understanding to benefit from the mathematics lectures. Arthur Wright alleged that when he arrived as a Fellow in the late 1860s many students did not bother to attend lectures.[43] Peill claimed in 1851 that lectures were 'adapted to the

---

[37] *Report* (1852), 178.
[38] Winstanley (1947), 308.
[39] The details are given in *Report* (1852), 178, 355.
[40] *Select Committee* (1867), 235; *Student's Guide* (1862), 44–5 contains a description of college lectures in general.
[41] *Select Committee* (1867), 230–1.
[42] *Dial* (Lent 1909), 247–8; see also *ibid.* (Easter 1916), 8–10; and *CR* (2.5.1924), 307.
[43] *Report* (1852), 356; *Dial* (Easter 1916), 9–10.

needs of the students', but Wright criticised them because students of all levels and abilities were expected to attend the same lectures.[44]

This situation was altered by the reforms which Pirie and Wright introduced in the late 1860s and 1870s: students were only required to attend lectures which were relevant for their university examinations, and the number of lectures was substantially increased to make better provision for students at different levels of understanding.[45] Wright and Pirie clearly managed to win the other Fellows over to their new ideas, and their reforms appear to have been successful. In general terms the relationship between college and university teaching was not resolved before the first world war;[46] but essentially it was a problem for which no final solution was possible, and which each subsequent generation of academics up to the present day has had to tackle in the light of shifting circumstances.

The reform of the lecture system is just one example of the college's concern to improve its academic standards and reputation at this time. In 1864, as has been shown, it introduced entrance scholarships.[47] In January 1873 it set up a committee to investigate 'the causes which result in the present low state of the College and to suggest measures for removing them and increasing the general usefulness of the College'.[48] The committee's proposals, which were adopted by the governing body in May of that year, were for a wide programme of changes, including improvements in college facilities and services, in order to make Queens' more attractive to potential stduents; and it also suggested a number of measures to lift educational standards.[49] All candidates for admission were to be interviewed by the senior tutor before being accepted; and men reading for the ordinary, or pass degree had to pass the Previous examination — a preliminary examination of relatively elementary standard introduced by the university in 1822 — at the second attempt or leave the college.[50] As incentives, candidates for minor scholarships were to receive free dinners from the college on the

---

[44] *Report* (1852), 178; *Dial* (Easter 1916), 8 – 10. Solomon Atkinson claimed in 1825 that lectures in the college in Milner's time were useless from an educational point of view and were only attended because they were compulsory, Atkinson (1825), 501.

[45] *CR* (2.5.1924), 307; *Dial* (Lent 1909), 247 – 8; (Easter 1916), 10 – 11. The precise date of the reforms is not clear: both Pirie and Wright were Fellows in the late 1860s, but the changes may only have begun when Pirie became a tutor in 1870. In 1916 Queens' was said to have seven college lecturers, and to provide four university lecturers, *Dial* (Easter 1916), 14.

[46] A point made by T. C. Fitzpatrick in 1915, *CR* (20.1.1915), 146 – 7. He also spoke of the need to find a balance between the demands of teaching and research.

[47] Above, p. 239.

[48] CB (1832 – 88), 7.1.1873.

[49] For what follows, *ibid.*, 17.5.1873.

[50] For a brief account of the previous examination, see Roach, 'University of Cambridge', 240, 245.

day of their examinations; more college prizes were awarded for classics; and the college undertook to bear the costs of lecture rooms and examinations, which had hitherto fallen on the tutors (and therefore presumably been paid for by the students in their tutorial fees, which were separate from the college accounts). It was now accepted 'as a principle' that the money from vacant fellowships should be paid into the scholarships fund. Further reforms in the 1880s to make the college more attractive to students have been described above;[51] they were part of the same process of improvement. In 1907 there was further tightening up on the level of performance required of candidates for both pass and honours degrees in the university's preliminary examinations if they wished to remain in residence.[52]

The last major area of confrontation between the external reformers and the university and college conservatives came with the second wave of parliamentary reforms in the late 1870s and early 1880s. An act of 1877 established statutory commissioners for both universities to enquire into the revenues and finances of the universities and colleges: it was intended that the latter should be made to contribute financially to the proposed expansion of university teaching — the creation, in effect, of a body of university lecturers — and that fellowships and other college emoluments should be attached to university offices.[53] The changes to college statutes in 1882, including those of Queens', were the other principal feature of the commissioners' efforts to professionalise academic life.[54]

It was inevitable that these proposals for what amounted to the taxing of college revenues to maintain lectureships would be opposed. The university had already taken some steps in this direction: in 1870 Queens' had declared its willingness to contribute towards the stipends of the proposed new Cavendish professor of experimental physics, and of other new university teachers and demonstrators, as well as to a fund for a building and apparatus. But it quibbled at the way in which the university had assigned its contribution, and was prepared to pay only in proportion to other colleges, according to a fixed ratio of the divisible income.[55] There was similar opposition to the statutory commissioners' assessments: Queens' protested that they had not given due weight to the colleges' financial needs for their own educational and other

---

[51] Above, chapter 17.
[52] CB (1889 – 1937), 11.10.1907.
[53] For a brief account, see Roach, 'University of Cambridge', 264 – 5; for a full summary, Winstanley (1947), 263 – 359.
[54] Above, p. 226.
[55] It also refused to contribute to funds for building an examination hall and for increasing the stipends of university professors, CB (1832 – 88), 6.1.1870. For the creation of the Cavendish chair, see Tanner (1917), 103. Campion thought a fixed percentage of each college's revenues would be the best arrangement, CU Reporter (26.10.1870), 51.

purposes, and insisted that its own contribution should be assessed only on the income which remained after it had made provision for its maintenance 'as a place of education, learning and research'. It also complained that the assessments were too inflexible, and failed to take account of the variations in college income from property, the value of which had 'very generally depreciated' at that time because of the agricultural depression. Finally, it protested that the total sum levied from the colleges together was far too high. In 1881 the college petitioned that queen against the commissioners' proposals.[56] Queens' might attack the details, but it had to concede the principle of the reforms, and the expansion of the university's educational resources at the end of the 19th century was in no small measure due to the financial support of the colleges.

We have seen the changes introduced at Queens' in the years after 1850 to improve the academic standards of the students. If we cannot tell fully how successful these were, there is no doubting the sincerity and effort of the college Fellows who introduced them. It remains to ask what effect the 'Revolution of the Dons' had on the academic calibre of the college's fellowship.

A pronounced shortage of distinguished scholars perhaps helps to explain the low academic reputation which Queens' enjoyed in the middle years of the century. Probably its most distinguished scientist during those years was the mathematician Philip Kelland, senior wrangler in 1834 and briefly a Fellow before being elected professor of mathematics at Edinburgh in 1838, the first time that that university had appointed a professor with a wholly English education.[57] It also produced an eminent engineer: Osborne Reynolds, who was a Fellow for a short while after graduating in 1867 (he was placed 7th in the mathematical tripos), and became professor of engineering at Owens College in Manchester in 1868; this was one of the first chairs of its kind in England. Reynolds was elected an honorary Fellow of Queens' in 1882.[58]

But in the field of oriental languages the college maintained a distinguished tradition. While one of the university's principal functions had been to train the clergy, the teaching of Hebrew had been particularly important; in 1682 Queens' employed a Mr Robertson, 'a man learned in the Hebrew Tongue . . . to teach the whole College both Schollars and Fellows'; and in 1740 it is known to have employed a 'Hebrew Master'.[59] In the 18th century, Queens' could boast two

---

[56] CB (1832 – 88), 20.11.1880, 18.6.1881.
[57] DNB; *Proceedings of the Royal Society* xxix (1879), vii – x; Gunther (1969), 107.
[58] AC; Lamb (1913), xv, xxi.
[59] Book 39, f.6; CB (1734 – 87), f.22v. Neither of these names can be identified from AC. The standard of learning in oriental languages and Hebrew was high in the university in the 17th century, Wordsworth (1968), 162 – 3.

eminent orientalists in Simon Ockley, who was professor of Arabic from 1711 to 1720; and Joseph Carlyle, who held the same chair from 1795 till 1804.[60] The tradition continued there in the person of Samuel Lee, one of the greatest linguists of the 19th century and a prolific writer. Lee had been apprenticed to a carpenter when he was 12 years old, but he taught himself several languages and became something of a celebrity before he was discovered by the Church Missionary Society. This evangelical connection brought him to Queens' in 1814 at the age of 30 and he was successively professor of Arabic (from 1819 – 31) and Regius professor of Hebrew (1831 – 48), though he moved to Trinity on his election to the latter post.[61]

The late 19th century fellowship of the college — those who had helped to carry out the 'Revolution of the Dons' or who had been influenced by it — can be divided into two broad types in academic terms. The first group consists of those who, although gifted intellectually, chose to devote their lives to the college as teachers, administrators and moral guides; the second group, though showing no less enthusiasm for the new collegiate ideal, spent more effort in the field of scholarship and research. These are crude distinctions, admittedly, and there are some Fellows who do not quite fit the pattern. One such was George Pirie, a Fellow in the 1860s and 1870s, and a tutor, who with Arthur Wright was responsible for reforming college teaching and for many other improvements. Pirie seems to have maintained his academic interests, too, for in 1878 he was elected professor of mathematics at the university of Aberdeen.[62] Arthur Wright, in addition to his college duties and enthusiasms, especially the heavy load of college teaching which he took upon himself, made an important contribution to New Testament studies and the 'higher criticism'.[63]

Other notable scholars of the period included the theologians Ryle and Chase, both professors in the university;[64] and the college's reputation in oriental studies was maintained firstly by George Phillips, and by William Wright, who held the chair of Arabic from 1870 – 9. Wright had been educated at St Andrew's, and studied further at Hallé and Leyden; he was professor of Arabic at University College, London and Trinity College, Dublin before coming to Cambridge, and is said to have been a

[60] DNB; Wordsworth (1968), 163 – 4; Tanner (1917), 82. Ockley was not a Fellow; Carlyle was for a short while. The lives of both are of interest.
[61] AC; DNB; Lee (1896), 24 and passim; Milner (1842), 594; Tanner (1917), 77. Claudius Buchanan seems to have been the prime mover in Lee's coming to Queens', Pearson (1817), ii.344.
[62] AC; see also above, pp. 227 – 8.
[63] CR (2.5.1924), 307; Dial (Lent 1909), 246 – 50. Wright claimed that instead of the five hours of lecturing per week for which he was contracted, he regularly lectured for five hours each day, Dial (Easter 1916), 10. For this theological work, see above, pp. 285 – 6.
[64] See above, pp. 284 – 5.

conscientious teacher. He was also a member of the Old Testament revision committee.[65] R. H. Kennett's contribution to Old Testament studies has already been noted. He was Hebrew lecturer at Queens' from 1888 (the Semitic languages tripos had been established in 1878), and Regius professor of Hebrew from 1903.[66] The college also appointed an Assyriology lecturer in 1898: he was C. H. W. Johns, the college's chaplain, who was elected to a Bye-fellowship in 1903, was also a lecturer at King's College London, and published regularly. He was highly regarded in his field. The *Dial*'s notice of his election to the mastership of St Catharine's in 1909 drew attention to 'his kindly readiness to impart to others the stores of his learning, and to help and encourage younger students'.[67] The college's tradition of housing eminent orientalists has persisted to this day: the latest — and by no means the least — in the line is Sir Harold Bailey, emeritus professor of Sanskrit and a Fellow of Queens' since 1936.

The college also possessed a prominent classicist, A. B. Cook (Fellow, 1900 – 1952), the first occupant of the chair of classical archaeology at Cambridge in 1931. Cook's main interest was in ancient religious beliefs, and he was the author of a massive three-volume work on Zeus which demonstrated a 'fabulous command of every kind of material which could be brought to bear on the subject'. He was also said to have been 'an admirable lecturer, always clear, thorough, and entertaining, and he was supremely helpful to younger men, whether undergraduates or colleagues'.[68]

The other Fellows of this period were mainly concerned with college work. Ernest Temperley was a mathematician, but did not apparently do much research, being busy with teaching (mostly of private pupils) and bursarial duties. He planned to publish on mathematics — it is not

---

[65] For Phillips, see *DNB*. For Wright, see Tanner (1917), 82; *AC*; *CR* (30.5.1889), 362; *DNB*. In 1878 a student at Queens' was given a studentship of £50 a year for three years 'to enable him to prosecute his study of oriental languages in some home or foreign university', CB (1832 – 88), 8.6.1878. The first examinations in the oriental languages tripos were held in 1895; it was created out of the Semitic and Indian languages triposes established in the 1870s, Tanner (1917), 938, 942, 946. Phillips and Campion were supporters of the establishment of the Semitic languages tripos, and Phillips, who was responsible for bringing Wright to Queens', also played a leading rôle in the establishment of the Indian languages tripos, *CR* (11.2.1892), 192; *CU Reporter* (1.11.1871), 42; *DNB*; Gray, 259.

[66] Above, pp. 283 – 4; *AC*; *Dial* (Michaelmas 1910), 3 – 6; (Lent 1932), 5 – 8. Kennett also held private classes for students of other subjects who wished to study Hebrew.

[67] *Dial* (Michaelmas 1909), 304 – 7; and see *AC*; *DNB*.

[68] Seltman (1952), 239, 296 – 8, 301 – 2; *DNB* (from which the quotations are taken). Cook's monumental work appears in the novel *Mistress Masham's Repose* by T. H. White, who was an undergraduate at Queens' in the 1920s: one of the characters in this book 'would dream of impossible successes: imagining that the Master of Trinity had referred to him by name in a lecture, or that Dr. Cook had offered to mention him in a footnote to Zeus', White (1947), 25.

clear precisely what kind of work — but this scheme was halted by his death at the age of 39.[69] W. M. Coates, who followed Temperley as bursar, was also a mathematician, and did not pursue any original research. He was reckoned to be a good lecturer and coach, and a successful private tutor, and was active in moves to reform the mathematical tripos.[70] Andrew Munro was another mathematician who made no original contribution, but 'left lecture-notes on a wide variety of branches, arranged and indexed with minute care'.[71]

In the humanities there was the classicist J. H. Gray, seemingly more involved with college life and with university sports than with scholarship, although he did edit some texts; and he wrote a history of Queens', first published in 1898.[72] The college's first history don, R. G. D. Laffan, seems also to have regarded teaching as his primary function. He edited a book of selected documents of medieval European history intended for schools and colleges; and translated a French work on the origins of the House of Commons, because it was a recommended text for the Cambridge historical tripos and out of print in its French edition. Laffan published only one book of his own: a history of modern Serbia, which he researched and wrote in the most difficult circumstances imaginable, while serving as an army chaplain in Macedonia in 1917.[73] C. T. Wood wrote with a similarly pedagogic aim: a Hebrew grammar for students of the theological tripos; and a study of St Paul meant primarily for theological students but also for masters of senior forms in schools. His obituary in the college magazine in 1953 admitted that 'Academically he might perhaps be said to have started and not had time rather than not been able — to finish . . . Had he attended to Old Testament Studies with the vigour he gave to his innumerable other activities he would have made a great name as a scholar. But then his world would have lost many acts of kindness'.[74] It is an epitaph which would fit many of the late Victorian and Edwardian dons.

---

[69] CR (24.1.1889), 150 – 1, 154; *Dial* (Easter 1916), 11; Wright (1889), 8.
[70] CR (25.1.1912), 209; *Dial* (Lent 1912), 6 – 8.
[71] *Dial* (Michaelmas 1935), 8.
[72] *Dial* (Easter 1932), 9 – 12.
[73] Laffan (ed.) (1930), v; Pasquet (translated Laffan) (1964; original edition 1925), xiv; Laffan (1918). The book on Serbia was based on the notes of a series of lectures given to the troops in 1917 — a remarkable work, given the conditions in which it was written. The papers which Laffan read to the college's history society were on a wide range of subjects (perhaps reflecting the endurance of liberal educational values in historical studies against over-specialisation): on St John Fisher and Cambridge (given twice); Malta; Machiavelli; and the European tradition, QC History Society minutes, 13.11.1935, 28.4.1938, 2.6.1947, 10.5.1950, 5.3.1953.
[74] Wood (1913), v; Wood (1925), v; QC (1960 – 1), 6 – 7. For Wood's other books, see below, chapter 22, n. 40.

20

College finances in the 18th and 19th centuries[1]

Colleges had generally been prosperous in the early 17th century.[2] The financial difficulties caused by the Civil War, though severe, were short-lived.[3] There was a brief period of depression at the end of the century, but improving economic conditions and advances in agricultural methods leading to greater productivity during the 18th century meant continued prosperity for college landowners.[4] Colleges began to look to ways to raise their incomes, and so entry and renewal fines on leases increased during the 18th century, whereas they had tended largely to remain static before. There were new investments in stocks and shares, although not yet on a permanent or large-scale basis; and colleges began to use London bankers.[5]

Income and expenditure at Queens' rose steeply, and hand in hand, for much of the period.[6] Rental income remained steady, with only a slight increase, due largely to the acquisition of new property in the late 17th and early 18th centuries.[7] Most of the growth in income came from 'outside' receipts, principally from raising fines, in common with other colleges. A memorandum written by Henry James in 1708 stressed the need to secure the best possible deal from fines, and without doubt he struck a hard bargain with the tenants.[8]

[1] This survey is perforce largely impressionistic; college finances and accounts deserve a specialist study to themselves.
[2] For the general financial background to this period and a description of the college's financial administration see above, chapter 9.
[3] Twigg (unpublished thesis, 1983), 131 – 6, 176 – 7; above, pp. 58 – 60.
[4] Howard (1935), 66 – 7; Dunbabin (1986), *passim*.
[5] Howard (1935), 69 – 80; Dunbabin (1986), 276 – 8, 285 – 6.
[6] Below, appendix 12.
[7] The new properties were at Beccles (acquired 1662/3), Wyvelingham (1673), Everleigh (1674 — exchanged for Kingston in 1734), Eversden (a rent charge, 1674/5), Coveney (1676), Oakington (1681/2), Carmarthen (1701/2), and Haddenham (1718/9), Book 12; OPR, f.125; Book 6, fos.164v, 166v; Book 73, f.93; Book 80, fos.3, 5, 29, 57v, 84 (all second pagination); p. 19 (third pagination); CB (1734 – 87), fos.9v, 16; *VCH Wiltshire* xi. 138.
[8] Book 80, f.7v, and see f.6; *passim* for records of many leases and fines, and see also Book 29. In 1678 Queens' sought to eject its tenant at Haslingfield, Book 80, f.41 (second pagination); this may have been due to James' firmness, but we do not know. In 1771 it was decided that the hall and parlour could have an extra sack of coal per week thanks to the increase in fines and the abolition of fasting nights, CB (1734 – 87), f.86v. Note also the important rôle of 'outside' receipts in paying Fellows' dividends, above, chapter 6.

Most of the new properties were benefactions, either left directly to the college, or purchased with money given to it. Land was still thought the best and safest investment; Queens' does not seem to have taken much interest in the purchase of securities before the late 18th century.[9] Ferdinand Smythies, a Fellow of the college, gave it £1500 worth of bank stock several years before his death in 1725, but it was decided to sell this and buy property instead.[10]

Under Henry James, Queens' ran its estates and financial business diligently, with a keen eye for its rights and dues.[11] James felt that there had been too much loose financial administration in the past;[12] colleges were generally more conscientious in keeping written records of their holdings after 1660, to reduce the opportunity for error or fraud.[13] The memory of their vulnerability at times of crisis such as the Civil War made the need for such records all too apparent.

James may have been over-fussy, but colleges had to be alert if they were not to be cheated by their tenants;[14] moreover, he was haunted by the fear of imminent financial ruin unless careful precautions were taken. At some time during the 1680s he recorded in his notebook that it was very difficult for the college to break even on its annual accounts, and he believed it would run into debt quickly 'were it not for the absences of men from the College, or for that the number of 15 Priests [Fellows] is not compleat, or the schollarships not full, and we have noe way to be reliev'd but by the Focalia-Bill [sales of timber] which is a mere contingent thing'. He argued therefore that the bursars should be 'very carefull to retrench all unnecessary expences, especially that of the Audit; which of late yeares amounts to a scandalous sum, and exceeds the ability of our small Revenue as much as it does the measures of a laudable and honest hospitality for our Tenants'.[15] In 1682 he warned

---

[9] e.g. Book 8, fos.103v, 130, 131; see also Book 49.

[10] Book 29; Book 80, f.83 (second pagination). Another long-serving Fellow, David Hughes, who died in 1777, left a financial estate consisting almost wholly of bank annuities, Book 80, 30 (third pagination).

[11] See Book 80, *passim*.

[12] e.g. his memorandum concerning Haslingfield, where the farm and woods were traditionally leased separately, but to the same tenant, in order to have two renewal fines. In 1660 the two leases were renewed for a single fine, the first time this had happened; James reckoned this was because 'either Dr Martin was surpriz'd haveing forgot the affaires of the College or else in kindness to Mr Norwich [the tenant] (that he might not pay double fees) who had been likewise an old sufferer'. The same method was adopted by William Wells at the renewals of 1667 and 1675, Book 80, f.4 (second pagination); see also above chapter 9, n. 35.

[13] Dunbabin (1986), 283 – 5.

[14] c.f. Robert Plumptre, who in one known example does not seem to have been at all forceful: a dispute over the value of the college property (and hence over the level of its fine) at St Nicholas Court in Kent with the tenant there was allowed to drag on for many years, Box 16/2.

[15] Book 80, f.48 (second pagination).

that 'great repaires' undertaken in recent years had almost exhausted the college's reserves, and that the situation looked unlikely to improve for some time.[16]

Sequestration of the profits of vacant fellowships for general college purposes was increasingly common henceforth, and fellowships were regularly left vacant at times of financial hardship, principally to pay for building and repairs;[17] these had always required considerable capital outlay and placed an immense strain on resources, but they posed the only real threat to the college's financial stability before the end of the 18th century.

Further significant improvements in agricultural productivity, and hence in incomes from land, were achieved from the middle of the century by enclosing estates. Colleges followed the trend, although the impetus for enclosure was just as likely to come from the tenants.[18] The first reference to enclosures concerning property owned by Queens' is in 1779, when the college agreed to plans for enclosing property belonging to its living at Grimston in Norfolk;[19] but the movement was particularly strong in the early 19th century.[20] Though obviously beneficial, enclosures were extremely costly: an act of parliament was required for each one, and there might be other expenses in fighting for the college's own rights against other interested parties.[21] In 1809 Milner observed in a letter to Lord Hardwicke that 'the expences of some enclosures in which the College have been concerned, have proved so very unexpected and enormous, as to make the Society at present in no very good humour in general with Commissioners, Surveyors, etc. and also disposed to receive their reports and promises with considerable reserve'.[22]

Hardwicke was seeking to enclose the college's property at Little Eversden, where he was tenant, but was strongly opposed by Milner, who feared that he was trying to take advantage. Queens' managed to

---

[16]   *ibid.*, fos.38v, 80v – 81 (second pagination). It is not clear what these repairs were.

[17]   e.g. CB (1734 – 87), fos.2v, 8, 12v, 30v, 47, 81v, 83, 85v, 99, 101, 108v, and *passim*; CB (1787 – 1832), 15.1.1795, 14.1.1796, 11.1.1798, and *passim*; Box 95, 'A State of the Case of Queen's College 1715'; below, p. 313. On one occasion in the late 18th century the practice was further justified on the grounds that there were often no good candidates for fellowships anyway, Box 95, documents on Hughes bequest. Other financial provisions included transferring money from other college funds to meet immediate debts, and borrowing, CB (1734 – 87), fos.3, 4v, 7, 8.

[18]   Howard (1935), 109; Dunbabin (1986), 286 – 7.

[19]   CB (1734 – 87), f.106v.

[20]   c.f. Howard (1935), 154 – 6, 163.

[21]   For illustrations of the costs, see Book 8, fos.154, 157, 160, 166v, 172v, 175v, 180, 197, 211, 213v, 216v, 255. At the start of the 19th century the sums involved were several hundreds of pounds, but the amounts increased and in 1834 over £2,000 was spent on various bills for the enclosure of Oakington. Other references to enclosures can be found in CB (1734 – 87), fos.97 – 97v.

[22]   Milner/Eversden papers (1810).

secure terms more favourable to its own interests, but it was a vigorous dispute.[23] The governing body voiced concern at the high costs of enclosure in January 1818, and in the following year the senior bursar, Joseph Jee, commented on Milner's reluctance to accept proposals for the enclosure of Oakington until full discussions had been held with the Fellows and the tenants concerned. Oakington was enclosed, but not until many years after Milner's death, and at vast expense.[24] By the mid-1830s Queens' had incurred debts of over £10,000, arising principally from enclosures.[25]

The peak of the enclosure movement coincided with the Napoleonic wars, a time of great economic instability in Britain. High agricultural prices and inflation during the wars were welcome to landlords, but they were followed after 1815 by an acute depression which persisted until the 1830s.[26] Wartime uncertainty created a recognised need for more astute financial management at Queens'. In 1797 it was resolved that the senior bursar should henceforth always be chosen from among the resident Fellows, and some of the lesser accounts were transferred to the butler's care.[27] The position of college butler was by no means a menial one: John Sharp, butler at Queens' for over forty years until his death in 1783, was instructed in August 1777 to 'carry on the business of the Bursarship' under the direction of the president until the annual appointment of college officers at Michaelmas, because of a sudden vacancy.[28] The senior bursarship had formerly been held largely by rotation among the Fellows, but from the middle of the 18th century it became more usual for bursars to remain in office for two or three years consecutively.[29] It was not until 1827, however, that the senior bursar was instructed formally to keep copies of all letters written by him on college business, and of the answers he received.[30]

The wars brought about an increase in taxation. By tradition colleges had been exempt from national taxes in the early modern period, and specific clauses of exemption are contained in many parliamentary acts of the 16th and 17th centuries which levied subsidies from other sections of the population.[31] This custom was broken rarely, and only at

[23] *ibid.*; CB (1787 – 1832), 22.3.1810, 8.1.1811, 19.3.1811; Box 15/27, /38, /39, /39a; Milner (1842), 452 – 3.
[24] CB (1787 – 1832), 13.1.1818; Joseph Jee's letter book, entry of 13.9.1819; CB (1832 – 88), 1.2.1833, 23.4.1833, 2.7.1833, 11.10.1833; Book 8, f.255.
[25] *Report* (1874), i.165.
[26] Howard (1935), 109 – 111; see also Dunbabin (1986), 275 – 7.
[27] Box 102.
[28] CB (1734 – 87), f.102v.
[29] Book 22.
[30] CB (1787 – 1832), 9.1.1827. In practice, many letters were kept before this time.
[31] Shadwell (1912), i.86, 90 – 2, 95, 153, 155 – 6, 165, 167 – 8, 174 – 5, 182, 199 – 200, 273 – 4, 288 – 9, 293, 296 – 8, 305 – 9, 313 – 4, 321 – 2, 330 – 1.

moments of great need and national crisis, such as war,[32] particularly the Civil War.[33] In the later 17th and early 18th centuries colleges were subject to such duties as hearth, window and poll taxes; in general they were taxed more often after the Restoration.[34] Tenants were often granted rebates for taxes which they paid on lands leased from the college.[35] But by the early 19th century the principle of exemption would appear to have been abandoned, for Queens' was paying substantial sums of money in property tax, and for the new income tax introduced to pay for the French wars.[36]

By the beginning of the century the college was unhappy with its financial position, and several fellowships were sequestered at about this time.[37] At a meeting in January 1800,

> 'It having appeared that on account of various deficiencies in payments of debts due to the College, and other unforeseen circumstances, the Bursar had been obliged to borrow considerable sums of Money at legal Interest, The Master and fellows approved of the measure, and at the same time, directed that such further sums should be borrowed in the same way upon the credit of the College, as may be found necessary'.[38]

In 1810 Milner was empowered to sell off stock, the profits of which had been intended for college repairs, 'on account of the necessities of the College', and it was also decided that all renewal fines should be increased by 50%.[39] In 1812 the college's needs forced it to sell £1,500 worth of consols.[40]

The two decades which followed Napoleon's defeat in 1815 were difficult years for the college, as agricultural prices fell.[41] In 1818 the

---

[32] In general, see Howard (1935), 64; Cooper, iv.20 – 1. For Queens', see Searle, 157, 159, 234 – 6. James I levied feudal aids for the marriages of his son and daughter in 1609 and 1613 respectively, Book 5, fos.129, 146; Book 24.

[33] Twigg (unpublished thesis, 1983), 135 – 6, 176 – 7; above, p. 59.

[34] Shadwell (1912), i.281, 290 – 1, 332 – 3; Cooper, iii.314 – 5, 501; Howard (1935), 64 – 5; Book 6, fos.183v – 184; Book 7, f.37 and *passim*; Book 8, f.4 and *passim*. However, beer brewed by colleges for their own consumption was not subject to excise in the late Stuart period, Shadwell (1912), i.290, 316 – 8.

[35] e.g. Book 6, fos.137v, 141, 164 – 164v, 165v, 169, 171, 190v, 193v, 194, 205v, 210v; Book 7, fos.37, 38v, 39, 60 – 60v, 89. Henry James complained that Queens' tenants were gaining exemptions from the college, but passing the taxes on to their subtenants, Book 80, f.8.

[36] e.g. Book 8, fos.145v, 148v, 154v, 157v, 163v, 168v, 171v, 175v, 178 – 9, 181 – 181v, 184 – 184v. See also Howard (1935), 126 – 7.

[37] CB (1787 – 1832), 11.1.1793, 16.1.1800, 15.1.1801; Book 8, f.155. Over £1,800 was raised by this method between 1796 and 1802.

[38] CB (1787 – 1832), 14.1.1800.

[39] *ibid.*, 9.1.1810.

[40] *ibid.*, 28.11.1812.

[41] Howard (1935), 115 – 6.

1 Old Court, built 1448 – 9.

2A Old Hall in use for May Ball, 1913.

2B Old Kitchens, 1912.

3 Old Hall — detail of roof, as repainted by G. F. Bodley, 1875.

4 President's Lodge and Long Gallery, c. 1890.

5 President's Lodge and Long Gallery.

6 Interior of Long Gallery.

7 Interior of Old Library.

8 Walnut Tree Court, c. 1855/60.

9A Essex Building, as originally planned.

B Essex Building, as built.

10 Old Chapel, pre 1890.

11 New Chapel, before completion of decoration.

12 River Front, Le Keux, c. 1837.

13 Queens' undergraduates manning trams during General Strike, 1926.

14 Tied Cottages for College Servants on site of present Fisher Building.

15 Fisher Building when new.

16 Planning the Erasmus Building:
A Rejected design by S. Dykes Bower

B Original version of design by Sir Basil Spence.

governing body made reference to the need to renew leases on the best possible terms, because of the 'very great expenses of several Enclosures which have lately taken place, as also the many peculiar difficulties of the present times'.[42] But the depression reduced the ability of tenants to pay, and in the 1820s Queens' was much troubled by defaulters, and was forced to go to law on several occasions.[43] Non-payment and delays in payment of rents were among the factors forcing the senior bursar to borrow large sums at interest. The governing body had no option but to approve this, and in 1826 it allowed him to borrow as much as necessary up to a total of £1,500.[44] In 1827 it was necessary to reduce the charges for leases because of falling corn prices.[45] There had also been problems with tenants felling timber without authorisation.[46]

Various financial restraints were ordered. In 1821 suppers at the annual audit were discontinued; a year later, four vacant fellowships were sequestered, fellow-commoners' fees were raised, and the senior bursar was ordered to demand all outstanding debts owed to the college by its MAs.[47] In 1823, on account of 'the depreciation of the value of Money', some small scholarships maintained out of fixed rent charges were amalgamated, being no longer substantial enough to support students as they stood. In 1828 the college cut back on the number of feasts held.[48] The difficulties continued, largely due no doubt to continued enclosures: the last was not until 1839.[49] In 1833 the senior bursar was empowered to borrow up to £1,000, and in both 1843 and 1844 he was permitted to borrow up to £2,000 on the best terms he could find.[50] Queens' was not the only college to experience such problems; their causes were common to all.[51]

After the mid-1830s, agricultural prices began to pick up once more, but it had become apparent that colleges would have to protect themselves against any future depression, and that the customary arrangements whereby property was let on long leases were inadequate

[42] CB (1787 – 1832), 13.1.1818.
[43] ibid., 20.6.1821, 6.11.1821, May 1822, 11.10.1823, 14.1.1824, 15.1.1824, 6.10.1824, and passim. Between 1816 and 1818 Queens' was in dispute with a London tenant over the level of fines, and unauthorised subletting; Milner was anxious for a settlement without the trouble and cost of a legal action, although he was quite prepared to go to court if necessary, Book 36. In 1820 the senior bursar, Joseph Jee, noted the depressed agricultural situation, and predicted that rents would come in slowly, Joseph Jee's letter book, entry of 26.12.1820.
[44] CB (1737 – 1832), 11.10.1826.
[45] ibid., 3.3.1827.
[46] Joseph Jee's letter book, entry of 1.1.1820. This was a perennial problem, of course, and its appearance here may be no more than coincidence.
[47] CB (1787 – 1832), 27.4.1821, 12.1.1822, 31.5.1822.
[48] ibid., 17.1.1823, 17.10.1828.
[49] At Abbotsley, CB (1832 – 88), 1.6.1839.
[50] ibid., 11.10.1833, 27.5.1843, 4.5.1844.
[51] Howard (1935), chapters VII – VIII.

for such crises.[52] In 1845, therefore, the governing body declared itself

> 'impressed with the conviction that the present system of letting the college property by beneficial leases is highly injurious to the permanent interests of the college and . . . desirous of introducing in place of the said system the mode of letting upon rack rent with a view of gradually effecting the said object'.[53]

This was a radical step: rack renting — letting property annually — gave landlords much more flexibility from one year to the next so that they could adjust to changing agricultural conditions. It was not a new expedient, for Queens' had considered it during the Napoleonic wars, but doubts had been expressed at the time as to its legality, and it had not caught on.[54] Innate conservatism generally had also played its part, and the decision of 1845 notwithstanding, some long leases continued to be renewed; it was not until the 1860s that all leases were made to run out. Similar changes took place at other colleges at the same time.[55]

Queens' sought a complete overhaul of its financial arrangements, of which the change in its leasing policy was but one part. In February 1845, a month after the decision to introduce rack renting, a governing body committee comprising the president, senior bursar, and five senior Fellows, was formed to examine the college's accounts, 'and to consider whether any and what alterations can be made in the mode of keeping them'.[56] The committee's report, which was presented in May 1846, calculated the college's average annual expenditure (excluding extra-ordinary expenses) at about £2,300, and its average annual income from 'outside' receipts and customary rents (but excluding sequestered fellowships) at some £700 less. A new schedule of rents was drawn up in order to compensate for this, and part of the Fellows' dividend money was appropriated for college use.[57]

Other measures of retrenchment followed over the next few years. In 1848 the president and senior bursar were instructed to investigate all

[52] *ibid.*, 111, 116.
[53] CB (1832 – 88), 16.1.1845; Gray, 255; c.f. Howard (1935), 178 – 9.
[54] Box 95, 'for opinion of Dr Adams'. Howard (1935), 115, notes the gradual extension of rack renting in the late 18th century. Box 102 contains a draft of 1802 concerning the success of a new, and unspecified measure adopted with regard to the Oakington estate, which some senior Fellows had thought 'a dangerous experiment'. Could this have been rack renting?
[55] CB (1832 – 88), 13.1.1846, 8.1.1850, 14.1.1851, 13.1.1852, 11.1.1853, 10.1.1854, 15.5.1854, 9.1.1855, 12.1.1857, 13.1.1857; *Report* (1874), i.164 – 5. In general, see Dunbabin (1975), 633.
[56] CB (1832 – 88), 17.2.1845, and ?October/November 1845.
[57] *ibid.*, 2.5.1846. The appropriation of part of the money received under the Corn Rent Act, which usually went towards the Fellows' dividend, had already begun, *ibid.*, 15.1.1846, 17.1.1846, and see 14.1.1847.

payments authorised by college orders but not by statute, and any payments supposedly made on college orders but for which no orders could be found.[58] The result was merely a fixing of the president's allowances and expenses, but in January 1849 he and the senior bursar were authorised to liquidate the college's debt of £10,200 by any suitable means, and in January 1851 there were further reforms: monthly audits were introduced, and the senior bursar was forbidden to pay any bills until permitted by the auditors.[59] It was also admitted that the system of account-keeping had 'rendered it impossible for the Society to understand their real position'. A committee was therefore created for the joint purpose of simplifying the accounts and paying off the college's debts.[60] The scheme put forward by the committee in April 1851 envisaged debt repayment over a period of 22 years, with part of the annual rental income to be set aside for this purpose; over £1,000 had already been received from the sale of property in London to the London, Brighton and South Coast Railway.[61] Fellowships continued to be sequestered; some college stock was sold; money was borrowed from various college funds; and costs were cut piecemeal here and there.[62]

This seems to have had some effect. In 1875 the governing body congratulated itself on 'the self denial of its members', especially with regard to the running out of beneficial leases and the consequent diminution of Fellows' dividends from fine money. It now hoped to repay the debts to various internal funds from which money had been borrowed, and to raise the 'educational efficiency' of the college. Money was to be diverted from its annual income in good years for repayment of debts, and to create a reserve fund for new college buildings, for founding new fellowships, or new studentships 'in specific departments of study' — in 1856 money had been set aside from the rents 'for the encouragement of Hebrew learning amongst members of the College' — or for 'otherwise increasing the educational efficiency of the College'.[63] In 1876 it purchased a new estate at Fulbourn.[64]

---

[58] ibid., 13.1.1848. The names of nine MAs had been struck off the boards for not paying their bills on 12.1.1848.

[59] ibid., 10.1.1849, 11.1.1849, 15.1.1851. There were some smaller cost-cutting measures: feasts on the queen's birthday were discontinued; expenditure on the president's lodge was restricted; and the amount spent on the garden was cut, 15.1.1851, 16.1.1851, and see 13.1.1857.

[60] ibid., 15.1.1851.

[61] ibid., 3.4.1851. For examples of rents set aside, see 16.1.1852, 13.1.1853; see also 4.1.1860, 5.5.1866, 9.1.1868.

[62] ibid., 12.1.1854, 22.11.1854, 11.1.1855, 22.5.1858, 6.1.1859, 28.12.1875. Some of the measures were petty: servants' salaries were fixed, and a quarterly gratuity paid to an ex-porter discontinued. The college relented over the gratuity subsequently, but gave him only half of the sum he had previously received, 10.1.1856, 14.5.1856, 11.10.1856, and see 11.10.1855.

[63] ibid., 11.10.1856, 28.12.1875, and see 2.1.1877, 1.1.1878, 31.12.1878.

[64] Gray, 263.

Such confidence must have been inspired by the thriving condition of British agriculture between the 1840s and early 1870s, from which college incomes benefited enormously, but after the mid-1870s there was a severe and prolonged depression, persisting until the turn of the century.[65] Colleges had remained dependent on their landed property. Until 1858 their ability to sell their land was restricted by law, and for the rest of the century the proceeds of such sales had to be lodged with the Board of Agriculture, with the nominal aim of reinvestment in land.[66] Almost all of the income of Queens' in 1871, as recorded by the royal commissioners, came from land let at rack rent, and only a very small amount from stocks, shares, and other investments.[67] Some of the old beneficial leases had not yet expired — Queens' was one of only seven colleges still to have lands out on such leases — and the survey predicted a further rise in income as these fell in; the last was due in 1883. The great debts incurred by enclosures early in the century had by now been substantially reduced, but they were still not inconsiderable, and the commissioners' study also showed Queens' lying 12th in the list of colleges in terms of income, a far decline from its relative position in the 16th century.[68]

The depression brought about a sharp decline in the yield from rented land, and colleges overall did not recover their income of the early 1870s until shortly before the first world war; the worst period came in the 1890s. Although it has been claimed recently that the general effect was 'perhaps no more than a check to an earlier rapid expansion' and 'a blow to confidence', the consequences of the depression were serious enough, and the blow did not fall evenly upon the colleges.[69] The full effects upon Queens' have yet to be calculated,[70] but the college conclusion books offer some insights into the governing body's state of mind. There is no sign of any anxiety until 1880, when it was necessary to reduce rents, but the college had had to do this in 1879 too, and perhaps in previous years.[71] In 1883 a committee was established to 'draw up a form for the college accounts' and to enlist professional assistance for this if necessary. A new system of accounting, prepared

[65] Howard (1935), 112, 174 – 84, 200 – 215; Dunbabin (1975), *passim*.
[66] Howard (1935), 189 – 90; Dunbabin (1975), 631; Shadwell (1912), iii.247 – 78. Queens' sold 35 acres of land to Corpus Christi in 1867, Bury (1952), 63.
[67] *Report* (1974), i.163 – 4. The incomes from lands amounted to over £6,700; those from stocks and shares to over £200. Note how incomes had risen since the 1840s, thanks to rack renting and improved agricultural conditions.
[68] *ibid.*, i. 164 – 5, 203 – 6; see Dunbabin (1975), 633; see below, appendix 13. Queens' was 10th in terms of income among the 12 colleges which replied to the royal commissioners in 1851, *Report* (1852), 196.
[69] Dunbabin (1975), 644 and *passim*; see also Engel (1978); Dunbabin (1978); Howard (1935), 226 – 41.
[70] Archival material from this period at Queens' is still largely unsorted.
[71] CB (1832 – 88), 11.10.1880.

principally by the junior bursar, Ernest Temperley, received the college's approval in 1885.[72] But it was necessary once again to sequester fellowships to pay the college's contribution to the university required by the recent reforms, and to supply deficits in the scholarships fund, the income of which had been much reduced by the depression; the governing body was anxious to maintain student numbers, which were sure to fall off without the lure of entrance scholarships. This problem was at its most acute in the 1890s, and it was not until 1909 that Queens' felt confident enough to stop transferring money into the scholarships fund from other college funds, indicating thereby the revived prosperity enjoyed throughout the university in the years immediately preceding 1914.[73]

[72] ibid., 16.6.1883, 6.10.1883, 3.10.1885; see also 12.1.1889, and CR (24.1.1889), 151. According to Arthur Wright, Temperley spent 'eight hours a day of nearly every vacation' for 'several years' in reordering the accounting system, Wright (1889), 5. In 1883 the college was still deducting money from its pre-dividend revenues to pay off debts to the trust funds, CB (1832 – 88), 9.1.1883.

[73] ibid., 14.6.1887, 16.1.1888, 6.10.1888; CB (1889 – 1937), 10.10.1894, 14.1.1895, 11.1.1896, 21.4.1898, 19.6.1909; see also 13.1.1896, 11.12.1896, for other measures employed. The Cambridge Review's obituary for W. M. Coates, who succeeded Temperley as bursar, praised his skills in that office, and his good relationship with the college's tenants, and claimed that 'it was in no small measure owing to his wisdom in tact that in the darkest days of agricultural depression not one acre of land belonging to the College went out of cultivation or was thrown on the hands of the landlords', CR (25.1.1912), 209.

21

The college buildings
in the 18th and 19th centuries

By the 18th century, some of the college's buildings were already very old, and often in need of repair and renovation. In 1685 it was recorded that

'all the first Court was stripp'd, the Sparrs which in many places were very bad new lin'd, all the upper Windowes made new and regular. The great Gate alter'd the Gate-House and Regent-Walk [probably the main path across Old Court] new laid with Freestone the bow window in the Hall repair'd with Freestone, and new glass there, the Dialls new-painted, the Cripple [a gap through the wall] betwixt the library and the Master's Bedchamber made new; that vast Summer [horizontal beam] in the Master's study, on which all the Sparrs of that building lean (being rotted at both ends) supported by two great peices [sic] of Timber, a Cupola new made etc. all which make the moneth's accounts swell to soe great a summe'.[1]

In 1743 the *London Evening Post* reported that 'Last Saturday Morning some Part of the old Building of Queen's College in Cambridge, was blown down by the Violence of the Wind'.[2]

At the beginning of the 19th century the college commissioned a surveyor's report on the condition of the 17th century building in Walnut Tree Court and learnt that it was 'certainly in a very bad State of Repair' both internally and externally; the report recommended an extensive and costly programme of renovation. The addition of a third storey to the building in 1778 – 82, following a fire, had compounded the problems, for the structure had not been reinforced to take the extra weight of this and the heavy roof, which was forcing the walls outwards in places.[3]

---

[1] Book 6, f.221, cited also in Gray, 212.
[2] *London Evening Post*, 7.4.1743. This reference was kindly supplied to the college by Dr J. M. Black.
[3] Box 101, report of 1804; Box 101 also contains another, undated, report, probably from the early 1820s, on the state of the roof; see also CB (1787 – 1832), 17.1.1823; above, pp. 132 – 3; CB (1734 – 87), fos.103, 108v – 109; Box 95, documents concerning Hughes bequest.

In addition to making repairs, the college also thought of extending and improving its buildings. In the early 1730s the interior of the hall was completely remodelled to the design of James Burrough, a Fellow — and later master — of Caius. Burrough has been variously described as 'a designer of purely local importance' and an 'amateur architect',[4] descriptions which, though not untrue in strict terms, do not do him justice: he was far from being unskilled in his art. With James Gibbs, he had already been involved in designing the senate house, and he was later to undertake several other projects in Cambridge.[5]

Burrough designed in the classical manner popular at the time; in the hall at Queens', this took the form of the black and gold wainscoting, with classical pillars, which survives to this day.[6] It was a Roman classical style, and much admired by contemporaries. Robert Plumptre thought it 'neat and elegant'; the antiquary William Cole described it in 1742 as 'elegantly fitted up according to the present tast[e], and is by now much the neatest Hall in any of the University'.[7] It is usually suggested that a flat ceiling was inserted below the roof at this time, but the appearance of attic windows in the roof in Loggan's view of 1685 suggests that a ceiling was already in place.[8]

In 1702 the college had built a new wooden bridge over the river from Cloister Court, but in 1748 it was decided to replace this with another of modern design.[9] The existing bridge may have been in a poor state of repair, but it is more likely that it was pulled down because of the college's enthusiasm for fashionable innovation. A leading contemporary bridge-builder and designer, William Etheridge, was commissioned to design the new bridge, and his plans and model were submitted in 1748. The bridge was built in 1749–50 by James Essex the younger, son of the carpenter who had worked on the hall under Burrough.[10]

Similar bridges may still be seen in several parts of the country; Essex is said to have built others of the type in and around Cambridge, and to have called them 'mathematical' bridges, apparently because of their 'geometrical' style of construction.[11] The Queens' bridge attracted some attention, as it was clearly intended to do, and still does. In 1753 it was described as 'one of the most curious pieces of Carpentery of this kind in

[4] Summerson (1963), 188; RCHM, lxxx.
[5] Colvin (1978), 168–70; Brooke (1985), 170–4; Summerson (1963), 188; RCHM, lxxx.
[6] W&C, ii.46; RCHM, cxxi, cxxv, 171–3.
[7] Book 73, fos.62–3, quoted in W&C, ii.46. Other references to the work in the hall can be found in Book 7, fos.170v, 174v–178v; CB (1734–87), f.7v.
[8] I owe this observation to Robin Walker.
[9] Book 7, f.37; W&C, ii.55; CB (1734–87), f.43.
[10] Book 73, f.63; Book 7, fos.236v, 237, 238–238v, 242; Colvin (1978), 300; Ruddock (1979), 30–2; W&C, iii.541.
[11] Ruddock (1979), 35, and chapter 3, passim. The bridge has twice been rebuilt since to the same design, RCHM, lxxxix, 179.

England'.[12] The college's second bridge, from the Fellows' garden to the grove, was taken down in 1793 and its materials sold.[13]

The younger Essex also aspired to architecture. He had studied under Burrough, and was to carry out many projects in Cambridge in the classical style which he learned from him, although his real enthusiasm was for Gothic architecture.[14] The classical structure which Essex designed for Queens', and was erected in c.1756 – 60, was one of his earliest commissions.[15] The clunch building of 1564 – 5 between the river and Silver Street was said to be 'very much decay'd', and was pulled down in 1756.[16] The building which Essex designed and constructed to replace it was described by Robert Plumptre as 'useful and ornamental',[17] and the college no doubt needed to replace the accommodation that it had lost, but the desire for display seems to have been paramount. Essex's building, which stands today, is only one wing of the vast structure which he planned to build along the whole river front, and which would have meant the demolition of the 15th century riverside range, and probably of the long gallery; some 25 feet of the 15th century building were sacrificed for the wing which was completed.[18]

The design was popular: a contemporary guide book observed that 'when the whole is completed, it will make an exceeding grand front', but building seems to have come to a halt in 1760.[19] We do not know the details of the arrangements made for funding the project, but in January 1758 the college agreed to borrow money to pay for it, at a rate of interest not exceeding 4%; and in the same year the president, William Sedgwick, lent it £1,000 of his own money in return for an annuity.[20]

---

[12] Carter (1753), 186; Carter was mistaken over the date of the bridge's construction. A mid-18th century guide book described it as 'a curious structure', Wordsworth (1874), 394. Dyer described it in 1814 as 'a white curious bridge of wood', Dyer (1814), ii.161. It may have been painted at this time: the accounts of 1756 contain an entry 'for Painting the Rails at the Bridge', Book 8, f.10v. But Robin Walker informs me that oak (the wood used for the bridge) turns white when it oxidises; and the bridge's present colour is due to recent staining.

[13] W&C, ii.53; CB (1787 – 1832), 10.1.1793.

[14] Colvin (1978), 297 – 300; W&C, iii.541.

[15] The pulling down of the clunch building which preceded it on the site was certainly in 1756; and in May of that year the college ordered that 'an Agreement be made with proper Artificers to erect our new Building by Measure upon the best Terms we can procure', CB (1734 – 87), f.56v. The accounts contain references to work on the foundations of the new building in 1756, Book 8, fos.10v, 12v.

[16] Book 73, f.63, cited in W&C, ii.18. Perhaps it was this building which had been damaged by wind in 1743.

[17] Book 73, f.63; W&C, ii.18. The Royal Commission on Historical Monuments describes it as 'a full and unashamed architectural use of white brick', RCHM, ci.

[18] W&C, ii.14, 18; Wordsworth (1874), 394.

[19] Wordsworth (1874), 393 – 4. According to Plumptre, the exterior was finished before Sedgwick's death in 1760, Book 73, f.63; W&C, ii.18. Essex seems to have been paid off in January 1761, CB (1734 – 87), f.61v.

[20] CB (1734 – 87), f.57v; Book 73, f.63; W&C, ii.18.

But there was a massive increase in the college's annual expenditure in the financial years 1757/8 to 1760/1, largely caused by the Essex building; by the early 1760s it was accumulating very heavy deficits on its annual accounts.[21] In an attempt to clear these, there was a flurry of borrowing, and a larger number than usual of vacant fellowships was sequestered; the college also sold off 'useless Plate' in its possession.[22] Financial equilibrium was largely restored by the later 1760s,[23] but there can have been no question of continuing with Essex's design, and over a century elapsed before another major building was undertaken.

The Victorian period saw a reaction against the artistic values of the previous century. A speaker to the Cambridge Architectural Society in 1861 described 18th century buildings in the university, including the Essex building, as

'examples of the stately tasteless monotony and heavy grandeur of the period, and mentioned it as a cause for hearty congratulation that they wanted money as much in the eighteenth century, as we do in the nineteenth, and so were unable to complete their extensive plans for the so-called "beautifying" the university according to the eighteenth century rage for uniformity'.[24]

At the end of the 19th century J. H. Gray wrote of the 'incongruity' of the Essex building with the other architecture at Queens', and he described the insertion of a false ceiling in the hall as an act of 'barbarism'.[25] In 1845 the *Ecclesiologist* had commented on 'the paganizing mania of the last century' which had inflicted such damage on the hall and chapel.[26]

The alterations to the interiors of these last two buildings in 1846 – 7 were the fruit of this new artistic sentiment. The work in the chapel has already been described; in the hall, the false ceiling was removed in 1846 and some of the decoration repaired. The oriel window, which had been ornamented with coats of arms in stained glass in 1819 – 22, was restored in 1854 and new stained glass was inserted.[27] The restoration and decoration of the fireplace, including the addition of the surrounding tiles designed by several distinguished artists in the pre-Raphaelite

---

[21] Book 12; Book 8, fos.10v – 29; below, appendix 12.
[22] CB (1734 – 87), fos.58v, 59v, 60, 62, 65 – 65v, 70, 73, 74, 78v, 80v; Box 95, case of John Lloyd, 1769.
[23] Book 12.
[24] *Ecclesiologist* xxii (1861), 405.
[25] Gray, 220.
[26] *Ecclesiologist* iv (1845), 142. The first sign of the Gothic revival at Queens' is the library extension of 1804; I owe this point to Robin Walker.
[27] Above, p. 273ff; W&C ii.47; Gray, 257 – 8; RCHM, 172; Robinson and Wildman (1980), 27; CB (1832 – 88), 14.1.1847; *Ecclesiologist* xv (1854), 414; and see *ibid.* xx (1859), 212.

style, took place in the early 1860s, when a new tiled and stone floor was also laid; this was done under Bodley's direction. The redecoration of the entire hall in 1875, even down to the designing of new high table furniture, was carried out partly by Bodley and partly by William Morris; in its aesthetic direction, this work paralleled that undertaken in the chapel.[28]

These restorations and alterations were prompted entirely by changing ecclesiastical and aesthetic fashions. The college's first new building of the century, the Friars building of 1886, was the result of the urgent need for additional undergraduate accommodation, although its design was strongly influenced by the artistic sensibilities of its time.[29] The idea was first discussed formally by the fellowship in January 1885, when the resident Fellows were set to consider if it were 'desirable to add a new block of buildings to the College', and if sufficient funds were available for its construction. The scheme was approved in June, and by the end of the year a design had been chosen and building contractors hired.[30] The college chose W. M. Fawcett to draw up the plans: he was a local architect, and an active member of the Cambridge Architectural Society, who worked on numerous university, college and town buildings, including the master's lodge of St Catharine's opposite the main gate of Queens', which was built in 1875. In the same year, Fawcett restored the east front of Queens'.[31] His work was 'marked by strong common sense' and his buildings were 'always practical and straightforward, and . . . generally pleasing'. He built in traditional styles: there was nothing radical or disconcerting about his designs.[32] The only opposition to the plan came from the president, George Phillips, who was reluctant to lose his second private garden on the proposed site of the new building, but his acceptance was secured by giving him exclusive use of the Fellows' kitchen garden during his tenure, after which it was to revert to the Fellows.[33]

Although Fawcett built in an uncontroversial style, the Friars building was not universally appreciated. The *Cambridge Review* thought it would

[28] *RCHM*, 172; *W&C* ii.47–8; Thompson (1967), 15, 69, 86, chapter 3; CB (1832–88), 29.12.1874, 11.10.1875; *Ecclesiologist* xxiv (1863), 362; xxviii (1867), 381. The fullest account and description is in Robinson and Wildman (1980), 1–2, 27–8. Note that not all of the fireplace tiles were inserted in the early 1860s: those of the two queens were added c.1875. I owe this point to Robin Walker, who is sceptical about Morris' involvement in the hall restorations; it is to be hoped that his thoughts on this subject will appear in print.
[29] See above, p. 234.
[30] CB (1832–88), 17.1.1885, 13.6.1885, 3.10.1885, 15.12.1885.
[31] *Builder* (2.12.1909), 19; *Ecclesiologist* xxi (1860), 40, 90, and following volumes, *passim*; CR (28.1.1909), 205; Gray, 262; CB (1832–88), 16.5.1874, 30.12.1874, 15.5.1875. Robin Walker tells me that Fawcett was guided by Loggan's late 17th century view.
[32] CR (28.1.1909), 205.
[33] CB (1832–88), 13.6.1885, 10.10.1885; *Dial* (Easter 1938), 5–6.

'ever be an eyesore to lovers of the backs', the main fault being 'its want of proportion'. Fawcett's obituary in the *Builder* did not even mention it, though it did refer to his restoration work at Queens' in 1875.[34] It was much taller than the other college buildings, but its style was taken from that of the pre-18th century buildings, and its incongruity of scale was reduced by the construction of the large new chapel in 1889 – 91.[35]

The rapid numerical expansion of the college in the early years of this century made further undergraduate accommodation essential. As early as 1888 the senior bursar had been instructed to write to Bodley's architectural partnership asking for designs 'for completing the east side of the Walnut Tree Court', to include a new gateway, student rooms, and a tutor's house, the whole to be 'of an inexpensive character'.[36] Nothing came of the scheme at this time: although astute financial management had made the Friars building possible despite the agricultural depression,[37] the college was certainly not able to finance another large new building, and the opening of Friars had made the shortage of student accommodation less acute.

Another difficulty concerned the proposed site, which was occupied by the college's almshouses. These could not be disturbed without the approval of the Charity Commissioners, and the college made several attempts to secure permission to demolish the almshouses and provide bigger pensions for the almswomen in compensation, which was finally granted in 1911.[38] There is a hint of a guilty conscience in the contemptuous remarks made about the almshouses in some quarters: the *Cambridge Review* spoke of 'a mean row of almshouses'; the *Dial* described them as 'as plain and ugly as only almshouses can be'.[39] Even before the Charity Commissioners gave their permission, Queens' had already approved the plans for the site drawn up by C. G. Hare, who had taken over Bodley's architectural practice after his death in 1907.[40] The new building, which was opened in 1912, was named after the college's first president, and contained 26 sets of rooms for under-graduates, a bursary, clerk's office, and guest room; like the Friars building, it was designed in imitation of older styles, in order to blend better with the other college buildings.[41] The *Cambridge Review* had some small criticisms to make, but described the overall effect as a 'happy

---

[34] CR (7.11.1889), 52; *Builder* (2.2.1909), 19.
[35] Gray, 264. For the chapel, see above, pp. 277 – 8.
[36] CB (1832 – 88), 14.12.1888.
[37] Largely thanks to Temperley's financial reorganisation, CB (1889 – 1937), 12.1.1889; *Dial* (Easter 1916), 11; CR (24.1.1889), 151; Wright (1889), 7; Gray, 264.
[38] CB (1889 – 1937), 5.12.1889, 10.10.1896, 21.9.1907, 28.9.1907, 17.2.1911, 29.5.1911, 17.6.1911.
[39] CR (13.12.1913), 265; *Dial* (Michaelmas 1912), 145.
[40] CB (1889 – 1937), 20.6.1910, 27.4.1911; Wodehouse (1976), 91.
[41] CR (13.2.1913), 265.

combination of reverence for the past with care for the present and future'; and the building was described in the *Dial* as 'extremely handsome' in 1912, although another writer in the same magazine the following year thought it characterless.[42]

There was one respect in which the Doket building was radically innovative: it introduced baths to Queens'. Hitherto, 'we had a metal tub in front of the fire in winter with hot water in a large can which the bedder had put to warm'.[43] The new baths were extremely popular, although they were only open at restricted times: from 7 till 8.30 in the morning and 3 till 6 in the afternoon.[44] College facilities were modernised in several other respects at about this time. Electric lights arrived in 1899;[45] the college's eight earth closets, behind the Friars building and in the west walk of Cloister Court, were replaced with water closets in 1909.[46] In 1907 it was decided to install telephones in the porter's lodge, the president's lodge, and the senior bursar's rooms; and a private telephone exchange was installed in 1914, with extensions to most of the Fellows' rooms and a pay telephone in the Bernard Room.[47] Also in 1914 gas rings were fitted throughout most of the college, replacing stoves which burnt methylated spirits.[48] After centuries in which many of the college's domestic arrangements had remained almost static, the pace of change must now have seemed rapid.

---

[42] CR (13.2.1913), 265; *Dial* (Michaelmas 1912), 145; (Lent 1913), 177–8. There was also the complaint that some of the lower rooms received little light, *Dial* (Lent 1913), 183. In 1913 the college sealed an indenture with King's 'to allow access of light and air to the rooms on the ground floor at the north end of the Doket Building', (CB 1889–1937), 8.3.1913.

[43] A. H. Noble (MS), 3; see also MS 79, 57; *Dial* (Michaelmas 1937), 14.

[44] CB (1889–1937), 9.10.1912; CR (24.10.1912), 46; *Dial* (Michaelmas 1912), 163. A story circulated that when plans for the Doket baths were being discussed by the Fellows, 'one elderly Don objected strongly that they were an extravagance, quite unnecessary, since the men were only up for eight weeks at a time', G. H. Harrison: letter. Such tales are told of other colleges too.

[45] CR (19.10.1899), 29. There had been gas lamps since 1835, CB (1832–88), 24.2.1835.

[46] *Dial* (Michaelmas 1909), 298; MS 79, 25; A. H. Noble (MS), 3; above, chapter 17, n. 163.

[47] CB (1889–1937), 18.4.1907, 13.1.1914; *Dial* (Easter 1914), 352; CR (29.4.1914), 392.

[48] CR (29.4.1914), 393; *Dial* (Easter 1914), 352.

22

The college and the first world war

In the summer vacation of 1914 the college mission camp was held on the Isle of Wight. One of the students who attended was G. B. Harrison, who had just completed his first year in the college; Harrison recalls

'At that time the heir to the Austrian Empire was murdered. Laffan, the expert in these matters, took a very serious view of it. He said it would mean great trouble. We took it rather lightly as at that time it was not uncommon for Kings and persons on the continent to be murdered'.[1]

Laffan was knowledgeable on Balkan affairs and had visited Serbia before the war; he understood only too well the patterns of recent history, and the likely consequences of the assassination at Sarajevo.[2] Within a few weeks, as he had probably predicted, Britain was at war; in Laffan's words

'The tension of uncertainty was over, and the nation as a whole, with many regrets, but with the fervour of crusaders, applauded its rulers' decision to enter the lists and to forge again the sword of Britain for the cause of European liberties and international justice'.[3]

It was a view shared by most of his contemporaries at Cambridge and elsewhere, who believed, instinctively, that Britain was honour-bound to intervene against German aggression.[4]

War broke out during the vacation, and a large number of undergraduates joined up soon afterwards in the first flush of patriotic enthusiasm. The student population of Queens' in the Michaelmas term of 1914 numbered 107, scarcely over half that of the previous year.[5] At this stage it was widely believed that the war would not last long. The

[1]   G. B. Harrison: letter.
[2]   Harrison (1985), 56; Laffan (1918), 46.
[3]   Laffan (1918), 187.
[4]   *British Universities* (1919), 4 – 7; Marwick (1965), 44 – 53.
[5]   CR (30.10.1913), 56; (28.10.1914), 38. Fifty-two students had matriculated in 1913; 35 did so in 1914. About 50% of the university's undergraduates (including those who would have come up for the first time in 1914) were said to be involved in war work of some sort at this stage.

governing body, in its formal conclusions, paid the matter little attention before 1915.[6] Although the Quaerists and the college Classical Society are known to have suspended their activities in the Michaelmas term of 1914, other college societies tried to continue as usual. The St Bernard Society continued its programme of debates and concerts, and the Kangaroos, with only three members left, attempted rather pathetically to continue their meetings in the usual boisterous style.[7] The *Dial*'s editorial in the Michaelmas term issue urged its readers to 'try and keep going as much of the old collegiate life as is fitting and possible', and hoped to continue publishing throughout the war.[8] The character of the college OTC was said to have changed: 'Absence from parade is regarded as a heinous offence, discipline is strictly enforced, officers are treated with all due deference and are even saluted'. There was a great deal of lecturing and training, and most of the students were keen, but the complaint was made that

> 'whereas quite a fair proportion of the College have done their duty by enrolling themselves in our body, yet there still remains a very small number of men who, though physically fit, prefer to spend their afternoons more selfishly and less healthily employed, rather than to prepare themselves for military duties at a time when the Country's need for men of their education is most pressing'.[9]

An early indication to those at Queens' that the conflict would not be over by Christmas, as many had believed and hoped, came among the extracts from the letters and diary of O. H. Best, a Queensman serving at the front, which were printed in the *Dial*. Best's diary entry of 21st September noted: 'It appears that Kitchener is making preparations for a war of years, not months'.[10]

By January 1915 student numbers had shrunk to 76; by the following October there were only 49, and the number continued to decline steadily to 29 in the autumn of 1916, and a low point of 12 in the Michaelmas term of 1917 and the beginning of 1918. Elsewhere in the university the rate of decline slowed in 1917 and numbers began to

---

[6] The only conclusion of the governing body relating to the war in 1914 concerned university and college dues from those on active service, CB (1889 – 1937), 12.10.1914, and see 16.1.1917. There was a similarly slow reaction by the university: it was not until June 1915 that men serving in the forces were given any allowance for their time spent on active service towards their degrees, Roach, 'University of Cambridge', 287.

[7] *Dial* (Michaelmas 1914), 5, 26 – 8; SBSM, *passim*; Kangaroo Club minutes, 17.10.1914. The last minuted meeting of the Kangaroos was in May 1915, though it was claimed subsequently that the club continued to meet until October of the following year, *ibid.*, 1.11.1919.

[8] *Dial* (Michaelmas 1914), 3; see also (Lent 1915), 2.

[9] *ibid.* (Michaelmas 1914), 17 – 19.

[10] *ibid.*, 9 – 13.

increase in the following year; Queens' was behind the general trend, but it had 27 students in the Michaelmas term of 1918, 98 by the following term, and 186 in the summer term of 1919.[11] Most of the other college personnel remained, apart from the college clerk and Laffan, who also went on active service.[12]

Queens' also had to provide accommodation and other facilities to various bodies of outsiders. There were soldiers and refugees in Cambridge from an early stage,[13] but there does not seem to have been any military presence in Queens', other than the OTC, until the beginning of 1915, when a number of soldiers from various regiments were billeted there.[14] Fifty men from the Royal Army Medical Corps occupied the college lecture rooms on the west bank of the river, and the president's wife, assisted by her husband and the vice-president, set up a canteen for them. Mrs Fitzpatrick also invited the men 'in small groups to tea and a game of croquet', and C. T. Wood organised cross-country runs for them on Saturday afternoons.[15] The St Bernard Society decided unanimously to elect all members of the armed forces resident in Queens' honorary members.[16]

Billeting continued in the college throughout the war: Cambridge became a training centre for new officers and a regular stream of cadets passed through.[17] An article in the Dial in 1916 portrayed these young men

'shaking chocolate-coloured army blankets on the turf, coveying hot shaving-water across the court in capacious washing-basins, or, most horrible of all, careering round Walnut Tree Court in gas helmets'.[18]

In June 1917 the governing body declared itself happy to receive up to 12 wounded men unfit for active service, in reply to a government circular; and towards the end of that year the rooms on one staircase were set aside for members of American universities on leave in England from service in France. As late as 1919 – 20 the college reserved rooms for naval officers, on condition that they all matriculated 'and are under

[11] CR (27.1.1915), 150; (5.5.1915), 283; (20.10.1915), 35; (27.10.1915), 52; (19.1.1916), 143; (10.5.1916), 291; (18.10.1916), 34; (8.11.1916), 84; (24.1.1917), 170; (2.5.1917), 304; (25.10.1917), 56; (24.1.1918), 204; (31.1.1918), 222; (2.5.1918), 356; (25.10.1918), 54; (31.1.1919), 182; (9.5.1919), 290.
[12] CB (1889 – 1937), 6.10.1915, 2.5.1916, 19.6.1916; Laffan (1918); above, p. 299.
[13] See Keynes (1976), 181 – 7; Roach, 'University of Cambridge', 287.
[14] Dial (Lent 1915), 9 – 10; (Michaelmas 1937), 15; CR (20.1.1915), 134.
[15] Dial (Lent 1915), 9 – 10.
[16] SBSM, 16.1.1915, and see also 31.10.1914, 28.2.1916; Dial (Lent 1915), 23.
[17] Dial (Easter 1915), 5; (Michaelmas 1916), 25; (Lent 1917), 15 – 19; CR (3.3.1915), 230; SBSM, 4.3.1916, 7.6.1917; CB (1889 – 1937), 11.10.1915.
[18] Dial (Michaelmas 1916), 26 – 7.

general College discipline'.[19] The military presence made the college more overcrowded than ever: in 1918, according to C. T. Wood, the officer cadets were sharing four to a set.[20]

In general the cadets were made welcome in the college, but there was some tension between them and the few remaining students, who seem to have looked down on them. An article in the *Dial* in 1916 put the cadets' point of view:

'What is necessary is to point out to the modern wartime undergraduate, that we are not outsiders, that we can appreciate this place. How we wish the University would realise this, that in spite of our khaki, our mud and our weird drills, we remain English gentlemen, men who, but for the call of war, would — most of us — have been either here or at Oxford, or have been there in the days before the war. We do not know the case of all the undergraduates here at present, we do not criticise their position, but we ask them to remember what we are and to treat us as such'.[21]

In June 1917 a heated argument broke out between the St Bernard Society, representing the undergraduates, and the Fellows over allowing the cox of the cadet's rowing eight to wear the college first May boat colours on the day of a race. The students were opposed to this, because the cadets were not members of the college; but the Fellows instructed the cadets that they might wear any colours they chose. The St Bernard Society debated whether the senior members had such authority in this matter, and it was 'clearly manifest that the House was enraged at what was considered the unlawful actions of the Fellows', but no further action was taken, for term ended on the following day, and the matter was apparently forgotten over the long vacation.[22]

This incident is just one aspect of a much broader desire to maintain as much of normality as was possible, difficult though this was. Normal academic life had been disrupted from the start, although the college seems not to have been particularly alarmed by the war situation before 1915. In January it implemented precautions against air raids in compliance with government orders: the chapel bell and college clock were silenced, and lights extinguished or at least diminished at night. The *Dial* commented: 'Within College the nights are very dark and silent. Dons occasionally collide around dark corners and mutually apologise. Undergraduates collide and don't apologise'. A college fire

[19]   CB (1889 – 1937), 16.6.1917, 20.11.1917, 10.3.1919, 29.4.1919, 2.3.1920, 11.5.1922; *Dial* (Easter 1919), 4. See also Howarth (1978), 25.
[20]   *Dial* (Michaelmas 1937), 16.
[21]   *ibid*. (Michaelmas 1916), 26.
[22]   SBSM, 7.6.1917.

brigade was also established, and the buildings were insured against damage from air raids.[23] Also in 1915, Queens' began to convert some of its stock into war bonds.[24] Financially, the situation was serious enough, although the position at Queens' is not yet clear, and the passing of emergency legislation in 1915 allowing colleges to amend their statutory restrictions to enable them to adjust to new financial conditions was clearly beneficial. In 1917 the governing body recorded its appreciation of the work of the senior bursar, Andrew Munro, 'in times of exceptional difficulty'.[25]

There were some wartime economies: the menu was reduced early in the war, and consumption of coal was restricted by not lighting unnecessary fires, which led to one Fellow appearing in hall in a greatcoat in the winter of 1914. In 1915 it was decided that towels were no longer to be provided by the college; and in 1916 termly charges on undergraduates were raised specifically to counter the price rises due to the war.[26] There were no serious shortages until 1917, when the government introduced voluntary food rationing: in response, Queens' instituted 'meatless days' on Tuesdays and Fridays, directed that no meat would be supplied at breakfast or lunch, and restricted the provision of other basic foodstuffs. A plot of land in the grove was dug for planting potatoes.[27] In 1915 the St Bernard Society had decided patriotically not to have beer served at its meetings, following the king's example in giving up alcohol; lemonade was substituted.[28]

College societies continued as best they could, but with increasing difficulty. The St Bernard Society continued to meet until 1917, but with diminishing frequency and small attendances, despite the presence of the cadets; the quorum for the society's business meetings had been reduced by half in 1915.[29] Debates were mostly on traditional and uncontroversial themes to divert attention from the war — such as 'this House believes in ghosts', 'the ideal life is that of a tramp', and 'low-lying countries are not conducive to a high type of character' — although

---

[23] *Dial* (Lent 1915), 11 – 12; (Easter 1915), 4; CBN (1889 – 1937), 5.6.1915, 19.6.1916, 16.6.1917, 25.4.1918.

[24] CB (1889 – 1937), 9.7.1915, 6.10.1915, 18.1.1916, 16.1.1917, 24.1.1917, 25.4.1918, 11.10.1918.

[25] *CR* (3.3.1915), 232; Roach, 'University of Cambridge', 287 – 8; CB (1889 – 1937), 12.10.1917. See Howard (1935), 241 – 2, for a discussion of the finances of St John's during the war.

[26] *Dial* (Michaelmas 1914), 30; CB (1889 – 1937), 11.10.1915, 11.1.1916.

[27] Marwick (1965), 191 – 200; Reports (1914 – 47), facing p. 1; *Dial* (Lent 1917), 4.

[28] SBSM, 10.6.1915.

[29] The last debate was on 10.3.1917, the last business meeting on 18.10.1917; the society revived in October-November 1918, SBSM. For the lowering of the quorum, see *ibid.*, 6.2.1915. In October 1914 two of the society's officers who were absent on war service were continued in their posts, but in January 1915 the members realised that this situation could continue no longer in view of 'the continuance of the war and the fact that no immediate end to the war was in sight', *ibid.*, 17.10.1914, 23.1.1915.

in 1916 there was a motion proposing that the war had 'revealed the existence of grave defects in the English scheme of education'.[30] The sports clubs also kept going for a while, but falling numbers made this increasingly difficult, and there are no signs of any sporting activity after the beginning of 1917.[31] The Christian Union struggled to survive, and though it lasted through certainly to the autumn of 1917, it may well have been at its last gasp by then.[32]

The undergraduates were intensely patriotic. In the early part of the war the *Dial* printed first-hand accounts of Queensmen serving at the front. One of these pieces, in 1915, relayed the experiences of a Queensman who had been captured, laying great stress on German barbarity. Other war news and casualty lists also featured in the magazine.[33] In its Easter term issue of 1915 the *Dial*'s editorial recognised the particular horrors of this war, and that no end to it was in sight, but it stressed that there was no alternative:

'If, at this University, men use religion and culture as a stalking-horse to preach peace at any price, Teutonic brotherhood and the "sparing" of Germany . . . — then remember the *Lusitania*; Remember that our own lads from Queens' were tortured by the foul gas at Ypres. Remember Justice'.[34]

A year after the outbreak of war, the *Dial* admitted that the early months had been

'a time of feverish excitement, indecision and bewilderment, much flag waving, little coherent thought and a blind groping to adapt oneself to a nightmare made reality'.

Now, people were 'more moderate in hopes and fears', but it was considered the duty of those who remained at home to keep civilised life going.[35] For a while, this was done, and in the spring of 1916 the *Dial* reported the continued success of the St Bernard Society, speculating

[30] *ibid.*, 7.11.1914, 14.11.1914, 5.12.1914, 30.1.1915, 13.2.1915, 27.2.1915, 30.10.1915, 13.11.1915, 27.11.1915, 29.1.1916, 12.2.1916, 12.3.1916, 18.11.1916, 10.3.1917, 22.11.1918.
[31] *Dial* (Lent 1915), 25 – 8; (Michaelmas 1915), 3, 16 – 17; (Lent 1916), 10 – 11; (Michaelmas 1916), 4, 37; (Lent 1917), 4, 21 – 2; QCBC minutes.
[32] *Dial* (Michaelmas 1915), 20 – 1; (Lent 1916), 11; (Lent 1917), 20; (Easter 1917), 22 – 3; (Michaelmas 1917), 9. The college mission appealed for more support in 1916, *ibid.* (Michaelmas 1916), 35.
[33] *ibid.* (Michaelmas 1914), 9 – 13; (Lent 1915), 5 – 9; (Easter 1915), 9 – 11; and *passim* for wartime years.
[34] *ibid.* (Easter 1915), 2 – 3.
[35] *ibid.* (Michaelmas 1915), 2.

that the war had somehow enhanced the college's corporate life.[36] A year later, the ideal had disintegrated:

'It is a curious fact, but not altogether inexplicable, that the smaller grows the number of men in residence, the greater is the hetero- geneous mass of scandals, jealousies and factions which stultify most of the current activities in the College . . . For what is it in these times to be President of such and such a Society or Captain of such and such a Club? It should be a position of utility, not ornament, and those who hold such positions should remember that we are all of us only here under sufferance, and that our proper course is to do our work of continuation humbly and in due consciousness of our own weakness, and above all in a spirit of mutual toleration and concession'.[37]

The college's senior members were no less patriotic.[38] Laffan's *The Guardians of the Gate*, a history of modern Serbia written in 1917, was typical of its time in portraying the Balkan conflict as a struggle between liberty and nationalism on the one hand, represented by Serbia, and the expansionist policy of the tyrannical central powers. The struggles of the Serbian people and their nation were portrayed in heroic terms; and the atrocities committed by the Austro-Hungarian forces and their allies following the invasion of Serbia were recounted with deep horror and condemnation.[39] Another Queens' clergyman, C. T. Wood, wrote in more general and spiritual terms: he believed that the war had brought

'a supreme challenge to repent . . . it now stands revealed what civilization means with God left out; what is the certain outcome of human greed and falsehood and materialism'.[40]

R. H. Kennett, in a university sermon in November 1916, rejected the view of the

---

[36] *ibid.* (Lent 1916), 9.
[37] *ibid.* (Lent 1917), 1 – 2. Note also C. T. Wood's remarks in 1916 on factionalism, above, p. 251. By 1917 there was throughout the country a growing war-weariness and questioning of the conduct of the war, Marwick (1965), 210 – 17.
[38] Although the evidence is of a rather different and more personal nature.
[39] Laffan (1918), *passim*.
[40] Wood (1916), 30 – 1. Wood's faith was not shaken, but in the light of the war's influence on popular attitudes towards death and the afterlife, he subsequently wrote a book, *Death and Beyond*, affirming his convictions gained from the Bible and 'reinforced . . . by many instinctive expressions of belief contained in letters from the Front'. He noted that although Christian thought had abandoned the old-fashioned belief in an everlasting hell, 'with it went a great deal more which we cannot afford to lose, especially the sense of the horror of sin', Wood (1920), v, vii.

'small minority . . . who affirm that the misery and bloodshed of this war is the direct consequence of our sins. Given German arrogance, German treachery and German ruthlessness, bloodshed and horror needs must be. But is it not certain that the bloodshed and the horror need not have been so great, and the thousands of those who have died for their country might have lived to serve it, if considerations of party politics had not prevented reasonable preparations being made for the threatened struggle?'.[41]

T. C. Fitzpatrick served as vice-chancellor from 1915 to 1917. In his speech summing up the events of the academic year 1916 – 17, he declared that

'No words of mine can express adequately our sorrow for this continued sacrifice, and our thankfulness that Cambridge men have played so noble a part in this long war for right and freedom. How great this part has been is to some extent indicated by the honours that have been won'.[42]

Such remarks were unfortunately open to misinterpretation as glorying in the slaughter. Yet Fitzpatrick was without doubt a sincerely compassionate man.[43] At the dedication service for the college's war memorial in 1921, an undergraduate recorded him being 'filled with emotion as he read the list of names' of the dead.[44] Four hundred and nine of the college's students (including those who had been expecting to come up for the first time in the autumn of 1914 but had instead joined up) served in the war: 67 were killed in action or died of their wounds, and another seven died of illness or accident; 121 were wounded, some more than once; ten were taken prisoner.[45] The proportion of deaths among Cambridge men who served as a whole was roughly similar: the officers — men from the élite social classes — suffered losses well above the average.[46] The shadow of this tragedy was to hang heavy over the survivors who returned to Cambridge when peace returned, and upon the new generation of undergraduates too young to have fought.

[41] CR (15.11.1916), 108.

[42] CU Reporter (2.10.1917), 38; he had made similar remarks in his speech of 1916, ibid., (2.10.1916), 38.

[43] For example, his support of fundraising on behalf of the Armenians in Turkey, and for the Syria and Palestine relief fund, CR (17.5.1916), 305; (24.5.1916), 319 – 20; (1.11.1917), 75. In 1919 he lent the local branch of the NSPCC the use of the president's lodge for its annual meeting, Granta (8.5.1919), 29. See also pp. 230, 282, n. 89, 342.

[44] Diary of H. C. Alexander.

[45] Carey (1921), 291 – 306, facing p. 536. This list includes only those who were students at Queens' at and after the outbreak of war, not former students.

[46] Winter (1985), 93 – 4, 97 – 8.

23

Aspects of college society, 1919 – 1939

Modernity

Student numbers rose sharply in Queens' at the end of the war, as those whose university careers had been interrupted returned. 'Like all other colleges we are crowded out', wrote the college's correspondent for the *Cambridge Review* in November 1919, 'and many of the first year live so far away that we only know of them through the residence list'.[1] Numbers remained high in 1919 – 20, but then began to fall slowly, approaching their pre-war level once more before the middle of the decade.[2]

The *Dial*'s editorial in its Michaelmas term issue of 1918 hoped for the return of the old college life, and that

> 'the broken strands of tradition will be gathered up and, interwoven with the fresh and better experience, will form the old fabric, yet new; a thing purged, but not to destruction'.[3]

Elsewhere, the student press emphasised the deliberateness of the return to tradition. In November 1919 the *Cambridge Review* reported that at Queens'

> 'Revival and reconstruction are going on zealously; old rules and minute books are being consulted everywhere for precedent and custom . . . In short the college seems to have settled down to general college routine, aided by the creditable efforts of the senior years'.[4]

College sports clubs and societies began to revive in 1918 – 19, although some took a while to emerge from their wartime hibernation. May Week returned to the social calendar in 1920, when Queens' held a May ball — a highly self-conscious return to pre-war style — and in 1922 the college sent a rowing eight to Henley for the first time, encouraged by the

---

[1] *CR* (7.11.1919), 74. There had been only one evening hall in 1918, but two halls were reintroduced in the following year, CB (1889 – 1937), 11.10.1918, 6.10.1919.
[2] *CR* (24.10.1919), 24; (22.10.1920), 23; (21.20.1921), 25; (20.10.1922), 22; (26.10.1923), 22.
[3] *Dial* (Michaelmas 1918), 2; see also (Michaelmas 1919), 1.
[4] *CR* (7.11.1919), 74 – 5.

Fellows, who probably saw it as another device to lay the ghost of the war.[5]

Normal university and college activities were thus resumed, but the 'tone and tempo' of the pre-war period could not be so easily recaptured.[6] Looking back on this time nearly twenty years later, C. T. Wood recalled that the students who had served in the war were

'at the same time eager to find out and keep old College ways and traditions, and yet very suspicious of all the pre-War generation and its beliefs'.[7]

One undergraduate who returned from wartime service, G. B. Harrison, has described post-war Cambridge as

'a strange mixture . . . Most of the undergraduates were adults; the freshmen direct from school were a timid minority. Moreover, there was a new breed, hitherto unthinkable — the married undergraduate who was not likely to take kindly to the old rules such as reporting himself to the college if he had not returned to his own home by 10 p.m., or requiring a chaperone if he wished to entertain a girl in his own room . . . Elderly dons and college porters were bewildered by the change and how to treat married students, especially those who had children'.[8]

The *Dial* commented in the summer of 1919 that the contemporary undergraduate was 'a much older and wiser person' who took his time at college seriously and was more hardworking and job-conscious, 'so that there is not much room for the old idea that one is here to meet people and enjoy oneself'.[9]

The old and new outlooks were bound to clash. A letter to the *Dial* in the Easter term of 1919 complained of the difficulty in getting men to join the Boat Club with so many studying hard for their examinations:

'I know that there are many men who are still suffering from the

[5]   *Dial* (Michaelmas 1918), 27; (Easter 1919), 22 – 4; (Michaelmas 1919), 32 – 7; (Easter 1920), 23 – 5, 30; (Michaelmas 1920), 18; (Michaelmas 1922), 2 – 3, 24 – 6; CR (5.3.1920), 261; *New Cambridge*, 25.1.1919, 1.2.1919; QCBC minutes, 28.2.1922 (and see 8.5.1922). Queens' had sent a scratch four to Henley in 1912 (Michaelmas 1912), 131; (Michaelmas 1913), facing p. 269. In 1921 there was a complaint that margarine was still supplied with commons instead of butter, which it had supplanted during the war, *Dial* (Michaelmas 1921), 44.
[6]   Howarth (1978), 21 – 2.
[7]   *Dial* (Michaelmas 1937), 16.
[8]   Harrison (1985), 120.
[9]   *Dial* (Easter 1919), 8.

ministrations of the Hun, and that it has been difficult in two terms to reach a pre-war standard, — but it is up to us now to re-establish and carry on the best sporting traditions of the College'.[10]

The ex-servicemen had gone by the mid-1920s, and college society in the decades between the wars retained many of the characteristics of the Victorian and Edwardian periods; but a steady flow of new social attitudes and ideas continued to challenge many traditional values. Students were more self-consciously modern than ever: the St Bernard Society debated the merits of 'the good old days', 'the Victorian age', 'Victorian morals', 'the present age', and 'old tradition', invariably coming down in favour of the values of the present day.[11] It supported unconventionality, living dangerously, and broadmindedness; and it discussed the achievements of civilisation, over-regulation and standardisation in modern life, modern journalism, modern architecture, and contemporary popular culture.[12]

The arrival of the motorcycle and motor car were prominent among the material manifestations of modernity; bicycles had been part of undergraduate life since the 1890s.[13] By the end of the 1920s motor vehicles were becoming a serious problem: they were numerous and noisy, and students tended to drive dangerously. *Varsity*, a student newspaper which commenced publication in 1931, contained many stories of accidents involving cars driven by undergraduates during the early 1930s.[14] Regulations to restrict the use of motor vehicles had first been introduced in 1909, and in 1925 the university authorities banned their use before 12.30 p.m. and after 8.30 p.m.; the rules were strictly enforced.[15] In October 1930 Queens' decided that only third-year men should be allowed to keep motor vehicles in Cambridge, a move which met with the support of the *Dial*; but in June of the following year all undergraduates were refused permission. Queens' was one of only five colleges enforcing a total ban at that time, although many of the others restricted permission to men from higher years.[16] Banning was a much-debated issue: it gave rise to an absurd letter of discontent to the *Dial* in 1933, in which a disgruntled athlete urged that since motor cars were not allowed, the Amalgamated Clubs should devise a scheme enabling

[10] *ibid.*, 29–30.
[11] SBSM, 14.1.1922, 4.3.1922, 31.10.1925, 6.3.1926, 29.10.1933.
[12] *ibid.*, 14.2.1920, 19.2.1921, 8.10.1921, 18.2.1922, 28.10.1922, 19.1.1924, 2.2.1924, 14.2.1925, 27.10.1928, 24.11.1928, 18.10.1930, 30.1.1932, 4.3.1933, 4.3.1935.
[13] Queens' built its first bicycle shed (for 48 bicycles) in 1909. In 1933 it required all students to have their name and college stamped on the frames of their bicycles, CB (1889–1937), 19.6.1909, 19.6.1933.
[14] *Varsity, passim*. I do not know of any such accidents involving Queensmen.
[15] Parker (1983), 165; Howarth (1978), 63; McGowan, 'Memories' (MS), 15.
[16] CB (1889–1937), 7.10.1930, 22.6.1931; *Varsity*, 7.11.1931; *Dial* (Michaelmas 1930), 3.

sports players to avoid 'the arduous bicycle ride or the somewhat lengthy tramp from the last bus stop to the Barton Road ground', suggesting the creation of a turning point for buses so that the bus route could be extended, or even a special college bus.[17]

One very noticeable clash between traditional and modern values occurred within the student body in the 1920s: it is referred to in one social history of the period as 'the long-standing war between the hearty and the aesthete'.[18] The origins of the conflict in Cambridge did indeed go back a long way — probably to the time when athleticism had first risen to prominence — but the aesthete was a new breed, not simply non-athletic and intellectual. Aestheticism was one aspect of a new enthusiasm for modern, avant-garde artistic and literary forms which arose during the decade, an enthusiasm which is evident in student magazines of the period, including the *Dial*.[19] More than ever, it seems, students felt the urge for display: aestheticism was expressed primarily in new and flamboyant styles of dress and the cultivation of 'arty' eccentricities.[20] One of those who fell under its spell for a while was Gilbert Harding, an undergraduate at Queens' in the mid-1920s, who recalled 'going through the awful phase of reading *fin de siècle* poetry' and buying 'a cloak with green silk lining and a slouch hat', the effect of which 'was to make me look like a replica of an advertisement for Sandeman's Port'. As a device to gain Harding a reputation for eccentricity and aestheticism the clothes failed, for nobody paid them any attention; and so 'I changed my tactics and affected a cloth cap', which was then 'the summit of eccentricity'.[21]

Aestheticism was deliberately at variance with the sporting ethos, and aesthetes and hearties held each other in contempt. The merits of their different ideals were the subject of some discussion among undergraduates. In 1925 the St Bernard Society debated a motion 'That this House does not applaud undergraduate attempts at aestheticism', which is of interest more for the arguments invoked than the result (the motion was carried by 20 votes to 14).[22] The proposer laid great stress on aestheticism's effeminacy, and speakers on both sides tended to concentrate on the question of dress, despite attempts by some participants to direct attention to the underlying mentality and ideology of aestheticism. Aesthetes were also attacked for their intellectual

[17] *Dial* (Easter 1933), 28 (and see *ibid.*, 27).
[18] Graves and Hodge (1971), 118.
[19] For illustrations of these changing tastes, see Howarth (1978), 69 – 78.
[20] e.g. *ibid.*, 61.
[21] Harding (1953), 44.
[22] SBSM, 14.11.1925. Other related motions were also debated: 'That the value of athleticism has been overestimated' (defeated 19 – 13); 'That the Intellectual gives more to the world than the mere Athlete' (carried 19 – 14); 'that the English have too little regard for intellect' (carried 22 – 15), *ibid.*, 27.10.1923, 12.2.1927, 11.2.1928.

snobbery, narrow outlook on life, and excessive individualism, all of which were felt to run counter to the athletic ideal.

In 1932 a defence of aestheticism appeared in the *Dial*. It was critical of fraudulent or over-extravagant aesthetes, but made no other concessions: a genuine aesthete, it was argued, appreciated beauty, 'and if he sees beauty where more ordinary people do not, then that is no discredit to him'. Once again, it was necessary to rebut the charge of effeminacy:

'all men are more or less effeminate, and it is no fault of theirs if they happen to be more so. Nor is it any reason to consider them inferior to other individuals. Further it has been observed that a faculty for or interest in art and effeminacy often go together'.

It was only natural, therefore, that

'many "aesthetes" may shew signs of a like for brighter colours in their dress as a woman does. Male dress is after all rather dull, and it is probably only a fear of being called effeminate or of making oneself conspicuous that deters men from adopting something more colourful.'

The article concluded with a plea for tolerance of individualism and non-conformity:

'It is probably better to try to be different, even if for no other motive, than to try to be always the same, always to do the correct thing, always to live in constant fear of dropping a brick'.[23]

The question of aestheticism had been raised in an article in the *Dial* in the previous term in the broader context of 'college spirit'. The article's author distinguished two principal trends of feeling in college life which he attributed to the influence of the public schools, where men learnt only 'to be one of a herd', and, in consequence, came up to Cambridge either totally imbued with this spirit or in violent reaction to it: they either

'soak themselves in the athletic cult . . . and thank Heaven that they no longer have to go to chapel; or else they scoff at all games . . . laugh at the idea of the college being a united body, and take a delight in saying what a rotten college it is'.

[23]   *Dial* (Lent 1932), 20 – 5.

The author argued that both types were slaves of the public school mentality, and that a more mature, considered compromise between extremes was needed:

'The college can only exist satisfactorily as a body of free individuals, living freely and individually, but finding the satisfaction of their social needs in the college community'.[24]

The college community

This conclusion was perhaps a forlorn effort to resurrect the Victorian collegiate ideal, parts of which had been eroded long since by growing student numbers and changing social fashions. The college was a close community still: many of the old Fellows remained and maintained the old familial pattern. But for the new generation of post-war undergraduates, some of them seemed figures from the remote past: one undergraduate of the early 1920s described C. T. Wood as 'a typical Victorian', almost as if a separate species. Though the same student thought J. H. Gray 'a dear old man and very wise', he also observed that 'most of the Queens' youth appear not to appreciate him'.[25] Several of the leading figures of the pre-war fellowship died in the early 1930s,[26] but 'their memories remained green' to the new generation of Fellows which succeeded them and continued to pursue their ideals.[27]

Despite the generation gap, there does seem to have been a genuine affection between students and dons for the most part.[28] When C. T. Wood took his BD degree at the Senate House in 1920

'A considerable contingent of Queens' men witnessed, or rather participated in the ceremony, which was enlivened by the unfurling of a banner — inscribed with what was apparently the Hebrew equivalent of "He's a jolly good fellow", and a cascade of balloons and pennies'.[29]

The only recorded exception to this pattern — and then only temporarily — was the novelist T. H. White, an undergraduate at Queens' in the mid-1920s:

[24] *ibid.* (Michaelmas 1931), 17 – 20.
[25] Diary of H. C. Alexander.
[26] T. C. Fitzpatrick (1906 – 31); J. H. Gray (1879 – 1932); R. H. Kennett (1888 – 1932); Andrew Munro (1893 – 1935). Arthur Wright, elected in 1867, had died in 1924.
[27] E. A. Maxwell, 'I Remember' (MS), 2; and in conversation.
[28] The evidence is limited, but all that there is — in the form of diaries, reminiscences, articles in the *Dial*, and society and club minutes — suggests this strongly.
[29] *Dial* (Michaelmas 1920), 2.

'My tutor was L. J. Potts, whom I disliked to the point of rage for about a year. It took me all that time to discover that he was going to be the great literary influence in my life, as well as being the most noble gentleman I ever met'.[30]

Potts encouraged White to become a creative writer when an undergraduate, and they remained lifelong friends.[31]

The custom of calling on the president and some of the other Fellows at least once a term after dinner in hall on Sundays was continued, and remained important. Sometimes there might even be breakfast or lunch parties. One undergraduate, after having lunch with J. H. Gray one Sunday, spent most of the afternoon in his rooms, 'and reaped the benefit of his fire, while reading Pickwick'.[32] Such gatherings consisted mostly of conversation: C. T. Wood, who was said to have been 'always prepared to offer counsel and cocoa to anyone who cared to see him', was known for telling ghost stories; when visiting A. D. Browne (elected Fellow 1921), the main topic of conversation was rowing.[33] R. G. D. Laffan is known to have encouraged parlour games on one occasion, and is the only Fellow known to have paid calls on students in their rooms; there is even an example of his paying a meeting of the Kangaroo Club 'an impromptu visit', when he 'livened the conversation by means of his inexhaustible store of perplexing and highly intellectual Limericks for half an hour'.[34]

Other customary forms of social intercourse between the two groups included the dons' debates in the St Bernard Society, an annual feature of the society's calendar. The subjects which they debated tended to be broad questions concerning modern society, or the state of education at Cambridge.[35] They seem to have remained enthusiastic about college sports: A. D. Browne, who as we have seen was a great rowing enthusiast, put his scientific skills at the service of the sport in 1932 when he took a slow-motion film of the college boat to analyse the mechanics of rowing, and also fitted apparatus within the boat to measure vibrations.[36] J. A. Venn (elected Fellow 1925; president

---

[30]   Quoted in Warner (1967), 35.
[31]   White (1984), 5; and *passim* for their collected correspondence.
[32]   The quotation is from the diary of H. C. Alexander; other references to the custom can be found in *ibid.*; Maxwell (MS), 1; McGowan (MS), 12 – 14; Bibby 'Reminiscences' (MS), 149; Harding (1953), 38.
[33]   McGowan (MS), 13 – 14. The quotation is from Harding (1953), 52.
[34]   Diary of H. C. Alexander; Kangaroo Club minutes, 14.2.1920. This surely indicates Laffan's insecurity and wish to be liked by students, see above, p. 232; below, p. 350.
[35]   CR (5.3.1920), 261; SBSM, 6.3.1926, 5.3.1927, 11.2.1928, 24.11.1928, 23.11.1929, 18.10.1930, 30.1.1932, 4.3.1933.
[36]   *Varsity*, 23.1.1932. For other illustrations of his enthusiasm for rowing, see McGowan (MS), 13 – 14; Harding (1953), 52.

1932 – 58) had worked with his father, the Caius mathematician John Venn, before the first world war on the design and construction of a cricket bowling machine, which bowled out the great Australian batsman Victor Trumper and other members of the Australian team when they tried it out in 1909.[37] C. M. Sleeman (elected Fellow 1912) used to go with undergraduates for an early morning swim in the river.[38]

Such interests and activities continued to maintain some community spirit, despite the pressures of change and size. Lesslie Newbigin, who came up in 1928, recalls that 'Queens' was a small college and it was easy to form friendships', but the sense of community must have been hindered by the fact that many undergraduates had to live out: all first years did so, and many second years, until the situation was eased by the opening of the Fisher building in 1936.[39] Both a physical and an institutional focus for college life were needed. The St Bernard Society had formerly fulfilled several of the functions of a JCR (Junior Common Room) committee, but had never been truly representative of the student body as a whole, although it had assumed that rôle at times.[40] In 1926 the governing body decided 'that there be a Junior Common Room', and that the Bernard Room (now also known as the Erasmus Room) should be adapted for that purpose.[41] This was in response to undergraduate calls for a common room, and it had also been suggested that the St Bernard Society should move into the old chapel; the society recognised that it did not represent all shades of opinion in the college, and gave up the room voluntarily.[42] The new common room was not very large, but the new Fitzpatrick Memorial Hall, opened in February 1937 on the other side of the river and created out of the old college lecture rooms, contained two JCRs — one a reading room, the other a games room — and remained in use until the early 1970s.[43]

This physical improvement was paralleled by an institutional shift. In 1927 the *Dial*, noting that the refitting of the Bernard Room met an old need, observed:

---

[37] Sales brochure (1909) in college library (unclassifed MS); Annan (1955), 287 and n. 16.

[38] *CR* (8.5.1931), 388. Gilbert Harding gained a different impression of Sleeman, feeling that he was nervous of students and 'could hardly wait for the end of term, when he would set off for the Alps and forget all about us', Harding (1953), 38.

[39] Newbigin (1985), 9; Harding (1953), 40; McGowan (MS), 3, 7, 9; Maxwell (MS), 1. Scholars were given rooms in college, e.g. Bibby 'Reminiscences' (MS), 137 – 8. For the Fisher building, see below, pp. 371 – 2.

[40] Above, pp. 242, 248, 250, 320.

[41] CB (1889 – 1937), 11.12.1926. The room was 're-furnished with arm-chairs, writing and tea-tables, carpets, a telephone box and a letter-rack. Tea and after-dinner coffee can be taken there', QC (1926 – 7), 2.

[42] SBSM, 16.10.1926, 26.10.1926, 21.1.1927, 22.1.1927, 12.3.1927.

[43] *Dial* (Lent 1937), 4; Browne and Seltman (1951), notes to plate 124; see also below, n. 45.

'we have been provided, in an incredibly short time, with all the amenities of a club smoking room. We should like to say thank you very much to the Committee of Dons who have done this for us, while we are confident that the undergraduate's standpoint will be competently represented under the scheme whereby the Committee of the United Clubs are responsible for the management of the room'.[44]

The United Clubs were far more representative of student sentiment than the St Bernard Society had been; but by the end of the 1930s there was a widespread call for further reforms in this direction. In 1939 about 150 students signed a petition calling for the establishment of a 'Representative Committee'. Their arguments were printed in the *Dial*: it was felt that as the college grew, its common social life was being destroyed; that 'cliques' had become too powerful; that there was insufficient contact between dons and students, between students of different years, between those who did and did not play games, and between those who did and did not work hard. The 'Representative Committee' was intended to counter this: it would centralise interest in the various college activities and give everyone a chance to participate in college life. It would be part of the United Clubs, since these were at the centre of college life; it would have control of the *Dial*, be closely linked with the college mission, and would revive the St Bernard Society; it would also help to inaugurate practical reforms, where nothing was being done because of student apathy.[45]

The governing body's reaction to these proposals is not recorded, and the outbreak of war soon afterwards made such questions irrelevant for the time being, but the scheme marked another important step towards a more autonomous, self-regulating student community. There are further signs of students' self-assertiveness in their complaints and suggestions concerning college catering. In 1927 the *Dial* published an undergraduate complaint about the allegedly shoddy dress of waiters in hall, who were said to be 'clad in lounge suits and soft collars', and the author of the complaint called for tails and stiff shirts. The college apparently made some changes in response, and, probably encouraged by this, a further complaint appeared in the following term concerning

---

[44] *Dial* (Lent 1927), 3 – 4.
[45] The college Socialist Club was involved in this call, but we do not know if it was the prime mover, *Dial* (Easter 1939), 10 – 12, 33. The call for reform was vague: one immediate practical proposal was that there should be a common room where students could 'go and talk (instead of whispering away among a lot of newspaper readers), play darts and have drinks and tea'; this suggests that the second common room in the Fitzpatrick Hall was not yet a games room, see above, n. 43.

the 'frayed and soiled' tablecloths, and calling for cork mats instead.[46] More serious was another letter to the college magazine in 1927 which advocated the formation of an undergraduate kitchen committee to consult with the head cook in order to relieve the monotony of the menus; both the cook and the steward were said to be sympathetic to the proposal in theory, but it was argued that it would be impractical, and the scheme does not seem to have come to anything.[47] In 1933 the *Dial* complained about compulsory hall, asking for permission to sign out; only evening meals were supplied in hall, and these were all paid for in advance.[48] In 1936 a kitchen committee was suggested again as a link between producers and consumers.[49] There is no known response to either of these two appeals. But there are no signs of any agitation against gate regulations, where battles had been fought and won before the first world war, and would be fought again in the 1960s: students might grumble about the restrictions, but most probably climbed into college when they came back late rather than pay a fine.[50]

Student life

The social composition of the undergraduate body remained relatively stable. After the first world war there was some state and local authority assistance available to the less wealthy, but this was still very limited. There was some expansion in the size of the student population immediately after the war, but relatively little thereafter.[51] During the inter-war decades Oxford and Cambridge took a higher proportion of students from the public schools of the Headmasters' Conference — there were fewer than 200 of these schools — than from the entire state system; indeed, the proportion from the former only fell below 50% in the early 1970s. Most boys whose parents could afford the fees could get in to Oxford and Cambridge at this time.[52] There has been much generalisation on these matters, but no detailed study of the social backgrounds of Cambridge undergraduates during the inter-war years

[46] *Dial* (Michaelmas 1927), 26; (Lent 1928), 38 – 9.
[47] *Dial* (Lent 1927), 52; Harding (1953), 39. According to Harding, food at Queens' was easily the best in the university in his time.
[48] *Dial* (Easter 1933), 27; for methods of payment, see e.g. Bibby, 'Reminiscences' (MS), 137 – 8; Harding (1953), 39; Maxwell (MS), 1.
[49] *Dial* (Lent 1936), 62; and see also (Easter 1936), 36 – 7.
[50] There is one reported example of a student spearing himself in the stomach on the spikes of the railings when climbing in, *Varsity*, 25.2.1933.
[51] Mowat (1968), 207, 210; Simon, *Educational Revolution*, 39, 56, 73, 80 – 1, 157 – 9, 218, 253; c.f. Roach, 'University of Cambridge', 292, 306; Howarth (1978), 64 – 8.
[52] Simon, *Educational Revolution*, 272 – 4; Branson (1975), 119 – 20; see below, appendix 16. Only 1.5% of the country's 18 – 20 age group were at a university (ancient or modern) in 1919 – 20, Branson, *loc. cit.*.

has yet been undertaken. Although C. T. Wood claimed in 1937 that many more students at Queens' were now helped by scholarships and financial grants of different kinds, and wrote of the gain to the college of having students from a greater variety of schools, there is no evidence of any significant social shift there.[53]

There is no doubt that life continued to be hard for many boys from poor backgrounds who were lucky enough to gain admission. The college's reserve fund for poor students was maintained, although it is not clear how often it was called upon.[54] One undergraduate in the 1930s has recorded that it was possible to collect scholarships and other money from a variety of sources at the same time, because there was no central account of cumulative awards, but this practice does not appear to have been widespread.[55] Abba Eban was only able to come into residence in 1934 because he had won a Kennett Scholarship in oriental languages which gave him 'the princely sum of £110 a year'.[56] T. H. White had to work as a private tutor for a year after leaving school before he could afford to come up, and had to return to tutoring in the vacations. At the end of his first year he won a college exhibition and shortly afterwards was recommended to the college for financial assistance 'on the grounds of his ability, industry, and economical habits'. When White was taken ill with tuberculosis and forced to intermit his course for a year, some of the college's Fellows clubbed together to raise enough money for him to go Italy to convalesce.[57] Gilbert Harding secured an outside scholarship, but this was never enough: he had to earn extra money by guiding tourists during the vacation, and resented not being able to visit the theatre or cinema as much as his wealthier friends; he could not afford to go to the college's May ball.[58]

There was no stigma attached to being dependent on grants and scholarships — college awards had great academic merit and were a mark of distinction — and both White and Harding were members of one of the college's leading clubs, the Cherubs. Harding, on his arrival at Queens'

'was mainly concerned with wondering what to say if people asked

---

[53] *Dial* (Michaelmas 1937), 16.
[54] CB (1889 – 1937), 15.7.1926, 28.2.1933, 7.12.1934, 8.10.1935.
[55] Bibby, 'Reminiscences' (MS), 137. But the government axe wrecked his plans to stay and do research, *ibid.*, 178; Bibby, 'Courtship' (MS), 13.
[56] Eban (1978), 14.
[57] Warner (1967), 33 – 4, 36, 37 – 8; White (1984), 252; Crutchley (1980), 18. Queens' later introduced improved medical facilities: from 1936 there was a college nurse; and in 1939 a health insurance scheme for students was started, CB (1889 – 1937), 26.11.1936, 5.12.1936; CB (1937 – 63), 5.12.1938, 27.2.1939; Reports (1924 – 39), February 1939.
[58] Harding (1953), 35 – 6, 39 – 40, 45 – 6, 54, 65 – 6. If Harding did overspend, then it was in order to keep up with the expected Cambridge style.

335

me why I was not wearing an old school tie. In those days, my school did not possess one. Even now it is pleasant to remember the relief I felt when, after a week or two, it became clear that nobody cared sufficiently about my lack of tie to make any comment at all'.[59]

The social ethos remained the same: Cambridge continued to incorporate social outsiders into its style and values. Abba Eban writes of 'a built-in defect — an élitist principle that had produced a society with no cross sections, no variety of shades and levels, so that reality could soon be lost in the sheltering ease', though in compensation, it provided a broad intellectual and cultural range.[60]

The 1920s often appear to have been a decadent age, but this impression is heightened by contrast with the world war which preceded the decade, and the great depression which concluded it. Certainly it is hard to draw any such conclusions concerning Cambridge society. It was in many ways an age of display, but this only confuses the issue. Oxford and Cambridge in the 1920 were 'two main hubs of advanced recreational fashion: they were not merely suburbs of London, as they afterwards became'.[61] Much of the evidence is subjective, and must be treated with care. For example, R. H. Kennett's remarks is his university sermon in May 1929 that 'The age in which we live in characterised by an almost feverish eagerness to grasp temporal pleasure, to make life yield its maximum of material enjoyment', could be a clergyman's Jeremiad from any period.[62] Undergraduate accounts tend to stress the fun and frivolity of life, rather than the work. An editorial in the *Dial* in 1928 admitted that 'The May Weeks are purple patches', but its description of the 'far more typical' aspects of student life comprised:

'the games of cricket and football, the wet days on the river, tea-parties with crumpets and Chelsea-buns, Bridge played until the small hours and then giving place to talk, the bedder's voice as we turn over in bed and decide to cut a lecture'.[63]

These are the aspects which memory recalls in later life: Lesslie

[59] Bibby, 'Reminiscences' (MS), 136 – 7; White (1984), 230; Harding (1953), 36 – 7, 51.
[60] Eban (1978), 15.
[61] Graves and Hodge (1971), 118 – 9. For some impressions of Cambridge life during the inter-war decades, see Howarth (1978), chapters 1, 4.
[62] CR (31.5.1929), 509 – 10. The two sides to the social life of Cambridge students are well summed up in this entry in H. C. Alexander's diary in June 1923: 'Last night the grove with fairy lights and Chinese lanterns in the trees was the prettiest thing in Cambridge but this morning the menials were swilling down the sick in Queens' Lane . . . and clearing up the crockery chucked out by the gallant drunk'.
[63] *Dial* (Easter 1928), 2.

Newbigin remembers that in his first year 'I did almost everything except work'; Gilbert Harding wrote that

'Whenever I try to remember what I liked most about Cambridge, I find myself desperately trying to fight through the conventional images; yet precious memories persist. Punts and gramophones on the river; bathing in Byron's Pool or loafing and sunbathing at the university bathing sheds; breakfast with other people, either in their rooms or mine; interminable talks, sherry parties, midnight gatherings'.

He regarded his time at Cambridge as 'the happiest three years of my life'.[64]

Some students certainly took their pleasures seriously. There was a call in the 1930s for Queens' to hold May balls more frequently: at that time they were held irregularly, whenever it was thought safe to take the financial risk, which was usually every three years or so. A letter to the *Dial* in 1933 thought that the annual May Week concert, a more serious event which that year had been attended by only one quarter of the college, should be given less frequently and instead there should be more May balls: 'Why should Queens' give a May Concert chiefly for the benefit of outsiders when fellow men are desirous of some other form of amusement?' Following the success of the 1937 ball, the *Dial* repeated this call, arguing that 'The status of a College is chiefly dependent on whether it holds an annual Ball or not'.[65] It would be rash to suggest that such views were typical: looking back over the college since his arrival in 1900, C. T. Wood wrote in 1937 that students in the post-war period took work more seriously than their predecessors, and he felt that fewer now came merely for social advantage.[66]

College societies proliferated in the early 1920s, most of them new rather than revivals of societies which had lapsed during the war.[67] The enthusiastic rush to form new societies resembles that of the late Victorian period, when they had first begun, and in 1923 the *Dial* observed, lightheartedly: 'A feature of this Michaelmas Term has been that no new Society has sprung up among us'.[68] They included a science club, agricultural study circle, dramatic society, history society, medical

64 Newbigin (1985), 8; Harding (1953), 36, 41. c.f. the diary of H. C. Alexander, where the working hours are recorded; more evidence of this kind is needed.
65 *Dial* (Easter 1933), 28 – 9 (and see (Lent 1934), 4); (Easter 1937), 25 – 8.
66 *Dial* (Michaelmas 1937), 16.
67 The only recorded revival is the Classical Society (1922), *Dial* (Michaelmas 1922), 2.
68 *Dial* (Michaelmas 1923), 1. When the Medical Society was established in 1926 the *Dial* found this regrettable, apparently because it felt that there were already enough societies, but it conceded that the growing number of medical students in the college justified the new society, *Dial* (Michaelmas 1926), 34.

society, and 'Query' society.[69] The activities of the Dramatic Society (1922) were confined to play readings and some acting out of scenes in students' rooms; there was talk of a full scale production in the hall, but this did not apparently occur.[70] The Query Society (1930) aimed 'to incorporate anything of educational value' within its activities and heard papers, and sometimes held debates on a wide variety of scientific, artistic, political, religious and other subjects.[71]

The societies began to fail in the 1930s, and by the middle of the decade many of them seem either to have closed down, or could no longer take the trouble to send reports of their activities to the college magazine. In 1933 the Scientific Society was reported to be at a low ebb.[72] The History Society was in difficulties at the same time, but effected a temporary revival by reconstituting itself as the Erasmus Society and broadening its range to include 'general discussion evenings' rather than just listening to academic papers. In the short term the change was successful, but by 1935 the society's future was again in doubt, though it managed to pull itself up again later in the year and continued to meet regularly until the war.[73] The St Bernard Society was less fortunate. Its decline had first been noted in 1929, when the *Dial* reported low attendances due to the 'many counter-attractions in the Lent Term to occupy people's Saturday nights'. It effected a revival in the following year by reducing the number of meetings; but during the early 1930s concern was repeatedly expressed at the indifference of the college to debates. In 1934 the freshmen's debate had to be abandoned owing to 'the grim determination of this year's freshmen to work all day and most of the night'. The usually popular dons' debate had also to be abandoned that year, and no debates at all were held after 1935.[74]

Why did the societies go into decline at this time? There may be some connection with the simultaneous rise of interest in politics — some socialists in Queens' thought the St Bernard Society flippant, for example.[75] A more significant reason may well have been the growth of

[69] *ibid*. (Lent 1922), 40, 43, 45 – 6; (Easter 1922), 34 – 5; (Michaelmas 1922), 2; (Michaelmas 1923), 29; (Lent 1924), 26; (Michaelmas 1926), 3 – 4; (Michaelmas 1930), 36; (Lent 1931), 23 – 4. The origins of the History Society are unclear, but it was in existence in 1922, diary of H. C. Alexander; *Dial* (Lent 1922), 41.
[70] *Dial* (Lent 1922), 40; (Michaelmas 1923), 29; (Lent 1924), 26.
[71] *ibid*. (Michaelmas 1930), 36; (Lent 1931), 23 – 4.
[72] *ibid* (Lent 1933), 33.
[73] *ibid* (Michaelmas 1933), 26 – 7; (Lent 1934), 21 – 3; (Lent 1935), 42 – 3; (Lent 1936), 51 – 2; History Society minutes, 27.10.1933, 6.2.1935, 6.2.1936, and *passim*.
[74] *Dial* (Lent 1929), 38; (Michaelmas 1930), 31; (Lent 1932), 31; (Michaelmas 1932), 22; (Lent 1934), 21; (Michaelmas 1934), 26; (Michaelmas 1935), 42; (Lent 1936), 46 – 7; SBSM, 21.11.1934, 14.11.1935, 27.10.1936, 17.11.1937. The concerts survived longer, and some attempts were made to revive the society through other activities.
[75] Bibby, 'Reminiscences' (MS), 164.

rival attractions and amusements in the town. The theatrical scene in Cambridge was more lively than in the 1920s, and there was the great advance of the cinema in the early 1930s: by 1936 there were ten cinemas in the town. The traditional forms of college-based entertainment could not hope to compete with these attractions.[76]

The college's clubs were determined to resurrect their pre-war glories, although there was some opposition — almost certainly official — to their revival in 1919.[77] The Kangaroos persisted in their customary vein: their minute books for the early 1920s display a somewhat smug, self-confident vulgarity, an urge to show off, as well as the fashionable affected *langueur* indicated in this 1922 minute: 'we went to bed feeling that life could still be enjoyed if only one went the right way about it'.[78] The Cherubs followed suit: 'Over beer and sandwiches we had many a merry meeting which always ended up in rowdyism. We were, therefore, somewhat unpopular with the college authorities'.[79]

Queens' was 'on the whole, a fairly quiet college' in the 1920s, with little ragging,[80] but there were sporadic outbreaks of rowdiness. The 'occasional habit of bread-throwing' in hall continued, and a St Bernard Society concert in 1932 was 'spoilt only by the disgraceful conduct of some hearty at the back, who considered that it enlivened the proceedings to shoot bread-pellets all over the hall'.[81] There was some vandalism. A circular from the junior bursar issued apparently at some time during the 1930s complained that:

> 'Considerable damage has been done to certain rooms in College through the playing of darts. Undergraduates are reminded that games which may cause damage must not be played in College rooms'.[82]

In 1939 a Queens' student was sent down as the result of an incident in which furniture had been thrown through the window of the provost's lodge in King's.[83]

The traditional 'rag' on November 5th each year, when under-graduates smashed street lights and engaged in running battles with police and university officers, remained a feature of the university

---

[76] Howarth (1978), 159–60. Note also this entry from the Kangaroo Club minutes, 9.11.1929: 'The meeting did not gain its full strength until rather later than usual, owing to the attractions of various dance-halls in the town'.
[77] See Kangaroo Club minutes, 6.2.1919; cf. C. T. Wood's remarks in 1916, above, p. 251.
[78] Kangaroo Club minutes, 20.5.1922, and *passim*.
[79] Harding (1953), 51.
[80] *ibid.*, 47–8.
[81] Maxwell (MS), 1; *Dial* (Lent 1932), 30–1.
[82] MS u/c-students.
[83] *Varsity*, 11.3.1939.

calendar until the 1950s; it was boisterous rather than violent, although it must have been rather rough. Students caught participating in these riots had been gated before the war, and the same penalty was presumably applied afterwards.[84] Disrespect for the police was common. In 1920 H. K. Cassels, an undergraduate of Queens', was reported for riding his bicycle at night without lights. The police account ran:

'I said "You have no light, Sir" and as he did not take any notice whatever I said "Stop". He did not do so and I ran and got in front of him and stopped him. I said "I called on you to stop". Cassels addressed Sergt. Dilley, who was there, and said "Did he say Stop?" Dilley said "yes". Cassels then said "You *are bloody liars*". He refused to give his name, wished I would lock him up and eventually gave me his card'.

Later that night he was stopped by another policeman, though again he tried to dodge past, and 'refused for nearly 10 minutes to give his name and address'.[85] In 1933 a student in the college lost his foundation scholarship 'in consequence of a confidential communication received from the Director of Public Prosecutions'.[86]

These should be regarded as isolated occurrences, perhaps; but there are indications of a worsening in student behaviour — at least, if the minute books of the Kangaroo Club are any guide. These show that by the early 1930s, the general tone of the club had descended to a very low level: the minutes had become vulgar and crude rather than witty; and its activities were more riotous and destructive than ever. The tutors often had to intervene to require meetings to disperse, and on occasions during the 1930s stronger measures were necessary to stop the club's behaviour from getting too far out of hand: in April 1932 both the Kangaroos and the Cherubs were gated for two weeks by the tutors for lighting a bonfire in one of the courts (one of their regular amusements). In 1933 the tutors put out a warning notice following an incident in which a number of objects, including some pieces of masonry, had been thrown from Queens' into the garden of the provost's lodge at King's; this observed that

'Recent Saturday nights have been marked by a certain amount of disorderly behaviour and noise at a very late hour. We have to warn members of the College that, should such disturbances continue, it

[84] In general, see Parker (1983), 142, 166–7; for Queens', see Harding (1953), 48; McGowan (MS), 16; above, p. 263. For 1950s examples see diary of J. B. Geyer. The problem seems to have persisted until at least 1960, GB, 19.4.1960.
[85] Letter inside TB (1895–1924).
[86] CB (1889–1937), 26.4.1933.

will, to our regret, be necessary to prohibit private or club dinners or to send individual gentlemen out of College into lodgings'.

This threat does not seem to have been taken very seriously, for it had no apparent effect on subsequent behaviour in either the short or long term. In November 1936 several members were gated for the rest of the term after an incident which saw a large number of objects, principally crockery (the smashing of which was almost a weekly ritual) thrown out of a college room into Silver Street; a woman passing by was struck on the shoulder by a coffee cup, and had to be dissuaded by the head porter from calling the police. In 1937 the club's annual dinner was banned by the tutors.[87]

There are isolated examples of the college tightening up its discipline, though their significance is hard to assess. In 1922 the governing body decided that no student should be allowed to come back into residence if he was more than one term in arrears in paying his bill; but in 1932 students were liable to rustication if their bills were unpaid by the division of term. In 1933 it was ordered that no more than one college sports team be permitted to visit Oxford in any one term, and no more than one team from Oxford was to come to play against Queens'; and also that 'in any arrangements made for a match with an Oxford College, the home College shall have the power to decide the hour by which the visiting team shall start on the return journey'.[88] In 1938, though, the college regulation that students' orders for wines and spirits must be countersigned by a tutor was abolished.[89] It may have been concern to maintain discipline that saw new tutorial procedures laid down in 1928, whereby the two tutors were to see all freshmen; all students were to be divided between them; they were to share responsiblity for student discipline with the dean; and were to meet with him and the president weekly to discuss any matters concerning students.[90]

Politics

Immediately after the end of the first world war, there was a vigorous reaction in Cambridge against pacifists and critics of the war; but there was also an equally strong determination to ensure that such a war should never happen again, and the League of Nations was supported

[87]   Kangaroo Club minutes, 23.4.1932, 14.5.1932, 11.2.1933 (and inserted copy of tutorial notice on following page), 21.11.1936, 25.11.1936, 13.2.1937, and *passim*.
[88]   CB (1889 – 1937), 9.10.1922, 5.12.1932, 31.5.1933.
[89]   CB (1937 – 63), 31.5.1938.
[90]   CB (1889 – 1937), 21.7.1928.

enthusiastically.[91] A Cambridge branch of the League of Nations Union was formed in 1919, and R. G. D. Laffan was one of its supporters.[92] Laffan had taken a strong line against the actions and ideals of the central powers during the war, but he was no less concerned for a just peace, and in a sermon in the college chapel in 1924 he bemoaned the fact that after the war Europe had

'met the naïve enthusiasm of the German people for a just peace with vindictive disbelief in their honesty and is now punished by the general wretchedness of Europe and having raised up in Germany a militarist and profiteer class'.[93]

Two other Fellows, C. M. Sleeman and C. T. Wood, were said to have had distinctly anti-war sentiments at this time, the former having recently moved across from an anti-pacifist position; T. C. Fitzpatrick though was of a different temper, with a strong belief in the necessity of serving one's country.[94] In 1922 a letter to the *Dial* complained that the university OTC was training with artillery and machine guns, which implied that nothing had been learnt from the experience of the war.[95]

Such attitudes are perhaps not likely to have been widespread, although it is hard to tell. Undergraduate society returned to its old, comfortable conservative attitudes. Students' main political enthusiasms during the 1920s were 'hostility to Bolshevism, suspicion of the motives of trade unions and Labour politicians, and a belief in the continuing utility and virtues of the British Empire'.[96] The St Bernard society continued to support conservative governments, to uphold typically conservative principles such as free trade and hereditary peerages, and to reject nationalisation of industries.[97] Though the society's debates were often poorly attended, and those on political themes especially so, there is no suggestion that the views which were affirmed there were unrepresentative: most undergraduates held instinctive political opinions, and probably saw little reason to debate

[91] Howarth (1978), 20 – 1, 23 – 4.
[92] SBSM, 18.10.1919.
[93] Reported in the diary of H. C. Alexander.
[94] *ibid.*.
[95] *Dial* (Michaelmas 1922), 39 – 40. There is an account of one student's experiences in the OTC in McGowan (MS), 4.
[96] Howarth (1978), 141 – 2. The St Bernard Society rejected the view that the British empire had passed its zenith in 1923, SBSM, 8.12.1923.
[97] SBSM, 22.11.1918, 1.11.1919, 24.1.1920, 22.1.1921, 28.1.1922, 25.11.1922, 24.11.1923, 17.1.1925, 28.11.1925, 2.2.1929, 9.3.1929; *CR* (7.11.1919), 75; *Dial* (Lent 1921), 28; (Michaelmas 1922), 20. The St Bernard Society did decide in a formal debate to continue to take the socialist *Daily Herald* in 1920, SBSM, 16.10.1920. In 1922 the History Society heard a paper on the House of Lords and the British constitution, which was said to have provoked much discussion, *Dial* (Lent 1922), 41.

them. But there was much informal discussion of political issues, nonetheless.[98] There were some socialist sympathisers in the college in the early 1920s, but there were in a very small minority, and most students had little time for them.[99]

The students' instinctive political beliefs and class outlook were amply demonstrated during the General Strike of May 1926. Many of them became strike-breakers, joining others from similar social backgrounds in helping to run essential services. They were genuine volunteers who

> 'accepted the prevailing middle-class assumption that this challenge from the trade unions put their whole way of life at risk. Many of them took it for granted that they were going into battle for a noble purpose: to protect the nation, the liberties of the people, and constitutional government from attack by wicked men. For though few believed that the miners were exactly wicked, they were believed to be misled by wicked men, by leaders who wanted to smash up everything that England stood for, and plunge us into anarchy'.

They were thrilled to be doing something out of the ordinary and exciting, and some even relished the prospect of a rough-house.[100]

Over half of the undergraduates at Cambridge registered for emergency duty, and their rôle in breaking the strike was a significant one.[101] Volunteers from Queens' were sent to Hull to operate the trams and to unload ships, and to London to drive buses; there was keen competition for places on these missions.[102] Gilbert Harding, an undergraduate at that time, thought that the strike

> 'came as a great boon to a large number of rather stupid undergraduates who were viewing the coming examinations with misgiving and alarm. I often wondered if there would have been so many volunteers if it had not been known that those with strike-breaking service to their credit, or discredit, would be leniently treated by the examiners'.[103]

Harding's sympathies were unfashionably with the strikers; his views

---

[98] Diary of H. C. Alexander.
[99] *ibid*. For socialism and communism in the university at this time, see Howarth (1978), 145 - 7. In 1919 the St Bernard Society had supported a call for higher wages, SBSM, 1.2.1919.
[100] Branson (1975), 192 - 3; Howarth (1978), 148.
[101] Howarth (1978), 148 - 151. Some Cambridge dons were critical of the government's handling of the strike, but it is not clear how many; and there was also staunch support for the government among other senior members, Martin (1926), 70, 86.
[102] There are accounts of their experiences in *Dial* (Easter 1926), 7 - 23; McGowan (MS), 9 - 11.
[103] Harding (1953), 47.

on the subject 'made me unpopular with some of the extreme hearties and I learnt that there was a movement to throw me in the river'.[104]

The strike soon collapsed, to the evident disappointment of those undergraduates who had not been able to take part in the fun. Those Queensmen who did participate did not meet with much trouble. One of the contingent which had driven London buses reported that: 'We arrived too late for any bloodshed. All the excitement had happened in the previous week, and we had nothing thrown at us beyond abuse and bad language'.[105] The Hull tramdrivers also suffered

'nothing worse than abuse . . . and the general attitude towards undergraduates was remarkable throughout. For, while several Hull men had their lives threatened, and others were forced to leave their trams, undergraduates seemed to amuse the strikers too much for them to be more than passively hostile as a rule'.[106]

Many from the middle classes welcomed the strike-breakers: C. W. N. McGowan recorded that when he arrived in Hull in a convoy of cars to work at the docks, 'the residents cheered as we passed . . . we felt as if we were relieving Ladysmith'.[107] The only accidents involving trams driven by undergraduates were due to their drivers' recklessness and what was described in the *Dial* as

'incredible carelessness for which those responsible showed no sense of shame. Power-points are not easy to negotiate, but that does not excuse attempts to carry them by sheer speed'.

McGowan recalled 'the sporting nature of the volunteer student drivers'.[108]

The Queensmen all seem to have had a thoroughly good time, and to have felt that the experience was well worth the effort: one of the Hull dock gangs even held a reunion dinner in Queens' the following month.[109] The accounts of the students' experiences which were printed in the *Dial* show almost no signs of any attempt to understand the

---

[104] *ibid.*, 47. This typifies the hearties' approach to politics. In 1931 the college's correspondent for the *Cambridge Review* observed: 'After the demoralizing effect of the General Election, our . . . athletes have abandoned their rowdy zeal for politics', *CR* (13.11.1931). See also *Dial* (Michaelmas 1933), 14–16.
[105] *Dial* (Easter 1926), 14.
[106] *ibid.*, 19, and c.f. p. 18: 'the departure of the would-be dockers on a three-mile tramp provoked some hostility, but the police soon cleared the streets'. The nature of the hostility is not specified.
[107] Howarth (1978), 149; McGowan (MS), 10.
[108] *Dial* (Easter 1926), 19–20; McGowan (MS), 10.
[109] *Dial* (Easter (1926), 15, 16–17; McGowan (MS), 11.

causes of the strike, or the aims of the strikers. Only one student commented on the strength of feeling, writing that 'both sides earnestly desired an agreement: and one of our deepest impressions must be the strikers' sincerity'.[110] For the rest, it was a rather grand game.

Politics in the 1930s

Despite the preponderance of strong conservative sentiments in the university, no doubt reinforced by the General Strike, there are some signs of increasing social concern among undergraduates in the late 1920s. The radical left was not yet in fashion, although less extreme socialists such as George Lansbury, the then leader of the Labour party, were quite popular in Cambridge. Lesslie Newbigin was drawn towards Lansbury's brand of socialism, 'but repelled by the intellectual style of the Marxists'.[111] But in the 1930s political attitudes changed dramatically: the great depression, the rise of fascism and the growing threat of war all led to mounting sympathy for left wing ideals, socialist and communist, although the extent of the latter may well have been exaggerated. Besides, most Cambridge men still remained true to their traditional tory instincts.[112]

These changes are clearer at university level than in an individual college, but it is possible to trace a much higher level of interest in politics in general, including left wing politics, in Queens' in the 1930s. Cyril Bibby, who came up in 1932, has recalled the vigour of university socialism at that time, and the intensity of political activity:

'we fervently attended large public meetings and seriously pondered in small study-groups; we demonstrated on open spaces and in the streets against war and against fascism; we were sometimes attacked by groups of right-wing student "toughs" '.[113]

Socialists were involved in the attempt to set up a more serious debating society to rival the St Bernard Society: the Phoenix Club, which is known to have met in 1934.[114]

The main domestic political issue was unemployment. This had been discussed by students in the 1920s too, but the problem was much more serious as the result of the depression.[115] Two articles in the *Dial* in 1936

[110]   *Dial* (Easter 1926), 20 – 1.
[111]   Howarth (1978), 147, 150 – 2; Newbigin (1985), 9.
[112]   Howarth (1978), 155 – 8, 209 – 11, 215 – 18; Graves and Hodge (1971), 254 – 5.
[113]   Bibby, 'Reminiscences' (MS), 151 – 2.
[114]   *Dial* (Lent 1934), 24; Bibby, 'Reminiscenses' (MS), 164.
[115]   The diary of H. C. Alexander shows students discussing unemployment in the early 1920s.

bore witness to undergraduate interest in the question, and demonstrated two main currents of thought regarding its eradication: the first
— the more moderate — recognised that unemployment was a long term
problem, and urged students (who benefited from the present industrial
order) to participate in voluntary and self-help schemes by, for example,
working at camps for the unemployed; it was felt that this would help to
break down class barriers.[116] The second article, which appeared the
following term, criticised the first for only attacking the symptoms of
unemployment, and argued that British capitalism could no longer
expand to provide new jobs, which under the present system would
only be created by war; socialism was urged as the sole solution.[117]
When the Jarrow March arrrived in Cambridge in 1936, left wing
students smuggled college blankets out of Queens' to the Corn
Exchange, where the marchers were to sleep.[118] By the end of the decade
Queens' had its own Socialist Club, which held regular lunchtime
discussions; but it also had a Conservative Club with some 60
members.[119] Socialism may have been an influential force in the college,
but there is nothing to suggest that it became a dominant one. A review
of Cyril Bibby's *The Evolution of Man and his Culture* in the *Dial* in 1938
which criticised the book's Marxist interpretation of history probably
reflected the view of the silent majority.[120]

There was much greater interest in foreign affairs, principally the
questions of war and fascism, which were of course closely connected.
Although this interest blossomed in the 1930s, students had been
interested in foreign affairs in the early 1920s, and we know of the
existence of an 'International Questions' discussion group in the college
at that time, which met weekly.[121] The question of the effectiveness of
the League of Nations was central to the debate on the likelihood of war.
In 1929 the History Society listened to a paper on the Pact of Paris and its
relation to the League's Covenant, and the discussion which followed
'lacked nothing in vigour'; in 1931 the St Bernard Society affirmed its
confidence in the League by a majority of over two to one.[122] In 1933
there was a study group at Queens' discussing the settlement of
international disputes and other contemporary issues, under the aegis
of the local branch of the League of Nations Union. In 1938 the History
Society considered the extent of the League's power and influence, and

[116] *Dial* (Lent 1936), 15 – 17. In 1935 the governing body gave £5 to the universities council for unemployed camps, CB (1899 – 1937), 8.2.1935.
[117] *Dial* (Easter 1936), 9 – 10.
[118] Bibby, 'Reminiscences' (MS), 154 – 5.
[119] *Dial* (Lent 1939), 69; (Easter 1939), 33 – 4.
[120] *ibid.* (Michaelmas 1938), 37 – 8; Bibby (1938), chapters xi – xii.
[121] McGowan (MS), 4, for the discussion group (1923/4); diary of H. C. Alexander for general interest.
[122] *Dial* (Michaelmas 1929), 31; SBSM, 21.11.1931 (by 23 votes to 9).

after a very lively discussion came to the gloomy conclusion that 'permanent peace and sovereign states were incompatible'.[123]

Questions relating more directly to war were also discussed. The Science Society's talk on chemical warfare in 1930 drew a large audience and was followed by 'considerable discussion'. Two years later a paper to the History Society on 'The Problem of War' again provoked a lengthy and vigorous discussion of disarmament and other related matters.[124] Also in 1932 a correspondent to the *Dial* protested at the methods used for collecting money on Armistice Day. He felt that a good cause was overshadowed by the intense competition between colleges to raise the largest sum and the rather forceful methods of collection which were sometimes employed:

'This is highly distasteful both to those many people who still hold this day sacred, and to those who wish that throughout the year we might be constantly reminded of the real, the lunatic and disgusting, aspect of war, which tends to be obscured by the hypocrisy of such spectacles as the popular Hendon Air Display or the Aldershot Tattoo, *prima facie* innocent entertainment, but really insidious militarist propaganda'.[125]

Although a debate in the St Bernard Society on the value of the OTC in schools attracted only a small audience in 1931, two years later a private debate in undergraduate rooms on the motion 'That this House would support strike action to prevent war' was said to have attracted 45 people, some from outside the college.[126] In a political editorial of 1934 the *Dial* noted the growing interest and concern expressed by Queensmen in political and international affairs:

'Bolivia's announcement that she would defy the established rules of war has raised a feeling of disgust and weariness at the folly of nations. Fresh events have provided us with food for thought, with subjects for conversation, have even prompted some among us to the unconscious bravery of wearing red ties and whispering anti-war propaganda in the ears of astounded army officers'.

But as the editorial also noted, Queens' sheltered its members from the 'jealousies and turmoils of a larger, more intriguing, yet less pleasant

---

[123] *Dial* (Lent 1933), 30 – 1; History Society minutes, 3.3.1938.
[124] *Dial* (Lent 1930), 51; (Lent 1932), 32; History Society minutes, 21.1.1932. For general remarks on pacifism in Cambridge, see Howarth (1978), 218 – 220, 225.
[125] *Dial* (Easter 1932), 28 – 9. For some of the stunts used to raise money, see *ibid.* (Michaelmas 1931), 30.
[126] SBSM, 28.3.1931; *Dial* (Lent 1934), 24.

world', and it suggested that students soon shrugged off the disturbing thoughts that this world provoked.[127]

There was public interest in fascism from an early date. In 1926 the History Society heard a paper by an Italian political leader who had been exiled by Mussolini.[128] But interest was most marked after the rise of the Nazis in Germany. In 1933 the college's League of Nations Union study group discussed Nazism and Italian fascism. In 1934 the Erasmus Society heard a paper on repression and anti-Semitism in the universities of central Europe (and especially Germany) since the war. The *Dial*'s Easter 1934 editorial observed that 'The eviction of Jews from Germany has caused some of us to shake our heads sadly', though it also noticed that the move 'has raised a murmur of approbation in others of us'. There was a further article on Nazism in the same issue.[129]

The civil war which broke out in Spain in 1936 intensified the fears of fascism and war. There was much sympathy for the Spanish republicans in Cambridge; and a paper on 'Spain' was one of the devices employed by the St Bernard Society to boost its flagging support in 1937, at which there was a good deal of political discussion.[130] In the same year the *Dial* carried an article on the threat of Japanese militarism; and in 1938 another on the Sino-Japanese war. Also in 1938 there was an article on the dispute between Germany and Czechoslovakia which was to lead to the Munich crisis. In 1939 the History Society heard a paper on 'The Austrian Republic 1918 – 1938' (the latter date being that of its annexation by Germany), and the college Conservative and Socialist clubs held a debate on conscription.[131]

The undergraduates studied these matters with great seriousness, and were profoundly influenced by them. The political content of the *Dial* grew steadily during the decade.[132] Abba Eban, who came up to Queens' in 1934, left Cambridge with a clearly defined system of political loyalties: he was a Zionist, democratic socialist, advocate of resistance to fascism, supporter of the Spanish republicans against Franco, and adherent of the League of Nations — 'All my future years were to fluctuate among those ideas'.[133] These issues served to politicise the student body in a way which had never happened before, but although they led undoubtedly to a growth in left wing sentiment, they also

[127] *Dial* (Easter 1934), 1 – 2.
[128] *Dial* (Easter 1926), 40. For anti-fascism in Cambridge in the 1930s, see Howarth (1978), 224 – 5.
[129] *Dial* (Lent 1933), 30 – 1; (Lent 1934), 21 – 2; (Easter 1934), 1, 13 – 17.
[130] Howarth (1978), 226; SBSM, 17.11.1937.
[131] *Dial* (Lent 1937), 22 – 3; (Lent 1938), 15 – 19, 20 – 3; (Easter 1939), 33; History Society minutes, 9.2.1939.
[132] Although it did initially have to defend itself against the charge of excessive concentration of politics, *Dial* (Easter 1936), 1 – 2.
[133] Eban (1978), 21 (he was also a Fellow of Pembroke for a while after graduating from Queens').

transcended the normal political divisions to a large extent. Even so, there are indications of growing enthusiasm for Soviet communism during the decade. In 1930 the college History Society heard a paper on Lenin, at which the speaker (who was not a Queensman) demonstrated 'very clearly the immense vitality and the entire lack of self-interest of the Bolshevist leader . . . The paper was followed by a very animated discussion'. In 1938 the *Dial* printed a student's account of a visit to the USSR which was strongly sympathetic to the Stalinist government: the author swallowed the party line on political trials without a qualm, treated the secret police in a lighthearted manner, and pointedly avoided answering the allegation that the Soviet state was undemocratic. In the same year the History Society held a debate on the motion 'That Socialism is a retrograde step in the development of liberty', culminating in a 'fierce and lengthy' discussion which must have comprised the policies of the USSR, but we have no further details.[134]

One can perceive other movements against conventional political creeds. In the 1920s there had been no doubt that the college supported the British empire wholeheartedly; but in 1937 the *Dial* published a poem which looked forward to the independence of Ceylon. In 1938 the History Society learnt about the background to recent constitutional reforms in India. Articles on the future of Palestine, written from opposing standpoints, had appeared in the *Dial* in 1936.[135]

All of these questions were brought together in the *Dial's* Lent term issue of 1939, which described itself as an 'International Dial', and was full of articles on such subjects as German expansion, Anglo-German relations, Palestine, the League of Nations, independence movements in British colonies, and China. The avowed purpose of the issue was to promote a better understanding of world affairs: the published articles expressed a wide range of opinion, and the editors made no apology for the political emphasis, which they regarded as 'a sign of the times'.[136] The following issue, while it contained no political articles, recognised in its editorial the imminence of war.[137]

Religion

The college's religious life took some while to get under way again after the war, with the exception of services in the chapel, which we must

[134] *Dial* (Lent 1930), 48; (Lent 1938), 6 – 13; History Society minutes, 23.11.1938 (although the attendance at this meeting was low).
[135] SBSM, 8.12.1923, 27.1.1927 (c.f. CR (5.3.1920), 261); *Dial* (Lent 1936), 11 – 14; (Easter 1936), 32 – 6; (Michaelmas 1937), 12; History Society minutes, 27.10.1938. Howarth (1978), 222 – 3, argues for growing scepticism in Cambridge about the morality and efficacy of the British empire during the 1930s.
[136] *Dial* (Lent 1936), 1 – 4, and *passim*.
[137] *ibid*. (Easter 1939), 3 – 4.

suppose had been conducted as usual throughout. The QCCU, the only religious body for which we have any information, made a slow start, in common with the other college societies, although it shared in the general revival in the autumn of 1919.[138] Many who had served in the trenches had had their religious faith severely shaken; but it has been argued that there was a high level of religious interest and enthusiasm in the university in the 1920s.[139]

At Queens' there is evidence of a diverse religious life ranging from evangelicalism to Anglo-Catholicism. There had been no marked clash between the high and low church outlooks in Queens' during the late Victorian and Edwardian periods, when the public reputation of the college, through the writings of its presidents and Fellows, was liberal and tolerant of diversity in religious practice; there do not seem to have been any notably high church Fellows in the college at that time. But high church feelings found a champion with the arrival of R. G. D. Laffan in 1913, whose impact can be seen clearly in the 1920s.[140] Laffan was a man of strong convictions, and not only in religious matters,[141] which could make him appear slightly ridiculous to those who did not share his views. 'It would do him a lot of good if he put aside his notions of his spiritual greatness and married', wrote one undergraduate in 1922.[142] He could be insecure, and sensitive to criticism: the same undergraduate recorded that he was 'much perturbed' when informed by the dean, C. T. Wood, that the college felt he mumbled hymn numbers and psalms, and 'also that the college blasphemes awfully because he rattles through the communion at an unseemly speed; he came in and grizzled to me about it, saying he tried to speak as if speaking to God'.[143] He was an enthusiast for confession, a subject which tended to crop up in his history lectures and supervisions.[144] In 1922 he established the Guild of St Bernard for those who believed that the 'most complete expression of Christianity' was to be found in 'the historic Faith and Practice of the Catholic Church': this held meetings and communion services.[145] Laffan became a Roman Catholic in 1933,

---

[138]   ibid. (Easter 1919), 24; (Michaelmas 1919), 34 – 6.
[139]   Marwick (1965), 218; Howarth (1978), 48 – 50.
[140]   After Laffan's conversion to Catholicism in 1933, the college appointed a chaplain who was not a Fellow: G. L. O. Jessop, son of the famous pre-war cricketer Gilbert Jessop, Brodribb (1974), 186; QC (1933 – 4), 4; (1935 – 6), 5.
[141]   See above, pp. 317, 323, 342.
[142]   Diary of H. C. Alexander. Laffan did marry in 1923, ibid.
[143]   ibid. Wood was relatively low church, and this difference posed problems for the college porter, whose duty it was to light the candles at services: he rarely knew until the last minute whether Laffan or Wood was to lead the service, and therefore whether he should light the candles (for Laffan) or not (for Wood), Harding (1953), 52 – 3.
[144]   Diary of H. C. ALexander.
[145]   Dial (Lent 1922), 42; his leadership of the Guild is also recorded in the diary of H. C. Alexander. Gilbert Harding joined it under Laffan's influence, having briefly espoused extreme low church views, Harding (1953), 55 – 6, 61.

which, since he had married ten years previously, forced him to give up the priesthood, to his great regret.[146]

At the other extreme was the evangelical QCCU, which despite the signs of revival in 1919 seems to have experienced difficulties in regaining its former strength. In 1921 it tried to win more support by stressing that it sought 'normal' people as members, and was not narrowly exclusive in its doctrine:

'No member of the Q.C.C.U. runs any risk of being expelled from it on grounds of "heresy" . . . It is gradually being realised that the *social* side of Christianity is to-day of most importance to the world. Consequently it is this aspect of religion with which the Union chiefly concerns itself. As a mere example of what is meant, I may state that one study-circle devoted an entire sitting to a discussion of The Ideal Public House'.[147]

A year later, its fortunes had risen a little, but it still reminded Queensmen that it was

'composed of perfectly normal people, and embraces every shade of opinion, so that no member of the College need feel that his views will not be met with sympathy'.[148]

But in 1923, following the success of that year's CICCU mission to the university, it was confident enough to take a firmer line and introduced 'some rather fundamental changes'. It had been felt that it was a 'Union' only in name

'and that having no definite membership it could achieve little in the way of fellowship. The membership has therefore been limited to those who can accept on [*sic*] the basis of their belief the principles and teaching of Jesus Christ'.[149]

There was some disappointment in the college at the passing of the old form, and T. C. Fitzpatrick was said to dislike the change.[150]

The CICCU missions to the university were sometimes very influential: Gilbert Harding was inspired by one to convert to

'extreme Protestantism . . . I gave up drinking and smoking and

---

[146]   D. W. Bowett in *Record* (1972 – 3); Maxwell (MS), 1.
[147]   *Dial* (Michaelmas 1921), 40.
[148]   *ibid.* (Michaelmas 1922), 36 – 7.
[149]   *ibid.* (Lent 1923), 37.
[150]   Diary of H. C. Alexander.

went to Keswick for the Convention for the Deepening of Spiritual Life. After a month or two of profound and rather pompous "spirituality" I found I was not cut out for that type of tub-thumping, after all'.[151]

The sources do not supply any more details of the history of the QCCU in the inter-war years, but we must assume that it adhered to the narrow and uncompromising doctrinal position set out by the CICCU during its jubilee celebrations in 1927, which rejected the 'higher criticism', the theory of evolution, and 'sacerdotalism', described Satan as 'a personal evil agency', and could not find any authority for the belief 'in the success of attempts by social or political action to make the world a better place'; nor could it 'be enthusiastic about schemes for bringing world peace by means of political bodies such as the League of Nations, or social uplift by methods of reform'.[152]

Occupying the middle ground was the Student Christian Movement (SCM), which had a lively branch at Queens' in the late 1920s. One undergraduate who was sceptical of Christianity at that time (though he went on to a distinguished career as a clergyman) was Lesslie Newbigin, who recalls of the SCM: 'I never felt that they were trying to "get at" me, as I did about the "evangelical" group'. The outlook and approach of the SCM was very different from that of the CICCU, and although there were many contacts between the two groups, their relationship was characterised by wariness of each other, especially on the part of the evangelicals. In Newbigin's time, evensong in the college chapel was

'the only place where the SCM and the CICCU could pray together, for the official evangelical view was that the SCM members were unbelievers. Even there, however, our divisions were published, for at the words "I believe" the SCM turned obediently towards the East while the CICCU stood firmly and resolutely facing one another across the chapel. It punctuated each act of worship with a moment of absurdity'.[153]

The 'muscular Christian' was still a recognisable type: one of Newbigin's contemporaries at Queens' was 'captain of the college rugby team, [and] leading member of the "Cherubs" (a group which the rest of us were tempted to regard as brainless toughs)', but 'the centre of his

---

[151] Harding (1953), 55.
[152] Howarth (1978), 49.
[153] Newbigin (1985), 9 – 10, 14. For the CICCU's view of the relationship, see Pollock (1953), 171 – 4, 195, 214 – 6.

life was a profound devotion to Christ. Prayer was his deepest being'.[154] In 1926 the captain of boats asked members of the Boat Club 'to continue the long standing tradition of the Club of attending Sunday evening in chapel'.[155]

The college mission, Queens' House, now at Rotherhithe, continued to be supported after the war. The governing body took over responsibility for its management in 1934, but by the end of the decade, though the house remained well organised and active, undergraduate support was failing, and in 1939 the governing body was forced to 'take such steps as are necessary to wind up and terminate the lease of the property'.[156] This is strange, for there was widespread interest in the relationship between religion and social issues among students in the 1930s. The debate was clearly linked to the rise of left wing political ideology: socialism and Christianity were by no means incompatible — members of the Queens' Socialist Club are known to have been supporters of Queens' House, for example[157] — but there were bound to be clashes. In 1934 Lesslie Newbigin returned to Queens' to address a meeting on the Christian attitude towards social abuses.[158] He was reported as arguing that the worlds of politics and economics were autonomous from the will of God, and that all that a Christian could hope to do was to enter those worlds and serve God in them.[159] An article which appeared in the *Dial* the following term reacted to these remarks with a fierce criticism of the church's historic relationship with social reform, arguing that Christianity had:

'militated positively against social progress; it still does so . . . the insistence of the Church on subjective spirituality . . . retards the realisation of the material standards which are an essential prerequisite for the growth of any true mental and moral culture for the masses perforce obsessed with the elementary problems of the next meal. Thus in Germany its fight for its own sectional interests keeps thousands from the revolutionary struggle, the only force which can

---

[154] Newbigin (1985), 10. But c.f. Kangaroo Club minutes, 16.11.1929.
[155] QCBC minutes, 18.10.1926.
[156] SBSM, 21.4.1922, *CR* (5.6.1931), 466; CB (1889 – 1937), 19.1.1934, 9.2.1934; CB (1937 – 63), 4.10.1939, 26.1.1940; Reports (1914 – 49), 145, 204 – 5. For the mission's work and the falling subscriptions from undergraduates and old members see entries in *QC* (1925 – 6) to (1938 – 9)
[157] *Dial* (Easter 1939), 33. The first debate of the socialist-inspired Phoenix Club in 1934 was on a motion that Christianity had no place in the socialist state, *ibid.* (Lent 1934), 24; Bibby, 'Reminiscences' (MS), 164.
[158] Newbigin was addressing the Ryle Society, founded in 1925 to 'emphasize the doctrines of the Church of England based on the appeal of the Reformation to the supremacy of Holy Scripture', *Dial* (Michaelmas 1926), 36 – 7.
[159] *Dial* (Lent 1934), 25.

overcome the barbarism of Hitler and save civilisation from the irreparable ruin and retrogression of war'.[160]

Another article in 1938 attacked the church as a barrier to human progress.[161] These were extreme positions, but vague echoes of these opinions may have sounded in many minds: religion could easily be associated with quietism, an increasingly unpopular position in the light of the depression, the rise of fascism, and the threat of war. Perhaps this may help to explain the demise of Queens' House.

[160] *ibid*. (Easter 1934), 23 – 5.
[161] *ibid*. (Michaelmas 1938), 31 – 6.

24

The college in the second world war

The reaction to the outbreak of war in 1939 was not characterised by the raucous jingoism which had been so typical of 1914: there was no less patriotism, but far less optimism that the war would soon be over; and the experiences of 1914–18 had demonstrated fully the horrors of modern warfare. The power of the enemy was not taken lightly; and his character was well understood. And the war had long been expected: L. J. Potts felt that it was 'fated to happen and nothing could have stopped it'.[1] Fatalism combined with a greater political maturity amongst students than in the years before 1914, and left them in no doubt of the trials ahead. It was a time for grim determination rather than boyish enthusiasm. We can gain little insight into the minds of Queens' undergraduates at this time. There were only two issues of the *Dial*, in Michaelmas 1939 and Lent 1940, which contain several articles on weaponry and military strategy, giving the magazine something of a martial flavour. There was also an article critical of one-party states, which was rather behind the times, and a piece advocating the use of Esperanto as a means of avoiding world crises — a similarly belated and forlorn plea. Not all opinion was in favour of the war: the *Dial* also printed an article in favour of pacificism (though it published an anti-pacifist rejoinder, too); and although the college's Socialist Club voted to support the war in 1939, there was some opposition.[2]

Again in contrast to 1914, the university was well prepared for the war. Some preliminary steps had been taken at the time of the Munich crisis in September 1938, and further plans were laid in the early months of 1939.[32] As early as May 1938 Queens' had set up a committee to 'consider and report on Air Raid Precaution plans', and A. D. Browne was appointed college air raid warden. Two air raid precaution (ARP) trenches, one in Walnut Tree Court, the other in the president's garden, were dug at the time of the Munich crisis; and during 1938–9 the ARP committee organised the purchase of blackout materials and sandbags

---

[1] In a letter of April 1940, White (1984), 110.

[2] *Dial* (Michaelmas 1939), 11–19, 21–7, 29–30, 43; (Lent 1940), 6–9, 18–26. Some members of the extreme left in Britain were hostile to the war until Germany invaded the USSR in 1941.

[3] For the universities in general, see Dent (1944), 137. For Cambridge, see Roach, 'University of Cambridge', 307. For Queens', see *Dial* (Michaelmas 1938), 5.

and the training of college staff in fire-fighting, and made arrangements to turn the wine cellar underneath the hall and the basement of the Doket building into shelters. L. J. Potts reckoned Queens' better prepared than most colleges by the outbreak of war.[4]

There was much subsequent expenditure on ARP throughout the war, and further precautionary measures were necessary. A blackout was strictly enforced after dark. Women guests were forbidden in college after 7 p.m. Although gate fines were abolished, students were 'reminded that it is a national duty not to wander about or congregate in the streets after dark', and were warned that a strict line would be taken with disorderly behaviour. The grove was closed to students between 1943 and 1945. Doors to college rooms were not to be sported and the gate onto the wooden bridge, usually closed at night, was now kept open, because of the dangers of fire. A fire-pump was purchased, and other fire-fighting precautions were taken. ARP duties were divided among senior and junior members.[5] One of the more absurd precautions, ordered by the military authorities in May 1942, required the sinking of a small covered shaft at the western foot of the wooden bridge, to be filled with explosives in the event of invasion, so that the bridge could be blown up and the enemy denied passage across the river. The scheme would have seemed less foolish at the beginning of the war, and was shelved only two weeks after the order had been issued.[6]

Many senior members of the university were called up for various kinds of war service, and four Fellows of Queens' were absent for the duration, including P. F. D. Tennant, a Fellow since 1933 and university lecturer in Scandinavian languages, who was press attaché at the British Legation in Stockholm; a fifth Fellow was absent for part of the war. At one blow, the college was thus deprived of its senior bursar and one of its tutors, as well as its steward and praelector, and at a time when administration, finance and catering were likely to become serious problems.[7] Those who remained had to take on other responsibilities: the president, J. A. Venn, became senior bursar (he had in addition been responsible for admissions for some years), and also served as vice-chancellor from 1941 – 3; L. J. Potts acted as sole tutor throughout the

---

[4] *Dial* (Michaelmas 1938), frontispiece; (Michaelmas 1939), 4 – 5; CB (1937 – 63), 12.5.1938, 31.5.1938, 7.10.1938, 16.11.1939; Reports (1914 – 49), 153; MS u/c-wartime(I); MS u/c-Drinkwater correspondence; QC (1938 – 9), 11.

[5] *Dial* (Michaelmas 1939), 1, 7 (and see 37 – 8); (Easter 1947), 7 – 8; CB (1937 – 63), 16.11.1939, 14.11.1940, 24.1.1941 (and see 17.10.1945), 15.5.1941, 13.11.1941, 19.11.1942, 22.1.1943, 21.6.1943, 20.10.1943, 17.11.1943, 15.11.1944, 8.12.1944, 14.11.1945; MS u/c-wartime(II); Reports (1914 – 49), 157.

[6] MS u/c-wartime(I).

[7] *Who's Who* (Tennant); *Dial* (Michaelmas 1939), 6; (Easter 1947), 5; CB (1937 – 63), 4.10.1939, 2.11.1939, 16.11.1939, 22.6.1942; MS u/c-wartime(IV).

war.[8]

In his vice-chancellor's report on the academic year 1941 – 2, Venn was grateful for the 'present-day measures of control and direction of man-power', instead of the 'haphazard enlistment' of the first world war, but even so the university's teaching staff had been reduced by more than half. With large numbers of students remaining in residence, their burden was increased, and with both seniors and juniors having civil defence and home guard duties in addition to their other work, it was clear to Venn that 'for both classes, the point is rapidly approaching when neither their little unappropriated time nor their physical endurance should be subjected to further demands'.[9] Potts wrote to his former pupil T. H. White in December 1941 that he was very busy, and rarely at home: 'It is just a matter of trying to keep one's feet from being swept away'. The university was 'surprisingly busy, trying to continue higher education while contributing to the war effort. The young men seem to appreciate our efforts, but they are inadequate to the demand and still more to the ideal'. As for academic work, he reported at the same time that 'my intellect, if not dead, sleepeth'; though it was said after the war that some of the college's Fellows had been able to continue their academic researches.[10] The burden seems to have weighed heavily on Potts: in 1947 he informed White that he was

'utterly sick of Cambridge . . . and find it a burden to deal with any human beings except my own domestic circle. I can't be bothered with any of my colleagues — with few exceptions they seem to me knaves or nit-wits . . . I got utterly worn out in the war — I never realised how much. But I really think I am getting better by degrees'.[11]

Some other college staff were also called up, and the shortage of manpower was felt particularly in the kitchens, which were already overburdened by the large number of evacuees in college; in hall, students had to pass the dishes down the table themselves instead of being waited on. The college paid regular bonuses to the staff in recognition of their increased duties, and some were given further cash

[8]   *QC* (1957 – 8), 2; CB (1937 – 63), 17.10.1945. The Universities and Colleges (Emergency Provisions) Act of 1939 allowed colleges to ignore statutory restrictions where it was necessary because of the war, which was of great value in financial and administrative matters, MS u/c-statutes; Reports (1914 – 49), facing p. 133; see also CB (1937 – 63), 17.10.1939, 2.11.1939, 16.11.1939, 25.4.1940.
[9]   *CU Reporter* (7.10.1942), 119.
[10] White (1984), 128; *Dial* (Easter 1947), 9.
[11] White (1984), 197.

gifts after the war.[12]

Student numbers did not at first drop as dramatically as they had in the previous war and for the early months at least business was more or less as usual. In April 1940 the governing body even granted permission for one of the Fellows to spend part of the Easter term at the Sorbonne.[13] Even in the academic year 1942 – 3 the university was still just over half of its pre-war size. But for much of the war there were hardly any third years resident, and there was a much reduced second year, as these students were called up. The call-up age was reduced from 20 to 18 in 1942, and from 1943 students in non-technical subjects were no longer allowed to defer. Those who remained were largely scientists and medical students. There were 117 arts students at Queens' in the Michaelmas term of 1939, and 91 in technical subjects; in 1944 the figures were 12 and 70 respectively. Entrance awards continued to be given, but their emoluments were deferred.[14] All students were required to perform military service of some sort while in Cambridge, in units such as the home guard, naval division, air squadron, or despatch rider service, in addition to such ARP duties as were demanded by the college; they often had to remain during the vacations to attend military training camps.[15]

The influx of evacuees meant that the college remained crowded, however. From the start of the war, the university took in students and staff from London university, and members of various government departments and RAF training units.[16] This had been foreseen as early as 1938, and in the summer of 1939 Queens' agreed to take 160 students from St Bartholomew's Medical School; the college was well prepared for their arrival in September.[17] It also played host to military cadets on 6-month courses in the university, some of whom had been accepted at Queens' as students before enlisting, but all of whom were matriculated members of the university. Other small military groups of various kinds passed through from time to time. In 1940 Queens' and other colleges had to cope at very short notice with hundreds of soldiers evacuated

[12] *Dial* (Michaelmas 1939), 7; (Easter 1947), 7; CB (1937 – 63), 9.5.1939, 4.10.1939, 17.10,1939, 8.12.1939, 11.10.1940, 16.10.1941, 10.10.1946; Reports (1914 – 49), 157, 163; MS u/c-wartime(I); Ms u/c-town and country planning.

[13] Dent (1944), 137 (for the universities in general); *Dial* (Michaelmas 1939), 5; CB (1937 – 63), 25.4.1940. The Fellow who went to Paris was C. T. Seltman, who returned to England in June 1940, as France fell to the Germans, QC (1939 – 40), 4.

[14] *Dial* (Easter 1947), 5 – 6, 9; Roach, 'University of Cambridge', 307; CU *Reporter* (7.10.1942), 119; (12.10.1943), 131; Dent (1944), 140 – 3; CB (1937 – 63), 4.10.1939; MS u/c-wartime(I).

[15] *Dial* (Easter 1947), 6 – 7; Roach, 'University of Cambridge', 307.

[16] Roach, 'University of Cambridge', 307.

[17] *Dial* (Michaelmas 1939), 4 – 5; CB (1937 – 63), 27.2.1939, 4.10.1939, 16.5.1940; MS u/c-correspondence with Financial Board.

from Dunkirk.[18]

The presence of the London students caused some problems at first. More Queens' students came back for the Michaelmas term in 1939 than had been expected, and the authorities had to suspend evacuations to the college. Accommodation was in short supply, and it was necessary for men to double up in college sets, although falling numbers thereafter eased the situation.[19] There was also some friction between the two groups of students: there seems to have been some dispute over use of the college sports ground; and an article in the *Dial* protested against the St Bartholomew's students accusing those at Queens' of 'irresponsibility' and of 'refusing to organise ourselves democratically and do our own administrative dirty work and of submitting complacently to a medieval discipline'.[20] But this seems soon to have blown over. In 1946, when the London students and staff left Cambridge, the governing body recorded 'our appreciation of the remarkably happy relations between us since their arrival . . . which must have been unique in the story of evacuation to Cambridge during the war'. In his obituary for J. A. Venn in 1958, L. J. Potts wrote that it was on the president's advice that the college had agreed to take members of St Bartholomew's in, which he described as 'wise advice indeed, as the College afterwards found when they compared their situation with that of many other colleges'. The visitors expressed their thanks to Queens' by creating two scholarships in clinical medicine at St Bartholomew's for graduates of Queens'.[21]

Many social activities were disrupted by the war. Some college societies persisted during the Michaelmas term of 1939: the St Margaret Society held informal and well attended concerts; and meetings of the Socialist Club were lively and similarly well supported. But other societies and clubs seem to have closed down from the beginning; there was no *Dial* either between the Lent term of 1940 and the Easter term of 1947.[22] On the other hand, the war also saw the formation of two new societies. The enigmatically titled 'D' Society was founded by the dean, H. St J. Hart, in 1940 with the aim of 'bringing together students in different faculties for discussions of a topic that was neither too technical

[18] *Dial* (Easter 1947), 6 – 8; CB (1937 – 63), 20.10.1942 (and see also 6.12.1940); MS u/c-wartime(I). In the Michaelmas term of 1944 the college contained 26 medical students, 40 cadets, and 82 of its own students, *Dial* (Easter 1947). 6.
[19] *Dial* (Michaelmas 1939), 5 – 6; QC (1938 – 9), 11; Reports (1914 – 49), 163. It appears that outsiders were always expected to share, and priority was given to Queensmen when more space was available.
[20] Rugby Club minutes, Michaelmas 1939; *Dial* (Michaelmas 1939), 1 – 3.
[21] CB (1937 – 63), 15.3.1946, 29.5.1946; *Dial* (Easter 1947), 16 (and see also 8); Reports (1914 – 49), 168, 184; QC (1957 – 8), 2.
[22] *Dial* (Michaelmas 1939), 39, 43; (1948), 68 – 9; History Society minutes; Kangaroo Club minutes (and see entry of 16.11.1948).

for the majority of them to understand without previous knowledge, nor too abstruse to kindle the general interest of its hearers'. While the college was populated mostly by scientists the society 'confined itself to . . . philosophy, current political affairs, literature and the other arts', but after the war its scope was extended to educate students of the humanities in scientific subjects.[23] The society survives to this day, now as the 'E' Society, but with the same purpose. The other new formation was a theatrical society, 'The Bats', which originated in 1942 out of a voluntary choir, produced a successful light revue and then disbanded; but it was refounded after the war, and is now one of the university's leading dramatic societies.[24]

There was less time or inclination for sports, but at least some of the sports clubs endeavoured to survive. In 1941 it was reported that 'The Amalgamated Clubs are continuing as best they may under present conditions'.[25] The Rugby Club persisted until 1944; the Boat Club seems to have continued right through the war. Both were badly hit by the demands of military service upon students, so that it was often difficult to raise teams and crews, and to train properly. The Boat Club combined with Corpus Christi for a while, the Rugby Club sometimes included London medical students in its teams, and both clubs recruited military cadets.[26]

The college's religious life was also inconvenienced. At the beginning of the war, it was decided not to elect any new organ scholar, and although this order was revoked not long afterwards, the employment of boys in the chapel choir was discontinued. Services after dark were held at first in the old chapel, where the blackout could be enforced properly, but plans were made to black out the new chapel in 1942. It was in that year too that Sunday morning services were discontinued, apart from holy communion, 'in view of the military duties now required of undergraduates'.[27]

There were many wartime shortages, and strict economies were necessary. Food was rationed, and everyone had to tighten their belts. The college's contracts with the local gas and electricity companies had to be renegotiated; and all orders for domestic items — right down to pillow cases, mops, and dusters — had to go through the Ministry of Works. In 1940 the university's Financial Board ordered colleges to cut down on the use of paper.[28] The health insurance scheme for students

---

[23] *Dial* (1948), 36 – 7.
[24] *ibid.*, 64 – 5.
[25] *QC* (1940 – 1), 8. There was a general effort to keep going during the first months of the war, *Dial* (Michaelmas 1939), 39 – 41. See also Dent (1944), 137 – 8.
[26] QCBC minutes; Rugby Club minutes.
[27] CB (1937 – 63), 2.11.1939, 16.5.1940, 30.5.1940, 28.5.1942, 22.6.1942, 19.1.1944; MS u/c-wartime(I).
[28] MS u/c-wartime(I), (III); MS u/c-stationery.

introduced in 1939 did not come into operation. In 1941 a new system of prepayment for meals was introduced eliminating optional meals to prevent waste; in 1942 the supply of crockery and cutlery to student rooms was discontinued; and in 1943 the college shoecleaning service was scrapped.[29]

Queens' was not damaged by the air raids, and Cambridge in general suffered little, but it was no longer possible to carry out routine maintenance: with the wartime shortage of materials and manpower, such matters now came under the control of the state and university authorities, and the amount which Queens' was allowed to spend on repairs was fixed by the Financial Board. Reconstruction and building were still strictly controlled at the end of the war, the aim being merely to provide the minimum work essential for the university and colleges to continue 'under something like reasonable conditions'. In 1946 Queens' had to apply to the Ministry of Works for permission to spend up to £600 on the internal decoration of its rooms, because 'Nothing [was] done during [the] war years and rooms have been occupied continuously, in some cases with two students in one set of rooms'.[30]

Orders were sent to the college's tenant farmers to plough up their glassland and sow it with specified crops; these directions continued in force after the war. Sheep were grazed on the Barton Road sports ground, and in October 1939 the governing body had decided to use 'all suitable flower-beds in the gardens and courts of the College' for growing vegetables.[31] Property at Oakington was taken over by the Air Ministry in 1939 for an airfield, and the college sold further land to the ministry in 1940. At the height of the panic caused by the rout of the allied armies in France in May 1940, the civil defence authorities issued notices to landowners and farmers on 'the importance of denying to the enemy the use of large fields etc. as aerodromes' by placing obstacles in them.[32]

The university's income did not suffer much during the war.[33] Queens' decided in November 1939 that 'in view of the satisfactory condition of the College finances', a War Reserve Fund should be established for 'any purpose agreed upon by the Governing Body'. Money was paid into this fund regularly each year — by 1945 there was nearly £8,500 — and it did not diminish until after the war, when it was

---

[29] Reports (1914 – 49), 163; MS u/c-sick benefit; MS u/c-student charges; CB (1937 – 63), 23.4.1942.

[30] Roach, 'University of Cambridge', 307; Dial (Easter 1947), 8; MS u/c-wartime(I), (III); QC (1955 – 6), 15. There was a large amount of repair and restoration work all over the college in 1951, probably catching up on work that it had been unable to carry out during the war and immediate post-war years, MS u/c-maintenance.

[31] MS u/c-wartime (IV); CB (1937 – 63), 4.10.1939.

[32] MS u/c-wartime (I); CB (1937 – 63), 4.10.1939, 26.1.1940, 29.2.1940; Times, 15.5.1940.

[33] Roach, 'University of Cambridge', 307.

employed to support other funds such as the scholarships fund.[34] Falling student numbers obviously led to some loss of income; but the general financial buoyancy of the time is suggested by the college's decision to create two new research fellowships in 1944.[35]

More than one hundred names of Queens' students are recorded on the war memorial in the chapel; and one member of the college staff was killed at home in Cambridge in an air raid.[36] The psychological burden of the war was immeasurable, not only on those who saw active service but on the whole nation which had endured the hardships and austerities at home. As in 1918, the society which emerged from the conflict was very different from that which had entered it; nor was the narrower world of the university any less affected.

[34]   CB (1937 – 63), 16.11.1939, 14.11.1940, 13.11.1941, 19.11.1942, 17.11.1943, 15.11.1944, 14.11.1945, 7.11.1946, 6.11.1947; Reports (1914 – 49), 143.
[35]   CB (1937 – 63), 15.5.1941, 26.4.1944.
[36]   Dial (Easter 1947), 8, 16; QC (1942 – 7), 14 – 16; (1947 – 8), 16.

25

The modern college (I)
— introduction; government; finance

Introduction: the historical problem

The most recent events and trends in the college's history are without
doubt the most difficult to describe adequately. There is the problem of
historical perspective: some events are still too recent for their
significance to be evaluated; the true direction of long-term trends may
not have revealed itself. The difficulty is made worse by a vast amount
of unsifted archival material which has to be read and the lack of
secondary literature to provide a context for research, so that often one
can do no more than describe, acting as chronicler rather than historian.
The rapidity of change in so many aspects of university and college life
since 1945 adds to the problem still further.

If the following survey of modern Queens' appears uneven in its
emphasis and sometimes impressionistic in its treatment, this is the
result of all these difficulties: certain aspects of college life are more
accessible than others, and appear more significant at the present
moment. The passage of time and the cumulative weight of scholarly
research will doubtless lead to different emphases and judgements, but
the importance of recording and interpreting these matters now is in no
way diminished by this consideration. A reviewer of J. H. Gray's history
of Queens' in 1899 wrote: 'It seems a pity that college historians dare not
write for posterity and tell what they know from personal experience'.[1]
This is a very important point, but even without extensive first-hand
experience it is imperative for a college historian to write of the most
recent happenings, for the description of them is in itself a historical
document, a perception and expression of its own times.

Government

The 'model' college created by the Victorian reformers was administered
by the Fellows through the traditional college offices, as it had always
been, relying on the fact that there were usually some amongst them

---

[1] CR (16.2.1899), 208.

with the aptitude and enthusiasm for such specialised business as financial management. The method worked well enough at that time, although the first signs of a movement towards greater specialisation were already discernible in the creation of new college offices, and closer definition of the rôles of older ones. In 1855 the office of steward was created, with responsibility for the kitchens.[2] In 1887 the post of junior bursar was formally defined: he was given responsibility for examining the state of the college grounds and buildings, and for the furniture and linen supplied to college rooms. He was authorised to carry out 'trifling repairs', but had to consult the senior bursar in the event of serious repair work being needed; he was also 'generally to assist the Senior Bursar'. There had been two bursars from the start of the college's history, one clearly an assistant to the other; and in practice some arrangement such as that now defined may have been in operation informally for a long time already.[3]

These trends did not develop rapidly at this stage, nor in the early 20th century. In 1932 the incoming president, J. A. Venn, was given formal responsibility for admissions, previously arranged by the senior tutor, and he was given clerical assistance for admissions work, an innovation reflecting the growing formality and complexity of this task.[4] Venn was later praised for his ability to delegate responsibility whilst he was president — it was no longer feasible for a head of house to oversee all the details of college business — although he was compelled to act as senior bursar during the second world war, and held the post again for much of the 1950s.[5] Immediately after the war the college began seriously to reconsider its administrative arrangements, which expansion and the pace of change were rapidly rendering out of date. It was felt that too much work had fallen upon individuals, and that too many trivial matters had been brought before the full governing body which could easily be delegated. In 1946 three governing body standing committees were established to deal with admissions, rooms, and scholarships; a fourth, for wages, was set up in 1948. By 1955 there was also a library standing committee; and by 1959 there were committees for investments, buildings, and the gardens.[6]

[2] CB (1832 – 88), 11.10.1855.
[3] ibid., 8.10.1887. For bursars in previous times see above, p. 77. Arthur Wright claimed that the first junior bursars in the modern sense were George Pirie and Ernest Temperley, Wright (1889), 5. Wright was always keen to stress the reforming achievements of his generation, although he may have disparaged some of their predecessors.
[4] CB (1889 – 1932), 7.3.1932, 1.11.1932; QC (1957 – 8), 2. For the admissions procedure before the first world war, see e.g. Student's Handbook (1902), 30.
[5] QC (1957 – 8), 2; CB (1937 – 63), passim (annual appointments of college officers).
[6] CB (1937 – 63), 10.10.1946, 8.10.1948; GB, 5.10.1955, 2.10.1959. Improved administrative efficiency is also suggested by the innovations of governing body minutes in 1954, and college minutes (papers presented to the governing body for discussion), in 1959.

In 1968 the governing body was again concerned at the 'great and continued increase in both the volume, and the intricacy, of the work of "running the College" in the conventional sense', as well as with the size of the governing body itself due to a great increase in the number of Fellows. It was suggested that a smaller college council or executive committee should be created to make most of the necessary decisions and reduce the need for such frequent meetings of the full fellowship. This procedure, which had long been employed by some colleges, was rejected in favour of redevelopment and expansion of the committee structure, because the latter was felt to be more flexible, and would involve many more Fellows in college administration.[7] The result of these discussions was a report in 1969 recommending the creation of a whole range of committees on almost every aspect of college life, and this forms the basis of college government today; the proposal for a college council surfaced again in 1977, but it was not taken up.[8] In this sense much of the late 19th century 'model' has been retained: all Fellows who are members of the governing body are still expected to be active participants in the running of Queens'; it is one way of reaffirming the college as a community.

But in bursarial matters especially the growing need for more 'professional' skills has become apparent, especially with the demands of expansion and modernisation of the college's fabric, and the increasingly unfavourable financial climate in general.[9] In 1969 it was decided to appoint a 'College Administrative Fellow', or assistant bursar, to 'provide assistance for certain College Officers, primarily the Junior Bursar and the Steward, and to provide help generally in the administration of the College'; his duties were to be 'tailored to existing needs' and would develop 'progressively'.[10] This post was nonetheless meant for a Fellow of the college, not for a 'professional', and as such it was very much a patchwork solution whereas something more fundamental was required. This became apparent in 1971, when the junior bursar resigned because he felt the job was getting on top of him and commented that the college was run essentially 'by a collection of part-time amateurs whose only qualifications for the various jobs are native common-sense, dedication, and willingness'; and although he noted the many advantages too of having Fellows in charge of administration, he felt that the arrival of a full-time professional administrator could not be delayed for long. The president, D. W. Bowett, also observed at this time that 'We appear to have reached a

[7] GB, 16.1.1968, 18.10.1968, 14.1.1969, 3.2.1969; CM 232, 237.
[8] CM 253, 521.
[9] See below, pp. 366 – 8, 369ff. The growing administrative burdens of the senior tutor are noted below, p. 412.
[10] GB, 14.11.1969, 5.12.1969.

stage when it is no longer reasonable to expect teaching Fellows, fulfilling Faculty teaching commitments and engaged in research programmes, to assume this burden of administration'.[11]

The outcome was that the posts of junior and assistant bursar were allowed to lapse, and were replaced by a 'full-time administrator', with the title of domestic bursar, who was to 'take charge of a variety of administrative tasks and allow Fellows to concentrate on their other duties'.[12] The experiment was not considered successful and the position was abolished in 1977. A new post of domus officer, a full-time professional appointment under the supervision of a part-time junior bursar who was a Fellow, was created in its stead, but lasted only for a short while until its holder resigned.[13] It was evident that either the senior or junior bursar would have to be full-time in order to take the pressure off the other, and a full-time junior bursar was appointed in 1979; the post was given to a Fellow who was an existing teaching officer of the college, but was nonetheless regarded as an administrative appointment first and foremost. The senior bursarship continued to be regarded as a part-time office.[14] Formally, this is the situation today, although the senior bursar's office has become ever more time-consuming. Queens' is fortunate to have Fellows with sufficient expertise to fill both of these positions, but this is pure chance, and it seems certain that the college will have to appoint a non-academic 'professional' to at least one of its bursarships in the near future.

Finance

Since the end of the first world war, and especially since the end of the second, the universities, including Oxford and Cambridge, have come to depend more and more upon state funding; the government is now indisputably their paymaster.[15] Colleges at the older universities rely on the state to pay students' fees, although they also derive income from their endowments; the latter, the traditional source of the colleges'

[11]   CM 318, 319.
[12]   The first (and only) assistant bursar left for an academic post elsewhere in 1972, CB, 11.1.1972, 10.3.1972, 9.6.1972, 14.7.1972; D. W. Bowett in *Record* (1972 – 3).
[13]   GB, 9.6.1977; CM 534, 573; MS u/c-staff(I); Dr K. E. Machin, personal communication.
[14]   CM 573; GB, 20.11.1978.
[15]   Green (1969), 184 – 8; Halsey and Trow (1971), 85 – 91. When Newnham proposed to apply directly to the University Grants Commission for financial assistance shortly after the second world war, and other colleges were canvassed for their reactions, Queens' declared itself 'extremely unwilling to make such an approach ourselves, on grounds affecting our autonomy', CB (1937 – 63), 13.1.1948.

income, is equally important today for their financial well-being, and even their survival.[16] Queens' is now among the poorer Cambridge colleges in terms of endowment income, and constantly emphasises its poverty. In the late 19th century, as we have seen, it occupied a relatively lowly position among the colleges in terms of income. In 1920 it was thirteenth out of 17 colleges listed by the royal commissioners, although its financial management appears to have been no different from that of most colleges, and there is no suggestion that the college was conscious of being badly off at that time.[17]

The senior bursar at the time of the first world war was Andrew Munro, and according to his obituary notice in the *Dial* in 1935 it was to him that Queens' owed much of its 'present prosperity'. On Munro's advice the college began to sell its farms after the war and invested in government stocks; and it accumulated large cash reserves.[18] Immediately before and after the second world war, Queens' seems to have been investing seriously in shop property — J. A. Venn reckoned in 1948 that investment income had been doubled thereby — and it was still pursuing this line in the mid-1950s. By 1960 there was only one farm left, and its contribution to the annual income of the college was very small.[19]

Queens' appears to have derived a satisfactory return from its investments at least up until the second world war, and possibly for longer. During the 1950s, however, it became apparent that the college had to be increasingly alert if it wished to keep up with the rate of change in the financial market. In 1956 its endowment income was only £15,800 *per annum*, and only three men's colleges had a lower income. In 1962 the president, A. ll. Armitage, claimed that Queens' relative position had 'deteriorated sharply' since 1950. In 1960 the bursar warned that the college was in a period of financial stringency, and its charges on students were already very high.[20] In 1955 a financial

---

[16] Benefactions continue to arrive in all sizes, and are invaluable, but irregular.

[17] Above, p. 308; *Report* (1922), 329 and *passim*. Student charges at Queens' in 1920 were very low, *ibid.*, 191. There are some indications of concern at the levels of income and expenditure in some areas immediately after the first world war, CB (1889–1937), 14.1.1919, 29.4.1919, 17.3.1923. The most recent published college accounts show Queens' in 22nd position out of 28 colleges in terms of external revenues, *CU Reporter* 14.3.1986 (Special No. 12). The question of college wealth and financial prosperity is far more complicated than this, but it provides a significant indicator.

[18] *Dial* (Michaelmas 1935), 7. For sale of farm property, see e.g. CB (1889–1937), 13.1.1920, 2.3.1920, 23.4.1920, 29.4.1920, 5.5.1920, 16.7.1920, 3.8.1920, 20.9.1920, 18.10.1920, and *passim*. Queens' was still selling off farmlands in the late 1920s, but the rate had slowed. It was also claimed that Fitzpatrick was influential in reorganising the college finances, Rackham (1937), 1.

[19] CB (1889–1937), 10.10.1933; CB (1937–63), 12.2.1938, 10.10.1947; GB, 5.10.1954, 3.12.1954, 1.2.1955, 25.2.1955, 19.4.1955, 5.10.1955; MS u/c-town and country planning; MS u/c-property; CM 26 (see also CM 590).

[20] The average collegiate income in 1956 was £44,000, but there was a very wide range, from £10,000 to £146,000, *QC* (1955–6), 3; GB, 16.2.1962; CM 12.

committee had been formed to advise the bursar on investments, and in 1959 Lazard Brothers were appointed to act as college investment advisors on all matters other than real estate; this led to some changes in investment policy. In 1960 the college reformed its outdated system of account-keeping; and in the following years efforts were made to increase charges and make savings wherever possible.[21]

But the situation was still gloomy in 1968, and the college was concerned at its inability to raise its income any further or to create any capital surplus on accounts such as the repairs and improvements fund.[22] The demands of modernisation and expansion during the 1960s had made heavy inroads into the college's resources. The senior bursar's report of 1981 was more gloomy still, forecasting major deficits on the college accounts, and the report concluded: 'the College is going rapidly into debt and substantial economies are necessary', even though this would 'have an effect, perhaps a profound effect, on College life as it exists at present'. A committee which had been established earlier in the year to look at possible economies 'speedily and carefully' was not quite so pessimistic, but the problem was undeniably serious, and substantial cost-cutting measures were imposed. As a result, the college remains in a position of severe financial retrenchment; and the present senior bursar's summary of the financial situation in June 1986 spoke of an uncertain future in which 'things are more likely to get worse rather than better', and argued for a firm grip on expenditure.[23] Proposed changes in government funding of student fees are even more threatening. These events are of enormous significance, and financial trends have influenced the college's history profoundly in many areas over the last three decades; they form an ever-present background to the changes described in the following chapters.

---

[21] GB, 11.1.1955, 11.2.1959, 13.3.1959, 21.4.1959, 15.1.1963, 18.10.1963, 11.3.1966, 1.3.1968, 21.5.1968; CM 5, 97, 215.
[22] GB, 15.11.1968.
[23] CM 663, 668, 995.

26

The modern college (II) —
college buildings in the 20th century

Repairs and restoration

The need for the restoration, repair or modernisation of the college's buildings, especially the older structures, has been a constant worry for its administrators in recent times.[1] Since the early 1960s, when the need for modernisation has become much more urgent, such work has at times imposed a considerable burden on the college's financial resources, and led it to seek outside grants and to set up college appeals.[2]

The first example serves as another illustration of changing architectural tastes. Between 1910 and 1926 the roofs of the buildings in Old Court were altered by removing the early 19th century battlements and clock tower and replacing the slates with tiles.[3] When the last battlements were taken down, the *Dial* expressed its delight at the demise of 'these excrescences of energetic but misguided Gothic revivalists'.[4]

Changes in aesthetic fashion were also in evidence when the college came to repair the 18th century Essex building shortly before the second world war. The building was in a vulnerable position: next to the road, where it was 'constantly plastered with mud by passing traffic', and presumably liable to damage from vehicles;[5] and, more significantly, alongside the river, and therefore subject to flooding and erosion. The problems which attended the college in its first centuries because of its riverside situation have been discussed above, in chapter 10; and both flooding and erosion of river walls have persisted throughout its subsequent history.[6] At the beginning of 1938 concern at widening

[1]   See for example *QC, Record, passim.*
[2]   e.g. CM 9, 11, 12, 21, 22, 25, 33, 43, 62, 76; GB, 16.5.1958 (and see 13.1.1959); *QC* (1959 – 60), 6. Other illustrations appear in this chapter.
[3]   T. C. Fitzpatrick paid for the work, *CR* (20.10.1910), 37; (12.11.1926), 88; CB (1889 – 1937), 20.6.1910, 21.10.1926; MS 79, 11; Rackham (1937), 1 – 2. Perhaps the work began with the repairs to the hall roof in 1909, *Dial* (Michaelmas 1909), 207.
[4]   *Dial* (Lent 1927), supplement, i.
[5]   *CR* (13.12.1913), 265.
[6]   For recent examples, see Walker in *Record* (1980), 6 – 7; (1981), 4; *Dial* (Easter 1947), 17; *CR* (22.11.1894), 82, 94; *QC* (1942 – 7), 5; (1948 – 9), 5 – 6; CM 45, 261, 566, 620 (and see 627); MS u/c-junior bursar; MS u/c-town and country planning; CB (1937 – 63), 24.10.1947; GB, 17.5.1978.

cracks in the riverside wall of the Essex building turned swiftly into serious alarm when examination of the wall's foundations revealed erosion so serious that steel tie-rods had to be inserted to tie it into the rest of the building and its base and foundations had to be underpinned, to prevent collapse.[7] The foundations must have been scoured by water currents ever since the building had been erected, but this serious erosion was thought to be of recent origin, caused by diversion of the current by new weirs upstream. The town corporation was responsible for this, and a legal action was prepared against it.

The Essex building was not universally popular: the Victorians had reacted against its 18th century style, and it seems that many of the 20th century Fellows of Queens' were of like mind. Venn commented in 1948 that its white brick facing contrasted 'unfortunately' with the red brick of the rest of the college, and the possibility of refacing it with the latter material was discussed at one stage.[8] Certainly the costs of repair in 1938 were considerable.[9] But the college took a surprising and indeed radical step in negotiating with the corporation to sell it 'a portion of the ground now occupied by the Essex Building' for the widening of the Silver Street bridge, and deciding to demolish the building itself and use the proceeds of the sale to construct a new building in the style of the recently erected Fisher building on the other side of the river and designed by the same architect. The corporation was happy with this arrangment, and plans for the new building were drawn up, but the scheme was vetoed by the Ministry of Transport.[10] The Essex building has continued to suffer from its vulnerable position, and has from time to time required other repairs and restoration work — most recently the replacement of the roof slates in 1985 — but it has never again been in danger of demolition.[11]

The president's lodge and long gallery have also given cause for concern from time to time during the present century. The gallery had been completely rendered from at least the late 17th century until shortly before the first world war, when the decaying rendering was pulled off and the building presented in the half-timbered style which it retains today, and which appears to have been its original appearance.

---

[7] Reports (1924 – 39), letters of 12.1.1938, 13.4.1938; *Varsity*, 23.4.1938, 30.4.1938; Maxwell (MS), 5; MS u/c-town and country planning; MS u/c-Drinkwater correspondence; *QC* (1937 – 8), 14.

[8] MS u/c-town and country planning; MS u/c-Drinkwater correspondence.

[9] Reports (1914 – 49), 143; MS u/c-wartime(I).

[10] *Varsity*, 21.10.1938; *Dial* (Michaelmas 1938), 8; CB (1937 – 63), 22.4.1938, 31.5.1938, 20.6.1938, 4.7.1938, 18.10,1938, 9.5.1939. Four Fellows voted against the scheme. For the lawsuit (which was resolved after the war), see also CB (1937 – 63), 4.10.1939, 7.12.1945, 9.2.1946; MS u/c-town and country planning.

[11] e.g. MS u/c-maintenance; MS u/c-junior bursar; *QC* (1950 – 1), 5; (1951 – 2), 6; CM 7, 17; Walker in *Record* (1983), 5; (1985), 16; (1986), 3.

Its interior was restored in 1923, when a new ceiling was inserted to the design of C. G. Hare, the architect of the Doket building.[12] The lodge in general continued to require repairs and restoration and needed constant watchfulness.[13] Serious problems were discovered in 1982, when a thorough investigation of the fabric of the gallery revealed that damp, fungus and beetles had caused great damage to its timber structure, necessitating the replacement of some beams and treatment of many others. Further investigations by a structural engineer discovered several major structural weaknesses, and many wood joints were reinforced internally with steel brackets and marine ply. The college was thrown suddenly into a desperate financial situation: these repairs and other alterations to the lodge at the same time were extremely expensive — over £343,000 was spent between 1982 and 1984 — and an appeal was launched to old members to raise money to cover these costs and those of repairs to other old parts of the college in the future.[14]

New buildings

Queens' has undertaken three major building projects since the first world war, and as in the later 19th century the main impetus for the work has been the pressure of student numbers. In December 1934 the college decided to erect a building of about 80 sets of rooms at a cost of no more than £55,000, and to ask G. C. Drinkwater, a London-based architect, to draw up plans. Drinkwater was the college's architectural adviser in this period, but the origin of his connection with Queens' is not recorded. The plans were approved in February 1935.[15] Because there was little room left on the East bank of the Cam it had been decided to build on the opposite side: a site which had from a very early stage in the college's life been occupied by outbuildings of different kinds, a garden, a grove of trees; and in more recent times tennis courts and a bicycle shed. The main structures there at the time of the decision to build were cottages which housed college servants and some students, and college lecture rooms converted out of former stables. There was also a builder's yard: this and the cottages were demolished, but much of the rest of the site was undamaged, for the new building curved

[12] CR (13.2.1913), 265; (30.1.1920), 172. Dial (Lent 1912), 48–9; CB (1889–1937), 27.4.1911, 17.3.1923; Walker in Record (1983), 6.
[13] MS u/c-Drinkwater correspondence; MS u/c-maintenance; CB (1937–63), 22.4.1938; QC (1948–9), 5–6.
[14] Walker in Record (1983), 6; (1984), 7–9; (1985), 15; appeal notice in Record (1985), 6; CM 766, 874.
[15] CB (1889–1937), 7.12.1934, 8.2.1935 (four Fellows dissenting); QC (1934–5), 17; Who Was Who (1941–50), (Drinkwater). For some of his other work at Queens', see MS u/c-Drinkwater correspondence; QC (1933–4), 14–15.

around one side of it.[16] The construction of the building, which was to be named after John Fisher, was financed by the sale of college investments, and it was opened in 1936.[17]

The Fisher scheme introduced squash courts and garages to Queens', and claimed to be innovatory in its material for roof insulation — a compound of aluminium and asbestos sheeting — but its style was steadfastly traditional.[18] Before the plans and elevation were made public it had been announced that the building would be similar in style to the residential block in Walnut Tree Court. Both the Friars and Doket buildings had been traditionalist; and Drinkwater was clearly following orders given him by the college.[19] But principally for this reason it has not been popular with architectural writers, and it was not much liked by contemporaries. The author of an article on the building in the *Cambridge Review* in October 1936 asked: 'Is there some lacuna in Cambridge culture that leaves us blind to the visual arts?' *Varsity* did not like it either, and was greatly relieved in 1938 that the plan to build another building of the same sort on the site of the Essex building fell through.[20] The Fisher building was known by some irreverently as 'Regina Terrace', an appellation which prefigures Pevsner's better known derision of it as 'looking exactly like a friendly block of flats at, say, Pinner'. Pevsner thought it 'a sadly insignificant range' in 'a timidly imitative style'; he felt the college had 'wasted a great opportunity here for a good contemporary building' which would 'in no way have interfered with existing collegiate structures of the past'.[21] The authors of *Cambridge New Architecture* have observed that while the distinctive brickwork of the college's old buildings has inspired some recent architectural projects in Cambridge, it 'has also presented a great temptation to dabblers in the picturesque, who designed the terrible Fisher Building'.[22] It is evident that the artistic sensibility of the college's governing body was not in general highly developed at that time, and the Fisher building is unremarkable — undistinguished, if one prefers — but for the most part it is not unattractive, and it has served its function well.

In the short term it solved the college's accommodation problem; and

[16] For the site see above, chapter 10; McGowan (MS), 5, 7; Keynes (1976), 2, 7 – 8, 92; Raverat (1960), 44, 85; Browne and Seltman (1951), plate 118; MS 79, 7, 19; White (1932), 40, 83 – 4, 86; CB (1889 – 1937), 21.1.1935, 4.2.1935, 22.2.1935, 3.5.1935. See *ibid.*, entries of 1935 – 6, for the construction of the building.

[17] Reports (1924 – 39), 1939; CM 10. Some capital was taken from other college funds, and invested in Fisher, with the room rents diverted to pay the interest.

[18] *Dial* (Lent 1936), 6; CB (1889 – 1937), 6.12.1935, 7.10.1936.

[19] *Dial* (Lent 1935), 2.

[20] Fowler and Fowler (1984), 313; *Varsity*, 2.12.1938.

[21] Crutchley (1980), 86; Pevsner (1970), 40, 138 – 9.

[22] *Cambridge New Architecture* (1965), 27.

in 1948 J. A. Venn said that 'No further building would be needed for 100 years'.[23] But he had not reckoned upon the great post-war expansion in student numbers, and by the mid-1950s it was becoming apparent that Queens' would have to build further student accommodation in the near future. In February 1955 the governing body began to explore the costs of such a project, and in the summer it inspected drawings by S. Dykes Bower, who restored the interior of the chapel in that year.[24] Dykes Bower's plan was for a five-storey building to house 49 students and one Fellow on a site at the western end of the Friars building, parallel to the river; the maximum cost allowed by the governing body for its construction was £100,000.[25] The problem of accommodation was considered acute: the new building would enable every undergraduate to spend two years in college, and remove the obligation for second year students to share — a return to the pre-war position.[26] Financial considerations were paramount, and the college appreciated that the necessarily substantial expenditure on the new building would make rigid economies necessary elsewhere when it was finished. A building fund was therefore established in November 1955, and an appeal sent out to old members.[27]

The next stage was to consider designs for the building. It was clear that several Fellows were unhappy with Dykes Bower's 'neo-Jacobean' scheme and there seems to have been a strong move in favour of something more modern; and so, early in 1957, the governing body decided to look at alternative designs.[28] After looking at the work of several architects, the college selected Basil Spence, who was well established, highly regarded, and unequivocally modern, best known for the new cathedral at Coventry. Spence was invited to submit drawings in the summer of 1957, and was formally appointed in January 1958.[29]

[23] MS u/c-town and country planning.

[24] GB, 1.2.1955, 22.7.1955; QC (1953 – 4), 6; Cambridge New Architecture (1965), 27. Dykes Bower seems to have been the college's architectural adviser at this time, as Drinkwater had been in the 1930s; Drinkwater was killed in an air raid in 1941, QC (1940 – 1), 5. For numbers at Queens' in this period see the college entries in Varsity Handbook, passim; CB (1937 – 63), 13.3.1948, 2.6.1950, 21.11.1950, 1.6.1951, 28.5.1962; GB, 5.10.1955; CM 98; MS u/c-town and country planning.

[25] GB, 22.7.1955.

[26] ibid., 18.10.1955, 1.11.1955; QC (1955 – 6), 2 – 4. The problem was partly offset by turning most of the sets in the Friars building into bedsits, see QC (1949 – 50), 4; (1950 – 1), 5.

[27] GB, 22.7.1955, 18.10.1955, 1.11.1955, 3.12.1955. By October 1956 the appeal had raised over £28,000; by January 1961, when the building was already in use, over £55,000. The total cost of the building was reckoned at about £115,000 in 1960, but in 1964 the final figure was given as £94,000, GB, 9.10.1956, 2.11.1960, JB-Erasmus.

[28] GB, 31.1.1957, 15.3.1957; Cambridge New Architecture (1965), 28.

[29] GB, 23.4.1957, 3.5.1957, 13.5.1957, 7.6.1957, 6.12.1957, 14.1.1958; Who Was Who (1971 – 80) (Spence).

The Fellows took a keen interest in the design of the new building. In 1957, when the governing body was considering alternative architects, 'there was also a detailed discussion about the preliminary instructions to be given to the chosen architect, but the view was widely expressed that he should be tied down as little as possible at this stage'.[30] Spence was therefore given a free hand; and although he was only appointed after the governing body had examined his designs, soon afterwards some Fellows expressed the wish 'for an opportunity to discuss points that some might regard as details but that the architect might regard as principles'.[31] His 'revolutionary design' for a five-storey L-shaped structure roughly on the same site that had been intended for the Dykes Bower building was made public early in 1958.[32] It provoked an immediate outcry because of its size and modernism, and because the published photograph misleadingly made it appear to be right next to the river. The governing body was greatly alarmed by this hostile reception, and the college magazine for that year attempted to reassure the old members on whom the success of the appeal for funds depended:

'There is every reason to suppose that the result will be a building which definitely improves the view from the Backs (at present the blank end wall and chimney stack of Friars' bulk too large in this prospect), is in real accord with the distinctive traditional character of the Queens' Buildings, and is at the same time a modern building'.

It was further emphasised that the governing body had not yet taken a final decision on the design: this was to be deferred until it could be seen from the architect's model how the building would look in relation to the rest of the college.[33] An earlier draft of this placatory notice had been far less compromising in tone, which presumably accounts for its rejection: this acknowledged the opposition of some old members, and promised not to be hasty in making its decision, but it also affirmed the inevitability of modern architecture not winning universal popularity. It stressed Spence's reputation, and the approval which had greeted his appointment and the college's decision 'to achieve a new building in a contemporary style suitable for Cambridge college architecture', and to follow the current move against the former fashion for 'more routine and derivative building'.[34]

The Fellows were now even more uneasy about the design, and asked

[30] GB, 13.5.1957.
[31] ibid., 31.1.1958.
[32] Varsity, 1.2.1958.
[33] QC (1956 – 7), 4.
[34] JB-Erasmus.

to see a model and further sketches; Spence also wished to make some alterations, and the governing body did not wish him to be hurried. Revised designs were approved in July 1958, but the college continued to dither during the following months. Spence was invited to dine at Queens' at the end of October to discuss the problem, and in his reply to the junior bursar wrote: 'I sincerely hope that before that time the College will have agreed to the latest design, because I am now convinced that this is the best that I can do'.[35] The college was still struggling to make up its mind about certain features of the building in the following year, although a scaled-down design for a structure of only three storeys was approved by the Royal Fine Arts Commission early in 1959; there was also concern about the cost of the project.[36] The Fellows even had difficulty in choosing a name for the new building, going through a good number of suggestions before deciding on 'Erasmus'.[37] Students were able to move into the building on time, in the autumn of 1960, and it was officially opened by the Queen Mother in June 1961; but for a few years afterwards it was plagued by problems with many of the internal fittings.[38]

Having decided to back a modern design in appointing Spence as architect, the Fellows seem to have been frightened by their own audacity; the outcry caused by publication of the original drawings at the beginning of 1958 clearly threw many of them into a panic. It has also been claimed that the earlier and exceedingly unattractive Dykes Bower design was only 'narrowly rejected' by the Fellows, and the governing body's great uncertainty regarding Spence's plans may have owed something to a persistent conservative faction.[39] The architect clearly felt that he did not enjoy the governing body's full confidence, and his task cannot have been an easy one.

Subsequent architectural critics have found it hard to understand what all the fuss was about. Pevsner commented that Spence was 'the target of much abuse for reasons now hard to understand' — the penalty for being a pioneer of modern architecture in the university, although his work would soon appear staid compared with some of the more daring designs which followed.[40] In the 1965 edition of *Cambridge New Architecture* the Erasmus building was described as 'Reassuringly massive in outline and warm in tone', and 'handsomely detailed and beautifully furnished', and was said to show 'all Sir Basil's skills in

[35] GB, 28.7.1958, 2.10.1958, 24.10.1958; MS u/c-Erasmus building.
[36] *Varsity*, 7.2.1959; GB, 2.10.1958, 27.1.1959, 11.2.1959, 24.2.1959, 13.3.1959, 21.4.1959, 1.5.1959, 3.6.1959, 26.6.1959; JB-Erasmus.
[37] GB, 18.7.1960, 2.11.1960, 3.12.1960.
[38] CM 32, 33; *Varsity*, 10.6.1961; JB-Erasmus.
[39] *Cambridge New Architecture* (1965), 28.
[40] Pevsner (1970), 44 – 6, 139 – 40.

siting the new next to the old' — indeed it was felt to be 'marred if anything by too great a desire to conform to the rest of Queens' '. The account concluded:

'It seems grotesque that this moderate, conformist design once caused such a furore among "Times" letter-writers, but in 1958 this was a test case for modern architecture in Cambridge, even though such battles had been won ten years or more earlier in the design, say, of primary schools'.[41]

By the middle of the 1960s Queens' was again looking to build student accommodation. In its appeal to old members for financial support for the Erasmus building in 1957, the college had insisted that it was not preparing to increase its student intake,[42] but the Robbins report, which envisaged a massive expansion of all the British universities, compelled it to reconsider the position, and during the early part of the 1960s it looked at ways of making better use of its existing facilities by conversion of other rooms into residential accommodation, splitting sets into bedsitters, or even constructing new garret bedrooms in the roofs of buildings as in the 17th century.[43] The main problem was lack of money — the early 1960s were a period of financial stringency for the college — but in January 1964 A. ll. Armitage reckoned the situation had improved sufficiently for the governing body to 'consider a major work plan over the next ten years to be financed out of Revenue', including not only the restoration and repairs already envisaged but also 'the problem of increased accommodation arising from the Robbins Report'.[44]

Later in the year a college development committee was set up to look at the whole range of questions, one of which was the provision of new buildings; and in May 1965 the governing body discussed possible sites for these. At this stage the college envisaged a residential block housing 120 undergraduates and over 20 graduates and research students, 'with some married accommodation', and it was also suggested that a new hall (a 'Village Hall') should be provided for general student use.[45] The plan was rapidly amended to provide for 200 undergraduates and over 30 graduates and research students (still with some married accommo-

---

[41] *Cambridge New Architecture* (1965), 28. McKean (1982), 21, merely notes the existence of the building and does not bother to pass comment; Rawle (1985), 124, observes that it blends well with its surroundings.

[42] QC (1955 – 6), 2 – 4.

[43] e.g. CM 74, 318; GB, 27.2.1963, 11.11.1963, 14.1.1964 (and see 21.4.1964).

[44] CM 107; and c.f. above, pp. 367 – 8, for the college's financial position in the early and late 1960s. For the question of student numbers during the decade see GB, 11.10.1965, 11.7.1966, 3.3.1967, 16.1.1968, 5.12.1969, 17.7.1970; CM 20, 82, 83, 98, 99, 100, 116, 286; Queens' entries in *Varsity Handbook, passim*.

[45] GB, 26.10.1964, 9.11.1964, 4.12.1964; CM 155.

dation), but the college development committee warned that 'Whilst this is the accommodation actually envisaged, it must be understood that implementation on that scale must depend on the help that the College receives from outside sources'.[46] There was a search for possible sources of money, but without much success, for in 1968 when the governing body discussed the new buildings again, the scale had been considerably reduced: there were now to be only about 50 rooms — the ideal of providing married accommodation had been abandoned — and an all-purpose hall at a cost of approximately £150,000 and the employment of professional fund-raisers was recommended.[47]

In the following year it became apparent that the college had at last found an outside sponsor, for it returned to a more ambitious scheme for 150 rooms, a new dining hall to seat 500, a multi-purpose hall, new JCR and graduate common room, and many other rooms for various social purposes.[48] The sponsor was the Cripps Foundation, a charitable trust created by the businessman and industrialist C. Humphrey Cripps, which had already funded the Cripps buildings at St John's and Selwyn.[49] The building at St John's, designed by Powell and Moya, was generally considered one of the more successful pieces of 1960s college architecture in Cambridge, and the same practice was selected for the new development at Queens'; the governing body examined their designs in June 1971.[50]

The costs of the entire undertaking were vast — by the time the final phase of Cripps Court is completed, they will have run into many millions of pounds — and with building costs rising rapidly in the early 1970s it was decided at an early stage of the planning to concentrate on the residential blocks first, and then to consider the remainder of the scheme in the light of future economic conditions.[51] These constraints meant many delays and the regular postponement of projected completion dates; great forbearance was needed by all the parties involved. Five of the six residential staircases were occupied in October 1974, and this concluded the first phase of the project; the new dining hall and kitchens were brought into use in January 1979, and the final residential staircase in 1981. The second phase was completed in 1983 with a new laundrette, toilets and meetings room. Phase three (the multi-purpose hall, squash courts and underground garage), designed

[46] CM 156; and see GB, 7.5.1965.
[47] CM 199, 222; GB, 8.2.1967, 16.4.1968.
[48] CM 261.
[49] GB, 11.6.1971; Who's Who (Cripps); Rawle (1985), 132, 148.
[50] Rawle (1985), 132; GB, 2.6.1971, 19.6.1971.
[51] GB, 11.6.1971, 19.6.1971, and see 10.11.1972. The main costs were borne by the Cripps Foundation, but some of the lesser costs — furnishing, for example — were paid for by the college, which launched a professionally directed appeal for the new development, D. W. Bowett in Record (1972–3).

by Bland and Brown, a local partnership, was begun in the summer of 1986 and is expected to take about three years to complete.[52]

A full assessment of the scheme is not possible at this stage. There have been, inevitably, some technical problems with the earlier phases, especially the flat roof, which was prone to leaking and had to be replaced in 1985.[53] There has also been some discolouring of the concrete surfaces, which is almost invariably the case with that material. Opinions of its architectural quality have varied enormously. There has been high praise: the Royal Institute of British Architects commended it in 1982; and the architectural correspondent of the *Observer*, a noted enthusiast for Powell and Moya designs, wrote that 'To my mind Cripps Court is easily the best piece of modern architecture by a British architect anywhere.'[54]

At the other extreme has been the predictable criticism of any new design. The building was savaged, perhaps inevitably, by the undergraduate press. While the first phase was still under construction in 1973, *Stop Press* thought it 'totally out of place. Erasmus building was sensitive and caused a furore — this one will rape the southern end of the Backs. Nobody seems to mind'. The *Varsity Handbook* of 1974 – 5 described it as 'a monstrous concrete sandwich disfiguring the Backs'; and five years later as 'a monstrosity . . . that resembles something Sir Charles Forte might have thrown up along the M4'.[55] These remarks might perhaps, but only partly, be written off as fashionable disdain for new design, and over-enthusiasm for literary effect. In Tom Sharpe's novel *Porterhouse Blue* an old Cambridge man revisiting the university 'pottered on through . . . Queens' over the wooden bridge and shuddered at the desecration of concrete that had been erected over the river',[56] an observation which may speak for many old members who resent the destruction of the old on such a massive scale. D. W. Bowett, in his comments on the development of the project in the 1976 issue of the college *Record*, admitted that 'A number of Queensmen have had reservations about the new Cripps Court and for that reason have felt unable to support the main College Appeal', and he expressed the hope

---

[52] *QC* (1970 – 1), 5; notes on new college development appeal in D. W. Bowett, P. G. Stein, J. M. Prentis, in *Record* (1972 – 3) — (1982); *Stop Press*, 19.10.1974, 16.2.1980 (and see 4.5.1973, 18.5.1973); Walker in *Record* (1984), 7; (1986), 3. Robin Walker informs me that Julian Bland of Bland and Brown worked with Powell and Moya during the construction of phase two. The new development was named, predictably, Cripps Court, GB, 15.5.1974, 7.6.1974, 12.7.1974. The new JCR was named after T. C. Fitzpatrick, the old Fitzpatrick Hall having been demolished to build Cripps Court; the long dining room next to the hall was named after A. ll. Armitage, a unique honour for a living Queensman, commemorating his work in inaugurating the project, CM 392.

[53] Walker in *Record* (1985), 15; (1986), 3.

[54] CM 725; Gardiner in *Observer* 11.5.1980.

[55] *Stop Press*, 9.2.1973; *Varsity Handbook* (1974 – 5), 46; (1979 – 80), 23.

[56] Sharpe (1976), 144.

that they would support the new special appeal for the old library instead.[57]

More serious critics have not been happy with the building either, feeling that it does not fit in well with its surroundings, and that it is inferior to the earlier Powell and Moya design for St John's, with which it has some stylistic similarities.[58] Cripps Court does appear to be too large for its site, but in itself it is a striking and attractive design, breaking with the convention of the last hundred years that new buildings at Queens' have to match the colours of the old college. To have built in brick yet again would, in D. W. Bowett's words, have made the new appear as 'a shoddy imitation of the old'.[59] But the layout of the buildings, and some of the internal features, are designed in imitation of the traditional college court, in an imaginative blend of old and new. The third phase is not part of this court, but it will complete the development of the site, and only then will a full appraisal of the scheme be possible; a more balanced view may prevail once the dust has settled.

---

[57] D. W. Bowett in *Record* (1976), 4.
[58] McKean (1982), 39; Rawle (1985), 124.
[59] D. W. Bowett in *Record* (1972 – 3).

27

The modern college (III) —
the curriculum; the library;
presidents and Fellows; religion

The curriculum

The expansion of the university syllabus which had begun in the late Victorian period continued apace after the first world war. The number of triposes grew, and great efforts were made to improve the level of teaching. The report of a royal commission in 1922 led to the creation of the modern system of faculty teaching and university lectureships, dealing a mortal blow to the influence of the colleges, which now became branches of the university teaching network, and were made to respond to changes introduced in the faculties.[1] This development was foreseen at Queens' in 1920, when the governing body decided, rather vaguely, that 'in view of the increase in the number of subjects of study in the University and the College it is desirable that there should be an increase in the number of Fellowships with a view to teaching and research'.[2]

One of the first of the new triposes to make an impact was English, introduced during the first world war and regarded with suspicion and scorn by traditionalists at first, although it soon established a reputation for academic distinction.[3] One of its first students was G. B. Harrison, who had returned to Queens' from war service. He had studied classics before the war, but was no longer interested in the endless translation exercises which that subject required and their 'demand for absolute accuracy', and he was full of enthusiasm for the new English tripos: 'There, I felt, lay the future of humane studies for the professions'. The college tutor in charge of enrolments was J. H. Gray:

> 'When I told him of my decision . . . he puffed his gills as of old, in indignation, and snorted with contempt at the 'Novel-reading Tripos'. He added that Queens' had no one to teach it or control it. But he gave in, warning me that if I started it I would have to look

[1] Roach, 'University of Cambridge', 290ff; Howarth (1978), chapter 2.
[2] CB (1889 – 1937), 19.6.1920.
[3] Howarth (1978), 116 – 124, 193 – 8.

after myself'.[4]

When Harrison obtained a first class degree in 1920, he wanted to remain in Cambridge as a don, but the English tripos was so new that no colleges had appointed any teaching Fellows in the subject. Gray even advised him to take another tripos, saying that Queens' would only consider him for a fellowship if he obtained a double first.[5] But in 1924 the college recognised the success and permanence of the new tripos by electing L. J. Potts to a fellowship and appointing him director of studies in English, a post which he held for 25 years.[6]

Other subjects for which Queens' had to make permanent provision by electing teaching Fellows were modern languages and medicine. The modern languages tripos had begun in 1886; it was first taken by a Queensman in 1897; and in 1928 the college introduced entrance scholarships and exhibitions in modern languages as well as English. But the tripos made limited progress even into the 1920s, and it was not until 1933 that Queens' appointed P. F. D. Tennant, a university lecturer in Scandinavian languages, to be its first Fellow in the subject.[7] Medicine was one of the oldest of university studies, although there had never been many formal students. Numbers increased after the first world war, and the course was restructured in the early 1930s; from the mid-1930s, therefore, Queens' always had a medical Fellow on its staff.[8] By the outbreak of the second world war, the college had three Fellows in the new, or reformed, subjects, whilst retaining a full complement of those in the older triposes. In relative terms this represented a major expansion.[9]

Since the second world war this growth has continued apace. Law, another of the oldest university subjects, and economics, a new tripos dating from 1910, were catered for at Queens' by new teaching appointments in 1945 and 1952 respectively, and henceforth these fellowships were regarded as an essential part of the teaching complement.[10] But there has also been considerable expansion within the boundaries of existing subjects in terms of the number of 'teaching'

[4] Harrison (1985), 119–20. See *ibid.*, 120–5, for the early years of the tripos.
[5] *ibid.*, 126.
[6] Potts was not a university lecturer at the time of his appointment, *QC* (1959–60), 3–4; CB (1889–1937), 9.10.1926.
[7] Tanner (1917), 951, 957; above, p. 292; *Who's Who* (Tennant); CB (1889–1937), 18.6.1928 (I know of no reference to these scholarships before this date); Roach, 'University of Cambridge', 281; Howarth (1978), 114–6.
[8] Roach, 'University of Cambridge', 301; *QC* (1934–5), 1; *QC, passim.*
[9] There were fourteen Fellows, including the president, in 1939, *QC* (1938–9), 3.
[10] *Record* (1984), 3; Tanner (1917), 981; *QC* (1950–1), 3. The law studied in the early days of the university had of course been civil, or Roman, law, not the English common law which makes up much of the present-day course.

Fellows appointed: the most significant aspect of this has been the increase in scientific Fellows.[11] In 1925 Queens' had ten Fellows: six were trained in the arts, and four in the sciences. There were two classicists, J. H. Gray and A. B. Cook, but otherwise no more than one Fellow in any subject. By the outbreak of the second world war, the college had a full complement of 14, nine in arts, five in science, and by the beginning of the 1950s the arts Fellows outnumbered scientists by two to one; but by the early 1960s the gap had narrowed, with 13 arts Fellows and 9 scientists.

The most dramatic expansion has been since this time, together with a fundamental shift in the balance of subjects. In 1972 there were 17 science Fellows, 16 in arts; in 1986 there are 21 and 17 respectively.[12] The number of Fellows has risen in almost every one of the principal teaching subjects, with the exception of classics, which is confined to a single Fellow these days, and for various reasons the number in a given subject rarely remains constant for long. The most significant area of expansion has been within the various branches of natural sciences, from one Fellow in the early 1950s to ten in 1986; this in itself explains the shift in balance between arts and sciences, since the other subjects in both disciplines have each tended to grow at roughly the same rate.

Of course, the college's teaching needs are not supplied by its own teaching Fellows alone: much is done on an exchange basis with other colleges and by outside supervisors; there are external directors of studies in several of the smaller subjects; and increasing use is being made of research Fellows and research students. Still, the composition of the college's fellowship remains a good guide to its teaching priorities. The distribution of subjects among students is closely linked to this changing composition by a complicated mechanism of cause and effect, but it reflects the same pattern: in recent years there has been a close balance between arts and sciences among the students, reflecting the picture for the university as a whole.[13]

It is not easy to pass an authoritative judgement upon the academic standards of Queens' students throughout the whole of this period. In the half century before the first world war the college was very slightly above the university average for the proportion of its students who took honours instead of pass degrees — that is to say, just under 50%.[14] In 1937 C. T. Wood wrote that he thought there had been a great

---

[11]   In these examples, subjects such as land economy, industrial relations, and economics have been grouped within the category of arts subjects, according to the conventional distinction. By 'teaching' Fellows are meant all except, research, retired, and honorary Fellows; in other words, including presidents and professorial Fellows, and some bye-Fellows.

[12]   QC (1925 – 6), 1; (1939 – 40), 1; (1950 – 1), 3; (1960 – 1), 1; Record (1972 – 3); (1986), 1.

[13]   CM 208, 272, 286, 298, 476, 749, 806, 957.

[14]   CR (23.1.1908), 179; (30.1.1908), 196; Grave (1983), 115 – 6; see also CR (6.2.1908), 212.

improvement in academic standards since 1919; certainly the quality of entrance scholars rose after the late 1920s, thanks to increased remuneration of scholarships and improved methods of assessing candidates.[15] The general impression must be that during this period Queens' was of moderate academic distinction — an average college. The Cambridge academic system was still geared mainly to the most gifted candidates, and the ambitious and intelligent students were likely to be successful in any college. The rewards of such success were considerable, and not solely within the academic world: Abba Eban soon found out after arriving at Queens' in 1934 that

> 'the academic ambition of Cambridge students was to achieve a First in each part of the examinations held at the end of the second and third years. A Double First was a distinction that pursued its holder all his life, a dignity by which he was known in private and sometimes even introduced in public'.[16]

The impression of moderate academic performance overall at Queens' persists beyond the second world war. In its percentage of students taking first class or upper second class degrees, Queens' was well in the middle of the college lists during the early to mid-1960s, and well below the university average in 1970, though performance in tripos is not the exclusive measure of academic achievement.[17] By the early 1970s there were signs of improvement. The official view put out in the *Cambridge Admissions Prospectus* when it first began to take entries from the colleges in 1974 was that Queens' examination performances were 'always respectable and occasionally brilliant', a formula repeated annually in the *Prospectus* until 1978, when they were described as 'always respectable and often — increasingly often nowadays — brilliant'; the students' *Varsity Handbook* commented on the college's 'high academic reputation' in 1980.[18] By 1980 Queens' was well above the university average, and since then it has maintained a high ranking in the tripos 'league table' and a good reputation at large.[19] These most recent successes have been due largely to the admission of women in 1980: throughout the university colleges which have become co-residential have experienced a substantial improvement in the academic calibre of their applicants, and it is still too early to predict with any accuracy

[15] *Dial* (Michaelmas 1937), 16; Reports (1914 – 49), 95, and see 125.
[16] Eban (1978), 16 – 17.
[17] *Varsity*, 12.10.1963, 10.10.1964, 8.10.1966, 14.10.1967; CM 722.
[18] *Varsity*, 14.10.1972; *Cambridge Admissions Prospectus* (1974), 94 – 5; (1978), 89; *Varsity Handbook* (1980 – 1), 30. The entries in the official prospectus are contributed by the college, which is hardly likely to undervalue its academic standard.
[19] CM 722, 784, 873, 1018; *Stop Press*, 4.10.1983; *Varsity Handbook* (1982 – 3), 29; *Cambridge Admissions Prospectus* (1982), 43; GB, 14.11.1984.

whether this improvement at Queens' will persist as a long-term trend.

The library

The college's archives contain few references to the library between the beginning of the 18th century (the concluding point of the discussion in chapter 8) and the 20th; from these we can perceive a constant concern for the security of books, and a steady stream of benefactions.[20] In late Victorian times the library was in a good state: only three colleges were said to have more books in 1881.[21] The expansion of the curriculum and the great increase in student numbers after this time not only made books more significant as a medium of undergraduate education, but also placed greater demands on the resources of college libraries. The library in Queens' depended still on benefactions, and these were increasingly insufficient to meet student needs. R. G. D. Laffan encouraged his history students to donate books in order to build up the library's collection in that subject, and the college History Society also contributed.[22] In 1948 *Varsity* described the Queens' library as having few books for contemporary student needs, and although the conversion of the old chapel into an undergraduate library in 1951 supplied much-needed space for books, the college was still unable to keep abreast of rising needs.[23] A report to the governing body in 1965 showed that official college expenditure on books over the past six years 'has fallen seriously behind that of other Colleges of roughly comparable financial standing . . . and has not even kept pace with the continuing rise in book prices'. The report also observed, as if such an observation were needed, that a good college library providing 'both adequate coverage for Tripos subjects . . . and a fair range of other books' was 'one of the greatest benefits a College can offer its students'. It noted too that the library was running out of shelf space.[24]

In the same year the committee for the college development plan had

---

[20] For security, see e.g. CB (1734 – 87), f.79v; and modern examples, CM 49; GB, 27.2.1963, 15.3.1963, 16.4.1963. The benefactions are too numerous to note here: many are small. One of the most significant was that of the 18th century Fellow David Hughes in 1777, see above, p. 203.

[21] *CR* (9.3.1881), 210 – 11.

[22] *Record* (1972 – 3); History Society minutes. The levy on Fellows (see above, p. 105) was revived in the early 19th century, CB (1787 – 1832), 13.1.1803; but it is not clear when it had lapsed, and I do not know its subsequent history.

[23] *Varsity*, 21.2.1948. For the conversion of the old chapel, see *QC* (1950 – 1), 7 – 8; *Varsity*, 11.10.1947; *Cambridge New Architecture* (1955), 27; MS u/c-maintenance.

[24] CM 158; GB, 14.1.1964 (and see 12.2.1965). Cambridge, with its range of university, faculty and college libraries, was and is very much better supplied with books than the modern universities, Halsey and Trow (1971), 92.

suggested that the governing body consider 'removing the under-graduate part of the Library from its present site to be incorporated in a building scheme', or at least 'overflow of the Library into Walnut Tree Court'.[25] No action was taken immediately, but the situation worsened in more than one respect, for in 1967 the librarian wrote to the president of the pressing need for more space, and the official librarian's report three years later called for the appointment of a part-time assistant to deal with the growing burden of library administration.[26] The latter request was granted, but the problem of space remained. Although there was a library development committee of the governing body, when this met in 1971 with the committee for developing those old parts of the college which would become redundant after the completion of the new buildings, 'it became clear that whole-hearted support would not be forthcoming for any of the proposals for expansion which the Library Development Committee had in mind'.[27]

There has been no subsequent progress, although the governing body recognised the need for 'urgent steps' to resolve the library's difficulties in 1984, and the matter is about to be raised again at the time of writing.[28] It is a sad omission — the library is the only student facility in the college not to have been developed significantly during the last two decades, and must surely be one of the college's foremost priorities for the future.

Fellows

The massive numerical expansion of the college fellowship which has been noted above in the context of the curriculum has slowed considerably in the last few years; the numbers can probably be expected to remain more or less static over the next few. The principal reason for this is financial. The new system of university lectureships developed after the first world war made it possible for colleges to recruit non-stipendiary Fellows from among university teaching officers whose salaries were paid by the university; but for this a college such as Queens', with relatively limited capital resources, would not have been able to expand.[29] Some other fellowships have been created from benefactions in this century, but such benefactions are infrequent, and

[25] CM 155.
[26] CM 200(a), 278.
[27] CM 328; see also GB, 2.10.1970.
[28] GB, 27.2.1984.
[29] See *Statutes* (1925), 13 – 14, for the new categories of Fellows.

very large sums of money are required to maintain a fellowship.[30]

Signs of difficulty in maintaining sufficient Fellows for the college's teaching needs with the funds available were apparent in 1948 when Queens' appointed a Fellow in classics for a probationary period of two years with the proviso that the appointment should not be renewed for more than another three years thereafter 'unless the Governing Body shall have ascertained by enquiry in the Faculty of Classics that he is likely to be appointed to a University teaching post in the near future'.[31] The problem became particularly acute with the rapid expansion of the student population in the early and mid-1960s, when there was considerable discussion of the matter: Queens' insisted that in order to prevent the wealthier colleges from stealing a march on the others, each college should have 'a reasonable proportion of Fellows who are University teaching officers in the commoner teaching subjects'. But it resisted suggestions of a fixed quota system, even while recognising that it would undoubtedly gain from such a system, on the grounds that colleges were 'institutions of independent education, with initiatives and policies of their own'. College teaching was felt to 'offer support to potential university teaching officers through research fellowships before University appointments become available. College teaching and college research fellowships thus do much to ensure the high calibre of the junior university appointments in Cambridge'.[32] In essence, this was the age-old battle for college autonomy against the influence of the university refought.

At this time only about two thirds of the Fellows of Queens' were university teaching officers — the others had to be maintained out of college funds — and this situation gave rise to some concern.[33] In 1964 it was announced that the college already had 'extensive' exchange teaching arrangements with other colleges, 'particularly in some arts subjects';[34] but this was increasingly insufficient, and more fellowships were needed. Since Queens' could not afford to fund these out of its own resources, outside assistance was sought: in the 1960s the Central

[30] e.g. T. C. Fitzpatrick left £10,000 to found one or more fellowships, but the money was not apparently utilised until the 1960s, CR (12.2.1932), 242; Reports (1914 – 49), 65; CM 150. In 1974 the Godfrey Mitchell Charitable Trust gave £10,000 towards founding an engineering fellowship; in 1984 the William Colton Foundation endowed a research fellowship; and in the same year another research fellowship was endowed by Osaka Gakuin university of Japan, CM 412, 843, 883, 902; GB, 16.3.1984.

[31] CB (1937 – 63), 21.6.1948.

[32] CM 64 (and see 66), 127; GB, 24.4.1962. There was already a quota system for professors, e.g. GB, 11.1.1955.

[33] Thirteen Fellows out of 23 were in university posts in October 1960; 19 out of 29 in December 1962, CM 79. It is usual to renew the fellowships of university teaching officers for as long as they hold their office, e.g. CM 871.

[34] CM 127. In 1958 Queens' had been keen to extend its teaching resources without appointing more Fellows, GB, 5.12.1958.

Electricity Generating Board supported a research fellowship, and half of another research Fellow's salary was paid by industry. This practice appears to have lapsed in the course of the 1970s, but in 1983 it was again suggested the the college's 'pressing need' for research Fellows might be met by an appeal to industry.[35] No teaching fellowships were supported in this way — though research Fellows have always done some teaching for the college — and such methods of funding could only benefit the scientific subjects, where there seems anyway to have been an adequate supply of university teaching officers for the most part.

The main difficulty was in the arts, but not exclusively. In 1974 the president, D. W. Bowett, noted that the shortage of college teaching was acute in two scientific subjects: mathematics and medicine; and in three arts subjects: law, modern languages and history.[36] The problem was partially resolved by setting up joint fellowships with other colleges: one each in history and law with Trinity; another in history with Girton; in mathematics with Magdalene; and in English with Trinity Hall. Such arrangements usually lapsed as soon as their holders received university or other positions.[37]

Such *ad hoc* practices could only stem the tide for a time. Although the governing body sanctioned an increase in the number of Fellows from 30 to 35 in 1979, and the creation of a fellowships fund was suggested,[38] the sudden financial crisis of the early 1980s forced the college into a totally different policy. A committee established to explore possible cuts in expenditure recommended in 1981 the 'utmost restraint' in replacing Fellows, argued that three existing vacancies should be filled 'only to meet exceptional circumstances', and urged the consideration of all possible alternatives before appointing anyone who did not hold a university teaching office to a fellowship, since such an appointment was reckoned to cost the college three times as much as that of a Fellow with such an office.[39]

The non-university teaching officer (or NUTO) had been vulnerable even before the financial crisis. In 1979 one Fellow whose university office had expired was reappointed to his fellowship only because he held a major college administrative post. In 1984 it was decided that the appointment of NUTOs to the retiring age should carry 'an obligation to

[35] CM 110, 117, 277, 766; GB, 21.4.1964, 22.7.1964, 29.7.1968, 4.12.1970, 11.6.1971, 5.10.1971.
[36] In *Record* (1974). See also GB, 21.2.1973, 11.6.1976. For problems in the sciences, see CM 360(1).
[37] But in a few cases new appointments were made, CM 359, 380; *Record* (1974); (1975); GB, 16.3.1973, 24.4.1973, 15.6.1973, 15.1.1974, 13.2.1974, 16.4.1974, 15.5.1974, 6.12.1974, 14.2.1975, 14.3.1975, 11.6.1976, 3.11.1976, 3.12.1976, 11.3.1977, 19.4.1977, 11.5.1977, 2.12.1977.
[38] GB, 17.5.1979; CM, 612, 629.
[39] CM 668.

undertake major College office if requested to do so by the Governing Body'.[40] In March 1986 only four members of a governing body of 37 were NUTOs.[41]

The other vulnerable category of Fellows in this period of financial retrenchment has been that of the research Fellows. These fellowships — 'to which young graduates may be elected under conditions of research', and tenable for three years — were first created under the revised statutes of 1925, although no appointment was made until 1936.[42] In recent years the college has endeavoured to make two elections each year, or to maintain approximately six research Fellows in residence at a given moment.[43] Several present teaching Fellows at Queens' were formerly research Fellows of the college. Financial pressures in recent years have on occasions led to recommendations that no new elections be made, although the rate of appointment has largely been maintained.[44] But the rôle of the research Fellow has begun to alter. In 1977 the college teaching committee warned the governing body to ensure that research Fellows did not accumulate too many teaching commitments, and laid down an upper limit in hours per week, but in 1984 the governing body discussed the purpose of research fellowships and their benefits to the college; and more recently, research fellowships have been advertised in specific subjects where there is a particular teaching need.[45]

The fellowship has changed in another respect, by the gradual erosion of the late Victorian ideal of a lifetime spent in the service of the college. The obitary in the *Record* in 1973 for R. G. D. Laffan, who had retired twenty years earlier, described him as 'a notable friend of a long succession of Queens' men', who 'gave himself to his College', held numerous college offices, and 'diffused a pre-1914 atmosphere of dignity, courtesy and consideration'.[46] These remarks were coloured by the experiences of student unrest in the late 1960s, though they are an essentially true portrayal of the late Victorian ideal, which was continued by the new generation of Fellows elected during the 1920s and 1930s: men such as E. A. Maxwell (1932 – 74; now a life Fellow), L. J.

---

[40] CM 588, 849, 870; GB, 5.10.1984; c.f. CM 802. See also CM 512, 869; GB, 1.10.1976, 11.1.1977, 15.3.1985.
[41] *Record* (1986), 2.
[42] *Statutes* (1925), 14; CB (1889 – 1937), 8.6.1936.
[43] e.g. GB, 18.5.1956, 22.6.1956, 31.5.1956, 31.3.1958, 13.3.1959, 1.5.1959, 9.11.1964, 25.1.1966, 14.10.1966, 3.12.1966; CM 549; fellowship lists in *QC, passim* and *Record, passim*. There are six at the time of writing. Selection procedures have varied: sometimes the fellowships have been open; sometimes restricted to college members. Sometimes there has been no restriction on subject; sometimes a tight definition, CM 321, 693; GB, 5.10.1979. See also CM 964.
[44] GB, 2.12.1977; CM 549, 945 (and see 964).
[45] CM 545 (and see 513), 876; GB, 5.10.1984, 7.12.1984.
[46] *Record* (1972 – 3).

Potts (1924 – 60), and J. A. Ramsay (1934 – 76, now a life Fellow) — teachers, counsellors and friends to undergraduates, and diligent college administrators in several capacities.[47]

The most prominent examples from this period are those of H. St J. Hart (1936 – 79, now a life Fellow) and A. D. Browne (1921 – 77). Hart held numerous college positions, and only in the last few years before his retirement did he relinquish all college office in order to concentrate fully on his academic work. He was 'one of a small group of College Officers upon whom the whole life of a College depended. He supported practically every College activity and for many years knew every man in the College by name'.[48] Browne

'dedicated sixty years of his life to this College. He never married, and, until ill-health forced him to give up his rooms in College, the College was his home and his whole life. He had other interests certainly . . . But for him the real world was the College and its members . . . he affected to despise research as a waste of time, since he regarded the proper task of a don as teaching undergraduates. One quickly learnt that he was unimpressed by academic or worldly distinctions, at least so far as dons were concerned, and, basically, this was because he judged a man almost entirely by what service he gave to the College'.[49]

Both this type of don and the ideal which he represented have faded since the second world war — its last classic representative was M. M. Bull (1957 – 81, retired; died 1985), 'a Queensman through and through', who forsook research to devote himself to teaching and other college activities.[50] However, it should by no means be assumed that the 'good college man' had necessarily to be interested only in teaching and not in research. The old collegiate tradition is not dead by any means, but it is no longer so deep or so all-encompassing. Its decline is due in part to changes in the outlook of Fellows themselves, but owes much more to changes among the students which began at least as far back as the 1920s, but have gathered pace since 1945; these are described elsewhere in this book.[51] Since the second world war the academic profession has been increasingly mobile, and many more college

[47] QC (1959 – 60), 3; D. W. Bowett in Record (1974), (1976), 4 – 5.
[48] D. W. Bowett in Record (1972 – 3); (1980), 5. Browne was the last of the Fellows under the old statutes for whom there was no retiring age, but he gradually gave up his college offices.
[49] D. W. Bowett in Record (1978), 8. After his poor health forced him to move out of Queens', Browne still lived nearby, and took a keen interest in college affairs, D. W. Bowett in Record (1972 – 3); (1974); (1975); (1976), 5.
[50] D. W. Bowett in Record (1982), 3; B. A. Callingham in Record (1985), 2 – 3.
[51] Above, chapters 17, 23; below, chapter 28.

Fellows have moved on to higher positions at other universities; this has been a major contributor to the demise of the late Victorian ideal.[52] In addition, most Fellows nowadays tend to be non-resident and married. Few choose to dine on high table in the evenings — once an important feature of the college's social life.[53] The substantial proportion of younger Fellows at Queens' are products of the new social awareness which began to influence students in the 1960s, and see their rôle in different terms. That complete identification with the life of the college in all its aspects no longer appears to be necessary, or even desirable in many cases. The old concept of the college community has not vanished, but it is considerably changed.

Presidents

The early chapters of T. H. White's novel Darkness at Pemberley, a thriller published in 1932, are set in a Cambridge college which is only too obviously modelled on Queens', and certainly parts of the college are described with great accuracy. Both the president and senior tutor of the college in White's story are cocaine addicts, and another of the dons is a murderer and a highly sophisticated criminal. These characters were not meant to portray real persons, although White's lawyers compelled him to secure written permission from anybody whom he might have libelled before the book was published.[54] Indeed, T. C. Fitzpatrick, president when White was an undergraduate in the 1920s and at the time Darkness at Pemberley was conceived, was as far from being notorious as one could get. He was, as we have seen, the typical 'good college man', diligent, loyal, sincere, and Christian. He was also generous, paying for the alterations in Old Court between 1910 and 1926, and leaving the college £10,000 to endow fellowships — and it was rumoured among the undergraduates that he had been elected 'because the college, which was a poor one, always looked for a man with private means to be its head'.[55]

T. H. White suggested that the same mercenary motive was behind the election of J. A. Venn to succeed Fitzpatrick in 1932: 'I suppose the idea is that he also must eventually leave £10,000 to the college. But is'nt [sic] it rather long to have to wait another thirty or forty years?'[56] It is scarcely credible that the governing body should have elected for

---

[52] D. W. Bowett in Record (1972 – 3); see QC and Record, passim, for notices of regular promotions. Government cuts in higher education in the 1980s have now severely curtailed much of this mobility.

[53] CM 336.

[54] White (1932); (1984), 16, 134; Warner (1967), 50.

[55] Above, pp. 230, 324; chapter 18, ns. 67, 89; Rackham (1937), 1 – 2, 4; Harding (1953), 39; above, chapter 26, n. 3; above, this chapter, n. 30.

[56] White (1984), 34; the misspelling is one of White's idiosyncrasies.

financial reasons somebody who was not deemed to be suitable for the position in every other respect, although Venn's election does appear to have come as a surprise to many outside the college. Fitzpatrick died in October 1931, but the Fellows did not elect Venn until the following spring. The *Cambridge Review* alleged that there was a fierce dispute within the college, but in fact it had decided to postpone the election from the start because Venn, who was already seen as the obvious candidate, was travelling abroad.[57] He was chosen no doubt for the traditional reason that he was the most able administrator and 'good college man' available — we do not know if the Fellows considered going outside Queens' for a president, as they had with Venn's three predecessors. He was also the fourth member of the Venn family to become a Fellow of Queens', the first being Henry Venn in the 18th century; and he was the ninth generation of that family to graduate from Oxford and Cambridge. They were a remarkably talented branch of what Lord Annan has called the 'intellectual aristocracy': a predominantly but not exclusively academic élite maintained and strengthened by intermarriage which became particularly prominent in and after the Victorian period when dons were permitted to marry, and which included many famous Cambridge names.[58]

Yet in one important respect his election marked a decisive break with tradition: Venn was not in holy orders. Admittedly, he was not the first layman to be president of Queens' — that distinction had fallen to Joshua King — but whilst King's election may in that respect be seen as an aberration, Venn's was a conscious break with the past. Under the college's revised Victorian statutes it had been possible to elect a layman as president provided that there was a two-thirds majority among the Fellows — only a simple majority was required for a clergyman — but the revision of 1925 made no such distinction, although a two-thirds majority was now required for any candidate.[59] Venn only became a Fellow in the year that these statutes were approved. He was still the junior Fellow when Fitzpatrick died, and it cannot have been often that a junior Fellow has risen straight to the position of head of house; but at the age of 48 he was elderly for a junior Fellow even if he did now become the youngest head of house in Cambridge.[60] Historically, he was by no means young for a president of Queens', of whom hardly any have been over fifty at the time of their election. The tendency to elect

---

[57] CR (22.1.32), 188; (22.4.1932), 322; CB (1889–1932), 31.10.1931; E. A. Maxwell, in conversation. For the president's stipend in recent times, see CM 197, 197A, 301; GB, 11.6.1982. In practice, it is now highly unlikely that anyone who is not a university professor will be elected president, unless the college's financial position improves dramatically.

[58] Annan (1955), 274–6.

[59] CR (22.4.1932), 322; *Statutes* (1883), 9; (1925), 9.

[60] *Dial* (Easter 1932), 3–4; CR (22.4.1932), 322.

older men as college masters is a recent one, born of the Victorian reforms, and has not been followed by Queens'.

Other presidential traditions have begun to crumble more recently. Fitzpatrick and Venn both died in office after long service, but these days presidents are not necessarily expected to remain until the retiring age, or until promoted to the episcopal bench: they are more likely to remain in office for a decade or so before moving on to other academic or secular positions. A. ll. Armitage inaugurated the new trend when he left Queens' to become vice-chancellor of Manchester university in 1970. His successor, D. W. Bowett, resigned in 1982 to devote more time to his academic and professional work as an international lawyer, but he has remained a Fellow of the college — something which has never happened before, and a potentially significant innovation.[61] It is still much too soon to judge if these new trends will evolve into tradition.

Religion

The formal religious life of the college has also altered in recent times. The customary religious practice of worship in the college chapel has declined just as churchgoing in society at large has done. There was a strong religious revival in the university during the late 1940s and 1950s; and the decline may have set in since then.[62] At the time of writing, attendance levels tend to be very low; and in April 1986 the dean of chapel sent out a circular to all college members encouraging Christians and non-Christians alike to attend: 'All are welcome — observers and participators — and with whatever degree of participation', and the valuable rôle of the chapel in bringing the college community together in a shared act of worship was also stressed.[63] But the underlying trend is not encouraging.

The importance of the chapel to the college is not seriously diminished by such purely numerical considerations; it must be judged by other values.[64] Nonetheless, the degree to which the college should be responsible for it and the college's religious life in general has inevitably been called into question in the light of falling attendances and financial

---

[61] QC (1968 – 9), 3; Stop Press, 18.11.1981; Record (1983), 2.

[62] For the religious revival, see Roach, 'University of Cambridge', 311; Vaizey (1977), 123. In the mid-1950s the CICCU is known to have discouraged its members from attending college chapel, diary of J. B. Geyer; and its members have by and large stayed away in recent years too. Many Christian students, not just the evangelicals, prefer to worship at churches in the town, and so there need not be any close correlation between the level of religious enthusiasm in the university as a whole and attendance at college chapels.

[63] Copy deposited among the miscellaneous college history papers.

[64] See Hebblethwaite (1985), 171 – 5.

pressures. The statutes require the appointment of a dean in holy orders and the conduct of daily morning and evening services during full term; the appointment of an additional chaplain, which had been required since the 1883 statutes, was made optional by the revisions of 1955.[65] This was in response to an already falling demand, and also because it was likely to become increasingly difficult to secure a second Fellow in holy orders who could take the chaplaincy on in addition to his other college duties; hitherto this had not been a problem.[66] But for the relaxation of the rules, the college would soon have been compelled to make an additional appointment, at great extra expense.

In practice, chaplains were appointed for most of the 1960s, when there was only one teaching Fellow in orders; but during the early 1970s the dean of chapel had to rely on part-time, outside assistance, and called for a full-time appointment.[67] In view of its financial problems, the college decided to look for a chaplain with sufficient academic qualification to carry out some college teaching: two such appointments have been made; and the college now employs a lay chaplain who is also a university teaching officer.[68] The most recent suggestion is that Queens' should employ a deaconess, which would also solve the pastoral problem arising from the college's current lack of a woman tutor.[69] Yet these are all temporary expedients, and the question of the religious facilities which the college should provide for its members still awaits a long-term solution.

[65] *Statutes* (1883), 33 – 4; (1933), 24 – 5; (1955), 17; see also above, pp. 282 – 3.
[66] For an isolated example of difficulty, see chapter 23, n. 140.
[67] GB, 13.3.1959, 26.6.1959, 12.7.1974, 9.7.1976, 11.10.1976; CM 395, 447; *QC* (1962 – 3), 3; (1966 – 7), 3.
[68] CM 532, 595, 692, 706, 709, 764; GB, 11.5.1977, 9.6.1977, 7.12.1979, 15.1.1980, 20.4.1982, 19.5.1982, 25.5.1983; D. W. Bowett in *Record* (1978), 7; (1980), 4; A. C. Spearing in *Record* (1983), 4; (1984), 5.
[69] CM 993, and see 968.

28

The modern college (IV)
— students and student life

Admissions

The introduction of state aid for students on a very limited scale after the first world war did not make a substantial difference to the social composition of the student body at Cambridge. Since the passing of the Butler Education Act in 1944 Britain has had a fully subsidised educational system at all levels, and this has made a profound difference to the class basis of student society; yet change has come surprisingly slowly. In 1961 – 2 only 21% of Cambridge undergraduates were from schools maintained by the state, as opposed to those where fees were paid by parents; in the newer universities, the proportion was over 70%.[1] In 1983 44% of those accepted for places at Cambridge were from maintained schools, 56% from the independent sector, and the figures for Queens' were almost identical. In 1985 half the admissions to Cambridge were from independent schools, compared to 20% in universities nationally.[2]

There is perhaps nothing sinister in this: the Cambridge colleges aim to recruit the most able students, and they seem to do their best to be fair. But the independent schools have a great advantage over the state sector: they are generally better able to prepare their pupils for university entrance because of superior facilities and knowledge of how the Oxbridge admissions system works through their extensive contacts with the colleges; a high proportion of their graduate teachers may be products of the older universities. Many state schools simply do not encourage their brighter pupils to apply, under the apprehension that the system is weighted against them.[3]

There are two good pre-war examples of the value of such contacts at Queens'. In 1932 we find T. H. White, newly appointed to be head of English at Stowe, writing to his former director of studies L. J. Potts for advice on the 'background of general literary acquaintance' required of

---

[1]   Robbins (1966), 62; see also Kalton (1966), 96 – 9.
[2]   CM 753; *Reporter* (27.11.1985), 2 – 3. There is also a strong regional bias towards London and the South East — 47% in 1985, *Reporter, loc. cit.*
[3]   See e.g. Robbins (1966), 63; Kalton (1966), 47.

prospective Cambridge candidates, and how this could best be supplied. Ten years earlier C. W. N. McGowan's mother had written to T. C. Fitzpatrick to enquire about the possibility of her son obtaining a place at Queens': Fitzpatrick's reply was discouraging, but Mrs McGowan received a more hopeful response when a teacher at her son's school, who had been a student at Christ's during Fitzpatrick's time there, wrote to press the boy's claims. McGowan still had to secure admission on academic merit, but without the schoolteacher's assistance he would probably not have tried.[4] In contrast, John Vaizey, who arrived at Queens' in 1948 and was only the second boy from his school to go Cambridge, chose his college with a pin from a book in a public library.[5]

In recent years Queens' has shown itself anxious to encourage applicants from a wider range of schools and social backgrounds. Recognition of the problem dates from the 1960s. In 1963 the governing body discussed proposals for Cambridge to join UCCA, the new central admissions scheme for all universities, which might mean abandoning its separate admissions procedure and entrance examination. It saw no reason to change: 'In particular, it was felt that the College already had a reasonable representation of undergraduates coming from day schools' — 56% of the current first year — and it was also believed that the existing admissions procedure 'enabled us in any case to take boys after two years of Sixth Form work from any type school, provided that they were of standard'.[6] The Oxbridge entrance system, with its interviews and examinations during the Michaelmas term, favoured candidates who were able to remain at school for an extra term after taking their A-levels: many of the independent schools possessed the teaching resources required for this additional coaching, whereas many state schools were handicapped by a relative shortage of staff. Moreover, boys from less well-to-do backgrounds often could not afford to stay on for the extra term. Cambridge did join UCCA soon afterwards, but retained its own admissions procedure.[7]

By 1968 Queens' was less confident. In November a governing body committee described admissions procedure as an 'area of special difficulty'. Whilst it believed the general level of applicants to be 'satisfactory', the committee recommended improving contacts with schools by visits from Fellows or the creation of special short-term schoolmaster fellowships at Queens'; and it urged that particular

[4] White (1984), 30; McGowan (MS), 1–2.
[5] Vaizey (1977), 116.
[6] GB, 11.11.1963.
[7] GB, 15.2.1963, 21.2.1964, 8.5.1964; Green (1969), 126.

attention to be paid to building up 'first-rate connections' with schools which did not provide post A-level teaching for Oxbridge or only prepared their pupils for two A-levels instead of the normal three, 'and also with Comprehensive Schools in general'. It was unhappy with the efficacy of scholarship examinations, although it maintained the need for entrance examinations in principle.[8]

In the 1970s Queens' began to rely much more on A-level results, headmaster's reports, and interviews as a basis for admission; but it was not yet prepared to abandon the examination system. In the early 1980s there was a mounting tendency to give pre A-level candidates offers conditional upon their attaining certain specified grades in their A-levels. The extension of this practice was urged by the admissions committee in 1983 as a means of encouraging applications from mantained schools. Although the college was still not ready to abolish the separate examination, the mood shifted suddenly in the following year when Oxford abandoned the old system; and in the face of this competition it was felt that the post A-level examination had outlived its usefulness. It has now been abolished: none of the 1987 intake of students will have experienced it.[9]

This development has gone hand in hand with further moves to improve the college's links with state schools. In 1980 the admissions committee recommended the abolition of existing *ad hoc* arrangements whereby prospective candidates visited Cambridge throughout the year and met Fellows informally to talk about the university and the college, on the grounds that only schools familiar with the system sent such candidates, and there were very few from the 'less sophisticated schools'; in addition, it took up a lot of Fellows' time. It was suggested that instead Queens' should follow the lead of other colleges and hold open days, to which selected schools would be invited to send likely candidates. The committee pursued the question again three years later, warning that 'there are people within the maintained sector who could be serious Cambridge candidates but who are unaware or in awe of the admissions procedure', and calling for the furthering of contacts with maintained schools. In 1984 the open days were reported a success, and many new contacts had been made with schools.[10] This work continues: the great weight of tradition cannot be lifted overnight, and the full effects of the changes will not be known for several years to come.

---

[8] CM 237. This concern was connected with the student agitation of 1968, which included consultation with students on admissions policy as one of its demands, see below, p. 408.
[9] CM 282, 317, 755, 821; GB, 12.1.1971, 17.1.1984, 14.11.1984. Dr K.E. Machin, personal communication.
[10] CM 649, 755, 853.

Careers

In the late 19th century, it was usual for Cambridge students to enter the church or one of the older professions, but not to go into trade or industry, against which there was a good deal of social prejudice.[11] This at least is the general impression, but little research has been done on the subject. One reason for this is the difficulty of compiling sufficient evidence of students' subsequent careers. At Queens' there is a good deal of material in the various college magazines, which list the occupations of former students; but this is far from comprehensive, because the magazines relied on information supplied by the old members themselves, and the careers of a great many went unrecorded. This is true even now, and there is the additional complication that many do not remain in the same type of job throughout their working lives. It is only possible to advance tentative conclusions with regard to the college, although in recent times more reliable information has been available regarding the university as a whole.

An analysis of the careers of all 57 Queensmen who had matriculated in 1912 was published in the 1937 – 8 edition of the *Dial*.[12] Of the 49 who were still alive, ten were clergymen, five schoolmasters, three doctors and three farmers; academic life, journalism, newspaper proprietorship, colonial administration, the armed forces, and commerce had each claimed two; and there were single representatives in accountancy, the home civil service, banking, the law, and secretarial work. The professions of another 9 were unknown. These proportions are not surprising, with the exception of law; and the *Dial* commented that in fact 8 men were barristers or solicitors, but only one regarded law as his principal occupation.

There is no such complete summary for any of the inter-war years, although a survey published in 1946 of university men who had graduated shortly before the second world war showed a continuing leaning towards many of the traditional professions, apart from the church. The more successful students academically tended to keep away from industry; and commerce was the occupation in which most sons did not follow their fathers.[13] The position altered dramatically within a few years of the end of the second world war: a survey of Cambridge graduates from the years 1952 – 3 carried out in the early 1960s showed that the two most popular occupations were teaching and industry, with

---

[11] For this social prejudice see above, pp. 241, 289. More research is needed on 19th century career patterns. See also Roach, 'University of Cambridge', 288.
[12] *Dial* (1937 – 8), 11. 56 matriculations are recorded for that October at Queens' by the *Cambridge Review*, CR (24.10.1912), 37; but there were sometimes a few more later in the year. The *Dial* seems to have believed that it had covered all of that year's intake.
[13] Below, appendix 16; Sanderson (1972), 283.

about 24% each; medicine and commerce each had 8%; 6% were clergymen; 5% were lawyers; and 9% public servants.[14] Figures published in 1985 for Cambridge graduates of 1984 showed industry (14%), postgraduate study (15%), and 'Vocational study and training' (12%) the largest single groups of occupation; 8% were teachers or on teacher-training courses; 3% in public service; 5% in banking and insurance; 6% in accountancy; 8% in 'Other Commerce'; 5% solicitors, and smaller proportions in various other fields. Sadly, 14% were either unemployed or 'not in permanent employment', showing the extent of the recession in the mid-1980s.[15] There is no comparable data for Queens' graduates at any of these periods, but no reason to expect the picture there to be significantly different.[16]

Graduate students

The student body has never consisted exclusively of undergraduates; but the considerable growth in the university's graduate population is a recent phenomenon. Cambridge first offered PhD courses in 1919, since when there has been an increasing number of research students, most noticeably after the second world war.[17] More recently, the number of post-graduate courses of all kinds has risen, and the graduate population has grown accordingly.

This has meant that colleges have had to make greater provision for the welfare of their graduate students. In the 1930s Queens' was already offering some research grants; and the mathematics don Andrew Munro, who died in 1935, left money to endow an annual studentship 'for advanced study or research'.[18] In 1958 the college appointed a tutor for research students; in 1983 the increase in the number of other graduate students made the appointment of a second graduates' tutor necessary.[19] A succession of graduate common rooms in different parts of the college also bears witness to the enlargement of this community.[20]

In recent times graduates have come to be regarded more and more as a distinct student group, entitled to special privileges on account of their status and maturity.[21] In the early 1960s there was a special BA table in

[14] Craig (1963), 85 – 7; Sanderson (1972), 353 – 4.
[15] Oxbridge Careers Handbook (1986), 35.
[16] The information supplied by old members about themselves in recent issues of the Record seems to bear this out.
[17] Howarth (1978), 86; Roach, 'University of Cambridge', 303, 312.
[18] CB (1889 – 1937), 18.6.1934, 17.11.1934, 20.6.1936.
[19] GB, 25.7.1958; A. C. Spearing in Record (1984), 5.
[20] e.g. CM 36, 177; GB, 18.4.1961, 3.5.1961, 3.11.1961, 7.12.1961, 22.2.1966, 3.5.1968, 15.11.1968; Record (1976), 16. The most recent of these rooms was extended this year.
[21] There are signs of such consideration before the first world war, above, p. 266.

hall on Saturday nights which was served food of high table standard; and in 1961 approval was given for a dinner for research students to be held during the Christmas vacation 'at which Lady guests might be invited' — the last concession was well in advance of undergraduate privileges in this direction.[22] By the middle of the decade the college was concerned at the alienation of graduates from college life. Graduate, and especially research students were seen as important to the college

'because they form an essential element in our shop-window. More immediately the need is for a source of Research Fellows, and ultimately Teaching Fellows, most immediately for help in supervision of undergraduates'.

By 1966 they formed almost 14% of the student body at Queens'.[23] Proposals for greater interaction between graduates and Fellows through such means as joint buffet lunches and after-dinner symposia were swiftly approved in consequence, and the hope was expressed that some Fellows 'might at times look in for coffee' to the graduates' common room.[24]

The question of graduate accommodation was an associated problem. In the mid-1960s the governing body was concerned that Queens' had no flats for married research students. It also became increasingly difficult to house graduate students in college. Initially, it was hoped to provide additional graduate accommodation in the new building scheme, but this idea was abandoned and in 1968 the college began to look at house property instead.[25] The problem has worsened since. In 1981 statistics presented to the governing body showed that Queens' provided a lower proportion of its graduates with accommodation than any other Cambridge college. Although efforts have been made to house more graduates in college, this has not kept pace with the increase in numbers during the 1980s; the shortage has been monitored with concern.[26] The college is in a difficult position: it can only increase graduate accommodation in Queens' by compelling more undergraduates to share; property in Cambridge is now extremely expensive,

[22] CM 36; GB, 18.4.1961, 3.5.1961, 3.11.1961.
[23] CM 170, 172, 177; *Varsity*, 29.10.1966; *QC* (1965 – 6), 26.
[24] GB, 11.1.1966, 22.2.1966 (see also 14.5.1980); CM 172, 177; *QC* (1965 – 6), 26.
[25] GB, 6.12.1963, 3.5.1968; CM 170, 172, 177, 223, 224, 229; above, pp. 376 – 7; *QC* (1965 – 6), 26. More recently, graduates have moved into college houses formerly occupied by staff.
[26] CM 660, 696, 812; GB, 30.9.1983, 9.11.1983, 2.12.1983. There were 95 graduates in 1976 – 7; and 173 in 1985 – 6. They now make up about one third of junior members, CM 812, 957; see also *Record* (1986), 14.

although attempts have been made to buy more college houses; and there is stiff opposition from the town council to any increase in student accommodation in residential areas.[27] A new building project would be very expensive indeed, yet may be the only solution if the college wishes to keep its present high level of graduate numbers. It is a very serious situation: student accommodation in Cambridge is in short supply generally, and rents are very high, with no sign of improvement.[28]

Plans to integrate graduates more closely into college life have been more successful, despite the large number living out of college. This has been due primarily to the development of the graduates' common room, not only through expansion of facilities, but also the growth in social activities which has gone hand in hand with it. The Graduates' Club was formally reorganised as a Middle Combination Room (MCR) in 1975, and graduates are represented on the governing body and some college committees.[29] A governing body committee on graduate entertainment in 1976 noted that although the new MCR facilities in Cripps Court had 'proved successful in integrating them [graduates] into the College', there was still some dissatisfaction with many arrangements, and the committee felt that senior members should give 'some kind of hospitality' to graduates, for they generally saw less of the Fellows than undergraduates. This was the origin of the successful scheme for inviting graduates in small groups to dine with the Fellows on high table, introduced in 1977.[30] The notices written by successive secretaries of the MCR committee for the college *Record* have generally expressed gratitude to those Fellows who have been most involved in graduate affairs; but the difficulty of maintaining a coherent graduate community in view of the shortage of college accommodation, increased numbers, and the different lifestyle of graduates, especially research students, has also been a recurrent theme.

---

[27] Although the college is attempting to buy more houses, e.g. CM 941, 1000. For local authority opposition, see e.g. CM 702, 797. The new development of the boathouse site, now under way, also provides some accommodation for married graduates, although there was local opposition to these plans too, GB, 25.5.1983, 22.7.1983, 15.3.1985, 15.5.1985, 7.6.1985; CM 787, 917, 926; *Stop Press*, 4.10.1983, 10.2.1984, 18.1.1985; local residents' circular among documents collected for the college history (I am grateful to Andy Cosh for supplying me with a copy of this circular). An attempt to buy a large warehouse site in central Cambridge fell through because Queens' could not match the price offered by commercial developers, GB, 25.5.1983. Similarly the university's asking price for a former nurses' hostel on the site of the old Addenbrooke's hospital was far too high.

[28] The question was raised by the MCR before the governing body at the beginning of the Michaelmas term 1986, see CM 1037; GB, 5.12.1986.

[29] For the general development of graduate activities, see the relevant entries in *QC* and *Record*. For the formation of the MCR see also GB, 12.7.1974, 14.3.1975.

[30] CM 495, 510, 522; *Record* (1977), 15; (1978), 14; GB, 1.10.1976, 11.1.1977.

Student society since 1945

The following pages seek to chronicle and explain the many substantial changes in student life and attitudes in the postwar era. In particular, they concentrate on the student agitation which influenced the college profoundly in the late 1960s and early 1970s. These events are described at length because of their great significance in college and university history: if the later 19th century witnessed the 'Revolution of the Dons', recent decades have seen nothing less than a student revolution.

The 1940s and 1950s

College society in the years immediately after the war was dominated by the prevailing mood of austerity.[31] Rationing continued for several years; and conscription was retained well into the 1950s.[32] As in 1919, the university welcomed back many students who had gone off to war; these too found it difficult to readjust to the petty regulations of college life designed for boys rather than men.[33] But one historian of the university has observed that 'The post-1945 generation was much more serious and hard-working than its post-1918 predecessor'.[34] There is perhaps an indication of this at Queens' in the outlook adopted by the Kangaroo Club when it re-formed in 1948 with the expressed intention of toning down 'the Bacchanalian reputation of yore': although it did not forswear alcohol, its meetings now began at 10.00 in the evenings, apparently to allow members to get in two hours' academic work after hall; and the club's minute books reveal a generally improved standard of behaviour.[35]

In the early 1950s this outlook began to alter. Attlee's Labour government had been replaced by a Conservative administration. The

---

[31] Vaizey (1977), 120.

[32] In 1945 Queens' recorded its preference for the performance of peacetime national service by its students before coming up — so that they would be more mature, perhaps, or just for administrative convenience? CB (1937 – 63), 28.2.1945.

[33] According to one Queensman who was there; this information came to me indirectly. I have not been able to discover just how widespread or strongly felt such sentiments were.

[34] Roach, 'University of Cambridge', 311. Roach suggests: 'Perhaps the increased difficulty of gaining admission has made men more studious, while the growing dependence of undergraduates on grants and scholarships has tended to level off social extremes . . . everyone now has his living to earn and views life a little more soberly in consequence'. *loc. cit.* This is only a hypothesis. There has been almost no research on postwar Cambridge as yet.

[35] *Dial* (1948), 30; Kangaroo Club minutes (K5). College societies of all kinds began to revive in 1947 – 8, QC (1947 – 8), 16; *Dial* (Easter 1947), 44; (Michaelmas 1947), 4, 6 – 7, 49; (1948), 64 – 6, 68 – 9, 82; (Lent 1949), 7, 40, 46 – 7; (Easter 1949), 13 – 14; (Lent 1953), 12; *Varsity*, 21.2.1948.

older ex-servicemen from the war had all gone, and 'The chinless wonder from the peacetime army was there again with the evening dress, May balls, backless gowns — a conscious revival of a mythicized 1920s', more interested in high living than ideas. There are a few slight — but only slight — hints at Queens' of more boisterous behaviour and more interest in socialising in style.[36]

Perhaps also some students, especially those from less privileged backgrounds, were coming to expect more of the university. John Vaizey complained that he was taught economics 'by a carpet-bagger who came down once a week from London, while the lectures were dull, with no revelation of the mysteries I had hoped to penetrate'. He also emphasized 'the isolation, the loneliness and the shyness which dominate the Cambridge lives of those who are not from one of the bigger schools and who lack some important inner resources'.[37] This sense of dissatisfaction with Cambridge is absent from the reminiscences of earlier generations of Queensmen in the late 19th and 20th centuries — it is necessary to go back to Arthur Wright's contempt for the mid-Victorian college to find any comparable criticisms. The incipient frustration of some members of Vaizey's generation was to grow into a major movement of protest in the 1960s.

There are signs of a more modern, independent lifestyle among students in the postwar decades. Before the war students required the college's permission to keep electrical equipment such as wireless sets in their rooms; but in 1959 the junior bursar informed Basil Spence that rooms in his new building ought to contain space for the wirelesses and gramophones which most undergraduates now possessed. The United Clubs set up a college record library in 1961. Television had arrived in 1948, by courtesy of Pye Ltd, who donated two to each college. In the early 1960s colleges took action to reduce the number of motor cars kept in Cambridge by students.[38] Students no longer wished to be waited on so extensively: in the 1920s bedmakers and their assistants had cleared lunch and tea as well as cleaning rooms first thing in the morning; Gilbert Harding claimed that his bedmaker even boiled the kettle for his tea.[39] According to John Vaizey the old styles of living and eating broke down after the war; certainly the process was well advanced by the late 1950s. The Erasmus building was intended to give undergraduates 'full freedom for private study, concentration and work, for separate and

---

[36] Vaizey (1977), 125. For hints of changes at Queens', Kangaroo Club minutes (K5); GB, 11.3.1955, 22.7.1955; 27.4.1956; 7.12.1961.

[37] Vaizey (1977), 116 – 8.

[38] MS u/c-junior bursar; JB-Erasmus; CB (1937 – 63), 11.6.1948; GB, 20.5.1955, 22.7.1955, 19.4.1960, 17.5.1961, 2.10.1964 (and see 19.11.1954, 21.6.1963); *Dial* (1948), 11; CM 130.

[39] Harding (1953), 58 – 9; Maxwell (MS), 2. See also MS u/c-junior bursar; MS u/c-staff(III).

individual development and social life'; and it had much improved domestic facilities.[40] A college laundrette was installed in 1963 — 'a sign of the times' in the words of the senior bursar — and a second followed towards the end of the decade. Also in 1963 the governing body decreed that undergraduates 'wishing to undertake any time consuming non-academic occupations, whether paid or unpaid', had to secure tutorial permission first.[41]

Such changes undermined much of the old Victorian ideal of the college community: it was a tradition which had become fixed and could no longer adjust quickly enough to changing student expectations. Dons and students found their outlooks diverging. An article in *Varsity* in 1948 alleged that there was 'little contact' between Fellows and students at Queens', which was one of the few colleges without a JCR (Junior Combination Room) committee to represent the students. The college was said to suffer 'from the general lack of corporate life in the modern university', and it was hoped that the revival of college societies would 'stimulate the college unity'.[42] The author was harking back to a golden age, for many students did not share that old commitment to the college community — at least not in its old form — and preferred to organise their own social life; this tendency was visible already before the war. The *Dial* could no longer rely on a steady flow of contributions, and complained in 1950 that 'Too many people spend too little time in their Colleges'; it ceased publishing a few years later. The St Bernard Society went into decline: its minutes commented in 1956 on 'the normal apathy attendant on College societies', and the fashion for running them down.[43] Many elements of the older style endured, even if perhaps in muted form: students might still spend an evening after hall with A. D. Browne 'talking mainly about the college', though in general the custom of calling on Fellows on Sunday evenings was rapidly dying out.[44] The old commitment to sports was undiminished: on his first day in Cambridge in 1953 J. B. Geyer was advised by his tutor to take up some sport such as rowing.[45] Early signs of resentment at the unofficial privileged status enjoyed by sportsmen appeared in an article in *Varsity* in 1961 describing the visit of the Queen Mother to Queens' to open the Erasmus building. The proceedings were said to have been carefully planned by the college to the extent of determining which students the Queen Mother should be allowed to meet: when she visited the library 'selected undergraduates were presented to her. All were sportsmen',

---

[40] Vaizey (1977), 115; QC (1955 – 6), 2 – 4; (1960 – 1), 5; JB-Erasmus.
[41] *Varsity*, 5.10.1963; QC (1962 – 3), 4; (1968 – 9), 4, 10; GB, 11.11.1963.
[42] *Varsity*, 21.2.1948.
[43] *Dial* (Lent 1950), 1 (see also *Varsity*, 21.2.1948); SBSM, 24.10.1956.
[44] Diary of J. B. Geyer; E. A. Maxwell, in conversation.
[45] Diary of J. B. Geyer.

and there was a similar occurrence later in the visit.[46] But the real challenges to the old order and style were still several years in the future.

The 1960s

The most striking new feature of student life at Queens' in the 1960s and early 1970s was rising discontent at the failure of the college authorities to move with the times, leading to agitation when students felt that their feelings were ignored by the Fellows. The college today is the product of that confrontation, which marked one of the single most important social and ideological changes in its history.

The discontent was in part political. As ever, political trends nationally exerted great influence on students' attitudes. In the later 1940s Labour support was strong at Cambridge, but this diminished in the following decade. The powerful spirit of the cold war led to far less sympathy for communism than in the 1930s: John Vaizey, dissatisfied with his teaching in economics, arranged for supervisions with the distinguished economist Joan Robinson, but recorded that 'my tutor, who denounced her as a communist, refused to pay her'.[47] The *Dial* showed no interest in politics in the early 1950s. The St Bernard Society, which struggled throughout the decade, found that college members were more interested in other subjects.[48] Perhaps this was because debating was no longer felt to be a worthwhile exercise. But a small, committed number regularly attended the society's informal discussion groups, which addressed many contemporary problems: cultural, moral and political. There was also a college economics group, founded in the early 1950s to talk about the political and economic issues of the day.[49]

The impression of widespread apathy may have been more characteristic of the early to mid-1950s than the later part of the decade, when there are signs of renewed interest in the world and its affairs. *Varsity*, the Cambridge undergraduates' weekly newspaper with a largely conventional outlook which concentrated mainly on university events and cultural matters during the 1950s, began in the early 1960s to cover issues of political and social concern, and problems which confronted

[46] *Varsity*, 10.6.1961.
[47] Vaizey (1977), 119 – 20, 125. The extreme right was also unfashionable: in the early 1960s there are isolated instances of individuals at Queens' with such views, but they were clearly regarded as oddities, *Varsity* 21.1.1961, 23.2.1963.
[48] SBSM, *passim*; for the difficulty of keeping the society going, see also *Dial* (Easter 1947), 44; (Michaelmas 1947), 45; (Lent 1949), 40; (Easter 1949), 29; (Lent 1950), 38 – 9; (Lent 1951), 30; (Easter 1951), 33; (February 1952), 32; Diary of J. B. Geyer.
[49] SBSM, *passim*; *Dial* (Lent 1951), 31; (May 1952), 23; Vaizey (1977), 121.

young people in particular. Its reporting of university events at this time reveals growing agitation among Cambridge students for a more liberal atmosphere and relaxation of old rules. The growing politicisation and radicalisation of the students led to political demonstrations becoming part of the Cambridge scene in the second half of the 1960s.

In Queens' too the limited evidence available from the recorded proceedings of the St Bernard Society suggests a more progressive outlook from the later 1950s, greater questioning of the Cambridge educational system and its relevance to the outside world, and some renewed interest in contemporary moral and political questions such as the value of the United Nations, the likelihood of a third world war, the rôles of the USA and USSR in world politics, devolution, the English legal system, racism, civil disobedience, the welfare state, trades unions, Rhodesia, political oppression in Franco's Spain; and also matters such as apartheid and pacifism in the informal discussion groups.[50] This should not be exaggerated: the St Bernard Society's debate on the inevitability of World War Three in 1959 was described as 'dull and uninspired'; and in the early 1960s, when for a short while many of the motions for debate were more serious and relevant to contemporary issues, the meetings were not noticeably well-attended.[51] But even if the timing and extent of the change cannot be determined, the increased interest in such matters is indisputable. No institution, no established code of values was immune to question and to challenge.

As the decade progressed, the questioning and the challenging grew.[52] In 1967–8 militant student protests began to break out all over Europe and North America, most famously in Paris in May 1968 when the French government was nearly brought down. Militancy was often the work of a minority (though it could be a substantial one), but it could only flourish in an environment of increased radicalism and sympathy for many of the militants' aims. Traditional youthful rebelliousness and the old student ambivalence towards authority had often been expressed in the past in high-spirited and sometimes violent behaviour, but were now given a new cause and a sharper focus. Students now saw themselves as a distinct social group (not a social class) distinguished by its youth. The generation gap was recognised as a perennial feature of

[50] SBSM, *passim*; QC, *passim*, entries for St Bernard Society. The questioning of the educational system is significant, but not surprising: there had been a major debate since the war on the failure of the universities to move with the times and on the reshaping of the old 'liberal education' to meet modern needs, see e.g. Moberley (1949); Butterfield (1962); Niblett (1974). The debate is by no means concluded. There no longer seems to be any consensus on the purpose of the universities.

[51] QC (1959–60), 22; SBSM, *passim*.

[52] The general discussion which follows is derived from Green (1969), 323–335; MacRae (1967); Zweig (1963); Cockburn and Blackburn (eds.) (1969), essays by Cockburn and Stedman Jones; Martin *et al.* (1969), essays by G. Martin, Shelston, Rock and Heidensohn, Hatch, Gellner, Crick, Sparrow.

society: parents and teachers were locked in their experiences of the 1930s, the second world war and the cold war which followed it; and their children were no longer prepared to take all that they said on trust. The young generation found new reference groups outside those of their class — liberation movements in the third world, anti-apartheid campaigners, and the like; protest movements were characteristic of the age. Students travelled more, learnt more about the world at first hand. There was a cultural and moral upheaval in the 1960s, most prominently in music, dress and the visual arts. Young people looked for alternative spiritual values to counter what were seen as the materialistic, hypocritical social and political order built up by older generations, and questioned the whole framework of advanced industrial society. They regarded higher education as a right rather than a privilege — in Britain this echoed the widespread expansionist enthusiasm which had been triggered earlier in the decade by the Robbins report on the universities — and they were scornful of a university system which purported to train their critical faculties but would not allow these to be applied to its own institutional regulations and values. They were disillusioned with organisations of all kinds, especially political. The threat of nuclear destruction devalued conventional politics, especially the British two-party system — the Campaign for Nuclear Disarmament was an important early protest movement — and the Labour government of the early 1960s, which had promised so much but was thought to have achieved very little, was felt to have betrayed the promise of progress which had been so enticing at the begining of the decade. Attitudes towards the USA grew ambivalent as a result of the Vietnam war, the focal point of much of the discontent. Young people, bursting with indignation and impatience, demanded in particular the right to be heard. This broad change in consciousness among the young world-wide is arguably one of the most significant historical phenomena of modern times.

Queens' and the student revolt

For students at Queens', as for many of their counterparts in Britain, Europe, and the United States, the year 1968 marked a turning point. Trouble broke out publicly for the first time in February, when an article in *Varsity* alleged that there was a 'major crisis of confidence' in the college, with students protesting against remarks in a recent issue of *Granta* on college discipline, which, although they had been unattributed in the magazine, were believed to have been made by the senior tutor of Queens'.[53] The suddenness and vehemence of the protest

[53] *Granta* (3.2.1968), 14 – 16; *Varsity*, 10.2.1968, and see 17.2.1968.

suggests strongly that there had been a good deal of discontent simmering in the college for some time. A letter to *Varsity* the following week by the president of the United Clubs and over 240 other students at Queens' deplored the newspaper's 'sensational and overgeneralised treatment' of 'the alleged crisis of confidence in this college', but the situation can only be adequately described as one of 'crisis'. In the same week, it was alleged by *Varsity* that the president, A. ll. Armitage, was rushing the final draft of the constitution of a new Queens' JCR committee through the governing body. Urgent discussions were held informally between dons and student representatives to try to defuse the dispute; and a general meeting of the junior members was called to discuss it. Certainly many students saw it as a major issue; and a governing body committee later described it with typical understatement as 'a time of sudden difficulty for the College'.[54]

The senior tutor protested that not only had he been misquoted by *Granta*, but his remarks had been taken out of context — the two comments unofficially attributed to him were: 'If you want freedom you go to a provincial University where you can sleep with 20 black women every night, smoke pot till you're blue in the face and nobody gives a damn', and 'My College is one big happy family: it's difficult to manage at times, but I try to be a good father to them all'. He pointed out that he had been discussing the extreme attitudes which hypothetical senior tutors might adopt, not expressing personal opinions. But he did express the hope that Queens' veered more towards the latter stance: 'I would maintain the value of the phrase "in loco parentis" as a function of a tutor'. This question was really the crux of the dispute, for it focused upon the whole question of don-student relations, the college community, and the tutorial function. The concept of the college as a large family — the ideal of the late Victorian reformers — had become distasteful to many students. In the words of one group of 'radical'[55] students at Queens', such an outlook was 'not . . . conducive to a real University community. Paternal repression does not produce responsible and aware citizens'.[56]

The issue was raised further by the same group in a broadsheet to the junior members which expressed their dissatisfaction with the way the college was run:

'The tutorial position "in loco parentis" is clearly unsuited to the

[54] *Varsity*, 10.2.1968, 17.2.1968; K. E. Machin papers; CM 237.
[55] This term requires explanation, as does the use of 'moderate' which appears below. Many in the late 1960s would have thought the 'moderate' ideals radical; whereas many today might find the 'radical' proposals moderate. Both are relative positions, to each other and to their historical context. Moreover, both groups had a great deal of common ground.
[56] *Varsity*, 10.2.1968.

creation of a community in which responsible individuals help to formulate the laws circumscribing their own activities. In contemporary usage, the term "in loco parentis" is obsolete. Few parents attempt to legislate for their children in the restrictive manner practised by some colleges . . . As individuals we are obliged to express opinions and take action on ethical matters if the benefits we gain from higher education are to find their social fulfilment'.[57]

More specifically, in a letter to the president and Fellows on 19th February, just over a week after the *Varsity* article, over 30 students, including the same radical group but expressing the concerns of many more junior members, argued that 'Certain aspects of the present institutional arrangements seem to have the effect of obstructing the dialogue of communication in the college', and urged a reform of tutorial methods. It was felt that the proposed introduction of a JCR committee — Queens' had not had one before — would certainly help to improve relations between Fellows and students,[58] but to enable this to work effectively three additional reforms were proposed: first, a temporary committee to discuss admissions, to include one student elected by the JCR ('We feel that the students would welcome the opportunity to discuss problems of admission and the difficulties of achieving a varied student community'); second, a standing committee on student discipline, also to include JCR representatives ('We feel that a wider structure to investigate matters of discipline would reduce the possibility of discontent over disciplinary decisions such as has arisen in other colleges in the recent past'); third, the president and one other member of the JCR committee should attend governing body meetings as observers ('This would enable the Governing Body, if they so desired, to hear the views of the students at first hand, and also permit students a better understanding of the processes of college government, which at present seem very remote').[59]

These requests appear innocuous by today's standards, but they were radical in the context of their time. Nothing like this had ever happened in the college before. The governing body replied the following day that such matters should be discussed by the proposed new council of the College Union and JCR committee.[60] The council of the union, to be elected by the students, but to include some Fellows chosen by the governing body, was intended to act as the undergraduates' representa-

---

[57] K. E. Machin papers.
[58] The ratio of teaching Fellows to undergraduates was about 1:15, which put Queens' about in the middle of the list of colleges marked in terms of staff/student ratio, CM 209.
[59] K. E. Machin papers.
[60] *ibid.*

tive and policy-making body and as a liaison committee with the governing body; its senior officers were to be the senior officers of the JCR committee, an arrangement which has often led to the two bodies being confused — in fact, the JCR was meant to operate as an administrative arm, or working committee. These new 'representative functions' distinguished the council from the old committee of the United Clubs, which it was to replace.[61]

But at this stage, in February 1968, the College Union was still on the drawing board. The governing body was concerned by the strength of undergraduate discontent, and realised the need for immediate action. At the beginning of March it established a committee to review all administrative and tutorial arrangements and college regulations. A letter was sent to all students informing them of this and of the governing body's 'intention to consult the junior members' on these matters.[62] The principle of consultation was not new, for the governing body had sent out questionnaires on previous occasions, but its use on this occasion and the need to publicise it was highly significant. The Fellows also decided later in the month that the activities of all college societies should be recorded in the college magazine — hitherto this had included entries for all the sports clubs, but only the St Bernard and St Margaret societies and the Bats of the others — and it was suggested that students be consulted as to how they wanted such activities presented. In April, the governing body agreed to seek student opinion on the priorities of the college development plan.[63]

These were necessary palliatives while the fundamental issues of relations between students and Fellows were discussed. The governing body did not in fact regard the college's regulations as unreasonable, though it accepted that their presentation might be improved. The question of gate hours was also discussed at this time.[64] The Fellows were reminded of the strength of student militancy over political issues on 25th April, when an announcement in that afternoon's issue of the *Cambridge News* that Enoch Powell was coming to Cambridge to speak to the university's Heraldic Society at Clare and would be dining first in Queens' resulted in some 200 students from all over the university turning out spontaneously to demonstrate outside Queens' in defiance of a proctorial ban on demonstrations. The visit was cancelled. On the same evening a general meeting of the United Clubs approved the new constitution for the council of the union and JCR committee. One of the student 'radicals' described the vote as

[61] *QC* (1967 – 8), 28.
[62] GB, 1.3.1968; K. E. Machin papers.
[63] GB, 15.3.1968, 16.4.1968.
[64] *ibid*. 16.4.1968, and see 29.7.1968.

'a decisive blow for student representation in the university. The one alarming thing was that only 50 to 60 people turned up, although the meeting was well publicised. But despite the obvious apathy, we've certainly taken an important step along the path towards a fully democratic administration'.[65]

The low attendance may also have been due partly to a general understanding that the new constitution was not a contentious issue, was tacitly accepted by most of the college, and therefore did not require much debate; certainly the general climate of opinion at this time was strongly in support of reforms.

Much progress was made during the next few months. In May the governing body accepted the proposed College Union constitution. Elections to the council of the union and the JCR committee were held soon afterwards, and were 'warmly contended'.[66] In June the governing body responded to a letter of complaint about the college kitchens from the incoming JCR committee by instituting a survey of undergraduate feeling on the subject — it was felt that

'While there was inherent difficulty in reaching certain policy conclusions now, and while it was desirable that the Governing Body should avoid the impression of stalling on these issues, it might be wiser to wait and see precisely what the undergraduates wanted'.[67]

At the same time, the governing body accepted in principle that women guests should be allowed to dine in hall, thereby resolving a long-standing student grievance; and it discussed plans for a proposed 'College Centre', which was to include improved social facilities for junior members.[68]

The new undergraduate institutions came into existence officially before the start of the Michaelmas term, and one of the Fellows on the council of the union reported to the governing body soon afterwards that 'the undergraduates were adopting a most responsible attitude in the exercise of their new powers', although there was some unease among the Fellows at calls for a college bar and discos.[69] The governing

---

[65] *Varsity*, 27.4.1968.
[66] GB, 21.5.1968; *QC* (1967 – 8), 28; CM 253 (and see 258); CU papers. The council's terms of reference were 'to collate, inform and express opinions of members of the College *in statu pupillari* on matters pertaining to their participation in College life and to co-operate with the Governing Body . . . in all such matters', and 'to provide a framework for the organisation of extra-curricular activities and amenities', CM 253.
[67] GB, 21.6.1968; see also CM 226; CU papers.
[68] GB, 21.6.1968; see also below, p. 438.
[69] GB, 18.10. 1968 The bar came a year later, see below, pp. 413 – 41, 418. Discos did not arrive until the opening of the new JCR in Cripps Court in the mid-1970s, *Record* (1977), 12.

body remained concerned at the strength of feeling among under-graduates about the way that the college was run, but the suggestion by one Fellow that high table guest nights should not be held in hall but in a separate dining room 'on the ground that it might cause friction with the undergraduates' was thought to be an overreaction.[70]

The honeymoon period did not last long, and the council of the union was soon pressing for changes to many of the petty regulations governing college life. In November, after holding an open meeting of the undergraduates, a series of proposals was submitted to the governing body 'with a view to extending the personal freedom of junior members of the College, thereby bringing their situation more into line with others of their generation'. There were five main points: first, they called for gate regulations to be abolished and students to be allowed unrestricted access either through issuing keys or appointing a night porter to let them into college.[71] This proposal had been supported by over three quarters of the 100 students present at the open meeting. One undergraduate had recently fallen on the spikes of the college railings when climbing in and required several stitches in his arm. The undergraduate president of the union was quoted by the *1/- Paper*, a radical student newspaper published largely from Queens', as saying that 'In no other country does the exterior of a college or university look like a concentration camp'. Certainly this was an issue on which most undergraduates felt very strongly.

A similar majority of students at the open meeting had voted that it should not be compulsory to wear gowns when visiting college officers, directors of studies or supervisors in the college. For most this was an irksome, outdated obligation; for some the gown was a 'symbol of student elitism and separation in Cambridge'. The third question was that of 'music hours', the periods when the playing of musical instruments or records was permitted. More than half of those present at the open meeting had voted for their total abolition, although all had agreed that care should be taken not to disturb others. Fourth, it was unanimously agreed by the meeting that students should not need to get intermediate exeats from their tutors in person — all students going

---

[70] GB, 18.10.1968.

[71] Before the first world war, students returning to college after 11.00 were fined. In 1948 Queens' abolished gate fines, but not gate hours. In 1952 it approved altering the locking-up time for licensed lodgings from 10.00 to 11.00. In 1957, after complaints, the college gates were opened until 11.00. In 1963 the requirement for undergraduates to sign in when returning to college between 11.00 and midnight was abolished. In 1966 Queens' became the third college to introduce an 'open gates' system, allowing each undergraduate living in college six free late leaves per term (meaning the freedom to return after midnight but before 2.00). By 1968, therefore, the gates were in effect closed at 12.00, above, p. 266; CB (1937 – 63), 6.2.1948, 14.2.1948, 8.3.1952; *Dial* (1948), 12; *Varsity*, 2.2.1957, 15.10.1966; GB, 12.2.1957, 27.1.1959, 11.11.1963.

away from Cambridge other than on day trips during term time were supposed to secure such formal permission. Finally, the council of the union urged 'that forms of neckwear other than collar and tie be allowed in Hall'.[72]

The governing body agreed to the second, fourth and fifth of these proposals without hesitation, and referred the question of noise back to the council for further discussion. It claimed to be sympathetic to the extension of gate hours in principle, was willing for entry to be 'unrestricted but not unsupervised', and suggested an extension allowing college members to enter and leave Queens' between midnight and 2.00, with a night porter letting them in between 2.00 and 6.00, when the gates opened again (thought it wished to consult university regulations first to ensure that this was permitted, and to consult other colleges, since such a move would go far beyond the existing general arrangements). The new gate regulations came into operation in January 1969.[73] The concessions were greeted enthusiastically by the 1/- Paper: 'This time the dons have given in. But whether they will do again, when faced with demands for representation and the integration of High Table, remains to be seen'.[74]

At the end of November the committee on administrative and tutorial arrangements presented an interim report to the governing body. This referred to 'The problem of fully effective interchange of information and opinions, at both formal and informal levels in and also between most or perhaps all sectors of the resident population of the College'; and also to 'Marked changes in attitude and opinion which in recent years have taken place, often inconspicuously, among resident Members', senior and junior. In the light of this, several reforms were proposed. It was felt that since tutors now had more administrative duties than in the past, and the personal side of their relationships with their pupils had become more important and difficult, more tutors should be appointed, and the burden of administrative work shouldered by the senior tutor should also be reduced. The dean's rôle was to be divided between two officers: a dean with responsibility for the chapel and college religious life, and a dean of college with a 'general advisory and counselling function to all members of the College parallel to and in co-operation with the Tutors and Directors of Studies'. The new tutorial arrangements were approved in February 1969.[75]

The committee also welcomed the current dialogue with the junior members over new college regulations. It believed that when a new set

---

[72] CM 235; 1/- Paper, 8.11.1968. For some background to the question of gowns, see also CM 57, 141; GB, 7.12.1961; SBSM, 14.10.1964.
[73] GB, 15.11.1968; Varsity, 1.2.1969. Draft regulations on noise are in CM 243.
[74] 1/- Paper, 22.11.1968.
[75] CM 237; GB, 6.12.1968, 3.2.1969.

of regulations was issued, it should be made clear that students had no special privileges with regard to the law of the land; but that, in an emergency, they could seek advice from tutors and other Fellows, even in more serious cases such as drug-peddling[76] and theft (although the remarks were probably meant mainly for students arrested at demonstrations and other protests). The committee felt that the governing body should become involved in the cases of students who were arrested, and they should have the right to be assisted or at least heard by the Fellows or the tutors. It also noted the importance of 'personal and private contacts of many different kinds' within the college in the 'in some ways difficult circumstances of today', and recommended that 'agreed conventions' should be established for making governing body decisions known to students whilst protecting the governing body's confidentiality. In February of the following year it was decided that individual members of the governing body might ask for the rule of confidentiality to be waived when discussing particular issues.[77]

The College Union also pressed for improved facilities: in January 1969 it called for a second laundrette, described as 'a basic amenity', and a college centre (with bar) in the Fitzpatrick Hall; the college centre was regarded as a particularly urgent need.[78] This was not the first time the question of a college bar had been raised. In 1957 undergraduates had asked for a bar to serve beer and coffee for a few hours in the early evening — the governing body would not countenance the sale of spirits — and this was opened in the late autumn of 1958. At the end of its first full term in use (the Lent term 1959) it was reckoned a great success socially, but in the following term it was closed down temporarily because it was no longer so popular in the light summer evenings; and in January 1960 it was closed down entirely 'except for special occasions', until demand increased. In 1967 the question was aired again, but the governing body decided that 'practical difficulties' were too great to re-establish it.[79] In February 1969 the Fellows agreed to a

---

[76] It is not clear how widespread drug-taking was, nor what kinds of drugs were used. In 1967 the senior tutor announced that Queens' was to follow the practice of some other colleges and issue statements to all undergraduates describing college policy on illegal drug-taking and suggesting how they could get help. In 1968 the governing body approved a donation to the Cambridge Association for the Prevention of Drug Addiction. In 1972 police raided a room in Queens' (with tutorial permission) to arrest two students for taking cannabis. In 1974 it was reported to the governing body that an undergraduate had been convicted of possessing cannabis: he had signed an undertaking not to use drugs again or to allow them to be used in his rooms, and the governing body agreed that no further disciplinary action was necessary. There was a similar instance soon afterwards, GB, 24.7.1967, 1.3.1968, 15.5.1974, 7.6.1974; *Varsity*, 25.11.1972.

[77] CM 237; GB, 21.2.1969.

[78] CM 248, 249.

[79] GB, 6.12.1957, 21.11.1958, 21.4.1959, 1.5.1959, 29.1.1960, 24.7.1967; QC (1957 – 8), 9.

college bar, subject to the details being worked out satisfactorily; and to a second laundrette.[80]

The governing body also made efforts to address the complaints about catering facilities which had been forwarded to it the previous June. Poor catering was a traditional grievance. In 1948 college meals at Queens' were said to be relatively expensive but always edible, with some variety; however, in 1957 the meals were said to be particularly cheap. In 1968 an undergraduate was quoted as saying that meals were very poor, and described waiter service in evening hall as 'a ridiculous waste of time and money with no atmospheric merit whatsoever'.[81] The incoming JCR committee in June 1968 referred to 'the perpetual stream of complaints about the food which have been expressed in the JCR Suggestion Book'. It called for 'the immediate employment of a professional caterer to enquire into the economics and general running of the College Kitchens', for more self-service meals, greater variety of dishes, and the introduction of meal tickets rather than the antiquated system of prepayment under which students had to sign out if they did not wish to take meals and were not allowed to do this very often.[82] As we have seen, the governing body delayed its response until it had gauged undergraduate feelings by means of a questionnaire at the start of the autumn term; it was recognised that the kitchens 'had been going through a bad patch administratively, but it was hoped that the worst of the storm had passed'.[83] When the governing body tackled the matter again in January 1969, it granted some concessions: an effort was to be made to improve hall service; third-year undergraduates were to be allowed to sign out three times per week; and in February it was agreed that, as an experiment, self-service evening meals would be supplied in the Erasmus Room, paid for with meal tickets. The idea of under-graduates dining on high table with the Fellows was rejected.[84]

Although the governing body was moving hesitantly in some areas of reform, much progress had been made. The official view of the College Union after its first few months in operation, expressed in the college magazine, was that the new representative bodies — the council and the JCR committee — had 'been largely concerned . . . with social and general amenities in College and have proved valuable additional means of communication between the Governing Body and the resident members' — a vague but confident summary of the achievements to

---

[80] GB, 3.2.1969. See also *Varsity*, 1.2.1969.
[81] *Varsity*, 21.2.1948, 16.2.1957, 22.10.1966.
[82] CM 226. Signing out was also open to abuse, see GB, 17.2.1961.
[83] CU papers; GB, 21.6.1968.
[84] GB, 14.1.1969, 21.2.1969. The idea of Fellows and students eating together was resurrected in moderated form in 1971 – 2, CM 303, 340. It was really doomed to failure from the start, although formal halls during the long vacation term have in the last few years been 'mixed'.

date.[85] But amenities had been tackled with more success than the problem of communication had, and the underlying issues had not been resolved fully.

Discipline was one of the outstanding problems. The council of the union had been looking into the matter, but was 'overtaken by events',[86] in February, when the president and five members of the JCR committee resigned claiming that their rôle on the council of the union as student representatives was ignored by the dons, who treated them as 'mere mouthpieces to inform the students of decisions taken at a higher level'. The president of the JCR argued further that the council had never worked as a two-way channel of communication:

'The four dons plan the meetings, trying to dissolve our enthusiasm by typing statements, correcting minutes, and so on. They insist that we are there in our personal capacity, not as representatives'.

He continued that although the governing body had indeed approved several reforms the previous term, 'The students really had to hammer for them'.[87]

One of the reforms which he had foremost in mind in this context was the abolition of gate hours for men living in. Gate hours and their associated restrictions had become a prominent issue again at the end of January, when students from all over the university held a 40-hour sit-in in the Old Schools in solidarity with student protesters at the London School of Economics who had recently been served with writs — an event which led to widespread agitation throughout the country's universities.[88] Among the motions passed by the students on the first day of the sit-in was a demand for 'the immediate removal of spikes, railings and gates and all other restrictions on free movement', and they voted to remove colleges' spikes and railings during the night. Feelings were running high, and alarmed college authorities instituted emergency measures during the early evening, which were described in a broadsheet printed by the *1/- Paper* the following day: 'Hoses are prepared, gates of colleges all over Cambridge are locked and guarded, rusty firearms are produced and some porters are armed with axes'. This may seem sensationalist stuff, but is not altogether implausible in the light of the prevailing panic among colleges, who had suddenly to deal with a quite unforeseen and potentially violent situation. One measure adopted by many colleges was the recruiting of what the

---

[85]   QC (1967 – 8), 29.
[86]   GB, 21.2.1969.
[87]   *Varsity*, 22.2.1969. See also *1/- Paper*, 21.2.1969.
[88]   For the sit-in and associated events, see *Varsity*, 31.1.1969; *1/- Paper*, 31.1.1969, 1.2.1969; broadsheet published by *1/- Paper* on 31.1.1969 in K. E. Machin papers.

broadsheet described as 'Vigilantes'. At Queens' a Fellow organised students 'whose loyalties are in the right place', as he put it, to defend its railings: these students consisted of 'Cambridge rowdies . . . (mostly Boat Club and Rugger Club)', who were 'plied with beer' by dons 'to provide the necessary atmosphere of reason and moderation'; some of them were alleged to have joined a crowd on the lawn outside the senate house seeking to intimidate the students at the sit-in.[89] Whether because of this threat, or for some other reason, no attempt was made on college railings.

This incident can only have added to the tensions which led to the resignation of the six council and JCR committee members in February. One particular catalyst was the accusation of 'sharp practice' levelled against the undergraduate members of the council over the question of visiting hours for students' guests. The question had not arisen in the previous year, and the reforms so far achieved had represented what the president of the council called 'the sum total of changes in substance of the college regulations envisaged by the Council of the Union'; but since this time, student opinion had moved on, and an open meeting had called for an extension of visiting hours for guests similar to the extension of gate hours for college members. The resigning JCR secretary commented: 'We represent this opinion to the Council and are accused of sharp practice'.[90] It was as if the implementation of reforms was to regarded as a 'one-off' practice, and the possibility of further improvements was not to be allowed.

Five members of the JCR committee did not resign, and disapproved of their colleagues' action: they saw it as 'petulance', bringing the College Union into disrepute, and argued that the JCR committee and the union

'cannot function properly if meetings of the latter are treated by some of the undergraduates as confrontations where no real discussion can take place and where no account is to be taken of the views and experience of others'.[91]

This is the first sign of a split between 'moderates'[92] and 'radicals'. It could only weaken the reform movement, which until then had presented a united front in public. The division seems to have been apparent privately for some time. The resigning members of the council announced their intention to 'stand again on a radical platform,

[89] *1/- Paper* broadsheet of 31.1.1969 in K. E. Machin papers.
[90] *Varsity*, 22.2.1969.
[91] *ibid.*
[92] See n. 55.

including demands for major structural reforms within the college'.[93] The 'moderates' opposed this tactic also, believing that the JCR committee should serve out its term in office in accordance with its original mandate, and should in particular 'confine itself to internal matters affecting the welfare of its electors'. If there were to be major changes to the structure of college government, this should be 'through the informed deliberation of all interested parties'. The resignations and re-elections were felt to have 'already disrupted and postponed reforms. Furthermore, an unnecessary and damaging situation of don-student confrontation has been provoked'.[94]

Five of the six 'radicals' were re-elected unopposed, the 'moderates' claiming that there was no point in contesting an election which they had not sought. The sixth, whose special function on the committee was the establishment of the college's new bar, was defeated by the landlord of the Anchor, a pub on Silver Street opposite the college. He had been nominated by some of his regulars from Queens' — 'a group of hearties', according to the 1/- Paper — and permitted to stand by a loophole in the JCR constitution which did not restrict candidates to college members. But the validity of his election was challenged nonetheless, and he did not take up the post. One of the 'moderate' committeemen who had not resigned described the college's attitude towards the election as 'too flippant'.

Both sides claimed that the result represented a victory for their principles. The 'radicals' had stood on a platform of abolition of the college union as presently constituted, student and worker representation at the college's decision-making level, and open governing body meetings. This they now hoped to implement. The 'moderates' refused to regard the result as a mandate for any new programme, and the 1/- Paper warned that 'Right-wing dons and conservative students . . . are hoping to direct the left into reformist activity'.[95]

These matters were debated at an open meeting in early March, which decided to keep the council of the union, but called for open meetings of the governing body (except for such classified topics as the appointment of staff and Fellows) with student and staff representatives; and the publication of full agenda and minutes of both the governing body and its committees. The student and staff representatives were to have speaking rights only at this stage, but it was decided that the college should change its statutes to allow them voting rights. The meeting also called upon the college to accept the right of its employees to engage in free collective bargaining, and voted that college members and their

[93]   1/- Paper, 21.2.1969.
[94]   Varsity, 1.3.1969; K. E. Machin papers.
[95]   1/- Paper, 28.2.1969; Varsity, 1.3.1969.

guests should be free to enter or leave Queens' at any time. These motions all received decisive majorities. Smaller, but nonetheless conclusive majorities carried proposals for the Fellows' private dining room, the Munro Room, to become an open common room for all college members; and for student participation in the formulation of admissions policy; and there was a close vote in favour of the recommendation that students, Fellows, and staff, should eat the same food in hall 'as a single community, dons and undergraduates having the option of eating together or separately'. This was a very clear mandate for further substantial reform, and demonstrates how much 'radicals' and 'moderates' had in common. The only hiccup in the proceedings occurred about two thirds of the way through the meeting, when 'a bunch of sportsmen burst in and proceeded to jeer from the back'.[96]

Procedural complications meant that these resolutions were not *formally* presented to the governing body until early June,[97] meaning that the matter had to drag on over the summer vacation — in fact it was abandoned by the Fellows in a successful exercise of what one senior member described in another context as 'the standard ploy of playing for time'.[98] Looking over the first year of the council of the union's operations in July 1969, the governing body noted its success in improving college facilities, and it was believed to have provided a useful channel of communication; but it was admitted that the council had failed as a 'consultative body'. It was hoped that the council for 1969 – 70 'with a new undergraduate representation' would be more satisfactory: the 'moderates' of February were now firmly in control of the JCR and the council, and could be expected to be more malleable.[99] But the governing body had also decided in May, before formal notification of the result of the March open meeting but clearly in response to it, that there should be a closer relationship between governing body committees and the college union, 'perhaps with undergraduates being allowed to make representations direct to the Committees'. This was a way of heading off the demand for student representation on the governing body itself.[100] In the meantime, the Fellows pursued plans for the new college bar and congratulated themselves on the success of the new laundrette. The bar was ready for the Michaelmas term and was an immediate success; the Fellows' tactics seemed to have led to a discernible improvement in relations with junior members.[101]

[96]   *1/- Paper*, 14.3.1969; CM 259.
[97]   GB, 13.3.1969, 14.3.1969; CM 259.
[98]   CU papers.
[99]   GB, 18.7.1969; CU papers.
[100] GB, 30.5.1969.
[101] GB, 5.5.1969, 30.5.1969, 3.10.1969; QC (1968 – 9), 4.

Clearly the governing body was too optimistic. It may have outman-oeuvred the student representatives on the council of the union after the March open meeting, but it had done nothing to remove the grievances which that meeting had articulated so forcefully. In November conflict over guest hours erupted again. The council of the union issued a questionnaire to junior members, and after studying the replies recommended that the rules should be altered so that guests accompanied by a member of college could enter Queens' between midnight and 2.00, whilst unaccompanied guests could leave at any time — in other words, permitting overnight guests in students' rooms for the first time. The council stressed that its proposals represented something of a compromise between the different views expressed, for most students wanted unrestricted entry for their guests, and there was widespread dissatisfaction with existing arrangements, which were not only inconvenient, but seen as 'an unwarranted interference with the liberty of the individual'. It emphasised too that the mere extension of existing guest hours from midnight until 2.00 would not be satisfactory.[102]

Yet this is precisely what the governing body decided upon, although there was considerable discussion of the matter; and it also decreed that guests entering or leaving between midnight and 2.00 must be accompanied by a member of the college. It felt that a complete relaxation of the rules would cause too much disturbance, place too great a burden on college staff, and would be incompatible with existing regulations concerning overnight guests in college guest rooms, though it was prepared to make it easier for students to accommodate such guests (the council of the union, however, had argued that noise and guest rooms were separate issues). The college was not 'analogous to a block of flats', the governing body pointed out, but was 'accommodation subsidised for academic uses'.[103]

The Fellows clearly misjudged the mood of the college: perhaps the apparent tactical success following the March open meeting had left them complacent; perhaps some felt there had been too much appeasement. Yet they should have heeded the clear warnings of the 'moderate' council of the union. The 1/- Paper was furious, even by its own customarily vehement standards. This was 'a case history of classic Governing Body intransigence', it argued, pointing out that a proposal to abolish guest hours had been passed overwhelmingly in March, that the undergraduate members of the college union had been elected on the platform of abolition, and that two referenda of junior members had confirmed the call for reform, with three quarters of the students emphatically in support. The paper was particularly incensed at the

---

[102] CM 263. See also 1/- Paper, 28.11.1969; Varsity, 22.11.1969.
[103] GB, 14.11.1969; CU papers.

hypocrisy shown by Fellows who in the past had accused the 'radicals' of not representing student opinion, but now ignored an undeniably popular view. The question of representation of student wishes now appeared to many as a smokescreen employed by dons who were not interested in students' feelings. Moreover,

> 'What the Governing Body still fails to address itself to is *not* the "inconvenience" of being cooped up like chickens in an educational battery farm . . . but the principle of freedom of access to members of a community and their guests'.

Varsity, a more moderate publication, described the college's undergraduates as 'greatly angered' by the governing body's decision.[104]

An extraordinary general meeting of students on 25th November opposed the decision overwhelmingly, and voted

> 'That non-cooperative action on the new rule on guest hours be taken. That this action be non-violent, and should not disturb members of the College not participating in such action'.

The action was to be taken on the night of 29th – 30th November (a Saturday night) and to consist of college members and their guests gathering in Cloister Court after 2 a.m. in defiance of college rules. The mood of radicalism engendered by the Fellows' decision also led the meeting to call unanimously for the council of the union to investigate forthwith the question of student representation on the governing body.[105]

By its intransigence, the governing body had given a new lease of life to the 'radicals', and undermined the 'moderates' on the council of the union who were opposed to direct action and felt they had been let down. The council's president spoke to *Varsity* saying 'It's not our policy to advocate confrontation, and if the governing body does not cooperate we just have to sit by. It's a very difficult situation'. But the decision was welcomed by the *1/- Paper*, which regarded direct action as the only course open to students 'once all constitutional and democratic means at the disposal of the community have been violated by the decision making body'. This was the first time that direct action had been approved democratically within a Cambridge college, and the paper exhorted its readers at Queens' and elsewhere:

> 'Lets start on Saturday night. Lets show what we think of the small

---

[104] *1/- Paper*, 28.11.1969; *Varsity*, 22.11.1969.
[105] CM 266.

group of men who should presume to know better than us what is good for us, and who outrageously deny our independence as rational beings who *have* come of age'.[106]

The demonstration was held as planned: a crowd of students and guests gathered in Cloister Court and there was no trouble until a snowball was thrown through a window of the long gallery, whereupon the gathering soon dispersed. The 'moderates' on the council of the union apologised to the governing body for the damage, which was costly, and dissociated themselves from all that happened.[107]

This was a tame affair indeed in comparison with student agitation elsewhere, but it did mark a significant new development in the student revolt at Queens': it was the first time that the college's students had had to resort to direct action, going outside the normal channels and openly defying the regulations; and it came as a considerable shock to many of the college's senior members. Having been complacent hitherto, the governing body was now thoroughly alarmed. At a meeting a few days after the demonstration, the Fellows established a large committee to consider their tactics should there be any similar actions in the future, together with 'the whole nature of the College and the status of its regulations and of the Governing Body in the changing social environment'; the college's 'peace, order and government'; the causes of the disturbance; machinery for considering undergraduate requests; 'the need to achieve a stable and peaceful community in which discussions could take place'; and 'the possibility that there was within the College a group of people whose object was to disrupt the College'. There was a recognised need to prove to undergraduates that there were 'serious issues demanding consideration which the Governing Body was anxious to discuss', to show that it had a defensible point of view, and to involve students in the decision-making process.[108]

The draft arrangements for measures to deal with crisis situations in college which are reproduced in appendix 19 were drawn up at around this time, and the governing body committee's report in January 1970 certainly took a very grave view of the situation:[109]

'If the College Regulations are enforced firmly and fairly, with the wholehearted backing of the Governing Body, the Committee do not seriously apprehend a total breakdown of law and order within the College. But if this were to occur, the Committee believe that it might be necessary to close the College temporarily. A decision to close the

---

[106] *Varsity*, 29.11.1969; *1/- Paper*, 28.11.1969. See CM 266.
[107] K. E. Machin, in conversation; CM 266; see GB, 11.1.1972.
[108] GB, 5.12.1969.
[109] CM 268, from which the following account is taken.

College might have to be taken at very short notice and in circumstances which made it impossible to convene a meeting of the Governing Body'.

To prevent such a situation arising, the committee felt that tutors should avoid imposing heavy penalties for purely technical offences against college rules, and reserve them for serious ones: for example, those which threatened the college fabric, or made work or sleep difficult or impossible; victimisation, or violence. The question of noise disturbance was not felt to be a critical one at that stage; and another technical offence which the committee felt might be overlooked concerned students walking on the lawns of the college courts. It was feared that 'a form of Challenge' to the Fellows's authority might emerge with students walking 'ostentatiously' on the grass. Fellows were permitted to do so; junior members were forbidden, although the rule was often broken.[110] Now the committee suggested that Fellows too should refrain from walking on the grass for the time being:

'We do not think it likely that undergraduates who are prone to this kind of action will accept the explanation that to allow 450 people to walk on the lawns would ruin them, but to allow 30 Fellows to do so would not'.

On the deeper question of college government, the committee came out in favour of the existing constitution of the council of the union, but disliked the practice whereby the students called open meetings to press their case further whenever the governing body turned down union proposals. It called for formal machinery to ensure further discussion in such situations — in effect, an institutionalised version of the practice of stalling for time. It also recognised that the principle of student representation on the governing body was 'achieving substantial recognition elsewhere', but postponed a decision on what action should be taken on this, resurrecting instead the old idea that the admission of students to governing body committees would make the question redundant.

The report was approved by the governing body, and tutors were instructed to adopt a 'flexible approach' to the enforcement of college rules. The question of guest regulations was referred to the council of the union, it having been recognised that some reforms were inevitable in this area: there were already 'many illicit guests'. The governing body

---

[110] See e.g. CR (29.10.1879), 41; (12.11.1879), 72; (26.11.1879), 103; CB (1889 – 1937), 14.1.1895; GB, 8.5.1964.

was also pleased with the contingency plan for closing the college down in an emergency.[111]

The 'moderates' who controlled the council of the union were now trying to play down the degree of confrontation within the college. The council's report on the first year of the union's operations in the college magazine commented on the success of the new bar and laundrette — 'the major tangible results of the year' — although it also noted the relaxation of gate hours. It was more evasive on the subject of representation and communications:

> 'Throughout the year, undergraduates on the Council of the Union have learnt a great deal about the problems involved in running the College, and through the undergraduate representatives contact between senior and junior members was increased. There is still much room for improving the system and enhancing further communication, but it seems that the Union has got off to a good start'.[112]

The issue of representation was pushed further at an open meeting in February, when a relatively moderate proposal for student observers on the governing body with speaking rights who would be present only during the discussion of 'Union matters' was passed unanimously. This motion had the support of the students on the council, which explained to the governing body that 'students today take a greater interest in the running of their educational institutions than in the past, and they wish to become more involved in the taking of decisions which affect their lives'. However, the meeting also accepted a radical motion calling for student observers with voting rights. In the prevailing conditions, the Fellows had really no option but to accept the first proposal, but they would have nothing to do with the second. Even the first caused some anxiety in their ranks, especially with regard to confidentiality; and the governing body decided that, whilst accepting the principle of student representation, it should 'proceed cautiously and should avoid giving the impression of creating precedents which might later prove embarrassing'.[113]

The following month the governing body also accepted the council of the union's proposals that college guest rooms should be available to women guests. In May it decided that suggested increases in student charges should be discussed with the council; and in June, after reading the tutorial committee's annual report, it noted 'with satisfaction' the

---

[111]   GB, 13.1.1970.
[112]   QC (1968 – 9), 10.
[113]   CU papers; GB, 9.2.1970; *Varsity*, 7.2.1970, 14.2.1970; *Cambridge Evening News*, 13.2.1970.

evidence of junior members' 'fruitful participation' on that committee.[114] The governing body had finally discovered the advantages of co-operating with the 'moderates' on the council, and of being seen to do so. Both the outgoing president of the JCR and the incoming president of the college, D. W. Bowett (who took up office in the autumn of 1970), expressed their satisfaction with the arrangements and achievements so far, although such views were by no means shared by all of the student body.[115]

Although student agitation at Queens' had been confined to purely domestic issues, it had occurred amidst intense political feeling and awareness among students in general.[116] Politics entered the domestic scene in February 1970, when a student general meeting called on the governing body to disinvest from South Africa. The Fellows were concerned at such interference in their investment policy; but the council of the union dropped the matter when it learnt that the college had no investments in South African companies.[117]

Students took part in politics as individuals throughout this period. The most famous example of this is the so-called 'Garden House riot' in February 1970, an event which seems already to have entered the realm of university mythology. A 'Greek Week' had been organised in Cambridge by local travel agents and hotels and the *Cambridge Evening News* on behalf of the Greek tourist board. Greece was governed by a military dictatorship at that time, and there were several political demonstrations at the week's events, which culminated with a dinner at the Garden House hotel, and a demonstration outside. There are widely conflicting accounts of what took place, but some property was damaged; windows were broken; there were scuffles and a few injuries.[118] More significant than the demonstration was the indignant reaction to it among the public at large, fanned by the press. There was a widespread feeling that severe punishments were needed to set an example. Six students were arrested that night, and another nine subsequently; they included four Queensmen. Some were charged with relatively minor offences, but all were charged with the very serious offence of riotous assembly, which indicated that this was not to be

---

[114] CU papers; GB, 13.3.1970, 11.5.1970, 13.6.1970; CM 280.
[115] *Varsity*, 16.5.1970. See also *QC* (1969 – 70), 10. Bowett had been a Fellow of Queens' for ten years.
[116] See the extent of political coverage in *Varsity*, but especially that in the *1/- Paper*, which carried a large number of articles on international, national and local affairs: it sought to integrate university members more closely with the world about them.
[117] But the governing body said nothing about investments in companies trading in South Africa, GB, 13.3.1970, 21.4.1970. The matter was raised again, with a similar outcome, in 1974, CU papers; GB, 13.2.1974.
[118] This account of the demonstration, the reaction to it, and the trial, is drawn from *Varsity*, 6.11.1971; *Cambridge Evening News*, 14.2.1970 – 20.2.1970, 25.6.1970 – 4.7.1970; *the Cambridge Greek affair* (1970); *Criminal Appeal Reports* (1970), 499 – 511.

treated like any other demonstration which had got out of hand.

The fifteen were tried at Hertfordshire assizes in late June — after the end of the summer term — before Mr Justice Melford Stevenson, a judge known to give severe sentences. The radical left claimed that prominent Cambridge leftwingers at the demonstration had been singled out for exemplary punishment, which betrays a certain degree of paranoia; but this was clearly intended to be a test case, and there were many who hoped that it would curb student radicalism. After a trial lasting seven days, seven of the fifteen (including two of the Queensmen) were acquitted of all charges. The other eight were sentenced to varying terms of imprisonment, the two most severe — 18 months and 15 months — being imposed upon the other two Queensmen. The severity of the sentences came as a shock to most people, although it was not altogether surprising given the prevailing mood after the Garden House incident. One of the two Queensmen to be sentenced, Rod Caird, had expected a harsh sentence from the tone of the trial:

'It was after all a show trial whose purpose was evidently the passing of exemplary sentences. We were being used as scapegoats in an attempt to clamp down on the student movement: all the protestations of the judge to the contrary, it was a *political* trial'.[119]

Caird also refuted the view that the harshness of the judge was mainly responsible for the length of the sentences:

'a more realistic appraisal was that Stevenson was only responding to the hysterical demands for vengeance which had been expressed in establishment circles since the demonstration'.[120]

On appeal, the conviction of one of the eight was overturned; and the sentence of the second Queensman commuted to two years' probation. Caird, who served 12 months of his 18 month sentence, used his experiences to write a book on the British prison system.[121]

In the short term, the severe punishments meted out to the Garden House demonstrators took the wind out of the sails of Cambridge student activism. An open meeting of the College Union in Queens' at the end of February passed unanimously a motion condemning disciplinary action of any kind against those who had been arrested; but there were fewer than 40 students present, to the disappointment of the

[119] *Varsity*, 6.11.1971.
[120] Caird (1974), 89 – 90.
[121] *Criminal Appeal Reports* (1970), 499 – 511; Caird (1974).

'radicals'.[122] The governing body made no public response to the demonstration.[123] When the undergraduates voted against giving financial and other support to the Cambridge Students Union (CSU) in October, one of the principal arguments against it was its political (allegedly socialist) affiliations — a vote against the Queens' radicals, one of whom had just been elected president of CSU.[124] As Rod Caird noted,

'it is characteristic of student politics as a whole that they tend to adopt moral issues such as Greece, Vietnam, South Africa and the like for a time and then to drop them again after only a limited period of activism . . . students have not yet reached the stage of comprising an analytical and consistent political mass movement and are therefore only engageable in politics when something arises which is of such glaring clarity and is imbued with such simple moral overtones that they have little work to do in distinguishing right from wrong'.[125]

Yet the movement for domestic reform at Queens' pressed ahead. The question of guest hours was still under discussion, and the memory of November's demonstration in Cloister Court was still fresh.[126] The main obstacle appeared to be not the governing body but the college staff, especially the bedmakers. At a meeting between staff and a representative of the students on the evening of the Garden House demonstration, the former came out very strongly against overnight guests of either sex, and the student representative was subjected to a good deal of abuse.[127]

This typifies the limited understanding among students of the outlook of college staff. It was all very well for the former to call for free collective bargaining and staff representation on the governing body, but these were vague abstract issues to most of the staff; whereas the changes in

[122] This meeting also called for the college to disinvest from South Africa, and to give financial support to a dossers' squat in the town, CU papers; *Varsity*, 28.2.1970.
[123] Caird's mother wrote asking the president and senior tutor to sign a petition to the home secretary for clemency for her son. There was some hostility to this on the governing body, but the president promised to write to the home secretary separately; it was college policy to help members in trouble with the law, CM 290; GB, 2.10.1970.
[124] *Varsity*, 31.10.1970; GB, 17.7.1970, 12.11.1970. There were many subsequent debates on this matter and the related one of affiliation to the National Union of Students; and it was usually the right-wingers who wished to disaffiliate, although the question declined in importance as a serious political issue, *Varsity*, 19.2.1972 (and see 5.10.1963); *Stop Press*, 20.10.1972, 29.11.1975, 31.1.1976, 20.11.1976, 7.11.1981, 14.11.1981.
[125] *Varsity*, 6.11.1971.
[126] In the words of one student: 'We know that last term's demonstration did not go unnoticed by the dons. I think we have a reasonable chance of getting the rules altered', *Cambridge Evening News*, 13.2.1970.
[127] CU papers.

gate hours and the proposed alterations to guest regulations were more immediate and meant a great deal more work. The students overlooked the innate conservatism which characterises many college staff and which had been reinforced by college traditions. The customary view of college 'servants' in the late 19th and early 20th centuries was of 'fine old crusted characters' with 'an intense pride in the college. . . Indeed they gave you the idea that it was they who made the wheels go round, while the dons . . . looked on'.[128] Their political attitudes were typified by Herbert Holder, a buttery servant who died in 1931 after half a century's service at Queens': 'Like many men who are tolerant of persons, he was severely intolerant of opinions and classes, being an ardent conservative and nationalist, ever ready to pour sarcasm upon foreigners and self-styled progressives'.[129] When one left-wing student tried to organise the staff to demand improvements in their pay and conditions in the 1930s, some of the dons thought his activities 'rather unwise', but the staff reacted more strongly, regarding him as an 'interfering troublemaker'.[130]

After the students' rebuff by the bedmakers in 1970, the guest hours campaign came temporarily to a halt, and the reform programme in general slowed down during the following academic year (1970 – 1); in part, this was because the council of the union was preoccupied with rewriting the union's constitution.[131] The focus of complaint shifted towards the inadequacy of catering facilities, a grievance shared by all students, and there was a series of skirmishes with the governng body. In the Michaelmas term of 1970 and again in the spring of 1971 the union pressed for one self-service evening hall, reduced meal and 'kitchen fixed'[132] charges, and complete freedom to sign out of hall. The governing body would not at first countenance any such changes and persisted in its customary notion that all would be well if the service in the evening 'formal' halls was improved. It also pinned much faith in the new hall and kitchens proposed as part of the new building development, even though these would not come into operation for a long while. But it finally came to realise the strength of student feelings,

[128] *Dial* (Easter 1938), 8 – 9; for other examples, see *ibid.*, (Lent 1931), 8 – 9; (Michaelmas 1932), 8 – 10; (Easter 1935), 5 – 6; (Michaelmas 1937), 13 – 14; (Michaelmas 1947), 8 – 10; (1948), 17 – 18; (Lent 1953), 4.
[129] *ibid.*, (Lent 1931), 8 – 9. 'Never rich in money, he had become rich in sympathy, in understanding and in friendships', *ibid.*
[130] Bibby, 'Reminiscences' (MS), 156. In the 1950s and 1960s college staff became aware that they were poorly paid, and the college had to improve its wages to attract and keep them, e.g. GB, 22.7.1954, 5.10.1954, 18.10.1954, 20.10.1954, 1.11.1954, 14.2.1955, 19.7.1956, 24.10.1956, 6.12.1957, 18.7.1960, 17.1.1961, 1.2.1961, 23.5.1962, 22.7.1965.
[131] QC (1970 – 1), 11; GB, 4.12.1970, 10.5.1971. It also encountered some financial difficulties early in 1971, *ibid.*, 8.2.1971.
[132] The 'kitchen fixed charge' is a termly levy on all students, which subsidises the kitchens. The meals themselves are paid for separately.

and introduced many reforms for the start of the Michaelmas term 1971: fewer formal halls, more flexible lunch arrangements, improved service, self-service in the Erasmus Room at a more convenient hour, abolition of the requirement to dine on a fixed number of nights per week, and total freedom to sign out of hall; meal tickets arrived soon afterwards.[133]

There was a similar pattern of concern with material questions the following academic year: these concerned kitchen improvements and charges, rent rebates to undergraduates disturbed by the noise from the building site of the new development — even the speed and frequency of repairs to the laundrette.[134] Catering remained a major issue: a student general meeting in January 1972 protested about the increased charges and called for a committee of inquiry to look at the catering accounts; and so strong was feeling throughout the year that the governing body had to introduce a further series of improvements for the following Michaelmas. The administration was reorganised and a full time catering officer appointed; the three formal halls were reduced to one and a self-service evening hall was introduced. Efforts were made to improve the quality and choice of food; and there were now also to be fortnightly 'Superhalls' of five courses, with wine.[135]

It had taken repeated pressure from the students to attain these reforms; and perhaps owing to frustration arising from this, the whole question of intra-college relations and communication was brought to the fore again in 1972, together with that of guest and gate regulations.[136] Early in the year there was a proposal to abolish the existing representative structure of JCR committee and council of the union, and replace it with a college students union and a subordinate liaison committee of students and Fellows, although enthusiasm for the scheme soon evaporated. The council of the union heeded the warning: in the Michaelmas term it instituted a JCR newsletter to keep in touch with junior members; and encouraged the formation and revival of college societies.[137] It could also claim the credit for promoting the kitchen reforms, and for the governing body allowing undergraduate representatives onto two more of its committees; in addition, consultative

---

[133]   QC (1970 – 1), 11; GB, 4.12.1970, 8.2.1971, 12.3.1971, 20.4.1971, 14.7.1971, 22.10.1971, 12.11.1971; CU papers; CM 303, 306, 313, 315. There are also some signs of the governing body's confidence in 1971: it rejected any relaxation of rules with regard to undergraduates living out, and decided to maintain its present gate hours policy, GB, 8.2.1971, 20.4.1971, 12.11.1971; CM 304.
[134]   GB, 12.11.1971, 11.1.1972, 16.2.1972, 10.3.1972, 18.4.1972, 3.10.1972; CU papers.
[135]   CU papers; College Union entry in Record (1972 – 3); CM 322, 340; Varsity, 7.10.1972. Despite increased charges, Queens' was said to be one of the cheaper colleges to eat in at this time, Varsity, 28.10.1972.
[136]   CU papers.
[137]   CM 326: College Union entry in Record (1972 – 3).

procedures over charges were agreed. It initiated 'Education Symposia' involving senior and junior members to discuss the relationship between educational theory and practice and especially 'to define more clearly the principles of higher education and to examine the role of the College within this framework'; these generated a good deal of interest among students and Fellows. The council was aware that the union was 'still very much in its infancy', but clearly pleased with what it had achieved, and confident that it was beginning to be accepted by the dons as an important college institution.[138] At the same time the governing body increased the number of tutors to make the tutorial rôle 'more meaningful'. There was a clear intention to escape the old-fashioned formality of the tutorial system, and it worked well. The *Cambridge University Prospectus* for 1973, written by students, observed that 'relations with senior members are good, Queens' having arguably the best set of Tutors of any Cambridge college'. This was enhanced by the rising proportion of relatively young Fellows in the college.[139] Relations were further improved by the governing body's decision in May 1972 'that funds be provided to a Committee of this year's Freshmen to provide appropriate entertainment to the new Freshmen next Michaelmas term', thus giving formal approval to the highly successful and subsequently much praised 'contact' scheme whereby a number of second-year students introduce the new first-years to Cambridge life during their first few days here.[140]

The old problem of guest regulations was finally tackled in 1973. The rules were already ignored by many students, but they were still technically liable to be fined.[141] In June 1973 the governing body allowed guests to stay overnight in students' rooms for up to three nights out of seven.[142] This was welcomed by the college, apart from some staff and a small group of evangelical Christians who were concerned that the new regulations might be abused 'for greater opportunities for promiscuous sex': they called for the prohibition of women guests overnight, reminded the college of its duty to provide moral guidance to students, and concluded with the dire warning that 'in past history, when people have forsaken opportunities to uphold the Law of God, the judgement

---

[138] CU papers; College Union entries in *Record* (1972 – 3), and (1974).

[139] D, W. Bowett in *Record* (1972 – 3); GB, 12.3.1971 (and see also CM 237, 836); *CU Prospectus* (1973), 61; (1975), 70; see also *ibid.* (1974), 63; (1983 – 4), 23. For an illustration of the old-style formality, see B. A. Callingham in *Record* (1985), 3.

[140] A similar system had been introduced in the late 1960s, but the new scheme was more extensive and sophisticated, and drawn up by the College Union, GB, 16.5.1972, 3.10.1972; CU papers; *CU Prospectus* (1979), 24; (1981 – 2), 31; K. E. Machin, in conversation.

[141] e.g. *Varsity*, 7.10.1972.

[142] *Stop Press*, 18.5.1973; CM 362; GB, 16.3.1973, 24.4.1973, 16.5.1973, 15.6.1973, 13.7.1973, 15.3.1974; College Union entry in *Record* (1974).

of God inevitably follows sooner or later'.[143]

This did not bring the disputes to an end. Increases in college charges upon students and the quality of catering were particular scenes of conflict, sometimes serious. In 1975 there was a rent strike as a protest about high charges in general, which was widely supported by all shades of political opinion in Queens' though not officially approved by the council of the union. The students also insisted on the right to inspect the college accounts in detail with a view to suggesting ways of taking some financial pressure off the junior members. The governing body agreed to this and a joint committee of dons and students was set up to look at the accounts. The rent strike was non-political — 'part of a struggle to ensure more consultation of students in the running of the college' — and one JCR committee member commented: 'Queens' has the potential to be the model of a college community. We're trying to see that it is'.[144] In 1976 the council of the union recorded in the college magazine that food was 'one of the most contentious issues of the year' because of compulsory levies to subsidise the kitchens and poor meals in overcrowded conditions.[145] These questions were still hotly debated when I was an undergraduate here in the late 1970s; and there was a particularly fierce reaction to increased kitchen charges in 1978 which led to student examination of the catering accounts and a governing body promise to grant a rebate should its estimates of necessary price levels prove inaccurate.[146]

These debates continually brought into question the efficacy of the council of the union as an instrument of change. The proposal to replace the existing machinery with a college students union was revived in 1974 at an open meeting which was 'constantly disrupted by people in dark glasses firing caps out of guns, and was packed with sports club members who had apparently been told that their money was to be taken away from them'.[147]

There was continued agitation for student representation on the

---

[143] This received a masterly reply from the dean of chapel, CU papers. It was argued in the 1960s that there was no evidence of increased promiscuity at British universities since 1945: though traditional sexual puritanism had been abandoned, students were thought to be more mature and responsible about such matters, Zweig (1963), 62-3, 66; MacRae (1967), 8-9; Stedman Jones in Cockburn and Blackburn (1969), 45.

[144] CU papers; Stop Press, 26.10.1974, 25.1.1975, 8.2.1975, 22.2.1975; 1/- Paper, January 1975, February 1975; GB, 21.2.1973, 14.3.1973. A left-wing member of the fellowship was appointed technical advisor to the joint committee examining the account.

[145] Record (1976), 10; see also College Union entry in Record (1975).

[146] There is a reference to the governing body's guarantee in Stop Press, 3.11.1978. The remarks on don-student relations at Queens' in CU Prospectus (1979), 24, may owe something to this dispute.

[147] Varsity, 18.5.1974. In 1982 there was a call for sovereign open meetings as another line of attack on this problem: under its present constitution the council is not obliged to implement open meeting resolutions, Stop Press, 5.11.1982.

governing body,[148] and in 1975 – 6 this question became significant once more. Some Fellows were at best indifferent to the existing machinery of consultation, and the *Cambridge University Prospectus* alleged that collective relations between dons and students were not good. There was much discussion of the question of student observers, and the governing body did at last establish a working party of Fellows and students to investigate the matter further in November 1976; but progress continued to be painfully slow and there was clearly much resistance to implementing reforms. Perhaps some Fellows hoped that the issue would be forgotten if the governing body stalled for time.[149] In March 1977 the council of the union passed a resolution reassuring Fellows that it had 'no intention whatsoever at the present time of seeking voting rights and full membership of the Governing Body for such of its members as may hereafter be given observer status on the Governing Body', presumably in the hope that this would speed up negotiations.[150] Draft regulations for four student observers, including extensive definition of the governing body's 'reserved business' from which they would be excluded, were ready by late 1977; the scheme came into operation in the following year, and was generally judged a success.[151]

This was almost the last great battle in the 1960s student revolt (the campaign for co-residence was still being fought, but soon to be won); and the high-minded idealism of the late 1960s was on the wane. In 1973 college politics were said to be 'characterised by apathy', and it was claimed that there was 'no strong sense of community'. The allegation of apathy has been levelled against Queens' ever since, coupled more recently with that of conservatism.[152] The union and JCR also began to change their outlook. The former's original terms of reference had been two-fold: representative and social,[153] and as many of the burning issues of the late 1960s were resolved it devoted more attention to the latter aspect, aiming to make the union the 'catalyst in the social life of the college'.[154] This was difficult because apathy among students appeared to be widespread, but the opening of the new JCR and bar in Cripps

---

[148] e.g. GB, 16.1.1973.
[149] CM 452, 467, 468, 473, 474, 485, 518, 527, 533, 546; GB, 13.1.1976, 20.4.1976, 11.6.1976, 9.7.1976, 3.11.1976, 11.1.1977, 11.3.1977, 8.7.1977; *Record* (1977), 12; *CU Prospectus* (1976), 70.
[150] GB, 9.6.1977.
[151] CM 546; GB, 30.9.1977, 9.11.1977, 16.3.1979; *Record* (1978), 13; (1979), 12; *CU Prospectus* (1978), 23.
[152] *CU Prospectus* (1973), 61; (1974), 63; (1978), 23; (1979), 24 – 5; (1980), 26; (1983 – 4), 23; *Varsity Handbook* (1978 – 9), 26.
[153] See n. 66.
[154] College Union entry in *Record* (1974). The union reckoned that students were increasingly apathetic and alienated from its work. But it was not just concerned with social events: it also founded a college group to visit old people in that year, *ibid.*

Court in 1975 livened up college life considerably: Queens' became widely known as 'a relaxed and friendly place', a reputation which it has retained to this day, despite occasional criticisms of the 'hearty' elements.[155] Over the next few years the JCR organised a growing number of social and cultural events and expanded its range of facilities for students; and for the most part it worked effectively with the Fellows over the many day-to-day administrative and practical difficulties which arose. These were its preoccupations.[156] Queens' had shed its old radical image.

Not all causes of conflict were removed: the kitchen fixed charge has continued to be a 'burning issue',[157] but the vast improvement in catering since 1979, when the dining hall and kitchens in Cripps Court came into use, has diluted the old hostility. And there is today perhaps a hint of reviving radicalism as the present government cuts the value of student grants. The College Union's report in the most recent issue of the *Record* contained this entry:

'Open meetings have been relatively well-attended although the issues have tended to be related more to government policies on grants and other topical external questions than to . . . [the union's] other roles, such as the organisation of the [college] shop and loans of JCR property'.[158]

What did the student revolt at Queens' achieve? If we compare it with contemporary agitation in many European universities and on the North American campuses — even with other British universities — it must seem a relatively moderate, mild-mannered business. If we view its achievements in the light of the situation today, when many of the changes for which the student reformers fought are taken for granted, it can be difficult to understand what all the fuss was about. But if taken in the proper context of the Cambridge of their time these changes do appear genuinely revolutionary — a revolution in college life at least as significant as that of the late 19th century. Students had colluded in the 'Revolution of the Dons'; this revolution was one of students against

155 College Union report in *Record* (1975); (1976), 11; *CU Prospectus* (1975), 69; (1976), 70; (1978), 23 – 4; (1979), 24; (1981 – 2), 31; (1983 – 4), 23; *Varsity Handbook* (1980 – 1), 30; (1983 – 4), 43.
156 *Record* (1977), 12; (1978), 13; (1979), 12; (1980), 12; (1981), 12; (1982), 10; (1983), 11; (1984), 14. See also *CU Prospectus* (1979), 24; *Varsity Handbook* (1978 – 9), 26; College Union entry in *Record* (1974); (1976), 10; CM 551; GB, 9.11.1977. Many of the changes are echoed in the annual editions of the *CU Prospectus*.
157 *Record* (1983), 19. See CM 436, 670, 677.
158 *Record* (1986), 13. There has also recently been a dispute over a student proposal that the college should award rent rebates to those junior members whose rooms overlook the building site for phase three of Cripps Court and are disturbed by noise from the site, CM 1038; GB, 5.12.1986.

dons. The word 'community' featured frequently in the students' demands: the college community they sought was not the familial one created by the Victorian reformers, but one based on partnership and democracy.[159] This new concept was incomprehensible to many Fellows who had been brought up in the old values, and they found it difficult to adjust. The governing body comprised many different shades of opinion, and it sometimes required adroit management to nudge it along the reformist path when this was seen to be necessary. Some of the apparent inconsistencies and changes in the governing body's tactics may have been the result of internal divisions. It is a tribute to the students' determination and deep sense of the injustice of the old order that they were able to achieve so much against the great weight of tradition, hostility and incomprehension among elements of the governing body, and the superior tactical awareness of many of the Fellows over inexperienced and transient student bodies.[160] The 'revolution' is not complete,[161] but even as it stands it is a great achievement, which has not received due recognition.

---

[159] The significance of this question of 'community' was recognised by D. W. Bowett in a college minute of 1971, in which he reminded the Fellows of the need to improve intra-college relations to recapture some community spirit: 'If the effort is not to be made, then the College will quite likely, in the long-term, degenerate into a Hall of Residence and the Fellowship into a luncheon club', annex to CM 303. The vehemence of the reaction against the old order hurt some long-established Fellows who were dedicated to the ideal of a college community but were seen to personify the paternalist system, see D. W. Bowett in Record (1980), 5; B. A. Callingham in Record (1985), 3; H. Chadwick in Record (1985), 14. At the other extreme, one left-wing Fellow of the college was an articulate supporter of student representation in university and college decision-making processes, and of the new communitarian ideal, 1/- Paper, 8.11.1968, 22.11.1968.

[160] This last feature is well demonstrated by the letters and memoranda in John Green's personal file on College Union matters from this period, which also reveals the high level of discussion behind the scenes, and the divisions within the fellowship. It is to be hoped that this and similar documents in the possession of other Fellows will find their way into the college archives in due course.

[161] Students do not yet have voting rights on the governing body (nor do research and bye-fellows) — much of the old power structure remains undamaged, therefore. Moves to include research Fellows on the governing body contemporary with the student troubles were talked out in 1969 – 70, GB, 14.1.1969; CM 268, 327 (and see 485). The proposal was raised again recently but seems to have got nowhere.

29

The admission of women

The entry for Queens' in the 1979 edition of the university's official admissions prospectus observed that 'After 531 years, the College has at last turned its back on monastic seclusion: from October 1980 Queens' will admit — and welcome — women as well as men'.[1] There had been women servants from a very early period in the college's history, and its presidents had been able to marry ever since the Reformation, but the movement for the education of women at the university began in the middle of the 19th century.[2] Many battles lay ahead, and many disappointments, and it was not until 1948 that women were admitted to full membership of the university. In the 1960s some graduate colleges became co-residential, and since the early 1970s the under-graduate colleges have followed suit with varying degrees of enthu-siasm: at the time of writing the last all-male college, Magdalene, has just announced its intention to admit women in the near future.[3]

The movement for the admission of women to Cambridge runs parallel to the campaign for female emancipation in general, and in their attitudes towards these matters both senior and junior members of Queens' in the 19th and 20th centuries have tended largely to adopt the conventional contemporary attitudes of their sex. In the late 19th century the St Bernard Society's frequent and popular debates on such subjects tended to result in a vote to keep women in their place, although there was always a measure of support for the contrary point of view.[4] Nineteenth century opinion polls taken at times of particularly strong agitation to allow women to take Cambridge degrees show Queens' students following the general university line in the massive opposition to the reform.[5]

Opposition was at least as marked among the college's senior members. In the senate house vote on degrees for women in 1897 none

---

[1] *Cambridge Admissions Prospectus* (1979), 92.
[2] See above, pp. 72, 124 – 5, for servants and presidents' wives.
[3] For the history of the women's movement in Cambridge, see McWilliams-Tullberg (1975); Bryant (1979), 62 – 3, 84 – 9. There are still two colleges for women students only.
[4] e.g. CR (17.11.1880), 88; (24.10.1883), 21; (2.2.1887), 178; (9.3.1887), 256; (26.10.1887), 38; (7.11.1889), 54; (20.2.1896), 221; SBSM, 29.1.1887, 22.10.1887, 2.11.1889, 11.2.1893, 15.2.1896; see also CR (15.11.1894), 75; SBSM, 27.1.1885, 10.11.1894.
[5] CR (7.5.1896), 290; (14.5.1896), 306; (3.6.1897), 390.

of the Fellows supported change, although the reformers mustered a good following in the university at large. This may have been due to the actions of H. E. Ryle, who had at first supported the admission of women, but then put his name to a fly-sheet signed by several who changed their minds shortly before the vote on the grounds that:

'The removal of a grievance which, after all, has pressed upon a comparatively small number of persons, can be bought at too high a price when considerably more than half the resident members of the Senate are known to be bitterly opposed to the measure'.

Acceptance of the reform would therefore be

'injurious to the best interests of the University, while the benefit conferred upon those for whom we are risking so much would be of doubtful value. They would find the University hostile instead of friendly'.

After the defeat of the proposals in the senate on this occasion, the question of degrees for women was lost for over twenty years.[6]

This did not mean that most dons were not interested in women's education at all, and some actively helped the new women's colleges at Girton and Newnham. Ernest Temperley of Queens' was lecturer in mathematics and physics at Girton between 1877 and 1887.[7] The line was drawn where it was felt that there was a risk of erosion of male privileges; it was for this reason that there was so much opposition to awarding women Cambridge degrees, and most men do not seem to have perceived any inconsistency in their position. The St Bernard Society voted in 1896 that women might be allowed degrees 'of such a kind as not to appropriate any privileges of the men already held by them'.[8] Yet in the early 20th century there was something of a shift in the college's outlook, with evidence of growing support among undergraduates both for women's suffrage and co-education.[9]

It was not easy for male students to meet girls of their own social class in Cambridge. Often they had to fall back on pleasant speculation: J. F. Williams recalled that one of his student contemporaries 'had an abundance of very good looking female cousins, whose photographs were greatly admired'.[10] Colleges imposed stern restrictions. G. B.

---

[6] CR (3.6.1897), 390; Fitzgerald (1928), 115 – 6.
[7] CR (24.1.1889), 150 – 1; Wright (1889), 5.
[8] SBSM, 15.2.1896; CR (20.2.1896), 221. See also (3.11.1898), 50.
[9] e.g. SBSM, 17.11.1906, 14.11.1908, 17.2.1912; Dial (Easter 1910), 353; CR (19.11.1908), 110; (22.2.1912), 300. See also above, pp. 246 – 7.
[10] MS 79, 63.

Harrison remembers that 'No man was allowed to entertain a woman in his rooms unless accompanied by a chaperone, and then not after 6 p.m. nor must he walk in the streets by night with a women'; and at a St Bernard Society debate which voted in favour of co-education for women in 1913 there were calls for freer social intercourse between male and female students. The first May ball in Queens', held just before the first world war and doubtless the result of the shift in attitudes in the early years of the century, provided one such social opportunity.[11]

After the war, the atmosphere may have relaxed a little, and there were many married students among the returning ex-servicemen, but the changes were relatively slight.[12] When the question of granting women equal privileges in the university was brought to the fore in 1920, it was again defeated in the senate house, though by a narrow margin; apparently a clear majority among the senior members of Queens' was still opposed to change.[13] The restrictions imposed by college regulations and social propriety remained firmly in force, and opportunities for Queens' students to meet girls were still limited, at least in the short term; students sometimes managed to dodge the regulations by pretending that their female companions were sisters or cousins.[14] The women's colleges tended to be stricter in this respect. In the mid-1930s Cyril Bibby's fiancée at Girton required special permission from her college to visit Queens' alone, and visits to Girton by men had to be notified to the college in advance; Queens' on the other hand is said to have had no rule against unnotified visits by women at this time.[15]

Not all contacts were discouraged: for example, in the late 1920s Lesslie Newbigin was one of the founders of a joint Queens'-Newnham group to sing Elizabethan madrigals, which seems to have been tolerated by the authorities.[16] Pressure mounted within Queens' in the early 1920s for more regular contact with the women's colleges. After 1919 the St Bernard Society regularly expressed the wish to arrange debates with the women's colleges, despite overwhelmingly deploring

[11] Harrison (1985), 54; SBSM, 1.3.1913; CR (6.3.1913), 358; above, p. 248.
[12] For married students after the first world war, see above, p. 326. There were also some married fellow-commoners in earlier times, e.g. above, p. 236.
[13] Seven out of twelve resident Queens' MAs who were on the voting roll of the senate (the fellowship was probably no more than nine at this time) opposed reform: two were in favour, and there were three abstentions, CR (18.2.1921), 248.
[14] Diary of H. C. Alexander; McGowan (MS), 14. The Kangaroos' minutes for the late 1920s and early 1930s contain much bragging about liaisons and sexual conquests; it is hard to know how seriously to take this, which is typical of the general vulgarity of the minutes of the time, Kangaroo Club minutes (K4).
[15] Bibby, 'Courtship' (MS), 6; 'Reminiscences' (MS), 172.
[16] Newbigin (1985), 8.

'the modern tendency towards the equality of the sexes' in 1921.[17] The motives of those who supported this innovation were not entirely idealistic: the proposer of a motion calling for termly debates with Newnham and Girton in 1922 argued 'that such a step would not only prove a source of much amusement but also would tend to give a greater breadth of opinion to our debates and he added [that] it would not in any way prejudice the position of men students in the University'.[18]

Although there were women in the audience for the St Bernard Society's revue in 1923, debates with Newnham and Girton did not take place until the middle of the following decade; opposition from the Queens' dons may have been responsible for this.[19] Even then, the debates were usually on frivolous subjects, implying that women were not expected to discuss serious matters: the debate held with Girton in February 1935 was on the motion that 'canned Art and tinned foods are undermining the moral and physical welfare of the British nation'; with Newnham a month later the motion was that 'Pandering to the Proletariat is the atrophy of Art'.[20] Of informal contacts between students of different sex, there is little that can be said, for as yet there is little published evidence on the subject.

Since the end of the second world war, all the traditional barriers to the meeting of the sexes have been broken down, but it was a long campaign, and many of the major battles were not won until the 1970s. In 1948 women were at long last awarded full membership of the university, but many conventional sexual prejudices remained within the men's colleges. The St Bernard Society again provides good illustrations of this, for although it held debates with Newnham frequently during the 1950s, they continued to be on light-hearted subjects, often on the theme of the 'battle of the sexes'. In 1952, for example, these were 'that Women should Spin and not Preach', and 'gentlemen do not prefer blondes'; in 1966, it was 'This House would change sex'.[21] In general, college clubs and societies held more events to which women were invited at this time.[22] The fellows maintained a

---

[17]   SBSM, 29.4.1919, 19.11.1921, 24.2.1923, 22.10.1927, 16.2.1929; *Dial* (Michaelmas 1921), 26; (Michaelmas 1927), 22.

[18]   SBSM, 11.3.1922.

[19]   *ibid.*, 25.2.1922, 1.12.1923. Female rôles in the revue's sketches were of course played by men.

[20]   *ibid.*, 9.2.1935, 11.3.1935; *Dial* (Lent 1935), 39–40. The socialist-inspired Phoenix Society originated at a debate with Girtonians in 1933, and took women debaters more seriously than the St Bernard Society, *Dial* (Lent 1934), 24; Bibby, 'Courtship' (MS), 8; 'Reminiscences' (MS), 164. Some college faculty societies invited women speakers at the beginning of the decade, *Dial* (Lent 1930), 47; (Lent 1932), 32.

[21]   *Dial* (Lent 1950), 38; (February 1952), 33; (May 1952), 26; SBSM, 15.10.1956, 24.1.1957, 6.2.1958, 26.11.1959, 4.2.1965, 28.10.1965, 3.2.1966, 1.11.1966; c.f. 19.10.1961.

[22]   e.g. History Society minutes, 1.3.1951; *Dial* (Lent 1953), 6; Kangaroo Club minutes (K5).

watchful eye over the process. In 1957 the governing body agreed to an undergraduate proposal to establish a bar in the Fitzpatrick Hall, but one of its conditions was that there should be 'No lady guests'. There was also some student agitation in the late 1950s for women to be allowed in college lodging houses until 11 p.m., which, though not meeting with any success at first, was permitted by new university regulations in 1959.[23]

By the 1960s the increasing involvement of women in university life and the wider relaxations of social restraints were placing the old conventions and regulations under pressure. Students began to challenge the authorities, and the question of greater social freedom was central to the agitation of the late 1960s and 1970s described above. In the early 1960s there was a widespread call among students of all-male colleges for women to be allowed to eat in hall. In 1962 a girl was smuggled into hall in Queens' for dinner, but was recognised and had to leave after the soup course. In 1968 an undergraduate from New Hall was alleged to have eaten a complete meal in Queens' in disguise without being recognised. She complained to *Varsity* that the food was awful 'And I didn't even meet any interesting people. I couldn't talk to anybody, could I?' Soon afterwards Queens' allowed women guests in hall as part of its broader programme of reform.[24]

Agitation to change guest regulations, a major issue of this period, has been described in the preceding chapter; the other great change in most recent times, representing virtually the culmination of the movement for women's rights, has been co-residence. In 1939, when Queens' replied to a circular from the vice-chancellor concerning plans for accommodating refugees from other universities in the event of war, it declared itself willing to take in outsiders of many kinds, but 'in the event of there being more women students than Newnham and Girton could house, the excess should not be accommodated in Queens' College as long as any of the College's own students remained in residence'. In the 1950s the governing body decided to permit conference parties including women to stay in the college.[25] Co-residence was called for by the radical 'slate' in the 1969 elections to the JCR committee, but not by their more moderate reformist opponents.[26] In fact, it does not seem to have become a major issue until the first men's colleges began to admit women in the early 1970s, although it had doubtless been discussed informally for some time.

The question first rose to prominence at Queens' in 1973, when *Stop*

[23] GB, 6.12.1957; *Varsity*, 2.2.1957, 25.4.1959.
[24] *Varsity*, 13.10.1962, 2.3.1968; GB, 18.10.1968 (and see 21.6.1968); CU papers. See also CM 26.
[25] CB (1937 – 63), 27.2.1939; GB, 22.7.1955, 5.10.1955.
[26] CU papers.

Press claimed that there was a 'gentleman's agreement' between the college and the Cripps Foundation that it would remain single-sex; this charge was hotly denied.[27] However, early in 1970 a governing body committee had rejected proposals for allowing women to stay overnight in students' rooms on the grounds that it 'would be likely to lead to considerable publicity, which could well jeopardise current development plans'.[28] Late in 1973 the college admitted in private to the JCR committee that it had no plans to become co-residential in the next four or five years at least: it was argued that co-residence was undesirable because it would embarrass the college in its relations with the Cripps Foundation, which would not want its generosity exploited in this way; and that the college was responsible to its old members, who had donated generously towards the development appeal and were strongly opposed to the admission of women. This information was 'leaked' to *Stop Press*, which proceeded to raise the issue in public once again.[29]

The president of the JCR committee had told *Stop Press* in May that it did not wish to press for co-residence at this time out of a desire not to put the governing body in an embarrassing situation,[30] but the publicity which the matter aroused at that time suggests that unofficial pressure for co-residence was growing,[31] and in November the council of the union set up a working party to discuss the admission of women. The working party's report was completed in February 1974; using the evidence of the few colleges to have become co-residential so far, it argued that co-residence would lead to 'a more relaxed atmosphere and a distinct improvement in courtesy and consideration among the student population' — a significant point perhaps in the light of the recent student troubles at Queens' — and that although the college's sporting strength might be affected a little, other activities such as music and drama were likely to benefit; moreover, academic standards would probably rise.[32] But the governing body dragged its feet: the report was not discussed properly until January 1975, when the general sentiment among the Fellows was that they should wait and see the long-term effects of co-residence in other colleges.[33]

There is an interesting parallel to these events of the early 1970s in the

---

[27] *Stop Press*, 4.5.1973, 18.5.1973. Schemes to include accommodation for married graduate students in the new development had been abandoned in the previous decade, see above, pp. 376 – 7.

[28] CM 263. See also *1/- Paper*, 28.11.1969.

[29] *Stop Press*, 11.11.1973; CU papers.

[30] *Stop Press*, 4.5.1973.

[31] The letter from the dean of chapel cited above, chapter 28, n. 143, assumed that the college would go co-residential in time.

[32] College Union entry in *Record* (1974); CU papers. See also GB, 15.3.1974, 6.12.1974, 14.1.1975, 17.1.1975; CM 421.

[33] GB, 14.1.1975, 17.1.1975; CM 421, 476.

efforts of some elements among the fellowship at the same time to secure greater college privileges for their wives. From the relaxation of college statutes allowing Fellows to marry in the 1860s and 1880s, Fellows' wives had played an important rôle in maintaining the college community by helping their husbands to entertain, a rôle which was expected of the Victorian and Edwardian wife; their assistance and their decorativeness were valued by colleges, but they had no rights or privileges therein.[34] This phenomenon of the 'academic wife' in Oxford and Cambridge has been the subject of recent academic discussion, from which it can be seen that, although many wives enjoyed their involvement with the college and had no complaints over their rôle, after the second world war frustration began to grow: they were expected to participate in their husbands' social duties, but were largely excluded from college social events, the academic social lifestyle being anyway heavily male-oriented; and their husbands had divided loyalties to college and family because of the social demands imposed by the former. This frustration seems to have grown steadily until the present day.[35]

One of the principal focal points of these grievances was the question of Fellows' wives dining on high table. In 1968 Queens' had agreed to admit women guests to high table together with the admission of women to lower hall, but this was not meant to extend to Fellows' wives.[36] The question was raised again in 1972 when there was concern about the low number of Fellows dining in college in the evenings. It was clear that some Fellows wanted no restrictions on bringing in women guests, especially wives, but there was also a strong body resolutely opposed to such a reform. At first it seemed that no solution was possible, but shortly afterwards a compromise was reached, with the abandoning of the custom that a Fellow did not bring his wife in to dine in favour of a new arrangement whereby Fellows agreed not to bring the same personal guest into dinner more than twice a term.[37] In the last few years wives have even attended college feasts, the last bastion of male preserve.[38]

Similar resistance hindered the movement for co-residence. In the Michaelmas term of 1975 the council of the union called for an immediate statement from the governing body that it approved co-residence in principle, for it was felt that the Fellows were stalling for

---

[34] See above, chapter 16. Note also this entry in a college magazine of the 1930s: 'The wives of Fellows and M.A.s of Queens' have presented the College with a banner embroidered with the College Arms', as an example of the customary wifely rôle, *QC* (1936 – 7), 12.

[35] Ardener (1984); Sciama (1984).

[36] GB, 18.10.1968. The new rule was meant to permit the invitation of women academics to dinner in the main — but Fellows' wives could be academics too.

[37] GB, 9.6.1972, 1.12.1972; CM 336, 342.

[38] This custom has been established *de facto*, but has not been welcomed in all quarters.

time.[39] The governing body had already taken legal advice concerning the implications of the 1975 Sex Discrimination Act and learnt that while the act did not prevent colleges from remaining single sex as far as students were concerned, the position regarding Fellows was less clear.[40] In March 1976, under the renewed pressure of undergraduate opinion, it was decided that Queens' should become co-residential as soon as possible after 1980 provided that the governing body was satisfied this would be in the best interests of the college, the university, and — rather pompously — the nation. It then dragged its feet again until the students called, in December 1977, for a detailed statement of its proposals and arrangmeents for co-residence instead of the existing vague policy statment. In February 1978 it was finally decided that women should be admitted to undergraduate and graduate courses from October 1981, and that a woman Fellow should also be appointed because the college might otherwise be at a disadvantage in attracting female applicants.[41]

In the autumn of 1978 the governing body decided to bring the date of co-residence forward by one year after its admissions committee had reported that both the number and quality of applicants to Queens' for 1979 had fallen, and that 'suddenly this year, all-male Colleges have started to lose applicants to the newly mixed colleges' — the movement towards co-residence was gathering speed throughout the university during the late 1970s. A vigorous propaganda campaign was launched to establish contacts with girls' schools, and some college facilities were improved in readiness for women students.[42] These plans proceeded successfully, but there was some unwelcome publicity shortly before the arrival of the first women entrants. In June 1980 the JCR committee organised a 'Stag Night' for college members, which included strippers — 'just a harmless piece of fun', in the words of one of the organisers, although feminist groups planning to demonstrate against it were warned that this might provoke 'unnecessary incidents . . . It is known that many members of the college sports clubs will be present, and it is likely that they will not take kindly to interference in their private event'.[43] The 'Stag Night' took place as planned, to the accompaniment of a peaceful demonstration — an unfortunate celebration of the worst features of the past, rather than a welcome to the future.

[39] CU papers; *Stop Press*, 29.11.1975. See also College Union entries in *Record* (1976), 10; (1977), 12.
[40] GB, 7.11.1973; CM 378, 421, 475, 476.
[41] GB, 12.3.1976, 2.12.1977, 15.2.1978, 17.3.1978; CM, 479, 547, 558; College Union entry in *Record* (1978), 13. The college was prepared to take a part-time woman tutor if necessary, GB, 13.7.1979.
[42] CM 579, 585, 644. See also GB, 17.3.1978.
[43] *Stop Press*, 3.5.1980, 7.6.1980. See also GB, 6.6.1980.

It is still too soon to try to gauge the effects of co-residence upon the college, except tentatively. The *Cambridge Prospectus*, written by students, described the transition as 'very smooth' in its 1981 – 2 edition; that of two years later observed that 'academic standards are rising and the "hearty" elements . . . are becoming more muted'.[44] The rise in academic standards is incontrovertible, although it remains to be seen how long it will last; the 'civilising' influence of co-residence is equally apparent to anybody who has been closely connected with the college on either side of the transition. The proportion of women students — usually about a third of undergraduates — is close to the national average, and they have contributed in full to every aspect of college life, although one consequence of co-residence has been to make the college more self-contained: Queens' was described as 'a bit insular' in the *Varsity Handbook* of 1983 – 4, a charge never levelled against college society before 1980.[45] The women students have integrated themselves into the older college values and style to the extent that their two principal 'dining' clubs, the Valkyries and the Scorpions, largely imitate the two main men's clubs in the college, the Kangaroos and Cherubs respectively, in terms of their various qualifications, social composition, and social manner. But there is also a Queens' Women's Group, founded in the second year of co-residence 'to provide a forum for discussion on a wide variety of topics, but principally those concerning women's position in society', it being felt important for women to meet 'and exchange views, which might otherwise go unaired in a College so predominantly male'.[46]

The opinions of an all-female student theatre group in the university in 1985 which included one undergraduate from Queens', might also be noted in this context: though the members had mixed views on women's place and achievements in Cambridge, the university was generally felt by them to be 'hierarchical, conservative and male-dominated at the top'.[47] Queens' itself has a tiny proportion of women Fellows — there have been only five since 1980, three of them short-term research Fellows. At the time of writing there are only three: two research Fellows (one of whom is shortly to leave), and one new teaching Fellow; and the college's pressing financial needs make it unlikely that many women will be appointed to teaching fellowships in the near future, owing to the scarcity of women university teaching

[44] *Cambridge University Prospectus* (1981 – 2), 31; (1983 – 4), 23.
[45] K. E. Machin in *Record* (1980), 5; J. T. Green in *Record* (1983), 4; *Varsity Handbook* (1983 – 4), 43.
[46] Entry for women's group in *Record* (1984), 19. See also the entries in (1983), 15; (1985), 23; (1986), 17.
[47] *Guardian*, 12.8.1985.

officers without other college attachments.[48] Amidst the great success of co-residence in Queens', this has been a significant disappointment to many.

[48]   GB, 5.12.1980, 11.2.1981.

Appendix 1

Matriculations and degrees, 1639/40 – 1664/5[1]

	university		Queens'	
	matric.	*BA*	*BA*	*MA*
1639/40	317	220	15	10
1640/1	299	188	22	10
1641/2	222	198	10	14
1642/3	45	175	3	8
1643/4	183	125	2	3
1644/5	311	171	15	3
1645/6	417	142	7	6
1646/7	331	87	3	3
1647/8	272	92	5	5
1648/9	276	164	10	4
1649/50	292	168	6	?
1650/1	254	157	19	7
1651/2	204	143	8	5
1652/3	183	124	6	3
1653/4	279	142	5	10
1654/5	243	143	8	10
1655/6	271	119	7	6
1656/7	298	162	9	8
1657/8	258	159	7	8
1658/9	267	167	8	3
1659/60	356	144	11	9
1660/1	295	169	14	8
1661/2	253	141	12	12
1662/3	279	118	5	9
1663/4	324	154	9	11
1664/5	266	168	5	10

[1] Information taken from Twigg (unpublished thesis, 1983), Appendix A; CUA Grace Books Z and H.

Appendix 2

Size of college fellowships, 1564 – 1727[1]

College	Number of Fellows				
	1564	*1621*	*1651*	*1672*	*1727*
Peterhouse	10	17	19	22	22
Clare	8	17	18	18	20
Pembroke	17	?	19	?	17
Caius	8	25	25	26	26
Trinity Hall	?	12	12	12	12
Corpus Christi	8	12	12	12	12
King's	?	?	?	?	?
Queens'	*15*	*19*	*19*	*19*	*20*
St Catharine's	13	6	6	6	8
Jesus	?	16	16	16	16
Christ's	11	13	13	13	15
St John's	43	54	54	52	60
Trinity	47	60	60	60	60
Magdalene	?	10	11	15	16
Emmanuel	–	14	14	14	15
Sidney Sussex	–	12	?	?	17

[1] Information taken fron contemporary accounts, recorded in Cooper, ii.206 – 8; Masson (1859), i.89 – 91; Langbaine (1651); Ivory (1672); Warren (1911), 344 – 5.

445

Appendix 3

Fellows ejected in the parliamentary purge of 1644 – 5[1]

College	No. ejected	Master (if ejected)
Trinity	49	Thomas Comber
St John's	32	William Beale
Queens'	22	*Edward Martin*
Pembroke	20	Benjamin Laney
Peterhouse	19	John Cosin
Jesus	16	Richard Sterne
Christ's	11	
Clare	9	Thomas Paske
Magdalene	9	
Caius	8	
King's	8	Samuel Collins
Sidney Sussex	6	
Corpus Christi	4	
Emmanuel	3	Richard Holdsworth
St Catharine's	1	Ralph Brownrigg
Trinity Hall	–	
TOTAL	217	

[1] Taken from Twigg (1983), 522. See also appendix 2.

Appendix 4

Presidents of Queens'

Andrew Doket	1448 – 84
Thomas Wilkinson	1484 – 1505
John Fisher	1505 – 8
Robert Bekynsaw	1508 – 19
John Jennyn	1519 – 26
Thomas Farman	1526 – 8
William Franklyn	1528 – 9
Simon Heynes	1529 – 37
William Mey	1537 – 53
William Glynn	1553 – 7
Thomas Peacock	1557 – 9
William Mey	1559 – 60
John Stokes	1560 – 8
William Chaderton	1568 – 79
Humphrey Tyndall	1579 – 1614
John Davenant	1614 – 22
John Mansell	1622 – 31
Edward Martin	1631 – 44
Herbert Palmer	1644 – 7
Thomas Horton	1647 – 60
Edward Martin	1660 – 2
Anthony Sparrow	1662 – 7
William Wells	1667 – 75
Henry James	1675 – 1717
John Davies	1717 – 32
William Sedgwick	1732 – 60
Robert Plumptre	1760 – 88
Isaac Milner	1788 – 1820
Henry Godfrey	1820 – 32
Joshua King	1832 – 57
George Phillips	1857 – 92
W. M. Campion	1892 – 6
H. E. Ryle	1896 – 1901
F. H. Chase	1901 – 5
T. C. Fitzpatrick	1906 – 31

J. A. Venn	1932 – 58
A. ll. Armitage	1958 – 70
D. W. Bowett	1970 – 82
E. R. Oxburgh	1982 –

Appendix 5

Status of Queens' students on entry, 1500 – 1751 (sample comprising names A – C only)[1]

Year	sizar	pensioner	Fellow-commoner	from other colleges	unknown	total
1500 – 19	–	1	–	–	13	14
1520 – 39	–	–	–	–	13	13
1540 – 59	24	25	1	4	6	60
1560 – 79	51	59	9	13	6	138
1580 – 99	45	61	23	5	2	136
1600 – 19	52	83	32	3	4	174
1620 – 39	73	60	18	5	2	158
1640 – 59	38	69	10	10	3	130
1660 – 79	37	34	16	7	1	95
1680 – 99	31	36	6	–	–	73
1700 – 19	13	25	4	3	2	47
1720 – 39	17	24	3	6	3	53
1740 – 51	8	10	3	1	–	22

[1] The figures are derived from AC.

Appendix 6

Numerical size of colleges[1]

College	number of Fellows and students						
	1564	*1574*	*1621*	*1641*	*1651*	*1672*	*1727*
Trinity	306	359	440	277	440	400	227
St John's	184	271	370	280	282	372	351
Christ's	136	157	265	163	166	206	73
King's	118	140	140	98	140	113	85
Clare	86	129	144	83	106	100	79
Queens'	65	122	230	124	190	c.120	64
Jesus	111	118	120	90	110	112	74
Peterhouse	61	96	140	55	106	86	58
Corpus Christi	32	93	140	108	126	145	46
Pembroke	48	87	140	80	100	c.100	61
Trinity Hall	51	68	56	59	60	68	55
Caius	48	62	180	172	209	140	100
Magdalene	—	49	90	96	140	118	45
St Catharine's	21	32	56	102	150	150	41
Sidney Sussex	—	—	140	100	210	122	44
Emmanuel	—	—	260	204	310	170	96
TOTAL	1267	1783	2911	2091	2848	2522	1449

[1] Sources as for appendix 2; and also Cooper, iii.315; Warren (1911), 347. These figures are all taken from contemporary accounts, The 1574 figures may refer to students only, but this is unclear.

450

Appendix 7

Geographical origins of Queens' students, 1500 – 1751 (sample comprising names A – C only)[1]

The geographical origin is known for 859 students of this group, distributed as follows (%):

Bedfordshire	3.3
Cambridgeshire	5.4
Essex	14.0
Hertfordshire	4.0
Huntingdonshire	3.1
Kent	3.7
Lancashire	2.7
Leicestershire	4.0
Lincolnshire	4.9
London	5.7
Middlesex	3.3
Norfolk	4.2
Nottinghamshire	2.3
Suffolk	10.7
Yorkshire	5.9
Other counties	22.8

[1] Figures derived from *AC*. The Queens' records are only thorough from 1569, *ibid.*, part i, p. viii.

Appendix 8

Examples of family connections with Queens'
over more than two generations[1]

(m/c = matriculated; adm. = admitted)

AYLMER

```
           John (BA 1540/1; Marian exile; bishop of London, 1577 – 94)
        ┌─────────────────────────┴───────────────────────────────┐
  Theophilus (m/c 1583)                                      Samuel (m/c 1583)
 ┌──────────┴──────────┐                        ┌────────────────┼────────────────┐
John              Theophilus                   John          Edward          Anthony
(m/c Jesus 1607)  (m/c Jesus 1607)                        (all adm. 1625)
```

BRAMSTON

```
            John (adm. Jesus 1593; chief justice King's Bench 1635)
        ┌────────────────┴─────────────────────────────────┐
   Mundeford (m/c 1632)                              Francis (m/c 1634)
 ┌────────┴─────────┐
George (adm. 1668)  William (adm. 1673)
                  ┌────────┴──────────┐
          William (adm. 1706)   John (adm. St Catharine's 1713)
```

connected Bramstons are: Anthony (m/c 1658), William (m/c 1639), and George (adm. 1720).

---

[1] Information taken from *AC*, part i (names A – C). This is not a comprehensive list, merely illustrative.

APPENDIX 8

CAPEL

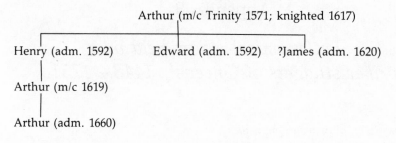

Arthur (m/c Trinity 1571; knighted 1617)

Henry (adm. 1592)   Edward (adm. 1592)   ?James (adm. 1620)

Arthur (m/c 1619)

Arthur (adm. 1660)

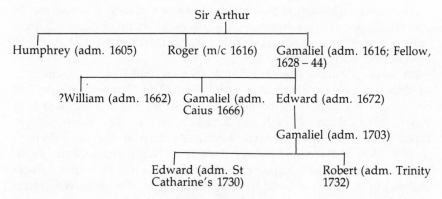

Sir Arthur

Humphrey (adm. 1605)   Roger (m/c 1616)   Gamaliel (adm. 1616; Fellow, 1628 – 44)

?William (adm. 1662)   Gamaliel (adm. Caius 1666)   Edward (adm. 1672)

Gamaliel (adm. 1703)

Edward (adm. St Catharine's 1730)   Robert (adm. Trinity 1732)

other Capels are: Gamaliel (MA 1584; Fellow, 1582 – 5; of London), Moses (m/c 1620; of London), and Thomas (m/c 1610; of Essex).

CROMWELL

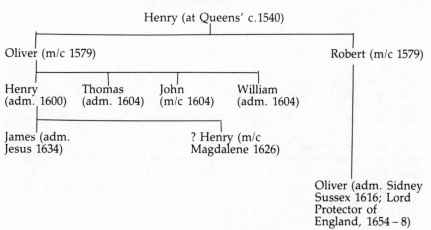

Henry (at Queens' c.1540)

Oliver (m/c 1579)   Robert (m/c 1579)

Henry (adm. 1600)   Thomas (adm. 1604)   John (m/c 1604)   William (adm. 1604)

James (adm. Jesus 1634)   ? Henry (m/c Magdalene 1626)

Oliver (adm. Sidney Sussex 1616; Lord Protector of England, 1654 – 8)

also: Henry Cromwell (mc/ 1580; of Huntingdonshire)

Appendix 9

Ecclesiastical offices held by former students of Queens', 1448 – 1751.

1. Before 1500 (all known Queensmen).[1]

(a) higher ecclesiastical positions: 14 canon's places; 2 deaneries; 19 prebend's places; three precentor's places; 3 archdeaconries; 2 treasurer's places; 12 miscellaneous other posts; 6 are known to have been monks (including 3 priors).

(b) lesser positions (parish livings): 46 men held 70 such positions at 61 different livings, distributed as follows: 11 in Cambridgeshire (7 of these were the cure of St Botolph's); 7 in Kent; 5 in Sussex; 4 each in Essex, Hampshire; 3 each in Suffolk (two at the same living), Lincolnshire, London, Norfolk, Middlesex (two at the same living), Surrey (two at the same living); 2 each in Northamptonshire, Nottinghamshire, Dorset, Yorkshire, Huntingdonshire, Somerset, Buckinghamshire; 1 each in Leicestershire, Lancashire, Cheshire, Worcestershire, Gloucestershire, Hertfordshire, Westmorland.

2. 1500 – 1751 (sample comprising names A – C only)[2]
(figures in brackets represent possible additional cases)

	no. of men	parish living	dean	prebend	arch-deacon	bishop	other	other ordained
					ecclesiastical offices held			
1500 – 19	3(2)	9(2)	1	6	1	–	5	3
1520 – 39	– (2)	– (2)	–	–	–	–	–	–
1540 – 59	10(2)	16(3)	–	3	2	1	–	–
1560 – 79	28(14)	52(25)	3	6(1)	2	3	5	5
1580 – 99	29(11)	53(12)	–	5	1	–	–	3
1600 – 19	40(14)	65(17)	–	3	–	–	2	10
1620 – 39	39(16)	59(21)	–	2	–	–	3(1)	8
1640 – 59	32(12)	46(17)	–	3	1	–	– (1)	4(1)
1660 – 79	33(4)	54(10)	–	6	1	–	2	4
1680 – 99	22(2)	39(3)	1	3	– (1)	–	5	10
1700 – 19	18(5)	45(8)	–	–	–	–	1	3
1720 – 39	21(2)	39(3)	–	1	1	–	1	3
1740 – 51	8	12(1)	–	–	1	–	2(2)	2(1)

[1] Information for the period before 1500 derived from Emden.
[2] Information for 1500 – 1751 derived from *AC*, part i. The column for men simply known to have been ordained includes ordained deacons. See also the lists in appendix 5 for the total number of students in the sample for these years.

Appendix 10

Scholars and bible-clerks at Queens', 1535/6 – 1639/40[1]

years	annual average
1535/6 – 39/40	5.4
– 44/5	5.8
– 49/50	10.4
– 54/5	10.4
– 59/60	9.4
– 64/5	25.0
– 69/70	34.6
– 74/5	30.8
– 79/80	29.0
– 84/5	34.2
– 89/90	28.6
– 94/5	34.0
– 99/1600	37.8
– 04/5	34.8
– 09/10	40.6
– 14/15	36.18
– 19/20	37.8
– 24/5	37.2
– 29/30	35.8
– 34/5	41.4
– 39/40	43.6

[1] Figures calculated from Books 3 – 6.

Appendix 11

Degree-taking, 1448 – 1751

Before 1500[1]

BA — 6
MA — 49 (these must therefore have taken the BA first)
BD — 22
DD — 12
In addition, there is one known bachelor of civil law, and one of canon law.

1500 – 1751 (sample comprising names A – C only)[2]
(figures in brackets represent possible additional examples)

	total	BA	MA	BD	DD	MB/MD	other	none
1500 – 19	14	9	9	5	3	—	—	5
1520 – 39	13	6	4	1	—	—	—	7
1540 – 59	60	11	7(1)	2	2	—	—	49
1560 – 79	138	62	38(1)	9(1)	4(1)	1	—	76
1580 – 99	136	62(3)	36(2)	9	5	(1)	—	71
1600 – 19	174	93(3)	71(4)	13(1)	7	1	2	78
1620 – 39	158	110(2)	77(1)	6(1)	3	1(1)	4	46
1640 – 59	130	72	49(1)	6	3	1	—	58
1660 – 79	95	52(6)	40(1)	6(1)	3	1	3	37
1680 – 99	73	51(4)	26(6)	4(1)	3	6(1)	2	18
1700 – 19	47	30(4)	22(4)	4	2	3	2	13
1720 – 39	53	29(4)	17(4)	2	1	1	4	20
1740 – 51	22	12(3)	9(3)	1	1	1	3	7

[1] Information for 1448 – 1499 derived from Emden.
[2] Information for 1500 – 1751 derived from *AC*, part i. The list includes some who entered Queens' having already taken degrees elsewhere (such as Fellows, but also some students): where an individual has proceeded to a higher degree for which another was first necessary, the taking of the earlier degree has been assumed and included in the table, even if not formally recorded in *AC*.

Appendix 12

College finances, 16 – 18th centuries[1]

1. Income and expenditure, 1534/5 – 1640/1
(* denotes that the accounts for some of these years are defective)

	average annual receipts (£)	average annual expenditure (£)
1534/5 – 1543/4	289.8	248.3
1544/5 – 1553/4	325.4*	303.8
1554/5 – 1563/4	433.0	354.0
1564/5 – 1573/4	436.7	381.1
1574/5 – 1583/4	418.5*	404.1
1584/5 – 1593/4	433.6	421.3
1594/5 – 1603/4	456.6	432.1
1604/5 – 1613/4	473.1	474.3
1614/5 – 1623/4	506.8	446.3
1624/5 – 1633/4	553.1	496.2
1634/5 – 1640/1	614.9	552.7

2. Variations in outside/external receipts (£)

1558/9	88	1566/7	52	1574/5	61	1582/3	70
1559/60	347	1567/8	57	1575/6	18	1583/4	99
1560/1	294	1568/9	137	1576/7	41	1584/5	102
1561/2	67	1569/70	134	1577/8	29	1585/6	65
1562/3	76	1570/1	82	1578/9	30	1586/7	46
1563/4	95	1571/2	162	1579/80	67	1587/8	49
1564/5	114	1572/3	110	1580/1	149	1588/9	77
1565/6	110	1573/4	60	1581/2	113	1589/90	81

3. Income and expenditure, 1660/1 – 1769/70

	average total annual receipts(£)	average rental income (£)	average annual expenditure (£)
1660/1 – 1669/70	550.3	423.6	546.1
1670/1 – 1679/80	640.3	453.2	653.3
1680/1 – 1689/90	704.4	493.5	694.4
1690/1 – 1699/1700	761.1	501.9	738.7
1700/1 – 1709/10	751.8	501.6	800.4
1710/11 – 1719/20	732.5	508.0	765.2
1720/1 – 1729/30	817.0	534.7	729.8
1730/1 – 1739/40	902.3	535.4	880.3
1740/1 – 1749/50	851.8	535.0	848.2
1750/1 – 1759/60	871.7	535.0	1175.0
1760/1 – 1769/70	1147.0	539.9	1318.2

[1] Figures compiled from Books 9 – 12.

Appendix 13

Incomes of Cambridge colleges, as presented to the crown, 1535 and 1546 (£)[1]

	1535	*1546*
Peterhouse	125	138
Michaelhouse	125	142
Clare	85	132
King's Hall	212	214
Pembroke	154	171
Gonville Hall	99	120
Trinity Hall	72	119
Corpus Christi	84	171
King's	751	1011
Queens'	*231*	273
St Catharine's	39	54
Jesus	88	130
Christ's	191	287
St John's	508	537
Magdalene	–	44

---

[1] Cooper, i.370 – 1; *Documents* (1852), i.108 – 274.

Appendix 14

Daniel Nichols' poem welcoming the restoration of Charles II in 1660[1]

'Twas Monarchy made thee and me be one,
Loyalty has been our Religion;
Joynt haters of the Tyrant and his train,
And faithfull subjects to our Sovereign.

Divines are fellow-soldiers, though in field
They never take up target, sword, or shield:
For whilst that others fight with swords and spears,
The Churches weapons are her prayers and tears.

These be the arms (dear Friend) which for our Prince
W'have taken up and brandish'd ever since
False subjects and an Act of Parliament
Forc'd Him to live abroad in banishment.
Whilst others for our King's Coronation,
And to reform a thing call'd Reformation
Have spilt their blood, lost estates, lives and health;
(Strange that this should be call'd a Commonwealth!)
Then thou and I with many a sigh and groan
Pray'd and believ'd Him to his Crown and Throne.
And still we'l preach and pray, and print and sing
Disgrace to Rebells, Glory to our King.

---

[1] Printed in Godman (1660), preface. The words 'thee' and 'dear Friend' in lines 1 and 9 seem to be addressed to Godman.

Appendix 15

The Plumptre family at Cambridge

(F = Fellow; Q = Queens'; St J = St John's; Pem = Pembroke; Cla = Clare;
K = King's)

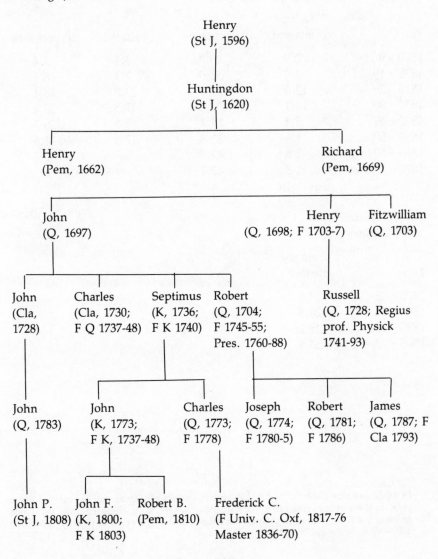

Henry
(St J, 1596)

Huntingdon
(St J, 1620)

Henry
(Pem, 1662)

Richard
(Pem, 1669)

John
(Q, 1697)

Henry
(Q, 1698; F 1703-7)

Fitzwilliam
(Q, 1703)

John
(Cla,
1728)

Charles
(Cla, 1730;
F Q 1737-48)

Septimus
(K, 1736;
F K 1740)

Robert
(Q, 1704;
F 1745-55;
Pres. 1760-88)

Russell
(Q, 1728; Regius
prof. Physick
1741-93)

John
(Q, 1783)

John
(K, 1773;
F K, 1737-48)

Charles
(Q, 1773;
F 1778)

Joseph
(Q, 1774;
F 1780-5)

Robert
(Q, 1781;
F 1786)

James
(Q, 1787; F
Cla 1793)

John P.
(St J, 1808)

John F.
(K, 1800;
F K 1803)

Robert B.
(Pem, 1810)

Frederick C.
(F Univ. C. Oxf, 1817-76
Master 1836-70)

Appendix 16

Size and social composition of the 19th century student body in Queens'

Average number of students[1]

Years	Fellow-commoners	pensioners	sizars	10-year men
1800 – 9	2.9	19.3	5.1	2.4
1810 – 19	6.0	31.0	7.1	8.4
1820 – 29	13.0	77.5	23.9	25.1
1830 – 39	13.1	92.4	27.3	30.2
1840 – 49	5.4	75.4	15.8	26.1
1850 – 59	1.6	35.8	17.6	21.6
1860 – 69	1.6	42.7	–	7.4
1870 – 79	1.3	43.1	–	–

Matriculations[2]

Years	average number
1876 – 85	17.6
1886 – 95	24.5
1896 – 1905	28.2
1905 – 13	54.1

[1] CU Cal.
[2] *Dial* (Michaelmas 1909), 299 – 303; *CR, passim*, entries usually at start of each academic year, but sometimes amended subsequently; where these disagree with the totals given in the *Dial*, I have relied upon the latter. c.f. the figures for university expansion 1800 – 99 in Stone (1975), 92.

Social composition of the Cambridge student body[3]

(a) 1752 – 1886:

	father's status	*son's status/career*
nobles	7.2%	4.7%
gentry	25.5	5.8
clergy	32.6	54.3
military	6.0	4.5
law	5.3	11.2
medicine	6.0	3.5
government	1.5	1.6
business	9.4	3.9
academic	3.3	9.1
plebeian	3.2	1.4

(b) 1937/8:

	father's occupation	*son's occupation*
commerce	32.5%	17.8%
scientific business	13.7	11.5
government	8.3	9.8
clergy	7.4	6.2
military	7.0	8.4
law	6.6	10.4
medicine	8.1	11.2
architecture	0.8	1.6
teaching	6.9	15.2
research	–	4.1
misc.	6.5	3.8

[3]   Anderson and Schnaper (1952), 6, 17.

Appendix 17

The 'ten year man'

Appendix 16 also shows a new category of student, the 'ten year man'. Although these became prominent only in the 19th century, they were an anachronistic feature of the old university, and already anomalous at the time of their numerical expansion. Under the university's Elizabethan statutes of 1570, men aged 24 or more without a university education could become non-resident members of the university for ten years and take the degree of bachelor of divinity at the end of that time.[1] The regulation had been introduced to counter the chronic shortage of 'qualified' clergy at the start of Elizabeth's reign caused by the disruptions to religious life during the previous decade or so. For some reason, nobody took advantage of it until the early 18th century, but the number of 'ten year men' grew steadily thereafter: they were usually clergymen seeking an easy way of acquiring a degree. The provision was criticised by 18th century reformers, and in the early 19th century the 'ten year men' were made to reside for three terms during their last two years, but this did not guarantee higher academic standards, and their number rose in line with the general expansion of the student population; the regulation was not abolished until the middle of the century.[2]

The earliest reference to 'ten year men' at Queens' is in 1770, when the college ordered that they should pay 10s per quarter in tuition fees.[3] Their numbers must have been small at this time. There were none in the late 1790s, but in 1802 there were two, and they began to increase thereafter; the last of them left in 1869, although numbers had been dwindling for some time.[4]

They do not seem to have been a particularly distinguished group, and mostly continued to serve as parish priests.[5] Not all were simply looking for an easy way to acquire a degree: George Ingram, who entered his name at Queens' in 1829, related 'how when he was reading

[1] Wordsworth (1874), 643; Gunning (1854), i.311.
[2] Wordsworth (1874), 643; Winstanley (1935), 69–71; Winstanley (1940), 153–4; Gunning (1854), i.311.
[3] CB (1734–87), f.84v.
[4] See appendix 16.
[5] For example, the careers of 23 of the 30 'ten year men' who were listed as members of Queens' in 1830 are known: all were ministers and chaplains; a few were schoolmasters, in addition, *CU Cal* (1830), names checked against *AC*.

for honours his poor wife died in child-bed of her first child and left him a widower with a little baby:- this calamity broke up his studies and he went abroad'.[6] William Scoresby, who enrolled in 1824, was a remarkable man: he was the son of a Whitby whaling captain, and had made his first Arctic voyage at the age of ten; he later became a captain himself. During his whaling expeditions he studied the flora and fauna of the Arctic world, and was a significant contributor to the development of 'Arctic science', as well as a notable explorer. He became a fellow of the Royal Society in 1825, the year of his ordination; while serving as a parish minister, he continued to be interested in scientific research, particularly electro-magnetism, and he was one of the founder members of the British Association in 1831.[7] But men such as this were untypical of 'ten year men' as a whole, and Scoresby would have been noteworthy in any case.

[6] Romilly (1967), 68.
[7] There is a full biography of Scoresby, by Stamp and Stamp (1975); and also a short account by a present Fellow of the college, Smith (1982). I am grateful to Rod Smith for drawing Scoresby to my attention

Appendix 18

Subjects for debate in the
St Bernard Society, 1886 – 1914

The society's minute books survive from 1884, but no debates are recorded in them until 1886. The list given here excludes the 'impromptu' debates and mock trials.

23.10.1886 'That this House would approve of some scheme of Imperial Federation'. Carried by 20 votes to 12.
6.11.1886 'That this House approves of the principles of Socialism'. Defeated 20 – 4.
20.11.1886 'That this House approves of the moderate use of tobacco'. Defeated 19 – 14.

29.1.1887 'That this House is in favour of the Franchise being extended to women'. Defeated 20 – 10.
12.2.1887 'That this House is of opinion that the French Revolution has in its effects been adverse to progress'. Carried by 8 votes.
22.10.1887 'That the opinion of this House is that degrees should be conferred by this University upon qualified women'. Defeated 28 – 21.
5.11.1887 'That it is the opinion of this House that the Hereditary Principle should disappear from the constitution of the House of Lords'. Defeated 23 – 14.
19.11.1887 'That it is the opinion of this House that the present policy of the Unionist Party is fatal to the best interests of this country'. Defeated 29 – 8; 1 abstention.

28.1.1888 'That the opinion of this House is that Philistinism is the prevailing characteristic of life and sentiment in this University at the present time'. Carried 26 – 5.
11.2.1888 'That this House approves of a system of cremation'. Carried 17 – 12.
18.2.1888 'That it is the opinion of this House that the influence of the Drama in England is a healthy one'. Carried 14 – 12; 10 abstentions.
3.3.1888 'That this House is in favour of a Republican form of Government'. Defeated 23 – 3
20.10.1888 'That it is the opinion of this House that the Present Race is not degenerate'. Carried 27 – 8.

APPENDIX 18

3.11.1888 'That any system of Free Education would be disastrous to the best interests of the nation'. Carried 19 – 11.
17.11.1888 'That this House does not believe in the adoption of vegetarianism as a system'. Carried 27 – 4.

2.2.1889 'That this House would deplore the abolition of the present system of Competitive Examination'. Defeated 22 – 16.
16.2.1889 'That the abolition of the so-called sports of Coursing and Horse-racing would be of permanent benefit to the community'. Carried 20 – 13.
2.3.1889 'That this House is of opinion that the House of Lords should be entirely remodelled and reformed'. Defeated 30 – 10.
19.10.1889 'That this House would welcome the introduction of a general system of cremation'. Carried 31 – 10.
2.11.1889 'That this House disapproves of woman's encroachments upon man's domains'. Carried 13 – 3.
23.11.1889 'That this House recognizes an improvement in current literature generally'. Defeated 9 – 6; 1 abstention.

25.1.1890 'That this House condemns the attempt to revive the Prize Ring'. Carried 17 – 7.
8.2.1890 'That this House is of opinion that Capital Punishment is in no way justifiable'. Defeated 23 – 8.
1.3.1890 That in the opinion of this House there should be no limit, except an economic one, to the education of the poorer classes'. Carried 19 – 4.
18.10.1890 'That this House disapproves of the recent annexations to the British Empire except in view of a speedy adoption of some system of Imperial Federation'. Defeated 38 – 2.
1.11.1890 'That the present mode of European dress is contrary to the principles of Health, Art and Economy'. Carried 19 – 9.
22.11.1890 'That there is nothing in the pursuit of Horse Racing incompatible with the character of a Gentleman'. Result unclear.

24.1.1891 'That English Society has deteriorated'. Defeated 12 – 10.
24.10.1891 'That the return of Mr. Gladstone to power would be a national disaster'. Carried 35 – 9.
7.11.1891 'That the abolition of compulsory Greek in the Examinations for the Arts degree at the University would be detrimental to the best interests of the nation'. 16 – 16; carried by the chairman's casting vote.
21.11.1891 'That this house would view with favour the universal practice of total abstinence from alcoholic drinks'. Carried 22 – 21.

30.1.1892   'That in the opinion of this House a Republic is the best form of government'. Defeated 20 – 5.

13.2.1892   'That in the opinion of this House tobacco smoking is injurious'. Carried 17 – 7.

5.3.1892   'That in the opinion of this House the Disestablishment and Disendowment of the Established Church would be a boon to the nation'. Defeated 17 – 10.

29.10.1892   'That this House would view with approval the abolition of the opium traffic in India'. Carried 16 – 4.

12.11.1892   'That in the opinion of this house the present system of free trade is opposed to the best interests of the United Kingdom'. Defeated 24 – 6.

26.11.1892   'That this House views with approval the return to power of the Liberal Party'. Defeated 32 – 12.

11.2.1893   'That in the opinion of this House the time has now come for placing women on an electoral equality with men'. Defeated 20 – 6.

25.2.1893   'That in the opinion of this House compulsory Chapel is undesirable'. Defeated 14 – 7.

28.10.1893   'That this house would welcome the outbreak of a European War'. Defeated 21 – 10.

11.11.1893   'That this house expresses its strong disapproval of the proposed Channel Tunnel'. Carried 22 – 16.

25.11.1893   'That this House considers the House of Lords to be worthy of the confidence of the country at large: and that the existence of the Upper Chamber is of the utmost importance as a safeguard of good government and social order'. Carried 30 – 15.

3.2.1894   'This house considers that in the interests of the working classes an eight hours labour bill should be passed'. Defeated 17 – 11.

3.3.1894   'That this House approves of modern Socialism'. Defeated 16 – 12.

27.10.1894   'That it is in the interests of civilized nations and Great Britain in particular that Japan and China be forthwith compelled to submit their dispute to arbitration'. Defeated 22 – 11.

10.11.1894   'That this House would welcome the removal of the artificial restrictions which prevent women from entering the trades and professions'. Carried 16 – 12.

24.11.1894   'That this House disapproves of the principle of payment of Members of Parliament'. Carried 24 – 6.

2.2.1895   'That this House looks with disapproval on all forms of gambling both in theory and practice'. Carried 36 – 8.

16.2.1895   'That in the opinion of this House the principal of State

Interference cannot with success be applied to all social questions'. Carried unamimously.

2.3.1895   'That in the application of the Gothenburg System rather than in any other lies the solution of the Temperance question'. Carried 20 – 14.

26.10.1895 'That this House welcomes the wave of reaction which has ejected the late Government'. Carried 42 – 8.

9.11.1895   'Suicide is justifiable'. 24 – 24; carried by the chairman's casting vote.

30.11.1895 'That some form of Conscription is desirable for England'. Carried 20 – 18.

1.2.1896   'Imperial Federation is the best solution of Imperial difficulties'. Carried 29 – 12.

15.2.1896   'That degrees be given to women, but of such a kind as not to appropriate any privileges of the men already held by them'. Carried 22 – 12.

29.2.1896   'That in the opinion of this House the Modern Novel makes for righteousness'. Defeated 38 – 15.

31.10.1896 'That the time has not yet come when the principles of compulsory arbitration can be applied to the solution of international disputes'. Carried 23 – 22.

14.11.1896 'That total abstinence is desirable from a moral and social standpoint'. Result unclear.

5.12.1896   'That the present mode of European dress is contrary to the principles of art, comfort and economy'. Defeated 23 – 20.

6.2.1897   ' 'Tis better to have loved and lost,
            Than never to have loved at all'. Carried 32 – 10.

20.2.1897   'That an army, generally speaking, is of greater importance to a country than a navy'. Defeated 22 – 5.

6.3.1897   'That England's future greatness depends on a steady adherence to true Conservative principles'. Carried 27 – 8.

20.11.1897 'That Trades Unionism is producing a harmful effect upon the National peace and prosperity'. Carried 22 – 6.

4.12.1897   'That in the opinion of this House "a fool is happier than a wise man" '. Carried 24 – 6.

29.1.1898   'That this House approves of the use of Tobacco'. Carried 35 – 6.

12.2.1898   'That this House would deplore the Disestablishment of the Church of England'. Defeated 15 – 13.

7.3.1898   'That in the opinion of this House the present race is degenerate'. Defeated 26 – 11.

29.10.1898 'That the high state of civilisation of the present century in England is not conducive to the true happiness of the English people'. Defeated 24 – 22.

12.11.1898 'That this House is in sympathy with the proposals of the Tsar of Russia with regard to International Disarmament'. Defeated 25 – 12.

26.11.1898 'That the game of Rugby football is superior to that of Association'. Carried 18 – 15.

28.1.1899 'That the behaviour of the undergraduates on the occasion of the Sirdar's visit to Cambridge was a disgrace to the University'. Defeated 16 – 12.

11.2.1899 'That the present government has fully justified the great confidence reposed in it by the country'. Carried 23 – 8.

11.3.1899 'That the true prosperity of this country is to be looked for in an adherence to the principle of free Trade'. Carried 24 – 8.

28.10.1899 'That in the opinion of this House a Tax ought to be imposed on Advertisements'. Defeated 24 – 14.

11.11.1899 'That this House would welcome a Permanent Tribunal of International Arbitration'. Carried 19 – 8.

25.11.1899 'That in the opinion of this House Capital Punishment ought to be abolished'. Carried 20 – 16.

10.2.1900 'That the House disapproves of gambling both in theory and in practice'. Carried 16 – 9.

24.2.1900 'That in the opinion of this House, in the place of conscription there should be a compulsory system of physical and military training in all public and private schools in the kingdom'. Result unclear.

10.3.1900 'That the House disapproves of local self-government as constituted in this country'. Defeated 19 – 13.

3.11.1900 'That the House disapproves of the Electioneering Methods of Mr. Chamberlain'. Defeated 21 – 13.

17.11.1900 'That the House regrets the influence of the Press'. Defeated 17 – 10.

24.11.1900 'That in the opinion of the House, Federation would be the solution of England's difficulties'. Carried 23 – 15.

16.2.1901 'That the House regrets the deterioration of the modern drama'. Defeated 22 – 13.

2.3.1901 'That in the opinion of the House the Licensing Laws require radical amendment'. Carried 20 – 15.

2.11.1901 'That specialization is the curse of a University education'. Defeated 22 – 20.

16.11.1901 'That the House considers that drastic measures should be taken for the repression of Anarchists'. Carried 18 – 16.

30.11.1901 'That this house would welcome the disappearance of the halfpenny press'. Carried 18 – 15.

1.2.1902 'That there is more to be said in favour of the Chinese than is usually expressed'. Carried 17 – 16.

15.2.1902 'That the House approves of Rudyard Kipling's last poem (the Islanders)'. Result unclear.

1.3.1902 'That it is time a lethal chamber be established for the idiot and incurable'. Carried 17 – 13.

1.11.1902 'That this house agrees with the recent attacks made upon the study of Classics'. Carried 22 – 21.

15.11.1902 'That in the opinion of this House the present Government is unworthy of the confidence of the country'. Defeated 49 – 11.

29.11.1902 'That in the opinion of this House vivisection should be abolished'. Defeated 17 – 12.

31.1.1903 'That in the opinion of this House Home Rule is the only solution of Ireland's difficulties'. Defeated 32 – 13.

14.2.1903 'That this House deplores the advance of civilization'. 15 – 15; carried by the chairman's casting vote.

21.2.1903 'That the present age is essentially inartistic'. Carried 23 – 17.

7.3.1903 'That this House regrets the fascination of the Footlights'. Carried 17 – 4.

31.10.1903 'That this House condemns Mr. Chamberlain's Fiscal Proposals'. Defeated 31 – 17.

14.11.1903 'That the decadent tendencies of modern fiction are patent and deplorable'. Carried 40 – 12.

28.11.1903 'That ambition has a better influence on man than love'. Defeated 27 – 5.

30.1.1904 'That the existing devotion to Sport is excessive and deplorable'. Defeated 19 – 16.

27.2.1904 'That this House would welcome compulsory arbitration in all international disputes'. Defeated 16 – 9.

29.10.1904 'That this House approves of the spread of Socialistic Ideas in England'. Carried 18 – 11.

12.11.1904 'That this House sympathises with the passive resistance movement'. Carried 34 – 3.

26.11.1904 'Common Sense is the most pressing need of the present day'. Carried 32 – 18.

28.1.1905 'This House would favour the introduction of Leasehold Marriages'. Defeated 22 – 6.
28.10.1905 'This House deplores the growth of journalism'. Carried 15 – 11.
11.11.1905 'The modern undergraduate is degenerate'. Defeated 35 – 17.
29.11.1905 'That instant war with Germany would be the best policy for this nation'. Defeated 'by a large majority'.

3.2.1906 Motion of confidence in the present government; defeated 23 – 4.
14.2.1906 'That this house deplores the growth of militarism'. Defeated by 4 votes.
27.10.1906 'That this house deplores the growth of Civilisation'. Defeated.
17.11.1906 'That in the opinion of this House the Modern woman claims more than is her due'. Defeated 18 – 8.
24.11.1906 'That this House deplores the growing Materialism of the Age'. Carried 20 – 14.

26.1.1907 'That this House would welcome the Abolition of Capital Punishment'. 15 – 15; carried by the chairman's casting vote.
9.2.1907 'That this House would welcome the Abolition of the House of Lords'. Defeated 42 – 12.
16.2.1907 'That in the opinion of this House Individual Freedom is an Ideal professedly aimed at by all, but desired by none'. Defeated 12 – 10.
25.2.1907 'That this House deplores the amount of specialization in the University'. Defeated 27 – 18.
26.10.1907 'That in the opinion of this House, Limericks and Diabolo have made England what she is'. Defeated 27 – 14.
16.11.1907 'That this house welcomes the rise of Socialism'. Defeated 18 – 16.
23.11.1907 'That in the opinion of this House, Beauty is Truth, Truth Beauty, that is all we know on earth and all we need to know'. Defeated 21 – 8.
30.11.1907 'That in the opinion of this House, a censor should be appointed for the half-penny dailies'. Defeated 35 – 9.

25.1.1908 'That this house approves of Vivisection'. 13 – 13; defeated by the chairman's casting vote.
8.2.1908 'That this House views with apprehension the introduction of an Old Age Pension Scheme'. Defeated 19 – 9.
22.2.1908 'That in the opinion of this House, the Simple Life is a Delusive Dream'. Defeated 19 – 18.

472

31.10.1908 'That in the opinion of this House, Conventionality is not opposed to true Progress'. Defeated 25 – 7.
14.11.1908 'That the Franchise be extended to Women', 19 – 19; carried by the chairman's casting vote.
28.11.1908 'That this House favours the extension of Municipal Trading'. Defeated 18 – 14.

30.1.1909 'That Suicide is sometimes justifiable'. Defeated 23 – 20.
6.3.1909 'That this House favours the abolition of the General Examination'. Carried 28 – 18.
20.10.1909 'That this House disapproves of the introduction of the Daylight Saving Bill'. Carried 23 – 15.
13.11.1909 'That this House deprecates our blind adherence to custom'. Defeated 23 – 10.
27.11.1909 'That this House deprecates the introduction of aeroplanes'. Defeated 26 – 11.

12.2.1910 'That we are none of us half awake'. Carried 33 – 16.
12.3.1910 'That this House is disgusted with the squalor of the middle classes'. Defeated by the chairman's casting vote.
29.10.1910 'That this House advocates compulsory military training for service in Imperial defence'. Carried 26 – 11.
12.11.1910 'That in the opinion of this House the barbarian state of life is preferable to modern civilization'. Defeated 24 – 12.
26.11.1910 'That in the opinion of this House debating is unprofitable'. Defeated 18 – 6.

28.1.1911 'That in the opinion of this House the state which advertising has reached in the present day is alarming'. Defeated 16 – 10.
4.3.1911 'That the present system of education in English boys' schools is in need of reform'. Carried 26 – 22.
4.11.1911 'That this house deplores the increasing power of the industrial classes'. Carried 19 – 12.
18.11.1911 'That a classical education is not suited to modern requirements'. Carried 20 – 11.
25.11.1911 'In the opinion of this house modern warfare is indefensible as a remedy for national disputes'. Defeated 19 – 12.

3.2.1912 'This house deplores the increasing output of books upon the modern market'. Defeated 16 – 11.
17.2.1912 'This House desires that suffrage be given to women on equal terms with men'. Carried 12 – 11.

2.3.1912   'The crying need of the present age is the restoration of individual liberty'. Defeated 24 – 16.

2.11.1912   'That this House pass a vote of censure on the present Government'. Carried 36 – 9.

16.11.1912 'That this House express its disapproval of the recent strikers'. Defeated 25 – 23.

30.11.1912 'In the opinion of this house the taxing of bachelors would be advantageous to the Country'. Carried 23 – 10.

1.2.1913   'This House deplores the growing conventionality of the age'. Carried 20 – 17.

15.2.1913   'That in the opinion of this house *class distinctions* will always be necessary to national existence'. Carried 19 – 9.

1.3.1913   'That this House looks forward to the fuller *co-education* of men and women in this University'. Carried 37 – 20.

25.10.1913 'That this House is of opinion that the provision of a tunnel between England and France has become a commercial necessity; and further holds that no danger to the country would be incurred thereby'. Carried 33 – 9.

19.11.1913 'That in the opinion of this House some form of compulsory military training is essential for national security'. Carried 20 – 15.

29.11.1913 'That in the opinion of this House the increasing control of the individual by the state is detrimental to the life of the nation'. Defeated 19 – 10.

31.1.1914   'That this House would welcome the abolition of the House of Commons'. 15 – 15; defeated by the chairman's casting vote.

14.2.1914   'That in the opinion of this House the present generation of undergraduates is degenerate'. Defeated 63 – 31.

28.2.1914   'That this House would welcome the passing of the Daylight Saving Bill'. Carried 27 – 16.

7.11.1914   'That this House abhors our Party System of Government'. Carried 12 – 8.

14.11.1914 'That the System of Education in this country is in urgent need of reform'. Carried 16 – 9.

5.12.1914   'That in the opinion of this House it is vain to attempt to organize humanity at the present time on a wider basis than that of the Nation'. Defeated 21 – 16.

Appendix 19

Contingency plans for dealing with student agitation, 1969 – 70

Situation	Precautionary measures	Measures during incident
A. Demonstration in college	1. Forbid demonstrations in Cloister Court. (on basis of 1 Dec. precedent) 2. Forbid demonstrations involving any breach of College Regulations or trespass upon College premises or likelihood of damage to College property. 3. Warn that participation in such demonstrations will led to disciplinary action. 4. Alert Porters and Tutors. Lock S.C.R., Library, etc.	1. Take names of *all* present (Fellows to wear M.A. gowns) 2. Request (a) strangers to leave (b) members to disperse 3. Summon police *only* if breach of peace or damage to property.
B. Demonstration in Hall	1. Instruct Kitchen staff to advise of situation *before* entry of Fellows.	1. Fellows do not enter if disturbance already exists and leave if it begins later.

		2. Kitchen staff note names.
		3. All service of meals stops.
C. Sit-in	1. Lock strategic parts of College such as S.C.R., Monro, Hall(?), Library, Kitchen.	1. Tutor, in company of Porter, warns that trespass must cease and calls on all to leave. Take names.
	2. Remove valuables from above.	2. Cut off heat, light and any other services.
	3. Prepare to disconnect heat, light and water.	3. If in Hall, cease all preparations of meals.
	4. Warn police but do *not* summon.	4. Station Porters at egress point to prevent persons, once having come out, from re-entering.
		5. Summon Police only if breach of peace, damage to property, etc.
D. Open meeting	1. Publish and circulate to College views of G.B. on issues involved.	1. Fellows to attend meeting, speak and *vote*.
	2. Detailed case prepared in advance and Fellows chosen to present it.	
	3. Prepare counter-proposals with emphasis on *consultation*. (a) through Council	

(b) with College staff affected.

4. Fellows to discuss informally with undergraduates, inviting support at meeting.

Tutorial enquiry

1. *All* persons whose names have been taken to be seen *individually* by own Tutor. Record made on file of gist of any admission of breach of Regulations *or* instructions given by College Officer.

2. Evidence to be collected and Tutorial decision reached on which persons to be disciplined.

3. Notice sent, summoning each person individually before 3 Tutors and advising of charges made.

4. Hearing before Tutors: student to be told of charges, allowed to call witnesses, hear any evidence against him and, if matter to be referred to G.B., told of this and of right to be heard in person by G.B.

5. Disciplinary decision communicated to student in person but told of right to appeal to G.B.

Sanctions

A. *Tutorial*

i) Fines for damage done
ii) Sent out of College into lodgings
iii) Rusticated for period (pref. G.B. decision)
iv) Sent down (must be G.B. decision)
v) Debarred from using dining facilities
vi) Warning

Repercussions	Reaction
A. (i) Non-payment of College Bill	Warn once, through Tutor, then proceed to other appropriate sanctions of greater gravity.
(ii) Refusal to leave rooms *or* use of another's rooms with his consent	Treat as Sit-in
Demonstration	Treat as Demonstration
(iii) As above	Treat as above
(iv) As above	Treat as above
(v) Forcibly enters Hall or Erasmus Room	(i) No meals to be served to him (ii) If passed food by others, *all* service of meals to stop (iii) Further sanctions of greater gravity
Cooks in own room	No reaction *unless* he offends against Reg. on Furnishings or Fire Risk

Bibliography of Unprinted Sources

(i) UNPUBLISHED ARTICLES AND DISSERTATIONS

Carter, A. H. C., Switsur, V. R., and Ward, A. P. (Cambridge Dendroclimatological Research Group), 'Dating of the Long Gallery, Queens' College by the Cambridge Dendroclimatological Research Group. Report to the President and Fellows of Queens' College', 1984.

Davis, V. G., 'The Life and Career of William Waynflete, Bishop of Winchester 1447–1486', University of Dublin PhD, 1985.

Gascoigne, J., ' "The Holy Alliance": The Rise and Diffusion of Newtonian Natural Philosophy and Latitudinarian Theology within Cambridge from the Restoration to the Accession of George III', University of Cambridge PhD, 1980.

Griffith, W. P., 'Welsh Students at Oxford, Cambridge and the Inns of Court during the Sixteenth and early Seventeenth Centuries', University of Wales PhD, 1982.

Mills, J. F., 'The Foundation Endowment and Early Administration of Magdalen College Oxford', University of Oxford BLitt, 1977.

Morgan, V., 'Country, Court and Cambridge University, 1558–1640: A Study in the Evolution of a Political Culture', University of East Anglia PhD, 1984.

Nelson, A., 'Queens' College Stage, 1540–1640', unpublished paper (copy in possession of Mr I. R. Wright).

Saveson, J. E., 'Some Aspects of the Thought and Style of John Smith, the Cambridge Platonist', University of Cambridge PhD, 1955.

Storey, R. L., 'The Universities in the Wars of the Roses', unpublished paper read to the Society for the History of the University of Cambridge on 22.10.1981; to appear in *The History of the University of Oxford*.

Twigg, J. D., 'The University of Cambridge and the English Revolution, 1625–1688', University of Cambridge PhD, 1983.

(ii) QUEENS' COLLEGE ARCHIVES

A. College Archives held in the University Library

Book 1 (*Journale*, 1484 – 1518).
Book 2 (*Journale*, 1518 – 35).
Book 3 (*Journale*, 1535 – 60).
Book 4 (*Journale*, 1560 – 87).
Book 5 (*Journale*, 1587 – 1621).
Book 6 (*Journale*, 1621 – 91).
Book 7 (*Journale*, 1691 – 1753).
Book 8 (*Journale*, 1753 – 1835).
Book 9 (Auditor's Book, 1534 – 46).
Book 10 (Auditor's Book, 1546 – 8, 1553 – 8).
Book 11 (Auditor's Book, 1558 – 1609).
Book 12 (Auditor's Book, 1610 – 42, 1660 – 1772).
Book 14 (*Computus Finalis*, 1532 – 1716).
Book 15 (Treasurer's Book, 1648 – 60).
Book 16 (Bursar's Book, 1632 – 3).
Book 17 (Bursar's Book, 1688 – 9).
Book 21 (Account Book, 1840 – 4).
Book 22 (General Acquittances, 1682 – 1783).
Book 24 (Bursar's Book, 1613 – 14).
Book 25 (Bursar's Book, 1625 – 6).
Book 26 (Bursar's Book, 1624 – 5)
Book 27 (Bursar's Book, 1636 – 7).
Book 27A (Tutor's Account Book, 1644).
Book 28 (Bursar's Book, 1647 – 8).
Book 29 (Bursar's Memo Book, early 18th century).
Book 32 (Audit Expenses and other notes on the accounts, 17th – 19th centuries).
Book 36 (Notes on Leases, early 19th century).
Book 39 (Account Book, 1677 – 1746; also some 19th century papers).
Book 40 (Wood Book, 1762 – 1826).
Book 41 (Lease Book I, 15th and early 16th centuries).
Book 42 (Lease Book II, 1530 – 1613).
Book 43 (Lease Book III, 1613 – 23).
Book 49 (orders concerning college lands and plate, 1615 – 1864).
Book 51 ('Index to Useful Particulars in College Books').
Book 58 (Building Accounts, 1820s).
Book 62 (*Codex Chadertonianus*: statutes).
Book 68 (*Status sive Declaracio*, 1546, 1557).
Book 76 ('Misc. A').
Book 77 ('Misc. B').
Book 78 (Rental, 1682 – 1725; also miscellaneous entries).

Book 79 (Statutes, and other miscellaneous material).

Book 80 ('Dr James' Book', late 17 – 18th centuries).

Book 81 (Correspondence concerning the Old Printing House, early 19th century).

Book 83 (Hughes Prizes, 1780 – 1833).

Book 86 (new fellows' oaths of allegiance, etc., 1715 – 1826).

Book 87 (Scott, John, *The Foundation of the Universitie of Cambridge*, Cambridge, 1618, presentation copy to the college).

Box 15 (documents concerning college property at Eversden).

Box 16 (college property, and miscellaneous documents).

Box 31 (royal letters and mandates, etc.).

Box 95 (case papers, 17th and 18th centuries).

Box 101 (papers concerning the college chapel and fabric).

Box 102 (miscellaneous documents, 16th – 19th centuries).

B. College Archives in the President's Lodge

Conclusion Book (1734 – 87).

Conclusion Book (1787 – 1832).

Conclusion Book (1832 – 88).

Conclusion Book (1889 – 1937).

Conclusion Book (1937 – 1963).

College Reports (1914 – 1949).

College Reports (1924 – 1939).

CU papers (President's personal correspondence with the College Union, 1968 – 75). These are to be distinguished from the formal, numbered memoranda submitted by the union to the governing body.

St Bernard Society minute book (1926 – 39).

C. College Archives in the Old Library

(i) Classified documents

Book 72 (notes for Robert Plumptre's history of Queens').

Book 73 (history of Queens', by Robert Plumptre).

Book 75 (Library Account Book).

MS 30 ('Andrew Doket's Inventory Book').

MS 73 (correspondence of Simon Patrick).

MS 77 (fair copy of Milner's lecture notes).

MS 79 (J. F. WIlliams' autobiographical reminiscences).

MS 80 (papers of George Gorham, Fellow, 1810 – 27).

MS 502 (miscellaneous documents, 1630s – 1650s).

MS 600 (lists of money and plate sent to Charles I in 1642).

MS index to Searle's History.

Old Parchment Register.

Registrum.

(ii) Unclassified documents
1707 student's lecture notes on lectures by Vigani.
Letter of William Sedgwick, 14.2.1736.
Joseph Jee's letter book (early 19th century).
Bibby, C., 'Correspondence of Courtship', and 'Reminiscences of a Happy Life' (MS autobiographical works).
C. W. N. McGowan, 'Memories of Queens' Sixty Years Ago' (MS reminiscences).
Promotional pamphlet for the bowling machine invented by J. and J. A. Venn, 1909.

(iii) Documents collected for college history
Harrison, G. B., letter and notes on Queens' in the early 20th century, containing additional material to the information in his published memoirs (Harrison (1985)).
MS reminiscences of Dr E. A. Maxwell.
Noble, A. H. 'Autobiography' (MS).
Correspondence with Miss D. M. Cannell concerning John Toplis.
Correspondence with Dr W. P. Griffith concerning the college's links with Wales in the 16th and 17th centuries.
Dean of chapel's circular to all members of college, April 1986.
Circular expressing local residents' opposition to the development on the college boathouse site, February 1986

D. College Archives in Room S2C

Uncatalogued MSS (miscellaneous bursarial documents roughly sorted by the author and arranged by subject alphabetically in 38 separate folders).
Legal Case 1932 – 4 concerning Pembroke and Queens' scholarships.
President's Records, 1907 – 8 (results of exams, etc.).
Scholarships, Exhibitions and Grants, 1895 – 1908.
Tutor's Book, 1878 – 87.
Tutor's Book, 1885 – 91.
Tutor's Book, 1889 – ?1916.
Tutor's Book, 1895 – 1924.
Tutor's Book, 1896 – 1903.
Tutor's Book, 1906.
Tutor's Book, 1910 – 14.

E. Junior Bursar's Files

Documents relating to the Erasmus Building (2 boxes).

F. Documents held in the Bursary

Governing Body Minutes, 1954 – .
College Minutes (papers presented to the governing body), 1959 – .

G. Documents held in the Tutorial Office

St Bernard Society Minutes.
(D1) 1884 – 1892.
(D2) 1893 – 1902.
(D3) 1902 – 1914.
(D4) 1914 – 1925.
(D7) 1956 – 1966.
Kangaroo Club Minutes.
(K1) 1895 – 1900.
(K2) 1911 – 1923.
(K4) 1929 – 1934.
(K5) 1935 – 1967.
Queens' College Rugby Club Minutes.
(R1) 1928 – 1945.
Queens' College Boat Club Minutes.
(B14) 1831 – 1842.
(B15) 1842 – 1853.
(B16) 1853 – 1863.
(B17) 1863 – 1877.
(B18) 1877 – 1891.
(B20) 1891 – 1913.
(B21) 1913 – 29, 1939 – 46.

H. Other Documents held in the College

— Collection of press cuttings concerning the BBC television series,
  'Queens': A Cambridge College', held by the senior tutor, Dr J. T.
  Green.
— Queens' College Club documents (including several printed ser-
  mons), held by the secretary of the Queens' College Club, Dr A. N.
  Hayhurst, but shortly to be transferred to the library.
— Dean's Chapel Book (1854 – 1944), held by the dean of chapel, the
  Rev B. L. Hebblethwaite.
— Minute Books of the Queens' College History Society (1930 – 60),
  held by the director of studies in history, Dr P. Spufford.
— K. E. Machin papers (miscellaneous documents relating to the
  student agitation of the late 1960s, belonging to Dr. K. E. Machin;
  photocopies of some of the documents cited are included in the file
  of documents received for the college history).

— College union papers and miscellaneous related documents belonging to Dr J. T. Green.

(iii) OTHER MANUSCRIPT SOURCES

A. Cambridge University Library and Archives

CUA University Grace Book Z (1620 – 45).
CUA University Grace Book H (1645 – 69).
CUA University Grace Book Θ (1669 – 1718).
CUA Vice-chancellor's court VC Ct.I.9.
CUA Vice-chancellor's court VC Ct.I.38.
CUA Vice-chancellor's court VC Ct.I.49.
CUA Vice-chancellor's court VC Ct.I.54.
CUA Vice-chancellor's court VC Ct.II.25.
CUA Collect. Admin. 13.
CUA CUR 7.
CUA CUR 18.
CUA CUR 78.
CUA CUR 82.
CUA Matr. 17.
CUL Add MS 20.
CUL Add MS 22.
CUL Baker MSS, vol. xxv.
CUL Baker MSS, vol. xxxiii.
CUL Baker MSS, vol. xxxvii.

B. Other Documents

PRO State Papers, SP28 (on microfilm in CUL).
BL [British Library] Harl. MS 7019 (I have used David Hoyle's notes from this).
New College, Oxford NCA 11, 704.

(iv) MISCELLANEOUS DOCUMENTS

Diaries of H. C. Alexander, 1921 – 4.
Diaries of J. B. Geyer, 1953 – 6 (on loan to the college).

Bibliography: Printed Sources

Academiae Cantabrigiensis ΣΩΣΤΡΑ. Sive, ad Carolum II reducem, De Regnis ipsi, Musis per ipsum feliciter restitutis Gratulatio, Cambridge, 1660.

A Full and and Impartial Account of all the late Proceedings in the University of Cambridge against Dr. Bentley, London, 1719.

Allen, P. S. (ed.), *Opus Epistolarum Des. Erasmi Roterodami*, vol. I, Oxford, 1906.

Allen, W. S., *Vox Latina*, Cambridge, 1965.

—— *Vox Graeca*, Cambridge, 1968.

Anderson, C. A., and Schnaper, M., *School and Society in England. Social Backgrounds of Oxford and Cambridge Students*, Washington, 1952.

Annan, N. G., 'The Intellectual Aristocracy', in J. H. Plumb (ed.), *Studies in Social History*, London, 1955.

Ardener, S., 'Incorporation and Exclusion: Oxford Academics' Wives', in H. Callan and S. Ardener (eds.), *The Incorporated Wife*, London, 1984.

Aston, T. H., Duncan, G. D., Evans, T. A. R., 'The Medieval Alumni of the University of Cambridge', *Past and Present* 86 (1980).

Atkinson, Solomon, 'Struggles of a Poor Student through Cambridge', *The London Magazine and Review*, April 1, 1825.

Aubrey, John, *Aubrey on Education* (ed. J. E. Stephens), London, 1972.

—— *Aubrey's Brief Lifes* (ed. O. L. Dick), London, 1972.

Ayandale, E. A., *The Missionary Impact on Modern Nigeria 1842 – 1914*, London, 1966.

Aylmer, G. E., 'The Economics and Finances of the Colleges and the University, c. 1530 – 1640', in J. K. McConica (ed), *The Collegiate University* (History of the University of Oxford iii), Oxford, 1986.

Bach, U., 'Bible-Clerks in Sixteenth-Century Cambridge', *Notes and Queries*, New Series 28, no. 1 (1981).

Bagley, J. J., *Margaret of Anjou Queen of England*, London, 1948.

Baker, Thomas, *History of the College of St. John the Evangelist, Cambridge* (ed. J. E. B. Mayor), Cambridge, 1869.

Ball, Thomas, *The Life of the Renowned Doctor Preston* (ed. E. W. Harcourt), Oxford, 1885.

Ball, W. W. R., *A History of the Study of Mathematics at Cambridge*, Cambridge, 1889.

—— *Notes on the History of Trinity College, Cambridge*, London, 1899

Barwick, Peter, *The Life of the Reverend Doctor John Barwick*, London, 1724.

Batho, G., 'Landlords in England', in Thirsk (1967).

Beddard, R. A., 'The Restoration Church', in J. R. Jones (ed.), *The Restored Monarchy 1660 – 1688*, London, 1979.

Bennet, H. S., *English Books and Readers 1603 to 1640*, Cambridge, 1970.

Best, G. F. A., *Temporal Pillars. Queen Anne's Bounty, the Ecclesiastical Commissioners, and the Church of England*, Cambridge, 1964.

Bibby, H. C., *The Evolution of Man and his Culture*, London, 1938.

Bligh, Reginald, *The Defence of the Rev. Reginald Bligh*, London, ?1780.

—— *Letters which passed between The Rev. Reginald Bligh, A.B. And Others*, London, 1781.

Boas, F. S., *University Drama in the Tudor Age*, Oxford, 1914.

Bowden, P., 'Agricultural Prices, Farm Profits, and Rents', in Thirsk (1967).

Bowdler, Charles (ed.), *The Case of the President of Queen's College, Cambridge*, London, 1821.

Bowes, R., *A Catalogue of Books printed at or relating to the University, Town & County of Cambridge from 1521 to 1893 with Bibliographical & Biographical Notes*, Cambridge, 1894.

Bradley, A. G., *Our Centenarian Grandfather 1790 – 1890*, London, ?1922.

Bradshaw, H., 'Notes of the Episcopal Visitation of the Archdeaconry of Ely in 1685', *CAS Communications* iii (1874 – 5).

Branson, N., *Britain in the Nineteen Twenties*, London, 1975.

Brawley, B., *Early American Negro Writers*, New York, facsimile edition, 1970.

Brink, C. O. *English Classical Scholarship*, Cambridge, 1986.

British Universities and the War. A Record and Its Meaning, London, 1919.

Brodribb, G., *The Croucher*, London, 1974.

Brooke, C. N. L., *A History of Gonville and Caius College*, Woodbridge, 1985.

Brown, F. K., *Fathers of the Victorians*, Cambridge, 1961.

Brown, W. Wells, *Three Years in Europe*, London, 1852.

Browne, A. D., and Seltman, C. T., *A Pictorial History of the Queen's College of Saint Margaret and Saint Bernard commonly called Queens' College Cambridge 1448 – 1948*, Cambridge, 1951.

Browne, G. F., *St Catharine's College*, London, 1902.

Brunskill, R., and Clifton-Taylor, A., *English Brickwork*, London, 1977.

Bryant, M., *The Unexpected Revolution*, London, 1979.

The Builder.

Burnet, Gilbert, *A Supplement from unpublished Manuscripts to Burnet's History of My Own Time* (ed. H. C. Foxcroft), Oxford, 1902.

Burrows, M., *Worthies of All Souls*, London, 1874.

Bury, J. P. T., *The College of Corpus Christi and of the Blessed Virgin Mary. A History from 1822 to 1952*, Cambridge, 1952.

Butterfield, H., *The Universities and Education Today*, London, 1962.

Buxton, J., and Williams, P. (eds.), *New College Oxford 1379 – 1979*, Oxford, 1979.

Byron, George (Lord), *Byron's Poems* (ed. V. DeS. Pinto), vol. i, London, 1963.

Caird, R., *A Good and Useful Life. Imprisonment in Britain Today*, London, 1974.

Calendar of the Patent Rolls, London (HMSO), 1901 – 86.

Calendar of State Papers (Domestic series), London (HMSO), 1856 – 1972.

Cam, H. M., 'The City of Cambridge', in *VCH Cambridgeshire* (1959).

Cambridge Admissions Prospectus, Cambridge, 1970/1 – .

Cambridge Evening News.

the Cambridge Greek affair, Cambridge, ?1970.

Cambridge New Architecture, Cambridge, 1965.

Cambridge in South London, London, 1910.

The Cambridge Review.

The Cambridge University Calendar, Cambridge, 1796 – 1950.

The Cambridge University Handbook, Cambridge, 1967/8 – .

Cambridge University: a prospectus by students, Cambridge, 1973 – 7; continued as *Cambridge students' prospectus*, Cambridge, 1978 – .

Cambridge University Reporter.

Campion, W. M., 'The Beauty of Holiness'. *A Sermon preached by the Rev. W. M. Campion, D.D. . . . September 27, 1892*, Cambridge, 1892.

Cannon, J., *Aristocratic Century. The peerage of eighteenth-century England*, Cambridge, 1984.

The Cantab (1898 – 9).

Carey, G. V. (ed.), *The War List of the University of Cambridge*, Cambridge, 1921.

Carter, Edmund, *The History of the University of Cambridge*, London, 1753.

Caspari, F., *Humanism and the Social Order in Tudor England*, New York, 1968.

Chadwick, W. O., *The Victorian Church*, London, 1970 – 2.

———— *The Reformation*, London, 1972.

———— 'Charles Kingsley at Cambridge', *The Historical Journal* xviii (1975).

Charlton, K., *Education in Renaissance England*, London, 1965.

———— 'Ages of admission to educational institutions in Tudor and Stuart England: a comment', *History of Education* 5 (1976).

Chase, F. H., *The Credibility of the Book of The Acts of the Apostles*, London, 1902.

———— *The Supernatural Element in our Lord's earthly Life in relation to Historical Methods of Study*, London, 1903.

Chaucer, G., *The Canterbury Tales* (transl. N. Coghill), London, 1960.

Chrimes, S. B., *Henry VII*, London, 1972.

Clark, J. W., and Hughes, T. M., *The Life and Letters of the Reverend Adam Sedgwick*, Cambridge, 1890.

Clarke, Samuel, *The Lives of Thirty-Two English Divines*, London, 1677.

The Clergyman's Intelligencer, London, 1745.

Clifton, R., 'Fear of Popery', in C. Russell (ed.), *The Origins of the English Civil War*, London, 1975.

Cobban, A. B., *The King's Hall within the University of Cambridge in the Later Middle Ages*, Cambridge, 1969.

—— 'Origins; Robert Wodelarke and St. Catharine's', in E. E. Rich (ed.)., *St. Catharine's College, Cambridge, 1473–1973*, Cambridge, 1973.

—— *The Medieval Universities: their development and organisation*, London, 1975.

—— 'The Medieval Cambridge Colleges: a Quantitative Study of Higher Degrees to c. 1500', *History of Education* 9 (1980).

Cockburn, A., and Blackburn, R. (eds.), *Student Power/Problems, Diagnosis, Action*, London, 1969.

Coleby, L. J. M., 'John Francis Vigani, First Professor of Chemistry in the University of Cambridge', *Annals of Science* 8 (1952).

—— 'Isaac Milner and the Jacksonian Chair of Natural Philosophy', *Annals of Science* 10 (1954).

Collinson, P., *The Elizabethan Puritan Movement*, London, 1967.

—— *The Religion of Protestants*, Oxford, 1982.

Colvin, H., *A Biographical Dictionary of British Architects 1600–1840*, London, 1978.

Cook, A. B., *Dominus in Refugium, A Sermon preached in Queens' College Chapel . . . 13 November 1927*, Cambridge, 1927 (copy in Queens' College Club MSS).

Cooper, C. H., *Annals of Cambridge*, Cambridge, 1842–1908.

—— 'Inventory of Plate sent to King Charles I by Queens' College, Cambridge, and Receipt for moneys advanced for his service by the President and Fellows, 1642', *CAS Communications* i (1851).

—— *Memorials of Cambridge*, Cambridge, 1860–6.

Cooper, C. H., and Cooper, T., *Athenae Cantabrigienses*, vol. i, Cambridge, 1858.

Costello, W. T., *The Scholastic Curriculum at Early Seventeenth-Century Cambridge*, Harvard, 1958.

Coward, B., *The Stuart Age*, London, 1980.

Cowper, H. (ed.), *Reports of Cases Adjudged in the Court of King's Bench*, London, 1783.

Cradock, P., *et al.*, *Recollections of the Cambridge Union 1815–1939*, Cambridge, 1953.

Cragg, G.R., *From Puritanism to the Age of Reason*, Cambridge, 1950.

Craig, C., *The Employment of Cambridge Graduates*, Cambridge, 1963.

Crawford, Charles, *Letters from Academicus to Eugenius on Various Subjects*, London, 1772.

Crawley, C., *Trinity Hall. The History of a Cambridge College 1350–1975*, Cambridge, 1976.

Cressy, D., 'The Social Composition of Caius College 1580–1640', *Past and Present* 47 (1970).

—— (ed.), *Education in Tudor and Stuart England*, London, 1975.

—— 'Educational Opportunity in Tudor and Stuart England', *History of Education Quarterly* 16 (1976).

—— 'School and College Admission Ages in Seventeenth-century England', *History of Education* 8 (1979).

The Criminal Appeal Reports.

Crummell, A., *1844 – 1894. The Shades and the Lights of a Fifty Years' Ministry. Jubilate*, Washington, 1894.

Crutchley, B., *To be a printer*, London, 1980.

Curtis, M. H., *Oxford and Cambridge in Transition, 1558 – 1642*, Oxford, 1959.

Darby, H. C., *The Draining of the Fens*, Cambridge, 1940.

—— *Medieval Cambridgeshire*, Cambridge, 1977.

Davies, Richard, *The General State of Education in the Universities*, Bath, 1759.

Dawson, J. E. A., 'The Foundation of Christ Church, Oxford and Trinity College, Cambridge in 1546', *Bulletin of the Institute of Historical Research* lvii (1984).

Defoe, Daniel, *A Tour through the Whole Island of Great Britain*, London, 1974.

de la Pryme, Abraham, *The Diary of Abraham de la Pryme*, Surtees Society lix (1869).

DeMolen, R. L., 'Ages of Admission to Educational Institutions in Tudor and Stuart England', *History of Education* 5 (1976).

Dent, H. C., *Education in Transition. A Sociological Study of the Impact of War on English Education, 1939 – 1943*, London, 1944.

Dewar, M., *Sir Thomas Smith: A Tudor Intellectual in Office*, London, 1964.

The Dial (college magazine).

Dickens, A. G., *The English Reformation*, London, 1967.

Dickens, Charles (the younger), *Dictionary of the University of Cambridge*, London, 1884.

The Dictionary of National Biography from the Earliest Times to 1900, London, 1885 – 1901.

The Dictionary of Scientific Biography, New York, 1970 – 80.

Documents relating to the University and Colleges of Cambridge, London (HMSO), 1852.

D'Oyly, G. (ed.), *The Life of William Sancroft, Archbishop of Canterbury*, London, 1821.

Drinkwater, G.C., 'Alterations at Queens' College, Cambridge', *CAS Communications* xxxvi (1934 – 5).

Dubbey, J. M., *The mathematical works of Charles Babbage*, Cambridge, 1978.

Du Bois, W. E. B., *The Souls of Black Folk*, London, 1905.

Duckett, T. E., *The Duckett Family History*, Frome/London, 1960.

Dunbabin, J. P. D., 'Oxford and Cambridge College Finances, 1871 – 1913', *Economic History Review* xxviii (1975).

—— 'Oxford College Finances, 1871 – 1913: A Reply', *ibid.* xxxi (1978).

'College Estates and Wealth 1660 – 1815', in L. S. Sutherland and L. G. Mitchell (eds.), *The Eighteenth Century* (History of the University of Oxford v), Oxford, 1986.

Duncan, G. D., 'The Property of Balliol College c. 1500 – c. 1640'.

—— 'An Introduction to the Accounts of Corpus Christi College', both in J. K. McConica (ed.), *The Collegiate University* (History of the University of Oxford iii), Oxford, 1986.

Dyer, G., *History of the University and Colleges of Cambridge*, London, 1814.

Eachard, John, *The Grounds & Occasions of The Contempt of the Clergy and Religion Enquired into*, Cambridge, 1670.

—— *Some Observations upon the Answer*, London, 1671.

Eban, A. S., *An Autobiography*, London, 1973.

The Ecclesiologist.

Edwards, G. M., *Sidney Sussex College*, London, 1899.

Eland, G. (ed.), 'The Annual Progress of New College by Michael Woodward — Warden 1659 – 1675', *Records of Buckinghamshire* xiii (1935).

Elliott-Binns, L. E., *The Early Evangelicals: A Religious and Social Study*, London, 1953.

Elton, G. R., *The Tudor Constitution*, Cambridge, 1972.

—— *England under the Tudors*, London, 1974.

—— *Reform and Reformation: England, 1509 – 1558*, London, 1977.

Emden, A. B., *A Biographical Register of the University of Cambridge to 1500*, Cambridge, 1963.

Engel, A. J., 'Oxford College Finances, 1871 – 1913: A Comment', *Economic History Review* xxxi (1978).

—— *From Clergyman to Don. The Rise of the Academic Profession in Nineteenth-Century Oxford*, Oxford, 1983.

Evelyn, John, *The Diary of John Evelyn* (ed. W. Bray), London, 1966.

Everett, W., *On the Cam*, London, 1869.

Everitt, A., 'The Marketing of Agricultural Produce', and

—— 'Farm Labourers', both in Thirsk (1967).

Farish, Charles, *Toleration of Marriage in the Universities recommended to the Attention of The Heads of Houses*, Cambridge, undated.

Feingold, M., 'Jordan Revisited: Patterns of Charitable Giving in Sixteenth and Seventeenth Century England', *History of Education* 8 (1979).

—— 'Oxford and Cambridge College Histories: An outdated Genre?', *History of Universities* i (1981).

—— *The mathematicians' apprenticeship. Science, universities and society in England, 1560 – 1640*, Cambridge, 1984.

Feyerharm, W. R., 'The status of the schoolmaster and the continuity of education in Elizabethan East Anglia', *History of Education* 5 (1976).

Fiennes, Celia, *The Journeys of Celia Fiennes* (ed. C. Morris), London, 1949.

Firth, C. H., *Oliver Cromwell and the Rule of the Puritans in England*, Oxford, 1953.

Firth, C. H., and Rait, R. S., *Acts and Ordinances of the Interregnum, 1642 – 1660*, London, 1911.

Fitzgerald, M. H., *A Memoir of Herbert Edward Ryle*, London, 1928.

Fontane, T., *Wanderungen durch England und Schottland*, Berlin, 1979.

Fowler, L., and Fowler, H. (eds.), *Cambridge Commemorated: An Anthology of University Life*, Cambridge, 1984.

Frank, R. G., 'Science, Medicine and the Universities of Early Modern England', *History of Science* 11 (1973).

Fuller, M., *The Life, Letters & Writings of John Davenant D.D.*, London, 1897.

Fuller, Thomas, *The History of the University of Cambridge* (ed. J. Nichols), London, 1840.

―――― *The History of the Worthies of England* (ed. P. A. Nuttall), London, 1840.

―――― *The Holy State and the Profane State* (ed. J. Nichols), London, 1841.

―――― *The Church History of Britain* (ed. J. Nichols), London, 1868.

Furneaux, R., *William Wilberforce*, London, 1974.

Gardiner, S., 'Masterpiece by the Cam', *The Observer*, 11.5.1980.

Garland, M. M., *Cambridge before Darwin. The Ideal of a Liberal Education, 1800 – 1860*, Cambridge, 1980.

Gascoigne, J., 'Politics, Patronage and Newtonianism: the Cambridge Example', *Historical Journal* 27 (1984).

―――― 'Mathematics and Meritocracy: The Emergence of the Cambridge Mathematical Tripos', *Social Studies of Science* 14 (1984).

―――― 'The Universities and the Scientific Revolution: The Case of Newton and Restoration Cambridge', *History of Science* xxiii (1985).

―――― 'Anglican Latitudinarianism and Political Radicalism in the late Eighteenth Century', *History* 71 (1986).

―――― 'Isaac Barrow's Academic Milieu', in M. Feingold (ed.), *Before Newton: The Life and Times of Isaac Barrow*, (forthcoming).

―――― 'The Holy Alliance': Politics, Religion and Science in Cambridge from the Restoration to the French Revolution, (forthcoming).

Gaskell, P., *Trinity College Library. The first 150 years*, Cambridge, 1980.

The Gentleman's Magazine.

Gillingham, J., *The Wars of the Roses*, London, 1981.

Girouard, M., *Life in the English Country House: A Social and Architectural History*, New Haven and London, 1978.

Godman, William, *The Son of Nobles*, London, 1660.

Goodman, A., *The Wars of the Roses*, London, 1981.

Goodman, A. W., *A Little History of S. Botolph's, Cambridge*, Cambridge, 1922.

The Granta.

Grave, W. W., *Fitzwilliam College Cambridge 1869 – 1969*, Cambridge, 1983.

Graves, R., and Hodge, A., *The Long Week-end. A Social History of Great Britain 1918 – 1939*, London, 1971.

Gray, A., 'On the Watercourse called Cambridge in Relation to the River Cam and Cambridge Castle', *CAS Communications* ix (1894 – 5).

Gray, A., and Brittain, F., *A History of Jesus College, Cambridge*, London, 1979.

Gray, J. H., *A Sermon preached in Queens' College Chapel . . . 15 November 1925*, Cambridge, 1925 (copy in Queens' College Club MSS).

————— *The Queens' College of St Margaret & St Bernard in the University of Cambridge*, Cambridge, revised edition, 1926.

Gray, T., *Correspondence of Thomas Gray* (ed. P. Toynbee and L. Whibley), Oxford, 1935.

Greaves, R. L., *Society and Religion in Elizabethan England*, Minneapolis, 1981.

Green, I. M., *The Re-Establishment of the Church of England, 1660 – 1663*, Oxford, 1978.

Green, V. H. H., *Religion at Oxford and Cambridge*, London, 1964.

————— *The Universities*, London, 1969.

————— *The Commonwealth of Lincoln College, 1427 – 1977*, Oxford, 1979.

Griffiths, O. M., *Religion and Learning: A Study in English Presbyterian Thought from 1662 to the foundation of the Unitarian Movement*, Cambridge, 1935.

Gunning, H., *Reminiscences of the University, Town, and County of Cambridge, from the Year 1780*, London, 1854.

Gunther, R. T., *Early Science in Cambridge*, London, facsimile edition, 1969.

Haig, A. G. L., *The Victorian Clergy*, London, 1984.

————— 'The Church, the Universities and Learning in Later Victorian England', *Historical Journal* 29 (1986).

Hall, C. P., and Ravensdale, J. R., *The West Fields of Cambridge*, Cambridge, 1976.

Haller, W., *The Rise of Puritanism*, Columbia, 1938.

Halsey, A. H., and Trow, M. A., *The British Academics*, London, 1971.

Hans, N., *New Trends in Education in the Eighteenth Century*, London, 1951.

Harding, G., *Along My Line*, London, 1953.

Harrison, G. B., *One Man in his Time. The Memoirs of G. B. Harrison, 1894 – 1984*, Palmerston North, 1985.

Harrison, William, *The Description of England* (ed. G. Edelen), Ithaca, 1968.

Harrison, W. J., *Life in Clare Hall Cambridge 1653 – 1713*, Cambridge, 1958.

Harvey, J., *English Medieval Architects. A Biographical Dictionary down to 1550*, Gloucester, 1984.

Haskins, C. H., *Studies in Medieval Culture*, Oxford, 1929.

Hausted, Peter, *A Sermon, Equally Pointing Forward, & Backward*, Cambridge, 1647.

Hayman, R. (ed.), *My Cambridge*, London, 1977.

Hebblethwaite, B. L., *Sermons from Queens' College Cambridge*, Oxford, 1985.

Hennell, M., *Sons of the Prophets. Evangelical Leaders of the Victorian Church*, London, 1979.

Heyck, T. W., *The Transformation of Intellectual Life in Victorian England*, London, 1982

Heywood, J., and Wright, T., *Cambridge University Transactions during the Puritan Controversies of the 16th and 17th Centuries*, London, 1854.

Hierurgia Anglicana, London, 1902.

Hill, C., *The Century of Revolution, 1603 – 1714*, Edinburgh, 1961.

—— *Puritanism and Revolution*, London, 1965.

Historical Manuscripts Commission, *Fifth Report of the Royal Commission on Historical Manuscripts*, Part I (Appendix), London, 1878.

—— *Calendar of the Manuscripts of the Most Hon. the Marquis of Salisbury, K.G.*, vol. ii, London, 1888.

Hoffman, J. G., 'The Puritan Revolution and the "Beauty of Holiness" at Cambridge', *CAS Proceedings* 72 (1984).

Holmes, G. *Augustan England. Professions, State and Society, 1680 – 1730*, London, 1982.

Horton, Thomas, *Sinne's Discovery and Revenge*, London, 1646.

—— *Wisdome's Judgment of Folly*, London, 1653 (*Thomason Tracts* E691(4)).

—— *Zion's Birth-Register Unfolded*, London, 1656.

Hoskins, W. G., *The Making of the English Landscape*, London, 1977.

Howard, H. F., *An Account of the Finances of the College of St John the Evangelist in the University of Cambridge 1511 – 1926*, Cambridge, 1935.

Howarth, T. E. B., *Cambridge Between Two Wars*, London, 1978.

Howell, T. B. (ed.), *A Complete Collection of State Trials*, vol. xx, London, 1814.

Hoyle, D. M., 'A Commons Investigation of Arminianism and Popery in Cambridge on the Eve of the Civil War', *Historical Journal* 29 (1986).

Hughes, P. (ed.), *Saint John Fisher: The Earliest English Life*, London, 1935.

Hunter, M., *Science and Society in Restoration England*, Cambridge, 1981.

Hutton, R., *The Restoration*, Oxford, 1985.

Ingram, R. A., *The Necessity of Introducing Divinity into the Regular Course of Academical Studies Considered*, Colchester, 1792.

—— *The Causes of the Increase of Methodism & Dissension, and of the Popularity of what is called Evangelical Preaching, and the Means of Obviating them*, London, 1807.

Innes, H. M., *Fellows of Trinity College, Cambridge*, Cambridge, 1941.

Ivory, John, *The Foundation of the University of Cambridge*, Cambridge, 1672.

Jackson, B., and Marsden, D., *Education and the Working Class*, London, 1966.

Jackson-Stops, G., 'The Building of the Medieval College', in Buxton and Williams (1979).

Jacob, E.F., *Essays in the Conciliar Epoch*, Manchester, 1953.

Jacombe, Samuel, *Moses his Death*, London, 1657.

James, Henry, *A Sermon Preached before the King at Newmarket, October 11. 1674*, London, 1674.

Jardine, L., 'The Place of Dialectic Teaching in Sixteenth-Century Cambridge', *Studies in the Renaissance* xxi (1974).

—— 'Humanism and the Sixteenth Century Cambridge Arts Course', *History of Education* 4 (1975).

Jebb, J., *The Works Theological, Medical, Political, and Miscellaneous, of John Jebb*, London, 1787.

Jenkins, H., and Caradog Jones, D., 'Social Class of Cambridge Alumni of the 18th and 19th Centuries', *British Journal of Sociology* 1 (1950).

Jordan, W. K., *Philanthropy in England, 1480–1660*, London, 1959.

—— *The Charities of Rural England, 1480–1660*, London, 1961.

Journals of the House of Lords.

Kalton, G., *The Public Schools*, London, 1966.

Kearney, H. F., *Scholars and Gentlemen: Universities and Society in Pre-Industrial Britain, 1500–1700*, London, 1970.

Kemp, Edward, *A Sermon Preached at St Maries in Cambridge . . . September the 6. 1668*, Cambridge, 1668.

Kennet, W., *A Register and Chronicle Ecclesiastical and Civil*, London, 1728.

Kennett, R. H., *The Church's Gain from Modern Thought as shown in Old Testament Study*, London, 1910.

Kenyon, J. P., *The Stuart Constitution 1603–1688*, Cambridge, 1966.

Keynes, M. E., *A House by the River*, Cambridge, 1976.

Knight, F., *University Rebel. The Life of William Frend (1757–1841)*, London, 1971.

Knowles, D., *The Religious Orders of England*, vol. iii, Cambridge, 1959.

Laffan R. G. D., *The Guardians of the Gate. Historical Lectures on the Serbs*, Oxford, 1918.

—— (ed. and transl.), *Select Documents of European History Vol. I. 800–1492*, London, 1930.

Lake, P., 'Robert Some and the Ambiguities of Moderation', *Archiv für Reformationsgeschichte* 71 (1980).

—— 'The Significance of the Elizabethan Identification of the Pope as Antichrist', *Journal of Ecclesiastical History* 31 (1980).

Lamb, H., 'Osborne Reynolds, 1842–1912', *Proceedings of the Royal Society of London*, Series A, lxxxviii, London, 1913.

Lamb, J. (ed.), *A Collection of Letters, Statutes, and other Documents . . . illustrative of the History of the University of Cambridge during the period of the Reformation*, London, 1838.

Lamont, W. M., *Godly Rule*, London, 1969.

?Langbaine, Gerard, *The Foundation of the Universitie of Cambridge*, London, 1651 (*Thomason Tracts* E628(15)).

Laslett, P., *The World we have lost*, London, 1971.

Lawson, J., and Silver, H., *A Social History of Education in England*, London, 1973.

Leader, D. R., 'Professorships and Academic Reform at Cambridge: 1488–1520', *Sixteenth Century Journal* xiv (1983).

—— 'Philosophy at Oxford and Cambridge in the Fifteenth Century', *History of Universities* iv (1984).

—— 'Teaching in Tudor Cambridge', *History of Education* 13 (1984).

Lee, A. M., *A Scholar of a Past Generation. A Brief Memoir of Samuel Lee, D.D.*, London, 1896.

Lee, S., *Dissent Unscriptural and Unjustifiable*, Cambridge, 1834.

—— *Some Remarks on the Dean of Peterborough's Tract, entitled 'Thoughts on the Admission of Persons, without Regard to their Religious Opinions, to Certain Degrees in the Universities of England'*, Cambridge, 1834.

—— *Dissent Unscriptural and Unjustifiable, demonstrated in a Second Letter to John Pye Smith, D.D.*, Bristol, 1835.

Le Neve, John, *Fasti Ecclesiae Anglicanae* (ed. T. D. Hardy), Oxford, 1854.

Letters and Papers, Foreign and Domestic, of the Reign of Henry VIII, vol. viii, London, 1885.

Levinz, C., *Les Reports de Sir Creswell Levinz*, London, 1702.

Lloyd, David, *Memoires of the Lives, Actions, Sufferings & Deaths of those Noble, Reverend, and Excellent Personages that Suffered . . . In our late Intestine Wars, From the Year 1637, to the Year 1660*, London, 1668.

Loggins, V., *The Negro Author*, New York, 1931.

The London Evening Post.

Lovatt, R., 'John Blacman: biographer of Henry VI', in R. H. C. Davis and J. M. Wallace-Hadrill (eds.), *The Writing of History in the Middle Ages*, Oxford, 1981.

MacCaffrey, W. T., *Queen Elizabeth and the Making of Policy, 1572–1588*, Princeton, 1981.

McConica, J. K., *English Humanists and Reformation Politics under Henry VIII and Edward VI*, Oxford, 1968.

Macfarlane, A., *Reconstructing Historical Communities*, Cambridge, 1977.

McFarlane, K. B., *Wycliffe and English Non-Conformity*, London, 1972.

MacGibbon, D., *Elizabeth Woodville (1437–1492). Her Life and Times*, London, 1938.

McKean, C., *Architectural Guide to Cambridge and East Anglia since 1920*, London, 1982.

McKenzie, D. F., 'A Cambridge Playhouse of 1638', *Renaissance Drama* 3 (1970).

McLachlan, H., *English Education under the Test Acts*, Manchester, 1931.

Macleane, D., *A History of Pembroke College Oxford*, Oxford, 1897.

MacRae, D. G., *et al.*, 'The Culture of a Generation: Students and Others', *Journal of Contemporary History* 2 (1967).

McWilliams-Tullberg, R., *Women at Cambridge*, London, 1975.

Mandell, William, *The Origin and the End of our Christian Calling*, Cambridge, 1819.

—— *A Sermon preached before the University of Cambridge . . . on the occasion of the death of the Rev. Charles Simeon, M.A.*, Cambridge, 1836.

Mangan, J. A., *Athleticism in the Victorian and Edwardian Public School*, Cambridge, 1981.

—— ' "Oars and the Man": Pleasure and Purpose in Victorian and Edwardian Cambridge', *British Journal of Sports History* 1 (1984).

Marsh, H., *A Reply to the Strictures of the Rev. Isaac Milner, D.D.*, Cambridge, 1813.

Martin, D. (ed.), *Anarchy and culture. The problem of the contemporary university*, London, 1969.

Martin, K., *The British People and the General Strike*, London, 1926.

Marwick, A., *The Deluge. British Society and the First World War*, London, 1965.

Masson, D., *The Life of John Milton*, vol. i, London, 1859.

Masters, R., *Memoirs of the Life and Writings of the late Rev. Thomas Baker, B.D.*, Cambridge, 1784.

The Book of Matriculations and Degrees . . . from 1851 to 1900, Cambridge, 1902.

Matthews, A. G., *Calamy Revised*, Oxford, 1934.

Mayor, J. E. B. (ed.), *Cambridge under Queen Anne*, Cambridge, 1911.

Mills, L. J., *Peter Hausted. Playwright, Poet, and Preacher*, Indiana, 1944.

Milner, Isaac, *A Plan of a Course of Experimental Lectures introductory to the Study of Chemistry and other Branches of Natural Philosophy*, Cambridge, ?1780.

—— *A Plan of a Course of Chemical Lectures*, Cambridge, 1784.

—— *Strictures on some of the Publications of the Rev. Herbert Marsh, D.D.*, London, 1813.

(Milner/Eversden Papers): collection of printed pamphlets and broadsheets concerning the dispute between Queens' and Lord Hardwicke over the enclosures of Great and Little Eversden, 1810; housed in the Rare Books Room of the Cambridge University Library, call no. Cam.a.810.3.

Milner, M., *The Life of Isaac Milner, D.D., F.R.S.*, London, 1842.

Moberly, W., *The Crisis in the University*, London, 1949.

Monk, J. H., *The Life of Richard Bentley, D.D.*, London, 1833.

Dictionary Catalog of the Jesse E. Moorland Collection of Negro Life and History, Howard University Library, Washington, D.C., Boston (Mass.), 1970.

Moorman, J. R. H., *The Grey Friars in Cambridge, 1225 – 1538*, Cambridge, 1952.

Morgan, J., *Godly Learning*, Cambridge, 1986.

Morgan, V., 'Cambridge University and "The Country", 1560 – 1640', in L. Stone (ed.), *The University in Society*, vol. i, London, 1975.

Morison, S. E., *The Founding of Harvard College*, Cambridge (Mass.), 1935.

Moses, W. J., *Black Messiahs and Uncle Toms*, Pennsylvania State University Press, undated.

Mowat, C. L., *Britain Between the Wars, 1918 – 1940*, London, 1968.

Mullinger, J. B., *The University of Cambridge*, Cambridge, 1873 – 1911.

Myers, A. R., *England in the Late Middle Ages*, London, 1971.

Neal, D., *The History of the Puritans or Protestant Non-Conformists*, London, 1754.

Newbigin, J. E. L., *Unfinished Agenda. An Autobiography*, Grand Rapids, 1985.

The New Cambridge (1919).

Newman, J. H., *The Idea of a University*, Oxford, 1976.

Nias, J. C. S., *Gorham and the Bishop of Exeter*, London, 1951.

Niblett, W. R., *Universities Between Two Worlds*, London, 1974.

Nicholls, J. (ed.), *The Progresses, and Public Processions, of Queen Elizabeth*, London, 1788.

—— *Literary Anecdotes of the Eighteenth Century*, London, 1812 – 16 (facsimile edition, New York, 1966).

—— *Illustrations of the Literary History of the Eighteenth Century*, London, 1817 – 58 (facsimile edition, New York, 1966).

O'Day, R., *The English Clergy: The Emergence and Consolidation of a Profession, 1558 – 1642*, Leicester, 1979.

—— *Education and Society, 1500 – 1800*, London, 1982.

Ogg, D., *England in the Reign of Charles II*, Oxford, 1967.

Orpen, P. K., 'Schoolmastering as a profession in the sixteenth century: the career patterns of the grammar schoolmaster', *History of Education* 6 (1977).

Oswald, A., 'Andrew Doket and his Architect', *CAS Proceedings* xlii

(1949).

Owen, D. M., 'James Yorke, Bishop of Ely, 1781 – 1808', *Report of the Society of the Friends of St. George's and the Descendants of the Garter*, (1967 – 8).

Owen, D. M., and Leedham-Green, E.S., *'Useful and Picturesque Officers'. Catalogue of an exhibition of university archives relating to the Esquire Bedells, 22 – 27 July 1981*, Cambridge, 1981.

The Oxbridge Careers Handbook 1986, Oxford, 1985.

Palin, W., *The History of the Church of England from the Revolution to the last Acts of Convocation, A.D. 1688 – 1717*, London, 1851.

Palmer, Herbert, *The Necessity and Encouragement of Utmost Venturing for the Churches Help: Together with The Sin, Folly, and Mischief of Self-Idolizing*, London, 1643.

—— *The Glasse of Gods Providence towards his Faithfull Ones*, London, 1644.

—— *The Duty and Honour of Church-Restorers*, London, 1646.

?Palmer, Herbert, *Scripture and Reason Pleaded for Defensive Armes*, London, 1643.

Parker, I., *Dissenting Academies in England*, Cambridge, 1914.

Parker, Richard, *The History and Antiquities of the University of Cambridge*, London, 1721.

Parker, R., *Town and Gown*, Cambridge, 1983.

The Parliamentary History of England, London, 1807.

Parr, Richard, *The Life of the most reverend Father in God, James Usher, late Lord Bishop of Armagh*, London, 1686.

Pasquet, D. (transl. R. G. D. Laffan), *An Essay on the Origins of the House of Commons*, London, 1964.

Patrick, Simon, *A Brief Account of the new Sect of Latitude-Men, together with some reflections upon the New Philosophy*, London, 1662.

—— 'A Sermon preached at the funeral of Mr John Smith', in John Smith, *Select Discourses*, Cambridge, 1673.

—— *The Auto-Biography of Simon Patrick, Bishop of Ely*, Oxford, 1839.

Patrides, C. A., *The Cambridge Platonists*, Cambridge, 1980.

Pearson, H., *Memoirs of the Life and Writings of the Rev. Claudius Buchanan, D.D.*, Oxford, 1817.

Peck, E. S., 'John Francis Vigani, First Professor of Chemistry in the University of Cambridge (1703 – 12), and his Materia Medica Cabinet in the Library of Queens' College', *CAS Communications* 34 (1932 – 3).

Peile, J., *Christ's College*, London, 1900.

Pepys, S., *The Diary of Samuel Pepys* (ed. R. Latham and W. Matthews), vol. i, London, 1970.

Pevsner, N., *The Buildings of England: Cambridgeshire*, London, 1970.

Pfeiffer, R., *History of Classical Scholarship from 1300 to 1850*, Oxford,

1976.

Piggin, F. S., *Making Evangelical Missionaries 1789 – 1858*, Sutton Courtenay, 1984.

Plumptre, Robert, *Hints Respecting some of the University Officers*, London, 1802.

Pollock, J. C., *A Cambridge Movement*, London, 1953.

Porter, H. C., *Reformation and Reaction in Tudor Cambridge*, Cambridge, 1958.

'The Tudors and the North American Indian', Hakluyt Society, 1983.

Porter, H. C., and Thomson D. F. S. (eds.), *Erasmus and Cambridge*, Toronto, 1963.

Porter, R., *English Society in the Eighteenth Century*, London, 1982.

—— 'The Natural Sciences Tripos and the "Cambridge School of Geology", 1850 – 1914', *History of Universities* ii (1982).

Powicke, F. M., *The Cambridge Platonists*, London, 1926.

Proceedings of the Royal Society.

Pryme, G., *Autobiographic Recollections of George Pryme, Esq. M.A.*, Cambridge, 1870.

Prynne, William, *Canterburies Doome*, London, 1646.

Queens' College (college record).

Queens' College Appeal (pamphlet printed for the college, 1961).

Queens' College Record.

The Queens' Courier (college magazine).

Querela Cantabrigiensis: A Remonstrance by way of Apologie for the banished Members of the late flourishing University of Cambridge, Oxford, 1647.

Rackham, H. (ed.), *Thomas Cecil Fitzpatrick. A Memoir*, Cambridge, 1937.

—— 'Christ's College', in J. P. C. Roach (ed.), *VCH Cambridgeshire* iii. (1959).

Rashid, S., 'The Growth of Economic Studies at Cambridge: 1776 – 1860', *History of Education Quarterly* 20 (1980).

Raverat, G., *Period Piece: A Cambridge Childhood*, London, 1960.

Rawle, T., *Cambridge Architecture*, London, 1985.

Ray, J., *Further Correspondence of John Ray* (ed. R. W. T. Gunther), London, 1928.

Raymond, Sir Thomas (ed.), *The Reports Of divers Special Cases Adjudged in the Courts of Kings Bench, Common Pleas & Exchequer, In the Reign of King Charles II*, London, 1696.

Report of Her Majesty's Commissioners appointed to inquire into the State, Discipline, Studies, and Revenues of the University and Colleges of Cambridge, London (HMSO), 1852.

Report of the Commissioners appointed to inquire into the Property and Income of the Universities of Oxford and Cambridge, London (HMSO), 1874.

Royal Commission on Oxford and Cambridge Universities. Report, London (HMSO), 1922.

Reynolds, E. E., *St. John Fisher*, Wheathampstead, 1972.

Roach, J. P. C., 'Liberalism and the Victorian Intelligentsia', *Cambridge Historical Journal* xiii (1957).

—— 'The University of Cambridge' in Roach (ed.) *VCH Cambridgeshire*, vol. iii, London, 1959.

—— 'Victorian Universities and the National Intelligentsia', *Victorian Studies* iii (1959).

Robbins, L. C. (Lord), *The University in the Modern World*, London, 1966.

Robb-Smith, A. H. T., 'Medical Education in Cambridge before 1600', in A. Rook (ed.), *Cambridge and its Contribution to Medicine*, London, 1971.

Robinson, D., and Wildman, S., *Morris & Company in Cambridge*, Cambridge, 1980.

Rolleston, Sir H., *The Cambridge Medical School*, Cambridge, 1932.

Romilly, J., *Romilly's Cambridge Diary 1832 – 42* (ed. J. P. T. Bury), Cambridge, 1967.

Rook, A., 'Medicine at Cambridge 1660 – 1760', *Medical History* 13 (1969).

Rose, P. L., 'Erasmians and Mathematicians At Cambridge In The Early Sixteenth Century', *Sixteenth Century Journal* viii (1977).

Rosenthal, J. T., 'The Universities and the Medieval English Nobility', *History of Education Quarterly* ix (1969).

—— *The Purchase of Paradise*, London, 1972.

—— 'The Fifteenth-Century Episcopate: Careers and Bequests', in D. Baker (ed.), *Sanctity and Secularity: the Church and the World*, Oxford, 1973.

Ross, C., *Edward IV*, London, 1974.

—— *Richard III*, London, 1981.

Rothblatt, S., 'The Student Sub-culture and the Examination System in Early 19th Century Oxbridge', in L. Stone (ed.), *The University in Society*, Princeton, 1975.

—— *Tradition and Change in English Liberal Education*, London, 1976.

—— *The Revolution of the Dons*, Cambridge, 1981.

—— 'Failure in Early Nineteenth-Century Oxford and Cambridge', *History of Education* 11 (1982).

Royal Commission on Historical Monuments, *An Inventory of the Historical Monuments in the City of Cambridge*, London (HMSO), 1959.

Ruddock, E., *Arch Bridges and their Builders 1735 – 1835*, Cambridge, 1979.

Russell, C., *Parliaments and English Politics, 1621 – 1629*, London, 1979.

Russell, E., 'The influx of commoners into the University of Oxford before 1581: an optical illusion?', *English Historical Review* xcii (1977).

Rye, W., *An Index to Norfolk Pedigrees*, Norwich, 1896.

—— *A Calendar of the Feet of Fines for Suffolk*, Ipswich, 1900.

Ryle, H. E., *Physical Science and the First Chapter of Genesis. A Sermon Preached at St. Luke's Church, Liverpool, On Sunday, September 20, 1896 On the occasion of the Visit of the British Association to Liverpool*, London, 1896.

—— *On Holy Scripture and Criticism. Addresses and Sermons*, London, 1904.

—— *On the Church of England. Sermons and Addresses*, London, 1904.

—— *Remember the Days of Old. Sermon preached in Westminster Abbey before the Members of the International Historical Congress*, Oxford, 1913.

Saltmarsh, J., *King Henry VI and the Royal Foundations*, Cambridge, 1972.

Salzman, L. F., *Building in England Down to 1540*, Oxford, 1967.

Sanderson, M., *The Universities and British Industry, 1850–1970*, London, 1972.

Sandys, J. E., *A History of Classical Scholarship*, vol. ii, Cambridge, 1908.

Sargent, J., *The Life of the Rev. T. T. Thomason, M.A.*, London, 1833.

Saveson, J. E., 'The Library of John Smith the Cambridge Platonist', *Notes and Queries* cciii (1958).

Scarisbrick, J. J., *Henry VIII*, London, 1971.

Scarr, M. M., *The Queen's College of Saint Margaret and Saint Bernard commonly known as Queens' College in the University of Cambridge*, Cambridge, 1983.

Schneider, B. R., *Wordsworth's Cambridge Education*, Cambridge, 1957.

Sciama, L., 'Ambivalence and Dedication: Academic Wives in Cambridge University, 1870–1970', in H. Callan and S. Ardener (eds.), *The Incorporated Wife*, London, 1984.

Scriba, C. J. (ed.), 'The Autobiography of John Wallis, F.R.S.', *Notes and Records of the Royal Society* xxv (1970).

Scruggs, O. M., 'Crummell, Alexander', in R. W. Logan and M. R. Winston (eds.), *Dictionary of American Negro Biography*, New York, 1982.

Searle, W. G., 'Catalogue of the Library of Queens' College in 1472', *CAS Communications* ii (1864).

—— *The History of the Queens' College of St Margaret and St Bernard in the University of Cambridge. 1446–1662*, Cambridge, 1867–71.

Seaver, P. S., *The Puritan Lectureships*, Stanford, 1970.

Special Report from the Select Committee on the Oxford and Cambridge Universities Education Bill, London, 1867.

Seltman, C., 'Arthur Bernard Cook 1868–1952', *Proceedings of the British Academy* xxxviii (1952).

Shadwell, L. L., *Enactments in Parliament specially concerning the Universities of Oxford and Cambridge*, Oxford, 1912.

Sharpe, T., *Porterhouse Blue*, London, 1976.

Shelton, John, *An Answer To A Letter of Enquiry into The Grounds and Occasions of the Contempt of the Clergy*, London, 1671.

The 1/- Paper.

Shrewsbury, J. F. D., *A History of Bubonic Plague in the British Isles*, Cambridge, 1971.

Shuckburgh, E. S., *Emmanuel College*, London, 1904.

Siderfin, Thomas (ed.), *Les Reports des divers special Cases Argue & Adjudge en le Court del Bank le Roy . . . En les premier dix ans apres le Restauration del son Tres-Excellent Majesty Le Roy Charles le II*, London, 1683.

Simon, B., *A Student's View of the Universities*, London, 1943.

―――― *The Two Nations and the Educational Structure, 1780 – 1870*, London, 1974.

―――― *The Politics of Educational Reform, 1920 – 1940*, London, 1974.

Simon, J., 'Social Origins of Cambridge Students 1603 – 1640', *Past and Present* 26 (1963).

―――― *Education and Society in Tudor England*, Cambridge, 1967.

Skinner, Q., *The foundations of modern political thought*, Cambridge, 1978.

Smith, A., 'Private schools and schoolmasters in the Diocese of Lichfield and Coventry in the seventeenth century', *History of Education* 5 (1976).

Smith, G., *The Coronation of Elizabeth Wydeville*, Gloucester, 1975.

Smith, G. C. M., *College Plays performed in the University of Cambridge*, Cambridge, 1923.

Smith, G. R., *Without Touch of Dishonour. The Life and Death of Sir Henry Slingsby 1602 – 1658*, Kineton, 1968.

Smith, M. H., 'Some Humanist Libraries in Early Tudor Cambridge', *Sixteenth Century Journal* v (1974).

Smith, R. A., 'From quarter-deck to pulpit', *The Geographical Magazine* liv (1982).

Sparrow, Anthony, *A Sermon concerning Confession of Sinnes and the Power of Absolution*, London, 1637.

Speck, W. A., 'Conflict in Society', in G. Holmes (ed.), *Britain after the Glorious Revolution 1689 – 1714*, London, 1969.

―――― *Stability and Strife: England 1714 – 1760*, London, 1977.

Stamp, T., and Stamp, C., *William Scoresby, Arctic Scientist*, Whitby, 1975.

Standish, John, *A Vindication of the Clergy*, London, 1672.

Statuta Collegii Reginalis, Anno 1559 A Regis Commissariis Reformata, Cambridge, 1850.

Statutes of Queens' College, 1882, as altered 1891, 1893, 1897.

Statutes of Queens' College in the University of Cambridge, Cambridge, 1925.

Statutes of Queens' College in the University of Cambridge 1926 as amended

1933, Cambridge, 1937.

Stettin-Pomerania, Philip Julius, Duke of, 'Diary of the Journey of Philip Julius, Duke of Stettin-Pomerania, through England in the year 1602' (ed. G. von Bülow and W. Powell, *Transactions of the Royal Historical Society*, new series vi (1892).

Stokes, H. P., *Corpus Christi*, London, 1898.

—— *The Mediaeval Hostels of the University of Cambridge*, Cambridge, 1924.

Stone, L., *An Elizabethan: Sir Horatio Palavicino*, Oxford, 1956.

—— 'The Educational Revolution in England 1540 – 1640', *Past and Present* 28 (1964).

—— *The Crisis of the Aristocracy*, Oxford, 1965.

—— (ed.), *The University in Society*, Princeton, 1975 (includes essay by Stone on 'The Size and Composition of the Oxford Student Body 1580 – 1909').

—— *The Family, Sex and Marriage in England 1500 – 1800*, London, 1977.

—— 'Ages of admission to educational institutions in Tudor and Stuart England: a comment', *History of Education* 6 (1977).

—— 'The Age of Admission to College in Seventeenth-Century England', *History of Education* 9 (1980).

Stop Press.

The Student's Guide to the University of Cambridge, London and Cambridge, 1862 – 93.

The Student's Handbook to the University and Colleges of Cambridge, Cambridge, 1902 – 66.

Summerson, J., *Architecture in Britain 1530 to 1830*, London, 1963.

Surtz, E., *The Works and Days of John Fisher*, Cambridge (Mass.), 1967.

Szechenyi, Stephen, Count, 'A Hungarian Magnate at Cambridge in 1787' (ed. H. Marczali), *Cambridge Historical Journal* iii (1929).

Tanner, J. R. (ed.), *The Historical Register of the University of Cambridge*, Cambridge, 1917.

Thirsk, J. (ed.), *The Agrarian History of England and Wales*, vol. iv, Cambridge, 1967.

Thomas, K., *Religion and the Decline of Magic*, London, 1971.

Thomason Tracts, E115(10), *A True Relation of the late Expedition into Kent . . . As also Newes from Cambridge*, London, 1642.

—— E115(14), *A true Relation of the manner of taking of the Earl of Northampton, and 60 Cavaliers . . . Also the taking of the Earl of Carlile, Dr. Beale, Dr. Martin, and Dr. Sterne, by the Parliaments Forces sent to Cambridge on Tuesday last*, London, 1642.

—— E494(11), *The Publick Intelligencer*, July 7 – 14, 1656.

—— 669.f.6(75), *Remarkable Passages from Nottinghamshire, Lichfield, Leicestershire, and Cambridge*, London, 1642.

503

Thompson, P., *The Work of William Morris*, London, 1967.

The Times.

The Times Higher Educational Supplement.

Trio, P., 'Financing of University Students in the Middle Ages: a New Orientation', *History of Universities* iv (1984).

Tulloch, J., *Rational Theology and Christian Philosophy in England in the Seventeenth Century*, vol. i, Edinburgh, 1872.

Twigg, G. I., *The Black Death: a Biological Reappraisal*, London, 1984.

Twigg, J. D., 'The parliamentary visitation of the University of Cambridge, 1644 – 1645', *English Historical Review* xcviii (1983).

—— 'The Limits of "Reform": Some Aspects of the Debate on University Education during the English Revolution', *History of Universities* iv (1984).

Tyacke, N., 'Puritanism, Arminianism and Counter-Revolution', in C. Russell (ed.), *The Origins of the English Civil War*, London, 1975.

Underwood, M. G., 'The Lady Margaret and her Cambridge Connections', *Sixteenth Century Journal* xiii (1982).

J. Vaizey, untitled essay in Hayman (1977).

Varley, F. J., *Cambridge during the Civil War*, Cambridge, 1935.

Varsity.

Varsity Handbook, Cambridge, 1947/8-.

Venn, H., *Academical Studies subservient to the Edification of the Church. A Sermon preached in The Chapel of Queen's College, Cambridge*, Cambridge, 1828.

—— (ed.), *The Life and A Selection from the Letters of the late Rev. Henry Venn, M.A.*, London, 1834.

Venn, J., *Annals of a Clerical Family*, London, 1904.

—— *Early Collegiate Life*, Cambridge, 1913.

Venn, J., and Venn, J.A., *Alumni Cantabrigienses*, Part i, Cambridge, 1922 – 7; Part ii, Cambridge, 1940 – 54.

Venn, J. A., *A Statistical Chart to illustrate The Entries at the various Colleges in the University of Cambridge, 1544 – 1907*, Cambridge, 1908.

—— *Oxford and Cambridge Matriculations 1544 – 1906*, Cambridge, 1908.

—— ('A Correspondent'), 'The Manor Farm. A Long Record Ended', *The Times* 15.5.1940.

The Victoria History of the Counties of England: Cambridgeshire and the Isle of Ely (ed. J. P. C. Roach), volume iii, London, 1959.

The Victoria History of the Counties of England: Wiltshire (ed. D. A. Crowley), vol. xi, London, 1980.

Vincent, W. A. L., *The Grammar Schools. Their Continuing Tradition, 1660 – 1714*, London, 1969.

Walker, John, *The Sufferings of the Clergy duriing the Great Rebellion*, London, 1862.

Wall, A., *The Ceremonies observed in the Senate-House of the University of Cambridge* (ed. H. Gunning), Cambridge, 1828.

Warner, S. T., *T. H. White*, London, 1967.

Warren, W., *Warren's Book* (ed. A. W. W. Dale), Cambridge, 1911.

Watson, R., *Anecdotes of the Life of Richard Watson, Bishop of Landaff*, London, 1818.

Webster, C., *The Great Instauration*, London, 1975.

Weiss, R., *Humanism in England during the Fifteenth Century*, Oxford, 1967.

White, J. F., *The Cambridge Movement. The Ecclesiologists and the Gothic Revival*, Cambridge, 1962.

White, R. J., *Dr. Bentley. A Study in Academic Scarlet*, London, 1965.

White, T. H., *Darkness at Pemberley*, London, 1932.

—— *Mistress Masham's Repose*, London, 1947.

—— (ed. F. Gallix), *Letters to a Friend. The Correspondence between T. H. White and L. J. Potts*, Gloucester, 1984.

Who's Who.

Who Was Who.

Wight, J. A., *Brick Building in England from the Middle Ages to 1550*, London, 1972.

Williams, J. F., 'A Collection of Essex Deeds at Queens' College, Cambridge', *Transactions of the Essex Archaeological Society* xx part i, (1933)

—— 'A Marriage Register at Queens' College, Cambridge', *CAS Communications* xl (1939 – 42).

—— 'A Medieval Squabble', *ibid.* liv (1960).

Williams, R., *The Long Revolution*, London, 1961.

Williamson, R., 'The Plague in Cambridge', *Medical History* i (1957).

Willis, R., and Clark, J. W., *The Architectural History of the University of Cambridge*, Cambridge, 1886.

Winstanley, D. A., *Personal and Party Government*, Cambridge, 1910.

—— *The University of Cambridge in the Eighteenth Century*, Cambridge, 1922.

—— *Unreformed Cambridge*, Cambridge, 1935.

—— *Early Victorian Cambridge*, Cambridge, 1940.

—— *Later Victorian Cambridge*, Cambridge, 1947.

Winter, J. M., *The Great War and the British People*, London, 1985.

Wodehouse, L., *British Architects 1840 – 1976*, Detroit, 1976.

Wolffe, B., *Henry VI*, London, 1983.

Wood, C. T., *A Hebrew Grammar*, London, 1913.

—— 'The Message of the War to the Clergy', in J. Plowden-Wardlow, et al., *Religious Reconstruction After the War. A Cambridge Programme*, London, 1916.

—— *Death and Beyond*, London, 1920.

——— *The Life, Letters and Religion of St. Paul*, Edinburgh, 1925.

Wordsworth, C., *Social Life at the English Universities in the Eighteenth Century*, Cambridge, 1874.

——— *Scholae Academiae. Some Account of Studies at the English Universities in the Eighteenth Century*, London, 1968.

Worthington, John, 'To the Reader', in John Smith, *Select Discourses*, Cambridge, 1673.

Wright, A., *In Memoriam Herberti Flowers, Pensionarii, Ernesti Temperley, A.M., Socii, Thesaurii, Tutoris, Coll. Regin. in Cant.*, Cambridge, 1889.

——— *A Sermon preached by the Rev. Arthur Wright, M.A. . . . October 18th, 1891*, Cambridge, 1891.

——— *Some New Testament Problems*, London, 1898.

——— *A Synopsis of the Gospels in Greek*, London, 1906.

Wright, I. R., 'An Early Stage at Queens' ', *Cambridge* 18 (1986).

Wright, J. M. F., *Alma Mater; or, Seven Years at the University of Cambridge*, London, 1827.

Wrightson, K., *English Society 1580 – 1680*, London, 1982.

Yates, T. E., *Venn and Victorian Bishops abroad*, Uppsala, 1978.

Yorke, P. C., *The Life and Correspondence of Philip Yorke Earl of Hardwicke*, Cambridge, 1913.

Zweig, F., *The Student in the Age of Anxiety*, London, 1963.

Index

academic profession,
  debt to 'crisis of faith', 276
  increasing mobility, 389 – 90
accommodation,
  fellow-commoners, 94, 236
  graduate, 399n, 399 – 400, 400n
  licensed lodgings, 236 – 7
  scholars', 260
  students, 236 – 7, 314, 315, 371 – 3
  passim, 376
Act of Supremacy, 28, 29
administration of Queens' after
  Second World War, 364 – 6
admission of women, 434 – 43
admissions, 394 – 6, 408, 418
advowsons, 165, 166n, 277
aestheticism, 328 – 9
Agar, Thomas, 96
agriculture, 300, 302, 305, 308, 361
Alane, Alexander, 29
Aldrich, Robert, 99n
Alexander, H. C., 232
Allen, A. S., 19
Allington, Charles, 184n
almshouses, 121 *and* n, 315
Alsop, George, 36n
amenities,
  college bars, 410 *and* n, 413 – 14,
  417, 418, 431, 438
  discos, 410 *and* n
  laundrettes, 403, 413, 414, 418,
  428
  modernisation in early 20th century, 316
  telephone, 316
  wireless and television, 402
Anderson, Edward, 222
Andrew, Richard, 6, 118 – 19
Anglicanism, *see* Church of England
Anne, Queen, 136, 155
Anne Neville, Queen, 11 *and* n
anti-Semitism, 348
Appleby, Ambrose, 53n
architecture,

Cripps Court, 378
criticism of 18th century buildings, 313
Erasmus building, 374, 375 – 6
Fisher building, 372
free-standing ranges, 132
Gothic revival, 272, 313n
long gallery, 131 – 2
St John's Cripps building, 377
Aristotelian philosophy, 98, 99, 147
Arminianism, 43, 45
Armitage, A. ll., 376, 378n, 392, 407
Arnold, Thomas, 223, 253n, 262
Ascham, Roger, 137
athleticism (*see also* sport), 252 – 62
Atkinson, Solomon,
  complains against mathematical
  tripos, 209
  and county restrictions on fellowships, 176n
  critic of private tuition, 208
  Fellows' income, 187n
  on pensioners and fellow-commoners, 194n
  seeks admission to Cambridge,
  205
  takes physical exercise, 195
Austyn, Thomas, 83
Ayerst, William, 190
Aylesbury, countess of, 135
Aylmer, John, 36

Bailey, Sir Harold, 298
Ball, Thomas, 132
Bankes, Caleb, 135
Bankes, Sir John, 135
Bardsey, George, 166 – 7, 168
Barnes, George, 220
Barnes, William (matriculated 1596),
  87n
Barnes, William (matriculated 1634),
  87n
Barrow, Isaac, 210
Barry, Thomas, 118

Barton Road sports ground, 255, 361
Beaufort, Lady Margaret,
    and Bekynsaw, 19, 65
    divinity, 15
    education of Henry VIII, 28
    endowments and foundations, 14, 17
    and Fisher, 17, 67
    humanism, 14
    Queens' College, 12, 135 – 6
    St John's College, 17, 28
    visits Cambridge, 18
    and Wilkinson, 18
Bedle, Capel, 96
bedmakers, 91, 124, 402, 426 – 7
Beevor, Thomas, 274
Bekynsaw, Robert, 19 and n, 64n, 65, 66n, 67
Belk, Michael, 168
benefactions,
    for chapel, 164 – 5
    fellowships created from, 385
    gifts of money, 118
    land and property, 118 – 19, 301
    objects of use, 117 – 18
    for purchase of livings, 164
    to endow scholarships, 74
    to library, 384 and n
    to maintain fellowships, 74
benefices,
    see also properties and benefices of Queens' College
    choice of incumbents, 277
    ecclesiastical authorities' responsibility for, 170
    increase in number of, 166
    value in decline, 88n
Benson, E. W., 270n
Bentley, Richard, 157, 179, 216
Bernard Room (see also Erasmus Room), 248, 250, 279, 316, 332
Best, O. H., 318
Bibby, Cyril, 345, 436
Bible, Protestants and, 26 and n
Bible Society, 177
bible-clerks, 90n, 455
Bickersteth, Robert, 268
bicycles, 327 and n
Bigland, Edward (matriculated 1637), 87n
Bigland, Edward, (matriculated c. 1591), 87n
Bland and Brown, architectural partnership, 378 and n

Bland, Julian, 378n
Bligh, Reginald, 190, 191
Boat Club,
    after First World War, 326 – 7
    chapel attendance, 353
    during Second World War, 360
    Fellows' interest in, 257 – 8, 258n
    precarious position in 19th century, 253 – 4, 254n
    boat clubs, appeal for support, 259 – 60, 260n
Bodley, G. F., 275 and n, 277 and n, 314
books,
    Cambridge University well supplied with, 384n
    handwritten, 104
    and invention of printing, 88, 104
Booth, William, 6
Bourdillon, Thomas, 162
Bower, S. Dykes, 373 and n, 375
Bowett, D. W., 365 – 6, 387, 392, 424 and n
Bretton, Lawrence, 99
Brightman, Thomas, 40
British Association, 465
Browne, A. D., 331, 355, 389 and n
Brown, W. Wells, 270
Bryan, Richard, 53n, 93, 145, 146
Bryan, Samuel, 119
Bucer, Martin, 33
Buchanan, T. C., 240
Buchanan, Claudius, 267, 297n
Buckby, William (matriculated 1610), 87n
Buckby, William (matriculated 1651), 87n
Buckingham, George Villiers, 1st Duke of, 42, 43 and n, 44, 83
buildings of Queens' College,
    bridges, 133, 311 and n, 312n
    chapel, see separate entry
    Cloister Court, 421
    Cripps Court, 377 – 9, 410n, 432n, 432 – 3
    Doket building, 237, 315 – 16, 316n
    Erasmus building, 373 – 6, 402 – 3
    Essex building, 131, 312, 313, 369 – 70
    Fisher building, 332
    Fitzpatrick hall, 438
    Friars building, 235, 236, 314 – 15
    hall, 311, 313

long gallery, 131, 132, 370 – 71
new buildings since First World
War, 371 – 9
Old Court, 130, 263
president's lodge, 130 – 31, 370
repairs and restoration, 310,
313 – 14, 369 – 71
temporary structures, 133
Walnut Tree court, 131, 132 – 3,
261, 277n, 311, 355
Bull, M. M., 389
Bullock, Henry,
and Erasmus, 24
health, 136 – 7, 138
leave of absence, 83
lecturer in mathematics, 100
and Reformation, 26
Burghley, William Cecil, 1st baron,
68, 70, 71, 81, 85
Burrough, James, 311, 312
butler, college, 303
Butler Education Act, 394
Byron, George Gordon Byron, 6th
baron, 156n, 172 – 3, 173n

Caird, Rod, 425, 426 *and* n
Caius College,
abolition of restrictions on Fel-
lows, 225
Burrough, 311
Gooch, 157
Green, 211
hygiene, 138
provenance of students, 86n
Venn, 183, 332
Caius, John, 83n
Calvinism, 43 – 4
Cam, river, 131, 134
Cambridge,
Civil War, 49, 50
Evelyn *et al* quoted on, 137 – 8
Hungarian's comments on, 126
unhealthy atmosphere, 137
visit of Queen Anne, 155
Cambridge Appointments Board,
289n
Cambridge Architectural Society,
272 – 3, 274, 275
Cambridge Camden Society, 272
Cambridge Inter-Collegiate Christian
Union,
attitude to missionary work,
280 – 81
discourages chapel attendance,

392n
doctrinal position, 352
dons support, 283 *and* n, 284n
mission to the university, 351
significance in religious life of
university, 279 – 80
Cambridge Platonist movement, 57,
92, 147 – 8, 154
Cambridge University
Cambridge Platonism, 148, 154n
chambers, 94
Erasmus on, 22, 23
execution of Charles I, 60
expansion in 16th century, 131
finance, 59, 127, 366
foundation, 4
introduction of new Fellows and
heads of colleges, 54
Jacobites, 155
lack of formal entrance procedure
in 18th century, 204 – 5
Lady Jane Grey, 35
lectureships, 15, 99
Earl of Manchester and, 55
loyalty to crown, 57, 150, 155, 160
mid-15th century population, 86n
mobility of Fellows, 78
national significance in 16th century, 67
petition against drainage of fens,
134
philosophy, 102
plague outbreaks, 139
poor rate on colleges, 59
professorships, 33, 102
provenance of students, 86
and Restoration, 141, 142
Richard III, 11
royal visits, 38, 136, 157
study of mathematics, 100
visitations, 29 – 30
well supplied with books, 384n
Whiggism 156 *and* n, 159
Cambridge University, religion,
Anglicanism, 143
Bible Society, 177
Catholic ceremonial under Mary
Tudor, 35
evangelical movement, 176
high church movements, 44, 148,
162
Lutheranism, 26
parliament examines state of, 47
Presbyterianism, 40

509

Protestantism, 35, 36, 38 – 9, 43
Puritanism, 41
Reformation, 28, 34
religious life in later 19th century,
276
Roman Catholicism, 151
Uniformity Act, 143 – 4
university preacher, 15
Cambridge University in wartime
Civil War, 48, 51, 52 – 3
evacuees in Second World War,
358
French Revolution, 159
Napoleonic Wars, 159, 160
O.T.C., 318, 319
prepared for Second World War,
355
Wars of the Roses, 7
Campaign for Nuclear Disarmament,
406
Campion, W. M.,
and Boat Club, 257
and Cambridge Architectural
Society, 274
dismisses immorality, 265
and educational reform, 291, 292
parochial work, 228
Queens' chapels, 274, 277
reform of conditions of fellowships, 224, 225, 226
religion, 282n, 286
restoration of St Botolph's, 273n
and St Bernard Society, 242
and students, 236 – 7, 241
subscriptions to sports clubs, 259
and value of Cambridge BA
degree, 242
and Wright, 227
Capel, Gamaliel, 85
Capel family, 93, 453
careers, 397 – 8
Carlyle, Joseph, 214n, 297
Cartesianism, 212
Cartwright, Thomas, 39 and n, 40
Cassels, H. K., 340
catering,
proposed undergraduate kitchen
committee, 334
Queens' food, 334n
student complaints about, 333,
414, 427, 428, 430
Catharine of Aragon, Queen,
Bekynsaw, 65
and Lambert, 79

marriage, 27, 28
precautions to avoid plague, 139
and Queens' College, 136
Catherine Parr, Queen, 32, 33
Caxton, William, 8
Cecil, William, 1st baron Burghley,
68, 70, 71, 81, 85
celibacy, 187 – 8, 225
Central Electricity Generating Board,
387
Chaderton, William, provenance,
64n
Chaderton, Wm,
bishop, 40, 64n, 66, 68
and Presbyterianism, 39 and n
president, 41, 70
president's lodgings, 72
and Rockrey, 40 and n
theologian, 67
chairs, 213, 214, 218
chancellors of the University,
Cromwell, 29
Fisher, 16 – 17
Gardiner, 31, 35
Gloucester, 177
Manchester, 60
Monmouth, 150
Newcastle, 156, 158
non-resident, 18
Northumberland, 35
St John, 60
Somerset, 33
chantries, 3 – 4, 117
Chantries Act, 32, 33
chapel, Queens' College,
in 18th century, 165
at Restoration, 143
benefactions, 117 – 18, 119, 164 – 5
burial vault beneath, 165
choirboys and organ scholar, 360
choral services reintroduced, 274
conversion into undergraduate
library, 278, 384
importance in Queens' devotional
life, 282
new chapel, 277n, 277 – 8, 282,
315
renovations and improvements,
164 and n
restoration, 273 – 4, 275, 277, 282,
373
restoration fund, 274
stained glass, 274 – 5
wedding services, 165 and n

chapels, high church movement and decoration of, 46
chaplains, 283 *and* n, 393
Chapman, Thomas, 88
Charles I,
  Arminianism, 43
  and Buckingham, 44
  Cambridge loyal to, 48
  and Capel, 85
  Civil War, 48
  execution, 60
  Queens' play performed before, 107
  and Roberts, 83n
  visits Cambridge, 48
Charles II,
  and college elections, 61
  and Davies, 157n
  demonstrations of loyalty, 150–51
  and James, 149
  mandates, 150
  permits limited freedom of worship, 143
  recommends Crawley, 150
  Restoration, 141, 142
  and Sparrow, 146, 148
  visits Queens', 136
Charles Stuart, Prince (*later* Charles I, *q.v.*), 127
Chase, F. H.,
  bishop of Ely, 258, 282
  involvement in religious activities, 283
  president, 229, 230
  and success of Queens', 235
  theologian, 285 *and* n, 297
Chase, Mrs F. H., 258
choristers, 265
Christian Union, Queens' College, 249, 261, 322
Christ's College,
  Fisher, 18, 19
  foundation of, 14
  gate tower, 130
  Lady Margaret Beaufort, 19
  permission for marriage of Fellows, 225
  well endowed, 116
Church of England,
  39 Articles, 163–4, 173
  Act of Supremacy, 28, 29
  Anglicanism at Restoration, 144
  Cartwright attacks, 39

Civil War, 51
conservatism, 162
evangelicalism, 173, 176–7
high church, 44, 46, 51, 144, 156, 162, 271–5
'higher criticism', 283, 284, 286
low church, 162
oath to royal supremacy, 34
prayer book, 33, 34
'Protestation' oath, 48
Queens' College, 45
return to Anglicanism, 143
strength of loyalty to, 151
Tory ideology and, 156
Westminster Assembly of Divines, 54
Wilberforce, 177
Church Missionary Society, 267
church, the,
  medieval concern for well-being, 10
  opportunity for advancement, 89–90
  university-trained men in cathedral positions, 90
cinema, 339
Civil War, 300, 304
Clare, countess of, 2
Clark, John, 227 *and* n
Clarke, Samuel, 56
clergy,
  demand for educated, 78
  demand for graduates, 90
  Fellows of Queens', 36, 37
  marriage permitted, 72
  Reformation, 27, 30
  subscription to 39 Articles, 163
  surplus in 18th century, 166
  taxation, 28, 29
  Uniformity Act, 144
  and university endowment, 117
Cleworth, T. H., 246
Clopton, Poley, 216n
clubs,
  see also Boat Club, Kangaroos *and* Societies
  Amalgamated Clubs, 254, 360
  Cherubs, 251 *and* n, 335, 339, 340, 352
  Chess, 255n
  Conservative, 346, 348
  dining, 250, 262, 442
  Phoenix, 345, 353, 437n
  'Ping-Pong', 255n

'Representative Committee' and United Clubs, 333
Rugby, 360
Socialist, 346, 348, 353, 359
subscriptions to sports, 259
university athletics, 258,
Walnut Tree Club, 264
Coates, W. M.,
  bursar, 309n
  committed Christian, 282n
  Conservative, 232
  involvement in religious activities, 283 *and* n
  mathematician, 299
  rugby player, 258
  and undergraduates, 229
coffee houses, 194
Coke, Henry, 119
Coldham, John, 52, 53n, 58
Cole, William, 311
Colet, John, 21
college community, 330 – 34
college offices,
  bursars, 303, 364, 365, 366
  dean, 412
  domus officer, 366 *and* n
  high steward, 363
colleges,
  academic obligations of fellow-commoners, 207
  advowsons, 165
  annual examinations introduced, 205
  arrival of upper classes, 89
  benefactions, 117
  buildings before 17th century, 94n
  buy up livings, 166
  chapels, 273
  community life, 403
  contributions to university expenditure, 295 – 6
  Erasmus on, 22
  exchange teaching arrangements among, 386
  family connections, 87
  growing popularity, 88n
  information for students, 235 *and* n
  libraries, 104 – 5
  medieval, 5, 104
  plays, 106, 107
  poor rate on, 59
  in reign of Elizabeth I, 67
  table showing numerical size of,

450
  town and, 126 – 9
  tutors, 91, 189
  visiting royalty and nobles, 135
Collyngwood, Roger, 83, 100
combination rooms, 183 *and* n
commencement, 97
Cook, A. B.,
  classicist, 298, 382
  evangelical, 282n
  interest in ancient religious beliefs, 298
  participates in debates, 231n
  and Quaerists, 249
  traveller, 228n
Corpus Christi College,
  boat club combines with Queens', 360
  Jegon, 92
  Parker, 32
  Queens' sells land to, 308n
  St Bernard's Hostel, 5, 111
  and St Botolph's, 5, 166, 277n
Cotton, John, 42
Covel, William, 39, 40 – 41
Cox, Thomas, 58
Cox, William, 85n
Craforth, John, 82
Cranmer, Thomas, 28
Crawford, Charles, 163, 200n, 200 – 201
Cripps, C. Humphrey, 377
Cripps Foundation, 377, 439
Cromwell, Oliver, 49, 58, 61
Cromwell, Richard, 61 – 2
Cromwell, Thomas, 29, 31, 35n
Cromwellian Protectorate, 141
Crowland, John, 78n
crown,
  and Dissolution, 30, 31, 32
  and elections to fellowships, 79 – 80, 189
  and leases of Queens' property, 116
  and maintenance of orthodoxy, 144 – 5
  mandates, 149 – 50, 151, 180n
  and presidential elections, 145 – 6, 148, 149, 179
  Queens' loyalty to, 155
  quit-rents, 35
  Reformation, 27
Crownfield, Henry, 190
Crummell, Alexander,

friends and patrons, 270 – 71
history, 268 – 70
literary works, 269n
to visit Liberia, 271n
Cummins, William, 96 – 7
curriculum (*see also* studies), 206, 208,
210, 380 – 84

Dampier, Thomas, 177
Darwinism, 276
Daubuz, Charles, 121
Davenant, Edward, 80, 83, 101, 102
Davenant, John,
admitted to fellowship, 81 – 2
bishop, 64n, 76
and Fuller, 82
gifts and bequests, 105, 166
origins, 64n
president, 43, 66 *and* n, 69 *and* n,
75, 81 – 2, 133
and Preston, 92n
theologian, 67
Davies, John,
appreciation of, 217n
classicist, 216, 217
president, 157, 180
Whig, 157
Davies, Richard,
advocates reform, 204, 218
critical of quality of medical teaching, 215
and holy orders, 168 – 9
interest in medicine and science,
212
and outside interference in elections, 189
and psychological consequence of
sizarship, 192
and tenure of fellowships, 185
debate, *see* St Bernard Society
Defoe, Daniel, 126
degree-taking, 456
degrees, 98, 103, 288, 434 – 5, 444
demonstrations,
in Cloister Court, 420 – 21
Garden House riot, 424 – 5
political, 405
students defy proctorial ban on,
409
dining, change in dining habits, 255
discipline, 263 – 5
gate regulations, 266
proposed standing committee on,
408

Queens' tightens up, 341
sports believed to promote, 256
students in lodgings, 236
disputations, 208, 209, 218
dissenting academies, 154 *and* n
dissolution of the monasteries,
30 – 31
Dixon, Henry, 239
dogs, 195
Doket, John, 5, 14
Doket, Andrew,
donates land, 6
and Elizabeth Woodville, 6, 9
Houses of York and Lancaster, 10
MA, 64n
president, 64 – 6 *passim*
Queens' College, 6, 9, 129
recommends successor, 66
rector of St Botolph's, 5, 6, 65,
169n
St Bernard's College, 3n
St Bernard's Hostel, 5
social origin, 6n
townsmen help, 126
Dowsing, William, 51
drama, 15th – 17th centuries, 106 – 9
dress,
of aesthetes, 328, 329
fellow-commoners' academic, 94,
196
livery of Queens' porter, 124
students' demands and complaints, 333, 411, 412
Drewell, John, 111
drink,
drunkenness, 262 *and* n
hard-drinking sportsmen, 261
new interest in, 220n
Drinkwater, G. C., 371 – 2, 373n
drug abuse, 413
Duffield, Thomas, 118
Dyer, George, 19n, 173

Eachard, John, 163
Eate, Thomas, 123
Eban, Abba, 335, 336, 348, 383
ecclesiastical offices held by former
students of Queens', 454
Ecclesiological Society, 272, 275
economics group, Queens', 404
Eden, Richard, 101
educational reform,
in 19th century, 287 – 9
at Queens', 290 – 96

Edward IV, 2, 3, 5, 8, 10
Edward VI, 33, 34, 35
Edwards, Thomas, 44, 136, 165
elections,
    disputed, 190, 221, 225n
    government interference, 61
    for vice-chancellorships, 156
Elizabeth, the Queen Mother, 375,
    403
Elizabeth I, 80, 136
    marriage of Fellows, 72
    religion in reign of, 37 – 41
    visits Cambridge, 38, 107
Elizabeth Woodville, Queen, 3n,
    8 – 9, 9n, 10, 11, 118
Elizabeth of York, Queen, 12, 79
Ely, Reginald, 6, 130
Emmanuel College, 39, 42, 57, 93,
    132n
employees of Queens', and free col-
    lective bargaining, 417
enclosure of property, 302 – 3, 305,
    308
English   Revolution   (1640 – 60),
    47 – 52, 108
episcopacy,
    abolished, 62
    Cambridge men, 17
    parliament and abolition of, 47
    parliament hopes to replace, 52
    and university endowment, 117
Erasmus, Desiderius, 19 – 24
    Fisher and, 17
    Greek scholar, 31
    ill health, 138
    and Luther, 25
    popular author, 16
    and Reformation, 26
    Renaissance humanism, 13
Erasmus Room, 332, 414, 428
Essex, James, the younger, 164, 165,
    311, 312
Essex, Robert Devereux, earl of, 35n,
    107, 135
Etheridge, William, 311
Eton College, 2nn, 5, 8
evangelicalism,
    attitude to learning, 176
    Bible Society a threat to, 177
    in decline, 178, 267
    hostility to, 214
    intolerance, 172
    Mandell, 220
    and Methodism, 173

and missionary work, 280
and Oxford Movement, 272
Pitt and, 176
in Queens', 163, 170 – 75 passim,
    178, 220, 267, 268, 270, 280
reactionary doctrine, 171
unpopularity of, 173
examinations,
    entrance scholarships, 239n
    preliminary, 295
    Previous, 294
    Queens' fellowship, 225 and n
    Queens' holds annual, 205
    university entrance, 292
exeats, students protest against
    applications for, 412
exhibitions, 238, 239 and n, 381

Fairclough, Samuel, 42
family connections with Queens',
    table of, 452 – 3
Fane William, 48
Farish, Charles, 168, 187, 188
Fawcett, W. M., 314, 315
Fawkes, Guy, 46
Fawne, John, 15, 85n, 99
feasts, 104, 305, 307n, 440
fellow-commoners,
    in 18th century, 193 – 4
    academic obligations of, 207
    accommodation, 94, 236
    Atkinson on, 194n
    in decline, 262
    degrees, 104
    examinations, 217
    fees raised, 305
    gowns, 94
    indiscipline, 196
    numbers decrease, 238
    ostentatious and expensive life of,
    196
    percentage of student population,
    194n
    private dinners, 198
    and prize in 'morals', 201
    proportion graduating, 207
    recreations, 195
    resigning Fellows admitted as,
    186, 187
Fellows,
    see also fellowships
    accepted character of, 183, 220,
    223, 231
    administration of Queens', 365

career expectations, 187
changing character of, 390
Christian commitment, 282
clerical qualification, 215, 218, 224, 226
college benefices, 167 – 9, 168n, 277
in debt, 187n
disputes at Queens' in 19th century, 221 – 3
duties, 74, 165
election, 225n
financial problems in maintaining, 386 – 8
gate regulations, 266
'higher criticism', 283
increase in numbers, 365, 382
indisciplined behaviour, 184
intruded Fellows at Restoration, 142, 146
involvement in sport, 257, 259
marriage restrictions lifted, 224, 226
non-resident, 185 – 6, 224, 226
oaths binding, 83 – 4, 155
politics, 232
as private tutors, 208
quarrels and misdemeanours, 84 – 5
of Queens', 183 – 91 *passim*, 220 – 23, 227 – 9, 232, 429
Queens' library, 105
reinstatement of ejected, 142
remuneration, 186 – 7
restrictions, 82, 84, 86, 189, 224
and 'Revolution of the Dons', 297
seek college privileges for their wives, 440
serve parishes close to Cambridge, 170
and Sex Discrimination Act, 441
and students, 231, 232, 403, 418
table of Fellows ejected in parliamentary purge, 446
and university teaching appointments, 386 *and* n
walking on the lawns, 422
war service, 356
women, 441, 442
fellowships,
see also Fellows
abolition of clerical restrictions, 276
Bye-fellowships, 185n

elections to, 78, 79 – 81, 209
eligibility for, 74 – 5
length of tenure, 185, 224 – 5, 225n, 78, 226
mathematics tripos, 189
new measures transform, 226
in new or reformed subjects, 381
numerical expansion slows down, 385
predominant disciplines in early 20th century, 292
reasons for resigning, 187
reforms in 19th century, 225
research, 388
seniority, 85n
sequestration of, 302 *and* n, 304, 305, 307, 309, 313
stipends and fees, 75 – 6
teaching, 381 – 2, 382n
vacant on financial grounds, 165
finance,
in 17th century, 300, 301 – 2
in 18th century, 300 – 301, 313
in 19th century, 304 – 9
allowances during times of plague, 139 – 40
books, 384
building and renovations, 133, 164, 312, 371, 372 *and* n, 373 *and* n, 374, 376
Civil War, 58 – 60
college servants, 123 *and* n, 124, 140
colleges, 58 – 60, 75 *and* n, 89, 110, 127, 295
Corn Rent Act, 112
cost of reception of Charles I, 136
dean of Queens', 165n
degree fees, 88
endowment income, 366 – 7
failure to graduate, 104
fellow-commoners, 196
Fellows, 75 – 6, 83, 386 – 8
funding from industry, 387
grants, 335
heads of colleges, 58
investment in land, 300 – 301
kitchen charges, 427 *and* n, 430, 432
levies on college lands, 127
'New System', 235
payment in kind, 112 – 13
pensioners, 196
price of property in Cambridge,

399 – 400
prosperity under Tudors and early Stuarts, 111
Queens' debts, 303
Queens' during First World War, 321
Queens' estates and revenues, 110 – 11
Queens' president, 58, 65 *and* n
Queens' War Reserve Fund, 361 – 2
rack renting, 306
renewal fines, 300, 301n, 304
rent strike, 430
rewards for recovery of stolen goods, 128
river dredging, 134
scholars and scholarships, 90, 91 *and* n, 238, 295
since end of First World War, 366 – 8
students, 93n, 239, 240, 335, 428, 430
students agitate against investment in South Africa, 424, 426
tables of income and expenditure, 16th – 18th centuries, 457 – 8
taxation, 303 – 4, 304n
tutorial fees, 295
university controls price levels, 127
university exemption from taxes, 159 – 60
fire,
    precautions against, 127
    watchmen, 125
fireworks, 263
First World War, 317 – 21 *passim*
Fisher, John,
    academic career, 16 – 19
    bishop, 64n
    chancellorship, 13
    Christ's College, 14, 19
    and Erasmus, 21, 22, 23
    execution, 28, 29, 35n
    humanism, 14, 15, 17, 99
    and Lady Margaret Beaufort, 14, 17, 67
    lodges at Queens', 65, 135
    and Luther, 25
    origins, 64n
    president, 67
    St John's College, 14, 19, 28
Fisher, Robert, 20

Fitzalan Henry, 89 *and* n
Fitzpatrick, T. C. and Queens' College Christian Union, 351
Fitzpatrick Memorial Hall, 332, 333n
Fitzpatrick, T.C., 330n
    and admission of McGowan, 395
    attitude to defence, 342
    chapel attendance, 278n
    Cripps Court JCR, 378n
    death of, 391, 392
    and First World War, 324 *and* n
    gifts and bequests to Queens', 369n, 386n, 390
    interest in college games, 258 *and* n
    involvement in religious activities, 283 *and* n
    ordained, 282n
    personality and interests, 231n, 390
    president, 229, 230 – 31
    and Queens' finances, 367n
    social outlook, 242
Fitzpatrick, Mrs T. C. 319
Fletcher, N. C., 264
floods, 125, 133 – 4
Forman, Thomas, 27
Fortrey, James, 135n
Framlingham, William, 24
Franklyn, William, 64n
Freer, Michael, 60n, 142
French Revolution, 160
    effect on freedom of debate, 177
    effect on political attitude of university, 232
    effect on reformist ideals, 159
    and evangelicalism, 173, 174
    political economy associated with, 218
Frend, William, 160, 160 – 61, 162
freshmen, 'contact' scheme, 429 *and* n
Fuller, Thomas, 57, 72, 82, 216n

gambling, 256
Garden House riot, 424 – 5
gardens, 131, 133, 355
Gardiner, Stephen, 31 – 2, 35
Garret, Robert, 137
gate regulations, 428 *and* n
    apply to students and Fellows, 266
    no agitation against, 334
    reformed, 411n, 412

student protest against, 415
undergraduate's accident, 334n, 411
undergraduates press for abolition, 266, 411
General Strike (1926), 343 – 4
George I, 156, 157
Gerey, George, 151
Geyer, J. B., 403
Gibbs, James, 311
Gibson, S. T., 274
Gibson, William, 227
Gilson, Younge, 198
Girton College, 387, 435, 436, 437 *and* n
Gloucester, William Frederick, 2nd duke of, 177 *and* n
Gloucester, Humphrey, duke of, 14
Gloucester, Richard, duke of (*later* Richard III, *q.v.*), 74
Glynn, William, 35, 37 *and* n, 64 *and* n, 66
Godfrey, Henry, 165n, 220, 221, 222 – 3, 267
Godfrey Mitchell Charitable Trust, 386n
Gonville College, 86n
Gooch, Thomas, 157
Goren, J. N., 274
Gorham, George C., 207n, 214, 268
governing body of Queens',
calls for closer relationship with College Union, 418
catering, 427 – 8
delaying tactics, 418
efforts to deal with undergraduate discontent, 409, 410 – 11, 414
and Garden House riot, 426
gate restrictions, 428n
and inspection of accounts by students, 430
and JCR, 415
measures to deals with student revolt, 421 – 2
opposed to students' open meetings, 422
proposed reform of, 408, 417 – 18
responsibility to students in event of law-breaking, 413
and Sex Discrimination Act, 441
and student representation on, 420, 422, 423, 428, 431 – 2
students and voting rights, 433n

undergraduate accommodation, 428n
and women guests, 423, 439
graffiti, 263n
Grand Remonstrance (1641), 47
grand tour, 154, 194
Gray, Thomas, 181, 189, 212
Gray, J.H.,
attitude of students to, 330
classicist, 258n, 299, 382
Conservative, 232
date of death, 330n
and expansion at Queens', 134 – 5
and Harrison, 380 – 81
his history, 228
and increase in student numbers, 257n
lecturer in history, 292n
and missionary work, 281
ordained, 228, 282n
relationship with undergraduates, 232, 331
sport and athletics, 257 *and* n, 258 *and* n, 259
and student misdemeanours, 265
Great St Mary's Church, 45
Green, George, 211
Greville, Sir Fulke, 76
Grey, Lady Jane, 35, 36
Grey, Sir John, 8
Grimston, William, 123
Grindal, Edmund, 115
guests,
call for extension of visiting hours, 416
evangelicals' attitude to, 429 – 30
overnight guests permitted, 429
regulations, 428
Guild of St Bernard, 350
Guilford, E. L., 260 – 61
Gunning, Henry, 159, 160 – 1

Haddon, John, 60n
Hadley, John, 212 – 13
Hammond, John, 164 *and* n
Harding, Gilbert,
eccentricity, 328
and General Strike, 343 – 4
his bedmaker, 402
on his time at Cambridge, 337
indigence, 335
influenced by CICCU, 351 – 2
joins Guild of St Bernard, 350n

517

old school tie, 335 – 6
on Sleeman, 332n
Hardwicke, Philip Yorke, 1st earl of, 158, 180, 181
Hardwicke, Philip Yorke, 2nd earl of, 158, 159
Hardwicke, Philip Yorke, 3rd earl of, 302
Hare, C. G., architect, 315, 371
Harrison, G. B., 255 – 6, 326, 380 – 81, 435 – 6
Harrison, William, 41
Hart, H. St J., 359, 389
Harvey, John, 102
Harvey, William, 101
Hausted, Peter, 45, 47 and n, 107 – 8
heads of colleges,
    increased stipends, 58
    permitted to marry, 72
    in service of state, 68
    status and power in 16th century, 67, 71 – 3
health and disease, 136 – 40
    plague, 22, 50, 121, 139
Henley Regatta, 325 – 6, 326n
Henry V, 8
Henry VI, 139
    Cambridge colleges, 1 – 2, 3, 6, 7 – 8
    Old Court, 130
    and Queens' College, 4, 7, 118, 135, 136
    scholar and theologian, 8
    and Wars of the Roses, 7
Henry VII, 10, 11 – 12, 17, 18, 135
Henry VIII,
    and Catharine of Aragon, 27
    and Catherine Parr, 33
    college incomes, 32
    death of, 33
    diplomacy and religious orthodoxy, 27
    Fisher and, 17
    humanists and, 21
    lodges at Queens', 135, 136
    Reformation, 27 – 8
    Regius professorships, 31
    taxation of clergy, 29
Herbert, George, 137
heresy, 4
Hewitt, George, 175 and n, 221
Heynes, Simon,
    authority, 70
    dispute with Maxwell, 84

marries, 72
prayer book, 34
president, 116n
Protestant, 27
Reformation, 28
in service of state, 65, 68
and town, 127
high table, 440 and n
Hills, Heigham, 53n
Hoare, John, 60n
Holder, Herbert, 427 and n
Holland, Henry Rich, 1st earl of, 80
Holy Trinity Church, 42, 46, 127n, 177
Hooper, H. D., 261
Horne, Thomas, 270
Horton, Thomas,
    oath of Engagement, 60
    petitions Cromwell, 58
    and Pindar, 61
    preacher, 62
    Presbyterianism, 62
    president, 57
    and Restoration, 62n, 141
    university visitor, 61
    withdraws from presidency, 142, 144
hostels, medieval, 4 – 5
Howard, Ephraim, 152 and n
Hubbersty, John, 221, 222
Huddleston, George, 52
Hughes, David
    benefactions and bequests, 203, 206 – 7, 301n, 384n
    Newcastle and, 158
    opposed to loyal address, 159n
humanism,
    16th century ruling classes, 88
    Bullock, 24
    and Dissolution, 30
    and drama, 106, 108
    Erasmus, 21, 24
    Fisher, 17
    Queensmen, 99
    and religious reform, 25
    Renaissance, 13 – 16
    and scholasticism, 103
Humphrey, duke of Gloucester, 14
Huntingdon, Theophilus Hastings, 7th earl of, 151n
hygiene,
    baths, 316 and n
    medieval sanitation, 138
    water closets, 261, 316

independent schools *see also* public
  schools *and* state schools, 394 – 5
indiscipline, 198 – 201
Ingaldesthorpe, Lady Joan, 75
Ingram, George, 464 – 5
Ingram, Robert, 174 – 5, 209, 218
interviews, for admission of candidates, 294
Isham, Gregory, 80

Jackson, John, 60n
Jacobinism, 155, 172, 174, 176
Jacombe, Samuel, 62 *and* n, 63n, 79n
James, Henry,
  and accession of William and
    Mary, 152
  bequest, 168n
  chamber pot for Caroline of Ans-
    pach, 136n
  character, 149, 179 *and* n, 180n,
    280
  defender of orthodoxy, 149 *and* n
  divinity chair, 164n
  financial adminstration, 300, 301,
    301 – 2, 304n
  moderator, 203
  nepotism, 190
  president, 148, 149, 157, 179 – 80
  receives Queen Anne, 155
  unmarried, 180
  visit from clergyman, 204 – 5
James I,
  and election of Queens' presi-
    dent, 69
  excessive use of mandates, 81
  levies feudal aids, 304n
  policy of religious comprehen-
    sion, 44
  Queens' play performed before,
    107
  supports Davenant's resignation,
    80
James II, 151
Jebb, John, 217
Jee, Joseph, 220, 222, 236, 303, 305
Jegon, John, 92 *and* n
Jennyn, John, 66n, 69 – 70
Jessop, G. L. O., 350
Jesus College,
  building materials, 130
  Civil War, 49
  rowing, 256
  theology, 10, 104
  Venn, 189

John XXII, Pope, 4
Johns, C. H. W., 283, 298
Johnson, William, 108
Jones, Ralph, 85
Jordan, Thomas, 171n
Josselin, John, 75, 119
Junior Common Room,
  Bernard Room adapted for, 332,
    and n
  committee, 407, 408, 409, 414 – 17
    passim, 428
  issue of co-residence, 438, 439
  newsletter, 428
  preoccupations since student
    revolt, 432
  and problem of communication
    with senior members, 415
  result of opening, 431 – 2
  'Stag Night', 441
  students appreciate, 332 – 3
justices of the peace, 127

Kangaroos,
  in 1920s, 339 *and* n
  activities, 250
  aim of, 250n
  deterioration in tone of, 340, 341
  during First World War, 318 *and* n
  earliest surviving minutes book,
    250n
  in early 20th century, 251n
  gambling proscribed, 256n
  Laffan visits, 331
  Sabbath day observance, 279n
  and St Bernard Society, 251
  standard of behaviour after
    Second World War, 401
  and women, 436n
Kelland, Philip, 296
Kemp, Edward, 46, 53n, 149n,
    164 – 5
Kennett, R. H.,
  dates, 330n
  and First World War, 323 – 4
  involvement in religious activi-
    ties, 283
  Old Testament critic, 283 – 4
  ordained, 282n
  personality, 229
  professor of Hebrew, 298 *and* n
  university sermon, 336
Kidman, Richard, 128 – 9
King, Richard, 138
King, Joshua,

Atkinson on, 211–12
attracted by evangelicalism, 268
mathematician, 211
president, 223, 391
suffers stroke, 274 *and* n
Tory, 232
vetoes admission of non-conformists, 271, 276
King's College, 88
aim of foundation, 1–2
Andrew Doket, 6
Edward IV, 8
Ely, 130
John Doket, 5, 14
lords of misrule, 106
and Queens', 130
Richard III, 11
royal visitors, 136
Simeon, 170
study of law restricted, 10
well endowed, 116
King's Hall, 32, 88, 130

Laffan, R. G. D.,
character, 232, 350
concern for library, 384
director of studies in history, 292
and First World War, 317, 319
and his students, 331 *and* n
obituary notice, 388
Queens' first history don, 299 *and*
n
Roman Catholic convert, 350–51
rugby player, 258 *and* n, 259
supports League of Nations, 342
The Guardians of the Gate, 323
unpopularity, 232
Lake, Edward, 46
Lambert, John, 27 *and* n, 79
Lammas, William, 123n
landowners,
education of sons of, 194
students from landowning
classes, 238
Lansbury, George, 345
Laplace, Pierre-Simon, marquis de,
210
Latin,
rule for Fellows, 82
spoken, 36, 82, 217
as spoken language, 217
statutory lectures in, 30
Laud, William, 44, 45, 46
Laudian faction, 44, 45

Laudianism, 45–8 *passim*
laundrettes, 413, 414
Lawson, John, 61
Leach, Thomas, 198
League of Nations, 341–2, 346–7
lectures, 99, 204, 293, 294 *and* n
lectureships, 15, 101, 205, 227n, 385
Lee, Samuel,
attitude to admission of non-conformists, 271n
and Cambridge Camden Society,
273
and Church Missionary Society,
267–8, 297
and church restoration,
274
history, 297
orientalist, 297
Leete, Thomas, 116
Leicester, Robert Dudley, earl of, 68,
80–81
Lennox, Ludovick Stuart, 2nd duke
of, 69
Leo, X, Pope, 26
libraries (*see also* Queens' College
library), 15–16
library of Queens' College, 384–5
astronomy, 100
benefactions, 105, 117
Bullock's collection, 24
during 15th–17th centuries,
104–6
geometry, 100
Hughes' bequest, 203
mathematics, 100
Smith's bequest, 105
Lloyd, John, 190, 198–9
Lloyd, William, 190, 191
lodgings, 236–7
president's, 72
Lollard movement, 4
Lorkins, Thomas, 101
Luther, Martin, 25, 26
Lutheranism, 18, 25–6

Macclesfield, Thomas Parker, 1st earl
of, 157
McGowan, C. W. N., 344, 395
Magdalene College, 43n, 49, 170,
387, 434
Manchester, Edward Montagu, 2nd
earl of, 51–55 *passim*, 58, 60, 142
and n, 148

Mandell, William,
  challenges Godfrey for presidency, 220 – 21
  and evangelical movement, 171 – 2
  and Jee, 222
  reprimanded, 221
  Simeon's funeral sermon, 178n, 221
  and Smith's lectures, 172n
  toasts United States, 175n
Manning, Owen, 158n, 189
Mansell, John, 44, 64n, 69, 101
Maplet, John, 102
Margaret of Anjou, Queen, 1, 2 – 3, 4, 6, 9
Marley, Thomas, 53n
marriage,
  academic life and ban on, 79
  of college servants, 123
  Farish advocates Fellows' right to, 188
  of Fellows, 72, 440
  of presidents, 434
  of priests, 72
  and resignation of fellowships, 186, 187
  wedding services performed, 165
Marsh, Herbert, 176n
Martin, Edward, 120
  benefaction, 119
  and Buckingham's chancellorship, 44n
  Civil War, 48, 50, 53
  dean of Ely, 136
  drafts petition to parliament, 143n
  experiences during English Revolution, 143
  geometry lecturer, 100
  guarantees position of Fellows, 142, 146
  leave of absence, 82n
  and living for Bardsey, 168
  and Palmer's bequest, 119
  president, 44 – 5, 47, 69, 96, 142
  property sequestered, 58
  provenance, 64n
  religion, 46, 53, 143, 144
martyrs, Catholic, 25
martyrs, Protestant, 27
Mary Tudor, reaction against Reformation during reign of, 34 – 7
Master(s) Francis, 150, 184

matriculations, 192, 444
Maxwell, Anthony, 84
Maxwell, E. A., 388
May balls, 248, 325, 337, 436
Mayhew, Anthony, 36
meals, dinner and supper at Queens', 255 – 6
medicine, 101
  at Queens', 215 – 16
  inoculation, 139n
  Medical Society, 337n
  Queens' medical facilities and insurance, 335, 360 – 61
Melancthon, Philip, 28
Melton, William, 14
merchants, and university endowment, 117
Meriton, George, 68, 107
Metcalfe, J. E., 240
Methodism, 173
Mey, John, 37, 38n
Mey, William,
  archbishopric, 64n
  Cecil consults, 70
  forced to resign, 35
  marries, 72
  prayer book, 34, 38
  president, 27n, 32, 38, 64n
  provenance, 64n
  in service of state, 65, 68
  visitations, 34, 38
Michaelhouse, 14, 16, 67, 99
Michell, John, 214 and n
Middleton, William, 70 – 71, 85 and n
Milne Street, 129 – 30
Milner, Isaac,
  abolition of sizars' duties, 193
  absentee, 183n
  act for BD degree, 211n
  appearance, 181n
  ascendancy over Fellows, 174
  attitude to private tutors, 208
  and Bible Society, 176n, 177
  Bligh and, 190, 191
  burial place, 165n
  Cambridge Philosophical Society, 214
  and candidates for fellowships, 189 and n, 190
  and Catholic emancipation, 172n
  character, 181, 182, 183, 211
  chemistry, 213
  dean of Carlisle, 176, 182 – 3

521

death of, 177
designs reading lamp, 213
disciplinarian, 201
enclosure of property, 302, 303
and Erasmus' corkscrew, 19n
evangelical movement, 170 – 76
passim, 267
examines two schoolboys, 205
financial administration, 304,
305n
glutton, 183
Gunning on, 213n
and Hewitt, 175
hypochrondria, 213n
idea of Fellow's main duty, 212
ill health, 182 *and* n
influence in Trinity Hall, 162
and Jacobinism, 161, 172
lecturer, 213
Lucasian professorship of mathematics, 211
popular preacher, 173
practical mechanics, 213
president, 129, 159, 193, 220
purge of non-conformists, 164n
reactionary, 159
St Botolph's 169n
and statute of county, 189n
on student indiscipline, 197
student numbers rise under presidency of, 204
and subscription to 39 Articles,
173
supports anti-slavery campaign,
182n
and transportation of Palmer, 162
vice-chancellor, 160, 182
Milner, Mary, 182
misdemeanours, 263 – 4
missionary work,
at Queens', 267 – 8, 281
Cambridge House, 281
Church Missionary Society, 267
college missions, 281n, 281 – 2,
317
in late 19th century, 280
Queens' House mission, 353
modernity, 325 – 9
Monmouth, James Scott, duke of,
150
Montaigne, George, 68 – 9, 107
Moore, John, 157n
More, St Thomas, 16n, 17 *and* n, 21,
25

Morley, William, 36
Morris, John, 6
Morris, William, 314
motor cars, 327, 402
Mountjoy, William Blount, 4th
baron, 20, 22, 82 – 3
Munro, Andrew,
bequest, 398,
conservative, 232 – 3
dates, 330n
his care for Queens', 258
mathematician, 299
senior bursar, 321, 367
traveller, 228n
vice-president, 228 – 9
Munro Room, 418
muscular Christianity, 281, 352
music,
college musical societies, 248
moratorium after 11 p.m., 263n
Queens' appoints choral scholar,
275
students protest against restrictions on playing, 441

Napoleon I, Emperor, 160
Napoleonic Wars, 160, 303, 304
Natley, Edward, 53n
Naylor, Martin, 161, 162
Needham, Gervase, 187n
Needham, Walter, 101, 215
New Hall, 438
'New System', 235, 236n
Newbigin, Lesslie, 336 – 7
attitude to Christianity, 352
and Christian attitude to social
abuses, 353 *and* n
friendships, 332
Queens'-Newnham madrigal
group, 436
and socialism, 345
Newcastle-under-Lyme, Thomas
Pelham-Holles, 1st duke of, 156,
158, 159
Newman, John Henry, 288 – 9
Newnham College, 366n, 435, 436,
437
Newton, Isaac, 210
Nicholl, C. B., 261
Nichols, Daniel, 141
text of poem welcoming Resto-
ration, 460
Noble, A. H., 261n
non-conformists,

admission to universities pressed for, 271, 276
dissenting academies, 154
Milner's attitude to, 172
in parish of Oakington, 170n
undergraduate attitude to, 278 – 9
non-university teaching officers, 387 – 8
Norfolk, Thomas Howard, 3rd duke of, 28, 31
Northumberland, Thomas Percy, 7th earl of, 33, 35 *and* n
Nunne, Robert, 139

Ockley, Simon, orientalist, 297
Officers' Training Corps, 245, 318, 319, 342
optimes, 209
Osaka Gakuin University, 386n
Oxford, John de Vere, 13th earl of, 11
Oxford Movement, 272
Oxford University,
  abandons post A-level examinations, 396
  academic refugees from, 4
  All Souls College, 121n
  Cardinal College, 28
  classics in 15th century, 14
  Edward IV and, 8
  humanism, 15
  Lady Margaret Beaufort's divinity lectureships, 15
  Lutheran cell, 26
  national significance in 16th century, 67
  Oxford Movement, 272
  Peter Martyr, 33
  public lectureships, 15
  reputation, 288
  state funding, 366
  Tory, 156
  Wars of the Roses, 7

pacifism, 355
Palmer, Herbert
  bequest to Queens', 119
  death of, 57
  election to fellowship, 81
  leaves of absence, 82 *and* n
  Presybyterianism, 44, 62
  president, 54 *and* n, 55 – 6, 58 *and* n
  tutor, 91, 93
Palmer, Thomas Fyshe, 161, 162, 164

and n, 174
Paman, Henry, 60
papacy, 27 – 8, 43
Parker, Matthew, 32
Parker's Piece, 254n
Parliament,
  and alienation of property, 167
  alteration of Queens' statutes, 224
  and Cambridge University, 52, 55, 58, 187 – 8, 271 – 2, 276, 287 – 8, 291, 295
  and Civil War, 48, 49, 50, 52 – 3
  and college elections, 81 *and* n
  Corn Rent Act, 112
  enclosure of property, 302
  imposes Anglicanism, 143
  and Laudianism 47, 48
  oath of Engagement, 60
  and Reformation, 27
  reforming acts, 271
  report on religious worship at Cambridge University, 46, 47
  Uniformity Act (1662), 143 – 4
  and university finances, 295
  University Tests Act, 276
  Westminster Assembly of Divines, 54
Parys, Thomas, 118
Patrick, Simon, 63n, 149n
  arrives at Queens', 54
  and Cambridge Platonism, 148
  Civil War, 51
  Covenant oath, 53
  haemorrhoids, 137
  and his tutors, 92
  and Horton, 57
  Jacombe recommends, 79n
  and John Smith, 92, 147
  a moderate, 62 – 3
  ordination, 62
  and presidential election, 145 – 7
  studious, 103
  as tutor, 91 – 2, 92n
Peacock, Reginald, 82n
Peacock, Thomas, 116
Peill, J. N., 224, 240 – 41, 274, 292 – 3
Pelham, John, 36
Pellett, Thomas, 216n
Pembroke, countess of, 2
Pembroke, College, 36, 348n
Penalties, *see also* fines
  corporal punishment, 95
  dismissal from university, 339
  and efforts to deal with crisis

situations during student agitation, 422
gating, 264, 340, 341
of John Lloyd, 200
loss of scholarship, 340
petition against severity of, 264
rustication, 200
Pennington, Isaac, lecturer, 212 – 13
pensioners,
in 18th century, 192 *and* n, 193n
examinations, 217
fee-paying, 89
increase in number of, 238
percentage of student population, 194n
proportion graduating, 104, 207
and sizars, 193
Perne, Andrew, 101
Pestell, Thomas, 97
Peter Martyr Vermigli, 33
Peterhouse,
Civil War, 49
Elizabeth I, 136
Ely, 130n
foundation, 4
Gray seeks assistance from, 189, 190
Perne's bequest, 101
Smith's library, 105
Some, 41, 101
Pevsner, Nikolaus, 372, 375
Peyton, William, 100
Philippe, John, 99
Phillips, George,
and Cambridge Camden Society, 273
and Old Testament criticism, 286n
opposes plan for Friars building, 314
orientalist, 297, 298n
president, 274
Queens' chapel window, 274
resists creation of more university professorships, 293
philosophy,
Aristotelian, 98, 99, 147
Cartesianism, 102
Pindar, Martin, 61, 62 *and* n
Pirie, George,
coaches Queens' boat, 258
educational reformer, 228, 294, 297
junior bursar, 364n
tutor, 294n

and Wright, 227
Pitt, William, the younger, 161, 176
plate, Queens' melts down, 172n
Plumptre, Anna, 181n
Plumptre, Annabella, 181n
Plumptre family, 180 – 81, 216, 461
Plumptre, Henry, 157, 181, 216 *and* n
Plumptre, James, 181n
Plumptre, Joseph, 190 – 91
Plumptre Robert,
academic reform, 217
attitude to private tutors, 208
Bligh and, 190, 191
death of, 171
dispute over college property, 301n
divinity chair, 164n, 203
and evangelical movement, 173
and expenses of fellow-commoner, 196
family, 180 – 81
and John Lloyd, 190, 199
Latin, 217
manuscript history of Queens', 182
opposed to marriage of Fellows, 188
politics, 158
president, 157, 163, 180, 181
reformer, 181
supports loyal address, 159n
unawareness, 200
Plumptre, Russell, 159n, 181, 216
pluralism, 66
politics,
18th century, 155 – 62
in 1930s, 345 – 9
communism, 349, 404
Conservatism, 404
demonstrations, 405
evangelists', 172
fascism, 348
immediately after First World War, 341 – 5
Nazism, 348
political outlook of University in 19th century, 232
renewed interest during 1950s, 405
socialism, 343, 345, 346, 404
student activism, 424 – 6
student attitude in early 20th century, 244 – 5, 246 – 7
university, 157 – 62

Whigs and Whiggism, 156, 157, 271
Pollard, G. C., 274
Ponet, John, 36n, 101
Post, Walter, 169
Potts, L. J.,
    director of English studies, 381 and n
    representative of late Victorian ideal, 389
    and St Bartholomew's medical students, 359
    sole tutor, 357
    and White, 331
Powell, Enoch, 409
Powell and Moya, architectural partnership, 377, 379
prayer book, 34, 59, 62
Presbyterianism, 39, 40, 44, 52, 55
Presbtyerians and 'Latitude' men, 148
presidents of Queens',
    18th and early 19th century, 179 – 83
    19th century, 229 – 31
    20th century, 390 – 92
    custom of calling on, 331
    list of, 447 – 8
    mid-15th to mid-17th centuries, 64 – 70
    permitted to marry, 72
Preston, John,
    achieves wealth, 76
    and Aristotelian philosophy, 99
    aspirations, 88 and n
    astrology, 102
    and Capel Bedle, 96
    high numbers at Queens', 153n
    insomniac, 137
    medicine, 101
    Puritan, 42 – 3, 93, 127n
    secret visit to Netherlands, 83
    student, 92
    studiousness, 103
    thinks of leaving Queens', 76 – 7
    tutor, 92n, 92 – 3, 132
printing, invention of, 88, 99, 104 – 5
prizes, 201, 206, 295
proctors, 60 – 61
properties and benefices of Queens' College,
    Beccles, 300n
    Carmarthen, 300n
    Coveney, 300n
    Everleigh, 300n
    Eversden, 300n
    Fulbourn, 307
    Grimston, 220, 302
    Haddenham, 300n
    Haslingfield, 300n, 301n
    Hickling, 166
    Little Eversden, 166, 168, 169, 170, 175, 278n, 302
    Newton Toney, 166, 168
    Oakington, 166, 170, 300n, 302n, 303, 306n, 361
    St Botolph's 166, 169n, 170, 175
    St Nicholas Court, 301n
    Sandon, 167, 175
    Seagrave, 167, 174
    Trimden, 167
    Wyvelingham, 300n
property,
    beneficial leases, 308
    rack rents, 306 and n, 308
    sale of land restricted, 308
prostitution, 198, 265
Protestantism,
    see also Reformation
    at Cambridge University, 35, 36, 38 – 9, 43
    Cambridge men leaders of, 26
    evangelical movement and early, 171
    and prayers for the dead, 119
    in reign of Elizabeth I, 37 – 9
    worship facilitated, 33
public schools,
    see also independent schools and state schools
    Arnold and reform of, 223, 253n, 262
    and 'college spirit', 329 – 30
    and moral purpose of athletics, 260n
    sport, 253
    university students from, 238 and n, 262
Puritanism,
    at Cambridge University, 41, 42
    opposition to theatre, 108
    Palmer, 55
    Preston, 93, 127n
Puritans, 39, 40, 41, 171
Pye Ltd, 402
Pypard, John, 83, 85

Queens' College, Mission to South

London, 281
Queens' House, Rotherhithe, 353, 354

Radnor, earl of, 167
rags, 263n, 339 – 40
Ramsay, J. A., 389
Randolph, Thomas, 108
Read, Thomas, 184
recreations,
  18th century, 195
  medieval, 95
Redman, John, 32
Reformation,
  Erasmus, 26
  Henrician, 27 – 33
  Luther triggers, 25
  marriage of heads of colleges, 72
  Queens' acquires land, 131
  and study at foreign universities, 83
  under Edward VI, 33 – 4
Regius professorships, 15, 31
religion,
  see also individual religions and sects
  after Restoration, 144, 147
  atrophy in, 163
  concern about heterodoxy, 144n
  during inter-War years, 349 – 54
  in 18th century, 162 – 70
  in later 19th century, 275 – 86
  in Queens' during Second World War, 360
  in recent times, 392 – 3
  religious education for undergraduates, 93n
  tolerance at Queens', 350
  Uniformity Act, 143, 144
  Worcester House declaration and freedom of choice, 143
Representative Committee of Queens', 333
restoration of the monarchy, verses to celebrate, 141, 460
'Revolution of the Dons', 432 – 3
Reynolds, Osborne, 296
Richard III,
  (as duke of Gloucester) endows Queens', 74
  benefactions, 110, 118
  and elections to fellowships, 79
  John Doket, 5
  Queens' College, 10, 11
  religious foundations and bene-

factions, 11
  seizes throne, 10
riots, town/gown, 263
Rob Roy boat club, 258
Robbins Report, 376, 406
Roberts, Robert, 123 – 4
Robinson, Joan, 404
Robinson, Nicholas, 107
Rockrey, Edmund, 40 *and* n, 41, 70, 85
Roman Catholicism,
  at Queens', 46
  and enforced celibacy in universities, 188
  hostility to, 43, 151, 172
  James II, 151
  martyrs, 25
  protection from, 93
  and Reformation, 33
Romilly, Joseph, 175n, 220n
Roos, Lady Margery, 75
Rosse, John, 125n
Royal Society, 57, 154, 214, 215, 465
Russell, Bertrand, *later* 3rd earl Russell, 249
Ryle, H.E.,
  bishop, 282
  and college missions, 292
  Fellow of King's, 230n
  involvement in religious activities, 280n, 283
  president, 229, 230
  religious thinking, 284 – 5
  and student misbehavior, 264
  and success of Queens', 235
  theologian, 284 *and* n, 285, 297
  attitude to admission of women, 435
Ryle, Mrs H. E., 230, 258n

St Bartholomew's medical school, Queens' takes evacuated students from, 358, 359
St Bernard Society, 242 – 8
  in 1950s, 404
  attitude to women, 434, 435, 436 – 7
  and Bernard Room, 250, 332
  conservative attitudes, 342
  in decline, 338, 403
  dons' debates, 231, 331
  during First World War, 318, 319, 320, 321n, 321 – 2
  factionalism, 251

and function of JCR committee, 332
paper on 'Spain', 348
Phoenix Club rivals, 345
politics, 342n, 346, 405
religion, 278–9
'Representative Committee' and, 333
rowdy behaviour, 339
subjects for debate, 256, 259, 327, 328 *and* n, 347, 466–74
supports higher wages, 343n
tries to act as focal point for Queens', 250
St Bernard's College, 3, 6
St Bernard's Hostel, 5, 6, 77, 111
St Botolph's Church, 277n
Campion, 228, 273n
Doket, 5, 6, 65
Milner, 182n
Preston, 42
restoration fund, 273
Walker, 273
Webster, 272
St Botolph's parish, 120
St Catharine's College, 26
foundation of, 3
Johns, 283, 298
Puritan emigration, 43n
and Queens', 129, 133, 254, 257
study of law restricted, 10
theology, 104
St George, Anthony, 60n
St John, Oliver, 60
St John's College,
16th century statutes, 17
and accession of William and Mary, 152
building materials, 130
Civil War, 49
Cripps building, 377, 379
Fisher, 19
foundation of, 14
gate tower, 130
Henry VIII and, 28
influential in elections, 214n
long gallery, 132n
performance of plays, 106, 108
Puritan emigration, 43n
Taylor, 34
well endowed, 116
Welsh students, 87n
Wigge, 132
St Margaret and St Bernard, College

of, 1
St Mark's Church, 278n
Salisbury, Robert Cecil, 1st earl of, 68, 69
Sandwich, Edward Montagu, 1st earl of, 158
scholars,
academic exercises to be performed, 206
and 'bible-clerks', 90n
domestic dutues of, 124
emoluments and duties, 90–91, 91n
live in college, 332
numbers rise, 90
percentage graduating, 207
percentage of student population, 194
scholars and bible-clerks at Queens', table of, 455
scholarships, 335
amalgamated, 305
effect of depression on income, 309
entrance, 239, 294
modern languages and English, 381
offered by Queens', 238–9, 292n
Queens' creates supernumerary, 239–40
spur to academic endeavour, 206
state, 239
waning attractiveness, 206
science,
early interest in, 100
expansion of, 288n
industry funds, 387
in late 17th century, 102
scientific tradition in Queens', 212, 213–4
triposes in natural and moral sciences, 291, 292
Scoresby, William, 465
Searle, W. G., 274
Second World War,
co-residence of evacuees not permitted, 438
Queens' College in, 355–62
Sedgwick, Adam, 214
Sedgwick, William,
appointment of Fellows, 186 *and* nn
congratulatory verses by, 158
ill health, 180 *and* n

527

interests, 212
lends money to Queens', 312
and non-resident Fellows, 185 – 6
performs marriage services, 165
and Post, 169
president, 157 – 8, 180
protégé of Hardwickes, 157n
Seltman, C. T., 358n
Selwyn College, Cripps building, 377
Senate House, 311, 434 – 5, 436 and n
servants,
butler, 123 – 4, 303
college, 123 – 6
of college heads, 71
day-labourers, 125, 134 – 5
of fellow-commoners, 196
gratuity to ex-porter, 307n
keep licensed lodgings, 237
marriage, 123
renumeration, 140, 193
shortage of manpower during
Second World War, 357
waiting at table, 193
weddings, 165
sexual promiscuity, 430n
Sharp, John, college butler, 303
Shute, Nathaniel, 168
Sidney Sussex College, 31, 39, 44, 61,
151
Silver Street, 129 and n, 199, 341, 417
Silver Street bridge, 370
Simeon Charles,
death of, 178
evangelical movement, 170, 171,
178
funeral sermon, 178n, 221
lectures in danger of suppression,
177
preacher, 173
sit-ins, 415, 416
sizars,
degrees, 91, 104
domestic duties, 89, 91
examinations, 217
improved position by 19th century, 192 – 3
misdemeanour, 198
numbers decrease, 238
percentage graduating, 207
percentage of student population,
194
Roberts becomes college butler,
123 – 4
Skelton, Thomas, 268

slavery, evangelical movement and
campaign against, 270
Sleeman, C. M., 332, 342
Slingsby, Henry, 94 – 5
Smith, Richard, 27n
Smith, John,
bequest to Queens', 100, 106
contentious sermon, 40
his library, 105 – 6
mathematics lecturer, 100
and Patrick, 62 – 3, 92 and n, 147
theologian, 57
tuberculosis, 138n
Smith, Sir James E., 172n
Smith, Sir Thomas,
benefactions and bequest, 105,
110, 111
Cecil consults, 70
Corn Rent Act, 112
fellowship for his nephew, 80
Greek scholar, 31 – 2
humanist and scholar, 100
leave of absence, 83
poverty, 76
revision of prayer book, 38
university visitor, 34
Smythies (or Smythes), Ferdinand,
150, 183 and n, 301
social intercourse, betweeen the
sexes, 435 – 7
societies of Queens' College, 242 – 8
Christian Union, 280 and n, 283,
350, 351
Classical, 249, 256, 337n
'D', 359 – 60
Dramatic, 337, 338
'E', 360
Erasmus, 248, 249, 278, 338, 348
History, 342n, 337, 347
Medical, 337n
'Pie Posse', 279 – 80
Quaerists, 31, 247n, 248 – 9, 249n,
278, 280n, 283
Query, 338
St Bernard, see separate entry
St Margaret, 248, 359
'The Bats', 360
Some, Robert, 39 and n, 41, 81, 101
Somerset, Edward Seymour, 1st
duke of, 33, 35n
Somerset, R. H. E. H., 250n
Somerseth, John, 6 – 7
Spanish civil war, 348
Sparrow, Anthony,

bishop of Exeter, 148, 282
Civil war, 48n, 53n
combination room panelling, 119n
crown intervention in presidential election, 145 – 6
high churchman, 144
Laudianism, 47
and Patrick, 147
president, 144, 147
and religious heterodoxy, 144n
resigns, 179
supports auricular confession, 46
Spence, Sir Basil, 373 – 5
sport,
    aestheticism at variance with sporting ethos, 328
    all-roundedness, 260n
    at universities, 253
    athleticism, 252 – 62, 281
    Barton Road sports ground, 255, 361
    in British educational system, 252
    changing attitudes in mid-19th century, 252 – 3
    character-building quality of, 261
    cricket, 252, 254, 255, 262
    croquet, 254
    darts, 339
    dons involvement in, 231, 256 – 9
    during First World War, 322
    during Second World War, 360
    enthusiasm for, 260, 403
    fives, 254
    Gray's involvement with, 299
    hockey, 255
    improved facilities at Queens', 257
    prize-fighting, 256
    quoits, 254
    racing, 256
    restrictions on matches against Oxford, 341
    rowing, 253 – 4, 255, 256, 257, 259 – 60
    rugby, 252, 254, 255, 256
    significance in university life, 257
    skating, 254n
    soccer, 254 – 5
    sporting revolution, 254, 256
    sportsmen's self-importance, 260
    tennis, 254, 255, 257
staff, college (see also servants), 427 and n
Staley, Thomas, 273

Stanbanke, Richard, 83
Stanley, James, 10
Starre, John, 125
state schools, see also independent schools and public schools, 394, 395, 396
statutes, Queens' revised, 226
Stevenson, Mr Justice Melford, 425
Stokedall, William, 123n
student agitation,
    19th and early 20th century, 265 – 6
    achievements of revolt, 432 – 3
    admissions policy, 396n
    anger against Fellows, 419 – 20
    campaign for co-residence, 431
    communication with senior members, 414
    contingency plans for dealing with, 475 – 8
    demonstration in Cloister Court, 420 – 21
    on discipline, 415
    for domestic reform, 414, 426 – 30, 432 – 3
    Garden House riot, 424 – 5
    for greater social freedom, 438
    guest regulations, 426 – 7
    impending violence, 415 – 16
    political, 404 – 5, 424 – 6
    sit-ins, 415, 416
student body in Queens', size and social composition in 19th century, 462 – 3
Student Christian Movement, 352
student revolt, at Queens', 406 – 33 passim
students (see also scholars and sizars)
    18th century, 192 – 202
    academic standards of Queens', 382 – 4
    accommodation for, 236 – 7, 371 – 3 passim, 376
    age, 95, 102, 262
    aristocrats, 180n
    choice of tutor, 204
    Christian worship, 392n
    clubs and societies, 242 – 52
    composition of population between 17th and 19th centuries, 194n
    discontent in 1960s, 404 – 6
    don's relationship with, 231, 232
    evangelical movement and rise in

number, 175
expansion of population from late
  19th century, 234
government funding of fees, 368
graduate, 398 – 401
identity as distinct social group,
  405 – 6
indiscipline, 96, 180n, 196 – 8,
  340 – 41
inter-War years, 334 – 41
lords of misrule, 106
married, 326, 436 *and* n
medieval student society, 95
middle class, 241
numbers, 153 – 4, 175, 189, 192,
  234, 317, 318 – 19, 325, 358, 359
poor, 123, 201, 238 – 40
in post-War decades, 402
prizes, 201, 206
protest movements, 406
provenance, 86
Queensmen in First World War,
  324 *and* n
reduction in number of ordinands, 276 *and* n
rent rebates, 432n
and Second World War, 358, 362
seek 'college community', 433
sexual promiscuity, 430n
social composition, 192 *and* n,
  237 – 42, 394
social intercourse between the
  sexes, 435 – 7
social origins, 87, 88
status of Queens' students on
  entry (1500 – 1751), 449
table of geographical origins, 451
studies
  in 18th century, 208 – 19
  astronomy, 214 *and* n
  classics, 216 – 17, 239
  geology, 214
  Greek, 21, 22, 30
  Hebrew, 307
  humanities, 13, 99
  Latin, 30
  law, 10, 103n, 217 – 18
  mathematics, 100, 202, 208 – 12
    passim, 239
  medicine, 215
  new and reformed, 381 – 2
  oriental languages, 296 – 7, 298n
  political economy, 218

range widens, 288, 291 – 2
scientific, 212 – 13
shift in balance, 382
theology, 10 *and* n, 22, 36, 103 *and*
  n
Sturbridge fair, 96, 97n, 140
Sturgeon, Thomas, 130
Suffolk, William de la Pole, 1st Duke
  of, 1
Syday, William, 118 – 19

Taylor, John, 34
teaching, in 18th century, 203 – 8
  passim
Temperley, Ernest, 228
  active worker for Queens', 228n
  committed Christian, 282n
  early death, 299
  fellowship, 228
  junior bursar, 257n, 364n
  lecturer at Girton, 435
  mathematician, 298 – 9
  new system of accounting,
    308 – 9, 309n
  oarsman, 257 – 8
'ten year man', 464 – 5
Tennant, P. F. D., 356, 381
thanksgiving days, 155
theatre,
  15th – 17th centuries, 106 – 9
  in 1920s, 339
Thomason, Thomas, 172, 209, 267
Thoresby, Ralph, 204
timber,
  college property, 59 *and* n
  for college repairs, 115
  felling, 117, 305
  financial asset, 301
  revenue from 113 – 14
Toplis, John, 210 – 11
Towers, John, 83
torn-gown relations, 126 – 9
Townson, Robert, 80, 81n
tractarianism, 272
Trinity College, 136
  Bentley, 157, 216
  Civil War, 51
  great gate, 130
  Herbert, 137
  influential in elections, 214n
  joint fellowships with Queens',
    387
  Lee, 297

530

lords of misrule, 106
performance of plays, 106, 108
profits from Dissolution, 31
Puritan emigration, 43n
Redman, 32
Sedgwick, 214
Trinity Hall,
considered an expensive college, 240
Gardiner, 31
joint fellowship with Queens', 387
Milner's influence in, 176n
permission for marriage of Fellows, 225
tenure of fellowships, 185n
Wrangham and Vickers, 162
triposes,
economics, 381
English, 380 – 81
law, 381 *and* n
mathematics, 189, 202, 208
medicine, 381
modern languages, 381
natural and moral sciences, 291, 292
new, 291
oriental languages, 298n
Trotter, Hugh, 84 *and* n, 110
Trumper, Victor, 332
Trumpington Street, 129
Tudway, Thomas, 157
Tunstall, Cuthbert, 136
Turner, J. W. C., 246 – 7
tutorial system,
in 16th century, 15
reform of, 429
tutors,
duties, 91, 93
importance of choice of, 204
Milner's power to appoint, 174
and misbehaviour of students, 264
new tutorial arrangements, 412
numbers, 189, 205, 429
outsiders as, 189
private, 207, 208, 210n
qualities desirable in, 91
Queens', 189n, 429
for research students, 398
responsibilities, 95, 96
tutorships, 227n
Tyndale, William, English New

Testament, 26
Tyndall, Francis, 116, 119
Tyndall, Humphrey,
benefaction, 119
family benefits from his office, 116
marries, 72
Middleton and, 71
non-resident, 66n
origins, 64n
president, 41, 43, 64, 68, 93
president's lodging, 72
quarrels with Fellows, 80
Tyndall, Jane, 72

UCCA, Cambridge joins, 395
undergraduates,
accommodation, 314, 315
after First World War, 326
and Bible Society, 177
and dons, 231, 232
evangelical movement, 170
and General Strike, 343
lodgings, 5, 332
medieval, 5
patriotism, 322
stability of social composition, 334
support women's suffrage and co-education, 435
termly charges raised, 321
unemployment
of graduates in 1960s, 398
undergraduate interest in problem of, 345 – 6
Union, Queens' College,
articulates grievances, 417 – 18
and co-residence, 439, 440
constitution, 410, 427
council of, 408, 409, 410, 428
and Garden House rioters, 425
guests, 419 – 20, 422
and improved amenities, 413, 414
kitchen reforms, 428
'moderates' and 'radicals', 420
original terms of reference, 431
proposal to replace with college students union, 430
'radicals' propose abolition of, 417
report on first year of operations, 423
and student representation on governing body, 423
431
Unitarianism, 164

universities,
    agitation throughout, 415
    Anglicanism obligatory, 143
    chantry act, 33
    crypto-Catholics, 47
    in decline, 86, 154
    education confers status, 88
    Grand Remonstrance (1641), 47
    in late medieval and early modern periods, 86
    lawyers benefit from study at continental, 83
    medieval lecterns destroyed, 105
    MPs for, 157
    relationship with industry, 289
    social revolution in 16th century, 88
Ustwayt, Richard, 79

Vaizey, John, 395, 402, 404
Valor Ecclesiasticus, 29
Vaughan, John, 99
Venn, J. A., not in holy orders, 391
Venn family, 391
Venn, Henry,
    cricketer, 252
    and evangelical movement, 171
    Fellow, 186, 189, 270, 391
    opinion of Fellows, 183 – 4
Venn, Henry (*grandson*), 267 *and* n, 270, 271
Venn, J. A., 359
    cricket bowling machine, 331 – 2
    and Crummell, 270
    dies in office, 392
    election to presidency, 390 – 91
    president, 364
    Queens' investment income, 367
    senior bursar, 356
    vice-chancellor, 356, 357
Venn, John, 183 – 4, 332
Vigani, John Francis, 102, 212, 215 – 16
visitations,
    after regicide, 60
    during Reformation, 30, 33 – 4
    in reign of Elizabeth I, 38
    in reign of Mary Tudor, 36, 70
    and supervision of college estates, 114 – 15

Walkden, Humphrey, 100
Walker, William, 273
Wallis, Garret, 80

Wallis, John, 57, 100 – 101, 101n
Walters, Henry, 168
Walton, Valentine, 49
Ward, Robert, 48, 108
Ward, Samuel, 44
Warham, William, 21, 22
Wars of the Roses, 7
Warwick, countess of, 11
Wasse, Joseph, 149n, 216 *and* n, 217
Watson, Richard, 274
Watson, Robert (16th c), 102
Watson, Robert (19th c), 291 – 2
Watson, Thomas, 35
Waynflete, William, 3n, 130n
Webster, Thomas, 272
Wellbore, Matthew, 97
Wells, John, 92
Wells, William, 148, 301n
Wemis, Lewis, 81 *and* n
Wenlock, Sir John, 1
Westminster Assembly of Divines, 54, 55, 56
White, T. H.,
    Darkness at Pemberley, 390
    financial help for, 335
    and his tutor, 330 – 31
    Mistress Masham's Respose, 298n
    seeks advice from Potts, 394 – 5
Whitford, Richard, 20, 82
Wigge, Gilbert, 132
Wilberforce, William, 173 *and* n, 176, 177, 182n
Wilkinson, Thomas, 18, 64n, 66n, 66 – 7, 118
William Colton Foundation, 386n
William Frederick, 2nd duke of Gloucester, 177 *and* n
William III *and* Mary, 152, 155
Williams, J. F., 258 – 9
Wodelarke, Robert, 3
Wolsey, Thomas, 16, 27, 136
women,
    admission to Queens', 434, 441
    all-female theatre group, 442
    college servants, 123, 124, 125, 434
    Fellows' wives, 440 *and* n
    full membership of the university, 437
    guests, 410, 429 – 30, 438
    illicit diners in hall, 438
    and improvements of academic standards, 383
    movement for university education of, 434

532

Queens' and co-residence, 439
Queens' Women's Group, 442
woman Fellow appointed, 441
Wood, C. T., 319
  anti-war sentiments, 342
  athletics, 258 *and* n
  celebrations at degree ceremony, 330
  complains of dining clubs, 262
  cricket, 262
  on dangers of factionalism, 251
  Death and Beyond, 323n
  and First World War, 319, 323, 336
  on Fitzpatrick, 230
  ordained, 282n
  participates in debates, 231n
  promotes the *Courier*, 252
  published works, 299
  religion, 283, 350n
  and students, 331, 335, 337
  'typical Victorian', 330
Wrangham, Francis, 162
wranglers, 209
Wray, Daniel, 157n, 194–5, 196, 210n

Wright, Arthur,
  attitude to chapel services, 282
  character, 228
  critical of lecture system, 294
  death of, 330n
  and educational reforms, 227, 228, 294, 297
  Fellow, 294n
  history, 227, 297
  influence on Queens', 228
  involvement in religious activities, 283
  lecturer, 297n
  'New system', 235–6
  ordained, 282n
  Queens' new chapel, 277
  theologian, 285, 298
  traveller, 228n
  a walker, 232
Wyche, Dame Alice, 75
Wyclif, John, 4, 82
Wykeham, William of, 1

Yale, Thomas, 37n
Yorke, Philip, 195, 207, 216

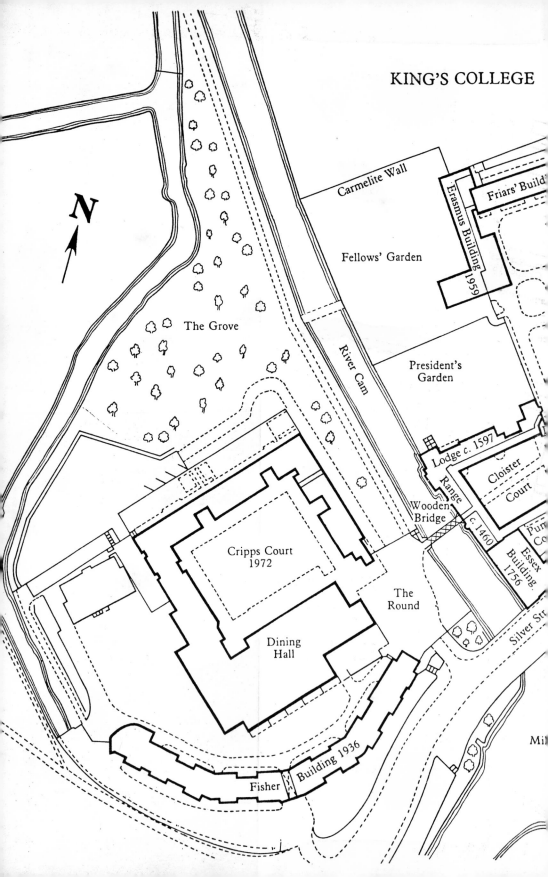

KING'S COLLEGE

N

Carmelite Wall

Fellows' Garden

Erasmus Building 1959

Friars' Build'

The Grove

River Cam

President's Garden

Lodge c. 1597

Cloister Court

Range

Wooden Bridge

c. 1460

Pur Co

Essex Building 1756

Cripps Court 1972

The Round

Dining Hall

Silver Str

Mil

Fisher

Building 1936